Microsoft® Office Ex 3

ILLUSTRATED, CourseCard Edition

COMPLETE

Microsoft®
Office
Specialist
Approved Courseware

Expert

Elizabeth Eisner Reding • Lynn Wermers

THOMSON
COURSE TECHNOLOGY™

Australia • Canada • Mexico • Singapore • Spain • United Kingdom • United States

Microsoft® Office Excel 2003—Illustrated Complete, CourseCard Edition

Elizabeth Eisner Reding, Lynn Wermers

Vice President, End User Publishing:
Nicole Jones Pinard

Managing Editor
Marjorie Hunt

Production Editors:
Aimee Poirier, Summer Hughes

QA Manuscript Reviewers:
Alex White, Chris Carvalho, Sean Franey

Senior Product Manager:
Christina Kling Garrett

Product Manager:
Jane Hosie-Bounar

Developmental Editors:
Kim Crowley, Barbara Clemens

Text Designer:
Joseph Lee, Black Fish Design

Associate Product Manager:
Emilie Perreault

Editorial Assistant:
Shana Rosenthal

Composition House:
GEX Publishing Services

ISBN-13: 978-1-4188-4296-3
ISBN-10: 1-4188-4296-6

The Illustrated Series Vision

Teaching and writing about computer applications can be extremely rewarding and challenging. How do we engage students and keep their interest? How do we teach them skills that they can easily apply on the job? As we set out to write this book, our goals were to develop a textbook that:

- works for a beginning student
- provides varied, flexible, and meaningful exercises and projects to reinforce the skills
- serves as a reference tool
- makes your job as an educator easier, by providing resources above and beyond the textbook to help you teach your course

Our popular, streamlined format is based on advice from instructional designers and customers. This flexible design presents each lesson on a two-page spread, with step-by-step instructions on the left, and screen illustrations on the right. This signature style, coupled with high-caliber content, provides a comprehensive yet manageable introduction to Microsoft Office Excel 2003—it is a teaching package for the instructor and a learning experience for the student.

About This Edition

New to this edition is a free, tear-off Excel 2003 CourseCard that provides students with a great way to have Excel skills at their fingertips!

Acknowledgments

Creating a book of this magnitude is a team effort. I would like to thank my husband, Michael, as well as Christina Kling Garrett, the project manager who experienced a true baptism-by-fire, Emilie Perreault, associate product manager, and my development editor, Kim Crowley, for her suggestions and corrections. I would also like to thank the production and editorial staff for all their hard work that made this project a reality.

Elizabeth Eisner Reding

I would like to thank Barbara Clemens for her insightful contributions and guidance. I would also like to thank Christina Kling Garrett for patiently answering and researching my endless questions.

Lynn Wermers

Preface

Welcome to *Microsoft Office® Excel 2003– Illustrated Complete, CourseCard Edition*. Each lesson in this book contains elements pictured to the right.

How is the book organized?

Two units on Microsoft Windows XP introduce students to basic operating system skills. The book is then organized into sixteen units on Excel, covering basic skills from creating, editing, and formatting worksheets, through advanced skills.

What kinds of assignments are included in the book? At what level of difficulty?

The lessons use MediaLoft, a fictional chain of bookstores, as the case study. The assignments on the light purple pages at the end of each unit increase in difficulty. Data Files and case studies, with many international examples, provide a great variety of interesting and relevant business applications. Assignments include:

- **Concepts Reviews** include multiple choice, matching, and screen identification questions.

- **Skills Reviews** provide additional hands-on, step-by-step reinforcement.

- **Independent Challenges** are case projects requiring critical thinking and application of the unit skills. The Independent Challenges increase in difficulty, with the first one in each unit being the easiest (most step-by-step with detailed instructions). Independent Challenges 2 and 3 become increasingly open-ended, requiring more independent problem solving.

- **E-Quest Independent Challenges** are case projects with a Web focus. E-Quests require the use of the World Wide Web to conduct research to complete the project.

- **Advanced Challenge Exercises** set within the Independent Challenges provide optional steps for more advanced students.

- **Visual Workshops** are practical, self-graded capstone projects that require independent problem solving.

Each 2-page spread focuses on a single skill.

Concise text introduces the basic principles in the lesson and integrates a real-world case study.

UNIT **C**
Excel 2003

Applying Colors, Patterns, and Borders

You can use colors, patterns, and borders to enhance the overall appearance of a worksheet and to make it easier to read. You can add these enhancements by using the Patterns or Borders tabs in the Format Cells dialog box or by using the Borders and Color buttons on the Formatting toolbar. You can apply color or patterns to the background of a cell, to a range, or to cell contents. You can also apply borders to all the cells in a worksheet or only to selected cells to call attention to individual cells or groups of cells. See Table C-4 for a list of border buttons and their functions. Jim asks you to add a pattern, a border, and color to the title of the worksheet to give the worksheet a more professional appearance.

STEPS

1. **Press** [Ctrl][Home] **to select cell** A1, **then click the** Fill Color list arrow **on the Formatting toolbar**
   The color palette appears.

   QUICK TIP
   Use color sparingly. Too much color can divert the reader's attention from the worksheet data.

2. **Click the** Turquoise color **(fourth row, fifth column)**
   Cell A1 has a turquoise background, as shown in Figure C-14. Cell A1 spans columns A through I because of the Merge and Center command used for the title.

3. **Right-click cell** A1, **then click** Format Cells **on the shortcut menu**
   The Format Cells dialog box opens.

4. **Click the** Patterns tab **if it is not already displayed**
   See Figure C-15. Adding a pattern to cells can add to the visual interest of your worksheet.

5. **Click the** Pattern list arrow, **click the** Thin Diagonal Crosshatch pattern **(third row, last column), then click** OK
   A border also enhances a cell's appearance. Unlike underlining, which is a text-formatting tool, borders extend to the width of the cell.

   QUICK TIP
   You can also draw cell borders using the mouse pointer. Click the Borders list arrow on the Formatting toolbar, click Draw Borders, then drag to create borders or boxes.

6. **Click the** Borders list arrow **on the Formatting toolbar, then click the** Thick Bottom Border **(second row, second column) on the Borders palette**
   It can be difficult to view a border in a selected cell.

7. **Click cell** A3
   The border is a nice enhancement. Font color can also help distinguish information in a worksheet.

   QUICK TIP
   The default color on the Fill Color and Font Color buttons changes to the last color you selected.

8. **Select the range** A3:I3, **click the** Font Color list arrow **on the Formatting toolbar, then click the** Blue color **(second row, third column from the right) on the palette**
   The text changes color, as shown in Figure C-16.

9. **Click the** Save button **on the Standard toolbar**

Clues to Use

Formatting columns or rows

You can save yourself time by formatting an entire column or row using any of the categories that appear in the Format Cells dialog box. You might, for example, want to format all the cells within a column to accept telephone numbers, social security numbers, zip codes, or custom number formats. Click the column or row heading—located at the top of a column or beginning of a row—to select the entire column or row. You can format a selected column or row by clicking Format on the menu bar, clicking Cells, then clicking the appropriate tab in the Format Cells dialog box.

EXCEL C-12 FORMATTING A WORKSHEET

OFFICE-262

Tips, as well as troubleshooting advice, right where you need them—next to the step itself.

Clues to Use boxes provide concise information that either expands on the major lesson skill or describes an independent task that in some way relates to the major lesson skill.

What online content solutions are available to accompany this book?

Visit www.course.com for more information on our online content for Illustrated titles. Options include:

MyCourse 2.0

Need a quick, simple tool to help you manage your course? Try MyCourse 2.0, the easiest to use, most flexible syllabus and content management tool available. MyCourse 2.0 offers you brand new content, including Topic Reviews, Extra Case Projects, and Quizzes, to accompany this book.

WebCT

Course Technology and WebCT have partnered to provide you with the highest quality online resources and Web-based tools for your class. Course Technology offers content for this book to help you create your WebCT class, such as a suggested Syllabus, Lecture Notes, Practice Test questions, and more.

Blackboard

Course Technology and Blackboard have also partnered to provide you with the highest quality online resources and Web-based tools for your class. Course Technology offers content for this book to help you create your Blackboard class, such as a suggested Syllabus, Lecture Notes, Practice Test questions, and more.

Is this book Microsoft Office Specialist Certified?

Microsoft Office Excel 2003—Illustrated Complete, CourseCard Edition covers the objectives for Microsoft Office Excel 2003 and Microsoft Office Excel 2003 Expert and has received certification approval as courseware for the Microsoft Office Specialist program. See the inside front cover for more information on other Illustrated titles meeting Microsoft Office Specialist certification.

The first page of each unit indicates which objectives in the unit are Microsoft Office Specialist skills. If an objective is set in red, it meets a Microsoft Office Specialist skill. A document in the Review Pack cross-references the skills with the lessons and exercises.

Every lesson features large, full-color representations of what the screen should look like as students complete the numbered steps.

Brightly colored tabs indicate which section of the book you are in.

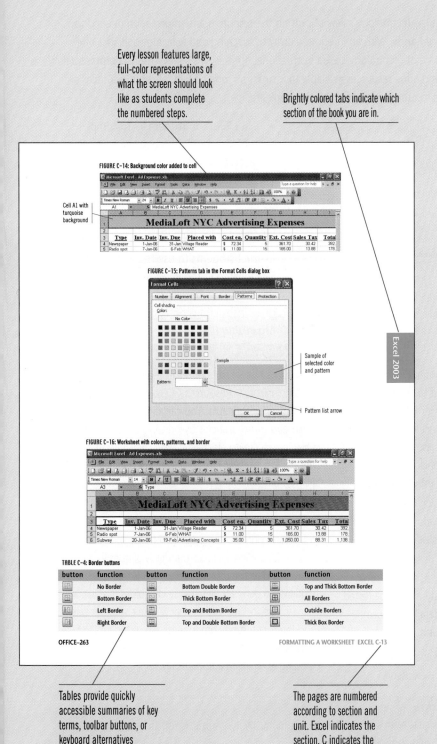

Tables provide quickly accessible summaries of key terms, toolbar buttons, or keyboard alternatives connected with the lesson material. Students can refer easily to this information when working on their own projects at a later time.

The pages are numbered according to section and unit. Excel indicates the section, C indicates the unit, 13 indicates the page.

v

Instructor Resources

The Instructor Resources CD is Course Technology's way of putting the resources and information needed to teach and learn effectively into your hands. With an integrated array of teaching and learning tools that offers you and your students a broad range of technology-based instructional options, we believe this CD represents the highest quality and most cutting edge resources available to instructors today. Many of these resources are available at www.course.com. The resources available with this book are:

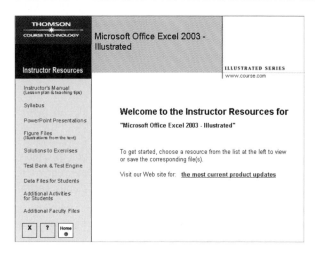

- **Data Files for Students**—To complete most of the units in this book, your students will need **Data Files**. Put them on a file server for students to copy. The Data Files are available on the Instructor Resources CD-ROM, and in the Review Pack, and can also be downloaded from www.course.com.

Instruct students to use the **Data Files List** located in the Review Pack and on the Instructor Resources CD. This list gives instructions on copying and organizing files.

- **Solutions to Exercises**—Solutions to Exercises contains every file students are asked to create or modify in the lessons and End-of-Unit material. A Help file on the Instructor Resources CD includes information for using the Solution Files. There is also a document outlining the solutions for the End-of-Unit Concepts Review, Skills Review, and Independent Challenges.

- **PowerPoint Presentations**—Each unit has a corresponding PowerPoint presentation that you can use in a lecture, distribute to your students, or customize to suit your course.

- **Instructor's Manual**—Available as an electronic file, the Instructor's Manual is quality-assurance tested and includes unit overviews, and detailed lecture topics with teaching tips for each unit.

- **Sample Syllabus**—Prepare and customize your course easily using this sample course outline.

- **Figure Files**—The figures in the text are provided on the Instructor Resources CD to help you illustrate key topics or concepts. You can create traditional overhead transparencies by printing the figure files. Or you can create electronic slide shows by using the figures in a presentation program such as PowerPoint.

- **ExamView**—ExamView is a powerful testing software package that allows you to create and administer printed, computer (LAN-based), and Internet exams. ExamView includes hundreds of questions that correspond to the topics covered in this text, enabling students to generate detailed study guides that include page references for further review. The computer-based and Internet testing components allow students to take exams at their computers, and also saves you time by grading each exam automatically.

SAM 2003 Assessment & Training

SAM 2003 helps you energize your class exams and training assignments by allowing students to learn and test important computer skills in an active, hands-on environment.

With SAM 2003 Assessment, you create powerful interactive exams on critical applications such as Word, Outlook, PowerPoint, Windows, the Internet, and much more. The exams simulate the application environment, allowing your students to demonstrate their knowledge and think through the skills by performing real-world tasks.

Designed to be used with the Illustrated series, SAM 2003 Assessment & Training includes built-in page references so students can create study guides that match the Illustrated textbooks you use in class. Powerful administrative options allow you to schedule exams and assignments, secure your tests, and run reports with almost limitless flexibility.

Contents

EXCEL 2003

Formatting a Worksheet — C–1

EXCEL 2003

Working with Charts — D-1

EXCEL 2003

Working with Formulas and Functions — E-1

EXCEL 2003

EXCEL 2003

EXCEL 2003

EXCEL 2003

EXCEL 2003

Read This Before You Begin

Software Information and Required Installation

This book was written and tested using Microsoft Office 2003 - Professional Edition, with a typical installation on Microsoft Windows XP plus installation of the latest Service Pack, and with Internet Explorer 6.0 or higher. Some of the exercises in this book assume that your computer is connected to the Internet. If you are not connected to the Internet, see your instructor for information.

Tips for Students

What are Data Files?

To complete many of the units in this book, you need to use Data Files. A Data File contains a partially completed document, so that you don't have to type in all the information in the document yourself. Your instructor will either provide you with copies of the Data Files or ask you to make your own copies. Your instructor can also give you instructions on how to organize your files, as well as a complete file listing, or you can find the list and the instructions for organizing your files in the Review Pack.

You will also need to create a Unit G folder at the same level as your other unit folders. There are no Data Files supplied for Unit G, but you will need to save the files you create in your Unit G folder.

Why is my screen different from the book?

Your Desktop components and some dialog box options might be different if you are using an operating system other than Windows XP.

Depending on your computer hardware and the display settings on your computer, you may also notice the following differences:

- Your screen may look larger or smaller because of your screen resolution (the height and width of your screen).

- Your title bars and dialog boxes may not display file extensions. To display file extensions, click Start on the taskbar, click Control Panel, click Appearance and Themes, then click Folder Options. Click the View tab if necessary, click Hide extensions for known file types to deselect it, then click OK. Your Office dialog boxes and title bars should now display file extensions.

- The colors of the title bar in your screen may be a solid blue, and the cells in Excel may appear different from the orange and gray because of your color settings

- Depending on your Office settings, your toolbars may be displayed on a single row and your menus may display a shortened list of frequently used commands. Office menus and toolbars can modify themselves to your working style by displaying only the most frequently used buttons and menu commands. To view buttons not currently displayed, click a Toolbar Options button at the end of either the Standard or Formatting toolbar. To view the full list of menu commands, click the double arrow at the bottom of the menu.

Toolbars in one row

Toolbars in two rows

In order to have your toolbars displayed in two rows, showing all buttons, and to have the full menus displayed, you must turn off the personalized menus and toolbars feature. Click Tools on the menu bar, click Customize, select the show Standard and Formatting toolbars on two rows and Always show full menus check boxes on the Options tab, and then click Close. This book assumes you are displaying toolbars in two rows and displaying full menus.

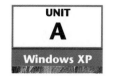

Getting Started with Windows XP

UNIT A — Windows XP

OBJECTIVES

Start Windows and view the desktop
Use the mouse
Start a program
Move and resize windows
Use menus, keyboard shortcuts, and toolbars
Use dialog boxes
Use scroll bars
Use Windows Help and Support Center
Close a program and shut down Windows

If you have a SAM user profile, you may have access to hands-on instruction, practice, and assessment of the skills covered in this unit. Log in to your SAM account and go to your assignments page to see what your instructor has assigned.

Microsoft Windows XP, or simply Windows, is an operating system. An **operating system** is a kind of computer program that controls how a computer carries out basic tasks such as displaying information on your computer screen and running other programs. Windows helps you save and organize the results of your work as **files**, which are electronic collections of data, with each collection having a unique name (called the **filename**). Windows also coordinates the flow of information among the programs, printers, storage devices, and other components of your computer system, as well as among other computers on a network. When you work with Windows, you use **icons**, small pictures intended to be meaningful symbols of the items they represent. You will also use rectangular-shaped work areas known as windows, thus the name of the operating system. This unit introduces you to basic skills that you can use in all Windows programs.

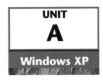

Starting Windows and Viewing the Desktop

When you turn on your computer, Windows XP automatically starts and the desktop appears (you may be prompted to select your user name and/or enter your password first). The desktop, shown in Figure A-1, is where you can organize all the information and tools you need to accomplish your computer tasks. On the desktop, you can access, store, share, and explore information seamlessly, whether it resides on your computer, a network, or on the **Internet**, a worldwide collection of over 40 million computers linked together to share information. When you start Windows for the first time, the desktop appears with the **default** settings, those preset by the operating system. For example, the default color of the desktop is blue. If any of the default settings have been changed on your computer, your desktop will look different from the one in the figures, but you should be able to locate the items you need. The bar at the bottom of the screen is the **taskbar**, which shows what programs are currently running. You click the **Start button** at the left end of the taskbar to perform such tasks as starting programs, finding and opening files, and accessing Windows Help. The **Quick Launch toolbar** often appears next to the Start button; it contains several buttons you can click to start Internet-related programs quickly, and another that you can click to show the desktop when it is not currently visible. Table A-1 identifies the icons and other elements you see on your desktop. If Windows XP is not currently running on your computer, follow the steps below to start it now.

STEPS

TROUBLE

If a Welcome to Microsoft Windows tour opens, move your mouse pointer over the Next button in the lower-right corner of the dialog box and click the left mouse button once; when you see the Do you want to activate Windows now? dialog box, click the No, remind me every few days option. See your instructor or technical support person for further assistance.

1. **Turn on your computer and monitor**

   When Windows starts, you may see an area where you can click your user name or a Log On to Windows dialog box. If so, continue to Step 2. If not, view Figure A-1, then continue on to the next lesson.

2. **Click the correct user name, if necessary, type your password, then press [Enter]**

   Once the password is accepted, the Windows desktop appears on your screen. See Figure A-1.

   If you don't know your password, see your instructor or technical support person.

Clues to Use

Accessing the Internet from the Desktop

Windows XP provides a seamless connection between your desktop and the Internet with Internet Explorer. Internet Explorer is an example of a **browser**, a program designed to access the **World Wide Web** (also known as the **WWW**, or simply the **Web**). Internet Explorer is included with the Windows XP operating system. You can access it on the Start menu or by clicking its icon if it appears on the desktop or on the Quick Launch toolbar. You can use it to access Web pages and to place Web content such as weather or stock updates on the desktop for instant viewing. This information is updated automatically whenever you connect to the Internet.

FIGURE A-1: Windows desktop

Icons (yours might be different)

My Documents

My Computer

My Network Places

Recycle Bin

Internet Explorer

My Briefcase

Outlook Express

Start button

Taskbar

Quick Launch toolbar

TABLE A-1: Elements of a typical Windows desktop

desktop element	icon	allows you to
My Computer		Work with different disk drives, folders, and files on your computer
My Documents folder		Store documents, graphics, video and sound clips, and other files
Internet Explorer		Start the Internet Explorer browser to access the Internet
Recycle Bin		Delete and restore files
My Network Places		Open files and folders on other computers and install network printers
My Briefcase		Synchronize files when you use two computers
Outlook Express		Send and receive e-mail and participate in newsgroups
Start button	start	Start programs, open documents, search for files, and more
Taskbar		Start programs and switch among open programs and files
Quick Launch toolbar		Display the desktop, start Internet Explorer, and start Outlook Express

Windows XP

Using the Mouse

A **mouse** is a handheld **input** or **pointing device** that you use to interact with your computer. Input or pointing devices come in many shapes and sizes; some, like a mouse, are directly attached to your computer with a cable; others function like a TV remote control and allow you to access your computer without being right next to it. Figure A-2 shows examples of common pointing devices. Because the most common pointing device is a mouse, this book uses that term. If you are using a different pointing device, substitute that device whenever you see the term "mouse." When you move the mouse, the **mouse pointer** on the screen moves in the same direction. You use the **mouse buttons** to select icons and commands, which is how you communicate with the computer. Table A-2 shows some common mouse pointer shapes that indicate different activities. Table A-3 lists the five basic mouse actions. Begin by experimenting with the mouse now.

STEPS

1. **Locate the mouse pointer on the desktop, then move the mouse across your desk or mouse pad**

   Watch how the mouse pointer moves on the desktop in response to your movements; practice moving the mouse pointer in circles, then back and forth in straight lines.

If the Recycle Bin window opens during this step, your mouse isn't set with the Windows XP default mouse settings. See your instructor or technical support person for assistance. This book assumes your computer is set to all Windows XP default settings.

2. **Position the mouse pointer over the** Recycle Bin icon

   Positioning the mouse pointer over an item is called **pointing**.

3. **With the pointer over the , press and release the** left mouse button

   Pressing and releasing the left mouse button is called **clicking** (or single-clicking, to distinguish it from double-clicking, which you'll do in Step 7). When you position the mouse pointer over an icon or any item and click, you select that item. When an item is **selected**, it is **highlighted** (shaded differently from other items), and the next action you take will be performed on that item.

4. **With selected, press and hold down the** left mouse button**, move the mouse down and to the right, then release the mouse button**

   The icon becomes dimmed and moves with the mouse pointer; this is called **dragging**, which you do to move icons and other Windows elements. When you release the mouse button, the item is positioned at the new location (it may "snap" to another location, depending on the settings on your computer).

5. **Position the mouse pointer over the , then press and release the** right mouse button

   Clicking the right mouse button is known as **right-clicking**. Right-clicking an item on the desktop produces a **shortcut menu**, as shown in Figure A-3. This menu lists the commands most commonly used for the item you have clicked. A **command** is a directive that provides access to a program's features.

6. **Click anywhere outside the menu to close the shortcut menu**

When a step tells you to "click," use the left mouse button. If it says "right-click," use the right mouse button.

7. **Position the mouse pointer over the , then quickly press and release the** left mouse button **twice**

   Clicking the mouse button twice quickly is known as **double-clicking**; in this case, double-clicking the Recycle Bin icon opens the Recycle Bin window, which displays files that you have deleted.

8. **Click the** Close button **in the upper-right corner of the Recycle Bin window**

WINDOWS XP A-4 GETTING STARTED WITH WINDOWS XP

OFFICE–4

FIGURE A-2: Common pointing devices

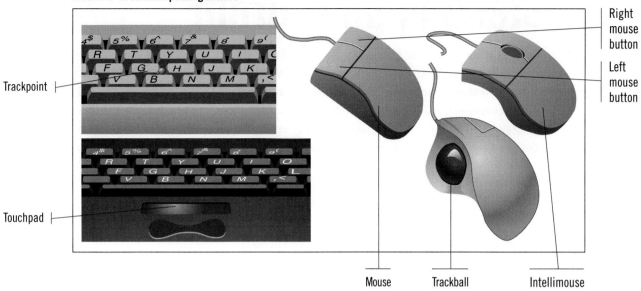

Trackpoint

Touchpad

Right mouse button

Left mouse button

Mouse   Trackball   Intellimouse

FIGURE A-3: Displaying a shortcut menu

Selected icon

Pointer positioned over icon

Shortcut menu

Open
Explore
Empty Recycle Bin
Create Shortcut
Properties

TABLE A-2: Common mouse pointer shapes

shape	used to
⩘	Select items, choose commands, start programs, and work in programs
I	Position mouse pointer for editing or inserting text; called the insertion point or Text Select pointer
⧗	Indicate Windows is busy processing a command
↔	Change the size of a window; appears when mouse pointer is on the border of a window
⇧	Select and open Web-based data and other links

TABLE A-3: Basic mouse techniques

technique	what to do
Pointing	Move the mouse to position the mouse pointer over an item on the desktop
Clicking	Press and release the left mouse button
Double-clicking	Press and release the left mouse button twice quickly
Dragging	Point to an item, press and hold the left mouse button, move the mouse to a new location, then release the mouse button
Right-clicking	Point to an item, then press and release the right mouse button

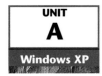

Starting a Program

Clicking the Start button on the taskbar opens the **Start menu**, which lists submenus for a variety of tasks described in Table A-4. As you become familiar with Windows, you might want to customize the Start menu to include additional items that you use most often. Windows XP comes with several built-in programs, called **accessories**. Although not as feature-rich as many programs sold separately, Windows accessories are useful for completing basic tasks. In this lesson, you start a Windows accessory called **WordPad**, which is a word-processing program you can use to create and edit simple documents.

STEPS

1. **Click the** Start button **on the taskbar**

   The Start menu opens.

2. **Point to** All Programs

   The All Programs submenu opens, listing the programs and categories for programs installed on your computer. WordPad is in the category called Accessories.

3. **Point to** Accessories

   > **QUICK TIP**
   > The left side of the Windows XP Start menu lists programs you've used recently, so the next time you want to open WordPad, most likely it will be handy in this list of recently opened programs.

   The Accessories menu, shown in Figure A-4, contains several programs to help you complete common tasks. You want to start WordPad.

4. **Click** WordPad

   WordPad starts and opens a blank document window, as shown in Figure A-5. Don't worry if your window does not fill the screen; you'll learn how to maximize it in the next lesson. Note that a program button appears on the taskbar and is highlighted, indicating that WordPad is open.

TABLE A-4: Start menu categories

category	description
Default	Displays the name of the current user; different users can customize the Start menu to fit their work habits
Internet Explorer / Outlook Express	The two programs many people use for a browser and e-mail program; you can add programs you use often to this list (called the "pinned items list")
Frequently used programs list	Located below Internet Explorer and Outlook Express, contains the last six programs used on your computer; you can change the number listed
All Programs	Displays a menu of most programs installed on your computer
My Documents, etc.	The five items in this list allow you to quickly access files you've saved in the three folders listed (My Documents, My Pictures, and My Music), as well as access My Computer, which you use to manage files, folders, and drives on your computer; the My Recent Documents list contains the last 15 files that have been opened on your computer
Control Panel / Connect To / Printers and Faxes	Control Panel displays tools for selecting settings on your computer; Connect To lists Internet connections that have been set up on your computer; and Printers and Faxes lists the printers and faxes connected to your computer
Help and Support / Search / Run	Help and Support provides access to Help topics and other support services; Search locates files, folders, computers on your network, and Web pages on the Internet; Run opens a program, file, or Web site by letting you type commands or names in a dialog box
Log Off / Turn Off Computer	End your Windows session; used when you are done using the computer and don't expect to use it again soon

FIGURE A-4: Cascading menus

Arrow indicates submenu

Click to open WordPad

Submenu

FIGURE A-5: WordPad program window

Document window

Program button indicates open program

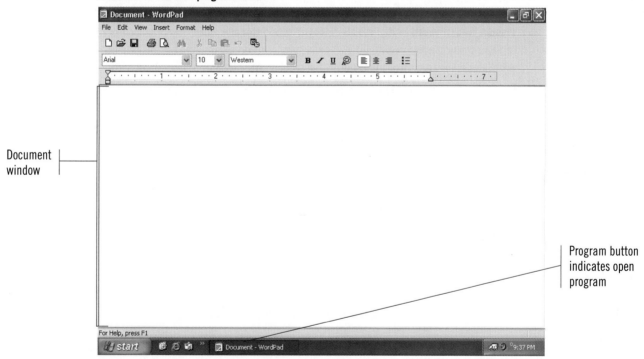

Clues to Use

Customizing the Start Menu

With Windows XP, you can change the way the Start menu looks and behaves by opening the Control Panel (click the Start button and then click Control Panel), switching to Classic view, if necessary, then double-clicking Taskbar and Start Menu. To get the look and feel of the classic Start menu from earlier versions of Windows, click the Start Menu tab and then click the Classic Start menu option button. You can then click the Customize button to add shortcuts to the Start menu for desired programs and documents, or change the order in which they appear. To preserve the Windows XP look of the Start menu but modify how it behaves, click the Customize button next to the Start menu and select the options you want.

Moving and Resizing Windows

One of the powerful features of Windows is the ability to open more than one window or program at once. This means, however, that the desktop can get cluttered with the various programs and files you are using. You can keep your desktop organized by changing the size of a window or moving it. You can do this by clicking the sizing buttons in the upper-right corner of any window or by dragging a corner or border of any window that does not completely fill the screen. Practice sizing and moving the WordPad window now.

1. **If the WordPad window does not already fill the screen, click the** Maximize button ☐ **in the WordPad window**

   When a window is **maximized**, it takes up the whole screen.

2. **Click the** Restore button ☐ **in the WordPad window**

   To **restore** a window is to return it to its previous size, as shown in Figure A-6. The Restore button only appears when a window is maximized.

3. **Position the pointer on the right edge of the WordPad window until the pointer changes to ↔, then drag the border to the right**

   The width of the window increases. You can change the height or width of a window by dragging any of the four sides.

> **QUICK TIP**
>
> You can resize windows by dragging any corner. You can also drag any border to make the window taller, shorter, wider, or narrower.

4. **Position the pointer in the lower-right corner of the WordPad window until the pointer changes to ↘, as shown in Figure A-6, then drag down and to the right**

   The height and width of the window increase proportionally when you drag a corner instead of a side. You can also position a restored window wherever you want on the desktop by dragging its title bar. The **title bar** is the area along the top of the window that displays the filename and program used to create it.

5. **Drag the** title bar **on the WordPad window up and to the left, as shown in Figure A-6**

   The window is repositioned on the desktop. At times, you might want to close a program window, yet keep the program running and easily accessible. You can accomplish this by minimizing a window.

> **QUICK TIP**
>
> If you have more than one window open and you want to quickly access something on the desktop, you can click the Show Desktop button ☐ on the Quick Launch toolbar. All open windows are minimized so the desktop is visible. If your Quick Launch toolbar isn't visible, right-click the taskbar, point to Toolbars, and then click Quick Launch.

6. **In the WordPad window, click the** Minimize button ☐

   When you **minimize** a window, it shrinks to a program button on the taskbar, as shown in Figure A-7. WordPad is still running, but it is out of your way.

7. **Click the** WordPad program button **on the taskbar to reopen the window**

   The WordPad program window reopens.

8. **Click the** Maximize button ☐ **in the upper-right corner of the WordPad window**

   The window fills the screen.

FIGURE A-6: Restored program window

Title bar ⊢

Sizing buttons

Drag to resize height and width proportionally

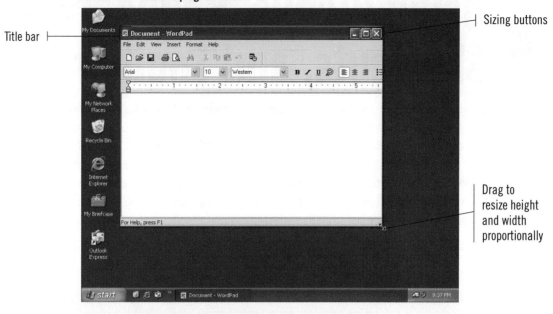

FIGURE A-7: Minimized program window

Indicates program is running but not in use

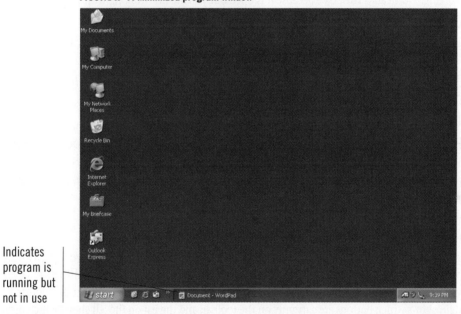

Clues to Use

More about sizing windows

Keep in mind that some programs contain two sets of sizing buttons: one that controls the program window itself and another that controls the window for the file with which you are working. The program sizing buttons are located in the title bar and the file sizing buttons are located below them. See Figure A-8. When you minimize a file window within a program, the file window is reduced to an icon in the lower-left corner of the program window, but the size of the program window remains intact. (*Note:* WordPad does not use a second set of window sizing buttons.)

Also, to see the contents of more than one window at a time, you can open the desired windows, right-click a blank area on the taskbar, and then click either Tile Windows Vertically or Tile Windows

Horizontally. With the former, you see the windows side by side, and with the latter, the windows are stacked one above the other. You can also click Cascade Windows to layer any open windows in the upper-left corner of the desktop, with the title bar of each clearly visible.

FIGURE A-8: Program and file sizing buttons

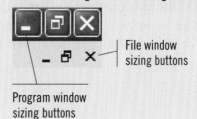

File window sizing buttons

Program window sizing buttons

Using Menus, Keyboard Shortcuts, and Toolbars

A **menu** is a list of commands that you use to accomplish certain tasks. Each Windows program also has its own set of menus, which are located on the **menu bar** under the title bar. The menus organize commands into groups of related tasks. See Table A-5 for a description of items on a typical menu. **Toolbar buttons** offer another method for executing menu commands; instead of clicking the menu and then the menu command, you click the button for the command. A **toolbar** is a set of buttons usually positioned below the menu bar. 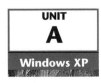 You will open My Computer, use a menu and toolbar button to change how the contents of the window appear, and then add and remove a toolbar button.

If you don't see the My Computer icon on your desktop, right-click the desktop, click Properties, click the Desktop tab, click the Customize Desktop button, click the My Computer check box, then click OK twice.

1. **Minimize WordPad, if necessary, then double-click the** My Computer icon 🖳 **on the desktop**

   The My Computer window opens. You now have two windows open: WordPad and My Computer. My Computer is the **active window** (or active program) because it is the one with which you are currently working. WordPad is **inactive** because it is open but you are not working with it.

2. **Click** View **on the menu bar**

   The View menu appears, listing the View commands, as shown in Figure A-9. On a menu, a **check mark** identifies a feature that is currently enabled or "on." To disable or turn "off" the feature, you click the command again to remove the check mark. A **bullet mark** can also indicate that an option is enabled.

3. **Click** List

   The icons are now listed one after the other rather than as larger icons.

[Alt][V] means that you should press and hold down the Alt key, press the V key, and then release both simultaneously.

4. **Press** [Alt][V] **to open the View menu, then press** [T] **to open the Toolbars submenu**

   The View menu appears again, and then the Toolbars submenu appears, with check marks next to the selected commands. Notice that a letter in each command on the View menu is underlined. These are **keyboard navigation indicators**, indicating that you can press the underlined letter, known as a **keyboard shortcut**, instead of clicking to execute the command.

5. **Press** [C] **to execute the Customize command**

   The Customize Toolbar dialog box opens. A **dialog box** is a window in which you specify how you want to perform a task; you'll learn more about working in a dialog box shortly. In the Customize Toolbar dialog box, you can add toolbar buttons to the current toolbar, or remove buttons already on the toolbar. The list on the right shows which buttons are currently on the toolbar, and the list on the left shows which buttons are available to add.

6. **Click the** Home button **in the Available toolbar buttons section, then click the** Add button **(located between the two lists)**

   As shown in Figure A-10, the Home button is added to the Standard toolbar.

7. **Click the** Home button **in the Current toolbar buttons section, click the** Remove button, **then click** Close **on the Customize Toolbar dialog box**

   The Home button disappears from the Standard toolbar, and the Customize Toolbar dialog box closes.

When you rest the pointer over a button without clicking, a ScreenTip often appears with the button's name.

8. **On the My Computer toolbar, click the** Views button list arrow 🖳 ▾, **then click** Details

   Some toolbar buttons have an arrow, which indicates the button contains several choices. Clicking the button shows the choices. The Details view includes a description of each item in the My Computer window.

FIGURE A-9: Opening a menu

Menu bar

Check mark

Bullet

Commands
in View
menu

Arrow
indicates
submenu

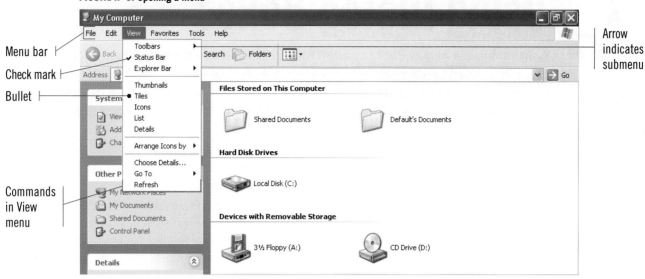

FIGURE A-10: Customize Toolbar dialog box

Buttons
you can
add to the
toolbar

Home
button is
added to
toolbar

Click to
move
selected
button to
toolbar

Home
button
listed here,
indicating
it is
currently
on the
toolbar

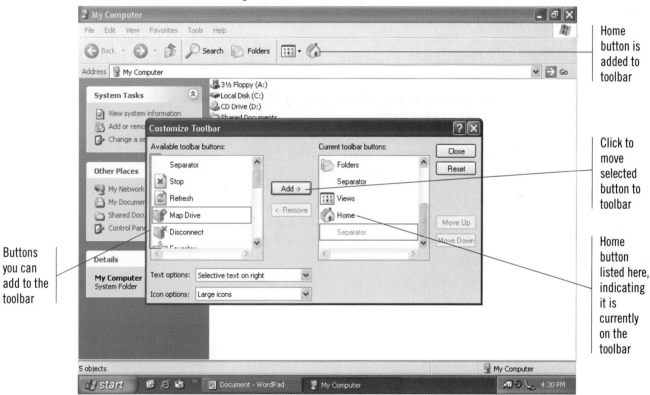

TABLE A-5: Typical items on a menu

item	description	example
Dimmed command	Indicates the menu command is not currently available	Recent File
Ellipsis	Indicates that a dialog box will open that allows you to select additional options	Save As...
Triangle	Opens a cascading menu containing an additional list of commands	Toolbars ▶
Keyboard shortcut	Executes a command using the keyboard instead of the mouse	Print... Ctrl+P
Underlined letter	Indicates the letter to press for the keyboard shortcut	Exit

UNIT
A
Windows XP

Using Dialog Boxes

A **dialog box** is a window that opens when you choose a menu command that needs more information before the program can carry out the command you selected. Dialog boxes open in other situations as well, such as when you open a program in the Control Panel. See Figure A-11 and Table A-6 for some of the typical elements of a dialog box. ░░░░ Practice using a dialog box to control your mouse settings.

STEPS

TROUBLE

If you don't see Printers and Other Hardware in the Control Panel window, you are using Classic view, not the default Category view. In the left pane, click Switch to Category view.

1. **In the left side of the My Computer window, click** Control Panel**; in the Control Panel window, click** Printers and Other Hardware**, then click the** Mouse icon 🖱

   The Mouse Properties dialog box opens, as shown in Figure A-12. **Properties** are characteristics of a computer element (in this case, the mouse) that you can customize. The options in this dialog box allow you to control the way the mouse buttons are configured, select the types of pointers that appear, choose the speed and behavior of the mouse movement on the screen, and specify what type of mouse you are using. **Tabs** at the top of the dialog box separate these options into related categories.

2. **Click the** Pointer Options tab **if necessary to make it the frontmost tab**

   This tab contains three options for controlling the way your mouse moves. Under Motion, you can set how fast the pointer moves on the screen in relation to how you move the mouse. You drag a **slider** to specify how fast the pointer moves. Under Snap To is a **check box**, which is a toggle for turning a feature on or off—in this case, for setting whether you want your mouse pointer to move to the default button in dialog boxes. Under Visibility, you can choose three options for easily finding your cursor and keeping it out of the way when you're typing.

3. **Under Motion, drag the** slider **all the way to the left for Slow, then move the mouse pointer across your screen**

   Notice how slowly the mouse pointer moves. After you select the options you want in a dialog box, you need to click a **command button**, which carries out the options you've selected. The two most common command buttons are OK and Cancel. Clicking OK accepts your changes and closes the dialog box; clicking Cancel leaves the original settings intact and closes the dialog box. The third command button in this dialog box is Apply. Clicking the Apply button accepts the changes you've made and keeps the dialog box open so that you can select additional options. Because you might share this computer with others, you should close the dialog box without making any permanent changes.

QUICK TIP

You can also use the keyboard to carry out commands in a dialog box. Pressing [Enter] is the same as clicking OK; pressing [Esc] is the same as clicking Cancel.

4. **Click** Cancel

   The original settings remain intact, the dialog box closes, and you return to the Printers and Other Hardware window.

FIGURE A-11: Elements of a typical dialog box

Text box ⊢

Option buttons ⊢

Command button ⊢

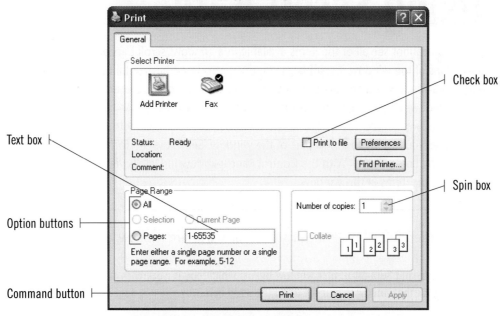

Check box

Spin box

FIGURE A-12: Mouse Properties dialog box

Tabs ⊢

Slider ⊢

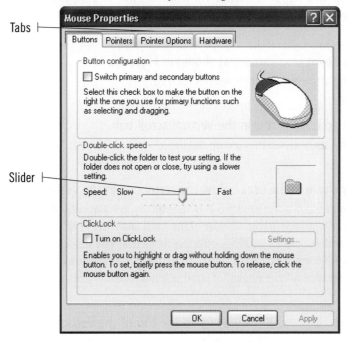

TABLE A-6: Typical items in a dialog box

item	description
Tab	A place in a dialog box that organizes related commands and options
Check box	A box that turns an option on (when the box is checked) and off (when it is unchecked)
Command button	A rectangular button with the name of the command on it
List box	A box containing a list of items; to choose an item, click the list arrow, then click the desired item
Option button	A small circle that you click to select a single dialog box option; you cannot select more than one option button in a list
Text box	A box in which you type text
Slider	A shape that you drag to set the degree to which an option is in effect
Spin box	A box with two arrows and a text box; allows you to scroll in numerical increments or type a number

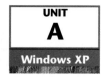

Using Scroll Bars

When you cannot see all of the items available in a window, scroll bars appear on the right and/or bottom edges of the window. **Scroll bars** are the vertical and horizontal bars along the right and bottom edges of a window and contain elements that you click and drag so you can view the additional contents of the window. When you need to scroll only a short distance, you can use the scroll arrows. To scroll the window in larger increments, click in the scroll bar above or below the scroll box. Dragging the scroll box moves you quickly to a new part of the window. See Table A-7 for a summary of the different ways to use scroll bars. ▅▅▅▅ With the Control Panel window in Details view, you can use the scroll bars to view all of the items in this window.

STEPS

> **TROUBLE**
> Your window might
> be called Printers
> and Faxes or some-
> thing similar, and
> the Printing link
> may appear as
> Troubleshoot print-
> ing, but you should
> still be able to com-
> plete the steps.

1. **In the left side of the Printers and Other Hardware window, under Troubleshooters, click Printing**

   The Help and Support Center window opens, which you'll work with further in the next lesson. For now, you'll use the window to practice using the scroll bars.

2. **If the Help and Support Center window fills the screen, click the Restore button 🗗 in the upper-right corner so the scroll bars appear, as shown in Figure A-13**

> **TROUBLE**
> If you don't see scroll
> bars, drag the lower-
> right corner of the
> Help and Support
> Center window up
> and to the left until
> scroll bars appear.

3. **Click the down scroll arrow, as shown in Figure A-13**

   Clicking this arrow moves the view down one line.

4. **Click the up scroll arrow in the vertical scroll bar**

   Clicking this arrow moves the view up one line.

5. **Click anywhere in the area below the scroll box in the vertical scroll bar**

   The view moves down one window's height. Similarly, you can click in the scroll bar above the scroll box to move up one window's height. The size of the scroll box changes to reflect how much information does not fit in the window. A larger scroll box indicates that a relatively small amount of the window's contents is not currently visible; you need to scroll only a short distance to see the remaining items. A smaller scroll box indicates that a relatively large amount of information is currently not visible.

6. **Drag the scroll box all the way up to the top of the vertical scroll bar**

   This view shows the items that appear at the top of the window.

7. **In the horizontal scroll bar, click the area to the right of the scroll box**

   The far right edge of the window comes into view. The horizontal scroll bar works the same as the vertical scroll bar.

8. **Click the area to the left of the scroll box in the horizontal scroll bar**

9. **Click the Close button ⊠ to close the Help and Support Center window**

   You'll reopen the Help and Support Center window from the Start menu in the next lesson.

FIGURE A-13: Scroll bars

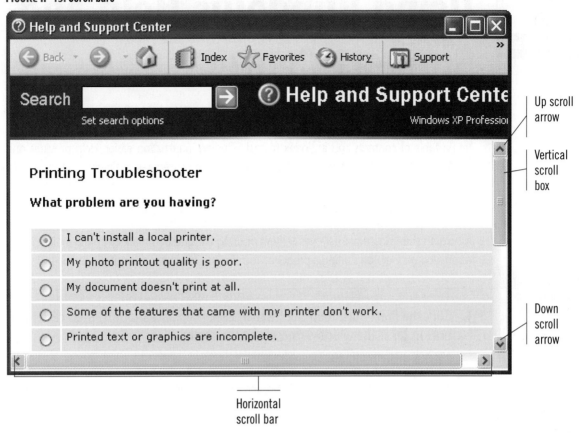

- Up scroll arrow
- Vertical scroll box
- Down scroll arrow

Horizontal scroll bar

TABLE A-7: Using scroll bars

to	do this
Move down one line	Click the down arrow at the bottom of the vertical scroll bar
Move up one line	Click the up arrow at the top of the vertical scroll bar
Move down one window height	Click in the area below the scroll box in the vertical scroll bar
Move up one window height	Click in the area above the scroll box in the vertical scroll bar
Move up a large distance in the window	Drag the scroll box up in the vertical scroll bar
Move down a large distance in the window	Drag the scroll box down in the vertical scroll bar
Move a short distance side-to-side in a window	Click the left or right arrows in the horizontal scroll bar
Move to the right one window width	Click in the area to the right of the scroll box in the horizontal scroll bar
Move to the left one window width	Click in the area to the left of the scroll box in the horizontal scroll bar
Move left or right a large distance in the window	Drag the scroll box in the horizontal scroll bar

Using Windows Help and Support Center

When you have a question about how to do something in Windows XP, you can usually find the answer with a few clicks of your mouse. The Windows Help and Support Center works like a book stored on your computer, with a table of contents and an index to make finding information easier. Help provides guidance on many Windows features, including detailed steps for completing procedures, definitions of terms, lists of related topics, and search capabilities. You can browse or search for information in the Help and Support Center window, or you can connect to a Microsoft Web site on the Internet for the latest technical support on Windows XP. You can also access **context-sensitive help**, help specifically related to what you are doing, using a variety of methods such as holding your mouse pointer over an item or using the question mark button in a dialog box. In this lesson, you get Help on starting a program. You also get information about the taskbar.

STEPS

1. **Click the Start button on the taskbar, click Help and Support, then click the Maximize button if the window doesn't fill the screen**

   The Help and Support Center window opens, as shown in Figure A-14. This window has a toolbar at the top of the window, a Search box below where you enter keywords having to do with your question, a left pane where the items matching your keywords are listed, and a right pane where the specific steps for a given item are listed.

2. **Click in the Search text box, type start a program, press [Enter], then view the Help topics displayed in the left pane**

   The left pane contains a selection of topics related to starting a program. The Suggested Topics are the most likely matches for your search text.

   > **QUICK TIP**
   > Scroll down the left pane, if necessary, to view all the topics. You can also click Full-text Search Matches to view more topics containing the search text you typed or Microsoft Knowledge Base for relevant articles from the Microsoft Web site.

3. **Click Start a program**

   Help information for this topic appears in the right pane, as shown in Figure A-15. At the bottom of the text in the right pane, you can click Related Topics to view a list of topics that are related to the current topic. Some Help topics also allow you to view additional information about important words; these words are underlined, indicating that you can click them to display a pop-up window with the additional information.

4. **Click the underlined word taskbar, read the definition, then click anywhere outside the pop-up window to close it**

5. **On the toolbar at the top of the window, click the Index button**

   The Index provides an alphabetical list of all the available Help topics, like an index at the end of a book. You can type a topic in the text box at the top of the pane. You can also scroll down to the topic. In either case, you click the topic you're interested in and the details about that topic appear in the right pane.

   > **QUICK TIP**
   > You can click the Favorites button to view a list of Help pages that you've saved as you search for answers to your questions. You can click the History button to view a list of Help pages that you've viewed during the current Help session.

6. **In the left pane, type tiling windows**

   As you type, the list of topics automatically scrolls to try to match the word or phrase you type.

7. **Double-click tiling windows in the list in the left pane and read the steps and notes in the right pane**

   You can also click the Related Topics link for more information.

8. **Click the Support button on the toolbar**

   Information on the Web sites for Windows XP Help appears in the right pane (a **Web site** is a document or related documents that contain highlighted words, phrases, and graphics that link to other sites on the Internet). To access online support or information, you would click one of the available options in the left pane.

9. **Click the Close button in the upper-right corner of the Help and Support Center window**

   The Help and Support Center window closes.

FIGURE A-14: Windows Help and Support Center

Help toolbar

Type keyword
or phrase
to search
for topics

Links for
popular
Help topics

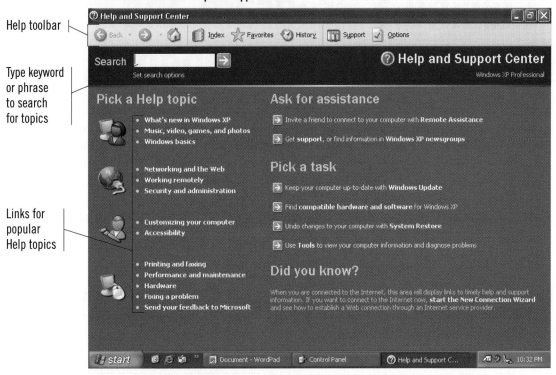

FIGURE A-15: Viewing a Help topic

Type search
text here

Left pane
contains
list of
Help topics
matching
your search
text

Click this
topic

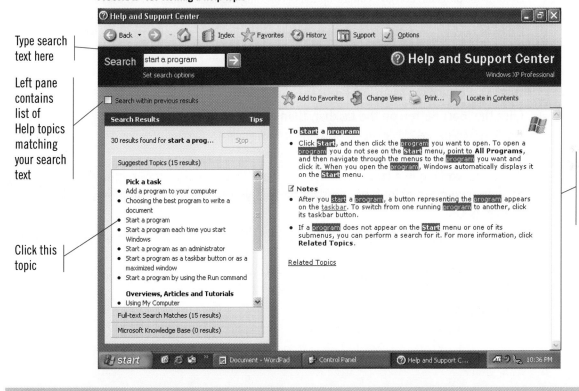

Right pane
contains
information
on the topic
you select

Clues to Use

Other forms of Help

The Help and Support Center offers information on Windows itself, not on all the other programs you can run on your computer. To get help on a specific Windows program, click Help on that program's menu bar. Also, to receive help in a dialog box (whether you are in Windows or another program), click the Help button ? in the upper-right corner of the dialog box; the mouse pointer changes to ⌖?. Click any item in the dialog box that you want to learn more about. If information is available on that item, a pop-up window appears with a brief explanation of the selected feature.

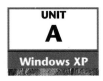

Closing a Program and Shutting Down Windows

When you are finished working on your computer, you need to make sure you shut it down properly. This involves several steps: saving and closing all open files, closing all the open programs and windows, shutting down Windows, and finally, turning off the computer. If you turn off the computer while Windows is running, you could lose important data. To **close** a program, you can click the Close button in the window's upper-right corner or click File on the menu bar and choose either Close or Exit. To shut down Windows after all your files and programs are closed, click Turn Off Computer on the Start menu, then select the desired option in the Turn off computer dialog box, shown in Figure A-16. See Table A-8 for a description of shut down options. ▃▃▃▃ Close all your open files, windows, and programs, then exit Windows.

STEPS

1. **In the Control Panel window, click the** Close button ☒ **in the upper-right corner of the window**

   The Control Panel window closes.

2. **Click** File **on the WordPad menu bar, then click** Exit

   If you have made any changes to the open file, you will be asked to save your changes before the program closes. Some programs also give you the option of choosing the Close command on the File menu in order to close the active file but leave the program open, so you can continue to work in it with a different file. Also, if there is a second set of sizing buttons in the window, the Close button on the menu bar will close the active file only, leaving the program open for continued use.

3. **If you see a message asking you to save changes to the document, click** No

   WordPad closes and you return to the desktop.

QUICK TIP

Complete the remaining steps to shut down Windows and your computer only if you have been told to do so by your instructor or technical support person. If you have been told to Log Off instead of exiting Windows, click Log Off instead of Turn Off Computer, and follow the directions from your instructor or technical support person.

4. **Click the** Start button **on the taskbar, then click** Turn Off Computer

   The Turn off computer dialog box opens, as shown in Figure A-16. In this dialog box, you have the option to stand by, turn off the computer, or restart the computer.

5. **If you are working in a lab, click** Cancel **to leave the computer running; if you are working on your own machine or if your instructor told you to shut down Windows, click** Turn Off, **then click** OK

6. **If you see the message "It is now safe to turn off your computer," turn off your computer and monitor**

   On some computers, the power shuts off automatically, so you may not see this message.

FIGURE A-16: Turn off computer dialog box

Click to leave
Windows
running but
reduce
computer's
power mode

Click to exit
Windows
safely and
turn off your
computer

Click to exit
Windows and
automatically
restart it

Click to return
to the desktop
without taking
any action

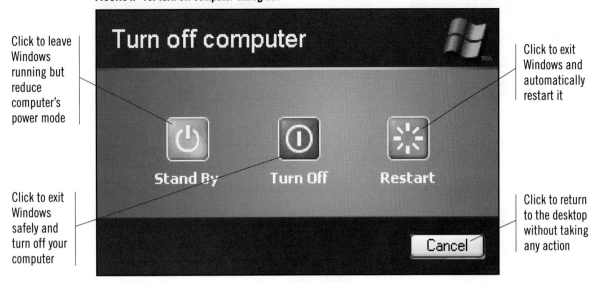

Clues to Use

The Log Off command

To change users on the same computer quickly, you can choose the Log Off command from the Start menu. When you click this command, you can choose to switch users, so that the current user is logged off and another user can log on, or you can simply log off.

Windows XP shuts down partially, stopping at the point where you click your user name. When you or a new user clicks a user name (and enters a password, if necessary), Windows restarts and the desktop appears as usual.

TABLE A-8: Turn off options

Turn off option	function	when to use it
Stand By	Leaves Windows running but on minimal power	When you are finished working with Windows for a short time and plan to return before the end of the day
Turn Off	Exits Windows completely and safely	When you are finished working with Windows and want to shut off your computer for an extended time (such as overnight or longer)
Restart	Exits Windows safely, turns off the computer automatically, and then restarts the computer and Windows	When your programs might have frozen or stopped working correctly

Practice

▼ CONCEPTS REVIEW

Identify each of the items labeled in Figure A-17.

FIGURE A-17

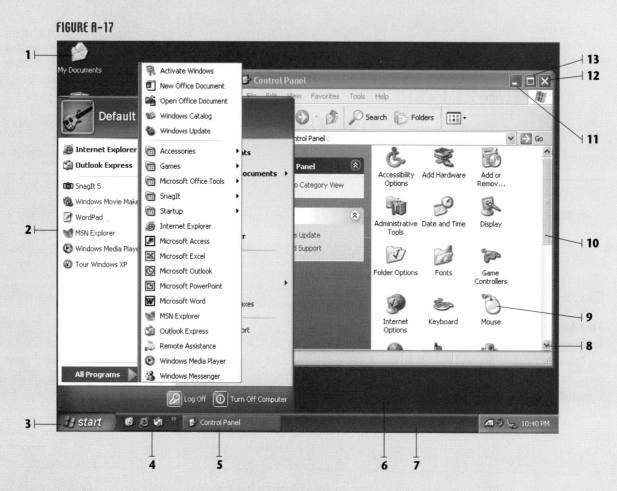

Match each of the statements with the term it describes.

14. Shrinks a window to a button on the taskbar
15. Shows the name of the window or program
16. The taskbar item you first click to start a program
17. Requests more information for you to supply before carrying out command
18. Shows the Start button, Quick Launch toolbar, and any currently open programs
19. An input device that lets you point to and make selections
20. Graphic representation of program

a. dialog box
b. program button
c. taskbar
d. Minimize button
e. icon
f. mouse
g. Start button

Select the best answer from the list of choices.

21. The term "file" is best defined as
- **a.** a set of instructions for a computer to carry out a task.
- **b.** an electronic collection of data.
- **c.** a collection of icons.
- **d.** an international collection of computers.

22. Which of the following is NOT provided by Windows XP?
- **a.** The ability to organize files
- **b.** Instructions to coordinate the flow of information among the programs, files, printers, storage devices, and other components of your computer system
- **c.** Programs that allow you to specify the operation of the mouse
- **d.** Spell checker for your documents

23. All of the following are examples of using a mouse, EXCEPT
- **a.** clicking the Maximize button.
- **b.** pressing [Enter].
- **c.** double-clicking to start a program.
- **d.** dragging the My Computer icon.

24. The term for moving an item to a new location on the desktop is
- **a.** pointing.
- **b.** clicking.
- **c.** dragging.
- **d.** restoring.

25. The Maximize button is used to
- **a.** return a window to its previous size.
- **b.** expand a window to fill the computer screen.
- **c.** scroll slowly through a window.
- **d.** run programs from the Start menu.

26. What appears if a window contains more information than can be viewed in the window?
- **a.** Program icon
- **b.** Cascading menu
- **c.** Scroll bars
- **d.** Check boxes

27. A window is active when
- **a.** you can only see its program button on the taskbar.
- **b.** its title bar is dimmed.
- **c.** it is open and you are currently using it.
- **d.** it is listed in the Programs submenu.

28. You can exit Windows by
- **a.** double-clicking the Control Panel application.
- **b.** double-clicking the Program Manager control menu box.
- **c.** clicking File, then clicking Exit.
- **d.** selecting the Turn Off Computer command from the Start menu.

▼ SKILLS REVIEW

1. Start Windows and view the desktop.
- **a.** Turn on the computer, select your user name, then enter a password, if necessary.
- **b.** After Windows starts, identify as many items on the desktop as you can, without referring to the lesson material.
- **c.** Compare your results to Figure A-1.

2. Use the mouse.
- **a.** Double-click the Recycle Bin icon, then click the Restore button if the window fills the screen.
- **b.** Drag the Recycle Bin window to the upper-right corner of the desktop.
- **c.** Right-click the title bar of the Recycle Bin, then click Close.

3. Start a program.
- **a.** Click the Start button on the taskbar, then point to All Programs.
- **b.** Point to Accessories, then click Calculator.
- **c.** Minimize the Calculator window.

4. Move and resize windows.
- **a.** Drag the Recycle Bin icon to the top of the desktop.
- **b.** Double-click the My Computer icon to open the My Computer window (if you don't see the My Computer icon, read the Trouble in the lesson on menus and toolbars for how to display it).
- **c.** Maximize the My Computer window, if it is not already maximized.

    d. Restore the window to its previous size.

    e. Resize the window until you see the vertical scroll bar.

    f. Minimize the My Computer window.

    g. Drag the Recycle Bin icon back to its original position.

5. Use menus, keyboard shortcuts, and toolbars.

    a. Click the Start button on the taskbar, then click Control Panel.

    b. Click View on the menu bar, point to Toolbars, then click Standard Buttons to deselect the option and hide the toolbar.

    c. Redisplay the toolbar.

    d. Press [Alt][V] to display the View menu, then press [B] to hide the status bar at the bottom of the window.

    e. Note the change, then use keyboard shortcuts to change the view back.

    f. Click the Up button to view My Computer.

    g. Click the Back button to return to the Control Panel.

    h. Click View, point to Toolbars, then click Customize.

    i. Add a button to the toolbar, remove it, then close the Customize Toolbar dialog box.

6. Use dialog boxes.

    a. With the Control Panel in Category view, click Appearance and Themes, click Display, then click the Screen Saver tab.

    b. Click the Screen saver list arrow, click any screen saver in the list, then view it in the preview monitor above the list.

    c. Click the Appearance tab in the Display Properties dialog box, then click the Effects button.

    d. In the Effects dialog box, click the Use large icons check box to select it, click the OK button to close the Effects dialog box, then click OK to close the Display Properties dialog box.

    e. Note the change in the icons on the desktop, minimizing windows if necessary.

    f. Right-click a blank area on the desktop, click Properties on the shortcut menu, click the Appearance tab, click the Effects button, click the Use large icons check box to deselect it, click OK, click the Screen Saver tab, return the screen saver to its original setting, then click Apply.

    g. Click the OK button in the Display Properties dialog box, but leave the Control Panel open and make it the active program.

7. Use scroll bars.

    a. In the left side of the Control Panel window, click Switch to Classic View, if necessary, click the Views button on the toolbar, then click Details.

    b. Drag the vertical scroll box down all the way.

    c. Click anywhere in the area above the vertical scroll box.

    d. Click the down scroll arrow until the scroll box is back at the bottom of the scroll bar.

    e. Click the right scroll arrow twice.

    f. Click in the area to the right of the horizontal scroll box.

    g. Drag the horizontal scroll box all the way back to the left.

8. Get Help.

    a. Click the Start button on the taskbar, then click Help and Support.

    b. Click Windows basics under Pick a Help topic, then click Tips for using Help in the left pane.

    c. In the right pane, click Add a Help topic or page to the Help and Support Center Favorites list.

    d. Read the topic contents, click Related Topics, click Print a Help topic or page, then read the contents. Leave the Help and Support Center open.

9. Close a program and shut down Windows.

    a. Click the Close button to close the Help and Support Center window.

    b. Click File on the menu bar, then click Close to close the Control Panel window.

    c. Click the Calculator program button on the taskbar to restore the window.

    d. Click the Close button in the Calculator window to close the Calculator program.

    e. If you are instructed to do so, shut down Windows and turn off your computer.

▼ INDEPENDENT CHALLENGE 1

You can use the Help and Support Center to learn more about Windows XP and explore Help on the Internet.

a. Open the Help and Support Center window and locate help topics on adjusting the double-click speed of your mouse and displaying Web content on your desktop.
If you have a printer, print a Help topic for each subject. Otherwise, write a summary of each topic.

b. Follow these steps below to access help on the Internet. If you don't have Internet access, you can't do this step.

i. Click a link under "Did you know?" in the right pane of the Help and Support Home page.

ii. In the left pane of the Microsoft Web page, click Using Windows XP, click How-to Articles, then click any link.

iii. Read the article, then write a summary of what you find.

iv. Click the browser's Close button, disconnect from the Internet, and close Help and Support Center.

▼ INDEPENDENT CHALLENGE 2

You can change the format and the actual time of the clock and date on your computer.

a. Open the Control Panel window; in Category view, click Date, Time, Language, and Regional Options; click Regional and Language Options; then click the Customize button under Standards and formats.

b. Click the Time tab, click the Time format list arrow, click H:mm:ss to change the time to show a 24-hour clock, then click the Apply button to view the changes, if any.

c. Click the Date tab, click the Short date format list arrow, click dd-MMM-yy, then click the Apply button.

d. Click the Cancel button twice to close the open dialog boxes.

e. Change the time to one hour later using the Date and Time icon in the Control Panel.

f. Return the settings to the original time and format, then close all open windows.

▼ INDEPENDENT CHALLENGE 3

Calculator is a Windows accessory that you can use to perform calculations.

a. Start the Calculator, click Help on the menu bar, then click Help Topics.

b. Click the Calculator book in the left pane, click Perform a simple calculation to view that help topic, then print it if you have a printer connected.

c. Open the Perform a scientific calculation topic, then view the definition of a number system.

d. Determine how many months you have to work to earn an additional week of vacation if you work for a company that provides one additional day of paid vacation for every 560 hours you work. (*Hint:* Divide 560 by the number of hours you work per month.)

e. Close all open windows.

▼ INDEPENDENT CHALLENGE 4

You can customize many Windows features, including the appearance of the taskbar on the desktop.

a. Right-click the taskbar, then click Lock the Taskbar to uncheck the command, if necessary.

b. Position the pointer over the top border of the taskbar. When the pointer changes shape, drag up an inch.

c. Resize the taskbar back to its original size.

d. Right-click the Start button, then click Properties. Click the Taskbar tab.

e. Click the Help button (a question mark), then click each check box to view the pop-up window describing it.

f. Click the Start Menu tab, then click the Classic Start menu option button and view the change in the preview. (*Note:* Do not click OK.) Click Cancel.

▼ VISUAL WORKSHOP

Use the skills you have learned in this unit to customize your desktop so it looks like the one in Figure A-18. Make sure you include the following:

- Calculator program minimized
- Vertical scroll bar in Control Panel window
- Large icons view in Control Panel window
- Rearranged icons on desktop; your icons may be different. (*Hint*: If the icons snap back to where they were, they are set to be automatically arranged. Right-click a blank area of the desktop, point to Arrange Icons By, then click Auto Arrange to deselect this option.)

Use the Print Screen key to make a copy of the screen, then print it from the Paint program. (To print from the Paint program, click the Start button on the taskbar, point to All Programs, point to Accessories, then click Paint; in the Paint program window, click Edit on the menu bar, then click Paste; click Yes to fit the image on the bitmap, click the Print button on the toolbar, then click Print in the Print dialog box. See your instructor or technical support person for assistance.)

When you have completed this exercise, be sure to return your settings and desktop back to their original arrangement.

FIGURE A-18

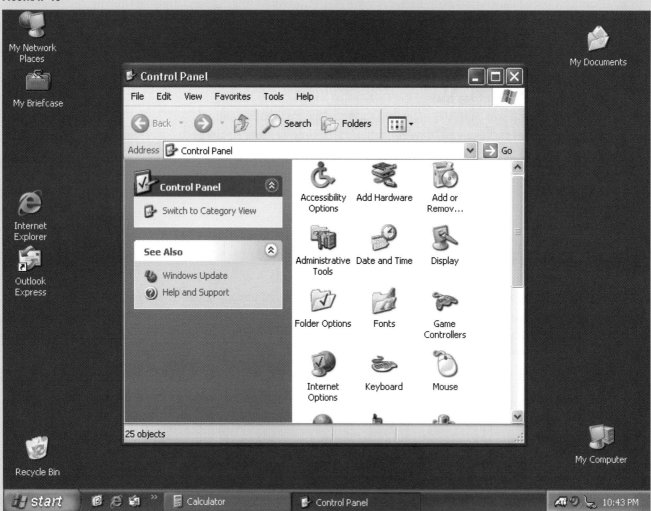

Working with Programs, Files, and Folders

OBJECTIVES

Create and save a WordPad document
Open, edit, and save an existing Paint file
Work with multiple programs
Understand file management
View files and create folders with My Computer
Move and copy files with My Computer
Manage files with Windows Explorer
Search for files
Delete and restore files

If you have a SAM user profile, you may have access to hands-on instruction, practice, and assessment of the skills covered in this unit. Log in to your SAM account and go to your assignments page to see what your instructor has assigned.

Most of your work on a computer involves using programs to create files. For example, you might use WordPad to create a resumé or Microsoft Excel to create a budget. The resumé and the budget are examples of **files**, electronic collections of data that you create and save on a disk. ▰▰▰ In this unit, you learn how to work with files and the programs you use to create them. You create new files, open and edit an existing file, and use the Clipboard to copy and paste data from one file to another. You also explore the file management features of Windows XP, using My Computer and Windows Explorer. Finally, you learn how to work more efficiently by managing files directly on your desktop.

Creating and Saving a WordPad Document

As with most programs, when you start WordPad, a new, blank document opens. To create a new file, such as a memo, you simply begin typing. Your work is automatically stored in your computer's random access memory (RAM) until you turn off your computer, at which point anything stored in the computer's RAM is erased. To store your work permanently, you must save your work as a file on a disk. You can save files either on an internal **hard disk**, which is built into your computer, usually the C: drive, or on a removable 3½" **floppy disk**, which you insert into a drive on your computer, usually the A: or B: drive, or on a **CD-ROM** or **Zip disk**, two other kinds of removable storage devices. (Before you can save a file on a floppy disk, the disk must be formatted; see the Appendix, "Formatting a Floppy Disk.") When you name a file, you can use up to 255 characters, including spaces and punctuation, using either upper- or lowercase letters. ⬛⬛⬛ In this lesson, you start WordPad and create a file that contains the text shown in Figure B-1 and save the file to the drive and folder where your Project Files are stored.

STEPS

1. **Click the** Start button **on the taskbar, point to** All Programs, **point to** Accessories, **click** WordPad, **then click the** Maximize **button** ◻ **if the window does not fill your screen**
   The WordPad program window opens. The blinking insertion point indicates where the text you type will appear.

2. **CType** Memo, **then press** [Enter] **to move the insertion point to the next line**

3. **Press** [Enter] **again, then type the remaining text shown in Figure B-1, pressing** [Enter] **at the end of each line**

4. **Click** File **on the menu bar, then click** Save As
   The Save As dialog box opens, as shown in Figure B-2. In this dialog box, you specify where you want your file saved and give your document a name.

5. **Click the** Save in list arrow, **then click** 3½ Floppy (A:), **or whichever drive contains your Project Files**
   The drive containing your Project Files is now active, meaning that the contents of the drive appear in the Save in dialog box and that the file will now be saved in this drive.

6. **Click in the** File name text box, **type** Memo, **then click the** Save button
   Your memo is now saved as a WordPad file with the name "Memo" on your Project Disk. The WordPad title bar contains the name of the file. Now you can **format** the text, which changes its appearance to make it more readable or attractive.

7. **Click to the left of the word** Memo, **drag the mouse to the right to highlight the word, then release the mouse button**
   Now the text is highlighted, indicating that it is **selected**. This means that any action you make will be performed on the highlighted text.

8. **Click the** Center button ≣ **on the Formatting toolbar, then click the** Bold button B **on the Formatting toolbar**
   The text is centered and bold.

9. **Click the** Font Size list arrow 10 ▾, **click** 16 **in the list, then click the** Save button 🖫
   A **font** is a set of letters and numbers sharing a particular shape of type. The **font size** is measured in points; one **point** is 1/72 of an inch in height.

FIGURE B-1: Text to enter in WordPad

Bold button

Center button

Press [Enter] three and four times (respectively) to insert blank lines

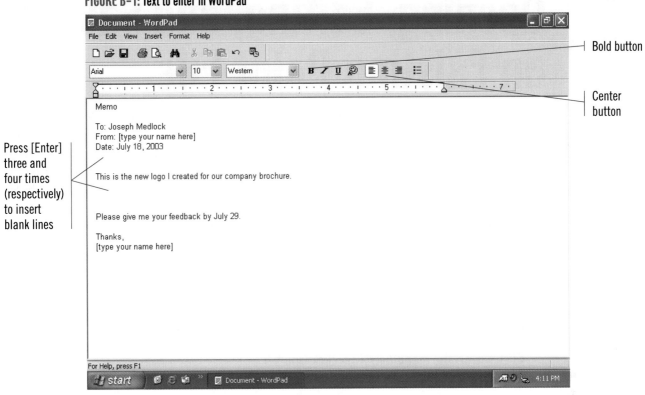

FIGURE B-2: Save As dialog box

Click to select the location in which to save the file

Type new filename here

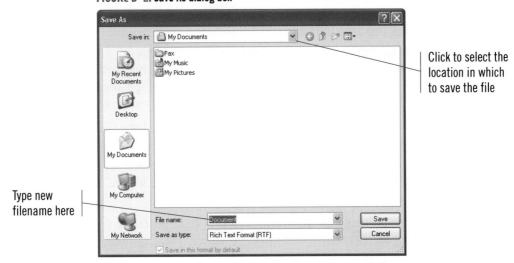

Opening, Editing, and Saving an Existing Paint File

Sometimes you create files from scratch, as you did in the previous lesson, but often you may want to work with a file you or someone else has already created. To do so, you need to open the file. Once you open a file, you can **edit** it, or make changes to it, such as adding or deleting text or changing the formatting. After editing a file, you can save it with the same filename, which means that you no longer will have the file in its original form, or you can save it with a different filename, so that the original file remains unchanged. ██████ In this lesson, you use Paint (a graphics program that comes with Windows XP) to open a file, edit it by changing a color, and then save the file with a new filename to leave the original file unchanged.

STEPS

1. **Click the Start button on the taskbar, point to All Programs, point to Accessories, click Paint, then click the Maximize button 🔲 if the window doesn't fill the screen**
   The Paint program opens with a blank work area. If you wanted to create a file from scratch, you would begin working now. However, you want to open an existing file, located on your Project Disk.

2. **Click File on the menu bar, then click Open**
   The Open dialog box works similarly to the Save As dialog box that you used in the previous lesson.

3. **Click the Look in list arrow, then click 3½ Floppy (A:)**
   The Paint files on your Project Disk are listed in the Open dialog box, as shown in Figure B-3.

QUICK TIP
You can also open a file by double-clicking it in the Open dialog box.

4. **Click Win B-1 in the list of files, and then click the Open button**
   The Open dialog box closes and the file named Win B-1 opens. Before you change this file, you should save it with a new filename, so that the original file is unchanged.

5. **Click File on the menu bar, then click Save As**

6. **Make sure 3½ Floppy (A:) appears in the Save in text box, select the text Win B-1 in the File name text box, type Logo, click the Save as type list arrow, click 256 Color Bitmap, then click the Save button**
   The Logo file appears in the Paint window, as shown in Figure B-4. Because you saved the file with a new name, you can edit it without changing the original file. You saved the file as a 256 Color Bitmap to conserve space on your floppy disk. You will now modify the logo by using buttons in the **Tool Box**, a toolbar of drawing tools, and the **Color Box**, a palette of colors from which you can choose.

7. **Click the Fill With Color button 🖌 in the Tool Box, then click the Light blue color box, which is the fourth from the right in the bottom row**
   Notice how clicking a button in the Tool Box changes the mouse pointer. Now when you click an area in the image, it will be filled with the color you selected in the Color Box. See Table B-1 for a description of the tools in the Tool Box.

8. **Move the pointer into the white area that represents the sky until the pointer changes to 🖌, then click**
   The sky is now blue.

9. **Click File on the menu bar, then click Save**
   The change you made is saved to disk, using the same Logo filename.

FIGURE B-3: Open dialog box

List of files

FIGURE B-4: Paint file saved with new filename

Name of file
appears in
title bar

Tool Box

Sky area to
fill with
light blue

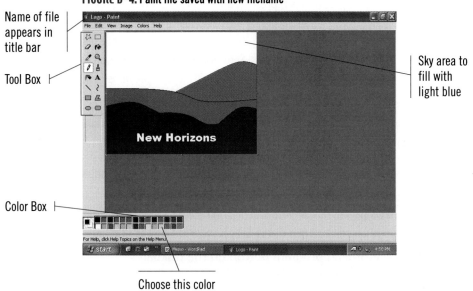

Color Box

Choose this color

TABLE B-1: Paint Tool Box buttons

tool	description
Free-Form Select button	Selects a free-form section of the picture to move, copy, or edit
Select button	Selects a rectangular section of the picture to move, copy, or edit
Eraser button	Erases a portion of the picture using the selected eraser size and foreground color
Fill With Color button	Fills a closed shape or area with the current drawing color
Pick Color button	Picks up a color from the picture to use for drawing
Magnifier button	Changes the magnification; lists magnifications under the toolbar
Pencil button	Draws a free-form line one pixel wide
Ellipse button	Draws an ellipse with the selected fill style; hold down [Shift] to draw a circle
Brush button	Draws using a brush with the selected shape and size
Airbrush button	Produces a circular spray of dots
Text button	Inserts text into the picture
Line button	Draws a straight line with the selected width and foreground color
Curve button	Draws a wavy line with the selected width and foreground color
Rectangle button	Draws a rectangle with the selected fill style; hold down [Shift] to draw a square
Polygon button	Draws polygons from connected straight-line segments
Rounded Rectangle button	Draws rectangles with rounded corners using the selected fill style; hold down [Shift] to draw a rounded square

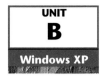

Working with Multiple Programs

A powerful feature of Windows is its capability to run more than one program at a time. For example, you might be working with a document in WordPad and want to search the Internet to find the answer to a question. You can start your **browser**, a program designed to access information on the Internet, without closing WordPad. When you find the information, you can leave your browser open and switch back to WordPad. Each open program is represented by a program button on the taskbar that you click to switch between programs. You can also copy data from one file to another (whether or not the files were created with the same Windows program) using the Clipboard, an area of memory on your computer's hard drive, and the Cut, Copy, and Paste commands. See Table B-2 for a description of these commands. ▰▰▰ In this lesson, you copy the logo graphic you worked with in the previous lesson into the memo you created in WordPad.

STEPS

1. **Click Edit on the menu bar, then click Select All to select the entire picture**
   A dotted rectangle surrounds the picture, indicating it is selected, as shown in Figure B-5.

2. **Click Edit on the menu bar, then click Copy**
   The logo is copied to the Clipboard. When you **copy** an object onto the Clipboard, the object remains in its original location and is also available to be pasted into another location.

QUICK TIP

To switch between programs using the keyboard, press and hold down [Alt], press [Tab] until you select the program you want, then release [Alt].

3. **Click the WordPad program button on the taskbar**
   WordPad becomes the active program.

4. **Click in the first line below the line that ends "for our company brochure."**
   The insertion point indicates where the logo will be pasted.

5. **Click the Paste button 📋 on the WordPad toolbar**
   The contents of the Clipboard, in this case the logo, are pasted into the WordPad file, as shown in Figure B-6.

6. **Click the WordPad Close button; click Yes to save changes**
   Your WordPad document and the WordPad program close. Paint is now the active program.

7. **Click the Paint Close button; if you are prompted to save changes, click Yes**
   Your Paint document and the Paint program close. You return to the desktop.

Clues to Use

Other Programs that Come with Windows XP

WordPad and Paint are just two of many programs that come with Windows XP. From the All Programs menu on the Start menu, you can access everything from games and entertainment programs to powerful communications software and disk maintenance programs without installing anything other than Windows XP. For example, from the Accessories menu, you can open a simple calculator; start Windows Movie Maker to create, edit, and share movie files; and use the Address Book to keep track of your contacts. From the Communications submenu, you can use NetMeeting to set up a voice and/or video conference over the Internet, or use the Remote Desktop Connection to allow another person to access your computer for diagnosing and solving computer problems. Several other menus and submenus display programs and tools that come with Windows XP. You can get a brief description of each by holding your mouse pointer over the name of the program in the menu. You might have to install some of these programs from the Windows CD if they don't appear on the menus.

FIGURE B-5: Selecting the logo to copy and paste into the Memo file

Dotted line
indicates
selected area

FIGURE B-6: Memo with pasted logo

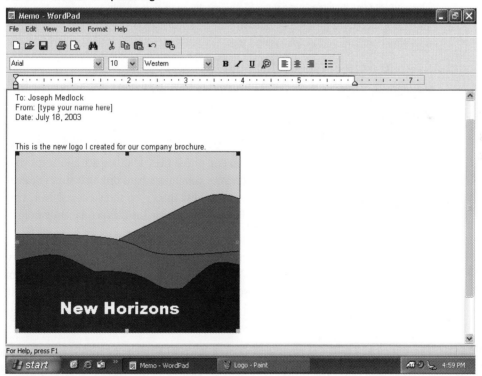

TABLE B-2: Overview of cutting, copying, and pasting

toolbar button	function	keyboard shortcut
Cut	Removes selected information from a file and places it on the Clipboard	[Ctrl][X]
Copy	Places a copy of the selected information on the Clipboard, leaving the file intact	[Ctrl][C]
Paste	Inserts whatever is currently on the Clipboard into another location within the same file or into another file (depending on where you place the insertion point)	[Ctrl][V]

Understanding File Management

After you have created and saved numerous files, the process of organizing and keeping track of all of your files (referred to as **file management**) can be a challenge. Fortunately, Windows provides tools to keep everything organized so you can easily locate the files you need, move files to new locations, and delete files you no longer need. There are two main tools for managing your files: My Computer and Windows Explorer.  In this lesson, you preview the ways you can use My Computer and Windows Explorer to manage your files.

DETAILS

Windows XP gives you the ability to:

- **Create folders in which you can save and organize your files**

  Folders are areas on a floppy disk (or other removable storage medium) or hard disk that help you organize your files, just as folders in a filing cabinet help you store and organize your papers. For example, you might create a folder for your work documents and another folder for your personal files. Folders can also contain other folders, which creates a more complex structure of folders and files, called a **file hierarchy**. See Figure B-7 for an example of how files can be organized.

- **Examine and organize the hierarchy of files and folders**

  You can use either My Computer or Windows Explorer to see and manipulate the overall structure of your files and folders. By examining your file hierarchy with these tools, you can better organize the contents of your computer and adjust the hierarchy to meet your needs. Figures B-8 and B-9 illustrate how My Computer and Windows Explorer list folders and files.

- **Copy, move, and rename files and folders**

  If you decide that a file belongs in a different folder, you can move it to another folder. You can also rename a file if you decide a different name is more descriptive. If you want to keep a copy of a file in more than one folder, you can copy it to new folders.

- **Delete files and folders you no longer need and restore files you delete accidentally**

  Deleting files and folders you are sure you don't need frees up disk space and keeps your file hierarchy more organized. The **Recycle Bin**, a space on your computer's hard disk that stores deleted files, allows you to restore files you deleted by accident. To free up disk space, you should occasionally check to make sure you don't need the contents of the Recycle Bin and then delete the files permanently from your hard drive.

- **Locate files quickly with the Windows XP Search feature**

  As you create more files and folders, you may forget where you placed a certain file or you may forget what name you used when you saved a file. With Search, you can locate files by providing only partial names or other facts you know about the file, such as the file type (for example, a WordPad document or a Paint graphic) or the date the file was created or modified.

- **Use shortcuts**

  If a file or folder you use often is located several levels down in your file hierarchy (in a folder within a folder, within a folder), it might take you several steps to access it. To save time accessing the files and programs you use frequently, you can create shortcuts to them. A **shortcut** is a link that gives you quick access to a particular file, folder, or program.

> **QUICK TIP**
>
> To browse My Computer using multiple windows, click Tools on the menu bar, and then click Folder Options. In the Folder Options dialog box, click the General tab, and then under Browse Folders, click the Open each folder in its own window option button. Each time you open a new folder, a new window opens, leaving the previous folder's window open so that you can view both at the same time.

FIGURE B-7: Sample file hierarchy

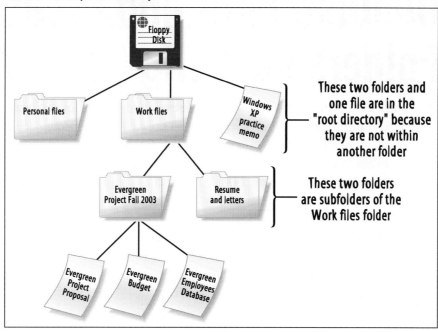

These two folders and one file are in the "root directory" because they are not within another folder

These two folders are subfolders of the Work files folder

FIGURE B-8: Evergreen Project folder shown in My Computer

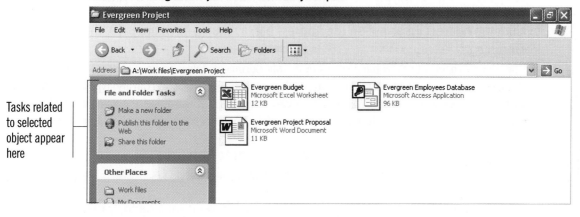

Tasks related to selected object appear here

FIGURE B-9: Evergreen Project folder shown in Windows Explorer

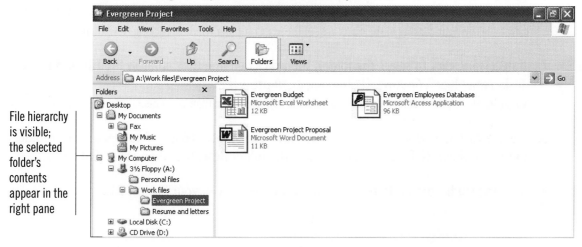

File hierarchy is visible; the selected folder's contents appear in the right pane

Viewing Files and Creating Folders with My Computer

My Computer shows the contents of your computer, including files, folders, programs, disk drives, and printers. You can click the icons to view that object's contents or properties. You use the My Computer Explorer Bar, menu bar, and toolbar to manage your files. See Table B-3 for a description of the toolbar buttons. ▰▰▰▰ In this lesson, you use My Computer to look at your computer's file hierarchy, then you create two new folders on your Project Disk.

STEPS

TROUBLE

If you do not see My Computer, click the Start button, and click My Computer. If you do not see the toolbar, click View, point to Toolbars, and click Standard Buttons. If you do not see Address bar, click View, point to Toolbar, and click Address Bar.

1. **Double-click the** My Computer icon 🖥 **on your desktop, then click the** Maximize button ⬜ **if the My Computer window does not fill the screen**

   My Computer displays the contents of your computer, as shown in Figure B-10. The left pane, called the **Explorer Bar**, displays tasks related to whatever is selected in the right pane.

2. **Make sure your Project Disk is in the floppy disk drive, then double-click the** 3½ Floppy (A:) icon

   The contents of your Project Disk appear in the window. Each file is represented by an icon, which varies in appearance depending on the program that was used to create the file. If Microsoft Word is installed on your computer, the Word icon appears for the WordPad files; if not, the WordPad icon appears.

TROUBLE

If you are in a lab you may not have access to the My Documents folder. See your instructor for assistance.

3. **Click the** Address list arrow **on the Address bar, as shown in Figure B-10, then click** My Documents

   The window changes to show the contents of the My Documents folder on your computer's hard drive. The Address bar allows you to open and view a drive, folder, or even a Web page. You can also type in the Address bar to go to a different drive, folder, or Web page. For example, typing "C:\" will display the contents of your C: drive, and typing "http://www.microsoft.com" opens Microsoft's Web site if your computer is connected to the Internet.

QUICK TIP

You can click the list arrow next to the Back or Forward buttons to quickly view locations you've viewed recently.

4. **Click the** Back button ◐ **on the Standard Buttons toolbar**

   The Back button displays the previous location, in this case, your Project Disk.

5. **Click the** Views button list arrow ▦ ▾ **on the Standard Buttons toolbar, then click** Details

   Details view shows not only the files and folders, but also the sizes of the files, the types of files, folders, or drives and the date the files were last modified.

6. **In the File and Folder Tasks pane, click** Make a new folder

   A new folder called "New Folder" is created on your Project Disk, as shown in Figure B-11. You can also create a new folder by right-clicking in the blank area of the My Computer window, clicking New, then clicking Folder.

QUICK TIP

You can also rename a folder or file by pressing [F2], typing the new name, then pressing [Enter].

7. **If necessary, click to select the folder, then click** Rename this folder **in the File and Folder Tasks pane; type** Windows XP Practice**, then press** [Enter]

   Choosing descriptive names for your folders helps you remember their contents.

8. **Double-click the** Windows XP Practice folder**, repeat Steps 6 and 7 to create a new folder in the Windows XP Practice folder, name the folder** Brochure**, then press** [Enter]

9. **Click the** Up button 🗁 **to return to the root directory of your Project Disk**

FIGURE B-10: My Computer window

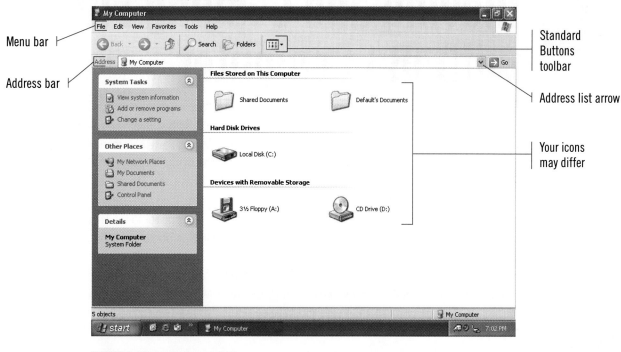

Menu bar

Address bar

Standard Buttons toolbar

Address list arrow

Your icons may differ

FIGURE B-11: Creating a new folder

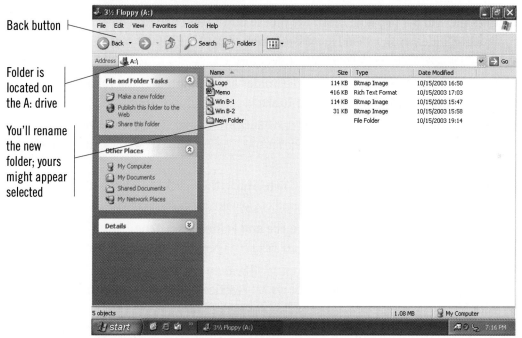

Back button

Folder is located on the A: drive

You'll rename the new folder; yours might appear selected

TABLE B-3: Buttons on the Standard Buttons toolbar in My Computer

button	function
Back button	Moves back one location in the list of locations you have recently viewed
Forward button	Moves forward one location in the list of locations you have recently viewed
Up button	Moves up one level in the file hierarchy
Search button	Opens the Search Companion task pane, where you can choose from various options to search for files, computers, Web pages, or people on the Internet
Folders button	Opens the Folders task pane, where you can easily view and manage your computer's file hierarchy
Views button	Lists the contents of My Computer using different views

Moving and Copying Files with My Computer

You can move a file or folder from one location to another using a variety of methods in My Computer. If the file or folder and the location to which you want to move it are both visible, you can simply drag the item from one location to another. You can also use the Cut, Copy, and Paste commands on the Edit menu, or right-click a file or folder and click the appropriate option on the menu that appears. Perhaps the most powerful file management tool in My Computer is the Common Tasks pane. When you select any item in My Computer, the Common Tasks pane changes to the File and Folder Tasks pane, listing tasks you can typically perform with the selected item. For example, if you select a file, the options in the Files and Folders task pane include "Rename this file," "Move this file," and "Delete this file," among many others. If you select a folder, file management tasks for folders appear. If you select more than one object, tasks appear that relate to manipulating multiple objects. You can also right-click any file or folder and choose the Send To command to "send" it to another location – most often a floppy disk or other removable storage medium. This **backs up** the files, making copies of them in case you have computer trouble (which can cause you to lose files from your hard disk). In this lesson, you move your files into the folder you created in the last lesson.

STEPS

1. **Click the** Win B-1 file**, hold down the mouse button and drag the file onto the** Windows XP Practice folder**, as shown in Figure B-12, then release the mouse button**
   Win B-1 is moved into the Windows XP Practice folder.

2. **Double-click the** Windows XP Practice folder **and confirm that the folder contains the Win B-1 file as well as the Brochure folder**

QUICK TIP

It is easy to confuse the Back button with the Up button. The Back button returns you to the last location you viewed, no matter where it is in your folder hierarchy. The Up button displays the next level up in the folder hierarchy, no matter what you last viewed.

3. **Click the** Up button ⬆ **on the Standard Buttons toolbar, as shown in Figure B-12**
   You return to the root directory of your Project Disk. The Up button shows the next level up in the folder hierarchy.

4. **Click the** Logo file**, press and hold down** [Shift]**, then click the** Memo file
   Both files are selected. Table B-4 describes methods for selecting multiple objects.

5. **Click** Move the selected items **in the File and Folder Tasks pane**
   The filenames turn gray, and the Move Items dialog box opens, as shown in Figure B-13.

6. **Click the plus sign next to My Computer if you do not see 3½ Floppy (A:) listed, click the** 3½ Floppy (A:) **drive, click the** Windows XP Practice folder**, click the** Brochure folder**, then click** Move
   The two files are moved to the Brochure folder. Only the Windows XP Practice folder and the Win B-2 file remain in the root directory.

7. **Click the** Close button **in the 3½ Floppy (A:) (My Computer) window**

FIGURE B-12: Dragging a file from one folder to another

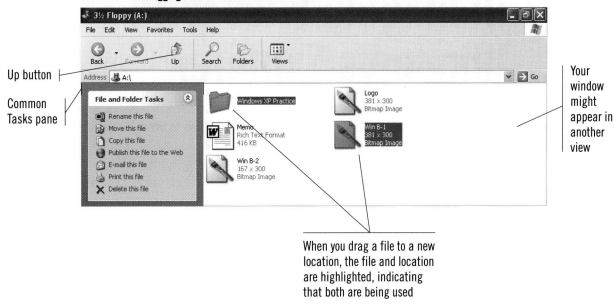

Up button

Common Tasks pane

Your window might appear in another view

When you drag a file to a new location, the file and location are highlighted, indicating that both are being used

FIGURE B-13: Moving files

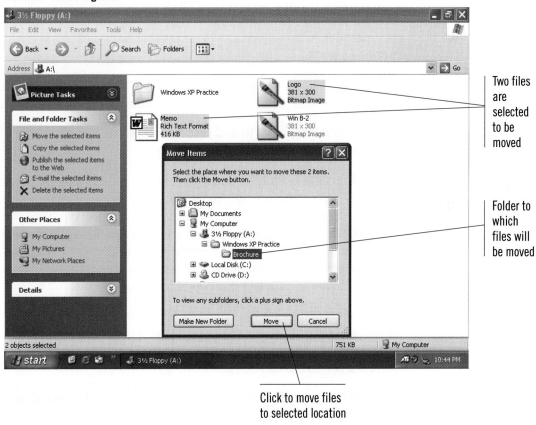

Two files are selected to be moved

Folder to which files will be moved

Click to move files to selected location

TABLE B-4: Techniques for selecting multiple files and folders

to select	do this
Individual objects not grouped together	Click the first object you want to select, then press and hold down [Ctrl] as you click each additional object you want to add to the selection
Objects grouped together	Click the first object you want to select, then press and hold down [Shift] as you click the last object in the list of objects you want to select; all the objects listed between the first and last objects are selected

Managing Files with Windows Explorer

As with My Computer, you can use Windows Explorer to copy, move, delete, and rename files and folders. However, in their default settings, My Computer and Windows Explorer look a little different and work in slightly different ways. In My Computer, the Explorer Bar displays the File and Folder Tasks pane when you select files or folders. In Windows Explorer, the Explorer Bar displays the Folders pane, which allows you to see and manipulate the overall structure of the contents of your computer or network while you work with individual files and folders within that structure. This allows you to work with more than one computer, folder, or file at once. Note that you can change the view in My Computer to show the Folders pane, and in Windows Explorer to view the File and Folder Tasks pane. ▓▓▓▓ In this lesson, you copy a folder from your Project Disk into the My Documents folder on your hard disk and then rename the folder.

STEPS

TROUBLE

If you do not see the toolbar, click View on the menu bar, point to Toolbars, then click Standard Buttons. If you do not see the Address bar, click View, point to Toolbars, then click Address Bar.

1. **Click the** Start button, **point to** All Programs, **point to** Accessories, **click** Windows Explorer, **then maximize the window if necessary**
   Windows Explorer opens, as shown in Figure B-14. The Folders pane on the left displays the drives and folders on your computer in a hierarchy. The right pane displays the contents of whatever drive or folder is currently selected in the Folders pane. Each pane has its own set of scroll bars, so that scrolling in one pane won't affect the other.

2. **Click** View **on the menu bar, then click** Details **if it is not already selected**
   Remember that a bullet point or check mark next to a command on the menu indicates that it's selected.

TROUBLE

If you cannot see the A: drive, you may have to click the plus sign (+) next to My Computer to view the available drives on your computer.

3. **In the Folders pane, scroll to and click** 3½ Floppy (A:)
   The contents of your Project Disk appear in the right pane.

4. **In the Folders pane, click the** plus sign (+) **next to 3½ Floppy (A:), if necessary**
   You click the plus sign (+) or minus sign (-) next to any item in the left pane to show or hide the different levels of the file hierarchy, so that you don't always have to look at the entire structure of your computer or network. A plus sign (+) next to an item indicates there are additional folders within that object. A minus sign (-) indicates the next level of the hierarchy is shown. Clicking the + displays (or "expands") the next level; clicking the – hides (or "collapses") it. When neither a + nor a – appears next to an icon, it means that the object does not have any folders in it, although it may have files.

5. **In the Folders pane, click the** Windows XP Practice folder
   The contents of the Windows XP Practice folder appear in the right pane, as shown in Figure B-15. Double-clicking an item in the Folders pane that has a + next to it displays its contents in the right pane and also expands the next level in the Folders pane.

TROUBLE

If you are working in a lab setting, you may not be able to add items to your My Documents folder. Skip, but read carefully, Steps 6, 7, and 8 if you are unable to complete them.

6. **In the Folders pane, drag the** Windows XP Practice folder **on top of the** My Documents folder, **then release the mouse button**
   When you drag files or folders from one drive to a different drive, they are copied rather than moved.

7. **In the Folders pane, click the** My Documents folder
   The Windows XP Practice folder should now appear in the list of folders in the right pane. You may have to scroll to see it. Now you should rename the folder so you can distinguish the original folder from the copy.

8. **Right-click the** Windows XP Practice folder **in the right pane, click** Rename **in the shortcut menu, type** Windows XP Copy, **then press** [Enter]

FIGURE B-14: Windows Explorer window

Left pane, known as the Folders list or the Explorer Bar

Your list of devices, folders, and files will differ

FIGURE B-15: Contents of Windows XP Practice folder

Windows XP Practice folder selected in left pane

Contents of Windows XP Practice folder appear in right pane

Your window might appear in a different view

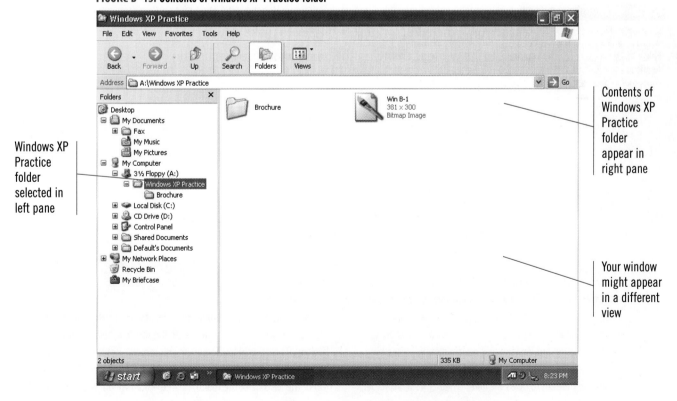

Searching for Files

After you've worked a while on your computer, saving, deleting, and modifying files and folders, you may forget where you've saved an item or what you named it. Or, you may want to send an e-mail to someone, but you can't remember how the name is spelled. You can use the **Windows XP Search** feature to quickly find any kind of object, from a Word document or a movie file to a computer on your network or a person in your address book. If you're connected to the Internet, you can use Search to locate Web pages and people on the Internet. ▰▰▰ In this lesson, you search for a file on your Project Disk.

STEPS

QUICK TIP

You can also start the Search Companion by clicking the Start button and then clicking Search. To change the way the Search tool works (such as whether the animated dog appears), click Change preferences at the bottom of the Search Companion pane.

1. **Click the** Search button 🔍 **on the Standard Buttons toolbar**

   The Explorer Bar changes to display the Search Companion pane, as shown in Figure B-16. Let's assume you can't remember where you placed the Logo file you created earlier. You know that it is a picture file and that it is somewhere on your floppy disk.

2. **In the Search Companion pane, click** Pictures, music, or video; **in the list that appears, click the** Pictures and Photos check box, **then type** Logo **in the All or part of the file name text box, as shown in Figure B-17**

3. **Click** Use advanced search options **to open a larger pane, click the** Look in list arrow, **click** 3½ Floppy (A:), **then click the** Search button **at the bottom of the Search Companion pane**

   The search results are displayed in the right pane and options for further searching are displayed in the Search Companion pane.

4. **Click the** Logo icon **in the right pane, click** File **on the menu bar, point to** Open With, **and then click** Paint

TROUBLE

If you don't like the way your clouds look, click Edit on the menu bar, click Undo, then repeat Step 5.

5. **Click the** Airbrush tool 🖌, **click the** white color box **in the Color box (the first one in the second row), then drag or click in the sky to make clouds**

6. **Save the file without changing the name and close Paint**

Clues to Use

Accessing files, folders, programs, and drives you use often

As you continue to use your computer, you will probably find that you use certain files, folders, programs, and disk drives almost every day. You can create a **shortcut**, an icon that represents an object stored somewhere else, and place it on the desktop. From the desktop, you double-click the shortcut to open the item, whether it's a file, folder, program, or disk drive. To create a shortcut on the desktop, view the object in My Computer or Windows Explorer, size the window so you can see both the object and part of the desktop at the same time, use the *right* mouse button to drag the object to the desktop, and then click Create Shortcuts Here. To delete the shortcut, select it and press [Delete]. The original file, folder, or program will not be affected. To **pin** a program to the Start menu, which places it conveniently at the top of the left side of the menu, open the Start menu as far as needed to view the program you want to pin, right-click the program name, and then click Pin to Start menu. To remove it, right-click it in its new position and then click Unpin from Start menu.

FIGURE B-16: Getting ready to search

Search
button

Search
Companion
pane

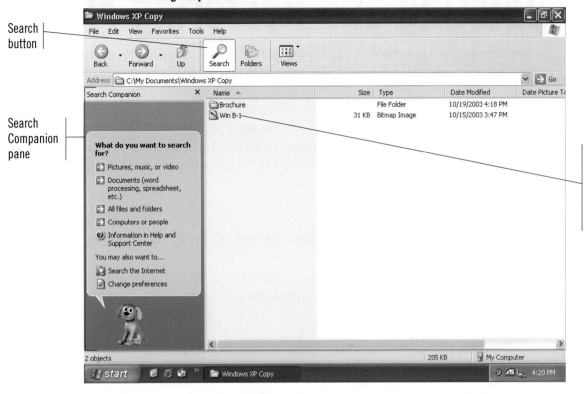

Contents of
right pane
won't change
until you
begin a
search

FIGURE B-17: Specifying search options

Select this
check box

Enter search
text here

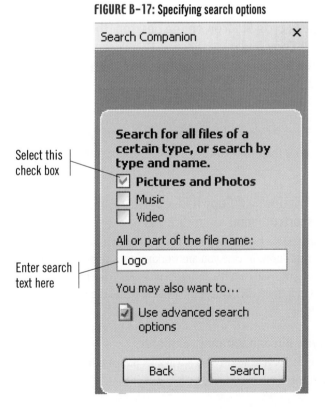

Deleting and Restoring Files

To save disk space and manage your files more effectively, you should **delete** (or remove) files you no longer need. There are many ways to delete files and folders from the My Computer and Windows Explorer windows, as well as from the Windows XP desktop. Because files deleted from your hard disk are stored in the Recycle Bin until you remove them permanently by emptying the Recycle Bin, you can restore any files you might have deleted accidentally. However, note that when you delete files from your floppy disk, they are not stored in the Recycle Bin – they are permanently deleted. See Table B-5 for an overview of deleting and restoring files. ▰▰▰▰▰ In this lesson, you delete a file by dragging it to the Recycle Bin, you restore it, and then you delete a folder by using the Delete command in Windows Explorer.

STEPS

1. **Click the** Folders button 📂, **then click the** Restore button 🗗 **on the Search Results (Windows Explorer) title bar**

   You should be able to see the Recycle Bin icon on your desktop, as shown in Figure B-18. If you can't see the Recycle Bin, resize or move the Windows Explorer window until it is visible.

2. **If necessary, select the** Windows XP Copy folder **in the left pane of Windows Explorer**

3. **Drag the** Windows XP Copy folder **from the left pane to the** Recycle Bin **on the desktop, as shown in Figure B-18, then click** Yes **to confirm the deletion, if necessary**

   The folder no longer appears in Windows Explorer because you have moved it to the Recycle Bin.

4. **Double-click the** Recycle Bin icon **on the desktop, then scroll if necessary until you can see the** Windows XP Copy folder

   The Recycle Bin window opens, as shown in Figure B-19. Depending on the number of files already deleted on your computer, your window might look different.

5. **Click the** Windows XP Copy folder, **then click** Restore this item **in the Recycle Bin Tasks pane**

   The Windows XP Copy folder is restored and should now appear in the Windows Explorer window.

6. **Right-click the** Windows XP Copy folder **in the right pane of Windows Explorer, click** Delete **on the shortcut menu, then click** Yes

   When you are sure you no longer need files you've moved into the Recycle Bin, you can empty the Recycle Bin. You won't do this now, in case you are working on a computer that you share with other people. But when you're working on your own machine, open the Recycle Bin window, verify that you don't need any of the files or folders in it, then click Empty the Recycle Bin in the Recycle Bin Tasks pane.

7. **Close the Recycle Bin and Windows Explorer**

   If you minimized the Recycle Bin in Step 5, click its program button to open the Recycle Bin window, and then click the Close button.

FIGURE B-18: Dragging a folder to delete it

Your desktop background and icons might differ

Drag the folder here

Folder located in the My Documents folder

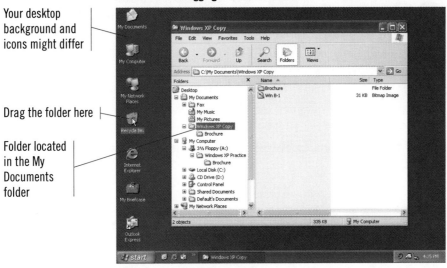

FIGURE B-19: Recycle Bin window

The buttons on your toolbar might differ

You may see more files and folders, and they may be displayed in a different view

Deleted folder

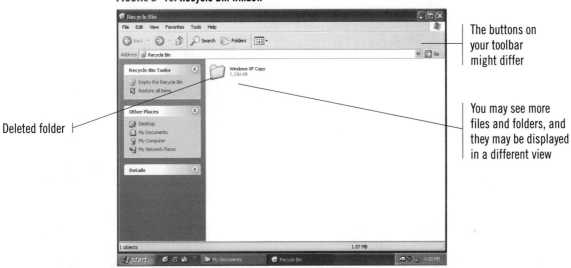

TABLE B-5: Methods for deleting and restoring files

ways to delete a file	ways to restore a file from the Recycle Bin
If File and Folder Tasks pane is open, click the file, then click Delete this file	Click Edit, then click Undo Delete
Select the file, then press [Delete]	Select the file in the Recycle Bin window, then click Restore this file
Right-click the file, then click Delete on the shortcut menu	Right-click the file in the Recycle Bin window, then click Restore
Drag the file to the Recycle Bin	Drag the file from the Recycle Bin to any other location

Clues to Use

Customizing your Recycle Bin

You can set your Recycle Bin according to how you like to delete and restore files. For example, if you do not want files to go to the Recycle Bin but rather want them to be immediately and permanently deleted, right-click the Recycle Bin, click Properties, then click the Do Not Move Files to the Recycle Bin check box. If you find that the Recycle Bin fills up too fast and you are not ready to delete the files permanently, you can increase the amount of disk space devoted to the Recycle Bin by moving the Maximum Size of Recycle Bin slider to the right. This, of course, reduces the amount of disk space you have available for other things. Also, you can choose not to have the Confirm File Delete dialog box open when you send files to the Recycle Bin. See your instructor or technical support person before changing any of the Recycle Bin settings.

Practice

▼ CONCEPTS REVIEW

Label each of the elements of the Windows Explorer window shown in Figure B-20.

FIGURE B-20

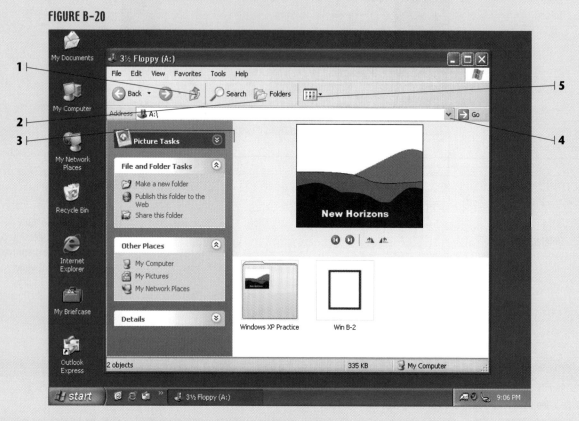

Match each of the statements with the term it describes.

6. Electronic collections of data
7. Your computer's temporary storage area
8. Temporary location of information you wish to paste into another location
9. Storage areas on your hard drive for files, folders, and programs
10. Structure of files and folders

a. RAM
b. Folders
c. Files
d. File hierarchy
e. Clipboard

Select the best answer from the list of choices.

11. To prepare a floppy disk to save your files, you must first make sure
    a. files are copied to the disk.
    b. the disk is formatted.
    c. all the files that might be on the disk are erased.
    d. the files are on the Clipboard.

12. You can use My Computer to
    a. create a drawing of your computer.
    b. view the contents of a folder.
    c. change the appearance of your desktop.
    d. add text to a WordPad file.

13. Which of the following best describes WordPad?
    a. A program for organizing files
    b. A program for performing financial analysis
    c. A program for creating basic text documents
    d. A program for creating graphics

14. **Which of the following is NOT a way to move a file from one folder to another?**
    a. Open the file and drag its program window to the new folder.
    b. In My Computer or Windows Explorer, drag the selected file to the new folder.
    c. Use the Move this file command in the File and Folder Tasks pane.
    d. Use the [Ctrl][X] and [Ctrl][V] keyboard shortcuts while in the My Computer or the Windows Explorer window.

15. **In which of the following can you, by default, view the hierarchy of drives, folders, and files in a split pane window?**
    a. Windows Explorer
    b. All Programs
    c. My Computer
    d. WordPad

16. **To restore files that you have sent to the Recycle Bin,**
    a. click File, then click Empty Recycle Bin.
    b. click Edit, then click Undo Delete.
    c. click File, then click Undo.
    d. You cannot retrieve files sent to the Recycle Bin.

17. **To select files that are not grouped together, select the first file, then**
    a. press [Shift] while selecting the second file.
    b. press [Alt] while selecting the second file.
    c. press [Ctrl] while selecting the second file.
    d. click the second file.

18. **Pressing [Backspace]**
    a. deletes the character to the right of the cursor.
    b. deletes the character to the left of the cursor.
    c. moves the insertion point one character to the right.
    d. deletes all text to the left of the cursor.

19. **The size of a font is measured in**
    a. centimeters.
    b. points.
    c. places.
    d. millimeters.

20. **The Back button on the My Computer toolbar**
    a. starts the last program you used.
    b. displays the next level of the file hierarchy.
    c. backs up the currently selected file.
    d. displays the last location you visited.

▼ SKILLS REVIEW

1. **Create and save a WordPad file.**
   a. Start Windows, then start WordPad.
   b. Type My Drawing Ability, then press [Enter] three times.
   c. Save the document as Drawing Ability to your Project Disk, but do not close it.

2. **Open, edit, and save an existing Paint file.**
   a. Start Paint and open the file Win B-2 on your Project Disk.
   b. Save the picture with the filename First Unique Art as a 256-color bitmap file to your Project Disk.
   c. Inside the picture frame, use [Shift] with the Ellipse tool to create a circle, fill it with purple, switch to yellow, then use [Shift] with the Rectangle tool to place a square inside the circle. Fill the square with yellow.
   d. Save the file, but do not close it. (Click Yes, if necessary to replace the file.)

3. **Work with multiple programs.**
   a. Select the entire graphic and copy it to the Clipboard, then switch to WordPad.
   b. Place the insertion point in the last blank line, paste the graphic into your document, then deselect the graphic.
   c. Save the changes to your WordPad document. Switch to Paint.
   d. Using the Fill With Color tool, change the color of a filled area of your graphic.
   e. Save the revised graphic with the new name Second Unique Art as a 256-color bitmap on your Project Disk.
   f. Select the entire graphic and copy it to the Clipboard.
   g. Switch to WordPad, move the insertion point to the line below the graphic by clicking below the graphic and pressing [Enter], type This is another version of my graphic: below the first picture, then press [Enter].
   h. Paste the second graphic under the text you just typed.
   i. Save the changed WordPad document as Two Drawing Examples to your Project Disk. Close Paint and WordPad.

4. **View files and create folders with My Computer.**
   a. Open My Computer. Double-click the drive that contains your Project Disk.
   b. Create a new folder on your Project Disk by clicking File, pointing to New, then clicking Folder, and name the new folder Review.
   c. Open the folder to display its contents (it is empty).
   d. Use the Address bar to view the My Documents folder.
   e. Create a folder in the My Documents folder called Temporary, then use the Back button to view the Review folder.
   f. Create two new folders in the Review folder, one named Documents and the other named Artwork.
   g. Click the Forward button as many times as necessary to view the contents of the My Documents folder.
   h. Change the view to Details if necessary.

5. **Move and copy files with My Computer.**
   a. Use the Address bar to view your Project Disk. Switch to Details view, if necessary.
   b. Press the [Shift] key while selecting First Unique Art and Second Unique Art, then cut and paste them into the Artwork folder.
   c. Use the Back button to view the contents of Project Disk.
   d. Select the two WordPad files, Drawing Ability and Two Drawing Examples, then move them into the Review folder.
   e. Open the Review folder, select the two WordPad files again, move them into the Documents folder, then close My Computer.

6. **Manage files with Windows Explorer.**
   a. Open Windows Explorer and view the contents of the Artwork folder in the right pane.
   b. Select the two Paint files.
   c. Drag the two Paint files from the Artwork folder to the Temporary folder in the My Documents folder to copy – not move – them.
   d. View the contents of the Documents folder in the right pane, then select the two WordPad files.
   e. Repeat Step c to copy the files to the Temporary folder in the My Documents folder.
   f. View the contents of the Temporary folder in the right pane to verify that the four files are there.

7. **Search for files.**
   a. Open the Search companion from Windows Explorer.
   b. Search for the First Unique Art file on your Project Disk.
   c. Close the Search Results window.

8. **Delete and restore files and folders.**
   a. If necessary, open and resize the Windows Explorer window so you can see the Recycle Bin icon on the desktop, then scroll in Windows Explorer so you can see the Temporary folder in the left pane.
   b. Delete the Temporary folder from the My Documents folder by dragging it to the Recycle Bin.
   c. Click Yes to confirm the deletion, if necessary.
   d. Open the Recycle Bin, restore the Temporary folder and its files to your hard disk, and then close the Recycle Bin. (*Note*: If your Recycle Bin is empty, your computer is set to automatically delete items in the Recycle Bin.)
   e. Delete the Temporary folder again by clicking to select it and then pressing [Delete]. Click Yes to confirm the deletion.

▼ INDEPENDENT CHALLENGE 1

You have decided to start a bakery business and you want to use Windows XP to create and organize the files for the business.

a. Create two new folders on your Project Disk, one named Advertising and one named Customers.
b. Use WordPad to create a letter inviting new customers to the open house for the new bakery, then save it as Open House Letter in the Customers folder.
c. Use WordPad to create a new document that lists five tasks that need to get done before the business opens (such as purchasing equipment, decorating the interior, and ordering supplies), then save it as Business Plan to your Project Disk, but don't place it in a folder.

▼ INDEPENDENT CHALLENGE 1 (CONTINUED)

d. Use Paint to create a simple logo for the bakery, save it as a 256-color bitmap named Bakery Logo, then place it in the Advertising folder.

e. Print the three files.

▼ INDEPENDENT CHALLENGE 2

To complete this Independent Challenge, you will need a second formatted, blank floppy disk. Write IC2 on the disk label, then complete the steps below. Follow the guidelines listed here to create the file hierarchy shown in Figure B-21.

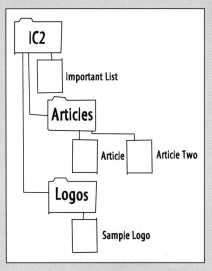

a. In the My Documents folder on your hard drive, create one folder named IC2 and a second named Project Disk 1.

b. Copy the contents of your first Project Disk into the new Project Disk 1 folder. This will give you access to your files as you complete these steps.

c. Place your blank IC2 disk into the floppy drive.

d. Start WordPad, then create a new file that contains a list of things to get done. Save the file as To Do List to your IC2 Disk.

e. Start My Computer and copy the To Do List from your IC2 Disk to the IC2 folder and rename the file in the IC2 folder Important List.

f. Copy the Open House Letter file from your Project Disk 1 folder to the IC2 folder. Rename the file Article.

g. Copy the Memo file from your Project Disk 1 folder to the IC2 folder in the My Documents folder and rename it Article Two.

h. Copy the Logo file from your Project Disk 1 folder to the IC2 folder and rename the file Sample Logo.

i. Move the files into the folders shown in Figure B-21.

j. Copy the IC2 folder to your IC2 Disk, then delete the Project Disk 1 and IC2 folders from the My Documents folder.

▼ INDEPENDENT CHALLENGE 3

With Windows XP, you can access the Web from My Computer and Windows Explorer, allowing you to search for information located not only on your computer or network but also on any computer on the Internet.

a. Start Windows Explorer, then click in the Address bar so the current location is selected, type www.microsoft.com, then press [Enter].

b. Connect to the Internet if necessary. The Microsoft Web page appears in the right pane of Windows Explorer.

c. Click in the Address bar, then type www.course.com, press [Enter], and then wait a moment while the Course Technology Web page opens.

d. Make sure your Project Disk is in the floppy disk drive, then click 3½ Floppy (A:) in the left pane.

e. Click the Back button list arrow, then click Microsoft's home page.

f. Capture a picture of your desktop by pressing [Print Screen] (usually located on the upper-right side of your keyboard). This stores the picture on the Clipboard. Open the Paint program, paste the contents of the Clipboard into the drawing window, clicking No if asked to enlarge the Bitmap, then print the picture.

g. Close Paint without saving your changes.

h. Close Windows Explorer, then disconnect from the Internet if necessary.

▼ INDEPENDENT CHALLENGE 4

Open Windows Explorer, make sure you can see the drive that contains your Project Disk listed in the left pane, use the right mouse button to drag the drive to a blank area on the desktop, then click Create Shortcuts Here. Then capture a picture of your desktop showing the new shortcut: press [Print Screen], located on the upper-right side of your keyboard. Then open the Paint program and paste the contents of the Clipboard into the drawing window. Print the screen, close Paint without saving your changes, then delete the shortcut when you are finished.

▼ VISUAL WORKSHOP

Recreate the screen shown in Figure B-22, which shows the Search Results window with the Memo file listed, one shortcut on the desktop, and one open (but minimized) file. Press [Print Screen] to make a copy of the screen, (a copy of the screen is placed on the Clipboard), open Paint, click Paste to paste the screen picture into Paint, then print the Paint file. Close Paint without saving your changes, and then return your desktop to its original state. Your desktop might have different icons and a different background.

FIGURE B-22

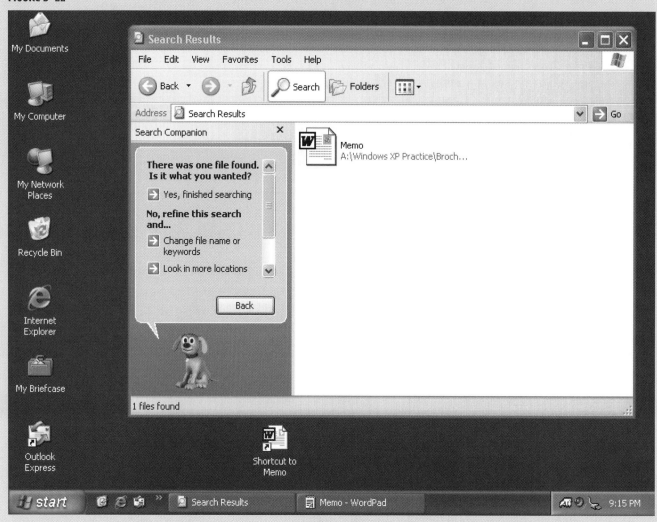

Formatting a Floppy Disk

A **disk** is a device on which you can store electronic data. Disks come in a variety of sizes and have varying storage capacities. Your computer's **hard disk**, one of its internal devices, can store large amounts of data. **Floppy disks**, on the other hand, are smaller, inexpensive, and portable. Most floppy disks that you buy today are 3 ½-inch disks (the diameter of the inside, circular part of the disk) and are already formatted. Check the package that your disk came in for the word "formatted" or "pre-formatted;" such disks do not require further formatting. If your package says "unformatted," then you should follow the steps in this appendix. In this appendix, you will prepare a floppy disk for use.

Formatting a Floppy Disk

In order for an operating system to be able to store data on a disk, the disk must be formatted. **Formatting** prepares a disk so it can store information. Usually, floppy disks are formatted when you buy them, but if not, you can format them yourself using Windows XP. To complete the following steps, you need a blank floppy disk or a disk containing data you no longer need. Do not use your Project Disk for this lesson, as all information on the disk will be erased.

STEPS

TROUBLE

This appendix assumes that the drive that will contain your floppy disks is drive A. If not, substitute the correct drive when you are instructed to use the 3 ½ Floppy (A:) drive.

1. **Start your computer and** Windows XP **if necessary, then place a 3 ½-inch floppy disk in drive A**

2. **Double-click the** My Computer icon 💾 **on the desktop**

   My Computer opens, as shown in Figure AP-1. This window lists all the drives and printers that you can use on your computer. Because computers have different drives, printers, programs, and other devices installed, your window will probably look different.

3. **Right-click the** 3 ½ Floppy (A:) **icon**

   When you click with the right mouse button, a shortcut menu of commands that apply to the item you right-clicked appears. Because you right-clicked a drive, the Format command is available.

TROUBLE

Windows cannot format a disk if it is write-protected; therefore, you may need to slide the write-protect tab over until it clicks to continue. See Figure AP-3 to locate the write-protect tab on your disk.

4. **Click** Format **on the shortcut menu**

   The Format dialog box opens, as shown in Figure AP-2. In this dialog box, you specify the capacity of the disk you are formatting, the File system, the Allocation unit size, the kind of formatting you want to do, and if you want, a volume label. You are doing a standard format, so you will accept the default settings.

5. **Click** Start, **then, when you are warned that formatting will erase all data on the disk, click** OK **to continue**

   Windows formats your disk. After the formatting is complete, you might see a summary about the size of the disk.

6. **Click** OK **when the message telling you that the format is complete appears, then click** Close **in the Format dialog box**

QUICK TIP

Once a disk is formatted, you do not need to format it again. However, some people use the Quick Format option to erase the contents of a disk quickly, rather than having to select the files and then delete them.

7. **Click the** Close button ⊠ **in the My Computer window**

   My Computer closes and you return to the desktop.

FIGURE AP-1: My Computer window

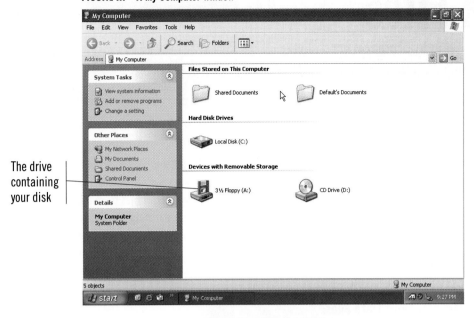

The drive containing your disk

FIGURE AP-2: Format dialog box

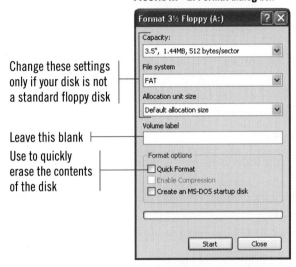

Change these settings only if your disk is not a standard floppy disk

Leave this blank

Use to quickly erase the contents of the disk

FIGURE AP-3: Write-protect tab

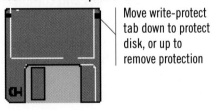

Move write-protect tab down to protect disk, or up to remove protection

3.5" disk

Clues to Use

More about disks

Disks are sometimes called **drives**, but this term really refers to the name by which the operating system recognizes the disk (or a portion of the disk). The operating system typically assigns a drive letter to a drive (which you can reassign if you want). For example, on most computers the hard disk is identified by the letter "C" and the floppy drive by the letter "A." The amount of information a disk can hold is called its capacity, usually measured in megabytes (MB). The most common floppy disk **capacity** is 1.44 MB. Computers also come with other disk drives, such as a **CD drives** and **Zip drives**. Such drives handle CDs and Zip disks, respectively. Both are portable like floppy disks, but they can contain far more data than floppy disks.

Data Files

Read the following information carefully!

It is very important to organize and keep track of the files you need for this book.

1. **Find out from your instructor the location of the Data Files you need and the location where you will store your files.**

   - To complete many of the units in this book, you need to use Data Files. Your instructor will either provide you with a copy of the Data Files or ask you to make your own copy.
   - If you need to make a copy of the Data Files, you will need to copy a set of files from a file server, stand-alone computer, or the Web to the drive and folder where you will be storing your Data Files.
   - Your instructor will tell you which computer, drive letter, and folders contain the files you need, and where you will store your files.
   - You can also download the files by going to www.course.com. A copy of a Data Files list is provided on the Review Pack for this book or may be provided by your instructor.

2. **Copy and organize your Data Files.**

   #### Floppy disk users

   - If you are using floppy disks to store your Data Files, the Data Files List shows which files you'll need to copy onto your disk(s).
   - Unless noted in the Data Files List, you will need one formatted, high-density disk for each unit. For each unit you are assigned, copy the files listed in the **Data File Supplied column** onto one disk.
   - Make sure you label each disk clearly with the unit name (e.g., Word Unit A).
   - When working through the unit, save all your files to this disk.

   #### Users storing files in other locations

   - If you are using a zip drive, network folder, hard drive, or other storage device, use the Data Files List to organize your files.
   - Create a subfolder for each unit in the location where you are storing your files, and name it according to the unit title (e.g., Word Unit A).
   - For each unit you are assigned, copy the files listed in the **Data File Supplied column** into that unit's folder.
   - Store the files you modify or create for each unit in the unit folder.

3. **Find and keep track of your Data Files and completed files.**

   - Use the **Data File Supplied column** to make sure you have the files you need before starting the unit or exercise indicated in the **Unit and Location column**.
   - Use the **Student Saves File As column** to find out the filename you use when saving your changes to a Data File that was provided.
   - Use the **Student Creates File column** to find out the filename you use when saving a file you create new for the exercise.

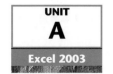

UNIT
A
Excel 2003

Getting Started with Excel 2003

OBJECTIVES

Define spreadsheet software
Start Excel 2003
View the Excel window
Open and save a workbook
Enter labels and values
Name and move a sheet
Preview and print a worksheet
Get Help
Close a workbook and exit Excel

If you have a SAM user profile, you may have access to hands-on instruction, practice, and assessment of the skills covered in this unit. Log in to your SAM account and go to your assignments page to see what your instructor has assigned.

In this unit, you will learn how to start Microsoft Office Excel 2003 and identify elements in the Excel window. You will also learn how to open and save existing files, enter data in a worksheet, manipulate worksheets, and use the extensive Help system. ▄▄▄ Jim Fernandez is the office manager at MediaLoft, a chain of bookstore cafés founded in 1988. MediaLoft stores offer customers the opportunity to purchase books, music, and movies while enjoying a variety of coffees, teas, and freshly baked desserts. Jim wants you, his assistant, to learn how to use Excel and help him analyze a worksheet summarizing budget information for the MediaLoft café in the New York City location.

Defining Spreadsheet Software

Microsoft Excel is an electronic spreadsheet program that runs on Windows computers. You use an **electronic spreadsheet** to produce professional-looking documents that perform numeric calculations rapidly and accurately. These calculations are updated automatically so that accurate information is always available. See Table A-1 for common ways spreadsheets are used in business. The electronic spreadsheet that you produce when using Excel is also referred to as a **worksheet**. Individual worksheets are stored within a **workbook**, which is a file with the .xls file extension. Each new workbook automatically contains three worksheets, although you can have up to 255 sheets. ░░░ Jim uses Excel extensively to track MediaLoft finances, and as you work with Jim, you will also use Excel to complete many tasks. Figure A-1 shows a budget worksheet that Jim created using pencil and paper, while Figure A-2 shows the same worksheet Jim created using Excel.

DETAILS

When you use Excel you have the ability to:

- ### Enter data quickly and accurately

  With Excel, you can enter information faster and more accurately than with pencil and paper. For example, in the MediaLoft NYC Café Budget, certain expenses, such as rent, cleaning supplies, and products supplied on a yearly contract (coffee, creamers, and sweeteners), remain constant for the year. You can copy the expenses that don't change from quarter to quarter, then use Excel to calculate Total Expenses and Net Income for each quarter by supplying the data and formulas.

- ### Recalculate data easily

  Fixing typing errors or updating data using Excel is easy, and the results of a changed entry are recalculated automatically. For example, if you receive updated expense figures for Quarter 4, you enter the new numbers, and Excel recalculates the worksheet.

- ### Perform a what-if analysis

  The ability in Excel to change data and quickly view the recalculated results makes it a powerful decision-making tool. For instance, if the salary budget per quarter is increased to $17,200, you can enter the new figure into the worksheet and immediately see the impact on the overall budget. Any time you use a worksheet to ask the question "what if?" you are performing a **what-if analysis**.

- ### Change the appearance of information

  Excel provides powerful features for making information visually appealing and easy to understand. For example, you can use boldface type and colored or shaded text headings or numbers to emphasize important worksheet data and trends.

- ### Create charts

  Excel makes it easy to create charts based on worksheet information. Charts are updated automatically as data changes. The worksheet in Figure A-2 includes a 3-D pie chart that shows the distribution of the budget expenses for the MediaLoft NYC Café.

- ### Share information with other users

  Because everyone at MediaLoft is now using Microsoft Office, it's easy for them to share worksheet data. For example, you can complete the MediaLoft budget that Jim started creating in Excel. Simply access the files you need or want to share through the network or from a disk, or through the use of online collaboration tools (such as intranets and the Internet), and make any changes or additions.

- ### Create new worksheets from existing ones quickly

  It's easy to take an existing Excel worksheet and quickly modify it to create a new one. When you are ready to create next year's budget, you can open the file for this year's budget, save it with a new filename, and use the existing data as a starting point. An Excel file can also be created using a special format called a **template**, which lets you open a new file based on an existing workbook's design or content. Excel comes with many prepared templates you can use.

FIGURE A-1: Traditional paper worksheet

MediaLoft NYC Café Budget					
	Qtr 1	Qtr 2	Qtr 3	Qtr 4	Total
Net Sales	56,000	84,000	72,000	79,000	291,000
Expenses					
Salary	17,200	17,200	17,200	17,200	68,800
Rent	4,000	4,000	4,000	4,000	16,000
Advertising	3,750	8,000	3,750	3,750	19,250
Cleansers	2,200	2,200	2,200	2,200	8,800
Pastries	2,500	2,500	2,500	2,500	10,000
Milk/Cream	1,000	1,000	1,000	1,000	4,000
Coffee/Tea	4,700	4,750	4,750	4,750	18,950
Sweeteners	650	650	650	650	2,600
Total Expenses	36,000	40,300	36,050	36,050	148,400
Net Income	20,000	43,700	35,950	42,950	142,600

FIGURE A-2: Excel worksheet

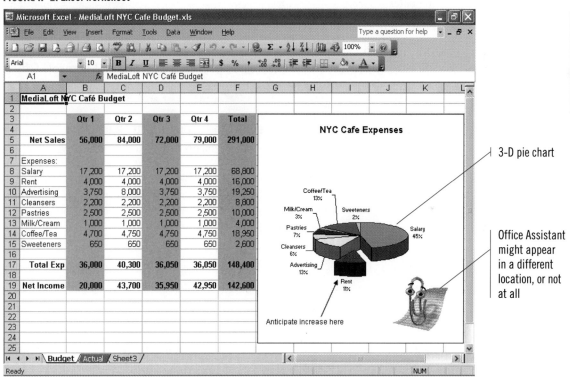

3-D pie chart

Office Assistant might appear in a different location, or not at all

Excel 2003

TABLE A-1: Common business uses for electronic spreadsheets

spreadsheets are used to	by
Maintain values	Calculating numbers
Represent values graphically	Creating charts based on worksheet figures
Create reports to summarize data	Creating workbooks containing multiple worksheets of related data, and numbering and printing the worksheets as consecutively numbered pages
Organize data	Sorting data in ascending or descending order
Analyze data	Creating data summaries and short lists using PivotTables or AutoFilters
Create what-if data scenarios	Using variable values to investigate and sample different outcomes

Starting Excel 2003

To start any Windows program, you use the Start button on the taskbar. A slightly different procedure might be required for computers on a network and those that use Windows-enhancing utilities. If you need assistance, ask your instructor or technical support person. Jim has asked you to work on the budget for the MediaLoft café in New York City, which he created using Excel. You begin by starting Excel.

STEPS

1. **Point to the** Start button [start] **on the taskbar**

   The Start button is on the left side of the taskbar. You use it to start programs on your computer.

> **QUICK TIP**
> You might also see Microsoft Office Excel 2003 listed on the left side of the Start menu, which you can also click to start Excel.

2. **Click** [start]

   Microsoft Office Excel is located on the All Programs menu, which is located at the bottom of the Start menu, as shown in Figure A-3.

3. **Point to** All Programs

   The All Programs menu opens. All the programs on your computer, including Microsoft Excel, are listed on this menu. Your All Programs menu might look different, depending on the programs installed on your computer.

4. **Point to** Microsoft Office

   A submenu displays listing all the Microsoft Office programs installed on your computer. See Figure A-4.

> **TROUBLE**
> If you don't see the Microsoft Office Excel 2003 icon, see your instructor or technical support person.

5. **Click the** Microsoft Office Excel 2003 program icon **on the Microsoft Office submenu**

   Excel opens and a blank worksheet is displayed. In the next lesson, you will learn about the elements of the Excel worksheet window.

6. **If necessary, click the** Maximize button [ ] **on the title bar**

   In the next lesson, you will learn about the elements of the Excel worksheet window.

FIGURE A-3: Start menu

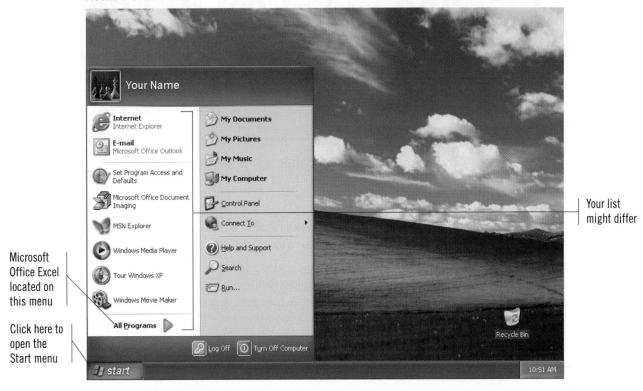

Microsoft Office Excel located on this menu

Click here to open the Start menu

Your list might differ

FIGURE A-4: All Programs menu

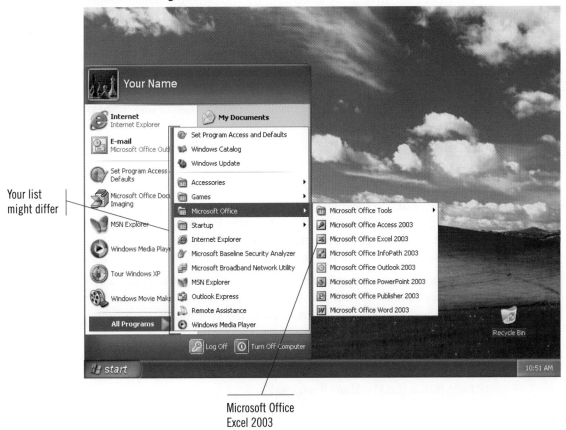

Your list might differ

Microsoft Office Excel 2003 program icon

Viewing the Excel Window

When you start Excel, the worksheet window appears on your screen. The **worksheet window** includes the tools that enable you to create and work with worksheets. ▓▓▓▓ You need to familiarize yourself with the Excel worksheet window and its elements before you start working on the budget worksheet. Compare the descriptions below to the elements shown in Figure A-5.

DETAILS

The elements of the Excel worksheet window include:

QUICK TIP

There are two sets of resizing buttons: one for the program and another for the active workbook. The program's resizing buttons are located on the title bar, while the workbook's resizing buttons appear below the program resizing buttons, on the menu bar (when the workbook is maximized).

- The **title bar** displays the program name (Microsoft Excel) and the filename of the open worksheet (in this case the default filename, Book1). As shown in Figure A-5, the title bar also contains a control menu box, a Close button, and resizing buttons, which are common to all Windows programs. The **control menu box** provides a menu of commands that allow you to move, size, open, or close the program window.

- The **menu bar** contains menus from which you select Excel commands. As with all Windows programs, you can select a menu command by clicking it with the mouse pointer or by pressing [Alt] plus the underlined letter in the menu command name. When you click a menu, only a short list of commonly used commands might appear at first; you can wait or click the double arrows at the bottom of the menu to see expanded menus with a complete list of commands.

- The **Name box** displays the active cell address. In Figure A-5, "A1" appears in the Name box, indicating that A1 is the active cell.

- The **formula bar** allows you to enter or edit data in the worksheet.

- The **toolbars** contain buttons for frequently used Excel commands. The **Standard toolbar** is located just below the menu bar and contains buttons that perform actions within the worksheet. The **Formatting toolbar**—beneath the Standard toolbar—contains buttons that change the worksheet's appearance. Each button contains an image representing its function. For instance, the Print button contains an image of a printer. To select any button, click it with the left mouse button.

QUICK TIP

You can always return to the Getting Started task pane by clicking the Home button 🏠 at the top of any task pane.

- The worksheet window contains a grid of columns and rows. Columns are labeled alphabetically (A, B, C, etc.) and rows are labeled numerically (1, 2, 3, etc.). The worksheet window displays only a small fraction of the whole worksheet, which has a total of 256 columns and 65,536 rows. The intersection of a column and a row is called a **cell**. Cells can contain text, numbers, formulas, or a combination of all three. Every cell has its own unique location or **cell address**, which is identified by the coordinates of the intersecting column and row. For example, the cell address of the cell in the upper-left corner of a worksheet is A1.

- A **task pane** is an organizational tool that allows you to perform routine tasks quickly and easily. The **Getting Started task pane** appears to the right of the worksheet window and lets you quickly open new or existing workbooks. The **Task pane list arrow** lets you choose from 12 different panes.

TROUBLE

If your screen does not display cells in orange and gray as shown in the figure, ask your technical support person to check your Windows color settings.

- The **cell pointer** is a dark rectangle that outlines the cell in which you are working. This cell is called the **active cell**. In Figure A-5, the cell pointer is located at A1, so A1 is the active cell. The column and row headings for the active cell are orange; inactive column and row headings are gray. To activate a different cell, just click any other cell or press the arrow keys on your keyboard to move the cell pointer elsewhere.

- **Sheet tabs** below the worksheet grid let you keep your work in a collection called a workbook. Each workbook contains three worksheets by default and can contain a maximum of 255 sheets. Sheet tabs allow you to name your worksheets with meaningful names. **Sheet tab scrolling buttons** help you display hidden worksheets.

- The **status bar** is located at the bottom of the Excel window. The left side of the status bar provides a brief description of the active command or task in progress. The right side of the status bar shows the status of important keys such as [Caps Lock] and [Num Lock].

FIGURE A-5: Excel worksheet window elements

Title bar
Control menu box
Menu bar
Standard toolbar
Formatting toolbar
Name box
Cell pointer highlights active cell
Formula bar
Sheet tab scrolling buttons

Close button
Resizing buttons
Task pane list arrow
Getting Started task pane lets you open or create a workbook
Worksheet window

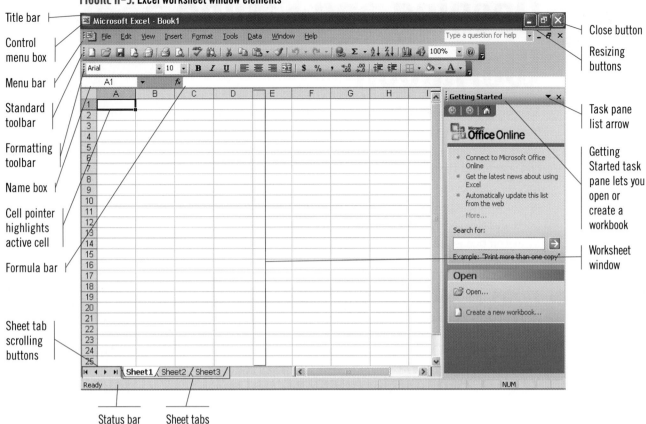

Status bar   Sheet tabs

Clues to Use

Working with toolbars and menus in Excel 2003

Although you can configure Excel so that your toolbars and menus modify themselves to conform to your working style, the lessons in this book assume you have turned off personalized menus and toolbars and are working with all menu commands and toolbar buttons displayed. When you use personalized toolbars, the Standard and Formatting toolbars appear on the same row and display only the most frequently used buttons, as shown in Figure A-6. To use a button that is not visible on a toolbar, you click the Toolbar Options button at the end of the toolbar, then click the button on the Toolbar Options list. As you work, Excel adds the buttons you use to the visible toolbars and drops the buttons you don't often use to the Toolbar Options list. Similarly, Excel menus adjust to your work habits, so that the commands you use most often appear on shortened menus. You can see all the menu commands by clicking the Expand button (double arrows) at the bottom of a menu. It is often easier to work with full toolbars and menus displayed. To turn off personalized toolbars and menus, click Tools on the menu bar, click Customize, then click the Options tab in the Customize dialog box. Select the Show Standard and Formatting toolbars on two rows and Always show full menus check boxes, then click Close. The Standard and Formatting toolbars appear on separate rows and display most of the buttons, and the menus display the complete list of menu commands. (You can also quickly display the toolbars on two rows by clicking a Toolbar Options button, then clicking Show Buttons on Two Rows.)

FIGURE A-6: Toolbars on one row

Toolbar Options buttons

UNIT
A

Excel 2003

Opening and Saving a Workbook

Sometimes it's more efficient to create a new workbook by modifying one that already exists. This saves you from having to retype information from previous work. Throughout this book, you will create new workbooks by opening a file from the location where your Data Files are stored, using the Save As command to create a copy of the file with a new name, then modifying the new file by following the lesson steps. Saving the files with new names keeps your original Data Files intact, in case you have to start the unit over again or you wish to repeat an exercise. Use the Save command to store changes made to an existing file. It is a good idea to save your work every 10 or 15 minutes and before printing. ▰▰▰ You want to complete the MediaLoft budget on which Jim has been working.

STEPS

QUICK TIP
If the task pane is not open, click View on the menu bar, then click Task Pane to display the Getting Started task pane.

1. **Click the** Open button ▣ **in the Getting Started task pane**
   The Open dialog box opens. See Figure A-7. You can also click the Open button ▣ on the Standard toolbar.

2. **Click the** Look in list arrow, **then click the drive and folder where your Data Files are located**
   The Look in list arrow lets you navigate to folders and disk drives on your computer. A list of your Data Files appears in the Open dialog box.

QUICK TIP
If you don't see the three-letter extension .xls on the filenames in the Open dialog box, don't worry. Windows can be set up to display or not to display the file extensions.

3. **Click the file** EX A-1.xls, **then click** Open
   The file EX A-1.xls opens. The Getting Started task pane no longer appears on the screen.

4. **Click** File **on the menu bar, then click** Save As
   The Save As dialog box opens, displaying the drive where your Data Files are stored. You can create a new folder from within the Save As dialog box by clicking ▣ on the dialog box toolbar, typing a name in the Name text box, then clicking OK. To open a file from a folder you create, double-click folders, or use the Look in list arrow in the Open dialog box to open the folder, click the filename, then click Open.

5. **In the File name text box, select the current filename if necessary, type** MediaLoft Cafe Budget, **as shown in Figure A-8, then click** Save
   Both the Save As dialog box and the file EX A-1.xls close, and a duplicate file named MediaLoft Cafe Budget opens, as shown in Figure A-9.

Clues to Use

Creating a new workbook

You can create your own worksheets from scratch by opening a new workbook. To create a new workbook, click the New button ▣ on the Standard toolbar. You can also use the Getting Started or New Workbook task panes to open a new workbook. Click the Go to New Workbook task pane button ▣ in the Getting Started task pane to open the New Workbook task pane, then click the Blank Workbook button ▣ to open a new workbook.

FIGURE A-7: Open dialog box

My Documents folder opens by default

Your files and folders appear here; your contents might differ

Selected filename will appear here

Look in list arrow

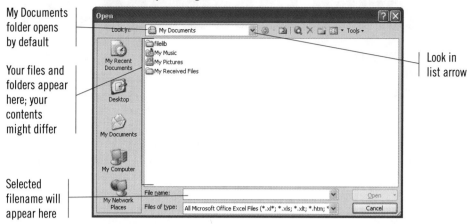

FIGURE A-8: Save As dialog box

Current drive or folder (yours might differ)

Your list of files might differ

Type new filename here

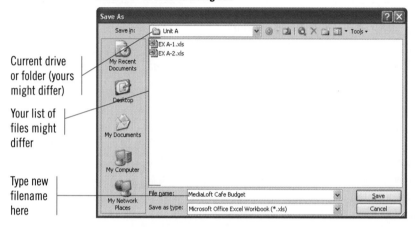

FIGURE A-9: MediaLoft Café Budget workbook

Orange column and row headers define the active cell

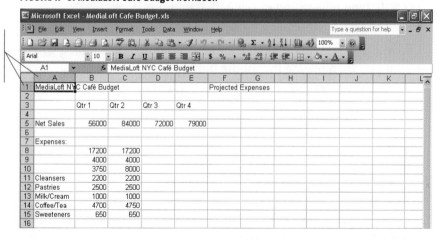

Clues to Use

Opening a workbook using a template

You can create a workbook by entering data and formats into a blank workbook, or you can use predesigned workbooks called templates that are included with Excel. Templates let you automatically create workbooks such as balance sheets, expense statements, loan amortizations, sales invoices, or timecards. Templates save you time because they contain labels, values, formulas, and formatting. To open a new workbook based on a template, click the Other Task Panes list arrow from the Getting Started task pane, then click New Workbook. Click the On my computer link under the Templates section, then click the Spreadsheet Solutions tab in the Templates dialog box. Click one of the samples, save it under a new name, then add your own information. You may need to have the Office CD available to install the templates. You can also find more templates by clicking the Templates home page link.

Entering Labels and Values

Labels help you identify the data in worksheet rows and columns, making your worksheet more readable and understandable. You should try to enter all labels in your worksheet before entering the data. Labels can contain text and numerical information not used in calculations, such as dates, times, or addresses. Labels are left-aligned by default. **Values**, which include numbers, formulas, and functions, are used in calculations. Excel recognizes an entry as a value when it is a number, or begins with one of these special symbols: +, -, =, @, #, or $. All values are right-aligned by default. When you ask Excel to total data in a column, it ignores those cells that have numbers within labels (such as 2006 Sales), and only totals those cells that contain values. When a cell contains both text and numbers, Excel recognizes the entry as a label. You notice that Jim's budget worksheet is missing some data. You want to enter labels identifying the rest of the expense categories, and the values for Qtr 3 and Qtr 4 into the MediaLoft Café Budget worksheet.

STEPS

1. **Click cell A8 to make it the active cell**
   Notice that the cell address A8 appears in the Name box. As you work, the mouse pointer takes on a variety of appearances, depending on where it is and what the program is doing. Table A-2 lists and identifies some mouse pointers. The labels in cells A8:A15 identify the expenses.

   TROUBLE
   If you notice a mistake in a cell entry after entering it, double-click the cell, use [Backspace] or [Delete], make your corrections, then press [Enter]. You can also click Edit on the menu bar, point to Clear, then click Contents to remove a cell's contents.

2. **Type Salary, as shown in Figure A-10, then click the Enter button ☑ on the formula bar**
   As you type, the word "Enter" appears in the status bar. Clicking the Enter button indicates that you are finished typing or changing your entry, and the word "Ready" appears in the status bar. Because the cell is still selected, its contents still appear in the formula bar. You can also confirm a cell entry by pressing [Enter], [Tab], or one of the keyboard arrow keys. These three methods also select an adjacent cell. To confirm an entry and leave the same cell selected, you can press [Ctrl][Enter]. If a label does not fit in a cell, Excel displays the remaining characters in the next cell to the right, as long as it is empty. Otherwise, the label is **truncated**, or cut off.

3. **Click cell A9, type Rent, press [Enter] to confirm the entry and move the cell pointer to cell A10, type Advertising in cell A10, then press [Enter]**
   The remaining expense values have to be added to the worksheet for Quarters 3 and 4.

4. **Click cell D8, press and hold down the left mouse button, drag ⊕ to cell E8 then down to cell E15, then release the mouse button**
   You have selected a **range**, which consists of two or more adjacent cells. The active cell is still cell D8, and the cells in the range are shaded in blue.

   QUICK TIP
   To enter a number that will not be used as part of a calculation, such as a telephone number, type an apostrophe (') before the number.

5. **Type 17200, press [Enter], type 4000 in cell D9, press [Enter], type 3750 in cell D10, press [Enter], type 2200 in cell D11, press [Enter], type 2500 in cell D12, press [Enter], type 1000 in cell D13, press [Enter], type 4750 in cell D14, press [Enter], type 650 in cell D15, then press [Enter]**
   You often enter data in multiple columns and rows; selecting a range makes working with data entry easier because pressing [Enter] makes the next cell in the range active. You have entered all the values in the Qtr 3 column. The cell pointer is now in cell E8.

   QUICK TIP
   The **AutoCalculate value** displays the sum of the selected values in the status bar.

6. **Type the remaining values for cells E8 through E15 as shown in Figure A-11**
   Before confirming a cell entry, you can click the Cancel button on the formula bar or press [Esc] to cancel or delete the entry.

7. **Click cell D8, type 17250, then press [Enter]**

8. **Press [Ctrl][Home] to return to cell A1**

9. **Click the Save button 🖫 on the Standard toolbar**
   You can also press [Ctrl][S] to save a worksheet.

FIGURE A-10: Worksheet with first label entered

Name box

Cancel button

Enter button

Formula bar

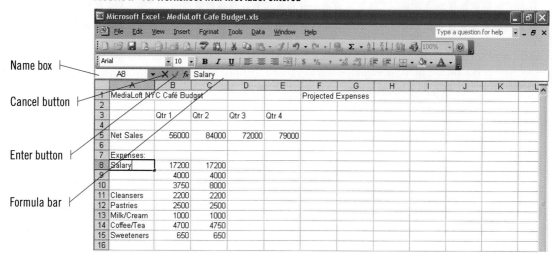

FIGURE A-11: Worksheet with new labels and values

Type these values

Labels entered

Values entered

AutoCalculate value

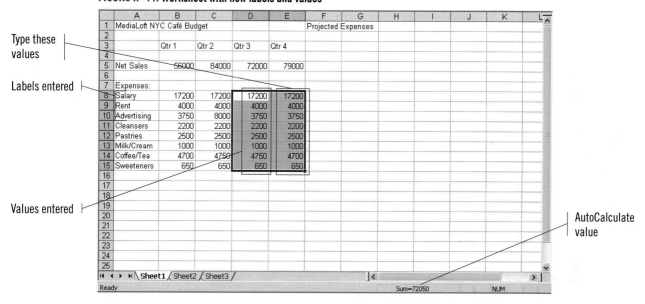

TABLE A-2: Commonly used pointers

name	pointer	use to
Normal	✛	Select a cell or range; indicates Ready mode
Copy	⬚⁺	Create a duplicate of the selected cell(s)
Fill handle	✚	Create an alphanumeric series in a range
I-beam	I	Edit contents of formula bar
Move	⬩	Change the location of the selected cell(s)

Clues to Use

Navigating a worksheet

With over a million cells available to you, it is important to know how to move around, or navigate, a worksheet. You can use the arrow keys on the keyboard (↑, ↓, ←, or →) to move a cell at a time, or use [Page Up] or [Page Down] to move a screen at a time. To move a screen to the left press [Alt][Page Up]; to move a screen to the right press [Alt][Page Down]. You can also use the mouse pointer to click the desired cell. If the desired cell is not visible in the worksheet window, use the scroll bars or the Go To command on the Edit menu to move the location into view. To return to the first cell in a worksheet, click cell A1, or press [Ctrl][Home].

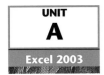

Naming and Moving a Sheet

Each workbook initially contains three worksheets, named Sheet1, Sheet2, and Sheet3. The sheet name appears on the sheet tab. When you open a workbook, the first worksheet is the active sheet. To move from sheet to sheet, you can click any sheet tab at the bottom of the worksheet window. The sheet tab scrolling buttons, located to the left of the sheet tabs, allow you to display hidden sheet tabs. To make it easier to identify the sheets in a workbook, you can rename each sheet and add color to the tabs. You can also organize them in a logical way. For instance, to better track performance goals, you could name each workbook sheet for an individual salesperson; then you could move the sheets so they appeared in alphabetical order. ▰▰▰▰ You have added data to Sheet1 of the budget workbook, which contains information on projected expenses. Jim tells you that Sheet2 contains data for the actual expenses. You want to be able to easily identify the actual expenses and the projected expenses, so you want to name the two sheets in the workbook, add color to distinguish them, then change their order.

STEPS

1. **Click the Sheet2 tab**

   Sheet2 becomes active; this is the worksheet that contains the actual quarterly expenses. Its tab moves to the front, and Sheet1 moves to the background.

2. **Click the Sheet1 tab**

   Sheet1, which contains the projected expenses, becomes active again. Once you have confirmed which sheet is which, you can assign them each a name that identifies their contents.

3. **Double-click the Sheet2 tab**

   Sheet 2 becomes the active sheet with the default sheet name of Sheet2 selected on the sheet tab.

4. **Type Actual, then press [Enter]**

   The new name automatically replaces the default name on the tab. Worksheet names can have up to 31 characters, including spaces and punctuation.

5. **Right-click the Actual tab, then click Tab Color on the shortcut menu**

   The Format Tab Color dialog box opens, as shown in Figure A-12.

6. **Click the red color (first column, third row), click OK, double-click the Sheet1 tab, type Projected, then press [Enter]**

   Notice that when you renamed Sheet1, the color of the entire Actual tab changed to red. You decide to rearrange the order of the sheets, so that Actual comes before Projected.

7. **Click the Actual sheet tab and hold down the mouse button, then drag it to the left of the Projected sheet tab**

   As you drag, the pointer changes to ⧖, the sheet relocation pointer, and a small, black triangle shows its position. See Figure A-13. The first sheet in the workbook is now the Actual sheet. To see hidden sheets, click the far left tab scrolling button to display the first sheet tab; click the far right navigation button to display the last sheet tab. The left and right buttons move one sheet in their respective directions.

8. **Click the Projected sheet tab, enter your name in cell A20, then press [Ctrl][Home]**

   Your name identifies your worksheet as yours, which is helpful if you are sharing a printer.

9. **Click the Save button 💾 on the Standard toolbar**

FIGURE A-12: Format Tab Color dialog box

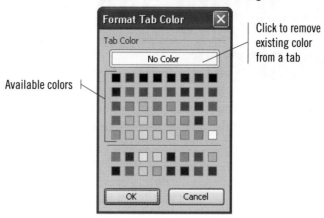

Click to remove existing color from a tab

Available colors

FIGURE A-13: Moving Actual sheet before Projected sheet

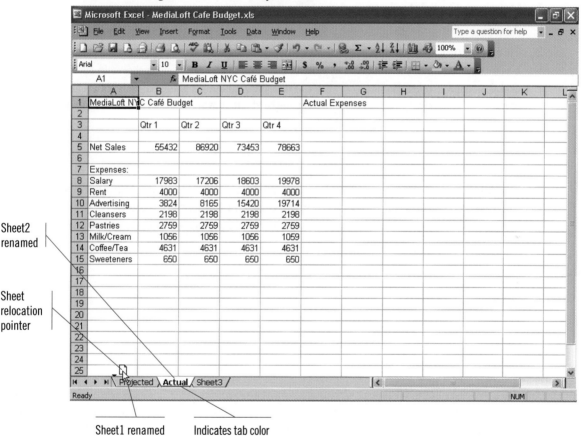

Sheet2 renamed

Sheet relocation pointer

Sheet1 renamed   Indicates tab color

Clues to Use

Copying worksheets

There are times when you may want to copy a worksheet. To copy it, press [Ctrl] as you drag the sheet tab, then release the mouse button before you release [Ctrl]. You can also move and copy worksheets between workbooks. You must have the workbook that you are copying to, as well as the workbook that you are copying from, open.

Select the sheet to copy or move, click Edit on the menu bar, then click Move or Copy sheet. Complete the information in the Move or Copy dialog box. Be sure to click the Create a copy check box if you are copying rather than moving the worksheet. Carefully check your calculation results whenever you move or copy a worksheet.

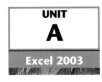

Previewing and Printing a Worksheet

After you complete a worksheet, you may want to print it to have a paper copy for reference or to give to others. You can also print a worksheet that is not complete to review your work when you are not at a computer. Before you print a worksheet, you should save any changes. That way, if anything happens to the file as it is being sent to the printer, you have your latest work saved. Then you should preview it to make sure it fits on the page the way you want. When you **preview** a worksheet, you see a copy of the worksheet exactly as it will appear on paper. See Table A-3 for a summary of printing tips. ▓▓▓▓ You are finished entering the labels and values into the MediaLoft budget. You have already saved your changes, so you preview the worksheet, then print a copy which you can review later.

STEPS

QUICK TIP
To print the work-sheet using existing settings without previewing it, click the Print button 🖨 on the Standard toolbar.

1. **Make sure the printer is on and contains paper**
   If a file is sent to print and the printer is off, an error message appears on your screen.

2. **Click the Print Preview button 🔍 on the Standard toolbar**
   A miniature version of the worksheet appears in the Print Preview window, as shown in Figure A-14. If your worksheet requires more than one page, you can click the Next button or the Previous button to move between pages. Because your worksheet is only one page, the Next and Previous buttons are dimmed to signify they are inactive.

3. **Click Print**
   The Print dialog box opens, as shown in Figure A-15.

4. **Make sure that the Active sheet(s) option button is selected in the Print what section and that 1 appears in the Number of copies text box in the Copies section**
   Adjusting the value in the Number of copies text box enables you to print multiple copies. You can also print a selected range by clicking the Selection option button.

QUICK TIP
After previewing or printing a work-sheet, dotted lines appear on the screen indicating individual page breaks in the printout. Page break positions vary with each printer.

5. **Click OK**
   A Printing dialog box appears briefly while the file is sent to the printer. Note that the dialog box contains a Cancel button. You can use it to cancel the print job while it is waiting in the print queue.

TABLE A-3: Worksheet printing tips

before you print	recommendation
Save the workbook	Make sure your work is saved before executing the command to print
Check the printer	Make sure that the printer is turned on and is online, that it has paper, and that there are no error messages or warning signals
Preview the worksheet	Check the formatted image for page breaks, page setup (vertical or horizontal), and overall appearance of the worksheet
Check the printer selection	Look in the Print dialog box to verify that the correct printer is selected
Check the Print what options	Look in the Print dialog box to verify that you are printing the active sheet, the entire workbook, or a range

FIGURE A-14: Print Preview window

Move to another page

Enlarge the screen image

Print the worksheet

Change print options

Zoom pointer

Return to worksheet

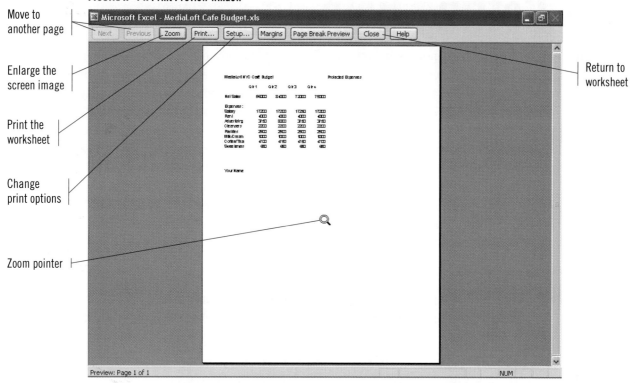

FIGURE A-15: Print dialog box

Your printer might differ

Prints the current worksheet

Indicates the number of copies to be printed

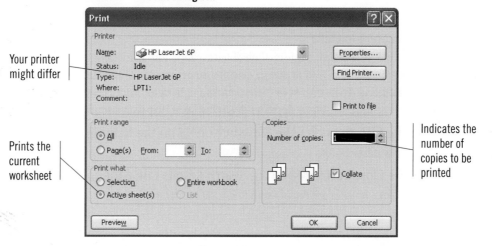

Excel 2003

Clues to Use

Using Zoom in Print Preview

When you are in the Print Preview window, you can enlarge the image by clicking the Zoom button. You can also position the Zoom pointer 🔍 over a specific part of the worksheet page, then click it to view that section of the page. Figure A-16 shows a magnified section of a document. While the image is zoomed in, use the scroll bars to view different sections of the page.

FIGURE A-16: Enlarging the preview using Zoom

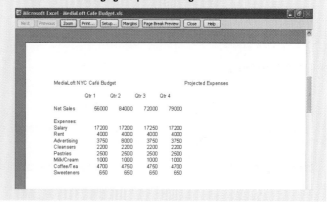

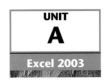

UNIT A

Excel 2003

Getting Help

Excel features an extensive **Help system** that gives you immediate access to definitions, how to complete tasks, explanations, and useful tips. The Help task pane lets you search the Microsoft online Help database stored on the Web or the Excel Help database stored on your computer. You can type a **keyword**, a representative word on which Excel can search your area of interest, or you can access a question-and-answer format to research your Help topic. In addition, you can press [F1] at any time to display the Help task pane and get immediate assistance. Alternately, the **Type a question for help box** on the menu bar is always available for asking questions. You can click in the text box and type a question at any time to display related Help topics. Questions from your current Excel session are stored, and you can access them at any time by clicking the Type a question for help list arrow, then clicking the question of interest. Jim wants you to find out more about formulas so you can work more efficiently with them. He suggests you find out more information by using the Microsoft Excel Help task pane.

STEPS

QUICK TIP

You can also display the Microsoft Excel Help task pane from any open task pane. To do this, click the Other Task Panes list arrow, then click Help.

1. **Click the** Microsoft Excel Help button ⊚ **on the Standard toolbar**

   The Excel Help task pane opens. You can get information by typing a keyword or question in the Search text box.

2. **Type** Create a formula **in the Search for text box**

   See Figure A-18.

3. **Click the** Start searching button →

   Excel searches for relevant topics from the Help files and displays a list of topics from which you can choose.

4. **Click** Create a formula

   A Help window containing information about creating formulas opens, as shown in Figure A-19. Microsoft Excel Help is an online feature that by default assumes you are connected to the Internet. If you are not connected to the Internet, then your search results might differ from Figure A-19. You may have fewer search results, reflecting those topics stored locally in the Excel Help database on your computer.

QUICK TIP

Clicking the Print button 🖨 in the Help window prints the information.

5. **Read the text, then click the** Close button ⊠ **on the Help window title bar**

   The Help window closes.

6. **Click the** Close button ⊠ **on the Search Results task pane to close it.**

   The task pane is no longer displayed in the worksheet window.

FIGURE A-18: Help task pane

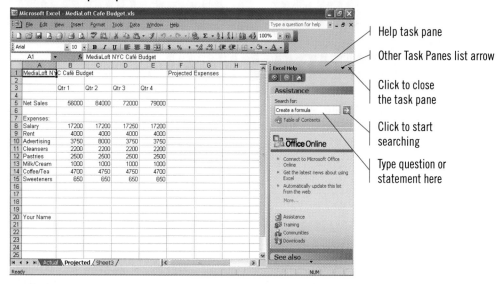

- Help task pane
- Other Task Panes list arrow
- Click to close the task pane
- Click to start searching
- Type question or statement here

FIGURE A-19: Help window

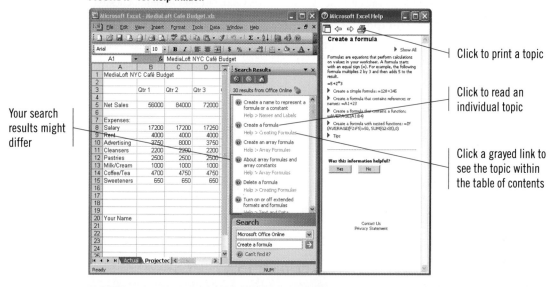

Your search results might differ

- Click to print a topic
- Click to read an individual topic
- Click a grayed link to see the topic within the table of contents

Clues to Use

Using the Office Assistant

If the Office Assistant is displayed, click it to access Help. If it is not displayed, click Help on the menu bar, then click Show the Office Assistant. (You may need to install additional components from your Microsoft Office CD in order to see the Office Assistant.) This feature provides help based on the text you type in the query box. To ask a question, click the Office Assistant. Type a question, statement, or word, as shown in Figure A-17, then click Search. The Search Results task pane searches the database and displays any matching topics. The animated Office Assistant provides Office Assistant Tips (indicated by a light bulb) on the current action you are performing. You can click the light bulb to display a dialog box containing relevant choices to which you can refer as you work. The default Office Assistant character is Clippit, but there are others from which you can choose. To change the appearance of the Office Assistant, right-click the Office Assistant, then click Options on the shortcut menu. Click the Gallery tab in the Options dialog box, click the Back and Next buttons until

you find an Assistant you want to use, then click OK. (You may need to insert your Microsoft Office CD to perform this task.)

FIGURE A-17: Office Assistant dialog box

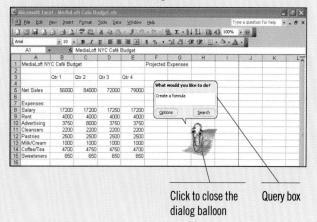

Click to close the dialog balloon

Query box

Excel 2003

Closing a Workbook and Exiting Excel

When you have finished working, you need to save the workbook file and close it. When you have completed all your work in Excel you need to exit the program. You can exit Excel by clicking Exit on the File menu. You have completed your work on the MediaLoft budget. You want to close the workbook, then exit Excel.

STEPS

1. **Click File on the menu bar**

   The File menu opens. See Figure A-20.

2. **Click Close**

   Excel closes the workbook, asking if you want to save your changes; if you have made any changes be sure to save them. You can also click the workbook Close button instead of clicking Close on the File menu.

QUICK TIP

To exit Excel and close several files at once, click Exit on the File menu. Excel prompts you to save changes to each open workbook before exiting the program.

3. **Click File on the menu bar, then click Exit**

   You can also click the program Close button to exit the program. Excel closes, and you return to the desktop.

Program
control
menu box

Workbook
control
menu box

Close
command

Microsoft Excel - MediaLoft Cafe Budget.xls

| File | Edit | View | Insert | Format | Tools | Data | Window | Help |

Type a question for help

	New...	Ctrl+N
	Open...	Ctrl+O
	Close	
	Save	Ctrl+S
	Save As...	
	Save as Web Page...	
	Save Workspace...	
	File Search...	
	Permission	▶
	Web Page Preview	
	Page Setup...	
	Print Area	▶
	Print Preview	
	Print...	Ctrl+P
	Send To	▶
	Properties	
	1 MediaLoft Cafe Budget.xls	
	2 EX A-1.xls	
	Exit	

NYC Café Budget

	D	E	F	G	H	I	J	K	L
1			Projected Expenses						
2									
3	Qtr 3	Qtr 4							
4									
5	72000	79000							
6									
7									
8	17250	17200							
9	4000	4000							
10	3750	3750							
11	2200	2200							
12	2500	2500							
13	1000	1000							
14	4750	4700							
15	650	650							
16									
17									
18									
19									
20									
21									
22									
23									
24									
25									

Actual \ **Projected** \ Sheet3

Ready

NUM

Your list
might differ

Exit command

Excel 2003

Practice

▼ CONCEPTS REVIEW

Label the elements of the Excel worksheet window shown in Figure A-21.

FIGURE A-21

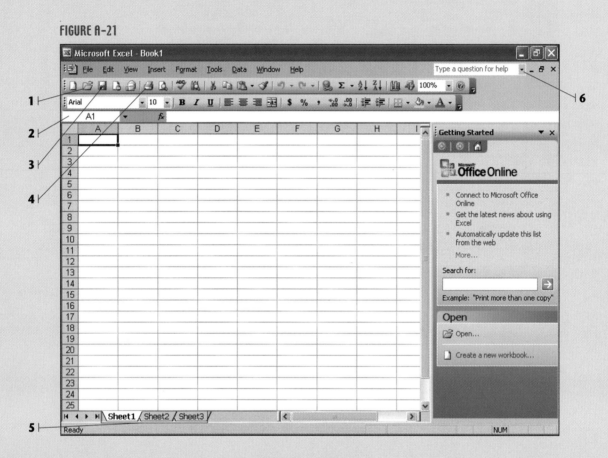

Match each term with the statement that best describes it.

7. Cell	a. Area that contains a grid of columns and rows
8. Worksheet window	b. The intersection of a column and row
9. Workbook	c. Allows you to enter or edit worksheet data
10. Name Box	d. Collection of worksheets
11. Cell pointer	e. Rectangle indicating the active cell
12. Formula bar	f. Displays the active cell address

Select the best answer from the list of choices.

13. The following key(s) can be used to confirm cell entries, except:

  a. [Enter].

  b. [Tab].

  c. [Esc].

  d. [Ctrl][Enter].

14. Each of the following is true about labels, except:

  a. They are left-aligned by default.

  b. They are not used in calculations.

  c. They are right-aligned by default.

  d. They can include numerical information.

15. An electronic spreadsheet can perform all of the following tasks, except:

  a. Display information visually.

  b. Calculate data accurately.

  c. Plan worksheet objectives.

  d. Recalculate updated information.

16. What symbol is typed before a number to make the number a label?

  a. '

  b. !

  c. "

  d. ;

17. You can get Excel Help in any of the following ways, except:

  a. Clicking Help on the menu bar, then clicking Microsoft Excel Help.

  b. Minimizing the program window.

  c. Clicking 🔘.

  d. Pressing [F1].

18. Each of the following is true about values, except:

  a. They can include labels.

  b. They are right-aligned by default.

  c. They are used in calculations.

  d. They can include formulas.

19. Which button is used to preview a worksheet?

  a. ▫

  b. ▫

  c. ▫

  d. ▫

20. Each of the following is true about the Help feature, except:

  a. You can use the Type a question for help text box.

  b. You can search your computer and Microsoft.com.

  c. You can change the appearance of the Office Assistant.

  d. It can complete certain tasks for you.

21. Which feature is used to enlarge a Print Preview view?

  a. Magnify

  b. Enlarge

  c. Amplify

  d. Zoom

▼ SKILLS REVIEW

1. Define spreadsheet software.

  a. Identify five disadvantages of using a nonelectronic spreadsheet.

  b. Identify five common business uses for electronic spreadsheets.

2. Start Excel 2003.

  a. Point to **All Programs** on the Start menu.

  b. Point to Microsoft Office, then click the **Microsoft Office Excel 2003** program icon.

  c. What appears when Excel opens?

3. View the Excel window.

   a. Identify as many elements in the Excel window without looking back in the unit.

   b. If the program and workbook are both maximized, which set of resizing buttons is used to minimize the workbook? (*Hint*: Would you use the upper or lower set?)

4. Open and save a workbook.

   a. Open the workbook EX A-2.xls from the drive and folder where your Data Files are located.

   b. Use the Create New Folder button in the Save As dialog box to create a folder called Toronto in the drive and folder where your Data Files are located.

   c. Save the workbook as MediaLoft Toronto Café in the Toronto folder where your Data Files are located.

   d. Close the file.

   e. Open it again from the new folder you created.

   f. Open a new workbook based on the Balance Sheet template: open the New Workbook task pane, click the On my computer link under the Templates section, display the Spreadsheet Solutions tab, then double-click Balance Sheet.

   g. Save the workbook as MediaLoft Balance Sheet in the drive and folder where your Data Files are stored, then close the workbook.

5. Enter labels and values.

   a. Enter the necessary labels shown in Table A-4. (The entry for "Water" should be in cell A4.)

   b. Enter the values shown in Table A-4.

   c. Clear the contents of cell A9 using the Edit menu, then type Tea in cell A9.

   d. Save the workbook using the Save button.

6. Name and move a sheet.

   a. Name the Sheet1 tab Inventory, then name the Sheet2 tab Sales.

   b. Move the Inventory sheet so it comes after the Sales sheet.

   c. Change the tab color of the Inventory sheet to yellow (third column, fourth row in the pallette).

   d. Change the tab color of the Sales sheet to aqua (fifth column, fourth row in the pallette).

TABLE A-4

	On-Hand	Cost Each	Sale Price
Water	32	10.03	
Coffee	52	13.71	
Bread	39	15.22	
Muffins	25	16.99	
Sweets	43	11.72	
Sodas	52	9.91	

7. Preview and print a worksheet.

   a. Make the Inventory sheet active.

   b. View it in Print Preview.

   c. Use the Zoom button to get a better look at your worksheet.

   d. Add your name to cell A11, then print one copy of the worksheet.

   e. Save the workbook.

8. Get Help.

   a. Display the Help task pane.

   b. Ask for information about defining a range.

   c. Print the information offered by the Help task pane using the Print button in the Help window.

   d. Close the Help window and task pane.

9. Close a workbook and exit Excel.

   a. Close the file using the Close command.

   b. Exit Excel.

▼ INDEPENDENT CHALLENGE 1

The Excel Help feature provides definitions, explanations, procedures, and other helpful information. It also provides examples and demonstrations to show you how Excel features work. Topics include elements such as the active cell, status bar, buttons, and dialog boxes, as well as detailed information about Excel commands and options.

    a. Start Excel and open a blank workbook using the Getting Started task pane.

    b. Display the Help task pane.

    c. Find information about displaying toolbar buttons.

Advanced Challenge Exercise

    ■ Display the Office Assistant, if necessary, using the Show Office Assistant command on the Help menu.

    ■ Click the Office Assistant, then type a question about saving a workbook in another file format. (*Hint*: You may have to ask the Office Assistant more than one question.)

    d. Print the information, close the Help window, then exit Excel.

▼ INDEPENDENT CHALLENGE 2

Spreadsheet software has many uses that can affect the way people work. The beginning of this unit discusses some examples of people using Excel. Use your own personal or business experiences to come up with five examples of how Excel can be used in a business setting.

    a. Start Excel.

    b. Write down five business tasks that you can complete more efficiently by using an Excel worksheet.

    c. Sketch a sample of each worksheet. See Table A-5, a sample payroll worksheet, as a guide.

    d. Open a new workbook and save it as **Sample Payroll** in the drive and folder where your Data Files are stored.

    e. Give your worksheet a title in cell A1, then type your name in cell D1.

    f. Enter the labels shown in Table A-5. Enter Hours Worked in column C and Hourly Wage in column E.

    g. Create and enter your own sample data for Hours Worked and Hourly Wage in the worksheet. (The entry for "Dale Havorford" should be in cell A4.)

    h. Save your work, then preview and print the worksheet.

    i. Close the worksheet and exit Excel.

TABLE A-5

Employee Name	Hours Worked	Hourly Wage
Dale Havorford		
Chris Wong		
Sharon Martinez		
Belinda Swanson		
Total		

▼ INDEPENDENT CHALLENGE 3

You are the office manager for Christine's Car Parts, a small auto parts supplier. Although the company is just three years old, it is expanding rapidly, and you are continually looking for ways to make your job easier. Last year, you began using Excel to manage and maintain data on inventory and sales, which has greatly helped you to track information accurately and efficiently. The owner of the company has just approved your request to hire an assistant, who will be starting work in a week. You want to create a short training document that acquaints your new assistant with basic Excel skills.

a. Start Excel.

b. Create a new workbook and save it as Training Workbook in the drive and folder where your Data Files are located.

c. Model your worksheet after the sample shown in Figure A-22. Enter a title for the worksheet in cell A1.

d. Enter your name in cell D1.

e. Create and enter values and labels for a sample spreadsheet. Make sure you have labels in column A.

f. Change the name of Sheet1 to Sample Data, then change the tab color of the Sample Data worksheet to another color.

g. Preview the worksheet, then print it.

Advanced Challenge Exercise

■ Open a workbook based on a template from the Spreadsheet Solutions tab in the Templates dialog box. (You may need to insert your Office CD in order to do this.)

■ Preview the worksheet, then print it.

■ Save the workbook as Template Sample.

h. Close the file(s) and exit Excel.

FIGURE A-22

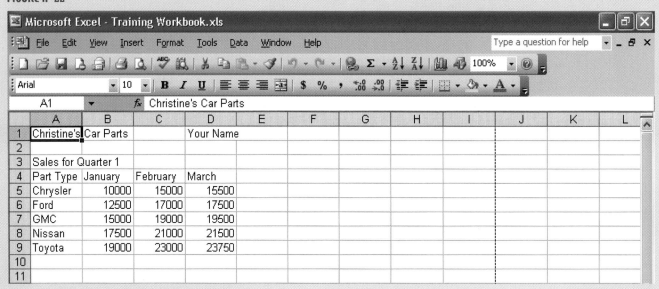

▼ INDEPENDENT CHALLENGE 4

You can use the World Wide Web to help make informed purchasing decisions. Your supervisor has just given you approval for buying a new computer. While cost is not a limiting factor, you do need to provide a list of hardware and software requirements. You can use data found on the World Wide Web, and use Excel to create a worksheet that details your purchase decision.

a. Connect to the Internet, then use your favorite search engine to find your own information sources on computer hardware and software you can purchase.

b. Locate data for the type of system you want by using at least two different vendor's Web sites. When you find systems that meet your needs, print out the information. Be sure to identify each system's key features, such as the processor chip, hard drive capacity, RAM, and monitor size.

c. When you are finished gathering data, disconnect from the Internet.

d. Start Excel, open a new workbook, then save it in the drive and folder where your Data Files are stored as New Computer Data.

e. Enter the manufacturers' names in columns and computer features (RAM, etc.) in rows. List the systems you found through your research, including the features you want (e.g., CD-ROM drive, etc.) and the cost for each system.

f. Indicate on the worksheet your final purchase decision by including descriptive text in a prominent cell. Enter your name in one of the cells.

g. Save, preview, then print your worksheet.

h. Close the file and exit Excel.

Excel 2003

▼ VISUAL WORKSHOP

Create a worksheet similar to Figure A-23 using the skills you learned in this unit. Save the workbook as **Carrie's Camera and Darkroom** in the drive and folder where your Data Files are stored. Type your name in cell A11, then preview and print the worksheet.

FIGURE A-23

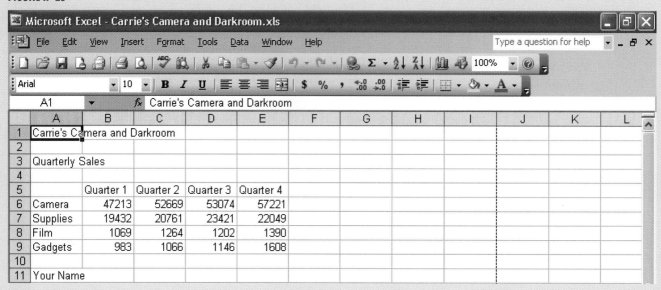

Building and Editing Worksheets

OBJECTIVES

Plan and design a worksheet
Edit cell entries
Enter formulas
Create complex formulas
Introduce Excel functions
Use Excel functions
Copy and move cell entries
Understand relative and absolute cell references
Copy formulas with relative cell references
Copy formulas with absolute cell references

If you have a SAM user profile, you may have access to hands-on instruction, practice, and assessment of the skills covered in this unit. Log in to your SAM account and go to your assignments page to see what your instructor has assigned.

Using your understanding of Excel basics, you can now plan and build your own worksheets. When you build a worksheet, you enter labels, values, and formulas into worksheet cells. Once you create a worksheet, you can save it in a workbook file and then print it. ▓▓▓ The MediaLoft Marketing Department has asked Jim Fernandez for an estimate of the average number of author appearances this summer. Marketing hopes that the number of appearances will increase 20% over last year's figures. Jim asks you to create a worksheet that summarizes appearances for last year and forecasts the summer appearances for this year.

Planning and Designing a Worksheet

Before you start entering data into a worksheet, you need to know the purpose and approximate layout of the worksheet. ▦▦▦▦ To increase store traffic and sales, MediaLoft encourages authors to come to stores and sign their books. Jim wants to forecast MediaLoft's 2006 summer author appearances. The goal, already identified by the Marketing Department, is to increase the year 2005 signings by 20%. Using the planning guidelines below, Jim works with you to plan this worksheet and create it in Excel.

DETAILS

In planning and designing a worksheet it is important to:

- **Determine the purpose of the worksheet and give it a meaningful title**

  You need to forecast summer appearances for 2006. Jim suggests you title the worksheet "Summer 2006 MediaLoft Author Events Forecast."

- **Determine your worksheet's desired results, or output**

  Jim needs to begin scheduling author events and will use these forecasts to determine staffing and budget needs if the number of author events increases by 20%. He also wants to calculate the average number of author events because the Marketing Department uses this information for corporate promotions.

- **Collect all the information, or input, that will produce the results you want**

  Jim helps you by gathering together the number of author events that occurred at four stores during the 2005 summer season, which runs from June through August.

- **Determine the calculations, or formulas, necessary to achieve the desired results**

  Jim states you will first need to total the number of events at each of the selected stores during each month of the summer of 2005. Then you will need to add these totals together to determine the grand total of summer appearances. Because you need to determine the goal for the 2006 season, the 2005 monthly totals and grand total are multiplied by 1.2 to calculate the projected 20% increase for the 2006 summer season. Jim suggests you use the Average function to determine the average number of author appearances for the Marketing Department.

- **Sketch on paper how you want the worksheet to look; identify where to place the labels and values**

  Jim suggests you put the store locations in rows and the months in columns. Jim creates a sketch, in which he enters the data and notes the location of the monthly totals and the grand total. Below the totals, he writes out the formula for determining a 20% increase in 2005 appearances. He also includes a label for the calculations of the average number of events. Jim's sketch of this worksheet is shown in Figure B-1.

- **Create the worksheet**

  Jim begins creating the worksheet for you, by entering the labels first, to establish the structure of the worksheet. He then enters the values—the data summarizing the events—into the worksheet. Finally, he enters the formulas necessary to calculate totals, averages, and forecasts. These values and formulas will be used to calculate the necessary output. The worksheet Jim creates is shown in Figure B-2.

FIGURE B-1: Worksheet sketch showing labels, values, and calculations

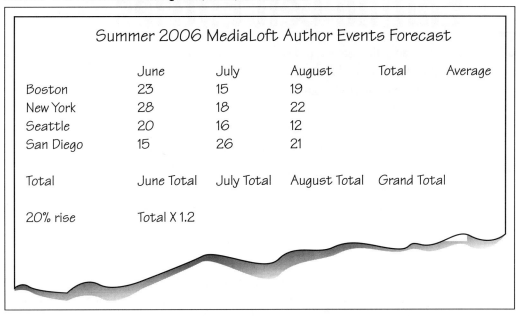

Summer 2006 MediaLoft Author Events Forecast

	June	July	August	Total	Average
Boston	23	15	19		
New York	28	18	22		
Seattle	20	16	12		
San Diego	15	26	21		
Total	June Total	July Total	August Total	Grand Total	
20% rise	Total X 1.2				

FIGURE B-2: Forecasting worksheet

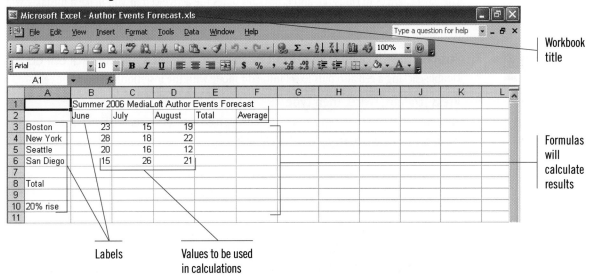

Editing Cell Entries

You can change the contents of a cell at any time. To edit the contents of a cell, you first select the cell you want to edit. Then you have two options: you can click the formula bar or press [F2]. This puts Excel into Edit mode. Alternately, you can double-click any cell and start editing. To make sure you are in Edit mode, look at the **mode indicator** on the far left of the status bar. After planning and creating the worksheet with Jim, you notice that he entered the wrong value for the August Seattle events, and that Houston should replace San Diego. You can edit these entries to correct them.

STEPS

QUICK TIP

In the Open dialog box, you can double-click the filename to open the workbook in one step.

1. **Start Excel, open the file** EX B-1.xls **from the drive and folder where your Data Files are stored, then save it as** Author Events Forecast

2. **Click cell** D5, **then click to the right of** 12 **in the formula bar**

   This cell contains August events for the Seattle store, which you want to change to reflect the correct numbers. Excel goes into Edit mode, and the mode indicator on the status bar displays "Edit." A blinking vertical line called the **insertion point** appears in the formula bar, and if you move the mouse pointer to the formula bar, the pointer changes to $\mathcal{I}$, which is used for editing. See Figure B-3.

QUICK TIP

The Undo button allows you to reverse up to 16 previous actions, one at a time.

3. **Press** [Backspace], **type** 8, **then click the** Enter button on the formula bar

   The value in cell D5 is changed from 12 to 18, and cell D5 remains selected.

4. **Click cell** A6, **then press** [F2]

   Excel returns to Edit mode, and the insertion point appears in the cell.

5. **Press and hold** [Shift], **press** [Home], **then release** [Shift]

   The contents of the cell is selected, and the next typed character will replace the selection.

6. **Type** Houston, **then press** [Enter]

   The label changes to Houston, and cell A7 becomes the active cell. If you make a mistake, you can click the Cancel button on the formula bar *before* confirming the cell entry. If you notice the mistake *after* you have confirmed the cell entry, click the Undo button on the Standard toolbar.

QUICK TIP

Double-clicking when the pointer is to the left of the cell's contents positions the insertion point to the left of the data.

7. **Position the** ✛ **pointer to the left of** 26 **in cell C6, then double-click cell** C6

   Double-clicking a cell also puts Excel into Edit mode with the insertion. point in the cell.

8. **Press** [Delete] **twice, then type** 19

   The number of book signings for July in Houston has been corrected. See Figure B-4.

9. **Click** **to confirm the entry, then click the** Save button **on the Standard toolbar**

FIGURE B-3: Worksheet in Edit mode

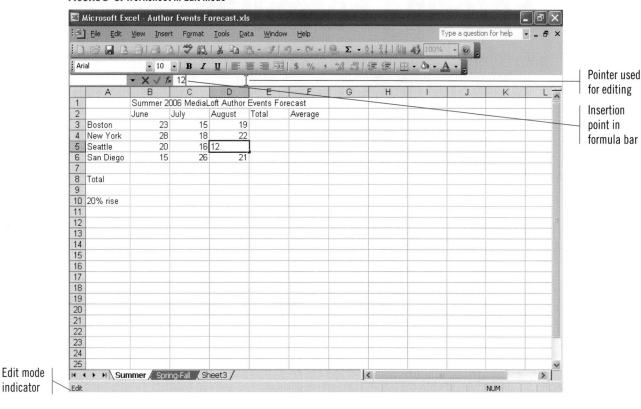

Pointer used for editing

Insertion point in formula bar

Edit mode indicator

FIGURE B-4: Edited worksheet

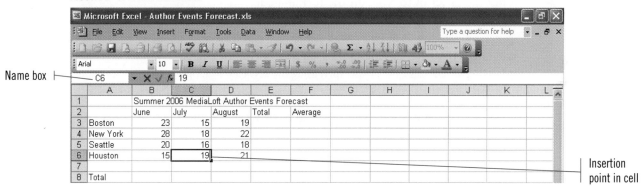

Name box

Insertion point in cell

Clues to Use

Recovering a lost workbook file

Sometimes while you are using Excel, you may experience a power failure or your computer may "freeze," making it impossible to continue working. If this type of interruption occurs, Excel has a built-in recovery feature that allows you to open and save files that were open at the time of the interruption. When you restart Excel after an interruption, the Document Recovery task pane opens on the left side of your screen displaying both original and recovered versions of the files that were open. If you're not sure which file to open (original or recovered), it's usually better to open the recovered file because it will have retained the latest information. You can, however, open and review all the versions of the file that were recovered and save the best one. Each file listed in the Document Recovery task pane has a list arrow with options that allow you to open the file, save the file, delete the file, or show repairs made to the file.

Entering Formulas

You use **formulas** to perform numeric calculations such as adding, multiplying, and averaging. Formulas in an Excel worksheet usually start with the equal sign (=), called the **formula prefix**, followed by cell addresses and range names. Arithmetic formulas use one or more **arithmetic operators** to perform calculations; see Table B-1 for a list of common arithmetic operators. Using a cell address or range name in a formula is called **cell referencing**. If you change a value in a cell, any formula containing that cell reference will be automatically recalculated using the new value. ▰▰▰▰▱▱▱ You need to total the values for the monthly author events for June, July, and August. You create formulas to perform these calculations.

STEPS

1. **Click cell B8**

   This is the cell where you want to enter the calculation that totals the number of June events.

2. **Type = (the equal sign)**

   Placing an equal sign at the beginning of an entry tells Excel that a formula is about to be entered, rather than a label or a value. "Enter" appears in the status bar. The total number of June events is equal to the sum of the values in cells B3, B4, B5, and B6.

   > **TROUBLE**
   >
   > If you type an incorrect character, press [Backspace], then type the correct character.

3. **Type b3+b4+b5+b6**

   Compare your worksheet to Figure B-5. Each cell address in the equation is shown in a matching color in the worksheet. For example, the cell address B3 is written in blue in the equation and is outlined in blue in the worksheet. This makes it easy to identify each cell in a formula.

   > **TROUBLE**
   >
   > If the formula instead of the result appears in the cell after you click ✓, make sure you began the formula with = (the equal sign).

4. **Click the Enter button ✓ on the formula bar**

   The result, 86, appears in cell B8. Cell B8 remains selected, and the formula appears in the formula bar. Excel is not case sensitive: it doesn't matter if you type uppercase or lowercase characters when you enter cell addresses. Typing cell addresses is only one way of creating a formula. A more accurate method involves **pointing** at cells using the mouse, then using the keyboard to supply arithmetic operators.

5. **Click cell C8, type =, click cell C3, type +, click cell C4, type +, click cell C5, type +, click cell C6, then click ✓**

   When you clicked cell C3, a moving border surrounded the cell. This **moving border** indicates the cell used in the calculation. Moving borders can appear around a single cell or a range of cells. The total number of author appearances for July is 68 and appears in cell C8. The pointing method of creating a formula is more accurate than typing, because it is easy to type a cell address incorrectly. You also need to enter a total for the August events in cell D8.

6. **Click cell D8, type =, click cell D3, type +, click cell D4, type +, click cell D5, type +, click cell D6, then click ✓**

   The total number of appearances for August is 80 and appears in cell D8. Compare your worksheet to Figure B-6.

7. **Click the Save button 🖫 on the Standard toolbar**

FIGURE B-5: Worksheet showing cells in a formula

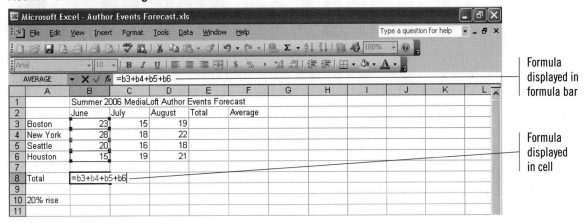

Formula displayed in formula bar

Formula displayed in cell

FIGURE B-6: Completed formulas

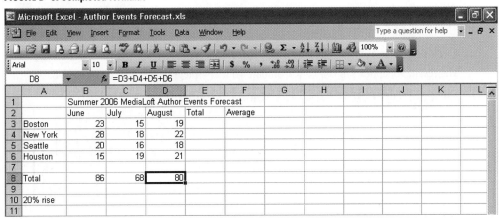

TABLE B-1: Excel arithmetic operators

operator	purpose	example
+	Addition	=A5+A7
–	Subtraction or negation	=A5–10
*	Multiplication	=A5*A7
/	Division	=A5/A7
%	Percent	=35%
^ (caret)	Exponent	=6^2 (same as 6^2)

Creating Complex Formulas

The formula you entered is a simple formula containing one arithmetic operator, the plus sign. You can create a **complex formula**—an equation that uses more than one type of arithmetic operator. For example, you may need to create a formula that uses addition and multiplication. You can use arithmetic operators to separate tasks within a complex equation. In formulas containing more than one arithmetic operator, Excel uses the order of precedence rules to determine which operation to perform first. You want to total the values for the monthly author events for June, July, and August, and forecast what the 20% increase in appearances will be. You can create a complex formula to perform these calculations.

STEPS

1. **Click cell B10, type =, click cell B8, then type *.2**

   This part of the formula calculates 20% of the cell contents by multiplying the June total by .2 (or 20%). Because this part of the formula uses multiplication, it is calculated first according to the rules of precedence.

   > **QUICK TIP**
   > Press [Esc] to turn off a moving border and deselect the range.

2. **Type +, then click cell B8**

   The second part of the formula adds the 20% increase to the original value of the cell. The mode indicator says Point, indicating you can add more cell references. Compare your worksheet to Figure B-7.

3. **Click the Enter button ✓ on the formula bar**

   The result, 103.2, appears in cell B10.

4. **Click cell C10, type =, click cell C8, type *.2, type +, click cell C8, then click ✓**

   The result, 81.6, appears in cell C10.

5. **Click cell D10, type =, click cell D8, type *.2, type +, click D8, then click ✓**

   The result, 96, appears in cell D10. Compare your completed worksheet to Figure B-8.

6. **Click the Save button 🖫 on the Standard toolbar**

Clues to Use

Order of precedence in Excel formulas

A formula can include several mathematical operations. When you work with formulas that have more than one operator, the order of precedence is very important. If a formula contains two or more operators, such as 4+.55/4000*25, the computer performs the calculations in a particular sequence based on these rules: Operations inside parentheses are calculated before any other operations. Exponents are calculated next, then any multiplication and division—from left to right. Finally, addition and subtraction are calculated from left to right. In the example 4+.55/4000*25, Excel performs the arithmetic operations by first dividing 4000 into .55, then multiplying the result by 25, then adding 4. You can change the order of calculations by using parentheses. For example, in the formula (4+.55)/4000*25, Excel would first add 4 and .55, then divide that amount by 4000, then finally multiply by 25.

FIGURE B-7: Elements of a complex formula

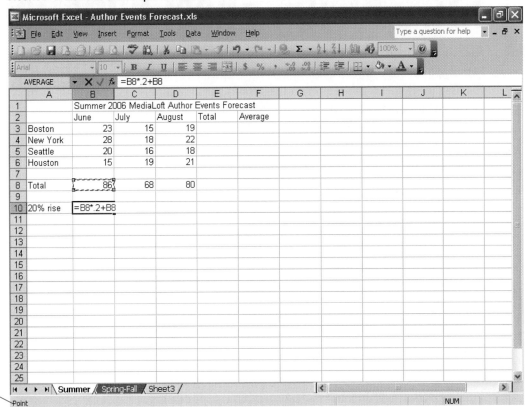

Mode indicator

FIGURE B-8: Multiple complex formulas

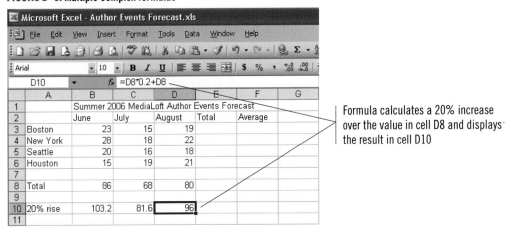

Formula calculates a 20% increase over the value in cell D8 and displays the result in cell D10

Clues to Use

Editing formulas

You edit formulas the same way you edit cell entries: you click the cell containing the formula then edit it in the formula bar; you can also double-click a cell or press [F2] to enter Edit mode, and then edit the formula in the cell. After you are in Edit mode, use the arrow keys to move the insertion point left or right in the formula. Use [Backspace] or [Delete] to delete characters to the left or right of the insertion point, then type or point to new cell references or operators.

Introducing Excel Functions

Functions are predefined worksheet formulas that enable you to perform complex calculations easily. Like formulas, functions always begin with the formula prefix = (the equal sign). You can type functions, or you can use the Insert Function button on the formula bar to select the function you need from a dialog box. The **AutoSum button** on the Standard toolbar enters the most frequently used function, SUM. A function can be used by itself within a cell, or as part of a formula. For example, to calculate monthly sales tax, you could create a formula that adds a range of cells (using the SUM function) and then multiplies the total by a decimal. ▰▰▰▰ You use the SUM function to calculate the grand totals in the worksheet.

STEPS

1. **Click cell E3**

   This is where you want the total of all Boston author events for June, July, and August to appear.

2. **Click the AutoSum button** Σ **on the Standard toolbar**

   The formula =SUM(B3:D3) appears in the formula bar and a moving border surrounds cells in the worksheet, as shown in Figure B-9.

3. **Click the Enter button** ✓ **on the formula bar**

   The result, 57, appears in cell E3. By default, AutoSum adds the values in the cells above the cell pointer. If there are one or fewer values there, AutoSum adds the values to its left—in this case, the values in cells B3, C3, and D3. The information inside the parentheses is the **argument**, or the information Excel uses to calculate the function result. In this case, the argument is the range B3:D3.

4. **Click cell E4, click** Σ **, then click** ✓

   The total for the New York events, 68, appears in cell E4.

5. **Click cell E5, then click** Σ

   AutoSum sets up a function to add the two values in the cells above the active cell, but this time the default argument is not correct.

6. **Click cell B5 and hold down the mouse button, drag to cell D5 to select the range B5:D5, then click** ✓

   As you drag, the argument in the SUM function changes to reflect the selected range, and a yellow **Argument ScreenTip** shows the function syntax. You can click any part of the Argument ScreenTip to display Help on the function.

7. **Click cell E6, type =SUM(, click cell B6 and drag to cell D6, then click** ✓

8. **Click cell E8, type =SUM(, click cell B8 and drag to cell D8, then click** ✓

9. **Click cell E10, type =SUM(, click cell B10 and drag to cell D10, click** ✓ **, then click the Save button** 💾 **on the Standard toolbar**

   Compare your screen to Figure B-10.

FIGURE B-9: Formula and moving border

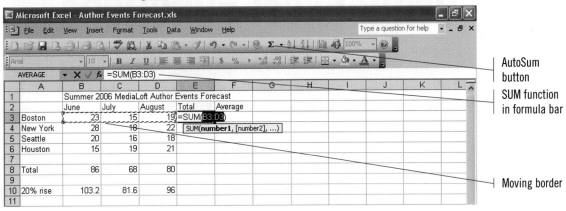

AutoSum
button

SUM function
in formula bar

Moving border

FIGURE B-10: Worksheet with SUM functions entered

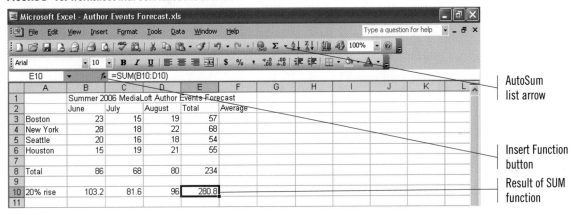

AutoSum
list arrow

Insert Function
button

Result of SUM
function

Clues to Use

Using the MIN and MAX functions

Other commonly used functions include MIN and MAX. You use the MIN function to calculate the minimum, or smallest, value in a selected range; the MAX function calculates the maximum, or largest, value in a selected range. The MAX function is included in the Most Recently Used function category in the Insert Function dialog box, while both the MIN and MAX function can be found in the Statistical category. These functions are particularly useful in larger worksheets and can be selected using the Insert Function button on the formula bar or the AutoSum list arrow on the Standard toolbar.

Using Excel Functions

Functions can be typed directly from the keyboard, or by using the Insert Function button on the formula bar. Clicking this button opens the Insert Function dialog box, which provides a guided method of choosing a function, describes what each function does, and helps you choose which cells to select to complete each equation. ▓▓▓▓ You need to use the AVERAGE function to calculate the average number of author events per store.

STEPS

TROUBLE
If the Office Assistant opens, click No, don't provide help now.

1. **Click cell F3, then click the** Insert Function button **fx** **on the formula bar**

   The Insert Function dialog box opens, as shown in Figure B-11. Here you can select a function from a list. See Table B-2 for frequently used functions. The function you need to calculate averages—named AVERAGE—appears in the Most Recently Used function category.

2. **Click** AVERAGE **in the Select a function list box, then click** OK

   The Function Arguments dialog box opens.

QUICK TIP
Modify a function's range by clicking the Collapse Dialog Box button, defining the range with your mouse, then clicking the Expand Dialog Box button to return to the Function Arguments dialog box.

3. **Type** B3:D3 **in the Number 1 text box, as shown in Figure B-12, then click** OK

   The value 19 appears in cell F3.

4. **Click cell F4, click** fx **to open the Insert Function dialog box, verify that** AVERAGE **is selected in the Select a function list, click** OK**, type** B4:D4**, then click** OK

5. **Click cell F5, click** fx**, click** AVERAGE **if necessary, click** OK**, type** B5:D5**, then click** OK

6. **Click cell F6, click** fx**, click** AVERAGE **if necessary, click** OK**, type** B6:D6**, then click** OK

   The result for Boston (cell F3) is 19; the result for New York (cell F4) is 22.66667; the result for Seattle (cell F5) is 18; and the result for Houston (cell F6) is 18.33333, giving you the averages for all four stores. See Figure B-13.

7. **Enter your name in cell A25, then click the** Save button **on the Standard toolbar**

8. **Click the** Print button **on the Standard toolbar**

TABLE B-2: Frequently used functions

function	description
SUM (argument)	Calculates the sum of the arguments
AVERAGE (argument)	Calculates the average of the arguments
MAX (argument)	Displays the largest value among the arguments
MIN (argument)	Displays the smallest value among the arguments
COUNT (argument)	Calculates the number of values in the arguments
PMT (rate, number of payments, loan amount)	Calculates loan payment amounts
IF (condition, if true, if false)	Determines a value if a condition is true or false
TODAY ()	Returns the current date using a date format

FIGURE B-11: Insert Function dialog box

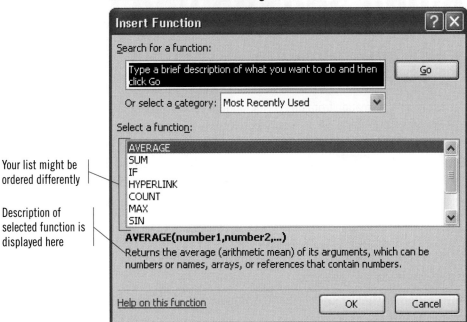

Your list might be ordered differently

Description of selected function is displayed here

FIGURE B-12: Function Arguments dialog box

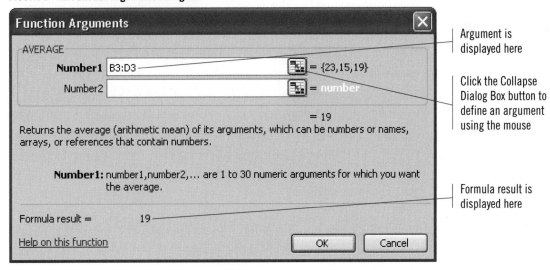

Argument is displayed here

Click the Collapse Dialog Box button to define an argument using the mouse

Formula result is displayed here

FIGURE B-13: Completed functions

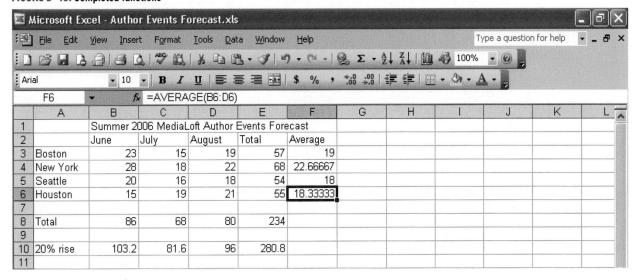

Copying and Moving Cell Entries

You can copy or move information from one cell or range in your worksheet to another using either the Cut, Copy, and Paste buttons, or the Excel drag-and-drop feature. When you cut or move information, the original data does not remain in the original location. You can also cut, copy, and paste labels and values from one worksheet to another. ■■●▪▪▪ You need to include the 2006 forecast for spring and fall author events. Jim has already entered the spring data in the second worksheet in the workbook, and asks you to finish entering the labels and data for the fall. You copy information from the spring report to the fall report.

STEPS

1. **Click the** Spring-Fall sheet tab **of the Author Events Forecast workbook**

   The store names in cells A6:A7 are incorrect.

2. **Click the** Summer sheet tab, **select the range** A5:A6, **then click the** Copy button 📋 **on the Standard toolbar**

   The selected range (A5:A6) is copied to the **Office Clipboard**, a temporary storage area that holds the selected information you copy or cut. A moving border surrounds the selected range until you press [Esc] or copy additional information to the Clipboard. The information you copied remains in the selected range.

TROUBLE
If the Clipboard task pane does not open, click Edit on the menu bar, then click Office Clipboard.

3. **Click the** Spring-Fall sheet tab, **select the range** A6:A7, **then click the** Paste button 📋 **on the Standard toolbar**

4. **Select the range** A4:A9, **then click** 📋

   The Clipboard task pane opens when you copy a selection to the already occupied Clipboard. You can use the Clipboard task pane to copy, cut, store, and paste up to 24 items. Each item in the pane displays its contents.

QUICK TIP
After you paste an item, the Paste Options button appears. If you move the pointer over it, the Paste Options list arrow appears, letting you choose whether to paste the contents with or without its formatting, or to paste only the formatting attributes.

5. **Click cell** A13, **click** [Boston New York Seattle Houston Total] **in the Clipboard task pane to paste the contents in cell A13, then click the** Close button ☒ **in the task pane title bar to close it**

   The item is copied into the range A13:A18. When pasting an item from the Clipboard into the worksheet, you only need to specify the upper-left cell of the range where you want to paste the selection. The Total label in column E is missing from the fall forecast.

6. **Click cell** E3, **position the pointer on any edge of the cell until the pointer changes to** ↖, **then press and hold down** [Ctrl]

   The pointer changes to the Copy pointer ↖.

7. **While still pressing** [Ctrl], **press and hold the left mouse button, drag the cell contents to cell** E12, **release the mouse button, then release** [Ctrl]

   As you dragged, an outline of the cell moved with the pointer, as shown in Figure B-14, and a ScreenTip appeared tracking the current position of the item as you moved it. When you released the mouse button, the Total label appeared in cell E12. This **drag-and-drop technique** is useful for copying cell contents. You can also use drag and drop to move data to a new cell.

TROUBLE
When you use drag and drop to move data into occupied cells, Excel asks if you want to replace the existing cells. Click OK to replace the contents with those of the cell you are moving.

8. **Click cell** C1, **position the pointer on the edge of the cell until it changes to** ↖, **then drag the cell contents to** A1

   You don't use [Ctrl] when moving information with drag and drop. You can easily enter the fall events data into the range B13:D16.

9. **Select the range** B13:D16, **then using the information shown in Figure B-15, enter the author events data for the fall into this range, then click the** Save button 💾 **on the Standard toolbar**

   The **AutoCalculate** area in the status bar displays "Sum=245," which is the sum of the values in the selected range.

FIGURE B-14: Using drag and drop to copy information

Copy button

Paste button

Copied cell

Outline of
copied cell

Drag-and-drop
pointer with
ScreenTip

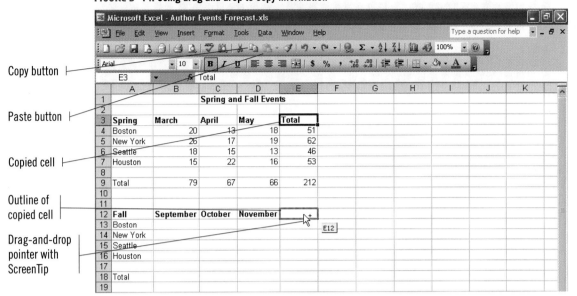

FIGURE B-15: Worksheet with fall author event data entered

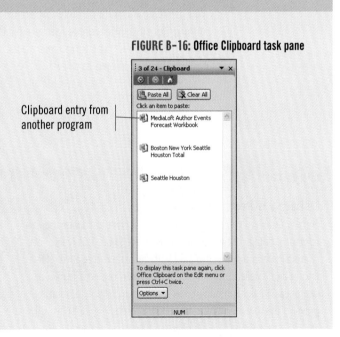

AutoCalculate displays
sum of selected range

Clues to Use

Using the Office Clipboard

The Office Clipboard, shown in the task pane in Figure B-16, lets you copy and paste multiple items such as text, images, tables, or Excel ranges within or between Microsoft Office applications. The Office Clipboard can hold up to 24 items copied or cut from any Office or Windows-compatible program. The Clipboard task pane displays the items stored on the Office Clipboard. You choose whether to delete the first item from the Clipboard when you copy the 25th item. The collected items remain on the Office Clipboard and are available to you until you close all open Office programs. You can specify when and where to show the Office Clipboard task pane by clicking the Options list arrow at the bottom of the Clipboard task pane.

FIGURE B-16: Office Clipboard task pane

Clipboard entry from
another program

Excel 2003

Understanding Relative and Absolute Cell References

As you work in Excel, you will often want to reuse formulas in different parts of the worksheet. This will save you time because you won't have to retype them. For example, you may want to perform a what-if analysis showing one set of sales figures using a lower forecast in one part of the worksheet and another set using a higher forecast in another area. But when you copy formulas, it is important to make sure that they refer to the correct cells. To do this, you need to understand relative and absolute cell references. ▰▰▰▰ Jim often reuses formulas in different parts of his worksheets to examine different possible outcomes, so he wants you to understand relative and absolute cell references.

DETAILS

- ### Use relative references when cell relationships remain unchanged

  When you create a formula that references other cells, Excel normally does not "record" the exact cell references, but instead the relationship to the cell containing the formula. For example, in Figure B-17, cell E5 contains the formula: =SUM(B5:D5). When Excel retrieves values to calculate the formula in cell E5, it actually looks for "the cell three columns to the left of the formula, which in this case is cell B5," "the cell two columns to the left of the formula," and so on. This way, if you copy the cell to a new location such as cell E6, the results will reflect the new formula location, and will automatically retrieve the values in cells B6, C6, and D6. This is called **relative cell referencing**, because Excel is recording the input cells *in relation to* the formula cell.

  In most cases, you will use relative cell references, which is the Excel default. In Figure B-17, the formulas in E5:E9 and in B9:E9 contain relative cell references. They total the "three cells to the left of" or the "four cells above" the formulas.

- ### Use absolute cell references when one relationship changes

  There are times when you want Excel to retrieve formula information from a specific cell, and you don't want that cell to change when you copy the formula to a new location. For example, you might have a price in a specific cell that you want to use in all formulas, regardless of their location. If you used relative cell referencing, the formula results would be incorrect, because Excel would use a different cell every time you copied the formula. Therefore you need to use an **absolute cell reference**, a reference that does not change when you copy the formula.

  You create an absolute cell reference by placing a $ (dollar sign) before both the column letter and the row number for the cell's address, using the [F4] function key on the keyboard. Figure B-18 displays the formulas used in Figure B-17. The formulas in cells B15 to D18 use absolute cell references to refer to a potential sales increase of 50%, shown in cell B12.

Clues to Use

Using a mixed reference

Sometimes when you copy a formula, you'll want to change the row reference, but keep the column reference the same. This type of cell referencing combines elements of both absolute and relative referencing and is called a **mixed reference**. When copied, the mixed reference C$14 changes the column relative to its new location, but prevents the row from changing. In the mixed reference $C14, the column would not change, but the row would be updated relative to its location. Like the absolute reference, a mixed reference can be created using the [F4] function key. With each press of the [F4] key, you cycle through all the possible combinations of relative, absolute, and mixed references ($C$14, C$14, $C14, C14).

FIGURE B-17: Location of relative references

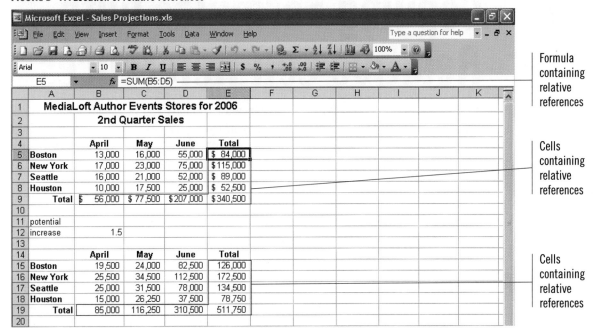

Formula containing relative references

Cells containing relative references

Cells containing relative references

FIGURE B-18: Absolute and relative reference formulas

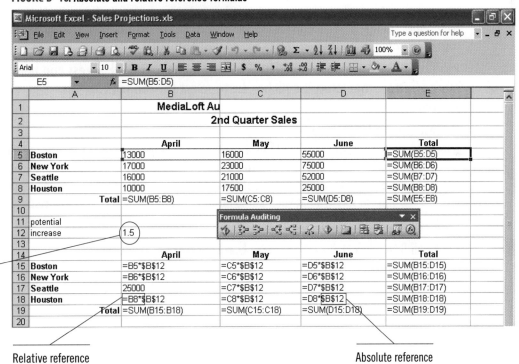

Cell referenced in absolute formulas

Relative reference

Absolute reference

Clues to Use

Printing worksheet formulas

As you create a worksheet, you may find it valuable to print the sheet showing the formulas rather than the cell contents. You can do this by clicking Tools on the menu bar, clicking Options, then clicking the View tab in the Options dialog box. Make sure a check is displayed in the Formulas check box, then click OK. When the Options dialog box closes, the cells are expanded to display the formulas, as shown in Figure B-18, and you can print the worksheet. To return the worksheet to its normal appearance, reopen the Options dialog box and deselect the Formulas check box.

Copying Formulas with Relative Cell References

Copying and moving formulas allows you to reuse formulas you've already created. Copying formulas, rather than retyping them, is faster and helps to prevent typing errors. You can use the Copy and Paste commands or the Fill Right method to copy formulas. ░▒▓▒░ You want to copy the formulas that total the author appearances by region and by month from the spring to the fall.

STEPS

1. **Click cell E4, then click the Copy button 🗐 on the Standard toolbar**

   The formula for calculating the total number of spring Boston author events is copied to the Clipboard. Notice that the formula =SUM(B4:D4) appears in the formula bar.

QUICK TIP

To specify components of the copied cell or range prior to pasting, click Edit on the menu bar, then click Paste Special. You can selectively copy formulas, values, and other more complex features.

2. **Click cell E13, then click the Paste button 🗐 on the Standard toolbar**

   The formula from cell E4 is copied into cell E13, where the new result of 59 appears. Notice in the formula bar that the cell references have changed, so that the range B13:D13 appears in the formula. This formula contains relative cell references, which tell Excel to copy the formula to a new cell, but to substitute new cell references so that the relationship of the cells to the formula in its new location remains unchanged. In this case, Excel adjusted the formula so that cells D13, C13, and B13—the three cell references immediately to the left of E13—replaced cells D4, C4, and B4, the three cell references to the left of E4. Notice that the lower-right corner of the active cell contains a small square, called the **fill handle**. You can use the fill handle to copy labels, formulas, and values. This option is called **AutoFill**.

3. **Position the pointer over the fill handle until it changes to ✚, press and hold the left mouse button, then drag the fill handle to select the range E13:E16**

   See Figure B-19.

4. **Release the mouse button**

   A formula similar to the one in cell E13 now appears in the range E14:E16. Again, because the formula uses relative cell references, cells E14 through E16 correctly display the totals for the fall author events. After you release the mouse button, the **AutoFill Options button** appears. If you move the pointer over it and click its list arrow, you can specify what you want to fill and whether or not you want to include formatting.

5. **Click cell B9, click Edit on the menu bar, then click Copy**

TROUBLE

If the Clipboard task pane opens, click the Close button. If the Office Assistant appears, right-click it, then click Hide.

6. **Click cell B18, click Edit on the menu bar, then click Paste**

   See Figure B-20. The formula for calculating the September events appears in the formula bar. You also need totals to appear in cells C18, D18, and E18. You could use the fill handle again, but another option is the Fill command on the Edit menu.

7. **Select the range B18:E18**

8. **Click Edit on the menu bar, point to Fill, then click Right**

   The rest of the totals are filled in correctly. Compare your worksheet to Figure B-21.

9. **Click the Save button 🖫 on the Standard toolbar**

FIGURE B-19: Selected range using the fill handle

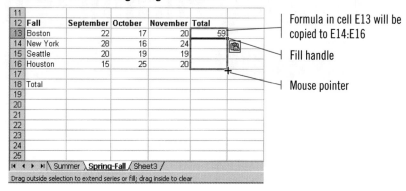

Formula in cell E13 will be copied to E14:E16

Fill handle

Mouse pointer

FIGURE B-20: Copied formula

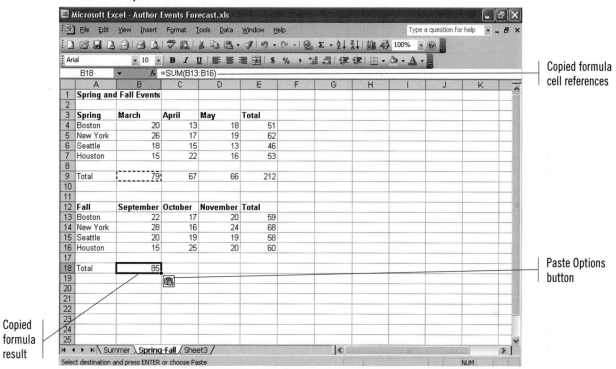

Copied formula cell references

Paste Options button

Copied formula result

FIGURE B-21: Completed worksheet with all formulas copied

12	Fall	September	October	November	Total
13	Boston	22	17	20	59
14	New York	28	16	24	68
15	Seattle	20	19	19	58
16	Houston	15	25	20	60
17					
18	Total	85	77	83	245
19					
20					
21					
22					
23					
24					
25					

Summer \ Spring-Fall / Sheet3 /
Ready

Clues to Use

Filling cells with sequential text or values

Often, you'll need to fill cells with sequential text: months of the year, days of the week, years, or text plus a number (Quarter 1, Quarter 2,...). You can easily fill cells using sequences by dragging the fill handle. As you drag the fill handle, Excel automatically extends the existing sequence. (The contents of the last filled cell appear in the ScreenTip.) Use the Fill Series command on the Edit menu to examine all of the available fill series options.

Copying Formulas with Absolute Cell References

When copying formulas, you might want a cell reference to always refer to a particular cell address. In such an instance, you would use an absolute cell reference. An absolute cell reference always refers to a specific cell address when the formula is copied. You create an absolute reference by placing a dollar sign ($) before the row letter and column number of the address (for example $A$1). ▰▰▰▰ The staff in the Marketing Department hopes the number of author events will increase by 20% over last year's figures. Jim asks you to add a column that calculates a possible increase in the number of spring events in 2006. You can then do a what-if analysis and recalculate the spreadsheet several times, changing the percentage by which the number of appearances might increase each time.

STEPS

1. **Click cell G1, type Change, then press [➔]**
   You can store the increase factor that will be used in the what-if analysis in cell H1.

2. **Type 1.1, then press [Enter]**
   The value in cell H1 represents a 10% increase in author events.

3. **Click cell G3, type What if?, then press [Enter]**

4. **In cell G4, type =, click E4, type *, click H1, then click the Enter button ☑ on the formula bar**
   The result, 56.1, appears in cell G4. This value represents the total spring events for Boston if there is a 10% increase. Jim wants you to perform a what-if analysis for all the stores.

> **QUICK TIP**
> Before you copy or move a formula, check to see if you need to use an absolute cell reference.

5. **Drag the fill handle to extend the selection from G4 to G7**
   The resulting values in the range G5:G7 are all zeros. When you copy the formula it adjusts so that the formula in cell G5 is =E5*H2. Because there is no value in cell H2, the result is 0, an error. You need to use an absolute reference in the formula to keep the formula from adjusting itself. That way, it will always reference cell H1. You can change the relative cell reference to an absolute cell reference by using [F4].

6. **Click cell G4, press [F2] to change to Edit mode, then press [F4]**
   When you press [F2], the range finder outlines the arguments of the equation in blue and green. When you press [F4], dollar signs appear, changing the H1 cell reference to an absolute reference. See Figure B-22.

7. **Click ☑, then drag the fill handle to extend the selection to range G4:G7**
   The formula correctly contains an absolute cell reference, and the value of G4 remains unchanged at 56.1. The correct values for a 10% increase appear in cells G4:G7. You complete the what-if analysis by changing the value in cell H1 to indicate a 20% increase in events.

8. **Click cell H1, type 1.2, then click ☑**
   The values in the range G4:G7 change to reflect the 20% increase. Compare your completed worksheets to Figure B-23. Because events only occur in whole numbers, the appearance of the numbers can be changed later.

9. **Enter your name in cell A25, click the Save button 🖫 on the Standard toolbar, click the Print button 🖨 on the Standard toolbar, close the workbook, then exit Excel**

FIGURE B-22: Absolute cell reference in cell G4

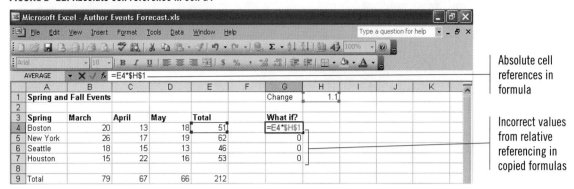

Absolute cell references in formula

Incorrect values from relative referencing in copied formulas

FIGURE B-23: Completed worksheets

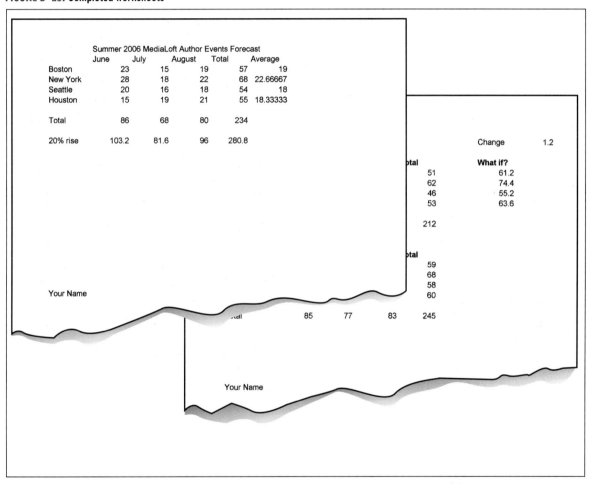

Clues to Use

Inserting and deleting selected cells

As you add formulas to your workbook, you may need to insert or delete cells, not entire rows or columns. When you do this, Excel automatically adjusts cell references to reflect their new locations. To insert cells, click Insert on the menu bar, then click Cells. The Insert dialog box opens, asking if you want to insert a cell and move the selected cell down or to the right of the new one. To delete one or more selected cells, click Edit on the menu bar, click Delete, and in the Delete dialog box, indicate which way you want to move the adjacent cells. When using this option, be careful not to disturb row or column alignment that may be necessary to make sense of the worksheet.

Practice

▼ CONCEPTS REVIEW

Label each element of the Excel worksheet window shown in Figure B-24.

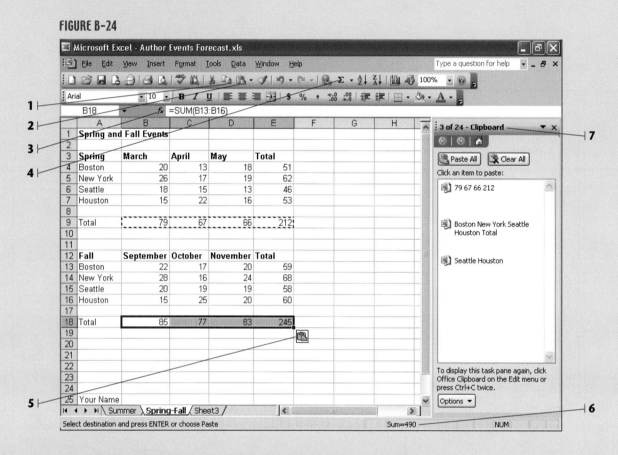

FIGURE B-24

Match each term or button with the statement that best describes it.

8. 🔲   **a.** A predefined formula that provides a shortcut for commonly used calculations

9. **Function**   **b.** A cell entry that performs a calculation in an Excel worksheet

10. **Formula**   **c.** Used to copy labels, formulas, and values

11. **Fill handle**   **d.** Adds the selected range to the Office Clipboard

12. 🔲   **e.** Used to paste cells

Select the best answer from the list of choices.

13. Which button is used to enter data in a cell?

a. [icon]   c. [icon]

b. [✕]   d. [✓]

14. What type of cell reference changes when it is copied?

a. Circular   c. Looping

b. Absolute   d. Relative

15. What character is used to make a reference absolute?

a. $ c. @

b. ^   d. &

▼ SKILLS REVIEW

1. Plan and design a worksheet.

a. Using the scenario of tracking quarterly sales at a formal-wear rental shop, determine what sort of output would be required.

b. Determine what kind of input would be required.

c. What sort of formulas might be needed?

d. Make a paper sketch of how the worksheet might look.

2. Edit cell entries.

a. Start Excel, open the workbook EX B-2.xls from the drive and folder where your Data Files are stored, then save it as **Office Furnishings**.

b. Change the quantity of Tables to **27**.

c. Change the price of Desks to **285**.

d. Change the quantity of Easels to **18**.

e. Enter your name in cell A40, then save the workbook.

3. Enter formulas.

a. In cell B6, use the pointing method to enter the formula **B2+B3+B4+B5**.

b. In cell D2, enter the formula **B2*C2**.

c. Save your work.

4. Create complex formulas.

a. In cell B8, enter the formula **(B2+B3+B4+B5)/4**.

b. In cell C8, enter the formula **(C2+C3+C4+C5)/4**.

c. Save your work.

5. Introduce Excel functions.

a. Delete the contents of cell B6.

b. In cell B6, use the AutoSum feature to calculate the sum of B2:B5.

c. Save your work.

6. Use Excel functions.

a. Enter the label **Min Price** in cell A9.

b. In cell C9, enter the function **MIN(C2:C5)**.

c. Enter the label **Max Price** in cell A10.

d. Create a formula in cell C10 that determines the maximum price of for the range C2:C5.

e. Save your work.

7. Copy and move cell entries.

a. Select the range **A1:C6**, then copy the range to cell A12.

b. Select the range **D1:E1**, then use drag and drop to copy the range to cell D12.

c. Move the contents of cell G1 to cell E9, then save your work.

Excel 2003

OFFICE-245

BUILDING AND EDITING WORKSHEETS EXCEL B-23

8. **Understand relative and absolute cell references.**

    a. Write a brief description of the difference between a relative and absolute reference.

    b. Provide a sketched example of a relative and absolute reference.

9. **Copy formulas with relative cell references.**

    a. Copy the formula in D2 into cells D3:D5.

    b. Copy the formula in D2 into cells D13:D16.

    c. Save the worksheet.

10. **Copy formulas with absolute cell references.**

    a. In cell E10, enter the value 1.375.

    b. In cell E2, create a formula containing an absolute reference that multiplies D2 and E10.

    c. Use the fill handle to copy the formula in E2 into cells E3:E5.

    d. Use the Copy and Paste buttons to copy the formula in E2 into cells E13:E16.

    e. Use the Delete command on the Edit menu to delete cells A13:E13, shifting the cells up.

    f. Change the amount in cell E10 to 3.45.

    g. Select cells A1:E1 and insert cells, shifting cells down.

    h. Enter Inventory Estimate in cell A1.

    i. Save, preview, print, and close the workbook, then exit Excel.

▼ INDEPENDENT CHALLENGE 1

You are the box office manager for the Young Brazilians Jazz Band, a popular new group. Your responsibilities include tracking seasonal ticket sales for the band's concerts and anticipating ticket sales for the next season. The group sells four types of tickets: reserved, general, senior, and student tickets.

The 2006–2007 season includes five scheduled concerts: Spring, Summer, Fall, Winter, and Thaw. You will plan and build a worksheet that tracks the sales of each of the four ticket types for all five concerts.

   a. Think about the results you want to see, the information you need to build into these worksheets, and what types of calculations must be performed.

   b. Sketch sample worksheets on a piece of paper to indicate how the information should be laid out. What information should go in the columns? What information should go in the rows?

   c. Start Excel, open a new workbook, then save it as Young Brazilians in the drive and folder where your Data Files are stored.

   d. Plan and build a worksheet that tracks the sales of each of the four ticket types for all five concerts. Build the worksheets by entering a title, row labels, column headings, and formulas.

   e. Enter your own sales data that shows that no concert sold more than 400 tickets, and the Reserved category was the most popular.

   f. Calculate the total ticket sales for each concert, the total sales for each of the four ticket types, and the total sales for all tickets.

   g. Name the worksheet Sales Data and color the worksheet tab red.

   h. Copy the Sales Data worksheet to a blank worksheet, name the copied worksheet 5% Increase, then color the sheet tab aqua.

   i. Modify the 5% Increase sheet so that a 5% increase in sales of all ticket types is shown in a separate column with an appropriate column label. See Figure B-25 for a sample worksheet.

   j. Enter your name in a cell in each worksheet.

   k. Save your work, preview and print the worksheets, then close the workbook and exit Excel.

FIGURE B-25

	A	B	C	D	E	F	G	H	I	J	K	L
1			2006-2007 Season									
2			Young Brazilians Jazz Band					Increase				
3								1.05				
4		Reserved	General	Senior	Student							
5	Concerts	Seating	Admission	Citizens	Tickets	Totals		What if?				
6	Spring	285	50	40	20	395		414.75				
7	Summer	135	25	35	20	215		225.75				
8	Fall	130	50	25	20	225		236.25				
9	Winter	160	100	30	20	310		325.5				
10	Thaw	250	75	35	20	380		399				
11	Total	960	300	165	100	1525		1601.25				
12												

▼ INDEPENDENT CHALLENGE 2

The Beautiful You Salon is a small but growing beauty salon that has hired you to organize its accounting records using Excel. The owners want you to track the salon's expenses using Excel. Before you were hired, one of the bookkeepers entered last year's expenses in a workbook, but the analysis was never completed.

a. Start Excel, open the workbook EX B-3.xls, then save it as **Beautiful You Finances** in the drive and folder where your Data Files are stored. The worksheet includes labels for functions such as the Average, Maximum, and Minimum amounts of each of the expenses in the worksheet.

b. Think about what information would be important for the bookkeeping staff to know.

c. Create your sketch using the existing worksheet as a foundation.

d. Create formulas in the Total column and row using the AutoSum function.

e. Rename Sheet1 **Expenses** and add a color to the sheet tab.

Advanced Challenge Exercise

■ Create formulas in the Average, Maximum, and Minimum columns and rows using the appropriate functions, dragging to select the range.

■ Create a formula using the COUNT function that determines the total number of expense categories listed per quarter.

f. Enter your name in a worksheet cell, then compare your screen to the sample worksheet shown in Figure B-26.

g. Preview the worksheet, then print it.

h. Save the workbook, then close the workbook and exit Excel.

FIGURE B-26

	A	B	C	D	E	F	G	H	I	J	K	L
1	Beautiful You Salon											
2												
3	Operating Expenses for 2006											
4												
5	Expense	Quarter 1	Quarter 2	Quarter 3	Quarter 4	Total	Average	Maximum	Minimum			
6	Rent	4750	4750	4750	4750	19000	4750	4750	4750			
7	Utilities	8624	7982	7229	8096	31931	7982.75	8624	7229			
8	Payroll	23456	26922	25876	29415	105669	26417.25	29415	23456			
9	Insurance	8355	8194	8225	8327	33101	8275.25	8355	8194			
10	Education	4749	3081	6552	4006	18388	4597	6552	3081			
11	Inventory	29986	27115	25641	32465	115207	28801.75	32465	25641			
12	Total	79920	78044	78273	87059	323296						
13												
14	Average	13320	13007.33	13045.5	14509.83							
15	Maximum	29986	27115	25876	32465							
16	Minimum	4749	3081	4750	4006							
17	Count	6										

▼ INDEPENDENT CHALLENGE 3

You have been promoted to computer lab manager at Learn-It-All, a local computer training center. It is your responsibility to make sure there are enough computers for students during scheduled classes. Currently, you have five classrooms: four with IBM PCs and one with Macintoshes. Classes are scheduled Monday, Wednesday, and Friday in two-hour increments from 9 a.m. to 5 p.m. (the lab closes at 7 p.m.), and each room can currently accommodate 32 computers.

You plan and build a worksheet that tracks the number of students who can currently use the available computers per room. You create your enrollment data. Using an additional worksheet, you show the impact of an enrollment increase of 25%.

- **a.** Think about how to construct these worksheets to create the desired output.
- **b.** Sketch sample paper worksheets to indicate how the information should be laid out.
- **c.** Start Excel, open a new workbook, then save it as **Learn-it-All** in the drive and folder where your Data Files are stored.
- **d.** Create a worksheet by entering a title, row labels, column headings, data, and formulas. Name the sheet to easily identify its contents.
- **e.** Create a second sheet by copying the information from the initial sheet.
- **f.** Name the second sheet to easily identify its contents.
- **g.** Add color to each sheet tab, then compare your screen to the sample shown in Figure B-27.
- **h.** Enter your name in a cell in each sheet.
- **i.** Save your work, preview and print each worksheet, then close the workbook and exit Excel.

FIGURE B-27

	A	B	C	D	E	F	G	H	I	J
1	Computer Lab Schedule - Increased enrollment									
2										
3	Monday	PC room #1	PC room #2	PC room #3	PC room #4	Mac room #1				
4	9:00	40	40	40	40	40				
5	11:00	40	40	40	40	40				
6	1:00	40	40	40	40	40				
7	3:00	40	40	40	40	40				
8	5:00	40	40	40	40	40				
9		200	200	200	200	200				
10										
11	Wednesday	PC room #1	PC room #2	PC room #3	PC room #4	Mac room #1				
12	9:00	40	40	40	40	40				
13	11:00	40	40	40	40	40				
14	1:00	40	40	40	40	40				
15	3:00	40	40	40	40	40				
16	5:00	40	40	40	40	40				
17		200	200	200	200	200				
18										
19	Friday	PC room #1	PC room #2	PC room #3	PC room #4	Mac room #1				
20	9:00	40	40	40	40	40				
21	11:00	40	40	40	40	40				
22	1:00	40	40	40	40	40				
23	3:00	40	40	40	40	40				
24	5:00	40	40	40	40	40				
25		200	200	200	200	200				

Actual \ **Increased** / Sheet3 /

Ready — NUM

▼ INDEPENDENT CHALLENGE 4

Your company is opening a branch office in Great Britain and your boss is a fanatic about keeping the thermostats at a constant temperature during each season of the year. Because she grew up in the United States, she is only familiar with Fahrenheit temperatures and doesn't know how to convert them to Celsius. She has asked you to find out the Celsius equivalents for the thermostatic settings she wants to use. She prefers the temperature to be 65 degrees F in the winter, 62 degrees F in the spring, 75 degrees F in the summer, and 70 degrees F in the fall. You can use the Web and Excel to determine the new settings.

a. Start Excel, open a new workbook, then save it as **Temperature Conversions** in the drive and folder where your Data Files are stored.

b. Use your favorite search engine to find your own information sources on calculating temperature conversions.

c. Think about how to create an Excel equation that can perform the conversion.

d. Create column and row titles using Table B-3 to get started.

e. In the appropriate cell, create an equation that calculates the conversion of a Fahrenheit temperature to a Celsius temperature.

f. Copy the equation, then paste it in the remaining Celsius cells.

TABLE B-3

Temperature Conversions		
Season	Fahrenheit	Celsius
Spring	62	
Winter	65	
Summer	75	
Fall	70	

Advanced Challenge Exercise

■ Copy the contents of Sheet1 to Sheet2.

■ In Sheet2, change the display so the formulas are visible, then print it.

g. Enter your name in one of the cells in each sheet, preview Sheet1, then print it.

h. Save the workbook, then close the files and exit Excel.

▼ VISUAL WORKSHOP

Create a worksheet similar to Figure B-28 using the skills you learned in this unit. Save the workbook as **Annual Budget** in the drive and folder where your Data Files are stored. Enter your name in cell A13, then preview and print the worksheet.

FIGURE B-28

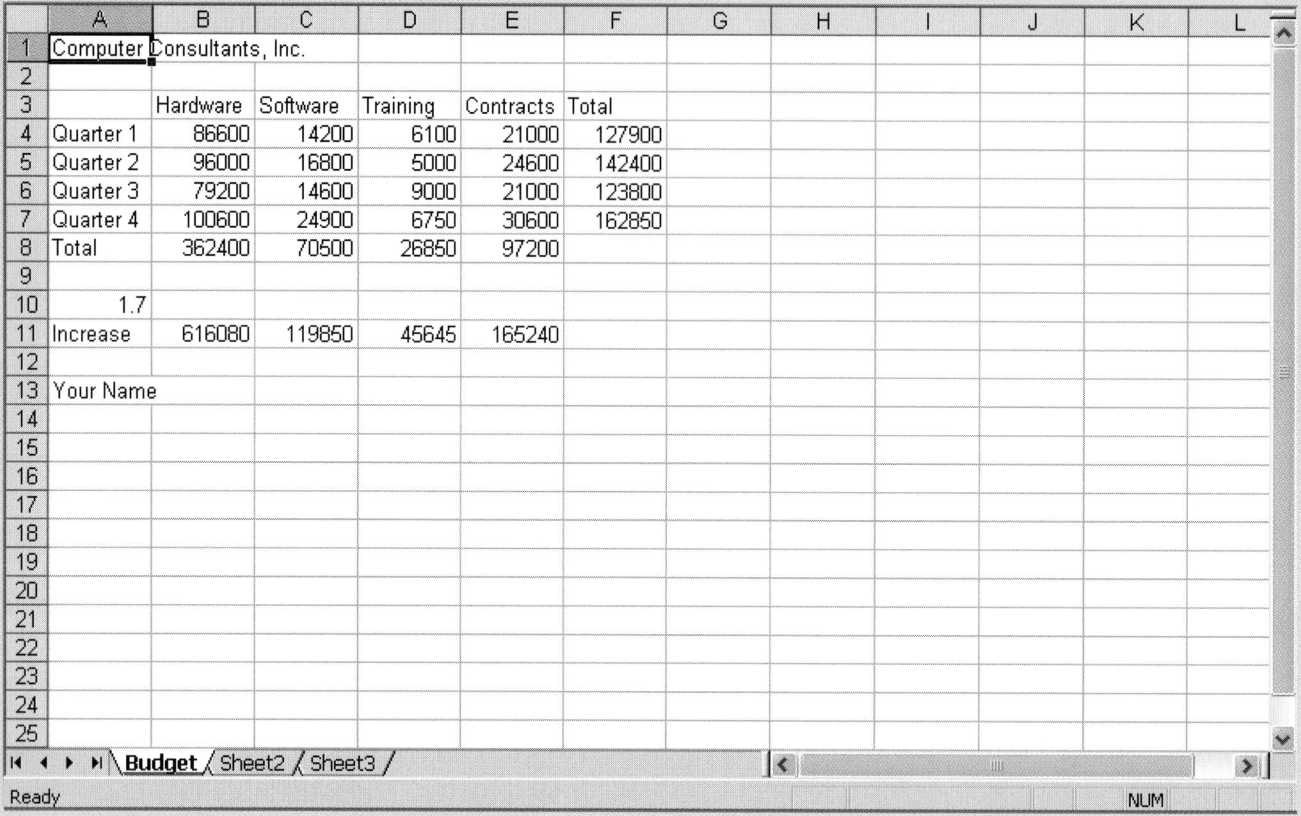

	A	B	C	D	E	F	G	H	I	J	K	L
1	Computer Consultants, Inc.											
2												
3		Hardware	Software	Training	Contracts	Total						
4	Quarter 1	86600	14200	6100	21000	127900						
5	Quarter 2	96000	16800	5000	24600	142400						
6	Quarter 3	79200	14600	9000	21000	123800						
7	Quarter 4	100600	24900	6750	30600	162850						
8	Total	362400	70500	26850	97200							
9												
10	1.7											
11	Increase	616080	119850	45645	165240							
12												
13	Your Name											
14												
15												
16												
17												
18												
19												
20												
21												
22												
23												
24												
25												

Budget / Sheet2 / Sheet3

Ready   NUM

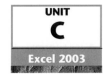

Formatting a Worksheet

OBJECTIVES

Format values
Use fonts and font sizes
Change attributes and alignment
Adjust column widths
Insert and delete rows and columns
Apply colors, patterns, and borders
Use conditional formatting
Check spelling

If you have a SAM user profile, you may have access to hands-on instruction, practice, and assessment of the skills covered in this unit. Log in to your SAM account and go to your assignments page to see what your instructor has assigned.

You can use Excel formatting features to make a worksheet more attractive, to make it easier to read, or to emphasize key data. You do this by using different colors and fonts for the cell contents, adjusting column and row widths, and inserting and deleting columns and rows. ▄▄▄ The marketing managers at MediaLoft have asked Jim Fernandez to create a workbook that lists advertising expenses for all MediaLoft stores. Jim has prepared a worksheet for the New York City store containing this information, which he can adapt later for use in other stores. He asks you to use formatting to make the worksheet easier to read and to call attention to important data.

Formatting Values

If you enter a value in a cell and you don't like the way the data appears, you can adjust the cell's format. A cell's **format** determines how labels and values appear in it, such as boldface, italic, with or without dollar signs or commas, and the like. Formatting changes only the way a value or label appears; it does not alter cell data in any way. To format a cell, first select it, then apply the formatting. You can format cells and ranges before or after you enter data. The Marketing Department has requested that Jim begin by listing the New York City store's advertising expenses. Jim developed a worksheet that lists advertising invoices, entered all the information, and now he wants you to format some of the labels and values. Because some of the changes might also affect column widths, you make all formatting changes before widening the columns.

STEPS

QUICK TIP

To save a workbook in a different location, you click File on the menu bar, click Save As, click the Save in list arrow in the Save As dialog box, navigate to a new drive or folder, type a new filename if necessary, then click Save.

1. **Start Excel, open the file** EX C-1.xls **from the drive and folder where your Data Files are stored, then save it as** Ad Expenses.

   The NYC advertising worksheet appears in Figure C-1. You can display numeric data in a variety of ways, such as with decimals or leading dollar signs. Excel provides a special format for currency, which adds two decimal places and a dollar sign.

2. **Select the range** E4:E32, **then click the** Currency Style button **$** **on the Formatting toolbar**

   Excel adds dollar signs and two decimal places to the Cost data. Excel automatically resizes the column to display the new formatting. Another way to format dollar values is to use the comma format, which does not include the dollar sign ($).

QUICK TIP

Select any range of contiguous cells by clicking the top-left cell, pressing and holding [Shift], then clicking the bottom-right cell. Add a row to the selected range by continuing to hold down [Shift] and pressing ↓; add a column by pressing →.

3. **Select the range** G4:I32, **then click the** Comma Style button **,** **on the Formatting toolbar**

   The values in columns G, H, and I display the comma format. You can also format percentages by using the Formatting toolbar.

4. **Select the range** J4:J32, **click the** Percent Style button **%** **on the Formatting toolbar, then click the** Increase Decimal button **.00** **on the Formatting toolbar to show one decimal place**

   The data in the % of Total column is now formatted with a percent sign (%) and one decimal place. You decide that you prefer the percentages rounded to the nearest whole number.

5. **Click the** Decrease Decimal button **.00** **on the Formatting toolbar**

   You can also apply a variety of formats to dates in a worksheet.

6. **Select the range** B4:B31, **click** Format **on the menu bar, click** Cells, **then if necessary click the** Number tab **in the Format Cells dialog box**

   The Format Cells dialog box opens with the Date category already selected on the Number tab. See Figure C-2.

7. **Select the format** 14-Mar-01 **in the Type list box, then click** OK

   The dates in column B appear in the format you selected. You decide you don't need the year to appear in the Inv. Due column. You can quickly open the Format Cells dialog box by right-clicking a selected range.

QUICK TIP

The 3-14-01 date format displays a single-digit date (such as 5/9/06) as does 9-May-06. The date format below it displays the same date as 5/09/06.

8. **Select the range** C4:C31, **right-click the range, click** Format Cells **on the shortcut menu, click** 14-Mar **in the Type list box in the Format Cells dialog box, then click** OK

   Compare your worksheet to Figure C-3.

9. **Click the** Save button **📁** **on the Standard toolbar**

FIGURE C-1: Advertising expense worksheet

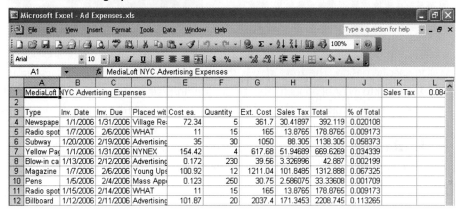

FIGURE C-2: Format Cells dialog box

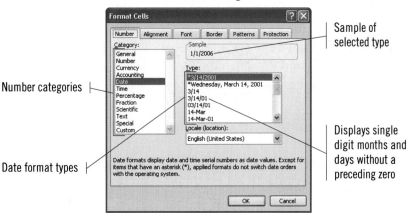

Number categories

Date format types

Sample of selected type

Displays single digit months and days without a preceding zero

FIGURE C-3: Worksheet with formatted values

Dates formatted to appear without year

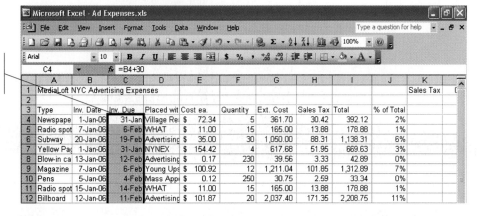

Clues to Use

Using the Format Painter

You can "paint" a cell's format into other cells by using the Format Painter button 🖌️ on the Standard toolbar. This is similar to using copy and paste to copy information, but instead of copying cell contents, you copy only the cell format. Select the cell containing the desired format, then click 🖌️. The pointer changes to ➕🖌️. Use this pointer to select the cell or range you want to contain the new format. You can paint a cell's format into multiple cells by double-clicking 🖌️, then clicking each cell that you want to paint with ➕🖌️. When you are finished painting formats, you can turn off the Format Painter by pressing [Esc] or by clicking 🖌️ again.

Using Fonts and Font Sizes

A **font** is the name for a collection of characters (letters, numerals, symbols, and punctuation marks) with a similar, specific design. The **font size** is the physical size of the text, measured in units called points. A **point** is equal to 1/72 of an inch. The default font in Excel is 10-point Arial. You can change the font, the size, or both of any worksheet entry or section by using the Format command on the menu bar or by using the Formatting toolbar. Table C-1 shows several fonts in different sizes. ▰▰▰ Now that the data is formatted, Jim wants you to change the font and size of the labels and the worksheet title so that they stand out more from the data.

STEPS

1. **Press** [Ctrl][Home] **to select cell A1**

2. **Right-click cell** A1, **click** Format Cells **on the shortcut menu, then click the** Font tab **in the Format Cells dialog box**
    See Figure C-4.

3. **Scroll down the** Font list **to see an alphabetical listing of the fonts available on your computer, click** Times New Roman **in the Font list box, click** 24 **in the Size list box, then click** OK
    The title font appears in 24-point Times New Roman, and the Formatting toolbar displays the new font and size information. The column headings should stand out more from the data.

4. **Select the range** A3:J3, **then click the** Font list arrow [Arial ▾] **on the Formatting toolbar**
    Notice that the font names on this font list are displayed in the font they represent.

QUICK TIP
Once you've clicked the Font list arrow, you can quickly locate a font in the list by typing the first few characters in its name.

5. **Click** Times New Roman **in the Font list, click the** Font Size **list arrow** [10 ▾] **on the Formatting toolbar, then click** 14 **in the Font Size list**
    Compare your worksheet to Figure C-5. Notice that some of the column headings are now too wide to appear fully in the column. Excel does not automatically adjust column widths to accommodate cell formatting; you have to adjust column widths manually. You'll learn to do this in a later lesson.

6. **Click the** Save button 🖫 **on the Standard toolbar**

TABLE C-1: Types of fonts

font	12 point	24 point
Arial	Excel	Excel
Playbill	Excel	Excel
Comic Sans MS	Excel	Excel
Times New Roman	Excel	Excel

FIGURE C-4: Font tab in the Format Cells dialog box

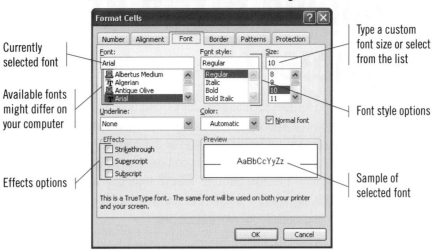

Currently selected font

Available fonts might differ on your computer

Effects options

Type a custom font size or select from the list

Font style options

Sample of selected font

FIGURE C-5: Worksheet with formatted title and labels

Font and size of active cell or range

Title appears in 24-point Times New Roman

Column headings now 14-point Times New Roman

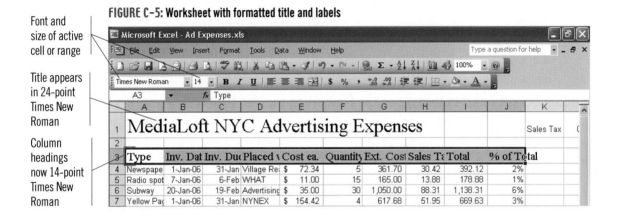

Clues to Use

Inserting and adjusting clip art

You can add clips to your worksheets to make them look more professional. A **clip** is an individual media file, such as art, sound, animation, or a movie. **Clip art** refers to images such as a corporate logo, a
picture, or a photo; Excel comes with many clips that you can use.
To add clip art to your worksheet, click Insert on the menu bar, point
to Picture, then click Clip Art. The Insert Clip Art task pane appears.
Here you can search for clips by typing one or more keywords
(words related to your subject) in the Search text box, then clicking
Search. Clips that relate to your keywords appear in the Clip Art task
pane, as shown in Figure C-6. Click the image you want. (If you have
a standard Office installation and have an active Internet connection,
you will have more images available.) You can also add your own
images to a worksheet by clicking Insert on the menu bar, pointing
to Picture, then clicking From File. Navigate to the file you want,
then click Insert. To resize an image, drag its lower-right corner. To
move an image, drag it to a new location.

FIGURE C-6: Results of Clip Art search

Changing Attributes and Alignment

Attributes are styling formats such as bold, italics, and underlining that you can apply to affect the way text and numbers look in a worksheet. You can also change the **alignment** of labels and values in cells to be left, right, or center. You can apply attributes and alignment options using the Formatting toolbar or using the Alignment tab of the Format Cells dialog box. See Table C-2 for a list and description of the available attribute and alignment toolbar buttons. Now that you have applied new fonts and font sizes to the worksheet labels, Jim wants you to further enhance the worksheet's appearance by adding bold and underline formatting and centering some of the labels.

STEPS

1. **Press [Ctrl][Home] to select cell A1, then click the Bold button B on the Formatting toolbar**
   The title appears in bold.

2. **Click cell A3, then click the Underline button U on the Formatting toolbar**
   Excel underlines the text in the column heading in the selected cell.

3. **Click the Italics button I on the Formatting toolbar, then click B**
   The word "Type" appears in boldface, underlined, italic type. Notice that the Bold, Italics, and Underline buttons are all selected.

4. **Click I**
   Excel removes italics from cell A3, but the bold and underline formatting attributes remain.

5. **Click the Format Painter button 🖌 on the Formatting toolbar, then select the range B3:J3**
   Bold formatting is added to the rest of the labels in the column headings. The title would look better if it were centered over the data columns.

6. **Select the range A1:J1, then click the Merge and Center button 🔳 on the Formatting toolbar**
   The Merge and Center button creates one cell out of the 10 cells across the row, then centers the text in that newly created large cell. The title "MediaLoft NYC Advertising Expenses" is centered across the 10 columns you selected. You can change the alignment within individual cells using toolbar buttons; you can split merged cells into their original components by selecting the merged cells, then clicking 🔳.

7. **Select the range A3:J3, then click the Center button ≡ on the Formatting toolbar**
   Compare your screen to Figure C-7. Although they may be difficult to read, notice that all the headings are centered within their cells.

8. **Click the Save button 🖫 on the Standard toolbar**

Clues to Use

Rotating and indenting cell entries

In addition to applying fonts and formatting attributes, you can rotate or indent cell data within a cell to further change its appearance. You can rotate text within a cell by altering its alignment. To change alignment, select the cells you want to modify, click Format on the menu bar, click Cells, then click the Alignment tab in the Format Cells dialog box. Click a position in the Orientation box, or type a number in the Degrees text box to change from the default horizontal alignment, then click OK. You can indent cell contents using the Increase Indent button 🔳 on the Formatting toolbar, which moves cell contents to the right one space, or the Decrease Indent button 🔳, which moves cell contents to the left one space.

FIGURE C-7: Worksheet with formatting attributes applied

Formatting buttons selected

Center button

Title centered across columns

Merge and Center button

Column headings centered, bold, and underlined

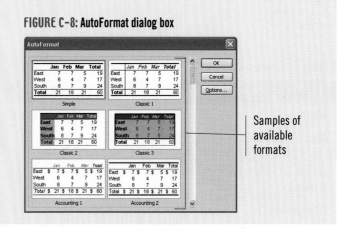

MediaLoft NYC Advertising Expenses

	A	B	C	D	E	F	G	H	I	J	K
1											Sales Tax
2											
3	Type	nv. Dat	nv. Due	aced wi	Cost ea.	Quantit	Ext. Cost	ales Ta	Total	of Tot al	
4	Newspape	1-Jan-06	31-Jan	Village Re:	$ 72.34	5	361.70	30.42	392.12	2%	
5	Radio spot	7-Jan-06	6-Feb	WHAT	$ 11.00	15	165.00	13.88	178.88	1%	
6	Subway	20-Jan-06	19-Feb	Advertising	$ 35.00	30	1,050.00	88.31	1,138.31	6%	
7	Yellow Pag	1-Jan-06	31-Jan	NYNEX	$ 154.42	4	617.68	51.95	669.63	3%	
8	Blow-in ca	13-Jan-06	12-Feb	Advertising	$ 0.17	230	39.56	3.33	42.89	0%	
9	Magazine	7-Jan-06	6-Feb	Young Ups	$ 100.92	12	1,211.04	101.85	1,312.89	7%	
10	Pens	5-Jan-06	4-Feb	Mass App	$ 0.12	250	30.75	2.59	33.34	0%	
11	Radio spot	15-Jan-06	14-Feb	WHAT	$ 11.00	15	165.00	13.88	178.88	1%	
12	Billboard	12-Jan-06	11-Feb	Advertising	$ 101.87	20	2,037.40	171.35	2,208.75	11%	

TABLE C-2: Attribute and alignment buttons on the Formatting toolbar

button	description	button	description
B	Bolds text	≡	Aligns text on the left side of the cell
I	Italicizes text	≡	Centers text horizontally within the cell
U	Underlines text	≡	Aligns text on the right side of the cell
⊞	Adds lines or borders	⊞	Centers text across columns, and combines two or more selected, adjacent cells into one cell

Clues to Use

Using AutoFormat

Excel has 16 predefined worksheet formats to make formatting your worksheets easier and to give you the option of consistently styling your worksheets. AutoFormats are designed for worksheets with labels in the left column and top rows, and totals in the bottom row or right column. To use AutoFormat, select the data to be formatted—or place your mouse pointer anywhere within the range to be selected (Excel can automatically detect a range of cells)—click Format on the menu bar, click AutoFormat, select a format from the sample boxes in the AutoFormat dialog box, as shown in Figure C-8, then click OK.

FIGURE C-8: AutoFormat dialog box

Samples of available formats

Adjusting Column Widths

As you continue formatting a worksheet, you might need to adjust column widths to accommodate a larger font size or style. The default column width is 8.43 characters wide, a little less than one inch. With Excel, you can adjust the column width for one or more columns by using the mouse or the Column command on the Format menu. Table C-3 describes the commands available on the Format Column menu. ▰▰▰ Jim notices that some of the labels in column A have been truncated and don't fit in the cells. He asks you to adjust the widths of the columns so that the labels appear in their entirety.

STEPS

1. **Position the pointer on the line between the column A and column B headings**

   The **column heading** is the orange box at the top of each column containing a letter. The pointer changes to ↔, as shown in Figure C-9. You position the pointer on the right edge of the column that you are adjusting. The Yellow Pages entries are the widest in the column.

QUICK TIP

To reset columns to the default width, click the column headings to select the columns, click Format on the menu bar, point to Column, click Standard Width in the Column Width dialog box, then click OK.

2. **Click and drag the ↔ pointer to the right until the column displays the Yellow Pages entries fully**

   You can use the **AutoFit** feature and your mouse to resize a column so it automatically accommodates the widest entry in a cell.

3. **Position the pointer on the column line between columns B and C headings until it changes to ↔, then double-click**

   Column B automatically widens to fit the widest entry, in this case, the column label.

4. **Use AutoFit to resize columns C, D, and J**

   You can also use the Column Width command on the Format menu to adjust several columns to the same width.

5. **Select the range F5:I5**

   Columns can be adjusted by selecting any cell in the column.

6. **Click Format on the menu bar, point to Column, click Width to open the Column Width dialog box, then move the dialog box, if necessary, by dragging it by its title bar so you can see the selected columns**

   The column width measurement is based on the number of characters in the Normal font (in this case, Arial).

TROUBLE

If "######" appears after you adjust a column of values, the column is too narrow to display the contents. Increase the column width until the values appear.

7. **Type 11 in the Column Width text box, then click OK**

   The column widths change to reflect the new setting. See Figure C-10.

8. **Click the Save button 🖫 on the Standard toolbar**

TABLE C-3: Format Column commands

command	description
Width	Sets the width to a specific number of characters
AutoFit Selection	Fits to the widest entry
Hide	Hide(s) column(s)
Unhide	Unhide(s) column(s)
Standard Width	Resets width to default widths

FIGURE C-9: Preparing to change the column width

Resize pointer between columns A and B

Row 2 button

Column D button

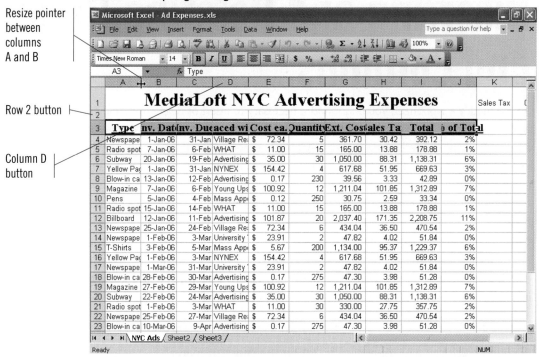

FIGURE C-10: Worksheet with column widths adjusted

Columns widened to display text

Columns widened to same width

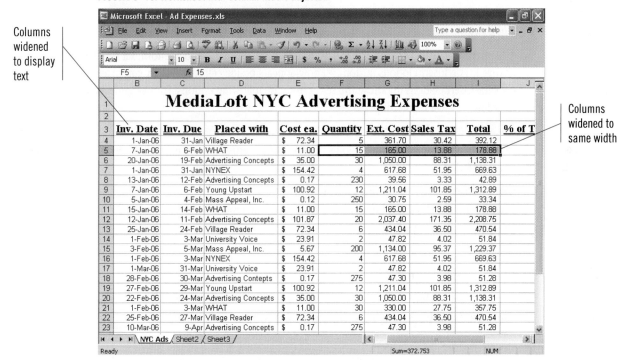

Clues to Use

Specifying row height

The Row Height command on the Format menu allows you to customize row height to improve readability. Row height is calculated in points, the same units of measure used for fonts. The row height must exceed the size of the font you are using. Normally, you don't need to adjust row heights manually. If you format something in a row to be a larger point size, Excel adjusts the row to fit the largest point size in the row. You can also adjust row height by placing the ✚ pointer under the row heading and dragging to the desired height.

Inserting and Deleting Rows and Columns

As you modify a worksheet, you might find it necessary to insert or delete rows and columns to keep your worksheet current. For example, you might need to insert rows to accommodate new inventory products or remove a column of yearly totals that are no longer necessary. Excel inserts rows above the cell pointer and inserts columns to the left of the cell pointer. When you insert a new row, the contents of the worksheet shift down from the newly inserted row. When you insert a new column, the contents of the worksheet shift to the right from the point of the new column. To insert a single row, you can also right-click the row heading immediately below where you want the new row, then click Insert. To insert multiple rows, drag across row headings to select the same number of rows as you want to insert. ██████ You have already improved the appearance of the worksheet by formatting the labels and values. Now Jim asks you to improve the overall appearance of the worksheet by inserting a row between the last row of data and the totals. Also, you have located a row of inaccurate data and an unnecessary column that you need to delete.

STEPS

1. **Right-click cell A32, then click Insert on the shortcut menu**

   The Insert dialog box opens. See Figure C-11. You can choose to insert a column or a row, or you can shift the data in the cells in the active column right or in the active row down. An additional row between the last row of data and the totals will visually separate the totals.

   QUICK TIP
   Inserting or deleting rows or columns can cause problems in formulas that contain absolute cell references. After adding rows or columns to a worksheet, be sure to proof your formulas.

2. **Click the Entire row option button, then click OK**

   A blank row appears between the totals and the Billboard data, and the formula result in cell E33 has not changed. The Insert Options button 🖉 now appears beside cell A33. When you place ℞ over 🖉, you can click the Insert Options list arrow and select from the following options: Format Same As Above, Format Same As Below, or Clear Formatting.

3. **Click the row 27 heading**

   Hats from Mass Appeal Inc. are no longer part of the advertising campaign. All of row 27 is selected, as shown in Figure C-12.

   QUICK TIP
   Use the Edit menu, or right-click the selected row and click Delete to remove a selected row. Pressing [Delete] on the keyboard removes the contents of a selected row; the row itself remains.

4. **Click Edit on the menu bar, then click Delete**

   Excel deletes row 27, and all rows below this shift up one row.

5. **Click the column J heading**

   The percentage information is calculated elsewhere and is no longer necessary in this worksheet.

6. **Click Edit on the menu bar, then click Delete**

   Excel deletes column J. The remaining columns to the right shift left one column.

7. **Click the Save button 🖫 on the Standard toolbar**

Clues to Use

Hiding and unhiding columns and rows

As you work with a worksheet, you may find that you need to make one or more columns or rows invisible. You can hide a selected column by clicking Format on the menu bar, pointing to Column, then clicking Hide. A hidden column is indicated by a black vertical line in its original position. You can display a hidden column by selecting the columns on either side of the black line, clicking Format on the menu bar, pointing to Column, and then clicking Unhide. (To hide/unhide one or more rows, substitute Row for the Column command.)

FIGURE C-11: Insert dialog box

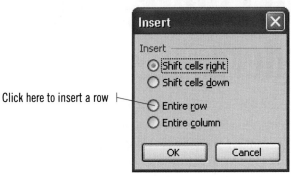

Click here to insert a row — Entire row

FIGURE C-12: Worksheet with row 27 selected

Row 27 heading

Inserted row

Insert Options button might appear in a different location, or not at all

20	Subway	22-Feb-06	24-Mar	Advertising Concepts	$	35.00	30	1,050.00	88.31	1,138
21	Radio spot	1-Feb-06	3-Mar	WHAT	$	11.00	30	330.00	27.75	357
22	Newspaper	25-Feb-06	27-Mar	Village Reader	$	72.34	6	434.04	36.50	470
23	Blow-in cards	10-Mar-06	9-Apr	Advertising Concepts	$	0.17	275	47.30	3.98	51
24	Radio spot	15-Mar-06	17-Mar	WHAT	$	11.00	25	275.00	23.13	298
25	Pens	15-Mar-06	14-Apr	Mass Appeal, Inc.	$	0.12	250	30.75	2.59	33
26	Yellow Pages	1-Mar-06	31-Mar	NYNEX	$	154.44	4	617.76	51.95	669
27	Hats	20-Mar-06	19-Apr	Mass Appeal, Inc.	$	7.20	250	1,800.00	151.38	1,951
28	Subway	20-Mar-06	19-Apr	Advertising Concepts	$	35.00	30	1,050.00	88.31	1,138
29	Newspaper	1-Apr-06	1-May	University Voice	$	23.91	2	47.82	4.02	51
30	Subway	10-Apr-06	10-May	Advertising Concepts	$	35.00	30	1,050.00	88.31	1,138
31	Billboard	28-Mar-06	27-Apr	Advertising Concepts	$	101.87	20	2,037.40	171.35	2,208
32										
33					$1,355.24		2034	17,987.90	1,512.78	19,500
34										
35										
36										

NYC Ads / Sheet2 / Sheet3 /

Ready   Sum=81782.06007   NUM

Clues to Use

Adding and editing comments

Much of your Excel work may be in collaboration with teammates with whom you share worksheets. You can share ideas with other worksheet users by adding comments within selected cells. To include a comment in a worksheet, click the cell where you want to place the comment, click Insert on the menu bar, then click Comment. A resizable text box containing the computer user's name opens in which you can type your comments. A small, red triangle appears in the upper-right corner of a cell containing a comment. If the comments are not already displayed, workbook users can point to the triangle to display the comment. To see all worksheet comments, as shown in Figure C-13, click View on the menu bar, then click Comments. To edit a comment, click the cell containing the comment, click Insert on the menu bar, then click Edit Comment. To delete a comment, right-click the cell containing the comment, then click Delete Comment on the shortcut menu.

FIGURE C-13: Comments in worksheet

20	Subway	22-Feb-06	24-Mar	Advertising Concepts	$	35.00
21	Radio spot	1-Feb-06	3-Mar	WHAT	$	11.00
22	Newspaper	25-Feb-06	27-Mar	Village Reader	$	72.34
23	Blow-in cards	10-Mar-06	9-Apr	Advertising Concepts	$	0.17
24	Radio spot	15-Feb-06	17-Mar		$	11.00
25	Pens	15-Mar-06	14-Apr		$	0.12
26	Yellow Pages	1-Mar-06	31-Mar		$	154.44
27	Subway	20-Mar-06	19-Apr		$	35.00
28	Newspaper	1-Apr-06	1-May	University Voice	$	23.91
29	Subway	10-Apr-06	10-May		$	35.00
30	Billboard	28-Mar-06	27-Apr		$	101.87
31						
32						$1,348.04
33						
34						

Jim Fernandez: Should we continue with these ads, or expand to other publications?

Jim Fernandez: We need to evaluate whether we should continue these ads.

NYC Ads / Sheet2 / Sheet3 /

Ready

FORMATTING A WORKSHEET EXCEL C-11

UNIT
C
Excel 2003

Applying Colors, Patterns, and Borders

You can use colors, patterns, and borders to enhance the overall appearance of a worksheet and to make it easier to read. You can add these enhancements by using the Patterns or Borders tabs in the Format Cells dialog box or by using the Borders and Color buttons on the Formatting toolbar. You can apply color or patterns to the background of a cell, to a range, or to cell contents. You can also apply borders to all the cells in a worksheet or only to selected cells to call attention to individual cells or groups of cells. See Table C-4 for a list of border buttons and their functions. Jim asks you to add a pattern, a border, and color to the title of the worksheet to give the worksheet a more professional appearance.

STEPS

1. **Press [Ctrl][Home] to select cell A1, then click the Fill Color list arrow on the Formatting toolbar**

   The color palette appears.

> **QUICK TIP**
> Use color sparingly. Too much color can divert the reader's attention from the worksheet data.

2. **Click the Turquoise color (fourth row, fifth column)**

   Cell A1 has a turquoise background, as shown in Figure C-14. Cell A1 spans columns A through I because of the Merge and Center command used for the title.

3. **Right-click cell A1, then click Format Cells on the shortcut menu**

   The Format Cells dialog box opens.

4. **Click the Patterns tab if it is not already displayed**

   See Figure C-15. Adding a pattern to cells can add to the visual interest of your worksheet.

5. **Click the Pattern list arrow, click the Thin Diagonal Crosshatch pattern (third row, last column), then click OK**

   A border also enhances a cell's appearance. Unlike underlining, which is a text-formatting tool, borders extend to the width of the cell.

> **QUICK TIP**
> You can also draw cell borders using the mouse pointer. Click the Borders list arrow on the Formatting toolbar, click Draw Borders, then drag to create borders or boxes.

6. **Click the Borders list arrow on the Formatting toolbar, then click the Thick Bottom Border (second row, second column) on the Borders palette**

   It can be difficult to view a border in a selected cell.

7. **Click cell A3**

   The border is a nice enhancement. Font color can also help distinguish information in a worksheet.

> **QUICK TIP**
> The default color on the Fill Color and Font Color buttons changes to the last color you selected.

8. **Select the range A3:I3, click the Font Color list arrow on the Formatting toolbar, then click the Blue color (second row, third column from the right) on the palette**

   The text changes color, as shown in Figure C-16.

9. **Click the Save button on the Standard toolbar**

Clues to Use

Formatting columns or rows

You can save yourself time by formatting an entire column or row using any of the categories that appear in the Format Cells dialog box. You might, for example, want to format all the cells within a column to accept telephone numbers, social security numbers, zip codes, or custom number formats. Click the column or row heading—located at the top of a column or beginning of a row—to select the entire column or row. You can format a selected column or row by clicking Format on the menu bar, clicking Cells, then clicking the appropriate tab in the Format Cells dialog box.

FIGURE C-14: Background color added to cell

Cell A1 with turquoise background

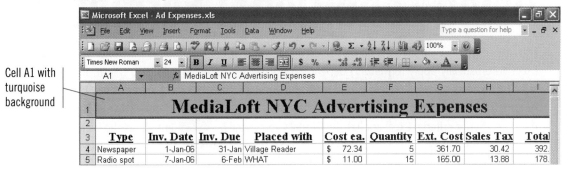

FIGURE C-15: Patterns tab in the Format Cells dialog box

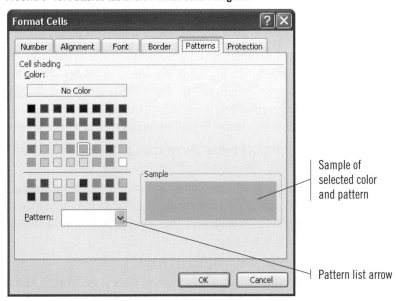

Sample of selected color and pattern

Pattern list arrow

FIGURE C-16: Worksheet with colors, patterns, and border

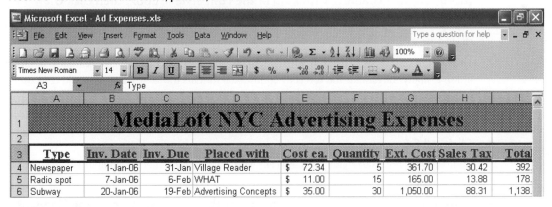

TABLE C-4: Border buttons

button	function	button	function	button	function
	No Border		Bottom Double Border		Top and Thick Bottom Border
	Bottom Border		Thick Bottom Border		All Borders
	Left Border		Top and Bottom Border		Outside Borders
	Right Border		Top and Double Bottom Border		Thick Box Border

Excel 2003

Using Conditional Formatting

Formatting makes worksheets look professional and helps distinguish different types of data. You can have Excel automatically apply formatting depending on specific values in cells. You might, for example, want advertising costs above a certain number to appear in red boldface and lower values to appear in blue. Automatically applying formatting attributes based on cell values is called **conditional formatting**. If the data meets your criteria, Excel applies the formats you specify. Jim wants the worksheet to include conditional formatting so that total advertising costs greater than $175 appear in boldface red type. He asks you to create the conditional format in the first cell in the Total cost column.

STEPS

1. **Click cell G4**

   Use the scroll bars if necessary, to make column G visible.

2. **Click Format on the menu bar, then click Conditional Formatting**

   The Conditional Formatting dialog box opens. Depending on the logical operator you've selected (such as "greater than" or "not equal to"), the Conditional Formatting dialog box displays different input boxes. You can define up to three different conditions, and then assign formatting attributes to each one. You define the condition first. The default setting for the first condition is "Cell Value Is" "between."

3. **Click the Operator list arrow to change the current condition, then click greater than or equal to**

   Because you changed the operator from "between," which required text boxes for two values, only one value text box now appears. The first condition is that the cell value must be greater than or equal to some value. See Table C-5 for a list of options. The value can be a constant, formula, cell reference, or date. That value is set in the third box.

4. **Click the Value text box, then type 175**

   Now that you have assigned the value, you need to specify what formatting you want for cells that meet this condition.

5. **Click Format, click the Color list arrow in the Format Cells dialog box, click the Red color (third row, first column), click Bold in the Font style list box, then click OK**

6. **Compare your settings to Figure C-17, then click OK to close the Conditional Formatting dialog box**

   The value in cell G4, 361.70, is formatted in bold red numbers because it is greater than 175, meeting the condition to apply the format. You can copy conditional formats the same way you would copy other formats.

7. **Verify that cell G4 is selected, click the Format Painter button 🖌 on the Standard toolbar, then drag ⊹🖌 to select the range G5:G30**

8. **Click cell G4**

   Compare your results to Figure C-18. All cells with values greater than or equal to 175 in column G appear in bold red text.

9. **Press [Ctrl][Home] to select cell A1, then click the Save button 🖫 on the Standard toolbar**

TABLE C-5: Conditional formatting options

option	mathematical equivalent	option	mathematical equivalent
Between	$X>Y<Z$	Greater than	$Z>Y$
Not between	$B>C<A$	Less than	$Y<Z$
Equal to	$A=B$	Greater than or equal to	$A>=B$
Not equal to	$A \neq B$	Less than or equal to	$Z<=Y$

FIGURE C-17: Completed Conditional Formatting dialog box

Operator list arrow

Enter value in the Value text box

Click to define format of cells that meet the condition

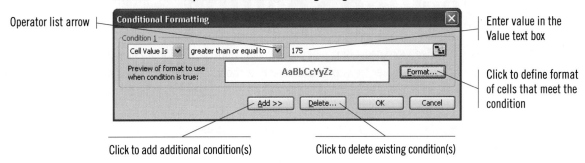

Click to add additional condition(s)

Click to delete existing condition(s)

FIGURE C-18: Worksheet with conditional formatting

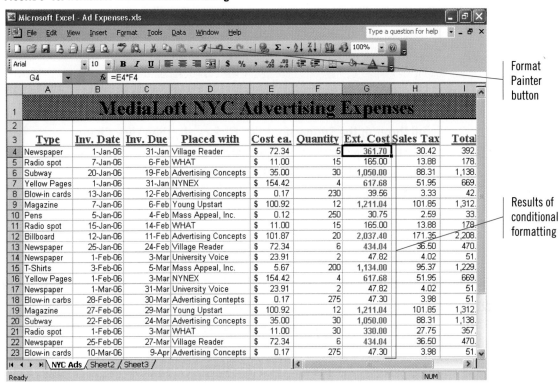

Format Painter button

Results of conditional formatting

Clues to Use

Deleting conditional formatting

Because it's likely that the conditions you define will change, you can delete any conditional format you define. Select the cell(s) containing conditional formatting, click Format on the menu bar, click Conditional Formatting, then click Delete in the Conditional Formatting dialog box. The Delete Conditional Format dialog box opens, as shown in Figure C-19. Select the check boxes for any of the conditions you want to delete, click OK, then click OK again. The previously assigned formatting is deleted—leaving the cell's contents intact.

FIGURE C-19: Delete Conditional Format dialog box

Delete Conditional Format

Select the condition(s) to delete:

☐ Condition 1
☐ Condition 2
☐ Condition 3

OK   Cancel

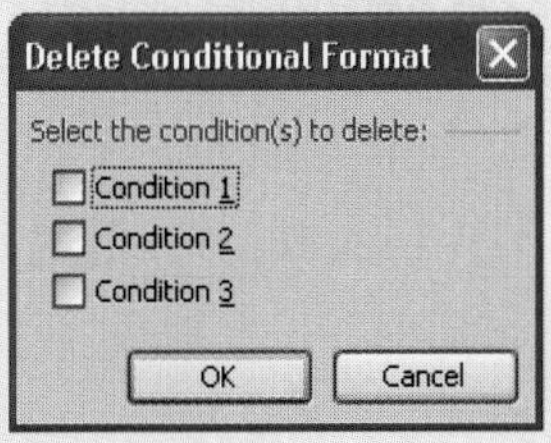

Checking Spelling

A single misspelled word can cast doubt on the validity and professional value of your entire workbook. Excel includes a spelling checker to help you ensure that the words in your worksheet are spelled correctly. The spelling checker scans your worksheet, displays words it doesn't find in its built-in dictionary, and when possible, suggests replacements. To check other sheets in a multiple-sheet workbook, you need to display each sheet and run the spelling checker again. Because the built-in dictionary cannot possibly include all the words that anyone needs, you can add words to the dictionary, such as your company name, an acronym, or an unusual technical term. The spelling checker will no longer consider that word misspelled. Any words you've added to the dictionary using Word, Access, or PowerPoint are also available in Excel. Because he will distribute this workbook to the marketing managers, Jim asks you to check its spelling.

STEPS

TROUBLE

If a language other than English is being used, the Spelling dialog box lists the name of that language in its title bar.

1. **Click the Spelling button 🔡 on the Standard toolbar**

   The Spelling: English (U.S.) dialog box opens, as shown in Figure C-21, with MediaLoft selected as the first misspelled word in the worksheet. For any word, you have the option to Ignore or to Ignore All cases that the spell checker flags, or to Add the word to the dictionary.

2. **Click Ignore All for MediaLoft**

   The spelling checker found the word "cards" misspelled and offers "crabs" as an alternative.

3. **Scroll through the Suggestions list, click cards, then click Change**

   The word "Concepts" is also misspelled, and the spelling checker suggests the correct spelling.

4. **Click Change**

   When no more incorrect words are found, Excel displays a message indicating that all the words on the worksheet have been checked.

5. **Click OK**

6. **Enter your name in cell A34, then press [Ctrl][Home]**

QUICK TIP

You can set **AutoCorrect** to correct spelling as you type. Click Tools on the menu bar, then click AutoCorrect Options.

7. **Click the Save button 🖫 on the Standard toolbar, then preview the worksheet**

8. **In the Preview window, click Setup to open the Page Setup dialog box, under Scaling click Fit to option button to print the worksheet on one page, click OK, click Print, then click OK**

   Compare your printout to Figure C-22.

9. **Click File on the menu bar, then click Exit to close the workbook without saving changes and exit Excel**

Clues to Use

Using e-mail to send a workbook

Once you have checked for spelling errors, you can use e-mail to send an entire workbook from within Excel. To send a workbook as an e-mail message attachment, open the workbook, click File on the menu bar, point to Send To, then click Mail Recipient (as Attachment). You supply the To and optional Cc information, as shown in Figure C-20, then click Send.

FIGURE C-20: E-mailing an Excel workbook

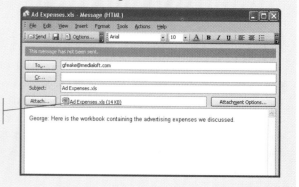

Workbook is automatically attached to message

FIGURE C-21: Spelling English dialog box

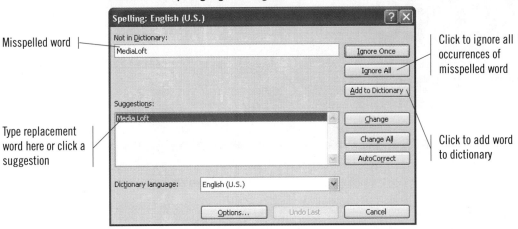

Misspelled word ⊣

Click to ignore all occurrences of misspelled word

Type replacement word here or click a suggestion

Click to add word to dictionary

FIGURE C-22: Completed worksheet

MediaLoft NYC Advertising Expenses

Sales Tax   0.0841

Type	Inv. Date	Inv. Due	Placed with	Cost ea.	Quantity	Ext. Cost	Sales Tax	Total
Newspaper	1-Jan-06	31-Jan	Village Reader	$ 72.34	5	361.70	30.42	392.12
Radio spot	7-Jan-06	6-Feb	WHAT	$ 11.00	15	165.00	13.88	178.88
Subway	20-Jan-06	19-Feb	Advertising Concepts	$ 35.00	30	1,050.00	88.31	1,138.31
Yellow Pages	1-Jan-06	31-Jan	NYNEX	$ 154.42	4	617.68	51.95	669.63
Blow-in cards	13-Jan-06	12-Feb	Advertising Concepts	$ 0.17	230	39.56	3.33	42.89
Magazine	7-Jan-06	6-Feb	Young Upstart	$ 100.92	12	1,211.04	101.85	1,312.89
Pens	5-Jan-06	4-Feb	Mass Appeal, Inc.	$ 0.12	250	30.75	2.59	33.34
Radio spot	15-Jan-06	14-Feb	WHAT	$ 11.00	15	165.00	13.88	178.88
Billboard	12-Jan-06	11-Feb	Advertising Concepts	$ 101.87	20	2,037.40	171.35	2,208.75
Newspaper	25-Jan-06	24-Feb	Village Reader	$ 72.34	6	434.04	36.50	470.54
Newspaper	1-Mar-06	3-Mar	University Voice	$ 23.91	2	47.82	4.02	51.84
T-Shirts	3-Feb-06	5-Mar	Mass Appeal, Inc.	$ 5.67	200	1,134.00	95.37	1,229.37
Yellow Pages	1-Feb-06	3-Mar	NYNEX	$ 154.42	4	617.68	51.95	669.63
Newspaper	1-Mar-06	31-Mar	University Voice	$ 23.91	2	47.82	4.02	51.84
Blow-in cards	28-Feb-06	30-Mar	Advertising Concepts	$ 0.17	275	47.30	3.98	51.28
Magazine	27-Feb-06	29-Mar	Young Upstart	$ 100.92	12	1,211.04	101.85	1,312.89
Subway	22-Feb-06	24-Mar	Advertising Concepts	$ 35.00	30	1,050.00	88.31	1,138.31
Radio spot	1-Feb-06	3-Mar	WHAT	$ 11.00	30	330.00	27.75	357.75
Newspaper	25-Feb-06	27-Mar	Village Reader	$ 72.34	6	434.04	36.50	470.54
Blow-in cards	10-Mar-06	9-Apr	Advertising Concepts	$ 0.17	275	47.30	3.98	51.28
Radio spot	15-Feb-06	17-Mar	WHAT	$ 11.00	25	275.00	23.13	298.13
Pens	15-Mar-06	14-Apr	Mass Appeal, Inc.	$ 0.12	250	30.75	2.59	33.34
Yellow Pages	1-Mar-06	31-Mar	NYNEX	$ 154.44	4	617.76	51.95	669.71
Subway	20-Mar-06	19-Apr	Advertising Concepts	$ 35.00	30	1,050.00	88.31	1,138.31
Newspaper	1-Apr-06	1-May	University Voice	$ 23.91	2	47.82	4.02	51.84
Subway	10-Apr-06	10-May	Advertising Concepts	$ 35.00	30	1,050.00	88.31	1,138.31
Billboard	28-Mar-06	27-Apr	Advertising Concepts	$ 101.87	20	2,037.40	171.35	2,208.75
				$ 1,348.04	1784	16,187.90	1,361.40	17,549.30

Your Name

Practice

▼ CONCEPTS REVIEW

Label each element of the Excel worksheet window shown in Figure C-23.

FIGURE C-23

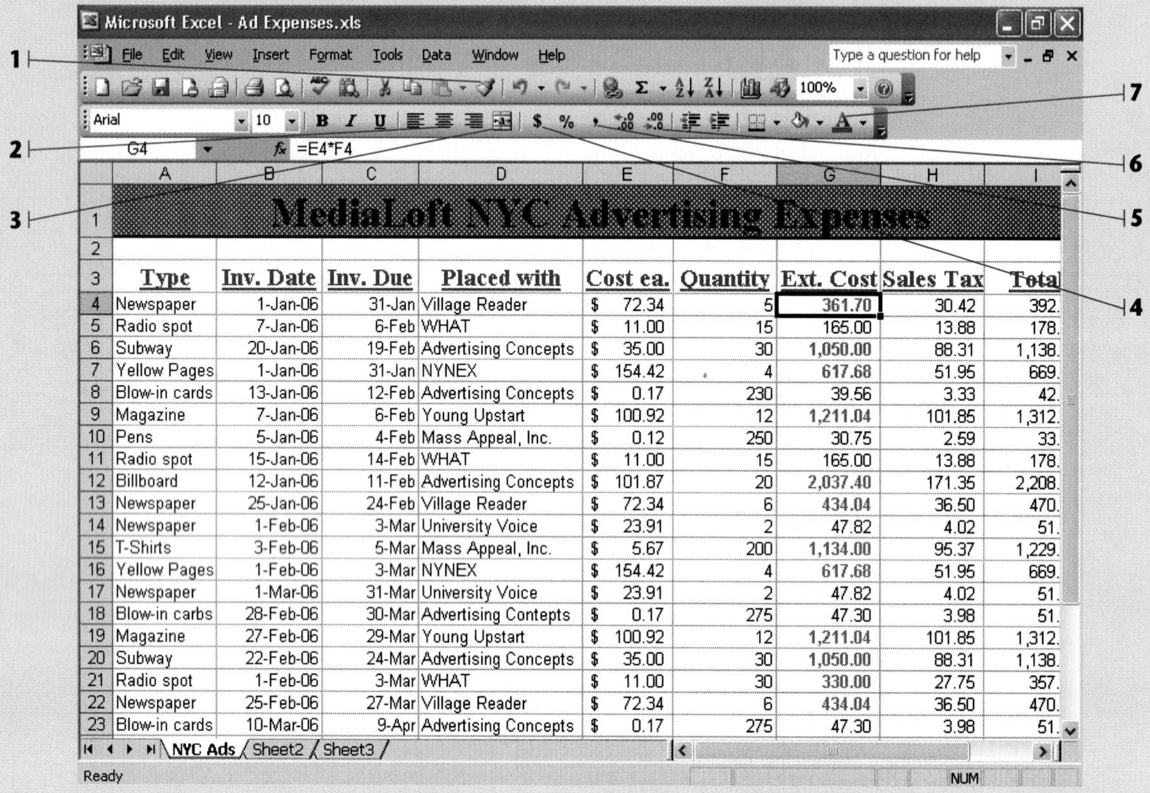

Match each command or button with the statement that best describes it.

8.  $

9. (button)

10. (button)

11. Cells command on the Format menu

12. Conditional Formatting

13. Delete command on the Edit menu

a. Changes appearance of a cell depending on result
b. Erases the contents of a cell
c. Used to check the spelling in a worksheet
d. Used to change the appearance of selected cells
e. Pastes the contents of the Clipboard into the current cell
f. Changes the format to Currency

EXCEL C-18 FORMATTING A WORKSHEET

OFFICE–268

Select the best answer from the list of choices.

14. **What is the name of the feature used to resize a column to its widest entry?**
    a. AutoResize
    b. AutoFormat
    c. AutoFit
    d. AutoAdjust

15. **Which button center-aligns the contents of a single cell?**
    a.
    b.
    c.
    d.

16. **Which button increases the number of decimal places in selected cells?**
    a.
    b.
    c.
    d.

17. **Which of the following is an example of the comma format?**
    a. 5555.55
    b. 55.55%
    c. 5,555.55
    d. $5,555.55

18. **How many conditional formats can be created in any cell?**
    a. 1
    b. 2
    c. 3
    d. 4

19. **Which feature applies formatting attributes according to cell contents?**
    a. AutoFormat
    b. Comments
    c. Conditional Formatting
    d. Merge and Center

20. **Each of the following operators can be used in conditional formatting, *except*:**
    a. Equal to.
    b. Greater than.
    c. Similar to.
    d. Not between.

▼ SKILLS REVIEW

1. Format values.

- **a.** Start Excel and open a new workbook.
- **b.** Enter the information from Table C-6 in your worksheet. Begin in cell A1, and do not leave any blank rows or columns.
- **c.** Save this workbook as **MediaLoft GB Sales** in the drive and folder where your Data Files are stored.
- **d.** Select the range of values in the Average Price column.
- **e.** Format the range using the Currency Style button.
- **f.** Apply the Comma format to the Average Price and Quantity data, and reduce the number of decimals in the Quantity column to 0.
- **g.** Insert formulas in the Totals column (multiply the Average Price by the Quantity).
- **h.** Apply the Currency format to the Totals data.
- **i.** Save your work.

TABLE C-6

MediaLoft Great Britain Quarterly Sales Projections			
Department	Average Price	Quantity	Totals
Sports	30	2250	
Computers	42	3185	
History	37	1325	
Personal Growth	29	2070	

2. Use fonts and font sizes.

- **a.** Select the range of cells containing the column labels.
- **b.** Change the font of the column labels to Times New Roman.
- **c.** Increase the font size of the column labels and the label in cell A1 to 14 point.
- **d.** Resize the columns as necessary.
- **e.** Save your changes.

3. Change attributes and alignment.

- **a.** Select the worksheet title **MediaLoft Great Britain**, then use the Bold button to apply the bold attribute.
- **b.** Use the Merge and Center button to center the title and the Quarterly Sales Projections labels over columns A through D.
- **c.** Select the label **Quarterly Sales Projections**, then apply underlining to the label.
- **d.** Add the bold attribute to the labels in the Department column.
- **e.** Use the Format Painter to paste the format from the data in the Department column to the Department and Totals labels.
- **f.** Add the italics attribute to the Average Price and Quantity labels.
- **g.** Select the range of cells containing the column titles, then center them.
- **h.** Return the underlined, merged and centered Quarterly Sales Projections label to its original alignment.
- **i.** Move the Quarterly Sales Projections label to cell D2 and change the alignment to Align Right.
- **j.** Save your changes.

4. Adjust column widths.

a. Use the Format menu to change the width of the Average Price column to **25**.

b. Use the AutoFit feature to resize the Average Price column.

c. Use the Format menu to resize the Department column to **18** and the Quantity column to **15**.

d. Change the text in cell C3 to **Sold**, then use AutoFit to resize the column.

e. Save your changes.

5. Insert and delete rows and columns.

a. Insert a new row between rows 4 and 5.

b. Add MediaLoft Great Britain's newest department—**Children's Corner**—in the newly inserted row. Enter **35** for the average price and **1225** for the number sold.

c. Add the following comment to cell A5: **New department**. Display the comment, if necessary.

d. Add a formula in cell D5 that multiplies the Average Price column by the Sold column.

e. Add a new column between the Department and Average Price columns with the title **Location**.

f. Delete the History row.

g. Edit the comment in cell A5 so it reads "New department. Needs promotion."

h. Save your changes.

6. Apply colors, patterns, and borders.

a. Add an outside border around the Average Price and Sold data.

b. Apply a light green background color to the labels in the Department column.

c. Apply a gold background to the column labels in cells **A3:E3**.

d. Change the color of the font in the column labels in cells A3:E3 to blue.

e. Add a 12.5% Gray pattern fill to the title in cell A1. (*Hint*: Use the Patterns tab in the Format Cells dialog box to locate the 12.5% Gray pattern.)

f. Enter your name in cell A20, then save your work.

g. Preview and print the worksheet, then close the workbook.

7. Use conditional formatting.

a. Open the file EX C-2.xls from the drive and folder where your Data Files are stored, then save it as **Monthly Operating Expenses**.

b. Create conditional formatting that changes a monthly data entry to blue if the value is **greater than 2500**, and changes the monthly data entry to red if the value is **less than 700**.

c. Create a third conditional format that changes the monthly data to green if a value is **between 1000 and 2000**.

d. Use the Bold button and Center button to format the column headings and row titles.

e. Make Column A wide enough to accommodate the contents of cells **A4:A9**.

f. Create formulas in cells F4:F9 and cells B11:F11. Use the Comma Style with no decimals in these cells.

g. AutoFit the remaining columns.

h. Use Merge and Center in row 1 to center the title over columns A–F.

i. Format the title in cell A1 using 14-point text. Fill the cell with a color and pattern of your choice.

j. Delete the third conditional format.

k. Enter your name in cell A20, then apply a green background to it and make the text color yellow.

l. Use the Edit menu to clear the cell formats from the cell with your name, then save your changes.

8. Check spelling.

a. Check the spelling in the worksheet using the spelling checker, correcting any spelling errors.

b. Save your changes, then preview and print the workbook.

c. Close the workbook, then exit Excel.

Excel 2003

▼ INDEPENDENT CHALLENGE 1

Beautiful You, a small beauty salon, has been using Excel for several months. Now that the salon's accounting records are in Excel, the manager would like you to work on the inventory. Although more items will be added later, the worksheet has enough items for you to begin your modifications.

a. Start Excel, open the file EX C-3.xls from the drive and folder where your Data Files are stored, then save it as **BY Inventory**.

b. Create a formula that calculates the value of the inventory on hand for each item.

c. Use an absolute reference to calculate the sale price of each item, using the markup percentage shown.

d. Add the bold attribute to the column headings.

e. Make sure all columns are wide enough to display the data and headings.

f. Change the On Hand Value and Sale Price columns so they display the Currency style with two decimal places.

g. Change the Price Paid column so it displays the Comma style with two decimal places.

h. Add a row under #2 Curlers for Nail Files, price paid $0.25, sold individually (each), with 59 on hand.

i. Verify that all the formulas in the worksheet are correct. Adjust any items as needed, and check the spelling.

j. Use conditional formatting to call attention to items with a quantity of 25 or fewer on hand. Use boldfaced red text.

k. Add an outside border around the data in the Item column.

l. Delete the row with #3 Curlers.

m. Enter your name in an empty cell, then save the file.

n. Preview and print the worksheet, compare your work to the sample shown in Figure C-24, close the workbook, then exit Excel.

FIGURE C-24

	A	B	C	D	E	F	G	H	I	J
1	Beautiful You Salon						markup ->	1.35		
2										
3	**Item**	**Price Paid**	**Sold by**	**On Hand**	**On Hand Value**	**Sale Price**				
4	#2 Curlers	13.80	box	53	$ 731.40	$ 18.63				
5	Nail Files	0.25	each	59	$ 14.75	$ 0.34				
6	Hair dryers	4.25	each	75	$ 318.75	$ 5.74				
7	Nail polish	3.92	each	62	$ 243.04	$ 5.29				
8	Conditioner	2.99	each	35	$ 104.65	$ 4.04				
9	Scrumptious shampoo	8.30	each	25	$ 207.50	$ 11.21				
10	Clips	2.25	box	33	$ 74.25	$ 3.04				
11	Pins	4.75	box	36	$ 171.00	$ 6.41				
12	#1 Curlers	2.10	box	37	$ 77.70	$ 2.84				
13	Jumbo conditioner	10.65	each	22	$ 234.30	$ 14.38				
14	#472 color	16.32	each	13	$ 212.16	$ 22.03				
15										
16										
17										
18										
19										
20	Your Name									
21										
22										
23										
24										
25										

| ◄ ◄ ► ►| \ Sheet1 / Sheet2 / Sheet3 /

Ready   NUM

▼ INDEPENDENT CHALLENGE 2

You volunteer several hours each week with the Community Action Center. You would like to examine the membership list, and decide to use formatting to make the existing data look more professional and easier to read.

   a. Start Excel, open the file EX C-4.xls from the drive and folder where your Data Files are stored, then save it as **Community Action**.

   b. Remove any blank columns.

   c. Format the Annual Revenue figures using the Currency format.

   d. Make all columns wide enough to fit their data and headings.

   e. Use formatting enhancements, such as fonts, font sizes, and text attributes to make the worksheet more attractive.

   f. Center-align the column labels.

   g. Use conditional formatting so that entries for Number of Employees that are greater than 50 appear in a contrasting color.

   h. Adjust any items as necessary, then check the spelling.

   i. Enter your name in an empty cell, then save your work.

   j. Before printing, preview the file so you know what the worksheet looks like, then print a copy. Compare your work to the sample shown in Figure C-25.

   k. Close the workbook, then exit Excel.

FIGURE C-25

	A	B	C	D	E	F	G
1	Community Action Center Members						
2							
3		Annual	Number of		Type of		
4	Member	Revenue	Employees	Status	Business		
5	Lisa's Photo Studio	$ 56,000.00	5	member	Restaurant		
6	Chip Technology	$ 492,600.00	175	member	Manufacturing, Microchips		
7	Computer Attic	$ 128,000.00	4	member	Computer Consultant		
8	Deluxe Auto Shop	$ 98,420.00	7	member	Automotive		
9	Front Office	$ 162,320.00	25	member	Employment Agency		
10	General Hospital	$ 1,154,000.00	480	member	Health		
11	Grande Table	$ 101,500.00	25	member	Restaurant		
12	Holiday Inn	$ 175,000.00	75	member	Hotel/Motel		
13	Midas Muffler	$ 106,000.00	22	member	Automotive		
14	Mill Shoppe	$ 346,000.00	165	member	Manufacturing, Furniture		
15	Reservation Inn	$ 272,000.00	42	member	Hotel/Motel		
16	State University	$ 975,630.00	422	member	Education		
17	Candy's Candy Shop	$ 100,500.00	3	non-member	Restaurant		
18	Dental Associates	$ 175,000.00	15	non-member	Health		
19	Dr. Rachel	$ 173,000.00	5	non-member	Health		
20	Dunkin' Donuts	$ 66,420.00	7	non-member	Restaurant		
21	Earl's Restaurant	$ 290,000.00	45	non-member	Restaurant		
22	First Federal Bank	$ 1,216,500.00	36	non-member	Bank		
23	Friendly Chevy	$ 289,000.00	17	non-member	Automotive		
24	Ken's Florist Shop	$ 89,900.00	10	non-member	Florist		
25	Moinako Mufflor	$ 107,900.00	24	non-member	Automotive		

Sheet1 / Sheet2 / Sheet3 /

Ready   NUM

▼ INDEPENDENT CHALLENGE 3

Classic Instruments is a Miami-based company that manufactures high-quality pens and markers. As the finance manager, one of your responsibilities is to analyze the monthly reports from your five district sales offices. Your boss, Joanne Bennington, has just asked you to prepare a quarterly sales report for an upcoming meeting. Because several top executives will be attending this meeting, Joanne reminds you that the report must look professional. In particular, she asks you to emphasize the company's surge in profits during the last month and to highlight the fact that the Northeastern district continues to outpace the other districts.

a. Plan a worksheet that shows the company's sales during the first quarter. Assume that all pens are the same price. Make sure you include:
  - The number of pens sold (units sold) and the associated revenues (total sales) for each of the five district sales offices. The five sales districts are: Northeastern, Midwestern, Southeastern, Southern, and Western.
  - Calculations that show month-by-month totals and a three-month cumulative total
  - Calculations that show each district's share of sales (percent of Total Sales)
  - Formatting enhancements to emphasize the recent month's sales surge and the Northeastern district's sales leadership

b. Ask yourself the following questions about the organization and formatting of the worksheet: How can you calculate the totals? What formulas can you copy to save time and keystrokes? Do any of these formulas need to use an absolute reference? How do you show dollar amounts? What information should be shown in bold? Do you need to use more than one font? Should you use more than one point size?

c. Start Excel, then build the worksheet with your own price and sales data. Enter the titles and labels first, then enter the numbers and formulas. You can use the information in Table C-7 to get started.

TABLE C-7:

Classic Instruments
1st Quarter Sales Report

		January		February		March		Total	
Office	Price	Units Sold	Sales	Units Sold	Sales	Units Sold	Sales	Units Sold	Sales
Northeastern									
Midwestern									
Southeastern									
Southern									
Western									

d. Save the workbook as Classic Instruments in the drive and folder where your Data Files are stored.
e. Adjust the column widths as necessary.
f. Change the height of row 1 to 30 points.
g. Format labels and values, and change the attributes and alignment if necessary.
h. Resize columns and adjust the formatting as necessary.
i. Add a column that calculates a 24% increase in sales dollars. Use an absolute cell reference in this calculation.
j. Create a new column named Increase in Sales that adds the projected increase to the Total Sales. (*Hint*: Make sure the current formatting is applied to the new information.)

Advanced Challenge Exercise

  - Use AutoFormat to add color and formatting to the data.
  - Insert a clip art image in an appropriate location, adjusting its size and position as necessary.

k. Enter your name in an empty cell.
l. Check the spelling, then save your work.
m. Preview, then print the file in landscape orientation.
n. Close the file, then exit Excel.

▼ INDEPENDENT CHALLENGE 4

After saving for many years, you now have enough funds to take that international trip you have always dreamed about. Your well-traveled friends have told you that you should always have the local equivalent of $100 U.S. dollars in cash with you when you enter a country. You decide to use the Web to determine how much money you will need in each country.

a. Start Excel, open a new workbook, then save it as Currency Conversions in the drive and folder where your Data Files are stored.

b. Enter column and row labels using the information in Table C-8 to get started.

c. Use your favorite search engine to find your own information sources on currency conversions.

d. Find out how much cash is equivalent to $1 in U.S. dollars for the following countries: Australia, Canada, France, Germany, Sweden, and the United Kingdom. Also enter the name of the currency used in each country.

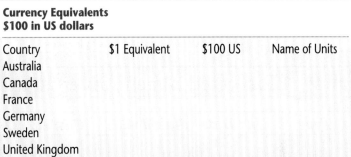

TABLE C-8

Currency Equivalents $100 in US dollars			
Country	$1 Equivalent	$100 US	Name of Units
Australia			
Canada			
France			
Germany			
Sweden			
United Kingdom			

e. Create an equation that calculates the equivalent of $100 in U.S. dollars for each country in the list, using an absolute value in the formula.

f. Format the entries in columns B and C using the correct currency unit for each country, with two decimal places. (*Hint*: Use the Numbers tab in the Format cells dialog box; choose the appropriate currency format from the Symbol list, using two decimal places.)

g. Create a conditional format that changes the font attributes of the calculated amount in the "$100 US" column to bold and red if the amount is equals or exceeds 500 units of the local currency.

h. Merge and center the title over the column headings.

i. Add any formatting attributes to the column headings, and resize the columns as necessary.

j. Add a background color to the title.

Advanced Challenge Exercise

- Apply the AutoFormat of your choice to the conversion table.
- Delete the conditional format in the $100 US column.
- If you have access to an e-mail account, e-mail this workbook to your instructor as an attachment.

k. Enter your name in an empty worksheet cell.

l. Spell check, save, preview, then print the worksheet.

m. Close the workbook and exit Excel.

▼ VISUAL WORKSHOP

Create the worksheet shown in Figure C-26, using skills you learned in this unit. Open the file EX C-5.xls from the drive and folder where your Data Files are stored, then save it as **Projected March Advertising Invoices**. Create a conditional format in the Cost ea. column so that entries greater than 60 appear in red. (*Hint*: The only additional font used in this exercise is Times New Roman. It is 22 point in row 1, and 16 point in row 3.) Enter your name in cell A20, spell check the worksheet, then save and print your work.

FIGURE C-26

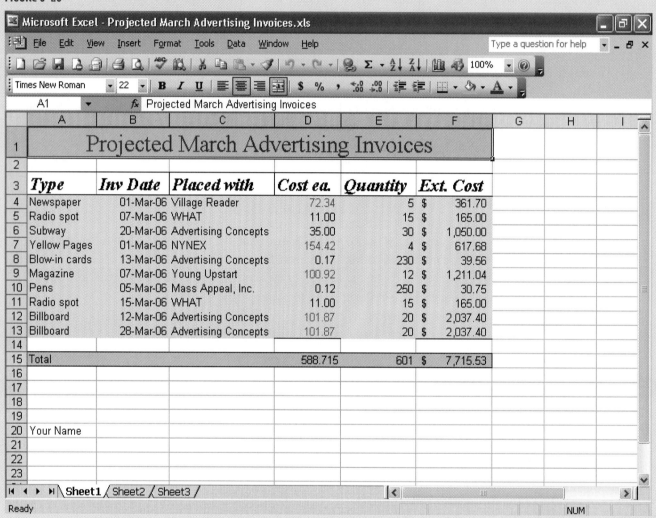

Working with Charts

OBJECTIVES

Plan and design a chart
Create a chart
Move and resize a chart
Edit a chart
Format a chart
Enhance a chart
Annotate and draw on a chart
Preview and print a chart

If you have a SAM user profile, you may have access to hands-on instruction, practice, and assessment of the skills covered in this unit. Log in to your SAM account and go to your assignments page to see what your instructor has assigned.

Worksheets provide an effective way to organize information, but they are not always the best format for presenting data to others. Information in a selected range or worksheet can easily be displayed as a chart. **Charts**, often called graphs, allow you to communicate the relationships in your worksheet data in readily understandable pictures. In this unit, you will learn how to create a chart, how to edit a chart and change the chart type, how to add text annotations and arrows to a chart, and how to preview and print a chart. ▒▒▒ For the annual meeting, Jim Fernandez needs you to create a chart showing the six-month sales history for the MediaLoft stores in the Eastern Division. He wants to illustrate the growth trend in this division.

UNIT D
Excel 2003

Planning and Designing a Chart

Before creating a chart, you need to plan the information you want your chart to show and how you want it to look. ▪▪▪▪▪ In early June, the Marketing Department launched a regional advertising campaign for the Eastern Division. The results of the campaign were increased sales during the fall months. Jim wants you to create a chart for the annual meeting that illustrates the growth trend for sales in MediaLoft's Eastern Division stores and to highlight this sales increase.

DETAILS

Jim wants you to use the worksheet shown in Figure D-1 and the following guidelines to plan the chart:

- **Determine the purpose of the chart and identify the data relationships you want to communicate graphically**

  You want to create a chart that shows sales throughout MediaLoft's Eastern Division from July through December. In particular, you want to highlight the increase in sales that occurred as a result of the advertising campaign.

- **Determine the results you want to see, and decide which chart type is most appropriate to use**

  Different charts display data in distinctive ways. Some chart types are more appropriate for particular types of data and analyses. How you want your data displayed—and how you want that data interpreted—can help you determine the best chart type to use. Table D-1 describes several different types of charts, the corresponding button on the Chart Type palette located on the Chart toolbar, and indicates when each one is best used. Because you want to compare data (sales in multiple locations) over a time period (the months July through December), you decide to use a column chart.

- **Identify the worksheet data you want the chart to illustrate**

  You are using data from the worksheet titled MediaLoft Eastern Division Stores shown in Figure D-1. This worksheet contains the sales data for the four stores in the Eastern Division from July through December.

- **Sketch the chart, then use your sketch to decide where the chart elements should be placed**

  You sketch your chart as shown in Figure D-2. You put the months on the horizontal axis (the **x-axis**) and the monthly sales figures on the vertical axis (the **y-axis**). The x-axis is often called the **category axis** because it often contains the names of data groups, such as months or years. The y-axis is called the **value axis** because it often contains numerical values that help you interpret the size of chart elements. (In a 3-D chart, the y-axis is referred to as the z-axis.) The area inside the horizontal and vertical axes is called the **plot area**. The **tick marks** on the y-axis create a scale of measure for each value. Each value in a cell you select for your chart is a **data point**. In any chart, a **data marker** visually represents each data point, which in this case is a column. A collection of related data points is a **data series**. In this chart, there are four data series (Boston, Chicago, Kansas City, and New York), so you include a **legend** to make it easy to identify them.

FIGURE D-1: Worksheet containing sales data

	A	B	C	D	E	F	G	H	I	J	K
	Microsoft Excel - MediaLoft Sales-Eastern Division.xls										
	A1		fx	MediaLoft Eastern Division Stores							
1	MediaLoft Eastern Division Stores										
2	FY 2006 Sales Following Advertising Campaign										
3											
4											
5		July	August	September	October	November	December	Total			
6	Boston	18,750	13,050	18,600	22,500	22,500	20,750	$116,150			
7	Chicago	17,200	18,200	17,250	19,500	18,600	19,500	$110,250			
8	Kansas City	12,150	11,500	15,350	18,100	17,050	17,500	$ 91,650			
9	NYC	19,500	16,250	18,900	20,500	22,000	23,800	$120,950			
10	Total	$ 67,600	$ 59,000	$ 70,100	$ 80,600	$ 80,150	$ 81,550	$439,000			
11											

Excel 2003

FIGURE D-2: Column chart sketch

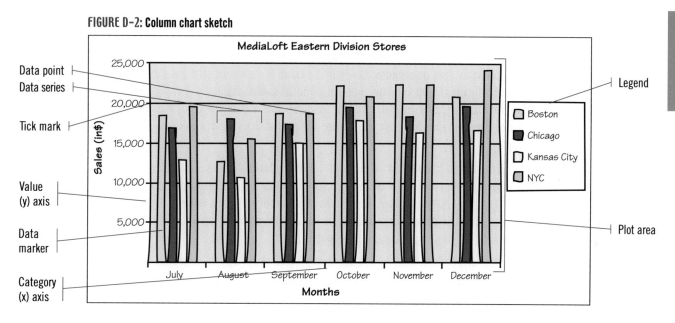

TABLE D-1: Commonly used chart types

type	button	description
Area		Shows how individual volume changes over time in relation to total volume
Bar		Compares distinct object levels over time using a horizontal format; sometimes referred to as a horizontal bar chart in other spreadsheet programs
Column		Compares distinct object levels over time using a vertical format; the Excel default; sometimes referred to as a bar chart in other spreadsheet programs
Line		Compares trends over even time intervals; appears similar to an area chart, but does not emphasize total
Pie		Compares sizes of pieces as part of a whole; used for a single series of numbers
XY (scatter)		Compares trends over uneven time or measurement intervals; used in scientific and engineering disciplines for trend spotting and extrapolation
Combination	none	Combines a column and line chart to compare data requiring different scales of measure

Creating a Chart

To create a chart in Excel, you first select the range containing the data you want to chart. Once you've selected a range, you can use the Excel **Chart Wizard** to lead you through the process of creating the chart. ▄▄▓▓ Using the worksheet containing the sales data for the Eastern Division, Jim asks you to create a chart that shows the growth trend that occurred.

STEPS

QUICK TIP
When charting any data, make sure all series are for the same time period.

1. **Start Excel, open the File** EX D-1.xls **from the drive and location where your Data Files are stored, then save it as** MediaLoft Sales-Eastern Division

   You want the chart to include the monthly sales figures for each of the Eastern Division stores, as well as month and store labels. You don't include the Total column and row because the monthly figures make up the totals, and these figures would skew the chart.

QUICK TIP
You can create a chart from noncontiguous cells by pressing and holding [Ctrl] while selecting each range.

2. **Select the range** A5:G9, **then click the** Chart Wizard button 📊 **on the Standard toolbar**

   The selected range contains the data you want to chart. The Chart Wizard opens. The Chart Wizard - Step 1 of 4 - Chart Type dialog box lets you choose the type of chart you want to create. The default chart type is a Clustered Column, as shown in Figure D-3. You can see a preview of the chart using your selected data by pressing and holding the Press and Hold to View Sample button.

3. **Click** Next **to accept Clustered Column, the default chart type**

   The Chart Wizard - Step 2 of 4 - Chart Source Data dialog box lets you choose the data to chart and whether the series appear in rows or columns. You want to chart the effect of sales for each store over the time period. Currently, the rows are appropriately selected as the data series, as specified by the Series in option button (located under the Data range). Because you selected the data before clicking the Chart Wizard button, Excel converted the range to absolute values and the correct range, =Sheet1!$A$5:$G$9, appears in the Data range text box.

4. **Click** Next

   The Chart Wizard - Step 3 of 4 - Chart Options dialog box shows a sample chart using the data you selected. The store locations (the rows in the selected range) are plotted against the months (the columns in the selected range), and Excel added the months as labels for each data series. A legend shows each location and its corresponding color on the chart. The Titles tab lets you add titles to the chart and its axes. Other tabs let you modify the axes, legend, and other chart elements.

5. **Click the** Chart title text box, **then type** MediaLoft Sales - Eastern Division

   After a moment, the title appears in the Sample Chart box. See Figure D-4.

6. **Click** Next

   In the Chart Wizard - Step 4 of 4 - Chart Location dialog box, you determine the placement of the chart in the workbook. You can display a chart as an object on the current sheet (called an **embedded chart**), on any other existing sheet, or on a newly created chart sheet. A **chart sheet** in a workbook contains only a chart, which is linked to the workbook data. The default selection—displaying the chart as an object in the sheet containing the data—will help Jim emphasize his point at the annual meeting.

QUICK TIP
If the Chart toolbar does not display, click View on the menu bar, point to Toolbars, and then click Chart.

7. **Click** Finish

   The column chart appears and the Chart toolbar opens, either docked or floating, as shown in Figure D-5. Your chart and the chart toolbar might be in different locations, and the chart may look slightly different. You adjust the chart's location and size in the next lesson. The **sizing handles**, the small squares at the corners and sides of the chart's border, indicate that the chart is selected. Any time a chart is selected, as it is now, a blue border surrounds the worksheet data range, a green border surrounds the row labels, and a purple border surrounds the column labels.

8. **Click the** Save button 💾 **on the Standard toolbar**

FIGURE D-3: First Chart Wizard dialog box

Selected chart

Clustered column chart is the default

Chart types

Chart sub-types for selected chart

Description of selected chart sub-type

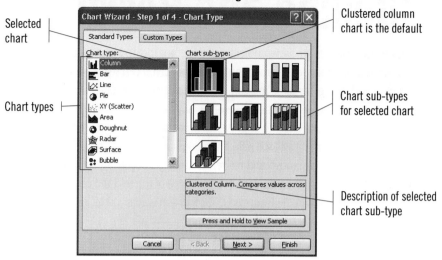

FIGURE D-4: Third Chart Wizard dialog box

Type the chart title here

Sample chart

Title added

Legend

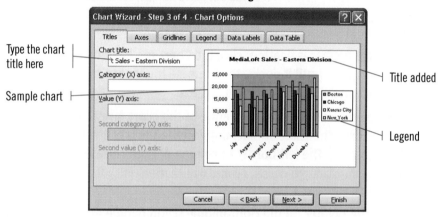

FIGURE D-5: Worksheet with column chart

Column labels

Title

Legend

Row labels

Data range

Selected chart object

Chart toolbar

Sizing handles

Month labels on the x-axis

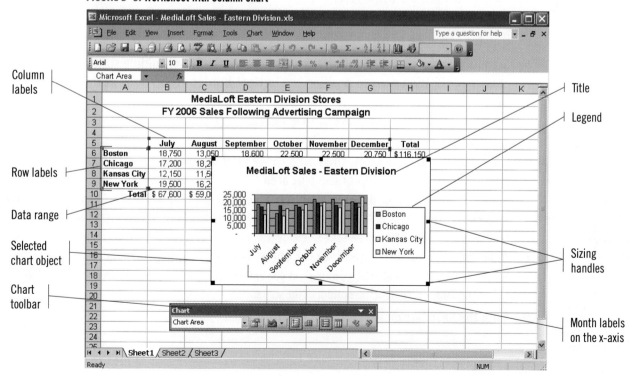

Moving and Resizing a Chart

Charts are graphics, or drawn objects, and are not located in a specific cell or at a specific range address. An **object** is an independent element on a worksheet. You can select an object by clicking within its borders to surround it with sizing handles. You can move a selected chart object anywhere on a worksheet without affecting formulas or data in the worksheet. However, any data changed in the worksheet is automatically updated in the chart. You can resize a chart to improve its appearance by dragging its sizing handles. You can even put a chart on another sheet, and it will still reflect the original data. Chart objects contain other objects, such as a title and legend, which you can move and resize. To move an object, select it, then drag it or cut and copy it to a new location. When you select a chart object, the name of the selected object appears in the Chart Objects list box on the Chart toolbar and in the Name box. Jim wants you to increase the size of the chart, position it below the worksheet data, and reposition the legend.

STEPS

QUICK TIP
If you want to delete a chart, select it, then press [Delete].

1. **Make sure the chart is still selected, then position the pointer over the chart**

   The pointer shape indicates that you can move the chart or use a sizing handle to resize it. For a table of commonly used chart pointers, refer to Table D-2. On occasion, the Chart toolbar obscures your view. You can dock the toolbar to make it easier to see your work.

2. **If the chart toolbar is floating, click the Chart toolbar's title bar, drag it to the right edge of the status bar until it docks, then release the mouse button**

   The toolbar is docked on the bottom of the screen.

3. **Place on a blank area near the edge of the chart, press and hold the left mouse button, using ✛, drag the chart until its upper-left edge is at the top of row 13 and the left edge of the chart is at the left border of column A, then release the mouse button**

   As you drag the chart, you can see a dotted outline representing the chart's perimeter. The chart appears in the new location.

QUICK TIP
Resizing a chart doesn't affect the data in the chart, only the way the chart looks on the sheet.

4. **Position the pointer on the right-middle sizing handle until it changes to ↔, then drag the right edge of the chart to the right edge of column H**

   The chart is widened. See Figure D-6.

5. **Position the pointer over the upper-middle sizing handle until it changes to ↕, then drag it to the top edge of row 12**

6. **Scroll down the screen, position the pointer over the lower-middle sizing handle until it changes to ↕, then drag to position the bottom border of the chart at the bottom border of row 25**

   You can move the legend to improve the chart's appearance. You want to align the top of the legend with the top of the plot area.

QUICK TIP
Placing the mouse pointer over a chart object displays a ScreenTip identifying it, whether the chart is selected or not. If a chart—or any object in it—is selected, the ScreenTips still appear and the name of the selected chart object appears in the Chart Objects list box on the Chart toolbar and in the Name box.

7. **Click the legend to select it, then drag the legend upward using so the top of the legend aligns with the top of the plot area**

   Sizing handles appear around the legend when you click it; "Legend" appears in the Chart Objects list box on the Chart toolbar as well as in the Name box, and a dotted outline of the legend border appears as you drag. Changing any label modifies the legend text.

8. **Click cell A9, type NYC, then click the Enter button on the formula bar**

   See Figure D-7. The legend changes to the text you entered. Because the chart is no longer selected, the chart toolbar no longer appears at the bottom of the screen.

9. **Click the Save button on the Standard toolbar**

FIGURE D-6: Worksheet with resized and repositioned chart

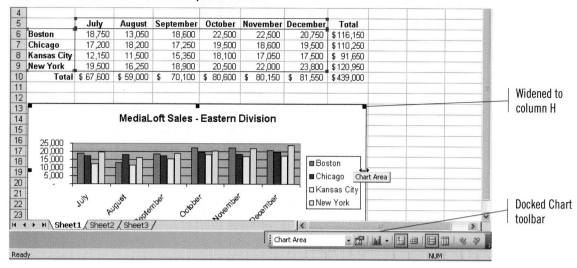

Widened to column H

Docked Chart toolbar

FIGURE D-7: Worksheet with repositioned legend

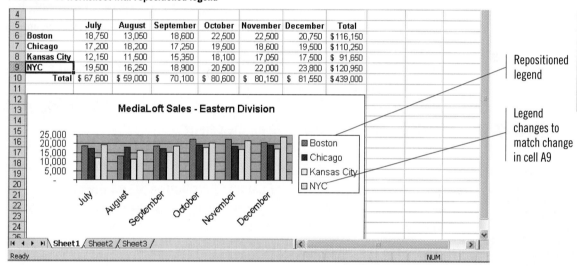

Repositioned legend

Legend changes to match change in cell A9

TABLE D-2: Commonly used pointers

name	pointer	use	name	pointer	use
Diagonal resizing	⤢ or ⤡	Change chart shape	I-beam	I	Edit chart text from corners
Draw	+	Create shapes	Move chart	✛	Change chart location
Horizontal resizing	↔	Change chart shape from left to right	Vertical resizing	↕	Changes chart shape from top to bottom

Clues to Use

Changing the location of a chart

Suppose you have created an embedded chart that you decide would look better on a chart sheet. You can make this change without recreating the entire chart. To change the location of a selected chart, click Chart on the menu bar, then click Location. If the chart is embedded, click the As new sheet option button, then click OK. If the chart is on its own sheet, click the As object in option button, then click OK.

Editing a Chart

Once you've created a chart, it's easy to modify it. You can change data values in the worksheet, and the chart is automatically updated to reflect the new data. You can also change a data point in a chart, and the corresponding data values in the worksheet are automatically updated. You can also easily change the type of chart displayed by using the buttons on the Chart toolbar. ⬛⬛⬛⬛ You look over your worksheet and realize the data for the Kansas City store in November and December is incorrect. After you correct this data, Jim asks you to see how the same data looks using different chart types.

STEPS

1. **If necessary, scroll the worksheet so that you can see both the chart and row 8 containing the Kansas City sales figures, click the** November Kansas City data point, **then click the data point again**

   Handles surround the data point. You can click and drag these handles to modify the plotted data value.

2. **Drag the upper handle until the ScreenTip displays 21000**

   The value in cell F8 displays 21000.

3. **Click cell** G8, **type** 23000, **then click the** Enter button ✅ **on the formula bar**

   The Kansas City columns for November and December reflect the increased sales figures. See Figure D-8. The totals in column H and row 10 are also updated.

4. **Select the chart by clicking a blank area within the chart border, then click the** Chart Type list arrow 📊▾ **on the Chart toolbar**

   The Chart Type buttons appear on the Chart Type palette. Table D-3 describes the principal chart types available.

5. **Click the** Bar Chart button 📊 **on the palette**

   The column chart changes to a bar chart. See Figure D-9. You look at the bar chart, take some notes, then decide to see if the large increase in sales would be better presented with a three-dimensional column chart.

6. **Click** 📊▾, **then click the** 3-D Column Chart button 📊 **on the palette**

   A three-dimensional column chart appears. You notice that the three-dimensional column format is more crowded than the two-dimensional format, but it gives you a sense of volume.

7. **Click** 📊▾, **then click the** Column Chart button 📊 **on the palette**

8. **Click the** Save button 💾 **on the Standard toolbar**

TABLE D-3: Commonly used chart type buttons

click to display a	click to display a	click to display a	click to display a
📊 area chart	🥧 pie chart	📊 3-D area chart	🥧 3-D pie chart
📊 bar chart	📊 (XY) scatter chart	📊 3-D bar chart	📊 3-D surface chart
📊 column chart	🍩 doughnut chart	📊 3-D column chart	📊 3-D cylinder chart
📊 line chart	⭐ radar chart	📊 3-D line chart	📊 3-D cone chart

FIGURE D-8: Worksheet with new data entered for Kansas City

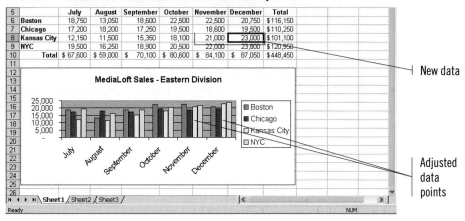

New data

Adjusted data points

FIGURE D-9: Bar chart

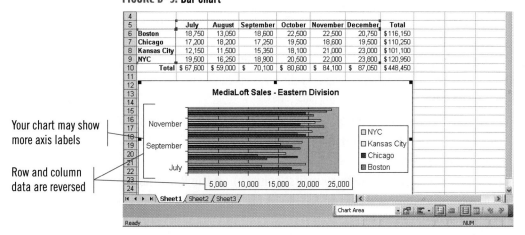

Your chart may show more axis labels

Row and column data are reversed

Clues to Use

Rotating a 3-D chart

In a three-dimensional chart, other data series in the same chart can sometimes obscure columns or bars. You can rotate the chart to obtain a better view. Click the chart, click the Corners object located at the tip of one of its axes, then drag the handle until a more pleasing view of the data series appears. See Figure D-10.

FIGURE D-10: 3-D chart rotated with improved view of data series

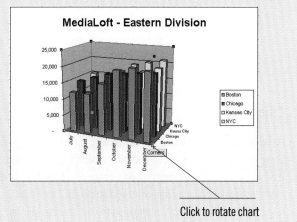

Click to rotate chart

Formatting a Chart

After you've created a chart using the Chart Wizard, you can easily modify its appearance. You can use the Chart toolbar and Chart menu to change the colors of data series and to add or eliminate a legend and gridlines. **Gridlines** are the horizontal and vertical lines in the chart that enable the eye to follow the value on an axis. ████ Jim wants you to make some changes in the appearance of the chart. He wants to see if the chart looks better without gridlines, and he wants you to change the color of a data series.

STEPS

1. **Make sure the chart is still selected**

   Horizontal gridlines currently extend from the value axis tick marks across the chart's plot area.

   > **QUICK TIP**
   > The Chart menu only appears on the menu bar when a chart or one of its objects is selected.

2. **Click Chart on the menu bar, click Chart Options, click the Gridlines tab in the Chart Options dialog box, then click the Major Gridlines check box for the Value (Y) axis to remove the check mark**

   The gridlines disappear from the sample chart in the dialog box, as shown in Figure D-11.

3. **Click the Major gridlines check box for the Value (Y) axis to reselect it, then click the Minor gridlines check box for the Value (Y) axis**

   Both major and minor gridlines appear in the sample. **Minor gridlines** show the values between the tick marks.

4. **Click the Minor gridlines check box for the Value (Y) axis, then click OK**

   The minor gridlines disappear, leaving only the major gridlines on the value axis. You can change the color of the columns to better distinguish the data series.

5. **With the chart selected, double-click any light blue column in the NYC data series**

   Handles appear on all the columns in the NYC data series, and the Format Data Series dialog box opens, as shown in Figure D-12.

6. **Click the fuchsia color (fourth row, first column) on the Patterns tab, then click OK**

   All the columns for the series become fuchsia, and the legend changes to match the new color. Compare your formatted chart to Figure D-13.

7. **Click the Save button** 🖫 **on the Standard toolbar**

Clues to Use

Adding data labels to a chart

There are times when your audience might benefit by seeing data labels on a chart. These labels can indicate the series name, category name, and/or the value of one or more data points. Once your chart is selected, you can add this information to your chart by clicking

Chart on the menu bar, clicking Chart Options, then clicking the Data Labels tab in the Chart Options dialog box. You can also apply formatting to data labels, or delete individual data labels.

FIGURE D-11: Chart Options dialog box

Sample chart appears without gridlines

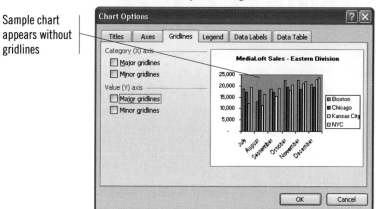

FIGURE D-12: Format Data Series dialog box

Sample of selected color

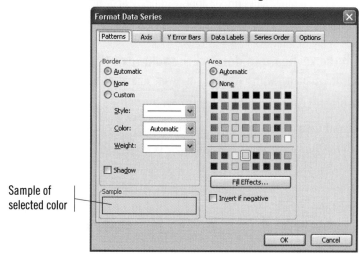

FIGURE D-13: Chart with formatted data series

Gridlines make it easy to follow axis values

New data series color

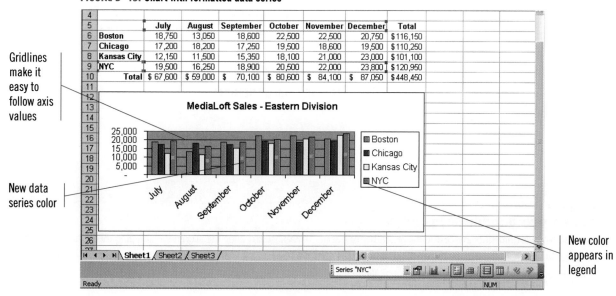

New color appears in legend

Enhancing a Chart

There are many ways to enhance a chart to make it easier to read and understand. You can create titles for the x-axis and y-axis, add graphics, or add background color. You can even format the text you use in a chart. Many enhancements can be made using the Chart toolbar buttons. These buttons are listed in Table D-4. ▓▓▓▓ Jim wants you to improve the appearance of the chart by creating titles for the category axis and value axis and adding a drop shadow to the chart title.

STEPS

1. **Click a blank area of the chart to select the chart, click** Chart **on the menu bar, click** Chart Options, **click the** Titles tab **in the Chart Options dialog box, then type** Months **in the Category (X) axis text box**

   Descriptive text on the category axis helps readers understand the chart. The word "Months" appears below the month labels in the sample chart, as shown in Figure D-14.

> **QUICK TIP**
> To edit the text, position the pointer over the selected text box until it changes to I, click the text box, then edit the text.

2. **Type** Sales (in $) **in the Value (Y) axis text box, then click** OK

   A selected text box containing "Sales (in $)" appears rotated 90 degrees to the left of the value axis. Once the Chart Options dialog box is closed, you can move the value or title to a new position by clicking an edge of the object then dragging it.

3. **Press** [Esc] **on the keyboard to deselect the value axis title**

   Next you decide that a border with a drop shadow will enhance the chart title.

4. **Click the** MediaLoft Sales – Eastern Division **chart title to select it**

> **QUICK TIP**
> The Format button 🔳 on the Chart toolbar opens a dialog box with the appropriate formatting options for the selected chart element. The ScreenTip for the button changes, depending on the selected object.

5. **Click the** Format Chart Title button 🔳 **on the Chart toolbar to open the Format Chart Title dialog box, make sure the** Patterns tab **is selected, then click the** Shadow check box **to select it**

   A border with a drop shadow appears in the sample area.

6. **Click the** Font tab **in the Format Chart Title dialog box, click** Times New Roman **in the Font list, click** Bold Italic **in the Font style list, click** OK, **then press** [Esc] **on the keyboard to deselect the chart title**

   A border with a drop shadow appears around the chart title, and the chart title text is reformatted.

7. **Click any one of the months (on the category axis), click** 🔳, **click the** Font tab **in the Format Axis dialog box if necessary, click** 8 **in the Size list if necessary, then click** OK

   The size of the category axis text decreases, making more of the plot area visible.

> **QUICK TIP**
> You can also double-click the text on the value axis to open the Format Axis Titles dialog box.

8. **Click any one of the sales values (on the value axis), click** 🔳, **click the** Font tab **if necessary, click** 8 **in the Size list, click** OK, **then press** [Esc] **on the keyboard to deselect the value axis**

   The text on the value axis becomes smaller. Compare your chart to Figure D-15.

9. **Click the** Save button 🔳 **on the Standard toolbar**

Clues to Use

Changing text alignment in charts

You can modify the alignment of axis text to make it fit better within the plot area. With a chart selected, double-click the axis text to be modified. The Format Axis dialog box opens. Click the Alignment tab, then change the alignment by typing the number of degrees in the Degrees text box, or by clicking a marker in the Degrees sample box. When you have made the desired changes, click OK.

FIGURE D-14: Sample chart with Category (X) axis text

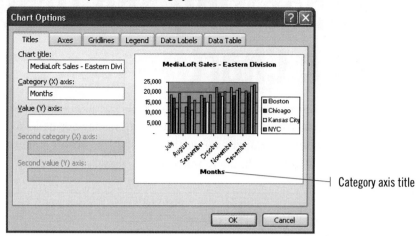

Category axis title

FIGURE D-15: Enhanced chart

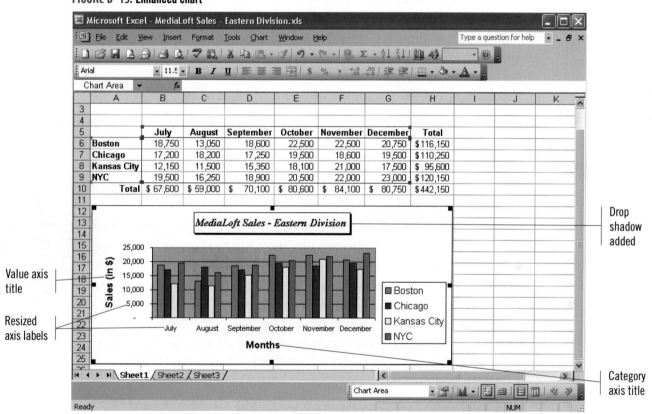

Value axis title

Resized axis labels

Drop shadow added

Category axis title

TABLE D-4: Chart enhancement buttons

button	use
	Displays the Format dialog box for the selected chart object
	Selects chart type (chart type on button changes to last chart type selected)
	Adds/deletes legend
	Creates a data table within the chart
	Charts data by row
	Charts data by column
	Angles selected text downward (clockwise)
	Angles selected text upward (counterclockwise)

Excel 2003

Annotating and Drawing on a Chart

You can add arrows and text annotations to point out critical information in your charts. **Text annotations** are labels that you add to a chart to further describe your data. You can draw lines and arrows that point to the exact locations you want to emphasize. ██████ Jim wants you to add a text annotation and an arrow to highlight the October sales increase.

STEPS

1. Make sure the chart is selected

To call attention to the Boston October sales increase, you can draw an arrow that points to the top of the Boston October data series with the annotation, "Due to ad campaign." With the chart selected, simply typing text in the formula bar creates annotation text.

2. Type Due to ad campaign, then click the Enter button ✔ on the formula bar

As you type, the text appears in the formula bar. After you confirm the entry, the text appears in a selected text box on the chart.

TROUBLE

If the pointer changes to I or ↔, release the mouse button, click outside the text box area to deselect it, select the text box, then repeat Step 3.

▶ 3. Point to an edge of the text box so that the pointer changes to ⇧

4. Drag the text box above the chart, as shown in Figure D-16, then release the mouse button

You can add an arrow to point to a specific area or item in a chart by using the Drawing toolbar.

QUICK TIP

To annotate charts, you can also use the Callout shapes in the AutoShapes menu on the Drawing toolbar.

5. Click the Drawing button ⊞ on the Standard toolbar if necessary to display the Drawing toolbar

The Drawing toolbar appears below the worksheet.

6. Click the Arrow button ↘ on the Drawing toolbar, then move the pointer over the chart

The pointer changes to ┼, and the status bar displays "Click and drag to insert an AutoShape." When you draw an arrow, the point farthest from where you start has the arrowhead.

QUICK TIP

You can also insert text and an arrow in the data section of a worksheet by clicking the Text Box button 🗎 on the Drawing toolbar, drawing a text box, typing the text, then adding the arrow.

▶ 7. Position ┼ under the t in the word "to" in the text box, press and hold the left mouse button, drag the line to the Boston column in the October sales series, then release the mouse button

An arrow appears, pointing to Boston October sales. The arrow is a selected object in the chart; you can resize, format, or delete it just like any other object. Compare your finished chart to Figure D-17.

8. Click ⊞ to close the Drawing toolbar

9. Click the Save button 🖫 on the Standard toolbar

Clues to Use

Adding an organizational chart or other diagram type

In addition to charts, annotations, and drawn objects, you can create a variety of diagrams. Diagram types include an Organization Chart, Cycle, Radial, Pyramid, Venn, or Target diagram. To insert a diagram, click Insert on the menu bar, then click Diagram. In the Diagram Gallery dialog box, click a diagram type, then click OK. The diagram appears on the worksheet as an embedded object with sizing handles, and the Diagram toolbar opens. You can edit placeholder text and use the Diagram toolbar buttons to insert or modify shapes, change the layout or diagram type, or select an AutoFormat. A selected diagram shape can be formatted using the Drawing toolbar buttons.

FIGURE D-16: Repositioning text annotation

Outline of repositioned annotation

Selected text annotation

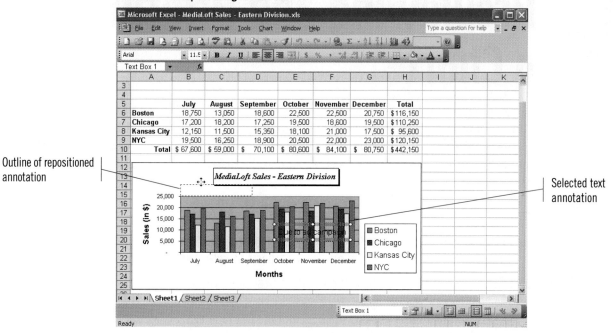

FIGURE D-17: Completed chart with text annotation and arrow

Repositioned text annotation

Arrow

Drawing toolbar

Boston October sales

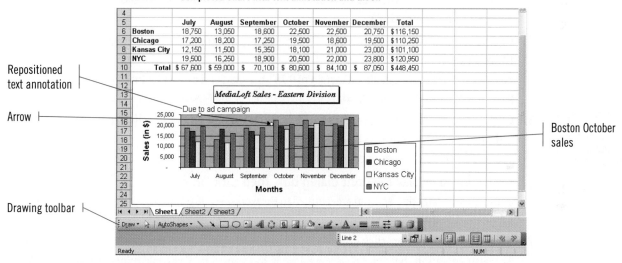

Clues to Use

Exploding a pie slice

Just as an arrow can call attention to a data series, you can emphasize a pie slice by exploding, or pulling it away from, the pie chart.
Once the pie chart is selected, click the pie to select it, click the
desired slice to select only that slice, then drag the slice away from
the pie, as shown in Figure D-18. After you change the chart type,
you may need to adjust arrows within the chart.

FIGURE D-18: Exploded pie slice

Eastern Division - 6 Months Sales

Slice pulled from pie

Previewing and Printing a Chart

After you complete a chart, you often need to print it. As with previewing a worksheet, previewing a chart lets you see what your chart looks like before you print it. You can print a chart by itself or as part of the worksheet. ▓▓▓▓ Jim wants a printed version of the chart for the annual meeting. He wants you to print the worksheet and the chart together, so that the shareholders can see the actual sales numbers for the Eastern Division stores.

STEPS

1. **Press [Esc] on the keyboard to deselect the arrow and the chart, enter your name in cell A35, then press [Ctrl][Home] on the keyboard to select cell A1**

QUICK TIP
The preview shows in color only if you have a color printer selected.

2. **Click the Print Preview button ◩ on the Standard toolbar**
   The Print Preview window opens. You decide the chart and data would fit better on the page if they were printed in **landscape** orientation—that is, with the text running the long way on the page. You use Page Setup to change the page orientation.

3. **Click Setup on the Print Preview toolbar to open the Page Setup dialog box, then click the Page tab, if necessary**

4. **Click the Landscape option button in the Orientation section, as shown in Figure D-19, then click OK**
   Because each page has a default left margin of 0.75", the chart and data will print too far over to the left of the page. You can change this setting using the Margins tab of the Page Setup dialog box.

QUICK TIP
The printer you have selected may affect the appearance of the preview screen.

5. **Click Setup on the Print Preview toolbar, click the Margins tab, click the Horizontally check box under Center on page, then click OK**
   The data and chart are positioned horizontally on the page. See Figure D-20.

6. **Click Print to display the Print dialog box, then click OK**
   The data and chart print, and you are returned to the worksheet. If you want, you can choose to preview (and print) only the chart.

7. **Select the chart, then click ◩**
   The chart appears in the Print Preview window. If you wanted to, you could print the chart by clicking the Print button on the Print Preview toolbar.

8. **Click Close on the Print Preview toolbar**

9. **Click the Save button ◩ on the Standard toolbar, close the workbook, then exit Excel**

FIGURE D-19: Page tab of the Page Setup dialog box

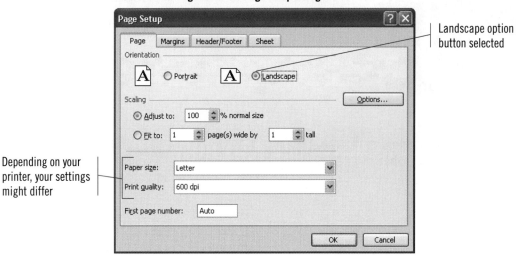

Landscape option button selected

Depending on your printer, your settings might differ

FIGURE D-20: Chart and data ready to print

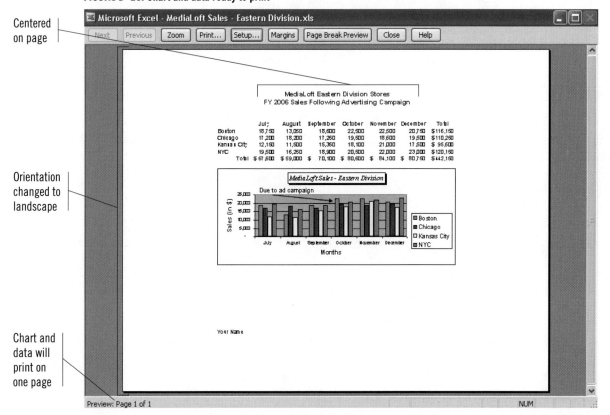

Centered on page

Orientation changed to landscape

Chart and data will print on one page

Clues to Use

Using the Page Setup dialog box for a chart

When a chart is selected, a different Page Setup dialog box opens than when neither the chart nor data is selected. The Center on Page options are not always available. To accurately position a chart on the page, you can click the Margins button on the Print Preview toolbar. Margin lines appear on the screen and show you exactly how the margins appear on the page. The exact placement appears in the status bar when you press and hold the mouse button on the margin line. You can drag the lines to the exact settings you want.

Practice

▼ CONCEPTS REVIEW

Label each element of the Excel chart shown in Figure D-21.

FIGURE D-21

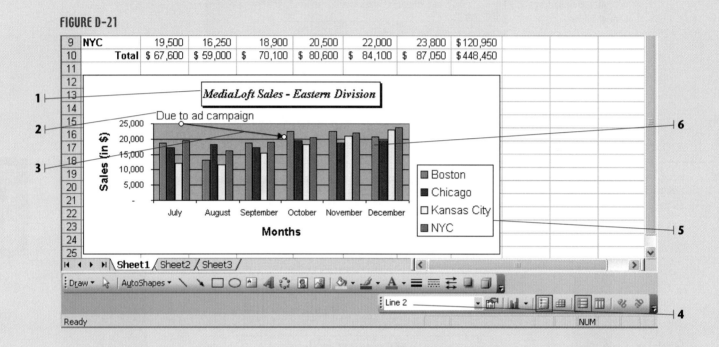

Match each chart type with the statement that best describes it.

7. Combination   **a.** Shows how volume changes over time

8. Column   **b.** Compares data as parts of a whole

9. Line   **c.** Displays a column and line chart using different scales of measurement

10. Area   **d.** Compares trends over even time intervals

11. Pie   **e.** Compares data over time—the Excel default

Select the best answer from the list of choices.

12. Which pointer is used to resize a chart object?
    a. I
    b. ↖↘
    c. ↔↕
    d. +

13. The object in a chart that identifies patterns used for each data series is a:
    a. Data point.
    b. Plot.
    c. Legend.
    d. Range.

14. The orientation of a page whose dimensions are 11" wide by 8½" tall is:
    a. Portrait.
    b. Longways.
    c. Landscape.
    d. Sideways.

15. What is the term for a row or column on a chart?
    a. Range address
    b. Axis title
    c. Chart orientation
    d. Data series

16. In a 2-D chart, the category axis is the:
    a. X-axis.
    b. Z-axis.
    c. D-axis.
    d. Y-axis.

17. In a 2-D chart, the value axis is the:
    a. X-axis.
    b. Y-axis.
    c. D-axis.
    d. Z-axis.

▼ SKILLS REVIEW

1. **Plan and design a chart.**
   a. Start Excel, open the Data File EX D-2.xls from the drive and folder where your Data Files are stored, then save it as MediaLoft Vancouver Software Usage.
   b. Sketch the type of chart you would use to plot this data.
   c. In what chart type is the y-axis referred to as the z-axis?
   d. What term is used to describe the visual representation of each data point?

2. **Create a chart.**
   a. Select the range containing the data and headings.
   b. Start the Chart Wizard.
   c. In the Chart Wizard, select a clustered column chart, then verify that the series are in rows, add the chart title Software Usage by Department, and make the chart an object on the worksheet.
   d. After the chart appears, save your work.

3. Move and resize a chart.

   a. Make sure the chart is still selected.

   b. Move the chart beneath the data.

   c. Resize the chart so it extends to column J.

   d. Use the Legend tab in the Chart Options dialog box to move the legend below the charted data.

   e. Resize the chart so the bottom is at the top of row 25.

   f. Save your work.

4. Edit a chart.

   a. Change the value in cell B3 to 6. Notice the change in the chart.

   b. Select the chart.

   c. Use the Chart Type list arrow to change the chart to a 3-D Column Chart.

   d. Rotate the chart to move the data.

   e. Change the chart back to a column chart.

   f. Save your work.

5. Format a chart.

   a. Make sure the chart is still selected.

   b. Use the Chart Options dialog box to turn off the displayed gridlines.

   c. Change the font used in the Category and Value labels to Times New Roman.

   d. Turn on the major gridlines for the value axis.

   e. Change the chart title's font to Times New Roman, with a font size of 18.

   f. Save your work.

6. Enhance a chart.

   a. Make sure the chart is selected, then select the Titles tab in the Chart Options dialog box.

   b. Enter Software as the x-axis title.

   c. Enter Users as the y-axis title.

   d. Change Production in the legend to Art. (*Hint*: Change the text entry in the worksheet.)

   e. Add a drop shadow to the chart title.

   f. Save your work.

7. Annotate and draw on a chart.

   a. Make sure the chart is selected, then create the text annotation Needs More Users.

   b. Position the text annotation beneath the chart title.

   c. Below the text annotation, use the Drawing toolbar to create an arrow that points to the area containing the Access data.

   d. Compare your work to Figure D-22.

   e. Save your work.

FIGURE D-22

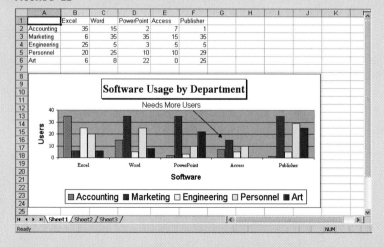

8. Preview and print a chart.

   a. In the worksheet, enter your name in cell A30.

   b. Preview the chart and data.

   c. Change the page orientation to landscape.

   d. Center the page contents horizontally and vertically on the page.

   e. Print the data and chart from the Print Preview window.

   f. Save your work.

   g. Preview only the chart, then print it.

   h. Close the workbook, then exit Excel.

▼ INDEPENDENT CHALLENGE 1

You are the operations manager for the Springfield Theater Group in Oregon. Each year the group applies to various state and federal agencies for matching funds. For this year's funding proposal, you need to create charts to document the number of productions in previous years.

   a. Sketch a sample worksheet on a piece of paper describing how you will create the charts. Which type of chart is best suited for the information you need to display? What kind of chart enhancements do you want to use? Will a 3-D effect make your chart easier to understand?

   b. Start Excel, open the Data File EX D-3.xls, then save it as **Springfield Theater Group** in the drive and folder where your Data Files are stored.

   c. Create a column chart for the data, accepting all Chart Wizard defaults.

   d. Change at least one of the colors used in a data series.

   e. Create at least two additional charts for the same data to show how different chart types display the same data. Each of these charts should be on its own chart sheet in the workbook.

   f. After creating the charts, make the appropriate enhancements. Include chart titles, legends, and value and category axis titles, using the suggestions in Table D-5.

   g. Add data labels.

   h. Enter your name in a worksheet cell.

   i. Save your work. Before printing, preview the workbook so you know what the charts look like. Adjust any items as necessary.

   j. Print the worksheet (charts and data).

   k. Close the workbook, then exit Excel.

TABLE D-5

suggested chart enhancements	
Title	Types and Number of Plays
Legend	Year 1, Year 2, Year 3, Year 4
Value axis title	Number of Plays
Category axis title	Play Types

▼ INDEPENDENT CHALLENGE 2

Beautiful You, a small beauty salon, has been using Excel for several months. One of your responsibilities at the Beautiful You salon is to re-create the company's records using Excel. Another is to convince the current staff that Excel can help them make daily operating decisions more easily and efficiently. To do this, you've decided to create charts using the previous year's operating expenses, including rent, utilities, and payroll. The manager will use these charts at the next monthly meeting.

a. Decide which data in the worksheet should be charted. Sketch two sample charts. What type of charts are best suited for the information you need to show? What kind of chart enhancements are necessary?

b. Start Excel, open the Data File EX D-4.xls from the drive and folder where your Data Files are stored, then save it as **BY Expense Charts**.

c. Create a column chart on the worksheet, containing the expense data for all four quarters.

d. Using the same data, create an area chart and one additional chart using any other appropriate chart type. (*Hint*: Move each chart to a new location on the worksheet, then deselect it before using the Wizard to create the next one.)

e. Add annotated text and arrows to the column chart that highlight any important data or trends.

f. In one chart, change the color of a data series, then in another chart, use black-and-white patterns only. (*Hint*: Use the Fill Effects button in the Format Data Series dialog box. Then display the Patterns tab. Adjust the Foreground color to black and the Background color to white, then select a pattern.)

g. Enter your name in a worksheet cell.

h. Save your work. Before printing, preview each chart so you know what the charts look like. Adjust any items as needed.

i. Print the charts.

j. Close the workbook, then exit Excel.

▼ INDEPENDENT CHALLENGE 3

You are working as an account representative at the Bright Light Ad Agency. You have been examining the expenses charged to clients of the firm. The Board of Directors wants to examine certain advertising expenses and has asked you to prepare charts that can be used in this evaluation.

a. Start Excel, open the Data File EX D-5.xls from the drive and folder where your Data Files are stored, then save it as **Bright Light**.

b. Decide what types of charts would be best suited for the data in the range A16:B24. Sketch three sample charts. What kind of chart enhancements are necessary?

c. Use the Chart Wizard to create at least three different types of charts that show the distribution of advertising expenses. (*Hint*: Move each chart to a new location on the worksheet, then deselect it before using the Wizard to create the next one.) One of the charts should be a 3-D pie chart.

d. Add annotated text and arrows highlighting important data, such as the largest expense.

e. Change the color of at least one data series.

f. Add chart titles and category and value axis titles. Format the titles with a font of your choice. Place a drop shadow around the chart title.

Advanced Challenge Exercise

- Explode a slice from the 3-D pie chart.
- Add a data label to the exploded pie slice.
- Change the alignment of labels on an axis.
- Modify the scale of the value axis in one of the charts. (*Hint*: Double-click the gridlines to open the Format Gridlines dialog box, then click the Scale tab.)

g. Enter your name in a worksheet cell.

h. Save your work. Before printing, preview the file so you know what the charts look like. Adjust any items as needed. Be sure the chart is placed appropriately on the page.

i. Print the charts, close the workbook, then exit Excel.

▼ INDEPENDENT CHALLENGE 4

Your company, Film Distribution, is headquartered in Montreal, and is considering opening a new office in the United States. Your supervisor would like you to begin investigating possible locations. You can use the Web to find and compare median pay scales in specific cities to see how relocating will affect the standard of living for those employees who move to the new office.

    a. Start Excel, open a new workbook, then save it as **New Location Analysis** in the drive and folder where your Data Files are located.

    b. Use your favorite search engine to find your own information sources on salary calculators, or cost-of-living calculators.

    c. Determine the median incomes for Seattle, San Francisco, Dallas, Salt Lake City, Memphis, and Boston. Record this data on a sheet named **Median Income** in your workbook. See Table D-6 below for suggested data layout.

    d. Format the data so it looks attractive and professional.

    e. Create any type of column chart, with the data series in columns, on the same worksheet as the data. Include a descriptive title.

    f. Remove the major gridlines in the Median Income chart.

    g. On a blank worksheet in the current workbook, determine how much an employee would need to earn in Seattle, San Francisco, Dallas, Memphis, and Boston to maintain the same standard of living as if the company chose to relocate to Salt Lake City and pay $75,000. Name the sheet **Standard of Living**.

TABLE D-6

location	income
Seattle	
San Francisco	
Dallas	
Salt Lake City	
Memphis	
Boston	

    h. Format the data so it looks attractive and professional.

    i. Create a 3-D column chart on the same worksheet as the data. Include a descriptive title.

    j. Change the color of the data series in the Standard of Living chart to bright green.

Advanced Challenge Exercise

    ■ Format the value axis in your chart(s) so that the salary income displays a 1000 separator (comma), but no dollar sign or decimal places.

    ■ Rotate the chart so you get a different view of the data.

    ■ Change the alignment of the category axis labels.

    k. Do not display the legends in your chart(s).

    l. Enter your name in a cell in your worksheet(s).

    m. Save the workbook. Preview the chart(s) and change margins as necessary.

    n. Print your worksheet(s), including the data and chart(s), making setup modifications as necessary.

    o. Close the workbook, then exit Excel.

▼ VISUAL WORKSHOP

Modify a worksheet, using the skills you learned in this unit and using Figure D-23 for reference. Open the Data File EX D-6.xls from the drive and folder where your Data Files are stored, then save it as **Quarterly Advertising Budget**. Create the chart, then change the chart to reflect Figure D-23. Enter your name in cell A13, save, preview, then print your results.

FIGURE D-23

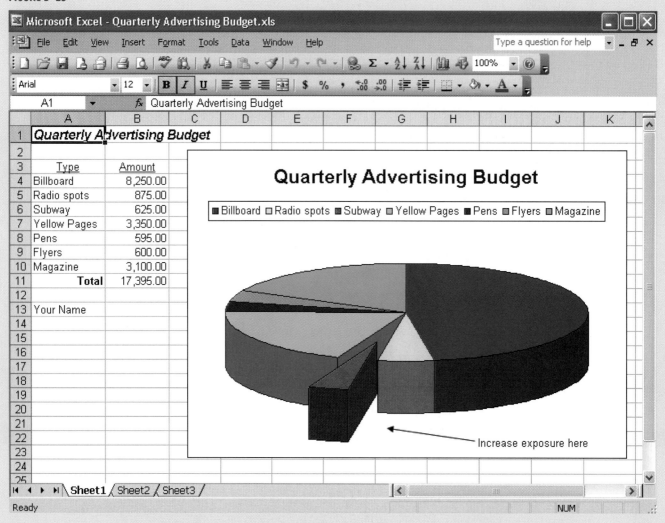

Working with Formulas and Functions

OBJECTIVES

Create a formula with several operators
Use names in a formula
Generate multiple totals with AutoSum
Use dates in calculations
Build a conditional formula with the IF function
Use statistical functions
Calculate payments with the PMT function
Display and print formula contents

If you have a SAM user profile, you may have access to hands-on instruction, practice, and assessment of the skills covered in this unit. Log in to your SAM account and go to your assignments page to see what your instructor has assigned.

Without formulas, Excel would simply be an electronic grid with text and numbers. Used with formulas, Excel becomes a powerful data analysis tool. As you learn how to analyze data using different types of formulas, including those containing functions, you will discover more ways to use Excel. In this unit, you will gain a further understanding of Excel formulas and learn how to use several Excel functions. Top management at MediaLoft has asked marketing director Jim Fernandez to analyze various company data. To do this, Jim creates several worksheets that require formulas and functions. Because management is considering raising salaries for store managers, Jim has asked you to create a report that compares the payroll deductions and net pay for store managers before and after a proposed raise.

Creating a Formula with Several Operators

You can create formulas that contain a combination of cell references (for example, Z100 or B2), operators (for example, * for multiplication or – for subtraction), and values (for example, 99 or 1.56). Formulas can also contain functions. You have used AutoSum to insert the SUM function into a cell. You can also create a single formula that performs several calculations. If you enter a formula with more than one operator, Excel performs the calculations in a particular sequence based on algebraic rules, called the **order of precedence** (also called the order of operations); that is, Excel performs the operation(s) within parentheses first, then calculates exponents, then any multiplication and division from left to right. Finally, it calculates addition and subtraction, from left to right. See Table E-1 for examples. ▰▰▰▰ Jim has received the gross pay and deductions for the monthly payroll and needs to complete his analysis. He has also preformatted, with the Comma style, any cells that are to contain values. He asks you to enter a formula for net pay that subtracts the payroll deductions from gross pay.

STEPS

QUICK TIP

You can learn more about the possible errors that Excel has flagged by clicking the cell, clicking the list arrow that appears, then choosing an option.

1. **Start Excel if necessary, open the Data File** EX E-1.xls **from the drive and folder where your Data Files are stored, then save it as** Company Data

    The green triangles in the cells indicate that the formulas differ from the surrounding formulas. In this case, the formulas are correct, so you can ignore the triangles. The first part of the net pay formula should go in cell B11.

2. **Click** Edit **on the menu bar, click** Go To, **type** B11 **in the Reference box, then click** OK

    Cell B11 is now the active cell. The Go To command is especially useful when you want to select a cell in a large worksheet.

3. **Type** =, **click cell** B6, **type** –, **then click the** Insert Function button *fx* **on the formula bar to open the Insert Function dialog box**

    You type the equal sign (=) to indicate that a formula follows. B6 references the cell containing the gross pay, and the minus sign (–) indicates that the next entry, a sum, is subtracted from cell B6. The Insert Function dialog box allows you to choose from a list of available functions or search for a specific function. See Figure E-1.

TROUBLE

If you make a mistake while building a formula, press [Esc] and begin again.

4. **Type** sum **in the Search for a function text box, click** Go, **click** SUM **in the Select a function list, then click** OK

    B6:B10 appears in the Number1 text box. You want to sum the range B7:B10.

QUICK TIP

Instead of using the Collapse Dialog Box and the Redisplay Dialog Box buttons, you can drag the dialog box out of the way and select the desired range on the worksheet to insert it in the formula.

5. **With the Number1 argument selected in the Function Arguments dialog box, click the Number1** Collapse Dialog Box button ▦, **select the range** B7:B10 **in the worksheet, click the** Redisplay Dialog Box button ▦, **then click** OK

    Collapsing the dialog box allows you to enter the range by selecting it. The net pay for Payroll Period 1 appears in cell B11.

6. **Copy the formula in cell B11 into cells C11:F11, then press** [Ctrl][Home] **to return to cell A1**

    The net pay for each column appears in row 11. See Figure E-2.

7. **Save the workbook**

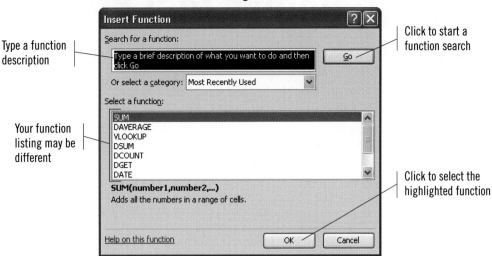

FIGURE E-1: Insert Function dialog box

Type a function description

Click to start a function search

Your function listing may be different

Click to select the highlighted function

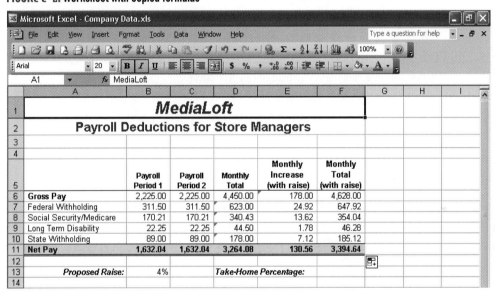

FIGURE E-2: Worksheet with copied formulas

TABLE E-1: Sample formulas using parentheses and several operators

formula	order of precedence	calculated result
=10–20/10–5	Divide 20 by 10; subtract the result from 10, then subtract 5	3
=(10–20)/10–5	Subtract 20 from 10; divide that by 10; then subtract 5	–6
=(10*2)*(10+2)	Multiply 10 by 2; add 10 to 2; then multiply the results	240

Clues to Use

Using Paste Special

You can use the Paste Special command to enter formulas and values quickly or even to perform quick calculations. Click the cell(s) containing the formula or value you want to copy, click the Copy button on the Standard toolbar, then right-click the cell where you want the result to appear. In the shortcut menu, click Paste Special, choose the feature you want to paste, then click OK.

Using Names in a Formula

To reduce errors and make your worksheet easier to follow, you can assign names to cells and ranges. You can also use names in formulas to make formulas easier to build. For example, the formula Revenue-Cost is much easier to understand than the formula A2-D3. When used in formulas, names become absolute cell references by default. Names can use uppercase or lowercase letters as well as digits. After you name a cell or range, you can use the name on any sheet in the workbook. If you move a named cell or range, its name moves with it. ▰▰▰▰ Jim wants you to include a formula that calculates the percentage of monthly gross pay that the managers would actually take home (their net pay) if they received a 4% raise. You decide to name the cells that you will use in the calculation.

STEPS

QUICK TIP

You can also assign names to ranges of cells. Select the range, click the name box, then type in the range name. You can also name a range by pointing to Name on the Insert menu, then clicking Define and typing the name.

1. **Click cell** F6, **click the** name box **on the formula bar to select the active cell reference, type** Gross_with_Raise, **then press** [Enter]

   The name assigned to cell F6, Gross_with_Raise, appears in the name box. Note that you must type underscores instead of spaces between words. Cell F6 is now named Gross_with_Raise to refer to the monthly gross pay amount that includes the 4% raise. The name box displays as much of the name as fits (Gross_with_...). The total net pay cell needs a name.

2. **Click cell** F11, **click the** name box, **type** Net_with_Raise, **then press** [Enter]

   The new formula uses names instead of cell references.

QUICK TIP

You can use the Label Ranges dialog box (Insert menu, Name submenu, Label command) to designate existing column or row headings as labels. Then instead of using cell references for the column or row in formulas, you can use the labels.

3. **Click cell** F13, **type** =, **click** Insert **on the menu bar, point to** Name, **click** Paste, **click** Net_with_Raise, **then click** OK

   The name is inserted and the color of the name matches the outline around the cell reference.

4. **Type** /, **click** Insert **on the menu bar, point to** Name, **click** Paste, **click** Gross_with_Raise, **click** OK, **then click the** Enter button ✔ **on the formula bar**

   The formula appears in the formula bar and the result, 0.7335, appears in the cell. Cell F13 needs to be formatted in Percent style.

QUICK TIP

To replace cell references in existing formulas with the corresponding names you have added, click Insert on the menu bar, point to Name, click Apply, click the name or names, then click OK.

5. **Select cell** F13 **if necessary, click** Format **on the menu bar, click** Style, **click the** Style name list arrow, **click** Percent, **then click** OK

   The result shown in cell F13, 73%, is rounded to the nearest whole percent, as shown in Figure E-3. A **style** is a combination of formatting characteristics, such as bold, italic, and zero decimal places. You can use the Style dialog box instead of the Formatting toolbar to apply styles.

6. **Enter your name in cell A20, save the workbook, then preview and print the worksheet**

Clues to Use

Defining and removing styles

To define your own style (such as bold, italic, 14 point numbers with commas and zero decimal places), select a cell, format it using the Formatting toolbar, open the Style dialog box and type a name for your style, then click Add. Later, you can apply all of your formatting characteristics by applying your new style from the Style dialog box. You can also use the Style dialog box to remove styles by selecting the cell that has a style and then selecting Normal in the Style name list.

FIGURE E-3: Worksheet formula that includes cell names

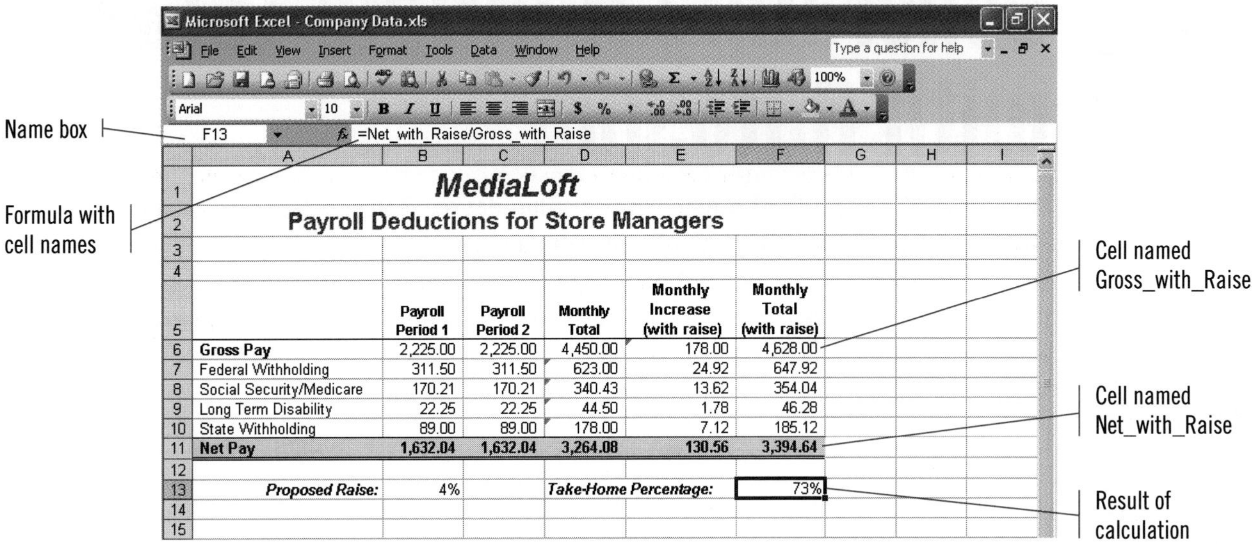

Name box

Formula with cell names

Cell named Gross_with_Raise

Cell named Net_with_Raise

Result of calculation

Clues to Use

Producing a list of names

You might want to verify the names you have assigned in a workbook and the cells they reference. To paste a list of names in a workbook, select a blank cell that has several blank cells beside and beneath it. Click Insert on the menu bar, point to Name, then click Paste. In the Paste Name dialog box, click Paste List. Excel produces a list of names that includes the sheet name followed by an exclamation point and the cell or range the name identifies. See Figure E-4.

FIGURE E-4: Worksheet with pasted list of names

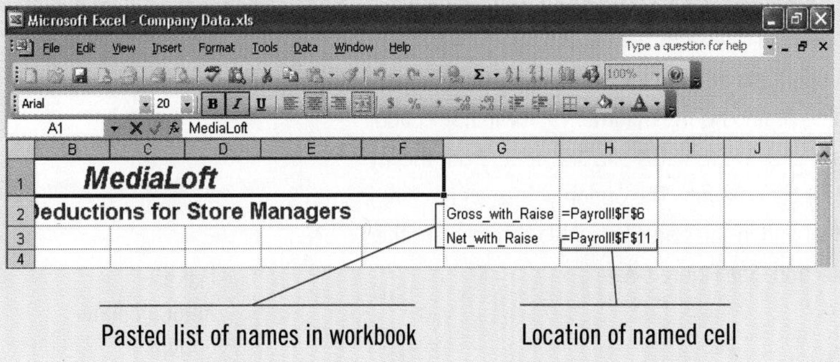

Pasted list of names in workbook

Location of named cell

Generating Multiple Totals with AutoSum

In most cases, the result of a function is a value derived from a single calculation. You have used AutoSum to produce a total of a single range of numbers; you can also use it to total multiple ranges. If you include blank cells to the right or at the bottom of a selected range, AutoSum generates several totals and enters the results in the blank cells. You can also use AutoSum to generate grand totals of worksheet subtotals. ▓▓▓▓ Maria Abbott, MediaLoft's general sales manager, has given Jim a worksheet summarizing store sales. He asks you to complete the worksheet totals.

STEPS

TROUBLE

If you select the wrong combination of cells, click a single cell and begin again.

1. **Click the** Sales sheet tab **to make the Sales sheet active, select the range** B5:E9**, press and hold** [Ctrl]**, then select the range** B11:E15

   To select nonadjacent cells, you must press and hold [Ctrl] while selecting the additional cells. Compare your selections with Figure E-6. Jim would like totals to appear in the last line of each selection.

2. **Click the** AutoSum button **Σ** **on the Standard toolbar**

   When the selected range you want to sum (B5:E9 and B11:E15, in this example) includes a blank cell with data values above it, AutoSum enters the total in the blank cell.

3. **Select the range** B5:F17**, then click** Σ

   Although Excel generates totals when you click the AutoSum button, it is a good idea to check the results.

QUICK TIP

Excel uses commas to separate multiple arguments in all functions, not just in SUM.

4. **Click cell** B17

   The formula bar reads =SUM(B15,B9). In this case, Excel ignores the data values and it totals only the sums. See Figure E-7. When generating grand totals, Excel separates the cell references with a comma.

5. **Enter your name in cell A20, save the workbook, then preview and print the worksheet**

Clues to Use

Quick calculations with AutoCalculate

To view a total quickly without entering a formula, just select the range you want to sum. The answer appears in the status bar next to SUM=. You also can perform other quick calculations, such as averaging or finding the minimum value in a selection: right-click in the status bar, and select from the list of function names. The option you select remains in effect and in the status bar until you make another selection. See Figure E-5.

FIGURE E-5: Using AutoCalculate

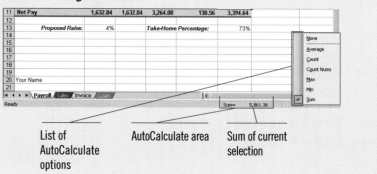

List of AutoCalculate options

AutoCalculate area

Sum of current selection

FIGURE E-6: Selecting nonadjacent ranges using [Ctrl]

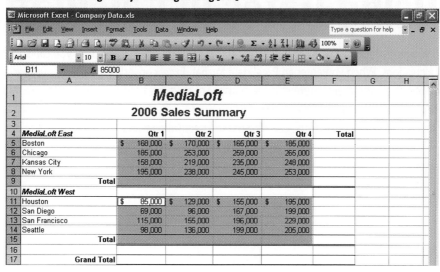

FIGURE E-7: Completed worksheet

Comma separates multiple arguments

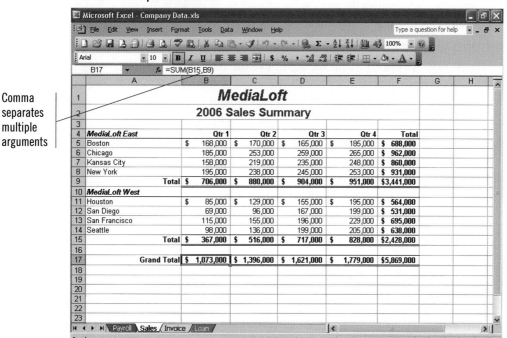

Using Dates in Calculations

If you enter dates in a worksheet in a format that Excel recognizes as a date, you can sort them and perform date calculations. When you enter an Excel date format, Excel converts it to a serial number so it can be used in calculations. A date's serial number is the number of days it is from January 1, 1900. Excel assigns the serial number of "1" to January 1, 1900 and counts up from there; the serial number of January 1, 2006, for example, is 38,718. When you format the cell with the serial number using a Date format, Excel displays the serial number as a date. ▰▰▰▰ Jim wants you to calculate the due date and age of each invoice on his worksheet. He reminds you to enter the worksheet dates in a format that Excel recognizes, so you can use date calculations.

STEPS

1. **Click the** Invoice sheet tab, **click cell** C4, **click the** Insert Function button *fx* **on the formula bar, type** date **in the Search for a function text box, click** Go, **click** DATE **in the Select a function list, then click** OK

   Your calculations need to be based on a current date of 4/1/06.

TROUBLE

If the year appears with four digits instead of two, your system administrator may have set a four-digit year display. You can continue with the lesson.

2. **Enter** 2006 **in the Year text box, enter** 4 **in the Month text box, enter** 1 **in the Day text box, then click** OK

   The Date function uses the format DATE(year, month, day). The date appears in cell C4 as 4/1/06. Your formula in cell E7 should calculate the invoice due date, which is 30 days from the invoice date. The formula adds 30 days to the invoice date.

3. **Click cell** E7, **type** =, **click cell** B7, **type** +30, **then click the** Enter button ✓ **on the formula bar**

   Excel calculates the result by converting the 3/2/06 invoice date to a serial date number, adding 30 to it, then automatically formatting the result as the date 4/1/06, as shown in Figure E-8. You can use the same formula to calculate the due dates of the other invoices.

QUICK TIP

You can also perform time calculations in Excel. For example, you can enter an employee's starting and ending time, then calculate how long he or she worked. You must enter time in an Excel time format.

4. **Drag the fill handle to copy the formula in cell E7 into cells E8:E13**

   Relative cell referencing adjusts the copied formula to contain the appropriate cell references. Now you are ready to enter the formula that calculates the age of each invoice. You do this by subtracting the invoice date from the current date. Because each invoice age formula must refer to the current date, you must make cell C4, the current date cell, an absolute reference in the formula.

5. **Click cell** F7, **type** =, **click cell** C4, **press** [F4] **to add the absolute reference symbols ($), type** –, **click cell** B7, **then click** ✓

   The formula bar displays the formula $C$4–B7. The numerical result, 30, appears in cell F7 because there are 30 days between 3/2/06 and 4/1/06. You can use the same formula to calculate the age of the remaining invoices.

QUICK TIP

You can also insert the current date into a cell by using the TODAY() function. The NOW() function inserts the current date and time into a cell. If you leave the argument area within its parentheses blank, it automatically displays today's date.

6. **Drag the fill handle to copy the formula in F7 to the range** F8:F13, **then press** [Ctrl][Home] **to return to cell A1**

   The age of each invoice appears in column F, as shown in Figure E-9.

7. **Save the workbook**

FIGURE E-8: Worksheet with calculated invoice due date

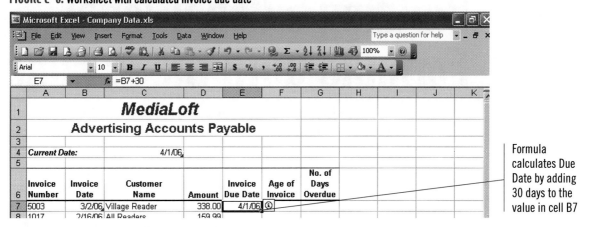

Formula calculates Due Date by adding 30 days to the value in cell B7

FIGURE E-9: Worksheet with copied formulas

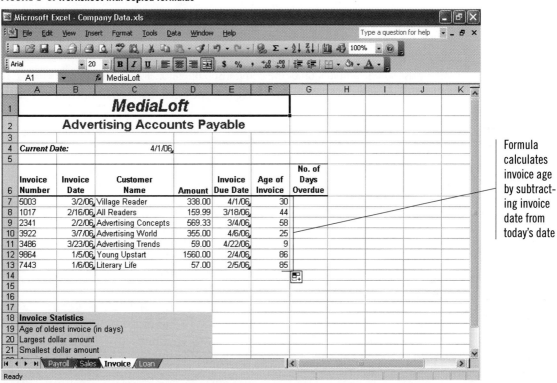

Formula calculates invoice age by subtracting invoice date from today's date

Clues to Use

Applying and creating custom number and date formats

When you use numbers and dates in worksheets or calculations, you can apply built-in Excel formats or create your own. To apply number formats, click Format on the menu bar, click Cells, then if necessary click the Number tab. In the Category list, click a category, then click the exact format in the list or scroll box to the right. To create a custom format, click Custom in the category list, then click a format that resembles the one you want. For example the value $3,789 uses the number format $#,### where # represents positive numbers. In the Type box, edit the symbols until they represent the format you want, then click OK. See Figure E-10.

FIGURE E-10: Custom formats on the Number tab in the Format Cells dialog box

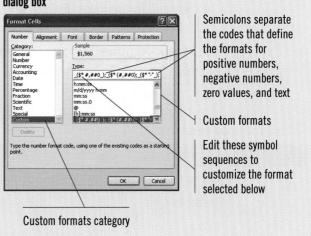

Semicolons separate the codes that define the formats for positive numbers, negative numbers, zero values, and text

Custom formats

Edit these symbol sequences to customize the format selected below

Custom formats category

Building a Conditional Formula with the IF Function

You can build a conditional formula using an IF function. A **conditional formula** is one that makes calculations based on stated conditions. For example, you can build a formula to calculate bonuses based on a person's performance rating. If a person is rated a 5 (the stated condition) on a scale of 1 to 5, with 5 being the highest rating, he or she receives an additional 10% of his or her salary as a bonus; otherwise, there is no bonus. A condition that can be answered with a true or false response is called a **logical test**. The IF function has three parts, separated by commas: a condition or logical test, an action to take if the logical test or condition is true, then an action to take if the logical test or condition is false. Another way of expressing this is: IF(test_cond,do_this,else_this). Translated into an Excel IF function, the formula to calculate bonuses would look something like this: IF(Rating=5,Salary*0.10,0). The translation would be: If the rating equals 5, multiply the salary by 0.10 (the decimal equivalent of 10%), then place the result in the selected cell; if the rating does not equal 5, place a 0 in the cell. When entering the logical test portion of an IF statement, you typically use some combination of the comparison operators listed in Table E-2. You are almost finished with the invoice worksheet. To complete it, you need to use an IF function that calculates the number of days each invoice is overdue.

STEPS

1. **Click cell G7, click the** Insert Function button ƒx **on the formula bar, enter** conditional **in the Search for a function text box, click** Go, **click** IF **in the Select a function list box, then click** OK

   You want the function to calculate the number of days overdue as follows: if the age of the invoice is greater than 30, calculate the days overdue (Age of Invoice − 30), and place the result in cell G7; otherwise, place a 0 (zero) in the cell.

2. **Enter** F7>30 **in the Logical_test text box**

   The symbol (>) represents "greater than." So far, the formula reads: if Age of Invoice is greater than 30 (in other words, if the invoice is overdue). The next part of the function tells Excel the action to take if the invoice is over 30 days old.

3. **Enter** F7−30 **in the Value_if_true text box**

   This part of the formula is what you want Excel to do if the logical test is true (that is, if the age of the invoice is over 30). Continuing the translation of the formula, this part means: take the Age of Invoice value and subtract 30. The last part of the formula tells Excel the action to take if the logical test is false (that is, if the age of the invoice is 30 days or less).

4. **Enter** 0 **in the Value_if_false text box, then click** OK

   The function is complete, and the result, 0 (the number of days overdue), appears in cell G7. See Figure E-11.

5. **Copy the formula in cell G7 into cells** G8:G13, **then press** [Ctrl][Home] **to return to cell A1**

   Compare your results with Figure E-12.

6. **Save the workbook**

TABLE E-2: Comparison operators

operator	meaning	operator	meaning
<	Less than	<=	Less than or equal to
>	Greater than	>=	Greater than or equal to
=	Equal to	<>	Not equal to

FIGURE E-11: Worksheet with IF function

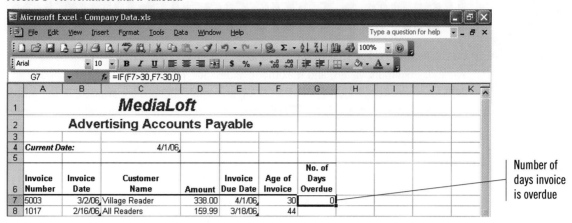

Number of days invoice is overdue

FIGURE E-12: Completed worksheet

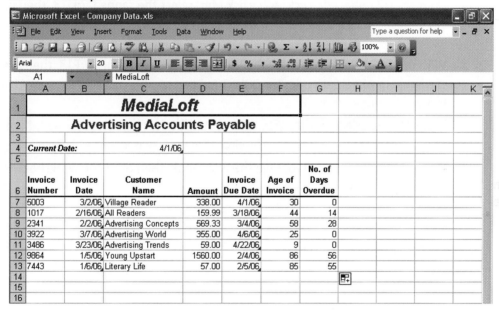

Clues to Use

Correcting circular references

A cell with a circular reference contains a formula that refers to its own cell location. If you accidentally enter a formula with a circular reference, a warning box opens alerting you to the problem. Click OK to display the Circular Reference toolbar or HELP to open a Help window explaining how to find the circular reference. In simple formulas, a circular reference is easy to spot. To correct it, edit the formula to remove any reference to the cell where the formula is located.

Using Statistical Functions

Excel offers several hundred worksheet functions. A small group of these functions calculate statistics such as averages, minimum values, and maximum values. See Table E-3 for a brief description of these commonly used functions. The AVERAGE, COUNT, MAX, and MIN functions are available in the AutoSum list as well as the Insert Function dialog box. ████ Jim wants to present summary information about open accounts payable, and he asks you to add some statistical functions to the worksheet. You decide to use the AutoSum list to insert these functions because it is faster and easier than typing them into the worksheet.

STEPS

1. **Click cell** D19, **click the** AutoSum list arrow Σ ▾ **and then click** Max

   The invoice age information is in cells F7:F13.

2. **Select the range** F7:F13, **then press** [Enter]

   The age of the oldest invoice (or maximum value in range F7:F13) is 86 days, as shown in Figure E-13. Jim needs to know the largest dollar amount among the outstanding invoices.

3. **With cell D20 selected, click** Σ ▾, **click** Max, **select the range** D7:D13, **then press** [Enter]

   The largest outstanding invoice, for 1560.00, is shown in cell D20. The MIN function finds the smallest dollar amount and the age of the newest invoice.

4. **With cell D21 selected, click** Σ ▾, **click** Min, **select the range** D7:D13, **then press** [Enter]

   The smallest dollar amount owed is 57.00, as shown in cell D21. Jim wants to know the age of the newest invoice.

5. **With cell D22 selected, click** Σ ▾, **click** Min, **select the range** F7:F13, **then press** [Enter]

   The newest invoice is 9 days old. The COUNT function calculates the number of invoices by counting the number of entries in column A.

6. **With cell D23 selected, click** Σ ▾, **click** COUNT, **select the range** A7:A13, **then press** [Enter]

   Cell D23 confirms that there are seven invoices. Compare your worksheet with Figure E-14.

7. **Enter your name in cell A26, save the workbook, then print the worksheet**

TABLE E-3: Commonly used statistical functions

function	worksheet action	function	worksheet action
AVERAGE	Calculates an average value	MAX	Finds the largest value
COUNT	Counts cells that contain numbers	MIN	Finds the smallest value
COUNTA	Counts cells that contain nonblank entries	MEDIAN	Finds the middle value

FIGURE E-13: Worksheet with age of oldest invoice

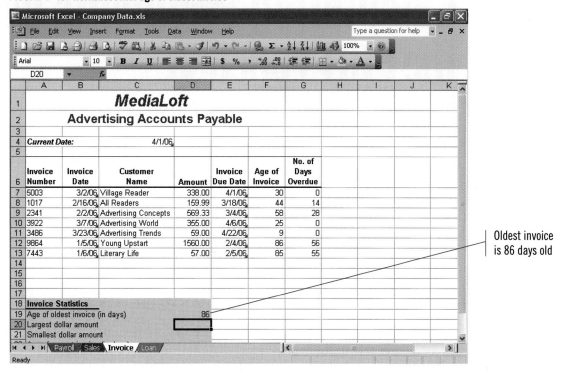

Oldest invoice
is 86 days old

FIGURE E-14: Worksheet with invoice statistics

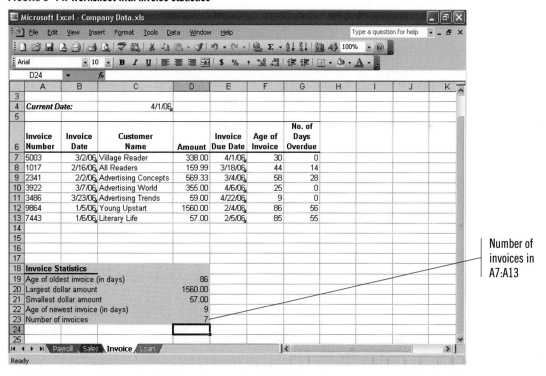

Number of
invoices in
A7:A13

Clues to Use

Using the COUNTA function

The COUNT function counts the number of cells that contain numeric data. If the cell entries that you are trying to count contain nonnumerical data (such as invoice numbers with text entries), the COUNT function does not work and displays a count of zero. There is another function, COUNTA, that counts the number of cells that are not empty and therefore can be used to count the number of entries that contain text.

Calculating Payments with the PMT Function

PMT is a financial function that calculates the periodic payment amount for money borrowed. For example, if you want to borrow money to buy a car, and you know the principal amount, interest rate, and loan term, the PMT function can calculate your monthly payment. Say you want to borrow $15,000 at 8.5% interest and pay the loan off in five years. The Excel PMT function can tell you that your monthly payment will be $307.75 The parts of the PMT function are: PMT(rate, nper, pv, fv, type). See Figure E-15 for an illustration of a PMT function that calculates the monthly payment in the car loan example. ▰▰▰▰▰ For several months, MediaLoft management has been discussing the expansion of the San Diego store. Jim has obtained quotes from three different lenders on borrowing $29,000 to begin the expansion. He obtained loan quotes from a commercial bank, a venture capitalist, and an investment banker. He wants you to summarize the information, using the Excel PMT function.

STEPS

1. **Click the** Loan sheet tab, **click cell** E5, **click the** Insert Function button f_x **on the formula bar, enter** pmt **in the Search for a function text box, click** Go, **click** PMT **in the Select a function list if necessary, then click** OK

2. **Move the Function Arguments dialog box so you can see row 5 of the worksheet; with the cursor in the Rate text box, click cell** C5 **on the worksheet, type** /12, **then press** [Tab]
   You must divide the annual interest by 12 because you are calculating monthly, not annual, payments.

3. **With the cursor in the Nper text box, click cell** D5; **click the** Pv text box, **click cell** B5, **then click** OK
   The FV and Type are optional arguments. Note that the payment of ($581.10) in cell E5 appears in red, indicating that it is a negative amount. Excel displays the result of a PMT function as a negative value to reflect the negative cash flow the loan represents to the borrower. To show the monthly payment as a positive number, you place a minus sign in front of the Pv cell reference in the function.

4. **Edit cell** E5 **so it reads** =PMT(C5/12,D5,–B5), **then click the** Enter button ☑
   A positive value of $581.10 now appears in cell E5. See Figure E-16. You can use the same formula to generate the monthly payments for the other loans.

5. **With cell** E5 **selected, drag the fill handle to fill the range** E6:E7
   A monthly payment of $895.44 for the venture capitalist loan appears in cell E6. A monthly payment of $1,296.43 for the investment banker loan appears in cell E7. The loans with shorter terms have much higher payments. You will not know the entire financial picture until you calculate the total payments and total interest for each lender.

6. **Click cell** F5, **type** =, **click cell** E5, **type** *, **click cell** D5, **then press** [Tab]; **in cell G5, type** =, **click cell** F5, **type** –, **click cell** B5, **then click** ☑

7. **Copy the formulas in cells** F5:G5 **into the range** F6:G7, **then return to cell** A1
   Compare your results with those in Figure E-17. You can experiment with different interest rates, loan amounts, or terms for any one of the lenders; the PMT function generates a new set of values automatically.

8. **Enter your name in cell A13, save the workbook, then preview and print the worksheet**

FIGURE E-15: Example of PMT function for car loan

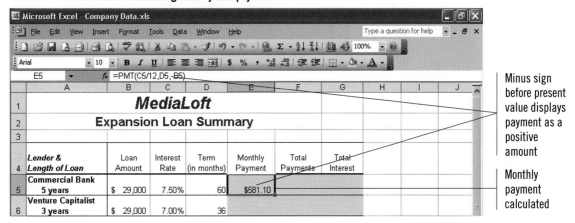

PMT(0.085/12, 60, 15000) = $307.75

| Interest rate per period (rate) | Number of payments (nper) | Present value of loan amount (pv) | Monthly payment calculated |

FIGURE E-16: PMT function calculating monthly loan payment

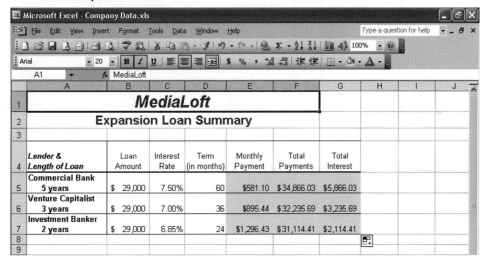

Minus sign before present value displays payment as a positive amount

Monthly payment calculated

FIGURE E-17: Completed worksheet

Clues to Use

Calculating future value with the FV function

You can use the FV (Future Value) function to determine the amount of money a given monthly investment will amount to, at a given interest rate after a given number of payment periods. The syntax is similar to that of the PMT function: FV(rate,nper,pmt,pv,type). For example, suppose you want to invest $1000 every month for the next 12 months into an account that pays 12% a year, and you want to know how much you will have at the end of 12 months (that is, its future value). You enter the function FV(.01,12,–1000), and Excel returns the value $12,682.50 as the future value of your investment. As with the PMT function, the units for the rate and nper must be consistent. If you made monthly payments on a three-year loan at 6% annual interest, you use the rate .06/12 and 36 periods (12*3). The arguments pv and type are optional; pv is the present value, or the total amount the series of payments is worth now. If you omit it, Excel assumes the pv is 0. The "type" argument indicates when the payments are made; 0 is the end of the period, and 1 is the beginning of the period.

UNIT
E
Excel 2003

Displaying and Printing Formula Contents

Excel usually displays the result of formula calculations in the worksheet area and displays formula contents for the active cell in the formula bar. However, you can instruct Excel to display the formulas directly in the worksheet cells in which they were entered. You can document worksheet formulas by first displaying the formulas, then printing them. These formula printouts are valuable paper-based worksheet documentation. Because formulas are often longer than their corresponding values, landscape orientation is the best choice for printing formulas. ████████ Jim wants you to produce a formula printout to submit with the Loan worksheet.

STEPS

1. **Click Tools on the menu bar, click Options, then click the View tab if necessary**

   The View tab of the Options dialog box appears, as shown in Figure E-18.

> **QUICK TIP**
>
> The worksheet formulas can also be displayed by selecting Formula Auditing Mode from the Formula Auditing option on the Tools menu.

2. **Under Window options, click the Formulas check box to select it, then click OK**

   The columns widen and retain their original formats. If the Formula Auditing toolbar is displayed, you can close it.

3. **Scroll horizontally to bring columns E through G into view**

   Instead of displaying formula results in the cells, Excel shows the actual formulas and automatically adjusts the column widths to accommodate them.

4. **Click the Print Preview button 🄰 on the Standard toolbar**

   The status bar reads Preview: Page 1 of 2, indicating that the worksheet will print on two pages. You want to print it on one page and include the row number and column letter headings.

> **QUICK TIP**
>
> All Page Setup options—such as Landscape orientation and Fit to scaling—apply to the active worksheet and are saved with the workbook.

5. **Click Setup in the Print Preview window, then click the Page tab if necessary**

6. **Under Orientation, click the Landscape option button; then under Scaling, click the Fit to option button and note that the wide and tall check boxes contain the number "1"**

   Selecting Landscape instructs Excel to print the worksheet sideways on the page. The Fit to option ensures that the document is printed on a single page.

> **QUICK TIP**
>
> To print row and column labels on every page of a multiple-page worksheet, click the Sheet tab, and fill in the Rows to repeat at top and the Columns to repeat at left in the Print titles section.

7. **Click the Sheet tab, in the Print section, click the Row and column headings check box to select it, click OK, then position the Zoom pointer 🔍 over column A and click**

   The worksheet formulas now appear on a single page, in landscape orientation, with row (number) and column (letter) headings. See Figure E-19.

8. **Click Print in the Print Preview window, then click OK**

   After you retrieve the printout, you want to return the worksheet to displaying formula results. You can do this easily by using a key combination.

9. **Press [Ctrl][`] to redisplay formula results**

   [Ctrl][`] (grave accent mark) toggles between displaying formula results and displaying formula contents.

10. **Save the workbook, then close it and exit Excel**

    The completed payroll worksheet is displayed in Figure E-3; the completed sales worksheet is displayed in Figure E-7; the completed invoice worksheet is shown in Figure E-14, and the completed loan worksheets are displayed in Figures E-17 and E-19.

FIGURE E-18: View tab of the Options dialog box

Select this option to view formulas

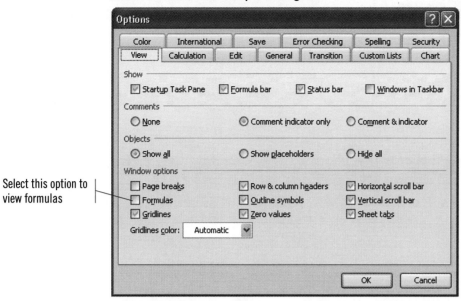

FIGURE E-19: Print Preview window

Column headings

Row headings

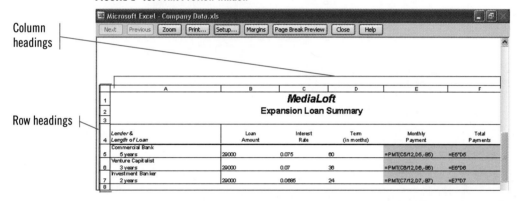

Clues to Use

Setting margins and alignment when printing part of a worksheet

You can set custom margins to print smaller sections of a worksheet. Select the range you want to print, click File on the menu bar, click Print, in the Print what section click Selection, then click Preview. In the Print Preview window, click Setup, then click the Margins tab. See Figure E-20. Double-click the margin numbers and type new ones. Use the Center on page check boxes to center the range horizontally or vertically. If you plan to print the range again, save the view after you print: click View on the menu bar, click Custom Views, click Add, then type a view name and click OK.

FIGURE E-20: Margins tab in the Page Setup dialog box

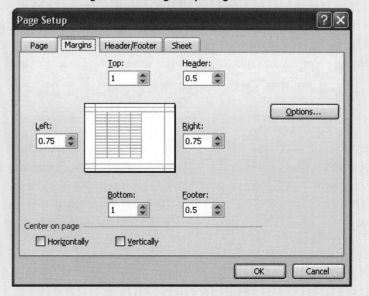

Practice

▼ CONCEPTS REVIEW

FIGURE E-21

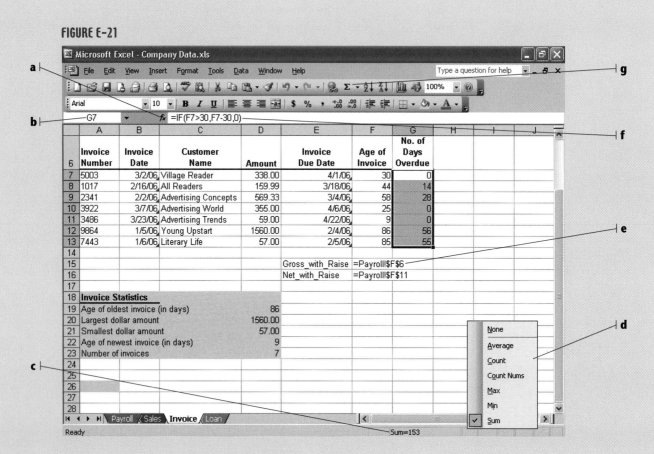

1. Which element points to the area where a name is assigned to a cell?
2. Which element points to a conditional formula?
3. Which element points to the AutoCalculate options?
4. Which element points to a list of the names assigned in the worksheet?
5. Which element do you click to insert a function into a worksheet?
6. Which element points to the result of an AutoCalculate option?
7. Which element do you click to enter a total of adjacent values into a blank cell?

Match each term with the statement that best describes it.

8. Style
9. COUNTA
10. test_cond
11. COUNT
12. pv

a. Function used to count the number of nonblank entries
b. A combination of formatting characteristics
c. Part of the PMT function that represents the loan amount
d. Part of the IF function in which the conditions are stated
e. Function used to count the number of numerical entries

Select the best answer from the list of choices.

13. **To generate a positive payment value when using the PMT function, you must:**
    a. Enter the function arguments as positive values.
    b. Enter the function arguments as negative values.
    c. Enter the interest rate divisor as a negative value.
    d. Enter the amount being borrowed as a negative value.

14. **When you enter the rate and nper arguments in a PMT function, you must:**
    a. Be consistent in the units used.
    b. Multiply both units by 12.
    c. Divide both values by 12.
    d. Use monthly units instead of annual units.

15. **To express conditions such as less than or equal to, you can use a(n):**
    a. Statistical function.
    b. PMT function.
    c. AutoCalculate formula.
    d. Comparison operator.

16. **Which of the following statements is false?**
    a. You can use only existing number and date formats in Excel.
    b. You can create custom number and date formats in Excel.
    c. Dates are stored in Excel as serial numbers.
    d. m/d/yy is an Excel date format.

▼ SKILLS REVIEW

1. **Create a formula with several operators.**
    a. Start Excel, open the Data File EX E-2.xls from the drive and folder where your Data Files are stored, then save the workbook as **Manager Bonuses**.
    b. On the Bonuses worksheet, select cell C13 using the Go To command.
    c. Enter the formula **.2*AVERAGE(C4:C10)**.
    d. Enter the formula **.1*C13** in cell **C14**.
    e. Use the Paste Special command to paste the values and formats in B4:B10 to G4:G10, then save your work.

2. **Use names in a formula.**
    a. Name cell C13 **Dept_Bonus**.
    b. Name cell C14 **Project_Bonus**.
    c. Select the range C4:C10 and name it **Base_Pay**.
    d. In cell E4, enter the formula **Dept_Bonus*D4+Project_Bonus**.
    e. Copy the formula in cell E4 into the range E5:E10.
    f. Format range E4:E10 with the Comma style, using the Style dialog box.
    g. Select the range E4:E10, if necessary, and name it **Bonus_Total**.
    h. In cell F4, enter a formula that sums Base_Pay and Bonus_Total.
    i. Copy the formula in cell F4 into the range F5:F10.
    j. Format range F4:F10 with the Comma style, using the Style dialog box.
    k. Save your work.

3. **Generate multiple totals with AutoSum.**
    a. Select range E4:F11.
    b. Enter the totals using AutoSum.
    c. Check the formulas in cells E11:F11 to make sure they are correct.
    d. Format range E11:F11 with the Currency style, using the Style dialog box.
    e. Enter your name in cell A18, save your work, then preview and print this worksheet.

4. Use dates in calculations.

  a. Make the Merit Pay sheet active.

  b. In cell D6, enter the formula B6+183.

  c. Copy the formula in cell D6 into the range D7:D14.

  d. Use the NOW function to insert the date and time in cell A3.

  e. In cell E18, enter the text Last Pay Date for Year, and in cell G18, use the Date function to enter the date 12/31/2006.

  f. Save your work.

5. Build a conditional formula with the IF function.

  a. In cell F6, use the Function dialog box to enter the formula IF(C6=5,E6*0.05,0).

  b. Copy the formula in cell F6 into the range F7:F14.

  c. Make sure the total in cell F15 is correct.

  d. Apply the Comma style with no decimal places to F6:F14.

  e. Save your work.

6. Use statistical functions.

  a. In cell C19, enter a function to calculate the average salary in the range E6:E14.

  b. In cell C20, enter a function to calculate the largest bonus in the range F6:F14.

  c. In cell C21, enter a function to calculate the lowest performance rating in the range C6:C14.

  d. In cell C22, enter a function to calculate the number of entries in range A6:A14.

  e. Apply the Comma style with no decimal places to C19:C22. Compare your results with Figure E-22.

  f. Enter your name into cell A28, then save, preview, and print the worksheet.

FIGURE E-22

18	**Department Statistics**		
19	Average Salary		30,560
20	Highest Bonus		1,825
21	Lowest Performance Rating		3
22	Number of Employees		9
23			
24			
25			
26			
27			
28			
29			
30			

Bonuses \ **Merit Pay** / Loan /

Ready

7. Calculate payments with the PMT function.

  a. Make the Loan sheet active.

  b. In cell B9, use the Insert Function dialog box to enter the formula PMT(B5/12,B6,−B4).

  c. In cell B10, enter the formula B9*B6.

  d. AutoFit column B, if necessary.

  e. In cell B11, enter the formula B10−B4.

  f. Enter your name in cell A15, then save, preview, and print the worksheet.

8. Display and print formula contents.

  a. Use the View tab in the Options dialog box to display formulas in the worksheet. If the Formula Auditing toolbar opens, you can close it.

  b. Adjust the column widths as necessary.

  c. Save, preview, and print this worksheet on one page in landscape orientation with the row and column headings.

  d. Redisplay the formula results in the worksheet, then resize columns as necessary.

  e. Close the workbook, then exit Excel.

▼ INDEPENDENT CHALLENGE 1

As manager of Mike's Ice Cream Parlor, you have been asked to create a worksheet that totals the monthly sales of all store products. Your monthly report should include the following:

- Sales totals for the current month for each product
- Sales totals for the last month for each product
- The percent change in sales from last month to this month

To document the report further, you decide to include a printout of the worksheet formulas.

a. Start Excel, open the Data File EX E-3.xls from the drive and folder where your Data Files are stored, then save it as **Mike's Sales**.

b. Use the TODAY function to enter today's date in cell A3.

c. Create and apply a custom format for the date entry.

d. Use AutoSum to enter totals for each week, and current month totals for each product.

e. Calculate the percent change in sales from the previous month for regular ice cream. (*Hint*: The formula in words would be (Current Month-Last Month)/Last Month.)

f. Copy the percent change formula down the column for the other products using AutoFill, then format the column with the Percent style using the Formatting toolbar.

g. Apply a Comma style with no decimal places to all weekly figures and totals, using the Formatting toolbar.

h. Enter your name into cell A15, then save, preview, and print the worksheet on a single page.

i. Display and preview the worksheet formulas, then print the formulas in landscape orientation on one page with row and column headings.

j. Close the workbook without saving the changes for displaying formulas, then exit Excel.

▼ INDEPENDENT CHALLENGE 2

You are an auditor with a certified public accounting firm. Fly Away, a manufacturer of skating products, has contacted you to audit its financial records. The management at Fly Away is considering opening a branch in Great Britain and needs its records audited to prepare the business plan. The managers at Fly Away have asked you to assist them in preparing their year-end sales summary as part of this audit. Specifically, they want to add expenses and show the percent of annual expenses that each expense category represents. They also want to show what percent of annual sales each expense category represents. You will include a formula calculating the difference between sales and expenses and another formula calculating expenses divided by sales. The expense categories and their respective dollar amounts are as follows: Building Lease $50,000; Equipment $208,000; Office $25,000; Salary $355,000; Taxes $310,000. Use these expense amounts to prepare the year-end sales and expenses summary for Fly Away.

a. Start Excel, open the Data File EX E-4.xls from the drive and folder where your Data Files are stored, then save the workbook as **Fly Away Sales**.

b. Name the cell containing the formula for total annual expenses **Annual_Expenses**. Use the name Annual_Expenses in cell C12 to create a formula calculating percent of annual expenses. Copy this formula as necessary and apply the Percent style. Add a formula that sums all the values for percent of annual expenses, which should equal 100%.

c. In cell D12, enter a formula calculating the percent of annual sales each expense category represents. Use the name **Annual_Sales** in the formula (cell B9 has been named Annual_Sales). Copy this formula as necessary and apply the Percent style. Include a formula that sums all the values for percent of annual sales.

d. Enter the formula calculating Net Profit in cell B19, using the names Annual_Sales and Annual_Expenses.

e. Enter the formula for Expenses as a percent of sales in cell B20, using the names Annual_Sales and Annual_Expenses.

f. Format cell B19 as Currency with two decimal places. Format cell B20 using the Percentage style with two decimal places. Widen the columns as necessary to display cell contents.

g. Enter your name into cell A22.

▼ INDEPENDENT CHALLENGE 2 (CONTINUED)

Advanced Challenge Exercise

- ■ Display the Formula Auditing toolbar and check the worksheet for errors.
- ■ Use the Formula Auditing toolbar to evaluate the formula in cell B20.
- ■ Close the Formula Auditing toolbar.

h. Save, preview, and print the worksheet.

i. Close the workbook, then exit Excel.

▼ INDEPENDENT CHALLENGE 3

As the owner of Custom Fit, a general contracting firm specializing in home-storage projects, you are facing a business challenge at your firm. Because jobs are taking longer than expected, you decide to take out a $10,000 loan to purchase some new power tools. You check three loan sources: the Small Business Administration (SBA), your local bank, and a consortium of investors. The SBA will lend you the money at 7% interest, but you have to pay it off in three years. The local bank offers you the loan at 7.75% interest over four years. The consortium offers you a 6.75% loan, but they require you to pay it back in two years. To analyze all three loan options, you decide to build a loan summary worksheet. Using the loan terms provided, build a worksheet summarizing your options.

a. Start Excel, open a new workbook, then save it as Custom Fit Loan Options in the drive and folder where your Data Files are stored.

b. Enter today's date in cell A3, using the TODAY function.

c. Using Figure E-23 as a guide, enter labels and worksheet data for the three loan sources.

FIGURE E-23

Loan Source	Loan Amount	Interest Rate	# Payments	Monthly Payment	Total Payments	Total Interest
SBA	10,000	7.00%	36			
Bank	10,000	7.75%	48			
Investors	10,000	6.75%	24			

Custom Fit / Loan Options — 9/18/2006

d. Enter the monthly payment formula for your first loan source (making sure to show the payment as a positive amount), copy the formula as appropriate, then name the range containing the monthly payment formulas Monthly_Payment.

e. Name the cell range containing the number of payments, Number_Payments.

f. Enter the formula for total payments for your first loan source using the named ranges Monthly_Payment and Number_Payments, then copy the formula as necessary.

g. Name the cell range containing the formulas for Total payments, Total_Payments. Name the cell range containing the loan amounts, Loan_Amount.

h. Enter the formula for total interest for your first loan source using the named ranges Total_Payments and Loan_Amount, then copy the formula as necessary.

i. Format the worksheet using formatting appropriate to the worksheet purpose, then enter your name in cell A14.

Advanced Challenge Exercise

- ■ Paste the range names for the worksheet starting in cell E9.
- ■ Name the cell range C5:C7 as Interest_Rate. Name the range G5:G7 as Total_Interest.
- ■ Delete the pasted list of names and paste the new list.

j. Save, preview, and print the worksheet on a single page. Print the worksheet formulas showing row and column headings using landscape orientation. Do not save the worksheet with the formula settings.

k. Close the workbook then exit Excel.

▼ INDEPENDENT CHALLENGE 4

You have been asked to research IRA rates for your company's human resources department. The company plans to deposit $4000 in the employees' accounts at the beginning of each year. You have been asked to research current rates at financial institutions. You will use the Web to find this information. You will use the rate information to determine the value of the deposited money after five years.

a. Open your browser, then go to the search engine of your choice and search for **IRA rates** in the search text box. Find IRA rates offered by three institutions for a $4000 deposit, then write down the institution name, the rate, and the minimum deposit in the table below.

b. Start Excel, open a new workbook, then save it as **IRA Rates** in the drive and folder where your Data Files are stored.

c. Enter the column headings, row headings, and, research results from the table below into your IRA Rates workbook.

IRA Worksheet

Institution	Rate	Minimum Deposit	Number of Years	Amount Deposited (Yearly)	Future Value
			5	4000	
			5	4000	
			5	4000	
Highest Rate					
Average Rate					
Highest Future Value					

d. Use the FV function to calculate the future value of a $4000 yearly deposit over 35 years for each institution, making sure it appears as a positive number. Assume that the payments are made at the beginning of the period, so the Type argument equals 1.

e. Use Excel functions to enter the highest rate, the average rate, and the highest future value into the workbook.

f. Enter your name in cell A15, then save, preview, and print the worksheet on a single page with one inch left and right margins.

g. Display and print the formulas for the worksheet on a single page using landscape orientation. Do not save the worksheet with the formulas displayed.

h. Close the workbook then exit Excel.

Create the worksheet shown in Figure E-24. (*Hints:* Use IF formulas to enter the bonus amounts. An employee with a performance rating of seven or higher receives a bonus of $1000. If the rating is less than seven, no bonus is awarded. The summary information in cells A15:C18 uses the SUM function and statistical functions.) Enter your name in cell A20, and save the workbook as **Bonus Pay**. Preview and then print the worksheet.

FIGURE E-24

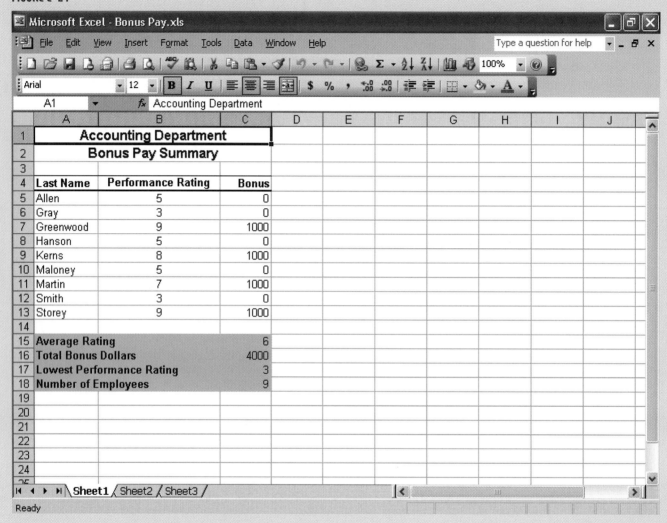

Managing Workbooks and Preparing Them for the Web

OBJECTIVES

Freeze columns and rows
Insert and delete worksheets
Consolidate data with 3-D references
Hide and protect worksheet areas
Save custom views of a worksheet
Control page breaks and page numbering
Create a hyperlink between Excel files
Save an Excel file as a Web page

If you have a SAM user profile, you may have access to hands-on instruction, practice, and assessment of the skills covered in this unit. Log in to your SAM account and go to your assignments page to see what your instructor has assigned.

In this unit you will learn several Excel features to help you manage and print workbook data. You will also learn how to prepare workbooks for publication on the World Wide Web. The MediaLoft Accounting Department asks its marketing director Jim Fernandez to design a timecard summary worksheet to track salary costs for hourly workers. When the worksheet is complete, the Accounting Department will add the rest of the employees and place it on the MediaLoft intranet site for review by store managers. Jim asks you to design a worksheet using some employees from the MediaLoft Houston store. He wants you to save the worksheet as a Web page for viewing on the company's intranet site.

Freezing Columns and Rows

As rows and columns fill up with data, you might need to scroll through the worksheet to add, delete, modify, and view information, and the column or row headings may scroll out of view. Looking at information without row or column labels can be confusing. In Excel, you can temporarily freeze columns and rows, so you can keep the headings in view as you scroll. **Panes** are the columns and rows that **freeze**, or remain in place, while you scroll through your worksheet. Jim asks you to check the total hours worked, hourly pay rate, and total pay for salespeople Paul Cristifano and Virginia Young. Because the worksheet is becoming more difficult to read as its size increases, you want to freeze the column and row labels.

STEPS

1. **Start Excel if necessary, open the Data File EX F-1.xls from the drive and folder where your Data Files are stored, then save it as** Timecard Summary

2. **Scroll through the Monday worksheet to view the data, then click cell** D6

    You select cell D6 because Excel freezes the columns to the left and the rows above the selected cell. You want to freeze columns A, B, and C as well as rows 1 through 5. By doing so, you can see each employee's last name, first name, and timecard number on the screen when you scroll to the right, and you can also read the labels in rows 1 through 5 when you scroll down.

3. **Click** Window **on the menu bar, then click** Freeze Panes

    A thin line appears along the column border to the left of the active cell, and another line appears along the row above the active cell, indicating that columns A through C and rows 1 through 5 are frozen.

4. **Scroll to the right until columns** A **through** C **and** L **through** O **are visible**

    Because columns A, B, and C are frozen, they remain on the screen; columns D through K are temporarily hidden from view. Notice that the information you are looking for in row 13 (last name, total hours, hourly pay rate, and total pay for Paul Cristifano) is readily available. Paul's data appears to be correct, but you still need to check Virginia Young's information.

5. **Scroll down until** row 26 **is visible**

    In addition to columns A through C, rows 1 through 5 remain on the screen. See Figure F-1. You are now able to verify Virginia Young's information. Even though a pane is frozen, you can click in the frozen area of the worksheet and edit the contents of the cells there, if necessary.

6. **Press** [Ctrl][Home]

    Because the panes are frozen, the cell pointer moves to cell D6, not A1.

7. **Click** Window **on the menu bar, then click** Unfreeze Panes

    The freeze lines no longer appear and the columns and rows are no longer frozen.

8. **Press** [Ctrl][Home] **to return to cell A1, then save the workbook**

Clues to Use

Viewing and arranging worksheets

In a multiple-sheet workbook, you can use the scrolling buttons to the left of the horizontal scroll bar. To scroll several tabs at once, press [Shift] while clicking one of the middle tab scrolling buttons. You can view multiple worksheets by clicking the sheet you want to view and then clicking New Window on the Window menu. Repeat this for each sheet you want to view. Each sheet becomes a button on the taskbar. To arrange the windows, click Arrange on the Window menu and choose a layout.

FIGURE F-1: Scrolled worksheet with frozen rows and columns

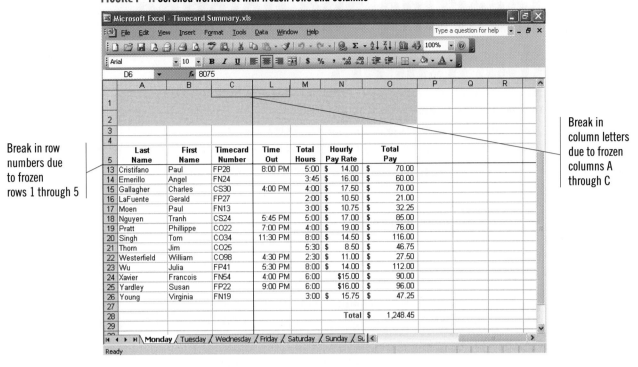

Break in row numbers due to frozen rows 1 through 5

Break in column letters due to frozen columns A through C

Clues to Use

Splitting the worksheet into multiple panes

Excel lets you split the worksheet area into vertical and/or horizontal panes, so that you can click inside any one pane and scroll to locate information in that pane while the other panes remain in place. See Figure F-2. To split a worksheet area into multiple panes, drag the split box (the small box at the top of the vertical scroll bar or at the right end of the horizontal scroll bar) in the direction you want the split to appear. To remove the split, move the pointer over the split until the pointer changes to a double-headed arrow ↔, then double-click.

FIGURE F-2: Worksheet split into two horizontal and two vertical panes

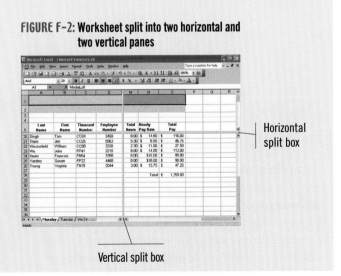

Horizontal split box

Vertical split box

Inserting and Deleting Worksheets

You can insert and delete worksheets in a workbook at any time. For example, because new workbooks open with only three sheets available (Sheet1, Sheet2, and Sheet3), you need to insert at least one more sheet if you want to have four quarterly worksheets in an annual budget workbook. You can do this by using commands on the menu bar or shortcut menu. Jim was in a hurry when he added the sheet tabs to the Timecard Summary workbook. He wants you to insert a sheet for Thursday and delete the sheet for Sunday because Houston workers do not work on Sundays.

STEPS

QUICK TIP
You can copy a selected worksheet by clicking Edit on the menu bar, then clicking Move or Copy Sheet. Choose the sheet you want the copy to precede, click the Create a copy check box, then click OK.

1. **Click the** Friday sheet tab, **click** Insert **on the menu bar, then click** Worksheet

   Excel inserts a new sheet tab labeled Sheet1 to the left of the Friday sheet.

2. **Double-click the** Sheet1 tab **and rename it** Thursday

   Now the tabs read Monday, Tuesday, Wednesday, Thursday, Friday, and Saturday. The tab for the Summary is not visible. You still need to delete the Sunday worksheet.

3. **Right-click the** Sunday sheet tab, **then click** Delete **on the shortcut menu shown in Figure F-3**

   The shortcut menu allows you to insert, delete, rename, move, or copy sheets; it also allows you to select all the sheets and change the tab color of a worksheet.

4. **Move the mouse pointer over any tab scrolling button, then right-click**

   Excel opens a shortcut menu of the worksheets in the active workbook. Compare your list with Figure F-4.

5. **Click** Monday **on the shortcut menu, then save the workbook**

Clues to Use

Grouping worksheets

You can group worksheets to work on them as a collection so that data entered into one worksheet is automatically entered into all of the selected worksheets. This is useful for data that is common to every sheet of a workbook such as headers and footers. Grouping worksheets can also be used to print multiple worksheets at one time. To group worksheets, press and hold [Ctrl] and click the tabs for the sheets you want to group. If the sheets that you want to group are adjacent, then click the first sheet and hold [Shift] while clicking the last sheet in the group.

FIGURE F-3: Worksheet shortcut menu

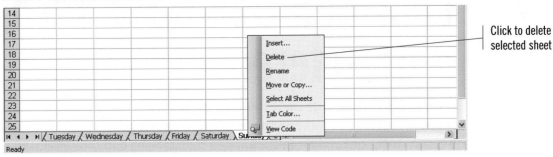

Click to delete
selected sheet

FIGURE F-4: Workbook with worksheets menu

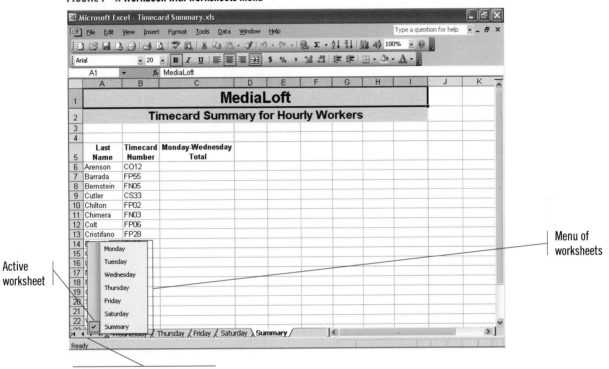

Menu of
worksheets

Active
worksheet

Right-click any tab scrolling button
to display the menu of worksheets

Clues to Use

Specifying headers and footers

As you prepare a workbook for others to view, it is helpful to provide as much data as possible about the worksheets, such as the number of pages, who created it, and when. You can do this easily in a **header** or **footer**, which is information that prints at the top or bottom of each printed page. Headers and footers are visible on the screen only in Print Preview. To add a header, for example, click View on the menu bar, click Header and Footer, then click Custom Header. You see a dialog box similar to that in Figure F-5. Both the header and the footer are divided into three sections, and you can enter information in any or all of them. You can type information, such as your name, and click the icons to enter the page number 🔲, total pages 🔲, date 🔲, time 🔲, file path 🔲, filename 🔲, or sheet name 🔲. You can insert a picture by clicking the Insert Picture icon 🔲, and you can format the picture by clicking the Format picture icon 🔲 and selecting formatting options. When you click an

icon, Excel inserts a symbol in the footer section containing an ampersand (&) and the element name in brackets. When you are finished, click OK, click the Print Preview button on the Header/Footer tab to see your header and footer, then click Close.

FIGURE F-5: Header dialog box

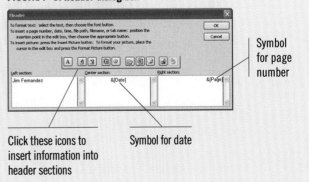

Symbol
for page
number

Click these icons to
insert information into
header sections

Symbol for date

Excel 2003

Consolidating Data with 3-D References

When you want to summarize similar data that exists in different sheets or workbooks, you can combine and display it in one sheet. For example, you might have departmental sales figures on four different store sheets that you want to **consolidate** on one summary sheet showing total departmental sales for all stores. The best way to consolidate data is to use cell references to the various sheets on a consolidation, or summary, sheet. Because they reference other sheets that are usually behind the summary sheet, such references effectively create another dimension in the workbook and are called **3-D references**. You can reference data in other sheets and in other workbooks. Referencing cells is a better method than retyping calculated results because the data values on which calculated totals depend might change. If you reference the values, any changes to the original values are automatically reflected in the consolidation sheet. ▰▰▰ Although Jim does not have timecard data for Thursday and Friday, he wants you to use the Summary sheet to consolidate the available data. He asks you to do this by creating a formula on the Summary sheet that adds the total pay data in the Monday, Tuesday, and Wednesday sheets. You want to freeze the panes to improve the view of the worksheet before initiating the 3-D reference.

STEPS

1. **On the Monday sheet, click cell D6, click Window on the menu bar, click Freeze Panes, then scroll horizontally to bring columns L through O into view**

2. **Right-click a tab scrolling button, then click Summary**
   Because the Summary sheet (which is the consolidation sheet) will contain the reference, the cell pointer must reside there when you initiate the reference.

   > **QUICK TIP**
   > If you have difficulty entering the formula references, press [Esc] and begin again.

3. **On the Summary sheet, click cell C6, click the AutoSum button Σ on the Standard toolbar, activate the Monday sheet, press and hold [Shift] and click the Wednesday sheet tab, click cell O6, then click the Enter button ✓ on the formula bar**
   The Summary sheet becomes active, and the formula bar reads =SUM(Monday:Wednesday!O6). See Figure F-6. Monday:Wednesday references the Monday, Tuesday and Wednesday sheets. The ! (exclamation point) is an **external reference indicator**, meaning that the cells referenced are outside the active sheet; O6 is the actual cell reference in the external sheets. The result, $168.80, appears in cell C6 of the Summary sheet, showing the sum of the total pay referenced in cell O6 of the Monday, Tuesday, and Wednesday sheets.

4. **In the Summary sheet, copy cell C6 into cells C7:C26**
   Excel copies the 3-D formula in cell C6. You can test a consolidation reference by changing one cell value on which the formula is based and seeing if the formula result changes.

5. **Activate the Monday sheet, edit cell L6 to read 6:30 PM, then activate the Summary sheet**
   The sum of Beryl Arenson's pay was automatically updated in the Summary sheet. See Figure F-7.

6. **Click View on the menu bar, click Header and Footer, click Custom Footer, enter your name in the Left section text box, click OK, then click OK**

7. **Preview the worksheet, then print it**

8. **Activate the Monday sheet, unfreeze the panes, then save the workbook**

FIGURE F-6: Worksheet showing total pay

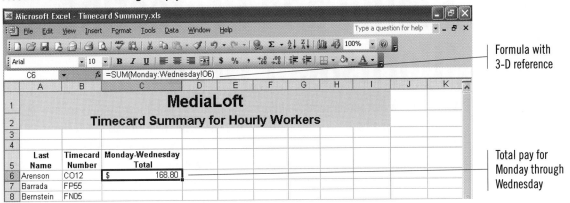

Formula with 3-D reference

Total pay for Monday through Wednesday

FIGURE F-7: Summary worksheet with updated total

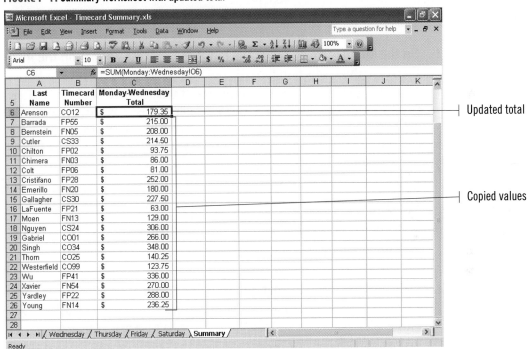

Updated total

Copied values

Clues to Use

Linking data between workbooks

Just as you can reference data between cells in a worksheet and between sheets, you can dynamically reference data between workbooks so that changes made in referenced cells in one workbook are reflected in the consolidation sheet in the other workbook. This dynamic referencing is called **linking**. To link a single cell between workbooks, open both workbooks, select the cell to receive the linked data, type = (the equal sign), select the cell in the other workbook containing the data to be linked, then press [Enter]. Excel automatically inserts the name of the referenced workbook in the cell reference. For example, if the linked data is contained in cell C7 of worksheet New in the Products workbook, the cell entry reads ='[Product.xls]New'!$C$7. To perform calculations, enter formulas on the consolidation sheet using cells in the supporting sheets. If you are linking more than one cell, you can copy the linked data to the Clipboard, select the upper-left cell in the workbook to receive the link, click Edit on the menu bar, click Paste Special, then click Paste Link.

Hiding and Protecting Worksheet Areas

Worksheets may contain sensitive information that you don't want others to view or alter. To protect such information, Excel gives you two options. You can **hide** the formulas in selected cells (or rows, columns, or entire sheets), and you can **lock** selected cells, in which case other people are able to view the data (values, numbers, labels, formulas, etc.) in those cells, but not change it. See Table F-1 for a list of options you can use to protect a worksheet. You set the lock and hide options in the Format Cells dialog box. Excel locks all cells by default, but this protection does not take effect until you activate the Excel protection feature on the Tools menu. A common worksheet protection strategy is to unlock cells in which data will be changed, sometimes referred to as the **data entry area**, and to lock cells in which the data should not be changed. Then, when you protect the worksheet, the unlocked areas can still be changed. ▰▰▰ Because Jim will assign an employee to enter the sensitive timecard information into the worksheet, he wants you to hide and lock selected areas of the worksheet.

STEPS

1. **On the Monday sheet, select the range** I6:L26, **click** Format **on the menu bar, click** Cells, **then click the** Protection tab

   Notice that the Locked box in the Protection tab is already checked, as shown in Figure F-8. The Locked check box is selected by default, meaning that all the cells in a new workbook start out locked. (Note, however, that cell locking is not applied unless the protection feature is also activated. The protection feature is inactive by default.) You do not want the Time In and Time Out cells to be locked when the protection feature is activated.

2. **Click the** Locked check box **to deselect it, then click** OK

   Excel stores time as a fraction of a 24-hour day. In the formula for total pay, hours must be multiplied by 24. This concept might be confusing to the data entry person, so you hide the formulas.

3. **Select range** O6:O26, **click** Format **on the menu bar, click** Cells, **click the** Protection tab, **click the** Hidden check box **to select it, then click** OK

   The data remains the same (unhidden and unlocked) until you set the protection in the next step.

4. **Click** Tools **on the menu bar, point to** Protection, **then click** Protect Sheet

   The Protect Sheet dialog box opens. The default options allow you to protect the worksheet while allowing users to select locked or unlocked cells only. You choose not to use a password.

5. **Make sure Protect worksheet and contents of locked cells is checked in the Protect Sheet dialog box, then click** OK

   You are ready to test the new worksheet protection.

6. **Click cell** O6

   The formula bar is empty because of the hidden formula setting.

7. **In cell O6, type** T **to confirm that locked cells cannot be changed, then click** OK

   When you attempt to change a locked cell, a message box reminds you of the protected cell's read-only status. See Figure F-9.

8. **Click cell** I6, **type** 9, **and notice that Excel allows you to begin the entry, press** [Esc] **to cancel the entry, then save the workbook**

   Because you unlocked the cells in columns I through L before you protected the worksheet, you can make changes to these cells. The Time In and Time Out data can be changed as necessary.

FIGURE F-8: Protection tab in Format Cells dialog box

Click to remove
check mark

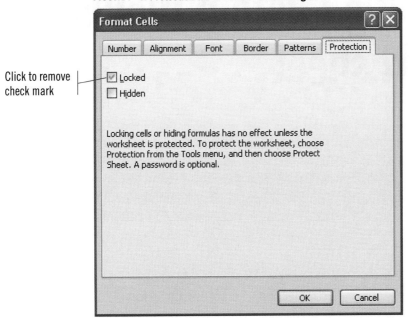

FIGURE F-9: Reminder of protected cell's read-only status

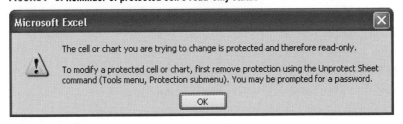

TABLE F-1: Options for hiding and protecting workbook elements

task	menu commands
Hide/Unhide a column	Format, Column, Hide or Unhide
Hide/Unhide a formula	Format, Cells, Protection tab, select/deselect Hidden check box
Hide/Unhide a row	Format, Row, Hide or Unhide
Hide/Unhide a sheet	Format, Sheet, Hide or Unhide
Hide/Unhide a workbook	Window, Hide or Unhide
Protect workbook	Tools, Protection, Protect Workbook, assign optional password
Protect worksheet	Tools, Protection, Protect Sheet, assign optional password
Unlock/Relock cells	Format, Cells, Protection tab, deselect/select Locked check box

(*Note*: Some of the hide and protect options do not take effect until protection is enabled. To enable protection, click Tools on the menu bar, point to Protection, then click Protect Sheet.)

Clues to Use

Changing workbook properties

You can also use a password to protect an entire workbook from being opened or modified by changing its file properties. Click File on the menu bar, click Save As, click Tools, then click General Options. Specify the password(s) for opening or modifying the workbook. To remove a workbook password, you can double-click the asterisks in the Password to open or Password to modify text boxes and press [Delete]. You can also use this dialog box to offer users an option to open the workbook in read-only format so that they can open, but not change it. Another way to make an entire workbook read-only is to right-click Start on the taskbar, then click Explore. Locate and right-click the filename, click Properties, click the General tab, then, in the Attributes section, select the Read-only check box.

Saving Custom Views of a Worksheet

A **view** is a set of display and/or print settings that you can name and save, then access at a later time. By using the Excel Custom Views feature, you can create several different views of a worksheet without having to create separate sheets. For example, if you often switch between portrait and landscape orientations when printing different parts of a worksheet, you can create two views with the appropriate print settings for each view. You set the display and/or print settings first, then name the view. ▰▰▰▰ Because Jim wants to generate several reports from his data, he asks you to save the current print and display settings as a custom view. To better view the data, he wants you to use the Zoom box to display the entire worksheet on one screen.

STEPS

QUICK TIP
After selecting the Zoom box, you can also pick a magnification percentage from the list or type the desired percentage.

1. **With the Monday sheet active, select range** A1:O28, **click the** Zoom list arrow **on the Standard toolbar, click** Selection, **then press** [Ctrl][Home] **to return to cell A1**

   Excel adjusts the display magnification so that the selected data fits on one screen. See Figure F-10.

2. **Click** View **on the menu bar, then click** Custom Views

   The Custom Views dialog box opens. Any previously defined views for the active worksheet appear in the Views box. In this case, Jim has created a custom view named Generic containing default print and display settings. See Figure F-11.

QUICK TIP
To delete views from the active worksheet, select the view in the Views list box, then click Delete.

3. **Click** Add

   The Add View dialog box opens, as shown in Figure F-12. Here, you enter a name for the view and decide whether to include print settings and hidden rows, columns, and filter settings. You want to include the selected options.

4. **In the Name box, type** Complete Daily Worksheet, **then click** OK

   After creating a custom view, you return to the worksheet. You are ready to test the two custom views. In case the views require a change to the worksheet, it's a good idea to turn off worksheet protection.

5. **Click** Tools **on the menu bar, point to** Protection, **then click** Unprotect Sheet

6. **Click** View **on the menu bar, then click** Custom Views

   The Custom Views dialog box opens, listing both the Complete Daily Worksheet and Generic views.

TROUBLE
If you receive the message "Some view settings could not be applied," repeat Step 5 to ensure that worksheet protection is turned off.

7. **Click** Generic **in the Views list, click** Show, **preview the worksheet, then close the Preview window**

   The Generic custom view returns the worksheet to the Excel default print and display settings. Now you are ready to test the new custom view.

8. **Click** View **on the menu bar, click** Custom Views, **click** Complete Daily Worksheet **in the Views list box if necessary, then click** Show

   The entire worksheet fits on the screen.

9. **Return to the Generic view, then save your work**

FIGURE F-10: Selected data fitted to one screen

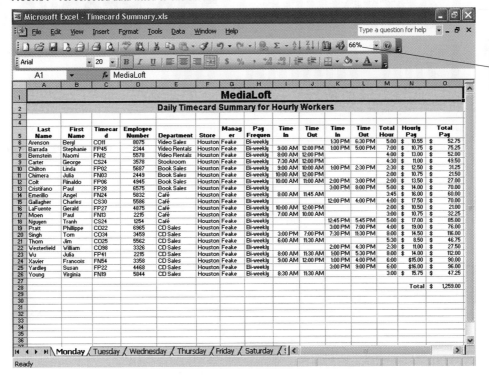

Zoom box showing current magnification

FIGURE F-11: Custom Views dialog box

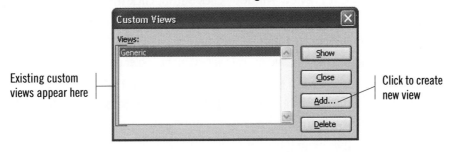

Existing custom views appear here

Click to create new view

FIGURE F-12: Add View dialog box

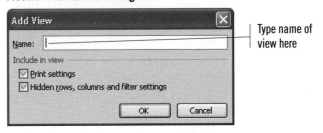

Type name of view here

Clues to Use

Creating a workspace

If you work with several workbooks at a time, you can group them so you can open them in one step by creating a **workspace**, a file with an .xlw extension. Then, instead of opening each workbook individually, you can open the workspace. To create a workspace, open the workbooks you wish to group and position and size them as you would like them to appear. Click File on the menu bar, click Save Workspace, type a name for the workspace file, then click Save. Remember, however, that the workspace file does not contain the workbooks themselves, so you still have to save any changes you make to the original workbook files. To have the workbooks automatically open in the workspace when you start Excel, place the workspace file in your XLStart folder (C:\Program Files\Microsoft Office\Office11\XLStart).

Controlling Page Breaks and Page Numbering

The vertical and horizontal dashed lines in worksheets represent page breaks. Excel automatically inserts a page break when your worksheet data doesn't fit on one page. These page breaks are **dynamic**, which means they adjust automatically when you insert or delete rows and columns and when you change column widths or row heights. Everything to the left of the first vertical dashed line and above the first horizontal dashed line is printed on the first page. You can override the automatic breaks by choosing the Page Break command on the Insert menu. Table F-2 describes the different types of page breaks you can use. ▄▄▄▄ Jim wants another report displaying no more than half the hourly workers on each page. To accomplish this, he asks you to insert a manual page break.

STEPS

1. **Click cell A16, click Insert on the menu bar, then click Page Break**

   A dashed line appears between rows 15 and 16, indicating a horizontal page break. See Figure F-13. After you set page breaks, it's a good idea to preview each page.

2. **Preview the worksheet, then click Zoom**

   Notice that the status bar reads "Page 1 of 4" and that the data for the employees up through Charles Gallagher appears on the first page. You decide to place the date in the footer.

3. **While in the Print Preview window, click Setup, click the Header/Footer tab, click Custom Footer, click the Right section box, then click the Date button** 📅

4. **Click the Left section box, type your name, then click OK**

   Your name, the page number, and the date appear in the Footer preview area.

5. **In the Page Setup dialog box, click OK, and while still in Print Preview, check to make sure that all the pages show your name, the page numbers, and the date, click Close, save the workbook, then print the worksheet**

6. **Click View on the menu bar, click Custom Views, click Add, type Half and Half, then click OK**

   Your new custom view has the page breaks and all current print settings.

7. **Make sure cell A16 is selected, then click Insert on the menu bar and click Remove Page Break**

   Excel removes the manual page break above or to the left of the active cell.

8. **Save the workbook**

FIGURE F-13: Worksheet with horizontal page break

Dashed line indicates horizontal break after row 15

	Last Name	First Name	Timecard Number	Employee Number	Department	Store	Manager	Pay Frequency	Time In	Time Out
6	Arenson	Beryl	CO11	8075	Video Sales	Houston	Feake	Bi-weekly		
7	Barrada	Stephanie	FP45	2344	Video Rentals	Houston	Feake	Bi-weekly	9:00 AM	12:00
8	Bernstein	Naomi	FN12	5578	Video Rentals	Houston	Feake	Bi-weekly	8:00 AM	12:00
9	Carter	George	CS24	3578	Stockroom	Houston	Feake	Bi-weekly	7:30 AM	12:00
10	Chilton	Linda	FP02	5687	Book Sales	Houston	Feake	Bi-weekly	9:00 AM	10:00
11	Chimera	Julia	FN03	2449	Book Sales	Houston	Feake	Bi-weekly	10:00 AM	12:00
12	Colt	Rinaldo	FP06	4945	Book Sales	Houston	Feake	Bi-weekly	10:00 AM	11:00
13	Cristifano	Paul	FP28	6575	Book Sales	Houston	Feake	Bi-weekly		
14	Emerillo	Angel	FN24	5832	Café	Houston	Feake	Bi-weekly	8:00 AM	11:45
15	Gallagher	Charles	CS30	5586	Café	Houston	Feake	Bi-weekly		
16	LaFuente	Gerald	FP27	4875	Café	Houston	Feake	Bi-weekly	10:00 AM	12:00
17	Moen	Paul	FN13	2215	Café	Houston	Feake	Bi-weekly	7:00 AM	10:00
18	Nguyen	Tranh	CS24	1254	Café	Houston	Feake	Bi-weekly		
19	Pratt	Phillippe	CO22	6965	CD Sales	Houston	Feake	Bi-weekly		
20	Singh	Tom	CO34	3459	CD Sales	Houston	Feake	Bi-weekly	3:00 PM	7:00
21	Thorn	Jim	CO25	5562	CD Sales	Houston	Feake	Bi-weekly	6:00 AM	11:30
22	Westerfield	William	CO98	3326	CD Sales	Houston	Feake	Bi-weekly		
23	Wu	Julia	FP41	2215	CD Sales	Houston	Feake	Bi-weekly	8:00 AM	11:30
24	Xavier	Francois	FN54	3358	CD Sales	Houston	Feake	Bi-weekly	9:00 AM	12:00
25	Yardley	Susan	FP22	4468	CD Sales	Houston	Feake	Bi-weekly		
26	Young	Virginia	FN19	5844	CD Sales	Houston	Feake	Bi-weekly	8:30 AM	11:30

TABLE F-2: Page break options

type of page break	where to position cell pointer
Both horizontal and vertical page breaks	Select the cell below and to the right of the gridline where you want the breaks to occur
Only a horizontal page break	Select the cell in column A that is directly below the gridline where you want the page to break
Only a vertical page break	Select a cell in row 1 that is to the right of the gridline where you want the page to break

Clues to Use

Using Page Break Preview

You can view and change page breaks manually by clicking View on the menu bar, then clicking Page Break Preview, or clicking Page Break Preview in the Print Preview window. (If you see a Welcome to Page Break Preview dialog box, click OK to close it.) You can drag the page break lines to the desired location. See Figure F-14. If you drag a page break to the right to include more data on a page, Excel shrinks the type to fit the data on that page. To exit Page Break Preview, click View on the menu bar, then click Normal.

FIGURE F-14: Page Break Preview window

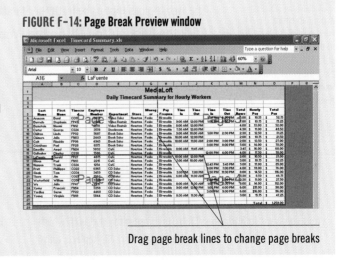

Drag page break lines to change page breaks

Creating a Hyperlink Between Excel Files

As you manage the content and appearance of your workbooks, you may want the workbook user to view information in another location. It might be nonessential information or data that is too detailed to place in the workbook itself. In these cases, you can create a **hyperlink**, an object (a filename, a word, a phrase, or a graphic) in a worksheet that, when you click it, displays, or "jumps to," another worksheet, called the **target**. The target can also be a document or a site on the World Wide Web. Hyperlinks are navigational tools between worksheets and are not used to exchange information. For example, in a worksheet that lists customer invoices, at each customer's name, you might create a hyperlink to an Excel file containing payment terms for each customer. Jim wants managers who view the Timecard Summary workbook to be able to view the pay categories for MediaLoft store employees. He asks you to create a hyperlink at the Hourly Pay Rate column heading. Users can click the hyperlink to view the Pay Rate worksheet.

STEPS

1. **Click cell** N5 **(the cell containing the text Hourly Pay Rate) on the Monday worksheet**

2. **Click the** Insert Hyperlink button **on the Standard toolbar, then click** Existing File or Web Page, **if it is not already selected**

    The Insert Hyperlink dialog box opens. See Figure F-15. The icons under Link to on the left side of the dialog box let you specify the type of location you want the link to jump to: an existing file or Web page, a place in the same document, a new document, or an e-mail address. Because you want the link to display a document that has been created, the first icon, Existing File or Web Page, is correct.

    > **QUICK TIP**
    > If you link to a Web page you must be connected to the Internet to test the link.

3. **Click the** Look in list arrow, **navigate to the location where your Data Files are stored if necessary, then click** Pay Rate Classifications.xls **in the file list**

    The filename you selected appears in the Address text box. This is the document users see when they click this hyperlink. You can also specify the ScreenTip that users see when they hold the pointer over the hyperlink.

4. **Click** ScreenTip, **type** Click here to see MediaLoft pay rate classifications, **click** OK, **edit the Text to display text box to show** Hourly Pay Rate, **then click** OK **again**

    Cell N5 now contains underlined blue text, indicating that it is a hyperlink. After you create a hyperlink, you should check it to make sure that it jumps to the correct destination.

    > **QUICK TIP**
    > To remove a hyperlink or change its target, right-click it, then click Remove Hyperlink or Edit Hyperlink.

5. **Move the pointer over the** Hourly Pay Rate text, **view the ScreenTip, then click once**

    Notice that when you move the pointer over the text, the pointer changes to ☝, indicating that it is a hyperlink, and the ScreenTip appears. After you click, the Pay Rate Classifications worksheet appears. See Figure F-16. The Web toolbar appears beneath the Standard and Formatting toolbars.

    > **QUICK TIP**
    > To print an entire workbook, click File on the menu bar, click Print, click to select the Entire workbook option button, then click OK.

6. **Click the** Back button **on the Web toolbar, save the workbook, then print the worksheet**

Clues to Use

Finding and replacing data and formats

You can easily change worksheet data by using the Find and Replace feature. Click Edit on the menu bar, click Replace, enter the text you want to find, press [Tab], then enter the text with which you want to replace it. Use the Find Next, Find All, Replace, and Replace All buttons to find and replace any or all occurrences of the specified text. You can specify a data format for your search criteria by clicking the Options button, clicking the Format list arrow, and selecting a format.

FIGURE F-15: Insert Hyperlink dialog box

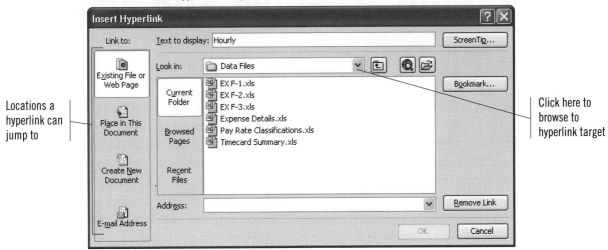

Locations a hyperlink can jump to

Click here to browse to hyperlink target

FIGURE F-16: Target document

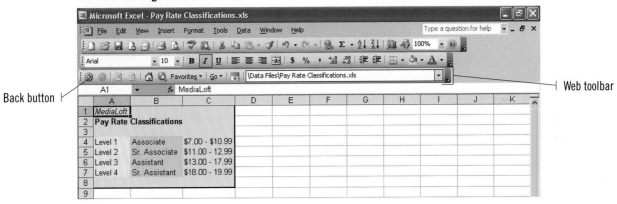

Back button

Web toolbar

Clues to Use

Using research services

You can access resources online and locally on your computer using the Research task pane. To open the Research task pane, click Tools on the menu bar, then click Research. The Search for text box allows you to specify a research topic. The task pane also has a drop-down list of the resources available to search for your topic. You can insert the information you find into your worksheet by moving your cursor over the information you want to insert, clicking the list arrow on the right, then clicking Insert, Copy, or Look Up. The research services feature will expand as more companies develop databases that are specifically designed for use in the Research task pane.

Saving an Excel File as a Web Page

One way to share Excel data is to place, or **publish**, the data on a network or on the Web so that others can access it using their Web browsers. The network can be an **intranet**, which is an internal network site used by a particular group of people who work together. If you post an entire workbook, users can click worksheet tabs to view each sheet. You can make the workbook interactive, meaning that users can enter, format, and perform data calculations. To publish an Excel document to an intranet or the Web, you must first save it in an **HTML (Hypertext Markup Language)** format. You can save your Excel file as a **single file Web page** that integrates all of the worksheets and graphical elements from the workbook into a single file. This file format is called MHTML. Incorporating the HTML and supporting files into one file makes it easier to publish your Excel file to the Web. Users who have IE 4.0 or higher can open a Web page saved in MHTML format. ▓▓▓▓▓ Jim asks you to save the entire Timecard Summary workbook in MHT format so he can publish it on the MediaLoft intranet for managers to view.

STEPS

1. **Click File on the menu bar, then click Save as Web Page**
   The Save As dialog box opens. By default, the Entire Workbook option button is selected. You want the title bar of the Web page to be more descriptive than the filename.

2. **Click Change Title**
   The Set Page Title dialog box opens.

3. **Type MediaLoft Houston Timecard Summary, then click OK**
   The new title appears in the Page title area.

4. **Click the Save in list arrow to navigate to the drive and folder where your Data Files are stored, change the filename to timesum, then click the Save as type list arrow and click Single File Web Page**
   The Save as type list box indicates that the workbook is to be saved as a Single File Web Page, which is in MHTML or MHT format. See Figure F-17.

5. **Click Save**
   A dialog box appears, indicating that the custom views you saved earlier will not be part of the HTML file.

6. **Click Yes**
   Excel saves the workbook as an MHT file in the folder location you specified in the Save As dialog box. The MHT file is open on your screen.

7. **Click File on the menu bar, click Web Page Preview, then if necessary maximize the browser window**
   The workbook opens in your default Web browser, showing you what it would look like if you opened the workbook on an intranet or on the Web. See Figure F-18.

8. **Click the Summary Sheet tab, then print the worksheet using your browser**

9. **Close the Web browser window, then close the timesum.mht workbook and the Pay Rate Classifications.xls workbook**

Clues to Use

Converting Excel files to other file types

You can use the Save As option on the File menu to save a workbook in a format that can be opened in earlier versions of Excel or in other spreadsheet programs. You can also use the Save As option to convert an Excel file to other file types such as XML, TXT (text file type), and CSV (comma-delimited file type).

FIGURE F-17: Save As dialog box

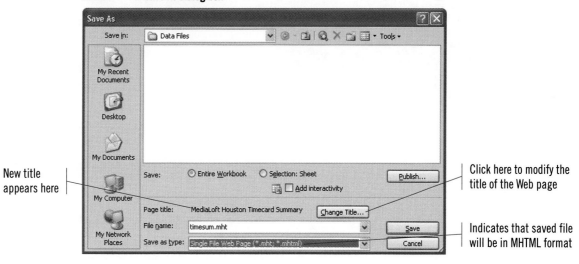

New title appears here

Click here to modify the title of the Web page

Indicates that saved file will be in MHTML format

FIGURE F-18: Workbook in Web page preview

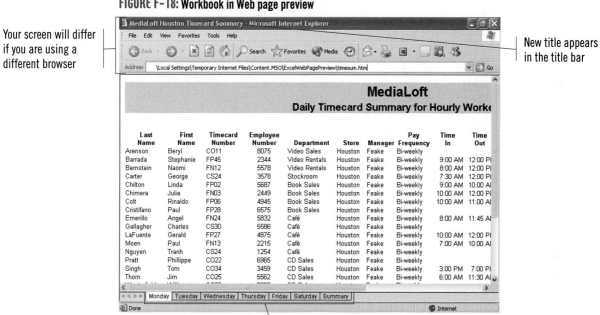

Your screen will differ if you are using a different browser

New title appears in the title bar

Sheet tabs allow users to view other sheets in their browser

Clues to Use

Holding Web discussions

You can attach a discussion comment to an Excel worksheet that you are going to save as an HTML document. This allows people viewing your worksheet on the Web to review and reply to your comments. To insert a discussion comment in Excel, click Tools on the menu bar, point to Online Collaboration, then click Web Discussions. This displays the Web Discussions toolbar. See Figure F-19. You can add comments that others can view on the Web by clicking the Insert Discussion about the Workbook button on the Web Discussions Toolbar. Your comments, which are stored on a discussion server, appear with the worksheet when it is saved and published as a Web document. People viewing your worksheet on the Web can reply by clicking the Discuss button on the Standard Buttons toolbar

in Internet Explorer to display the Discussions toolbar. Then they can click the Insert Discussion about the Workbook button. (*Note*: You must specify a discussion server to use this feature.)

FIGURE F-19: Web Discussion toolbar

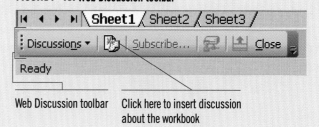

Web Discussion toolbar

Click here to insert discussion about the workbook

Practice

▼ CONCEPTS REVIEW

FIGURE F-20

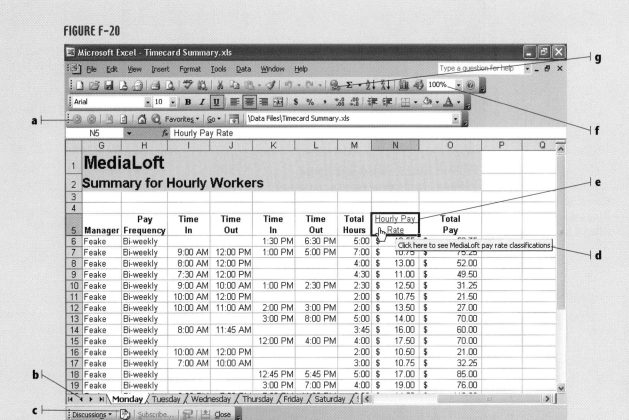

1. Which element points to a ScreenTip for a hyperlink?
2. Which element points to the Zoom box?
3. Which element points to a hyperlink?
4. Which element points to the Back button of the Web toolbar?
5. Which element do you click to insert a hyperlink into a worksheet?
6. Which element do you right-click to get a menu of the worksheets?
7. Which element do you click to insert a comment that can be viewed by others on the Web?

Match each term with the statement that best describes it.

8. Dashed line
9. Hyperlink
10. 3-D reference
11. 🖼
12. 🔧

a. Inserts a picture into header or footer
b. A navigational tool for use between worksheets or workbooks
c. Indicates a page break
d. Formats a picture in a header or footer
e. Uses values from different worksheets or workbooks

Select the best answer from the list of choices.

13. You can save frequently used display and print settings by using the _____ feature.
    a. HTML
    b. Custom Views
    c. View menu
    d. Save command

14. You can group several workbooks in a _____ so they can be opened together rather than individually.
    a. Workgroup
    b. Consolidated workbook
    c. Workspace
    d. Work unit

15. You can specify data formats in the Find and Replace dialog box by clicking the _____ button.
    a. Options
    b. Format
    c. Data
    d. Tools

16. You can group worksheets by pressing and holding _____ while clicking the sheet tabs that you want to group.
    a. [Alt]
    b. [Spacebar]
    c. [Ctrl]
    d. [F6]

▼ SKILLS REVIEW

1. **Freeze columns and rows.**
   a. Start Excel, open the Data File EX F-2.xls from the drive and folder where your Data Files are stored, then save it as San Francisco Budget.
   b. Activate the 2005 sheet if necessary, then freeze columns A and B and rows 1 through 3 for improved viewing. (*Hint*: Click cell C4 prior to issuing the Freeze Panes command.)
   c. Scroll until columns A and B and F through H are visible.
   d. Press [Ctrl][Home] to return to cell C4.
   e. Unfreeze the panes.
   f. Split the 2005 sheet into two horizontal panes. (*Hint*: Drag the Horizontal split box.) Remove the split by double-clicking over the split, then save your work.

2. **Insert and delete worksheets.**
   a. With the 2005 sheet active, use the sheet shortcut menu to insert a new sheet to its left.
   b. Delete the 2004 sheet, rename the new sheet 2007, and position it to the right of the 2006 sheet.
   c. Add a custom footer to the 2005 sheet with your name on the left side and the page number on the right side.
   d. Add a custom header with the worksheet name on the left side.
   e. Save and preview the 2005 sheet, compare your results to Figure F-21, then print it.

3. **Consolidate data with 3-D references.**
   a. In cell C22, enter a reference to cell G7.
   b. In cell C23, enter a reference to cell G18.
   c. Activate the 2006 worksheet.
   d. In cell C4, enter a reference to cell C4 on the 2005 worksheet.
   e. In the 2006 worksheet, copy the contents of cell C4 into cells C5:C6.
   f. Preview the 2006 worksheet, then use the Setup button to add your name to the left side of the footer.
   g. Print the 2006 worksheet, then save your work.

FIGURE F-21

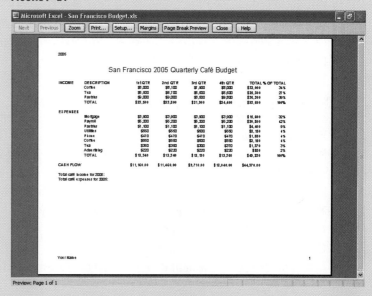

4. Hide and protect worksheet areas.

    a. On the 2005 sheet, unlock the expense data in the range C10:F17.

    b. On the 2005 sheet, hide the percent of total formulas in the range H4:H18 and the cash flow formulas in the range C20:G20.

    c. Protect the sheet without using a password.

    d. To make sure the other cells are locked, attempt to make an entry in cell D4. You should see the error message displayed in Figure F-22.

FIGURE F-22

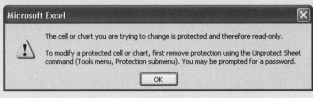

    e. Change the first quarter mortgage expense to $4000.

    f. Verify the formulas in column H and row 20 are hidden.

    g. Unprotect the worksheet.

    h. Save the workbook.

5. Save custom views of a worksheet.

    a. Set the zoom on the 2005 worksheet to fit the worksheet data to the screen.

    b. Make this a new view called Entire 2005 Budget.

    c. Use the Zoom box to change the magnification percentage of the worksheet to 200%. Save the worksheet at 200% as a new view called **200**.

    d. Use the Custom Views dialog box to delete the 200 view.

    e. Use the Custom Views dialog box to return to Generic view.

    f. Save the workbook.

6. Control page breaks and page numbering.

    a. Insert a page break above cell A9.

    b. Save the view as Halves.

    c. View the worksheet in Page Break Preview and modify the page break so it occurs after row ten. (*Hint*: Drag the page break line.)

    d. Return to the Halves view.

    e. Save the workbook.

7. Create a hyperlink between Excel files.

    a. On the 2005 worksheet, make cell A9 a hyperlink to the file Expense Details.xls.

    b. Test the link, then print the Expense Details worksheet.

    c. Edit the hyperlink in cell A9, adding a ScreenTip that reads Expense Assumptions.

    d. On the 2006 worksheet, enter the text Based on 2005 budget in cell A2.

    e. Make the text in cell A2 a hyperlink to cell A1 in the 2005 worksheet. (*Hint*: Use the Place in This Document button and note the cell reference in the Type the cell reference text box.)

    f. Test the hyperlink.

    g. Save the workbook and protect it with the password pass. (*Hint*: Use lowercase letters for the password.)

    h. Close and reopen the workbook to test the password. (*Hint*: If you cannot open the workbook, check that you are using lowercase letters.)

    i. Remove the password and save the workbook again.

8. Save an Excel file as a Web page.

    a. If you have access to a Web discussion server, attach a discussion comment to the 2005 worksheet with your name and the date you reviewed the budget. (If you don't have access to a discussion server, proceed to Step b.)

    b. Save the entire budget workbook as a Web page in MHT format with a title that reads Our Budget and the file named sfbudget.

    c. Preview the Web page in your browser. If your browser doesn't open automatically, check your taskbar.

    d. Test the worksheet tabs in the browser to make sure they work.

    e. Print the 2005 worksheet from your browser.

    f. Close your browser.

    g. Return to Excel, close the .mht document and the Expense Details.xls workbook, then exit Excel.

▼ INDEPENDENT CHALLENGE 1

As a new employee at SoftSales, a computer software retailer, you are responsible for tracking the sales of different product lines and determining which computer operating system generates the most software sales each month. Although sales figures vary from month to month, the format in which data is entered does not. You decide to create a worksheet tracking sales across platforms by month. Use a separate worksheet for each month and create data for three months. Use your own data for the number of software packages sold in the Windows and Macintosh columns for each product.

a. Start Excel, create a new workbook, then save it as **Software Sales Summary.xls** in the drive and folder where your Data Files are stored.

b. Add a fourth sheet by clicking Insert on the menu bar, then clicking Worksheet.

c. Drag the fourth sheet to the right of Sheet3.

d. Group the worksheets by clicking Sheet1, then press and hold [Shift] while clicking Sheet4.

e. With the worksheets grouped, use Table F-3 as a guide to enter the row and column labels that need to appear on each of the four sheets.

f. Rename Sheet1 to **January** by right-clicking the sheet name and entering the new name. Rename Sheet2 to **February**, Sheet3 to **March**, and Sheet4 to **Summary**.

g. Enter your own data, and formulas for the totals in the January, February, and March sheets.

h. Use the AutoSum function on the Summary sheet to total the information in all three monthly sheets.

i. Hide the Summary worksheet. (*Hint*: Select the Sheet command on the Format menu and choose Hide.)

j. Unhide the Summary worksheet. (*Hint*: Select the Sheet command on the Format menu and choose Unhide, then click OK.)

TABLE F-3

	Windows	Macintosh	Total
Games Software			
Combat Flight Simulator			
Safari			
NASCAR Racing			
Total			
Business Software			
Word Processing			
Spreadsheet			
Presentation			
Graphics			
Page Layout			
Total			
Utilities Products			
Antivirus			
File Recovery			
Total			

k. Group the worksheets again by clicking the January sheet then pressing and holding [Shift] while clicking the Summary sheet. Add headers to all four worksheets that include your name on the left, the sheet name in the center, and the date on the right.

l. Format the worksheet appropriately.

m. Save the workbook, preview and print the four worksheets, then exit Excel.

▼ INDEPENDENT CHALLENGE 2

You own PC Assist, a software training company located in Montreal, Canada. You have added several new entries to the August check register and are ready to enter September's check activity. Because the sheet for August includes much of the same information you need for September, you decide to copy it. Then you edit the new sheet to fit your needs for the September check activity. You use sheet referencing to enter the beginning balance and beginning check number. Using your own data, you complete five checks for the September register.

a. Start Excel, open the file EX F-3.xls from the drive and folder where your Data Files are stored, then save it as **Update to Check Register**. The expense amounts in the worksheet includes all taxes.

b. Delete Sheet2 and Sheet3, then create a worksheet for September by copying the August sheet and renaming it. If necessary, move the September sheet before the August sheet.

c. With the September sheet active, delete the data in the range A6:E24.

d. To update the balance at the beginning of the month, use sheet referencing from the last balance entry in the August sheet.

e. Generate the first check number. (*Hint*: Use a formula that references the last check number in August and adds one.)

f. Enter data for five checks using September 2006 dates. For the check number, use the number above it and add 1. Delete the balances in the range F11:F24.

g. Use the Find and Replace dialog box to change the beginning balance for August from **22000** to **27000**, formatted as a number with two decimal places. (*Hint*: The Options >> button allows you to change the data format.)

Advanced Challenge Exercise

■ Add a new worksheet to the workbook and name it **Statistics**.

■ Enter labels for August and September statistics into the Statistics worksheet using the table below as a guide.

August Statistics	
Number of Checks	
Average Check Amount	
Number of Classroom Expenses	
September Statistics	
Number of Checks	
Average Check Amount	
Number of Classroom Expenses	

■ Use 3-D references and the appropriate statistical functions to enter the number of checks, average check amount, and the number of classroom expenses for the months of August and September. (*Hint*: Use the Insert Function dialog box to enter the COUNT function for the number of checks, the AVERAGE function for the check averages, and the COUNTIF function with the criteria Classroom for the number of classroom expenses.)

■ Format the statistical information appropriately, add your name to the statistics worksheet footer, save the workbook, preview the worksheet, then print it in landscape orientation on a single page.

h. Add your name to the September sheet footer. Save the workbook, then preview and print the September worksheet. Close the workbook and exit Excel.

▼ INDEPENDENT CHALLENGE 3

You have decided to create a spreadsheet to track the long-distance phone calls made by you and your two roommates each month. You create a workbook with a separate sheet for each person and track the following information for each long-distance call: date of call, time of call, call minutes, city called, state called, area code, phone number, and call charge. Then you total the charges for each person and create a summary sheet of all three roommates' charges for the month. You are not sure what programs your roommates will be using to view the information so you also save the summary information in a text format.

a. Start Excel, create a new workbook, then save it as Monthly Long Distance in the drive and folder where your Data Files are stored.

b. Create a sheet for the first roommate. Enter column headings to track each call, then create two copies of the sheet and label the tabs.

c. Use your own data, entering at least three long-distance calls for each roommate.

d. Group the worksheets and create totals for minutes and charges on each roommate's sheet.

e. Create a summary sheet that shows each name and uses cell references to display the total minutes and total charges for each person.

f. On the summary sheet, create a hyperlink from each person's name to cell A1 of their respective worksheet. Enter your name on all worksheet footers, save the workbook, then print the four worksheets.

g. Create a workbook with the same type of information for the two people in the apartment next door. Save it as **Next Door.xls**. Enter your name on all worksheet footers, save the workbook, then print the three worksheets.

h. Arrange the two open workbooks in a tiled display on your screen. (*Hint*: Select the Arrange option on the Window menu.)

▼ INDEPENDENT CHALLENGE 3 (CONTINUED)

i. Use linking to create a 3-D reference that displays the neighbors' totals on your summary sheet so your roommates can compare their expenses with the neighbors'.

j. Create a workspace that includes the workbooks Monthly Long Distance and Next Door in the tiled layout. Name the workspace **Phonebill.xlw**. (*Hint*: Save Workspace is an option on the File menu.)

k. Hide the Next Door.xls workbook. (*Hint*: Hide is an option on the Window menu.)

l. Unhide the Next Door.xls workbook. (*Hint*: Unhide is an option on the Window menu.)

m. Change the workbook properties of the Next Door.xls workbook to Read-only.

n. Save the Summary sheet as a text file named Monthly Long Distance.txt. (*Hint*: Use the Save As command on the File menu.)

o. Close any open files and exit Excel.

▼ INDEPENDENT CHALLENGE 4

The creative director at WebProductions, a Web design company, is considering purchasing digital cameras for the New York and Montreal offices. You have been asked to research this purchase by comparing features and current prices in U.S. and Canadian currencies. You investigate online vendors and prepare a worksheet containing the following information about each camera: Manufacturer, Model, Zoom Lens Magnification, Megapixel Rating, Max Resolution, and Price in both U.S. and Canadian currencies. Your worksheet information will be protected but, because currency rates flucuate, the Canadian prices are unlocked. You use an online currency converter to calculate the price information in Canadian currency.

a. Find features and pricing (in U.S. dollars) for five digital cameras using the search engine of your choice. Also, search for a currency converter site, then convert the U.S. prices you found from the online vendors into Canadian currency.

b. Start Excel, create a new workbook, then save it as **Camera Research** in the drive and folder where your Data Files are stored, then enter the column headings shown in the table below.

Manufacturer	Model	Zoom Lens Magnification	Megapixel Rating	Max Resolution	Price $USD	Price $CAD

c. Enter the information you found on the Web into the worksheet. Some of the entries may include ranges of values.

d. Enter the information from the table into your Camera Research workbook. Name the worksheet **Online Vendors.**

e. Add a custom header that displays the sheet name centered on the printout.

f. Add a custom footer that includes your name on the left side of the printout.

g. Make the cells in the Manufacturer column hyperlinks to the manufacturer's Web site.

h. Use the Research task pane and the English (U.S. or Canada) thesaurus to find a synonym for **manufacturer**. Use the insert option in the Research task pane to replace the Manufacturer label in your worksheet with one of the listed synonyms.

i. Unlock the price information in the Canadian price column. Protect the worksheet without using a password. Save the workbook.

j. Save the workbook with the name **camera** in MHTML format for management's use and preview it in your Web browser.

k. Print the worksheet from your browser.

l. Exit your browser and return to the workbook in MHTML format.

Advanced Challenge Exercise

- Unprotect the worksheet, insert the company name, **WebProductions**, in cell A10 and create an e-mail link to it using your e-mail address.
- Insert a subject of **Digital Cameras** in the subject area.
- Add a ScreenTip of **Contact Us**.
- Preview the worksheet, then print it in landscape orientation on one page.

m. Close the workbook and exit Excel.

Excel 2003

▼ VISUAL WORKSHOP

Create the worksheet shown in Figure F-23, then save it as **Martinez**. Enter your name in the footer, save the workbook and print the worksheet. Save the workbook as a Single File Web page (MHTML) using the name **martinez**. Preview the worksheet in your Web browser, then print the sheet from the browser. Notice that the text in cell A1 is a hyperlink to the Our History worksheet; the graphic is from the Clip Gallery. If you don't have this graphic, substitute a graphic of your choice.

FIGURE F-23

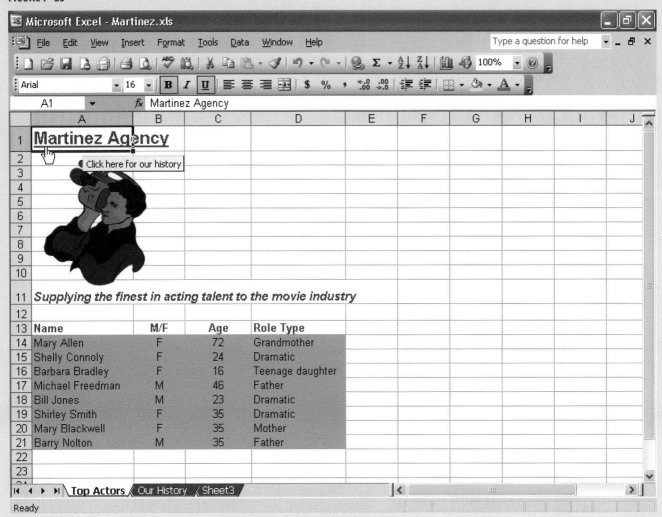

Automating Worksheet Tasks

OBJECTIVES

Plan a macro

Record a macro

Run a macro

Edit a macro

Use shortcut keys with macros

Use the Personal Macro Workbook

Add a macro as a menu item

Create a toolbar for macros

If you have a SAM user profile, you may have access to hands-on instruction, practice, and assessment of the skills covered in this unit. Log in to your SAM account and go to your assignments page to see what your instructor has assigned.

A **macro** is a set of instructions that performs tasks in the order you specify. You create macros to automate frequently performed Excel tasks. For example, if you usually enter your name and date in a worksheet footer, you can record the keystrokes in an Excel macro that enters the text and inserts the current date automatically when you run the macro. In this unit, you will plan and design a simple macro, then record and run it. Then you will edit the macro and explore ways to make it more easily available as you work. Jim Fernandez, the office manager for MediaLoft, wants you to create a macro for the Accounting Department. The macro needs to automatically insert text that identifies the worksheet as an Accounting Department document.

Planning a Macro

You create macros for tasks that you perform frequently. For example, you can create a macro to enter and format text or to save and print a worksheet. To create a macro, you record the series of actions or write the instructions in a special programming language. Because the sequence of actions is important, you need to plan the macro carefully before you record it. ▰▰▰▰▰ Jim wants you to create a macro for the Accounting Department that inserts the text "Accounting Department" in the upper-left corner of any worksheet. You work with him to plan the macro using the following guidelines:

DETAILS

- **Assign the macro a descriptive name.**

  The first character of a macro name must be a letter; the remaining characters can be letters, numbers, or underscores. Spaces are not allowed in macro names; use underscores in place of spaces. (Press [Shift][–] to enter an underscore character.) Jim wants you to name the macro "DeptStamp." See Table G-1 for a list of macros Jim might create to automate other tasks.

- **Write out the steps the macro will perform.**

  This planning helps eliminate careless errors. Jim writes a description of the macro he wants, as shown in Figure G-1.

- **Decide how you will perform the actions you want to record.**

  You can use the mouse, the keyboard, or a combination of the two. Jim wants you to use both the mouse and the keyboard.

- **Practice the steps you want Excel to record, and write them down.**

  Jim has written down the sequence of actions he wants you to include in the macro.

- **Decide where to store the description of the macro and the macro itself.**

  Macros can be stored in an active workbook, in a new workbook, or in the Personal Macro Workbook, a special workbook used only for macro storage. Jim asks you to store the macro in a new workbook.

TABLE G-1: Possible macros and their descriptive names

description of macro	descriptive name
Enter a frequently used proper name, such as Jim Fernandez	JimFernandez
Enter a frequently used company name, such as MediaLoft	Company_Name
Print the active worksheet on a single page, in landscape orientation	FitToLand
Add a footer to a worksheet	FooterStamp
Show a generic view of a worksheet using the default print and display settings	GenericView

Macro to create stamp with the department name

Name:	DeptStamp
Description:	Adds a stamp to the top left of the worksheet, identifying it as an Accounting Department worksheet
Steps:	1. Position the cell pointer in cell A1.
	2. Type Accounting Department, then click the Enter button.
	3. Click Format on the menu bar, then click Cells.
	4. Click the Font tab, under Font style, click Bold, under Underline, click Single, and under Color, click Red, then click OK.

Clues to Use

Macros and viruses

When you open an Excel workbook that has macros, you may see a message asking you if you want to enable or disable them. If you know your workbook came from a trusted source, click Enable macros. If you are not sure of the workbook's source, click Disable macros, because a macro may contain a **virus**, a destructive software program that can damage your computer files. If you disable the macros in a workbook, you will not be able to use them. For more information about macro security and security levels, type "About macro security" in the Type a question for help text box.

Recording a Macro

The easiest way to create a macro is to record it using the Excel Macro Recorder. You turn the Macro Recorder on, name the macro, enter the keystrokes and select the commands you want the macro to perform, then stop the recorder. As you record the macro, Excel automatically translates each action into program code you can later view and modify. You can take as long as you want to record the macro; a recorded macro contains only your actions, not the amount of time you took to record it. ▓▓▓▓▓ Jim wants you to create a macro that enters a department "stamp" in cell A1 of the active worksheet. You create this macro by recording your actions.

STEPS

1. **Start Excel, save the new blank workbook as My Excel Macros in the drive and folder where your Data Files are stored**

   You are ready to start recording the macro.

2. **Click Tools on the menu bar, point to Macro, then click Record New Macro**

   The Record Macro dialog box opens. See Figure G-2. The default name Macro1 is selected. You can either assign this name or enter a new name. This dialog box also lets you assign a shortcut key for running the macro and assign a storage location for the macro.

3. **Type DeptStamp in the Macro name text box**

4. **If the Store macro in list box does not display This Workbook, click the list arrow and select This Workbook**

TROUBLE

If the Stop Recording toolbar is not displayed, click View, point to Toolbars, then click Stop Recording.

5. **If the Description text box does not contain your name, select the existing name, type your own name, then click OK**

   The dialog box closes. A small Stop Recording toolbar appears containing the Stop Recording button 🔲, and the word "Recording" appears on the status bar. Take your time performing the steps below. Excel records every keystroke, menu selection, and mouse action that you make.

6. **Press [Ctrl][Home]**

   When you begin an Excel session, macros record absolute cell references. By beginning the recording in cell A1, you ensure that the macro includes the instruction to select cell A1 as the first step, in cases where A1 is not already selected.

7. **Type Accounting Department in cell A1, then click the Enter button 🟩 on the formula bar**

8. **Click Format on the menu bar, then click Cells**

TROUBLE

If your results differ from Figure G-4, clear the contents of cell A1, then slowly and carefully repeat Steps 2 through 10. When prompted to replace the existing macro at the end of Step 5, click Yes.

9. **Click the Font tab, in the Font style list box click Bold, click the Underline list arrow and click Single, then click the Color list arrow and click the red color (third row, first color on the left)**

   See Figure G-3.

10. **Click OK, click 🔲 on the Stop Recording toolbar, click cell D1 to deselect cell A1, then save the workbook**

    Compare your results with Figure G-4.

FIGURE G-2: Record Macro dialog box

Type macro name here

Reflects the computer user's name and the system date

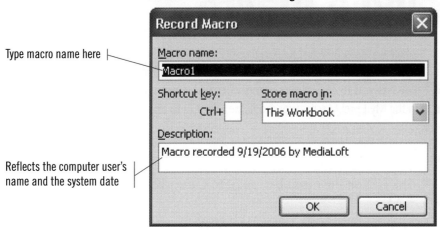

FIGURE G-3: Font tab of the Format Cells dialog box

Stop recording toolbar

Macro will apply these formatting attributes to the text

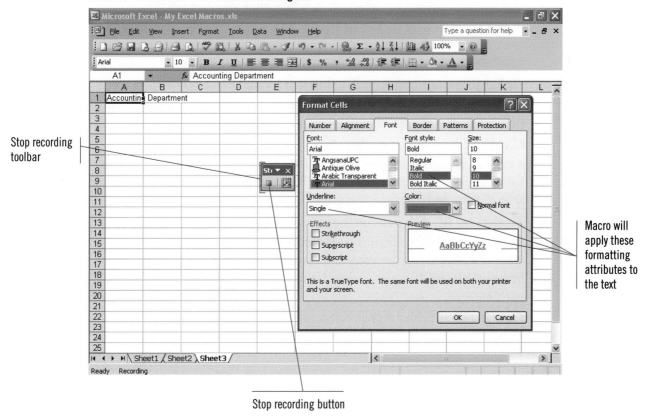

Stop recording button

FIGURE G-4: Accounting Department stamp

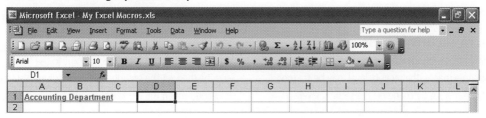

Running a Macro

Once you record a macro, you should test it to make sure that the actions it performs are correct. To test a macro, you **run,** or play, it. One way to run a macro is to select the macro in the Macros dialog box, then click Run. Jim asks you to clear the contents of cell A1 and then test the DeptStamp macro. After you run the macro in the My Excel Macros workbook, he asks you to test the macro once more from a newly opened workbook.

STEPS

1. **Click cell A1, click Edit on the menu bar, point to Clear, click All, then click any other cell to deselect cell A1**

   When you delete only the contents of a cell, any formatting still remains in the cell. By using the Clear All option on the Edit menu, you can be sure that the cell is free of contents and formatting.

> **QUICK TIP**
>
> To delete a macro, select the macro name in the Macro dialog box, click Delete, then click Yes to confirm the action.

2. **Click Tools on the menu bar, point to Macro, then click Macros**

   The Macro dialog box, shown in Figure G-5, lists all the macros contained in the open workbooks. If other people have used your computer, other macros may be listed.

3. **Make sure DeptStamp is selected, click Run, then deselect cell A1**

   Watch your screen as the macro quickly plays back the steps you recorded in the previous lesson. When the macro is finished, your screen should look like Figure G-6. As long as the workbook containing the macro remains open, you can run the macro in any open workbook.

> **QUICK TIP**
>
> To stop a macro while it is running, press [Esc] then click End.

4. **Click the New button 🗋 on the Standard toolbar**

   Because the new workbook automatically fills the screen, it is difficult to be sure that the My Excel Macros.xls workbook is still open.

5. **Click Window on the menu bar**

   A list of open workbooks appears underneath the menu options. The active workbook name (in this case, Book2) appears with a check mark to its left. The My Excel Macros.xls workbook appears on the menu, so you know it's open. See Figure G-7.

6. **Deselect cell A1, click Tools on the menu bar, point to Macro, click Macros, make sure 'My Excel Macros.xls'!DeptStamp is selected, click Run, then deselect cell A1**

   When multiple workbooks are open, the macro name in the Macro dialog box includes the workbook name between single quotation marks, followed by an exclamation point, indicating that the macro is outside the active workbook. Because you only used this workbook to test the macro, you don't need to save it.

7. **Close Book2.xls without saving changes**

   The My Excel Macros.xls workbook reappears.

Clues to Use

Setting macro security levels

If you get a security error message when attempting to open a workbook containing a macro, the security level may be set too high. You can enable macros by changing the security level for workbooks. Click the Tools menu, point to the Macro option, click Security, then set the security level to Medium. You must save, then close and reopen the workbook to activate the new security level.

FIGURE G-5: Macro dialog box

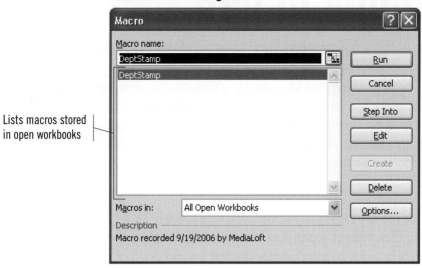

Lists macros stored in open workbooks

FIGURE G-6: Result of running DeptStamp macro

DeptStamp macro inserts formatted text in cell A1

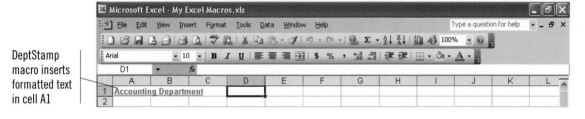

FIGURE G-7: Window menu listing open workbooks

Check mark indicates active workbook

Indicates this workbook is still open

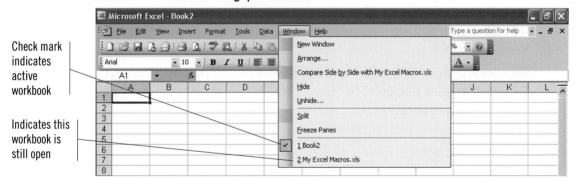

Clues to Use

Adding a digital signature to a macro

If the macro security level in Excel is set to High, only macros that are digitally signed from trusted sources can run. To sign a macro with a trusted digital signature, you need a valid certificate issued by a certificate authority. To digitally sign a macro with a certificate you have obtained, make sure the workbook containing it is open, then click the Tools menu, point to Macro, click Visual Basic Editor, select the macro in the module you want to sign in the Project Explorer (it will be in Module 1 unless you named the module), click the Tools menu, click Digital Signature, click Choose, select the certificate, then click OK twice.

Editing a Macro

When you use the Macro Recorder to create a macro, the program instructions, called **program code**, are recorded automatically in the **Visual Basic for Applications (VBA)** programming language. Each macro is stored as a **module**, or program code container, attached to the workbook. After you record a macro, you might need to change it. If you have a lot of changes to make, it might be best to rerecord the macro. But if you need to make only minor adjustments, you can edit the macro code directly using the **Visual Basic Editor**, a program that lets you display and edit your macro code. ▓▓▓▓ Jim wants you to modify his macro to change the point size of the department stamp to 14.

STEPS

TROUBLE
If the Properties window does not appear, click the Properties Window button 🔲 on the Visual Basic Editor toolbar.

1. **Make sure the My Excel Macros.xls workbook is open, click** Tools **on the menu bar, point to** Macro, **click** Macros, **make sure** DeptStamp **is selected, then click** Edit
   The Visual Basic Editor starts, showing the DeptStamp macro steps in a numbered module window (in this case, Module1).

2. **If necessary, maximize the window titled** My Excel Macros.xls – [Module1(Code)], **then examine the steps in the macro, comparing your screen to Figure G-8**
   The name of the macro and the date it was recorded appear at the top of the module window. Below that, Excel has translated your keystrokes and commands into macro code. When you open and make selections in a dialog box during macro recording, Excel automatically stores all the dialog box settings in the macro code. For example, the line .FontStyle = "Bold" was generated when you clicked Bold in the Format Cells dialog box. You also see lines of code that you didn't generate directly while recording the DeptStamp macro; for example, .Name = "Arial".

3. **In the line .Size = 10, double-click** 10 **to select it, then type** 14
   Because Module1 is attached to the workbook and not stored as a separate file, any changes to the module are saved automatically when you save the workbook.

4. **In the Visual Basic Editor, click** File **on the menu bar, click** Print, **click** OK **to print the module, then review the printout**

QUICK TIP
You can return to Excel without closing the module by clicking the View Microsoft Excel button 🔲 on the Visual Basic Editor toolbar.

5. **Click** File **on the menu bar, then click** Close and Return to Microsoft Excel
   You want to rerun the DeptStamp macro to make sure the macro reflects the change you made using the Visual Basic Editor.

6. **Click cell** A1, **click** Edit **on the menu bar, point to** Clear, **click** All, **deselect cell** A1, **click** Tools **on the menu bar, point to** Macro, **click** Macros, **make sure** DeptStamp **is selected, click** Run, **then deselect cell** A1
   Compare your results to Figure G-9. The department stamp is now in 14-point type.

QUICK TIP
Another way to start the Visual Basic Editor is to click Tools on the menu bar, point to Macro, then click Visual Basic Editor, or press [Alt][F11].

7. **Save the workbook**

FIGURE G-8: Visual Basic Editor showing Module1

Project Explorer with open module selected

Properties window showing properties for selected objects

Properties Window button

Comments appear in green preceded by an apostrophe

Code window

Font size line

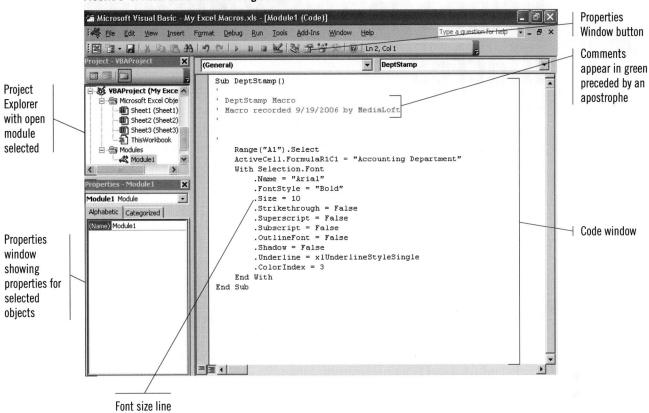

FIGURE G-9: Result of running edited DeptStamp macro

Font size enlarged to 14 point

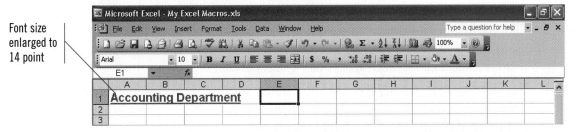

Clues to Use

Adding comments to Visual Basic code

With practice, you will be able to interpret the lines of macro code. Others who use your macro, however, might want to know the function of a particular line. You can explain the code by adding comments to the macro. **Comments** are explanatory text added to the lines of code. When you enter a comment, you must type an apostrophe (') before the comment text. Otherwise, the program tries to interpret it as a command. On the screen, comments appear in green after you press [Enter], as shown in Figure G-8. You also can insert blank lines as comments in the macro code to make the code more readable. To do this, type an apostrophe, then press [Enter].

Using Shortcut Keys with Macros

In addition to running a macro from the Macro dialog box, you can run a macro by using a shortcut key combination you assign to it. Using shortcut keys reduces the number of actions you need to take to run a macro. You assign shortcut key combinations in the Record Macro dialog box. ▄▄▄▓▓ Jim also wants you to create a macro called CompanyName to enter the company name into a worksheet. You will assign a shortcut key combination to run the macro.

STEPS

1. **Click cell B2**

    You will record the macro in cell B2. You want the macro to enter the company name anywhere in a worksheet. Therefore, you do not begin the macro with an instruction to position the cell pointer, as you did in the DeptStamp macro.

2. **Click Tools on the menu bar, point to Macro, then click Record New Macro**

    The Record Macro dialog box opens. Notice the option Shortcut key: Ctrl+ followed by a blank box. You can type a letter (A–Z) in the Shortcut key text box to assign the key combination of [Ctrl] plus that letter to run the macro. You use the key combination [Ctrl][Shift] plus a letter to avoid overriding any of the Excel [Ctrl] [letter] shortcut keys, such as [Ctrl][C] for Copy.

3. **With the default macro name selected, type CompanyName, click the Shortcut key text box, press and hold [Shift], type C, then, if necessary, replace the name in the Description box with your name**

    Compare your screen with Figure G-10. You are ready to record the CompanyName macro.

4. **Click OK to close the dialog box**

    By default, Excel records absolute cell references in macros. Beginning the macro in cell B2 causes the macro code to begin with a statement to select cell B2. Because you want to be able to run this macro in any active cell, you need to instruct Excel to record relative cell references while recording the macro.

    <table><tr><td>QUICK TIP</td></tr></table>
    If your Relative Reference button is already selected (pushed in), skip to Step 6.

5. **Click the Relative Reference button 📧 on the Stop Recording toolbar**

    The Relative Reference button is now selected. See Figure G-11. This button is a toggle and retains the relative reference setting until you click it again to turn it off or you exit Excel.

6. **Type MediaLoft in cell B2, click the Enter button ✅ on the formula bar, press [Ctrl][I] to italicize the text, click the Stop Recording button 🔳 on the Stop Recording toolbar, then deselect cell B2**

    MediaLoft appears in italics in cell B2. You are ready to run the macro in cell A5 using the shortcut key combination.

7. **Click cell A5, press and hold [Ctrl][Shift], type C, then deselect the cell**

    The company name appears in cell A5. See Figure G-12. Because the macro played back in the selected cell (A5) instead of the cell where it was recorded (B2), you know that the macro recorded relative cell references.

8. **Save the workbook**

FIGURE G-10: Record Macro dialog box with shortcut key assigned

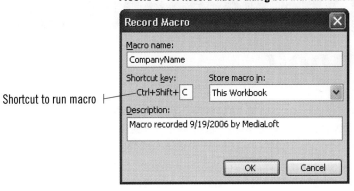

Shortcut to run macro

FIGURE G-11: Stop Recording toolbar with Relative Reference button selected

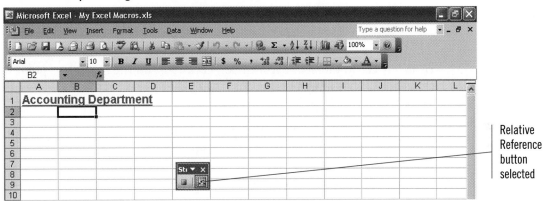

Relative Reference button selected

FIGURE G-12: Result of running the CompanyName macro

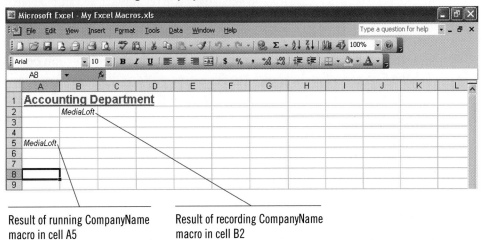

Result of running CompanyName macro in cell A5

Result of recording CompanyName macro in cell B2

Clues to Use

Running a macro from a hotspot on your worksheet

You can create a **hotspot** on your worksheet that runs a macro when you click it. To create a hotspot, first add an AutoShape to the worksheet: click AutoShapes on the Drawing toolbar, point to a shape category, and then click a shape. Drag across a worksheet area to create a shape, then type to add a label to the button, such as "Click to run Name macro." Right-click the button and click Assign Macro on the shortcut menu to choose the macro the button runs.

Using the Personal Macro Workbook

You can store commonly used macros in a **Personal Macro Workbook**. The Personal Macro Workbook is always available, unless you specify otherwise, and gives you access to all the macros it contains, regardless of which workbooks are open. The Personal Macro Workbook file is automatically created the first time you choose to store a macro in it. You can add additional macros to the Personal Macro Workbook by saving them there. By default, the Personal.xls workbook opens each time you start Excel, but you don't see it because Excel designates it as a hidden file. Jim often likes to add a footer to his worksheets identifying his department, the workbook name, the worksheet name, his name, and the current date. He wants you to create a macro that automatically inserts this footer. Because he wants to use this macro in future worksheets, he asks you to store this macro in the Personal Macro Workbook.

STEPS

1. **From any cell in the active worksheet, click** Tools **on the menu bar, point to** Macro, **then click** Record New Macro

   The Record Macro dialog box opens.

2. **Type** FooterStamp **in the Macro name text box, click the** Shortcut key text box, **press and hold** [Shift], **type** F, **then click the** Store macro in list arrow

   You have named the macro FooterStamp and assigned it the shortcut combination [Ctrl][Shift][F]. Notice that This Workbook is selected by default, indicating that Excel automatically stores macros in the active workbook. See Figure G-13. You also can choose to store the macro in a new workbook or in the Personal Macro Workbook.

3. **Click** Personal Macro Workbook, **replace the existing name in the Description text box with your own name, if necessary, then click** OK

   The recorder is on, and you are ready to record the macro keystrokes. If you are prompted to replace an existing macro named FooterStamp, click Yes.

4. **Click** File **on the menu bar, click** Page Setup, **click the** Header/Footer tab **(make sure to do this even if it is already active), click** Custom Footer, **in the Left section box, type** Accounting; **click the** Center section box, **click the** File Name button 🖺, **press** [Spacebar], **type** /, **press** [Spacebar], **click the** Tab Name button 🖼 **to insert the sheet name; click the** Right section box, **type your name followed by a comma, press** [Spacebar], **click the** Date button 🖬, **then click** OK **to return to the Header/Footer tab**

   The footer stamp is set up, as shown in Figure G-14.

5. **Click** OK **to return to the worksheet, then click the** Stop Recording button 🔲 **on the Stop Recording toolbar**

   You want to ensure that the macro can set the footer stamp in any active worksheet.

6. **Activate Sheet2, in cell A1 type** FooterStamp macro test, **press** [Enter], **press and hold** [Ctrl][Shift], **then type** F

   The FooterStamp macro plays back the sequence of commands.

7. **Preview the worksheet to verify that the new footer is inserted, then close the Preview window**

8. **Save the workbook, then print the worksheet**

QUICK TIP

If you see a message saying that the Personal Macro Workbook needs to be opened, open it, then begin again from Step 1. The Personal Macro Workbook file is usually stored in the Documents and Settings\ *username*\ Application Data\ Microsoft\Excel\ XLSTART folder under the name "PERSONAL.XLS" and opens when you open Excel.

FIGURE G-13: Record Macro dialog box showing macro storage options

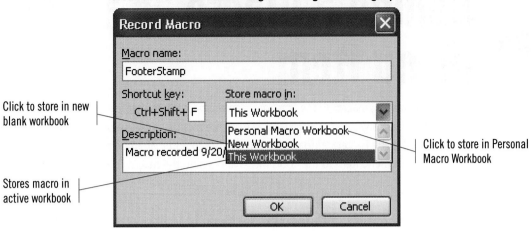

Click to store in new blank workbook

Click to store in Personal Macro Workbook

Stores macro in active workbook

FIGURE G-14: Header/Footer tab showing custom footer settings

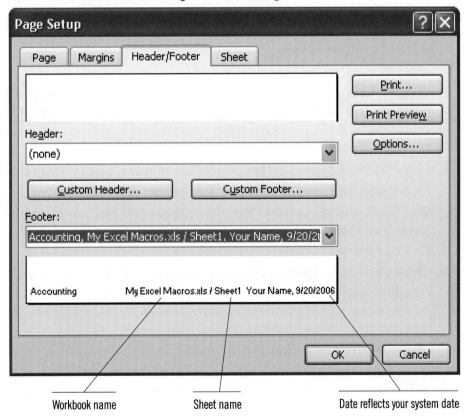

Workbook name

Sheet name

Date reflects your system date

Clues to Use

Working with the Personal Macro Workbook

Once you use the Personal Macro Workbook, it opens automatically each time you start Excel so you can add macros to it. By default, the Personal Macro Workbook is hidden as a precautionary measure so you don't accidentally delete anything from it. If you need to delete a macro from the Personal Macro Workbook, click Unhide on the Window menu, click PERSONAL.XLS, then click OK. To hide the Personal Macro Workbook, click Hide on the Window menu when the workbook is active.

Adding a Macro as a Menu Item

In addition to storing macros in the Personal Macro Workbook so that they are always available, you can add macros as items on any Excel menu available from the menu bar, just under the title bar. To increase the availability of the FooterStamp macro, Jim decides to add it as an item on the Tools menu. He wants you to add a custom menu item to the Tools menu and assign the macro to that menu item.

1. **With Sheet2 active, click** Tools **on the menu bar, click** Customize, **click the** Commands tab, **then under Categories, click** Macros

   See Figure G-15.

You may need to reposition the Customize dialog box to make the Tools option on the Worksheet menu bar visible.

2. **Click** Custom Menu Item **under Commands, drag the selection over** Tools **on the menu bar (the menu opens), then point just under the last menu option, but do not release the mouse button**

   Compare your screen to Figure G-16.

3. **Release the mouse button**

   Now, Custom Menu Item is the last item on the Tools menu.

4. **With the Tools menu still open, right-click** Custom Menu Item, **select the text in the Name box (&Custom Menu Item), type** Footer Stamp, **then click** Assign Macro

   Unlike a macro name, the name of a custom menu item can have spaces between words like all standard menu items. The Assign Macro dialog box opens.

5. **Click** PERSONAL.XLS!FooterStamp **under Macro name, click** OK, **then click** Close

   You have assigned the FooterStamp macro to the new menu command.

6. **Click the** Sheet3 tab, **in cell A1 type** macro menu item test, **press** [Enter], **then click** Tools **on the menu bar**

   The Tools menu appears with the new menu option at the bottom. See Figure G-17.

7. **Click** Footer Stamp, **preview the worksheet to verify that the footer was inserted, then close the Print Preview window**

   The Print Preview window appears with the footer stamp. Because others using your computer might be confused by the macro on the menu, it's a good idea to remove it.

8. **Click** Tools **on the menu bar, click** Customize, **click the** Toolbars tab, **click** Worksheet Menu Bar **to highlight it, click** Reset, **click** OK **to confirm, click** Close, **click** Tools **on the menu bar to make sure that the custom item has been deleted, then save the workbook**

Clues to Use

Adding a custom menu

You can create a custom menu on an existing toolbar and assign macros to it. To do this, click Tools on the menu bar, click Customize, click the Commands tab, click New Menu in the Categories list, then drag the New Menu from the Commands box to the toolbar. To name the new menu, right-click, then enter a name in the Name box. You can drag Custom Menu Items from the Commands tab of the Customize dialog box to the menu and then right-click each menu item to assign macros to them.

FIGURE G-15: Commands tab of the Customize dialog box

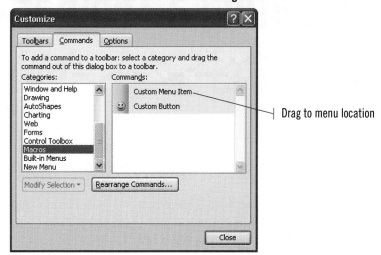

Drag to menu location

FIGURE G-16: Tools menu showing placement of the Custom Menu Item

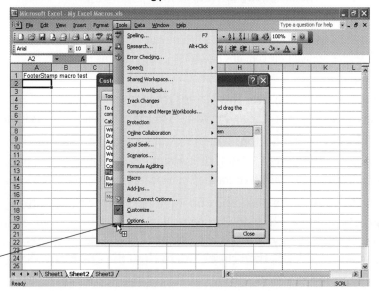

Pointer and line showing location at which to drop menu item

FIGURE G-17: Tools menu with new Footer Stamp item

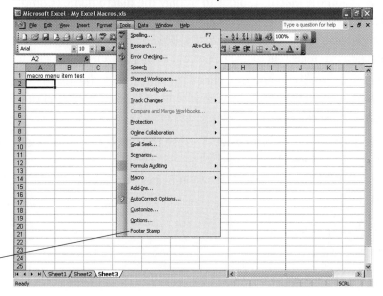

Added menu item

Creating a Toolbar for Macros

Toolbars contain buttons that let you single-click to issue commands you use frequently. You can create your own custom toolbars to organize commands so that you can find and use them quickly. Once you create a toolbar, you can add buttons to it so you can run macros by simply clicking the buttons. ▀▀▄▄▄ Jim asks you to create a custom toolbar called Macros that contains buttons to run two of his macros.

STEPS

1. **With Sheet3 active, click** Tools **on the menu bar, click** Customize, **click the** Toolbars tab, **then click** New

   The New Toolbar dialog box opens, as shown in Figure G-18. Under Toolbar name, a default name of Custom 1 is selected.

2. **Type** Macros, **then click** OK

   Excel adds the new toolbar named Macros to the bottom of the Toolbars list, and a small, empty toolbar named Macros opens. See Figure G-19. You cannot see the entire toolbar name. A new toolbar starts out small and expands to fit the buttons you assign to it.

3. **Click the** Commands tab **in the Customize dialog box, click** Macros **in the Categories list, then drag the** Custom button ☺ **over the new Macros toolbar and release the mouse button**

   The Macros toolbar now contains one button. You want the toolbar to contain two macros, so you need to add one more button.

4. **Drag the** ☺ **button over the Macros toolbar again**

   With the two buttons in place, you are ready to customize the buttons and assign macros to them.

5. **Right-click the left button** ☺ **on the Macros toolbar, select** &Custom Button **in the Name box, type** Department Stamp, **click** Assign Macro, **click** DeptStamp, **then click** OK

   With the first toolbar button customized, you are ready to customize the second button.

6. **With the Customize dialog box open, right-click the right button** ☺ **on the Macros toolbar, edit the name to read** Company Name, **click** Change Button Image, **click the** 🛉 **image (seventh row, first column), right-click** 🛉, **click** Assign Macro, **click** CompanyName **to select it, click** OK, **then click** Close **to close the Customize dialog box**

   The Macros toolbar appears with the two customized macro buttons.

7. **Move the mouse pointer over** ☺ **on the Macros toolbar to display the macro name (Department Stamp), then click to run the macro, click** cell B2, **move the mouse pointer over** 🛉 **on the Macros toolbar to display the macro name (Company Name), click to run that macro, then deselect the cell**

   Compare your screen with Figure G-20. The DeptStamp macro automatically replaces the contents of cell A1. Because others using your computer might be confused by the new toolbar, it's a good idea to remove it.

8. **Click** Tools **on the menu bar, click** Customize, **click the** Toolbars tab **if necessary, in the Toolbars window click** Macros **to highlight it, click** Delete, **click** OK **to confirm the deletion, then click** Close

9. **Save the workbook, print Sheet3, close the workbook, save changes to the Personal Macro Workbook if prompted, then exit Excel**

   The completed figure for Sheet1 is shown in Figure G-12.

FIGURE G-18: New Toolbar dialog box

Type toolbar name here

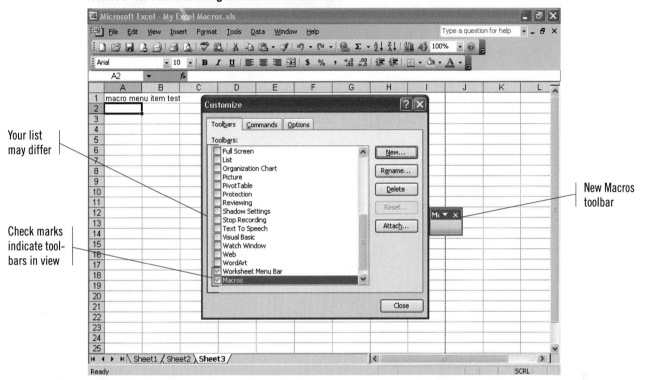

FIGURE G-19: Customize dialog box with new Macros toolbar

Your list may differ

Check marks indicate toolbars in view

New Macros toolbar

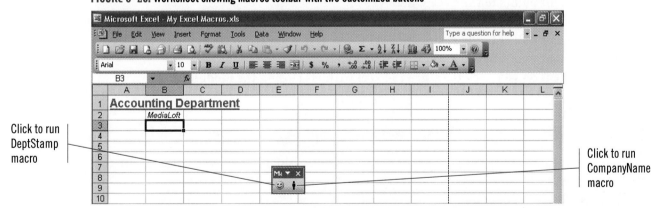

FIGURE G-20: Worksheet showing Macros toolbar with two customized buttons

Click to run DeptStamp macro

Click to run CompanyName macro

Clues to Use

Organizing macros

You can organize your workbooks containing macros by placing them in folders with names that describe the macro tasks. To rename a folder, right-click the folder, click Rename on the shortcut menu, then enter the new name.

Practice

FIGURE G-21

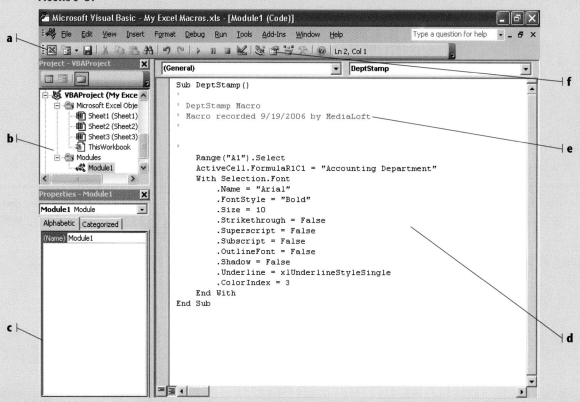

1. Which element points to a comment in the Visual Basic code?
2. Which element points to the Code window?
3. Which element points to the Properties Window button?
4. Which element points to the Project Explorer?
5. Which element points to the Properties window?
6. Which element do you click to return to Excel without closing the module?

Match each term or button with the statement that best describes it.

7. **Visual Basic Editor**
8. **Macro comments**
9. **Personal Macro Workbook**
10. ☺
11. ▦

    a. Used to add a custom button on a macros toolbar code
    b. Used to store commonly used macros
    c. Used to record relative cell references
    d. Used to make changes to macro code
    e. Statements that appear in green explaining the macro

Select the best answer from the list of choices.

12. **Which of the following is the best candidate for a macro?**
    a. One-button or one-keystroke commands.
    b. Nonsequential tasks.
    c. Seldom-used commands or tasks.
    d. Often-used sequences of commands or actions.

13. **You can open the Visual Basic Editor by clicking the _____ button in the Macro dialog box.**
    a. Edit
    b. Visual Basic Editor
    c. Modules
    d. Programs

14. **Commonly used macros should be stored in:**
    a. The Common Macro Workbook.
    b. The Personal Macro Workbook.
    c. The Master Macro Workbook.
    d. The Custom Macro Workbook.

15. **Which of the following is *not* true about editing a macro?**
    a. A macro cannot be edited and must be recorded again.
    b. You edit macros using the Visual Basic Editor.
    c. You can type changes directly in the existing program code.
    d. You can make more than one editing change in a macro.

16. **Why is it important to plan a macro?**
    a. Macros won't be stored if they contain errors.
    b. Macros can't be deleted.
    c. It is impossible to edit a macro.
    d. Planning helps prevent careless errors from being introduced into the macro.

17. **Macros are recorded with relative references:**
    a. Only if relative references are chosen while recording the macro.
    b. In all cases.
    c. Only if the Relative Reference button is selected.
    d. Only if the Absolute Reference button is not selected.

18. **You can run macros:**
    a. From the Macro dialog box.
    b. From shortcut key combinations.
    c. From custom menu commands.
    d. Using all of the above.

19. **To change the security level for workbooks on your computer you must:**
    a. Click Tools, then click Security.
    b. Click Edit, then click Security.
    c. Click Edit, point to Tools, then click Security.
    d. Click Tools, point to Macros, then click Security.

▼ SKILLS REVIEW

1. **Plan a macro.**
   a. You need to plan a macro that enters and formats your name, address, and telephone number in a worksheet.
   b. Write out the steps the macro will perform.
   c. Write out how the macro could be used in a workbook.

2. Record a macro.

   a. Start Excel, open a new workbook, then save it as Macros in the drive and folder where your Data Files are stored. You want to record a macro that enters and formats your name, address, and telephone number in a worksheet.

   b. Name the macro MyAddress, store it in the current workbook, and make sure your name appears as the person who recorded the macro.

   c. Record the macro, entering your name in cell A1, your street address in cell A2, your city, state, and ZIP code in cell A3, and your telephone number in cell A4.

   d. Format the information in 12-point Arial bold.

   e. Resize column A to fit the information entirely in that column.

   f. Add a border and make the text blue.

   g. Stop the recorder and save the workbook.

3. Run a macro.

   a. Clear cell entries and formats in the range affected by the macro.

   b. Check the security level for workbooks on your computer. (*Hint*: Click the Tools menu, point to Macro, then click Security.)

   c. Run the MyAddress macro to place your name and address information in cell A1.

   d. On the worksheet, clear all the cell entries and formats generated by running the MyAddress macro.

   e. Save the workbook.

4. Edit a macro.

   a. Open the MyAddress macro in the Visual Basic Editor.

   b. Locate the line of code that defines the font size, then change the size to 16 point.

   c. Edit an existing comment line to describe this macro's function.

   d. Save and print the module, then use the Close and Return to Microsoft Excel option on the File menu to return to Excel.

   e. Test the macro on Sheet1.

   f. Save the workbook.

5. Use shortcut keys with macros.

   a. Record a macro called NameStamp in the current workbook that enters your full name in italics in the selected cell of a worksheet. (*Hint*: You need to record a relative cell reference).

   b. Assign your macro the shortcut key combination [Ctrl][Shift][N] and store it in the current workbook, using your name as the creator.

   c. After you record the macro, clear the cell containing your name that you used to record the macro.

   d. Use the shortcut key combination to run the MyName macro.

   e. Save the workbook.

6. Use the Personal Macro Workbook.

   a. Using Sheet1, record a new macro called FitToLand and store it in the Personal Macro workbook. The macro should set the print orientation to landscape, with content scaled to fit on one page. If you are prompted to replace the existing FitToLand macro, click Yes.

   b. After you record the macro, activate Sheet2, and enter test data in row 1 that exceeds one page width.

   c. In the Page Setup dialog box, make sure the orientation is set to portrait and the scaling is 100% of normal size.

   d. Run the macro.

   e. Preview Sheet2 and verify that it's in Landscape view and that the test data fits on one page.

   f. Save the workbook.

7. Add a macro as a menu item.

   a. On the Commands tab in the Customize dialog box, specify that you want to use the Macros category to create a Custom Menu Item placing the Custom Menu Item at the bottom of the Tools menu.

   b. Rename the Custom Menu Item Fit to Landscape.

   c. Assign the macro PERSONAL.XLS!FitToLand to the command.

   d. Go to Sheet3 and make sure the orientation is set to portrait and the scaling is 100% of normal size. Enter test data in column A that exceeds one page in length.

   e. Run the Fit to Landscape macro from the Tools menu.

f. Preview the worksheet and verify that it is in landscape view and that the test data fits on one page.

g. Reset the Worksheet Menu bar.

h. Verify that the Fit to Landscape command has been removed from the Tools menu.

i. Save the workbook.

8. Create a toolbar for macros.

a. With the Macros.xls workbook still open, use the Toolbars tab of the Customize dialog box to create a new custom toolbar, titled My Info.

b. Display the Macros category on the Commands tab of the Customize dialog box, then drag the Custom Button to the My Info toolbar.

c. Drag the Custom Button to the My Info toolbar a second time to create another button.

d. Rename the first button My Address, and assign the MyAddress macro to it.

e. Rename the second button My Name, and assign the NameStamp macro to it.

f. Change the second button image to one of your choice.

g. On Sheet3, clear the existing cell data. Test the first macro button on the My Info toolbar. Select cell A7 and test the second macro button on the My Info toolbar.

h. Use the Toolbars tab of the Customize dialog box to delete the toolbar named My Info.

i. Save the workbook, print Sheet3, close the workbook, then exit Excel.

▼ INDEPENDENT CHALLENGE 1

As a computer-support employee of Boston Accounting Solutions, you need to develop ways to help your fellow employees work more efficiently. Employees have asked for Excel macros that can do the following:

- Delete the current row and insert a blank row.
- Delete the current column and insert a blank column.
- Place the department name of Accounting in a 12-point font in red in cell A1 (the width of A1 should be increased if necessary).

a. Plan and write the steps necessary for each macro.

b. Start Excel, save a blank workbook as Excel Utility Macros in the drive and folder where your Data Files are stored.

c. Create a macro for each employee request described above, name them DeleteRow, DeleteColumn, and DepartmentName, then save them in the Excel Utility Macros.xls workbook.

d. Add comment lines to each macro containing your name and describing the function of the macro, then return to Excel.

e. Use the Commands tab of the Customize dialog box to add three Custom Menu items to the Tools menu. Right-click each Custom Menu item to name the new menu items DeleteRow, DeleteColumn, and DepartmentName. Assign the macros you created in Step c to the new menu items.

f. Use the Toolbars tab of the Customize dialog box to create a new toolbar called Helpers.

g. Use the Commands tab of the Customize dialog box to drag three Custom buttons to the Helpers toolbar.

h. Right-click each toolbar button to name them DeleteRow, DeleteColumn, and DepartmentName. Assign the macros created in step c to the new toolbar buttons.

i. Right-click each toolbar button to change the button images.

j. Test each macro by using the Run command, the menu command, and the new toolbar button.

k. Delete the new toolbar, then reset the Worksheet Menu Bar on the toolbars tab of the Customize dialog box.

l. Save the workbook, print the module containing the program code for all three macros, then close the workbook and exit Excel.

▼ INDEPENDENT CHALLENGE 2

You are an analyst in the Atlantic Bank Loan Department. Every quarter, you produce a number of single-page quarterly budget worksheets. Your manager has informed you that certain worksheets need to contain a footer stamp indicating that the worksheet was produced in the loan department. The footer should also show the current page number out of the total number of pages, (for example, 1 of 5) and the workbook filename. It's tedious to add the footer stamp to the numerous worksheets you produce. You want to record a macro to do this.

a. Plan and write the steps to create the macro described above.

b. Start Excel, save a blank workbook as Footer Stamp in the drive and folder where your Data Files are stored.

c. Create the macro using the plan from Step a, name it footerstamp, assign it the shortcut key combination [Ctrl][Shift][H], and store it in the current workbook.

d. Edit the macro to add a descriptive comment line with your name.

e. Add the footerstamp macro to the Tools menu.

f. Create a toolbar titled Stamp, then add a button to the toolbar to run the macro.

g. Enter the text Testing Footer in cell A1. Test the macro using the shortcut key combination, then delete the footer. Test the macro using the menu command on the Tools menu, then delete the footer again. Test the new button on the Stamp toolbar.

h. Delete the new toolbar, then reset the Worksheet Menu Bar.

i. Save the workbook, print the module for the macro, close the module and the workbook, then exit Excel.

j. Create a folder named Macros in the drive and folder where your Data Files are stored then drag a copy of the Footer Stamp.xls file into the Macros folder.

k. Rename the folder Footer Macros.

l. Close the workbook, then exit Excel.

▼ INDEPENDENT CHALLENGE 3

You are an administrative assistant at the Sydney, Australia, branch of Computers Inc. A major part of your job is to create spreadsheets that project sales results in different markets. It seems that you are constantly changing the print settings so that workbooks print in landscape orientation and are scaled to fit on one page. You have decided that it's time to create a macro to streamline this process.

a. Plan and write the steps necessary to create the macro.

b. Start Excel, create a new workbook, then save it as Computers Inc Macro in the drive and folder where your Data Files are stored.

c. Create a macro that changes the page orientation to landscape and scales the worksheet to fit on one page. Name the macro LandFit, assign it the shortcut key combination [Ctrl][Shift][L], and store it in the current workbook.

d. Add the macro to the Tools menu.

e. Go to Sheet2 and enter the text Testing Macro in cell A1 and enter your name in cell A2. Enter test data in column A that exceeds one page in length. Test the macro using the new menu command.

f. Reset the Worksheet Menu Bar and go to Sheet3.

FIGURE G-22

g. Edit the macro to include the company name, Computers Inc, in the center header and add your name as a comment. Use Figure G-22 as a guide. Enter test data in row 1 that exceeds one page in width. Test the macro using the shortcut key combination, making sure the header was added.

h. Add a custom menu to the standard toolbar and name it Macros. Add a custom menu item to the new Macros menu, name the menu option Page Orientation, and assign the LandFit macro to it.

i. On Sheet3, delete the header and change the page orientation to portrait, then test the macro using the new menu.

▼ INDEPENDENT CHALLENGE 3 (CONTINUED)

j. Reset the standard toolbar.

k. Print the module for the macro.

Advanced Challenge Exercise

- Use the Help feature in Excel to research how digital certificates, used to sign a macro, are obtained and copy your findings into Sheet1.
- Use the Help feature to find the difference between class 2 and class 3 digital certificates and copy your findings into Sheet1.
- Use the Help feature to find the steps to digitally sign a file and copy the steps into Sheet1. Print Sheet1.

l. Save and close the workbook, then exit Excel.

▼ INDEPENDENT CHALLENGE 4

PC Assist, a software training company, has decided to begin purchasing its branch office supplies through online vendors. One of the products the company needs to purchase is toner for the Hewlett-Packard LaserJet 3100 printers in the offices. You have been asked to research vendors and prices on the Web. You want to create a workbook to hold office supply vendor information that you can use for various products. You want to add a macro to this workbook to find the lowest price of the product, format the information, and add a descriptive footer to the worksheet.

Using the search engine of your choice, find three online suppliers of toner for the company's printers and note their prices.

a. Start Excel, create a new workbook, then save it as **Office Supplies**.

b. Complete the table below with three online suppliers of office products you found in your search.

c. Enter three vendors and their prices from your table into your worksheet. Enter the Product name **Toner** in the cell next to Office Product.

d. Create a macro named **Toner** in the Office Supplies.xls workbook that can be activated by the [Ctrl][Shift][T] key combination. The macro should do the following:

Office Product	
Vendor	Price
Lowest Price	

- Find the lowest price for the office product and insert it to the right of the Lowest Price label.
- Boldface the Lowest Price text and the cell to its right that will contain the lowest value.
- Place a thick box border around all the information.
- Fill the information area with a light turquoise color.
- Add a footer with the company name **PC Assist** on the left and the workbook name on the right.

e. Clear all the formatting, the footer, and the lowest price from the worksheet.

f. Test the macro using the key combination [Ctrl][Shift][T].

g. Enter your name in cell A15, save your workbook, then print the results of the macro. Open the macro in the Visual Basic Editor, enter your name as a comment, then print the macro code.

Advanced Challenge Exercise

- Return to Excel and create a macro named **Toner_Average** that does the following:
  - Inserts a label **Average Price** under the Lowest Price label.
  - Finds the average toner price, inserts it under the lowest price, and formats it as a number with two decimal places.
  - Boldfaces the Average Price label and the average toner price.
- Delete the average toner price that was inserted by recording the Toner_Average macro. Do not delete the Average Price label.
- Make the Average Price label a hotspot that runs the macro when clicked. Run the Toner_Average macro using the hotspot.
- In the Visual Basic code for the Toner_Average macro, enter your name as a comment, then print the macro code.

h. Print the worksheet. Save and close the workbook, then exit Excel.

▼ VISUAL WORKSHOP

Create the macro shown in Figure G-23. (*Hint*: Enter the months using the default font size, then change the size to the size shown.) Test the macro, save the workbook as **Accounting Macro**, and then print the module.

FIGURE G-23

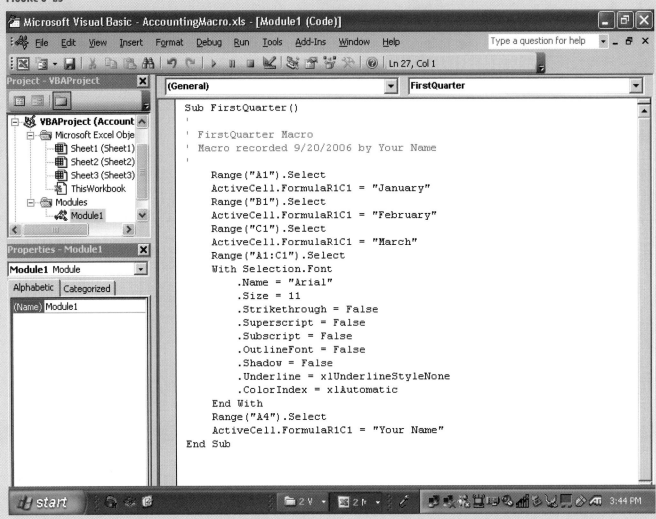

UNIT H
Excel 2003

Using Lists

OBJECTIVES

Plan a list

Create a list

Add records with the data form

Find records

Delete records

Sort a list on one field

Sort a list on multiple fields

Print a list

If you have a SAM user profile, you may have access to hands-on instruction, practice, and assessment of the skills covered in this unit. Log in to your SAM account and go to your assignments page to see what your instructor has assigned.

In addition to using Excel's spreadsheet features, you can also use Excel as a database. A **database** is an organized collection of related information, such as a telephone book, a card catalog, or a roster of company employees. A worksheet used as a database contains rows and columns of similarly structured data and is called a **list**. Using an Excel list, you can organize and manage worksheet information so that you can quickly find data for projects, reports, and charts. In this unit, you'll learn how to plan and create a list; add, change, find, and delete information in a list; and then sort and print a list. ▓▓▓▓ MediaLoft uses lists to analyze new customer information. MediaLoft marketing director Jim Fernandez has asked you to help him build and manage a list of new customers as part of the ongoing strategy to focus on the company's advertising expenses.

Planning a List

When planning a list, consider what information the list needs to contain and how you want to work with the data, now and in the future. As you plan a list, you should understand its most important components. A list is organized into rows called records. A **record** contains data about an object or person. Records are composed of fields. **Fields** are columns in the list; each field describes a characteristic about the record, such as a customer's last name or street address. Each field has a **field name**, a column label that describes the field. To plan your list, use the steps below. See Table H-1 for additional planning guidelines. If your list contains more records than can fit on one worksheet (that is, more than 65,536 records), you should consider using database software rather than spreadsheet software. ▓▓▓▓ Jim has asked you to compile a list of new customers. Before entering the data into an Excel worksheet, you plan the list using the following guidelines.

DETAILS

- **Identify the purpose of the list**

  Determine the kind of information the list should contain. Jim wants to use the list to identify how new customers found out about MediaLoft.

- **Plan the structure of the list**

  Determine the fields that make up a record. Jim has customer cards that contain information about each new customer. Figure H-1 shows a typical card. Each record will contain data for one customer. The fields in each record correspond to the descriptive information on the cards.

- **Write down the names of the fields**

  Field names appear in the first row of a list. Field names can be up to 255 characters long (the maximum column width), although shorter names are easier to see in the cells. Field names describe each piece of information. Jim's list will contain nine field names, each one corresponding to the nine pieces of information on each card.

- **Determine any special number formatting required in the list**

  Most lists contain both text and numbers. When planning a list, consider whether any fields require specific number formatting. For example, some zip codes begin with zero. Because Excel automatically drops a leading zero when entering numeric data, you must format zip code fields using a special format to display the full zip code. Jim's list includes a zip code field that needs this format.

FIGURE H-1: Customer record and corresponding field names

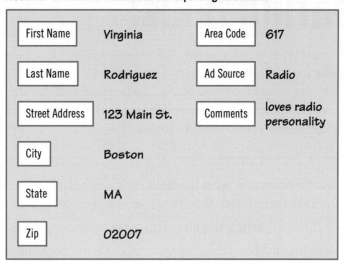

First Name	Virginia		Area Code	617
Last Name	Rodriguez		Ad Source	Radio
Street Address	123 Main St.		Comments	loves radio personality
City	Boston			
State	MA			
Zip	02007			

TABLE H-1: Guidelines for planning a list

worksheet structure guidelines	row and column content guidelines
Lists can be created from any contiguous range of cells on your worksheet	Plan and design your list so that all rows have similar items in the same column
A list should not have any blank rows or columns	Do not insert extra spaces at the beginning of a cell because that can affect sorting and searching
Data defined by your list can be used independently of data outside of the list on the worksheet	Instead of blank rows or columns between your labels and your data, use formatting to make column labels stand out from the data
Data can be organized on a worksheet using multiple lists to define sets of related data	Use the same format for all cells below the field name in a column

Creating a List

Once you have planned the list structure, the sequence of fields, and any appropriate formatting, you are ready to create the list. Table H-2 provides guidelines for naming fields. You then select the range and tell Excel that it is a list using a command on the Data menu. ████ Jim asks you to build a list with his customer information. You begin by entering the field names. After entering the field names, you enter the corresponding customer information, then create the list.

STEPS

1. **Start Excel if necessary, open the Data File EX H-1.xls from the drive and folder where your Data Files are stored, then save it as** New Customer List

2. **Rename Sheet1** Practice, **then if necessary maximize the Excel window**

QUICK TIP

If the field name you plan to use is wider than the data in the column, you can turn on Wrap Text on the Alignment tab in the Format Cells dialog box to stack the heading in the cell. You can also press [Alt][Enter] to force a line break while entering field names.

3. **Beginning in cell A1 and moving horizontally, enter each field name in a separate cell, as shown in Figure H-2**

   Field names are usually in the first row of the list. Don't worry if your field names are wider than the cells; you will fix this later.

4. **Select the field headings in range** A1:I1, **then click the** Bold button **B** **on the Formatting toolbar; with range A1:I1 still selected, click the** Borders list arrow, **then click the** Thick Bottom Border **(second column, second row)**

5. **Enter the information from Figure H-3 in the rows immediately below the field names, without leaving any blank rows**

   The data appears in columns organized by field name. The leading zeroes are dropped in the zip code column.

6. **Select** column F, **click** Format **on the menu bar, click** Cells, **on the Number tab under Category click** Special, **from the Type list click** Zip Code, **then click** OK

   The zip codes now have leading zeroes.

7. **Select the range** A1:I4, **click** Format **on the menu bar, point to** Column, **then click** AutoFit Selection

   Resizing the column widths this way is faster than double-clicking the column divider lines between each pair of columns.

QUICK TIP

If the List toolbar doesn't appear, click View on the menu bar, point to Toolbars, then click List.

8. **With A1:I4 selected, click** Data **on the menu bar, point to** List, **click** Create List, **make sure** My list has headers **is checked, click** OK, **then press** [Ctrl][Home] **to return to cell A1**

   The List toolbar appears and the list now has a blue border. See Figure H-4. **AutoFilter list arrows**, which let you display portions of your data, appear next to each column header. The blank last row of the list is the insert row, ready for new list data to be added.

TABLE H-2: Guidelines for naming fields

guideline	explanation
Use text to name fields	Numbers can be interpreted as parts of formulas
Do not use duplicate field names	Duplicate field names can cause Excel to enter and sort information incorrectly
Use descriptive names	Avoid names that might be confused with cell addresses, such as Q4

FIGURE H-2: Field names entered and formatted in row 1

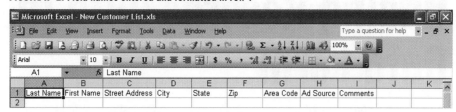

FIGURE H-3: Cards with customer information

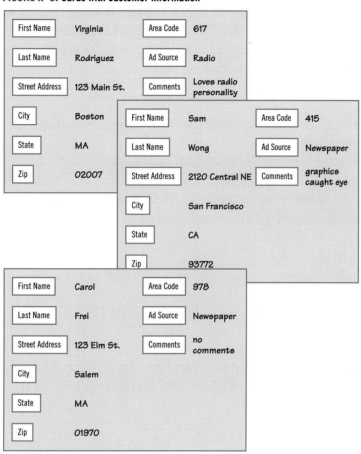

FIGURE H-4: List with three records

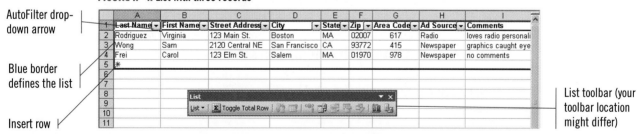

AutoFilter drop-down arrow

Blue border defines the list

Insert row

List toolbar (your toolbar location might differ)

Clues to Use

Filtering lists using AutoFilter

You can filter a list to show only the rows that meet specific criteria. For example, you might want to display only the records of customers in a certain zip code, or only residents of California. The AutoFilter list arrows, which automatically appear when you create a list, provide an easy way to apply a filter. The list arrows allow you to specify certain criteria for a field. For example, if you specify MA as the criteria in a State field, Excel displays only the records where MA is entered as the state. The AutoFilter options also include Sort Ascending and Sort Descending, which can be used to arrange your list data in increasing or decreasing order. Remember that a **filter** displays particular records, while a **sort** changes the order of records.

Adding Records with the Data Form

You can add records to a list by typing data directly into the last row of the list, which is called the **insert row**. Typing information in this row automatically adds the data to the list and expands the list's boundaries. You can also use a data form as a quick, easy method of data entry. A **data form** is a dialog box that displays one record at a time. You have entered all the customer records Jim had on his cards, but he receives the names of two additional customers. You decide to add the new customer information to the list using both methods: the data form and the insert row.

STEPS

1. **Make sure the New Customer List file is open, then activate** Sheet2 **and rename it** Working List

   Working List contains the nearly completed customer list.

QUICK TIP

You can also open a data form by clicking List on the List toolbar and then clicking Form.

2. **Select any cell in the customer list, click** Data **on the menu bar, then click** Form

   A data form containing the first record appears, as shown in Figure H-5.

3. **Click** New

   A blank data form appears with the insertion point in the first field.

TROUBLE

If you accidentally press [↑] or [↓] while in a data form and find that you displayed the wrong record, press [↑] or [↓] until you return to the desired record.

4. **Type** Chavez **in the Last Name box, then press** [Tab]

   The insertion point moves to the next field.

5. **Enter the rest of the information for Jane Chavez, using the information shown in Figure H-6**

   Press [Tab] to move the insertion point to the next field, or click in the next field box to move the insertion point there.

6. **Click** Close **to add Jane Chavez's record, then if necessary scroll down to view the end of the list**

   The record that you added with the data form appears at the end of the list.

QUICK TIP

Excel automatically extends formatting and formulas in lists.

7. **Click cell** A47, **enter** Ross, **press** [Tab], **then enter the rest of the information for Cathy Ross in the insert row using the information shown in Figure H-6**

8. **Return to cell A1, then save the workbook**

FIGURE H-5: Data form showing first record in the list

Current record number ⊢

Working List

Last Name:	Rodriguez
First Name:	Virginia
Street Address:	123 Main St.
City:	Boston
State:	MA
Zip:	2007
Area Code:	617
Ad Source:	Radio
Comments :	loves radio personality

1 of 44

New
Delete
Restore
Find Prev
Find Next
Criteria
Close

Total number of records

Click to open a blank data form for adding a record

FIGURE H-6: Information for two new records

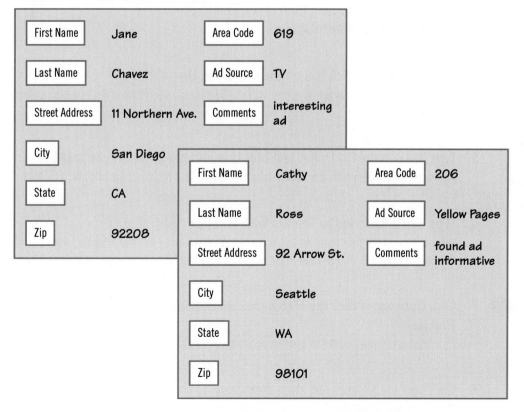

First Name	Jane	Area Code	619
Last Name	Chavez	Ad Source	TV
Street Address	11 Northern Ave.	Comments	interesting ad
City	San Diego		
State	CA		
Zip	92208		

First Name	Cathy	Area Code	206
Last Name	Ross	Ad Source	Yellow Pages
Street Address	92 Arrow St.	Comments	found ad informative
City	Seattle		
State	WA		
Zip	98101		

Finding Records

From time to time, you need to locate specific records in your list. You can use the Excel Find command on the Edit menu or the data form to search your list. You can also use the Replace command on the Edit menu to locate and replace existing entries or portions of entries with specified information. ▄▄▄▄▄ Jim wants to be more specific about the radio ad source, so he asks you to replace "Radio" with "KWIN Radio." He also wants to know how many of the new customers originated from the company's TV ads. You begin by searching for those records with the ad source "TV."

STEPS

TROUBLE
If you receive the message "No range was found that could be filtered," select cell A1, then repeat Step 1.

1. **Click cell A1 if necessary, click Data on the menu bar, click Form, then click Criteria**

   The data form changes so that all fields are blank and "Criteria" appears in the upper-right corner. See Figure H-7. In this dialog box, you enter criteria that specify the records you want to find. You want to search for records whose Ad Source field contains the label "TV."

2. **Click in the Ad Source text box, type TV, then click Find Next**

   Excel displays the first record for a customer who learned about the company through its TV ads. See Figure H-8.

QUICK TIP
You can also use comparison operators when searching using the data form. For example, you could specify >s in a Last Name field box to display those records with customer last names starting with the letter "s" or later in the alphabet. To display customers who live in a particular area of the country, you could enter >90000 in the Zip Code field box.

3. **Click Find Next and examine the Ad Source field for each found record until no more matching records appear, then click Close**

   There are six customers whose ad source is TV.

4. **Return to cell A1, click Edit on the menu bar, then click Replace**

   The Find and Replace dialog box opens with the Replace tab selected and the insertion point in the Find what box. See Figure H-9.

5. **Type Radio in the Find what text box, then click the Replace with text box**

   Jim wants you to search for entries containing "Radio" and replace them with "KWIN Radio."

6. **Type KWIN Radio in the Replace with text box**

   Because you notice that there are other list entries containing the word "radio" with a lowercase "r" (in the Comments column), you need to make sure that only capitalized instances of the word are replaced.

QUICK TIP
Be sure to clear this option for future searches in which you may not want to use it.

7. **Click Options >>, click the Match case check box to select it, click Options <<, then click Find Next**

   Excel moves the cell pointer to the first occurrence of "Radio."

8. **Click Replace All, click OK, then click Close**

   The dialog box closes. Excel made seven replacements. Note that in the Comments column, each instance of the word "radio" remains unchanged.

9. **Make sure there are no entries in the Ad Source column that read "Radio," then save the workbook**

FIGURE H-7: Criteria data form

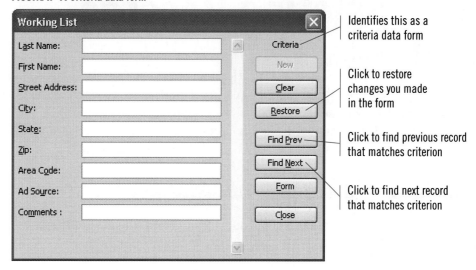

Identifies this as a criteria data form

Click to restore changes you made in the form

Click to find previous record that matches criterion

Click to find next record that matches criterion

FIGURE H-8: Finding a record using the data form

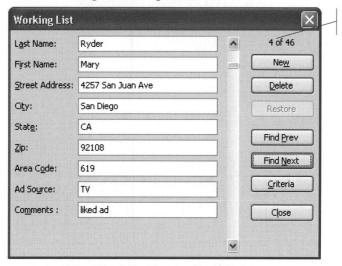

Record number of the displayed record

FIGURE H-9: Find and Replace dialog box

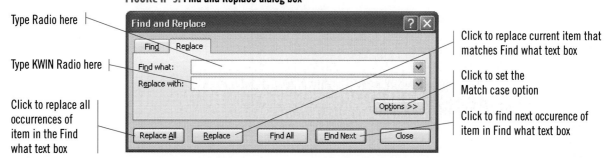

Type Radio here

Type KWIN Radio here

Click to replace all occurrences of item in the Find what text box

Click to replace current item that matches Find what text box

Click to set the Match case option

Click to find next occurence of item in Find what text box

Clues to Use

Using wildcards to fine-tune your search

You can use special symbols called **wildcards** when defining search criteria in the data form or Replace dialog box. The question mark (?) wildcard stands for any single character. For example, if you do not know whether a customer's last name is Paulsen or Paulson, you can specify Pauls?n as the search criteria to locate both options. The asterisk (*) wildcard stands for any group of characters. For example, if you specify Jan* as the search criteria in the First Name field, Excel locates all records with first names beginning with Jan (for instance, Jan, Janet, and Janice).

Deleting Records

You need to keep your list up to date by removing obsolete records. One way to remove records is to use the Delete button on the data form. You can also delete all records that share something in common—that is, records that meet certain criteria. For example, you can specify a criterion for Excel to find the next record containing zip code 01879, then remove the record by using the Delete button. If specifying one criterion does not meet your needs, you can set multiple criteria. ▰▰▰ Jim notices two entries for Carolyn Smith, and wants you to check the list for additional duplicate entries. You use the data form to delete the duplicate record.

STEPS

1. **Click Data on the menu bar, click Form, then click Criteria**
   The Criteria data form opens.

QUICK TIP

You can use the data form to edit records by finding the desired record and editing the data in the appropriate box.

2. **Type Smith in the Last Name text box, press [Tab] to move the insertion point to the First Name text box, type Carolyn, then click Find Next**
   Excel displays the first record for a customer whose name is Carolyn Smith. You decide to leave the initial entry for Carolyn Smith (record 5 of 46) and delete the second one, once you confirm that it is a duplicate.

3. **Click Find Next**
   The duplicate record for Carolyn Smith, number 40, appears as shown in Figure H-10. You are ready to delete the duplicate entry.

QUICK TIP

Clicking Restore on the data form undoes your changes when you are adding a new record, as long as you click it before you press [Enter] or click Close. Restore cannot restore deleted record(s).

4. **Click Delete, then click OK to confirm the deletion**
   The duplicate record for Carolyn Smith is deleted, and all the other records move up one row. The data form now shows the record for Manuel Julio.

5. **Click Close to return to the worksheet, if necessary scroll down until rows 41–46 are visible, then read the entry in row 41**
   Notice that the duplicate entry for Carolyn Smith is gone and that Manuel Julio moved up a row and is now in row 41. You also notice a record for K. C. Splint in row 43, which is a duplicate entry.

6. **Return to cell A1, and read the record information for K. C. Splint in row 8**
   After confirming the duplicate entry, you decide to delete the row.

7. **Click cell A8, click List on the List toolbar, then point to Delete**
   The delete options are displayed. See Figure H-11.

8. **Click Row**
   The duplicate record for K. C. Splint is deleted and the other records move up to fill in the gap.

9. **Save the workbook**

FIGURE H-10: Data form showing duplicate record for Carolyn Smith

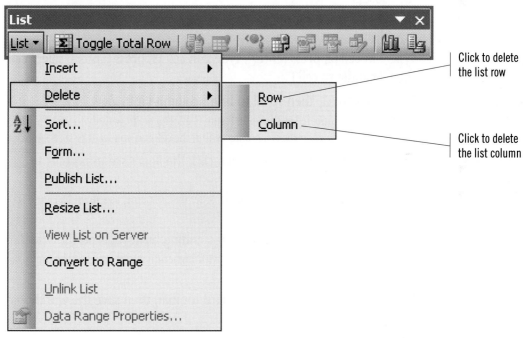

Working List

Last Name:	Smith
First Name:	Carolyn
Street Address:	921 Lopez Lane
City:	San Diego
State:	CA
Zip:	92102
Area Code:	619
Ad Source:	Newspaper
Comments :	likes ad prose

40 of 46

New
Delete
Restore
Find Prev
Find Next
Criteria
Close

Record 40 contains duplicate information for Carolyn Smith

Click to delete current record from list

FIGURE H-11: Delete options

List — Toggle Total Row

Insert ▶
Delete ▶   Row
Sort...   Column
Form...
Publish List...
Resize List...
View List on Server
Convert to Range
Unlink List
Data Range Properties...

Click to delete the list row

Click to delete the list column

Clues to Use

Deleting records using the worksheet

When you delete a record using the data form, you cannot undo your deletion. When you delete a record by deleting its row in the worksheet, however, you can immediately retrieve it. To do so, you can either use the Undo command on the Edit menu, click the Undo button on the Standard toolbar, or press [Ctrl][Z].

Sorting a List on One Field

Usually, you enter records in the order in which you receive the information, rather than in alphabetical or numerical order. When you add records to a list using the data form, Excel adds the records to the end of the list. You can change the order of the records any time using the Excel **sort** feature. You can use the sort buttons on the Standard toolbar to sort records by one field, such as zip code or last name. You can also use the Sort command on the Data menu to sort on more than one field, such as zip code and then, within each zip code, by last name. Because the data is a list, Excel changes the order of the records while keeping each record, or row of information, together. You can sort an entire list or any portion of a list, and you can arrange sorted information in ascending or descending order. In **ascending order**, the lowest value (the beginning of the alphabet, or the earliest date) appears at the top of the list. In a field containing labels and numbers, numbers come first. In **descending order**, the highest value (the end of the alphabet or the latest date) appears at the top of the list. In a field containing labels and numbers, labels come first. Table H-3 provides examples of ascending and descending sorts. Because Jim wants to be able to return the records to their original order following any sorts, he wants you to create a new field called Entry Order. You then perform several single field sorts on the list.

STEPS

QUICK TIP

Before you sort records, consider making a backup copy of your list or create a field that numbers the records so you can return them to their original order, if necessary.

1. **Click cell J1, enter the column heading** Entry Order, **then format cell J1 with a thick bottom border**

   The AutoCorrect options button appears after you enter the label because the list is expanded to include the new column.

2. **Type 1 in cell J2, press [Enter], type 2 in cell J3, press [Enter], select cells J2:J3, then drag the fill handle to cell J45**

3. **Return to cell A1, then scroll to bring column J into view**

   The records are numbered as shown in Figure H-12. You are now ready to sort the list in ascending order by last name. You must position the cell pointer within the column you want to sort before issuing the sort command.

QUICK TIP

If your sort does not perform as you intended, press [Ctrl][Z] immediately to undo the sort.

4. **Return to cell A1 if necessary, then click the** Sort Ascending button ⬇ **on the Standard toolbar**

   Excel rearranges the records in ascending order by last name, as shown in Figure H-13. You can also sort the list in descending order by any field.

5. **Click cell G5, then click the** Sort Descending button ⬆ **on the Standard toolbar**

   Excel sorts the list, placing those records with higher-digit area codes at the top. You are now ready to return the list to its original entry order.

6. **Click cell J1, click ⬇ on the Standard toolbar, then save the workbook**

   The list returns to its original order.

TABLE H-3: Sort order options and examples

option	alphabetic	numeric	date	alphanumeric
Ascending	A, B, C	7, 8, 9	1/1, 2/1, 3/1	12A, 99B, DX8, QT7
Descending	C, B, A	9, 8, 7	3/1, 2/1, 1/1	QT7, DX8, 99B, 12A

FIGURE H-12: List with Entry Order field added

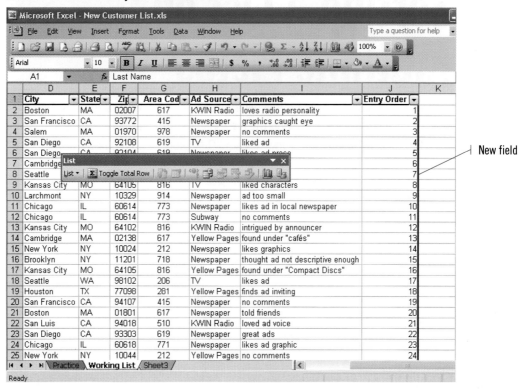

New field

FIGURE H-13: List sorted alphabetically by Last Name field

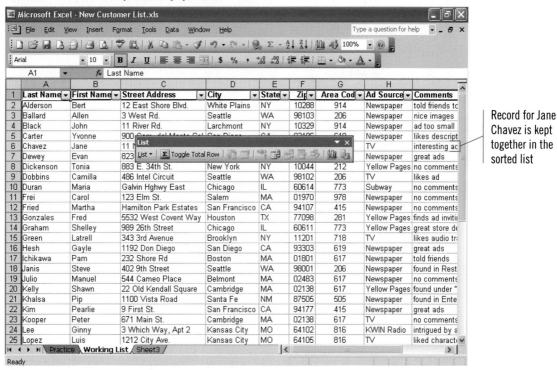

Record for Jane Chavez is kept together in the sorted list

Clues to Use

Sorting records using the AutoFilter

You can sort a list in ascending or descending order on one field using the AutoFilter list arrows next to the field name. Click the AutoFilter list arrow, then click Sort Ascending or Sort Descending to sort the list in the desired order. You may need to scroll up to the top of the list to see the sort commands.

Sorting a List on Multiple Fields

You can sort lists by as many as three fields by specifying **sort keys**, the criteria on which the sort is based. For example, you could sort first on the Ad Source field to reorder the records according to ad source, and then specify Last Name as a second sort key. The records would be sorted by Ad Source, and then within each ad source, by last name. You can enter up to three column headings in the Sort dialog box to specify the sort keys. It doesn't matter which cell is selected when you sort using the Sort dialog box. Jim wants you to sort the records alphabetically by state first, then within the state by zip code.

STEPS

QUICK TIP

You can include capitalization as a sort criterion by clicking Options in the Sort dialog box, then selecting the Case sensitive box. When you choose this option, lowercase entries precede uppercase entries.

1. **Click List on the List toolbar, then click Sort**

   The Sort dialog box opens, as shown in Figure H-14. You want to sort the list by state and then by zip code.

2. **Click the Sort by list arrow, click State, then click the Ascending option button to select it, if necessary**

   The list will be sorted alphabetically in ascending order (A–Z) by the State field. A second sort criterion will sort the entries within each state grouping.

3. **Click the top Then by list arrow, click Zip, then click the Descending option button**

   You could also sort by a third key by selecting a field in the bottom Then by list box.

4. **Click OK to perform the sort, return to cell A1, then scroll through the list to see the result of the sort**

   The list is sorted alphabetically by state in ascending order, then within each state by zip code in descending order. Compare your results with Figure H-15.

5. **Save the workbook**

FIGURE H-14: Sort dialog box

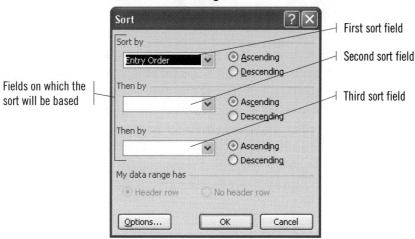

Fields on which the sort will be based

First sort field

Second sort field

Third sort field

FIGURE H-15: List sorted by two fields

First sort by state in ascending order

Second sort by zip code in descending order

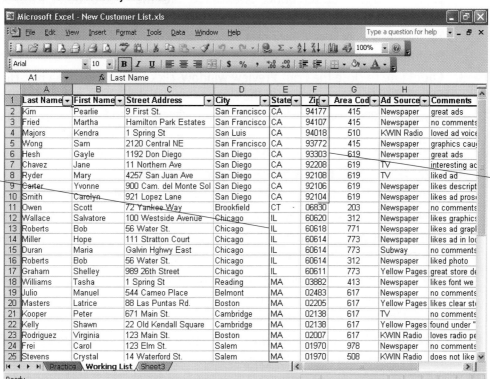

Clues to Use

Specifying a custom sort order

You can identify a custom sort order for the field selected in the Sort by box. Click Options in the Sort dialog box, click the First key sort order list arrow, then click the desired custom order. Commonly used custom sort orders are days of the week (Sun, Mon, Tues, Wed, etc.) and months (Jan, Feb, Mar, etc.); alphabetic sorts do not sort these items properly.

Printing a List

If a list is small enough to fit on one page, you can print it as you would any other Excel worksheet. If you have more columns than can fit on a portrait-oriented page, you can set the page orientation to landscape. Because lists often have more rows than can fit on a page, you can define the first row of the list (containing the field names) as the **print title**, which prints at the top of every page. Most lists do not have any descriptive information above the field names on the worksheet. To augment the information contained in the field names, you can use headers and footers to add identifying text, such as the list title or report date. If you want to exclude any fields from your list report, you can hide the selected columns from view so that they do not print. ⬛⬛⬛⬛ Jim has finished updating his list and would like you to print it. You begin by previewing the list.

STEPS

1. **Click the** Print Preview button 🔍 **on the Standard toolbar**

   The status bar reads Preview: Page 1 of 2. You want all the field names in the list to fit on a single page, but you need two pages to fit all the data.

2. **In the Print Preview window, click** Setup, **click the** Page tab **if necessary, click the** Landscape option button **under Orientation, click the** Fit to option button **under Scaling, double-click the** tall box **and type** 2, **click** OK, **then click** Next

   The list still does not fit on a single page. Because the records on page 2 appear without column headings, you want to set up the first row of the list, which contains the field names, as a repeating print title.

3. **Click** Close **to close the Print Preview window, click** File **on the menu bar, click** Page Setup, **click the** Sheet tab, **click the** Rows to repeat at top text box **under Print titles, click any cell in row 1, compare your Page Setup dialog box to Figure H-16, then click** OK

   When you select row 1 as a print title, Excel automatically inserts an absolute reference to a beginning row to repeat at the top of each page—in this case, the print title to repeat beginning and ending with row 1.

4. **Click** 🔍, **click** Next **to view the second page, then click** Zoom

   Setting up a print title to repeat row 1 causes the field names to appear at the top of each printed page.

5. **Click** Setup, **click the** Header/Footer tab, **click** Custom Header, **click the** Left section box **and enter your name, then click the** Center section box **and enter** MediaLoft -, **press** [Spacebar], **then click the** Filename button 📄

6. **Select the header information in the Center section box, click the** Font button 🅰, **change the font size to** 14 **and the style to** Bold, **click** OK, **click** OK **again to return to the Header/Footer tab, click** OK **to preview the list, then click** Close

7. **Save the workbook, print the worksheet, close the workbook, then exit Excel**

   Compare your printed worksheet with Figure H-17.

FIGURE H-16: Sheet tab of the Page Setup dialog box

Indicates that row 1 will appear at the top of each printed page

Turns gridline display on or off

Indicates which columns will appear at the left of each printed page

Displays row and column headings on printout

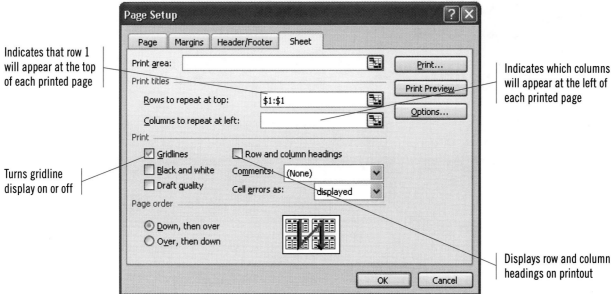

FIGURE H-17: Completed list

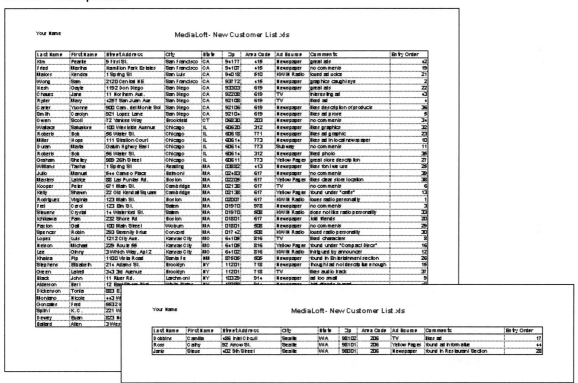

Clues to Use

Setting a print area

There are times when you want to print only part of a worksheet. To do this, select any worksheet range, then click File on the menu bar and click Print. In the Print dialog box, choose Selection under Print what, then click OK. If you want to print a selected area repeatedly, it's best to define a **print area**, which prints when you click the Print button on the Standard toolbar. To set a print area, click View on the menu bar, then click Page Break Preview. In the preview window, select the area you want to print. (If you see a Welcome dialog box, click OK.) Right-click the area, then select Set Print Area. The print area becomes outlined in a blue border. You can drag the border to extend the print area or add nonadjacent cells to it by selecting them, right-clicking them, then selecting Add to Print Area. When printing a print area that is part of a list, you must select Active sheet, rather than List, in the Print what section of the Print dialog box. To clear a print area, click File on the menu bar, point to Print Area, then click Clear Print Area.

Practice

▼ CONCEPTS REVIEW

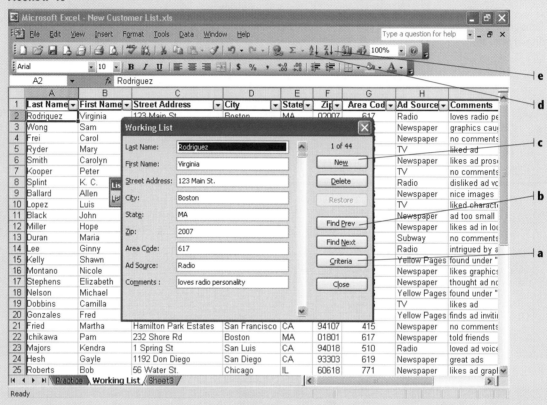

1. Which element do you click to sort a list in ascending order?
2. Which element do you click to sort a list in descending order?
3. Which element do you click to open a blank data form?
4. Which element do you click to search for records by specifying data in a field?
5. Which element do you click to find an earlier occurrence of a record that matches specified criteria?

Match each term with the statement that best describes it.

6. **Data form**
7. **Record**
8. **List**
9. **Field name**
10. **Sort**

a. Arrange records in a particular sequence
b. Organized collection of related information in Excel
c. Row in an Excel list
d. Used for entering data into a list
e. Label positioned at the top of the column identifying data

Select the best answer from the list of choices.

11. **Which of the following Excel sorting options do you use to sort a list of employee names in order from Z to A?**
    a. Absolute
    b. Ascending
    c. Alphabetic
    d. Descending

12. **Which of the following series appears in descending order?**
    a. 4, 5, 6, A, B, C
    b. 8, 6, 4, C, B, A
    c. 8, 7, 6, 5, 6, 7
    d. C, B, A, 6, 5, 4

13. **What color is the border that encloses a list on a worksheet?**
    a. Red
    b. Blue
    c. Green
    d. Yellow

14. **When printing a list on multiple pages, you can define a print title containing repeating row(s) to:**
    a. Include appropriate fields in the printout.
    b. Include the header in list reports.
    c. Include field names at the top of each printed page.
    d. Exclude from the printout all rows under the first row.

▼ SKILLS REVIEW

1. **Create a list.**
   a. Create a new workbook, then save it as **Employee List** in the drive and folder where your Data Files are stored.
   b. Enter the field names and records shown in the following table:
   c. Apply bold formatting to the field names and center the field names in the columns.

Last Name	First Name	Years Employed	Position	Full/Part Time	Training?
Lenon	Sarah	5	Video Sales	F	Y
Marino	Donato	3	CD Sales	P	N
Khederian	Jay	4	Video Sales	F	Y
Jones	Cathy	1	Video Sales	F	N
Rabinowicz	Miriam	2	CD Sales	P	Y

   d. Adjust the column widths to make the data readable.
   e. Select the field names and the records, then create a list from the selected range. Adjust the column widths, if necessary, to display the field names.
   f. Enter your name in the worksheet footer, then save and print the list.

2. **Add records with the data form.**
   a. Click any record in the list.
   b. Open the data form and add a new record for **Danielle Gitano**, a one-year employee in book sales. Danielle works full time and has not completed training.
   c. Use the insert row to add a new record for **George Worthen**. George works full time, has worked at the company five years in book sales, and has completed training.
   d. Use the insert row to add a new record for **Valerie Atkins**. Valerie works full time, has worked at the company three years in video sales, and has completed training.
   e. Save the file.

3. **Find and delete records.**

   a. Use the Find command to find the record for Cathy Jones.

   b. Delete the record.

   c. Use the Find command to find the record for Valerie Atkins.

   d. Delete the record.

   e. Save the file.

4. **Sort a list on one field.**

   a. Sort the list in descending order by years employed.

   b. Sort the list alphabetically in descending order by training.

   c. Sort the list alphabetically in ascending order by position.

   d. Sort the list alphabetically in ascending order by last name.

   e. Save the file.

5. **Sort a list on multiple fields.**

   a. Sort the list first in ascending order by years employed and then alphabetically in descending order by last name.

   b. Check the list to make sure the records appear in the correct order.

   c. Sort the list alphabetically in ascending order, first by whether or not the employees have completed training and then by last name.

   d. Check the list to make sure the records appear in the correct order.

   e. Save the file.

6. **Print a list.**

   a. Add a header that reads Employee Information in the center, then format the header in bold.

   b. Add the file name to the center section of the footer.

   c. Use the Margins tab in the Page Setup dialog box to add top and bottom margins of one inch.

   d. Select all of the information in the worksheet and change the font size to 16.

   e. Use the Sheet tab of the Page Setup dialog box to add column A as a print title that repeats at the left of each printed page.

   f. Save the workbook, then print the list.

   g. Close the workbook, then exit Excel.

▼ INDEPENDENT CHALLENGE 1

You own Personalize IT, an advertising firm located in New Zealand. The firm sells specialty items imprinted with the customer's name and/or logo such as hats, pens, mugs, and T-shirts. Plan and build a list of order information with eight records using the items sold. Your list should contain at least five different customers. (Some customers may place more than one order.)

   a. Prepare a list plan that states your goal, outlines the data you need, and identifies the list elements.

   b. Sketch a sample list on a piece of paper, indicating how the list should be built. Which of the data fields should be formatted as labels? As values?

   c. Start Excel, create a new workbook, then save it as Personalize IT in the drive and folder where your Data Files are stored. Build the list by first entering Personalize IT as the worksheet title in cell A1, then enter the following field names in the designated cells:

   d. Enter eight data records using your own data.

   e. Select the range A2:E10 and create a list. Adjust the column widths as necessary.

   f. Enter Subtotal in cell F2, Total in cell G2, Tax in cell H2, and .125 in cell I2 (the 12.5% Goods and Services tax). Make sure the new items are added to the list range.

   g. Enter formulas to calculate the subtotal (Quantity*Cost) in cell F3 and the total (including tax) in cell G3. Copy the formulas down the columns.

   h. Format the Cost, Subtotal, and Total columns as currency. Adjust the column widths as necessary.

   i. Add a new record to your list using the data form. Add another record using the insert row.

Cell	Field name
A2	Customer Last
B2	Customer First
C2	Item
D2	Quantity
E2	Cost

▼ INDEPENDENT CHALLENGE 1 (CONTINUED)

j. Sort the list in ascending order by Item using the Sort Ascending button on the Standard toolbar.

k. Enter your name in the worksheet footer, then save the workbook.

l. Preview the worksheet, print the worksheet on one page, close the workbook, then exit Excel.

▼ INDEPENDENT CHALLENGE 2

You are taking a class titled Television Shows: Past and Present at a local community college. The instructor has given you an Excel list of television programs from the '60s and '70s. She has included fields tracking the following information: the number of years the show was a favorite, favorite character, the show's length in minutes, least favorite character, and comments about the show. The instructor has included data for each show in the list. She has asked you to add a field (column label) and one record (a show of your choosing) to the list. Because the list should cover only 30-minute shows, you need to delete any records for shows longer than 30 minutes. Also, your instructor wants you to sort and format the list as needed before printing. Feel free to change any of the list data to suit your tastes and opinions.

a. Start Excel, open the file EX H-2.xls from the drive and folder where your Data Files are stored, then save it as **Television Shows of the Past**.

b. Add a field called **Rating** in column G. The list formatting should be extended to include the new column and your worksheet should look like Figure H-19. Complete the Rating field for each record with a value of 1–5 with 5 being the highest, that reflects the rating you would give the television show.

FIGURE H-19

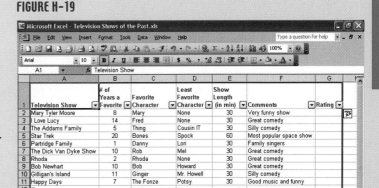

c. Use the data form to add one record for a 30-minute show to the list. Make sure to enter information in every field.

d. Use the data form to delete any records having show lengths other than 30. (*Hint*: Use the comparison operator <> in the Show Length field to find records not equal to 30.)

e. Make any formatting changes to the list as needed and save the list.

f. Sort the list in ascending order by show name.

g. Enter your name in the worksheet footer, save the workbook, then print the list.

h. Sort the list again, this time in descending order by the number of years the show was a favorite.

i. Add a centered header that reads **Television Shows of the Past: '60s and '70s**.

j. Save the workbook, preview it, then print the list.

Advanced Challenge Exercise

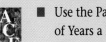

■ Use the Page Break Preview view to create a print area that prints only the first two columns, Television Show, and # of Years a Favorite. Print the print area. (*Hint*: You must change the "Print what" setting in the Print dialog box from List to Active sheet.)

■ Add the third column, Favorite Character, to the print area using the shortcut menu option, then print the print area.

k. Save the workbook, close the workbook, then exit Excel.

▼ INDEPENDENT CHALLENGE 3

You are the assistant manager at Nite Owl Video in Brisbane, Australia. You have assembled an Excel list of the most popular Australian films your store rents, along with information about the Australian Film Institute (AFI) award they won, the release dates, and the film genres. Your customers have suggested that you prepare an in-store handout listing the films with the information sorted in different ways.

a. Start Excel, open the file EX H-3.xls from the drive and folder where your Data Files are stored, then save it as
Best Films.

b. Sort the list in ascending order by Genre. Sort the list again in ascending order by Film Name.

FIGURE H-20

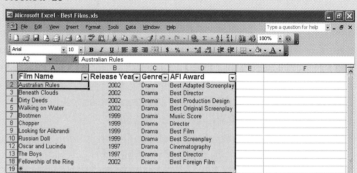

c. Sort the list again using two fields, this time in descending order by Release Year, then in ascending order by Genre.

d. Enter your name in the worksheet footer, then save the workbook.

e. Use the data form to add a record to the list with the following information: Film Name: Fellowship of the Ring; Release Year: 2002; Genre: Drama; AFI Award: Best Foreign Film.

f. Use the data form to find and delete the record for the film *Passion*.

g. Use AutoFilter to display only dramas. (*Hint*: Click the AutoFilter list arrow in the Genre column and select Drama.) Compare your list to Figure H-20.

h. Redisplay all films. (*Hint*: Click the AutoFilter list arrow in the Genre column and select All.)

Advanced Challenge Exercise

- Create your own sort order of: Drama, Comedy, Thriller, Suspense for the Genre column. (*Hint*: You must create a custom list using Options on the Tools menu and the Custom Lists tab.)
- Sort the list in ascending order on the Genre field using your custom sort order. You need to clear all sort fields except the first key sort field in the Sort dialog box.

i. Save the workbook, print the list, close the workbook, then exit Excel.

▼ INDEPENDENT CHALLENGE 4

Your local newspaper has decided to start publishing the top-selling MP3 titles. They want to list the best-selling titles in the genres of Pop, Hip Hop, Country, and Classical. You have been asked to research the bestselling MP3 music along with price information. You create a list to hold the information about the top two titles for each genre. Using AutoFilter, you then display titles by the type of music and sort the list.

a. Go to the search engine of your choice and research the top selling MP3 titles in the categories of Pop, Country, Hip Hop, and Classical.

b. Complete the table below with the MP3 title information you found in your search.

Title	Artist	Genre	Price

c. Start Excel, enter your name in the worksheet footer of the new workbook, then save the workbook as **MP3 Titles**.

d. Use your table to enter the top two titles for each of the four music categories, along with the artist and price information, into your Excel worksheet. Save the workbook.

e. Create a list that contains the MP3 information.

f. Use AutoFilter to display only the Pop titles. (*Hint*: Click the AutoFilter arrow in the Genre column and select Pop.)

g. Use AutoFilter to display all the records. (*Hint*: Click the AutoFilter arrow in the Genre column and select All.)

h. Use the data form to delete both Pop records.

i. Use the AutoFilter to sort the list in ascending order by price. (*Hint*: Click the AutoFilter arrow in the Price column and select Sort Ascending.)

j. Save the workbook, print the list, close the workbook, then exit Excel.

▼ VISUAL WORKSHOP

Create the worksheet shown in Figure H-21. Save the workbook as **Famous Jazz Performers** in the drive and folder where your Data Files are stored. Once you've entered the field names and records, sort the list using two fields. The first sort should be in ascending order by Contribution to Jazz, and the second sort should be in ascending order by Last Name. Change the page setup so that the list is printed in landscape orientation on one page and centered on the page horizontally. Add a header that is centered, formatted in bold with a size of 16, and reads Famous Jazz Performers. Enter your name in the worksheet footer. Save the workbook, preview and print the list, close the workbook, then exit Excel.

FIGURE H-21

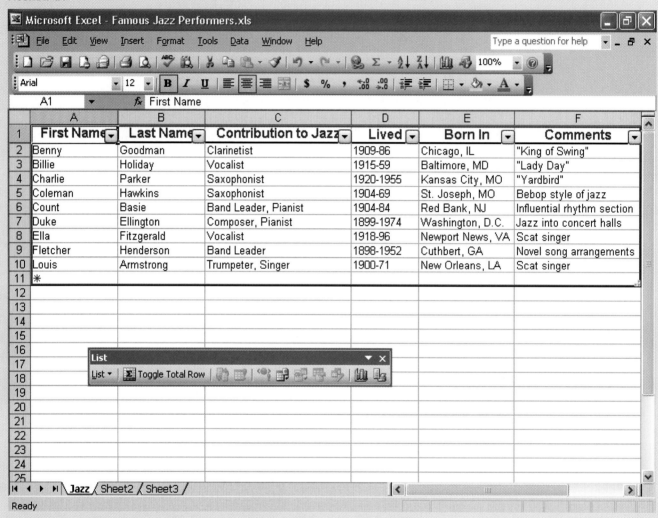

UNIT I
Analyzing List Data

OBJECTIVES

Retrieve records with AutoFilter
Create a custom filter
Filter a list with Advanced Filter
Extract list data
Create subtotals using grouping and outlines
Look up values in a list
Summarize list data
Use data validation for list entries

If you have a SAM user profile, you may have access to hands-on instruction, practice, and assessment of the skills covered in this unit. Log in to your SAM account and go to your assignments page to see what your instructor has assigned.

There are many ways to analyze or manipulate list data with Excel. One way is to filter a list so that only the rows that meet certain criteria are retrieved. In this unit, you will retrieve records using AutoFilter, create a custom filter, and then filter a list using the Advanced Filter feature. In addition, you will learn to insert automatic subtotals, use lookup functions to locate list entries, and then apply database functions to summarize list data that meet specific criteria. You'll also learn how to restrict entries in a column by using data validation. Jim Fernandez, the marketing director for MediaLoft, recently conducted a survey for his department. The survey results have been entered into an Excel workbook and Jim wants you to analyze and summarize the customer data.

Retrieving Records with AutoFilter

In an Excel list, you can use the AutoFilter feature to **retrieve** (search for and list) records that meet criteria you specify. AutoFilter **filters** out, or hides, data that fails to meet your criteria. You can filter records based on a specific field, such as Country, and then request that Excel retrieve only those records having a specific entry in that field. For example, you can filter a customer list to retrieve names of only those customers residing in Canada. You can use an AutoFilter to display records containing the highest or lowest values in a field or use a custom AutoFilter to display records in which a field value matches a value you specify. ⬛⬛⬛⬛ Jim is now ready to work with the survey information. He asks you to retrieve data for customers who live in Chicago, Illinois. He also asks for information about the customers who purchased the most merchandise. You will begin by creating a list from the customer data.

STEPS

1. **Start Excel, open the Data File** EX I-1.xls **from the drive and folder where your Data Files are stored, then save it as** Survey Data

2. **With the Filter sheet active, select the range** A1:M36, **click** Data **on the menu bar, point to** List, **click** Create List, **make sure My list has headers is checked, click** OK

   The List toolbar appears and list arrows appear to the right of each field name. The list arrows let you filter the data.

3. **Click the** City list arrow

   An AutoFilter list containing the different city options appears below the field name, as shown in Figure I-1. Because you want to retrieve data for only those customers who live in Chicago, you use Chicago as your **search criterion**.

   QUICK TIP
   You can filter the list further by applying another AutoFilter search criterion to the records.

4. **In the AutoFilter list, click** Chicago

   Only those records containing Chicago in the City field appear, as shown in Figure I-2. The row numbers for the matching records change to blue, as does the list arrow for the filtered field. Next, you want to retrieve information about those customers who purchased the most merchandise.

5. **Click the** City list arrow, **scroll up to the top of the list, then click** (All)

   You have cleared the previous filter, and all the records reappear.

   TROUBLE
   If the column label in cell A1 covers the column headers, making it difficult to find the appropriate columns, select A2 before scrolling.

6. **Scroll right until columns G through M are visible, click the** Purchases to Date list arrow, **then click** (Top 10...)

   The Top 10 AutoFilter dialog box opens. The default is to select the 10 records with the highest value. You need to display only the top two.

7. **Select** 10 **in the middle box, type** 2, **then click** OK

   Excel retrieves the records for the two customers who purchased the most merchandise, $3,200 and $2,530. See Figure I-3.

8. **Click the** Purchases to Date list arrow, **click** (All), **press** [Ctrl][Home]

   You have cleared the filter, and all the records reappear.

9. **Add your name to the right side of the footer, save the workbook, then print the list**

   The worksheet prints, using the existing print settings.

FIGURE I-1: Worksheet showing AutoFilter options

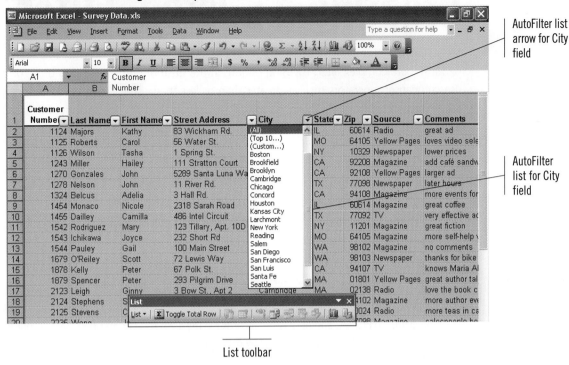

AutoFilter list arrow for City field

AutoFilter list for City field

List toolbar

FIGURE I-2: List filtered with AutoFilter

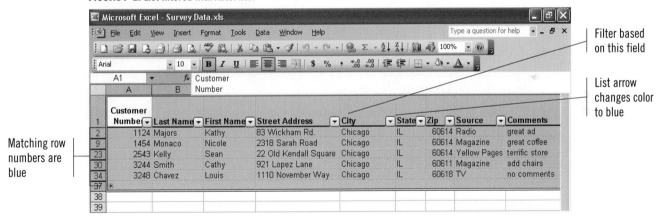

Filter based on this field

List arrow changes color to blue

Matching row numbers are blue

FIGURE I-3: List filtered with Top 2 AutoFilter criterion

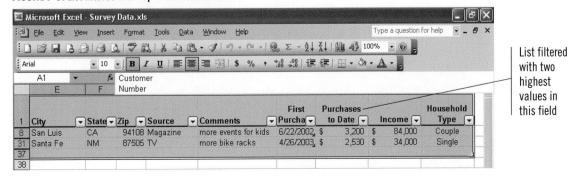

List filtered with two highest values in this field

Creating a Custom Filter

So far, you have used the AutoFilter command to filter rows based on an entry in a single column. You can perform more complex filters by using options in the Custom AutoFilter dialog box. For example, you can use comparison operators such as greater than or less than. ░▒▓▒ Jim wants to locate customers who reside west of the Rocky Mountains, in a family household, and who heard about MediaLoft through a magazine advertisement. He asks you to create a custom filter to list the customers satisfying these criteria.

STEPS

QUICK TIP
When specifying criteria in the Custom AutoFilter dialog box, use the ? wildcard to represent any single character and the * wildcard to represent any series of characters.

1. **Click the Zip list arrow, then click (Custom)**

   The Custom AutoFilter dialog box opens. Because all residents west of the Rockies have a zip code greater than 81000, that is your criterion.

2. **Click the Zip list arrow, click is greater than, press [Tab], then type 81000**

   Your completed Custom AutoFilter dialog box should match Figure I-4.

3. **Click OK**

   The dialog box closes, and only those records having a zip code greater than 81000 appear in the worksheet. Now, you narrow the list even further by displaying only those customers who live in a family household.

4. **Scroll right until columns G through M are visible, click the Household Type list arrow, then click Family**

   The list of records retrieved has narrowed. Finally, you need to filter out all customers except those who heard about MediaLoft through a magazine advertisement.

5. **Click the Source list arrow, then click Magazine**

   Your final filtered list now shows only customers in family households, west of the Rocky Mountains, who heard about MediaLoft through magazine ads. See Figure I-5.

6. **Preview, then print the worksheet**

   The worksheet prints using the existing print settings—landscape orientation, with your name in the footer, scaled to fit on a single page.

7. **Click Data on the menu bar, point to Filter, click Show All, then press [Ctrl][Home]**

   You have cleared the filter, and all the customer records reappear.

FIGURE I-4: Custom AutoFilter dialog box

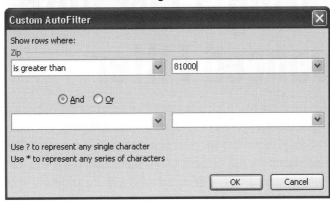

FIGURE I-5: Results of custom filter

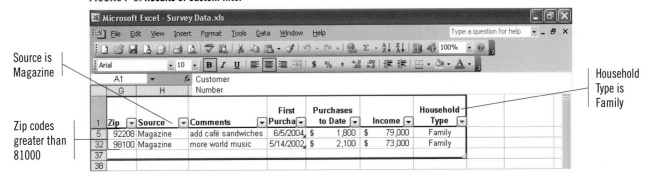

Source is Magazine

Zip codes greater than 81000

Household Type is Family

Clues to Use

And and Or logical conditions

You can narrow a search even further by using the And or Or buttons in the Custom AutoFilter dialog box. For example, you can select records for those customers with homes in California *and* Texas as well as select records for customers with homes in California *or* Texas. See Figure I-6. When used in this way, And and Or conditions are often referred to as **logical conditions**. When you search for customers with homes in California *and* Texas, you are specifying an And condition. When you search for customers with homes in either California *or* Texas, you are specifying an Or condition.

FIGURE I-6: Using the Custom AutoFilter dialog box

Multiple criteria

Click to find records matching both criteria

Click to find records matching one or the other criterion

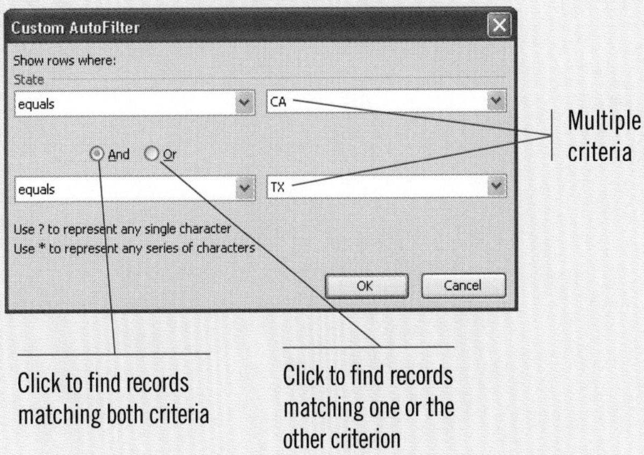

Filtering a List with Advanced Filter

The Advanced Filter command lets you search for data that matches complicated criteria in more than one column, using And and Or conditions. To use advanced filtering, you must define a criteria range. A **criteria range** is a cell range containing one row of labels (usually a copy of the column labels) and at least one additional row underneath the row of labels that contains the criteria you want to match. Jim wants to identify customers who have been doing business with the company since before May 1, 2002, and whose total purchases are less than or equal to $1000. He asks you to use the Advanced Filter command to retrieve this data. You begin by defining the criteria range.

STEPS

1. **Select** rows 1 through 6, **click** Insert **on the menu bar, then click** Rows; **click cell** A1, **type** Criteria Range, **then click the** Enter button ✓ **on the Formula bar**

   Six blank rows are added above the list. Excel does not require the label Criteria Range, but it is useful in organizing the worksheet. It is also helpful to see the column labels.

2. **Select range** A7:M7, **click the** Copy button 📋 **on the Standard toolbar, click cell** A2, **then click the Paste button** 📋 **on the Standard toolbar, then press** [Esc]

   Next, you want to list records for only those people who have been customers prior to May 1, 2002 and who have purchased no more than $1000.

   TROUBLE

   If the column labels make it difficult for you to drag the pointer to cell M7, try clicking M7 first; then drag the pointer all the way left to cell A7.

3. **Scroll right until columns H through M are visible, click cell** J3, **type** <5/1/2002 **(making sure there is no space between the < symbol and the 5), click cell** K3, **type** <=1,000, **then click** ✓

   This enters the criteria in the cells directly beneath the Criteria Range labels. See Figure I-7. Placing the criteria in the same row indicates that the records you are searching for must match both criteria; that is, it specifies an **And condition**.

4. **Click any cell in the list, click** Data **on the menu bar, point to** Filter, **then click** Advanced Filter

   The Advanced Filter dialog box opens, with the list range already entered. The default setting under Action is to filter the list in its current location rather than copy it to another location.

   TROUBLE

   If you did not get the filtered list of records, make sure the date in cell J3 has the same date format as the dates in the list range.

5. **Click the** Criteria Range text box, **select range** A2:M3 **in the worksheet (move the dialog box if necessary), then click** OK

   You have specified the criteria range and performed the filter. The filtered list contains 13 records that match both the criteria—the first purchase was before 5/1/2002 and the purchases to date total less than $1,000. See Figure I-8. You'll filter this list even further in the next lesson.

FIGURE I-7: Criteria in the same row

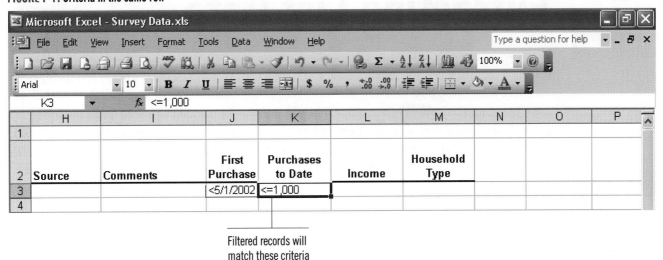

Filtered records will match these criteria

FIGURE I-8: Filtered list

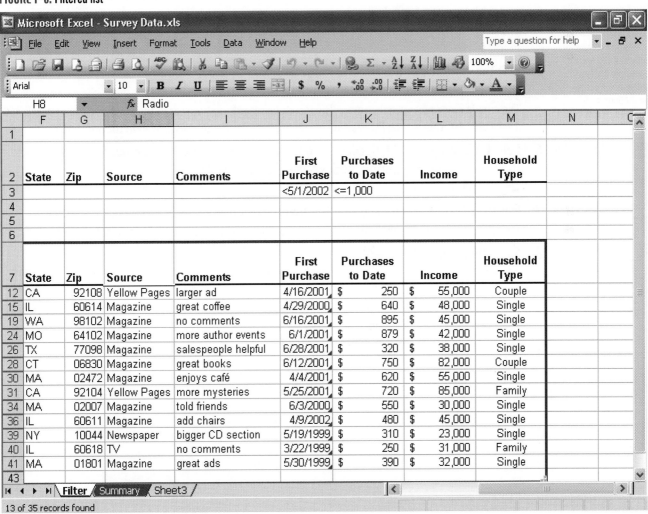

Extracting List Data

Whenever you take the time to specify a complicated set of search criteria, it's a good idea to extract the matching records. When you **extract** data, you place a copy of a filtered list in a range you specify in the Advanced Filter dialog box. That way, you won't accidentally clear the filter or lose track of the records you spent time compiling. ▤▤▤▤ Jim needs to filter the previous list one step further to reflect only those customers in the current filtered list who heard of MediaLoft through TV or a magazine ad. He asks you to complete this filter by specifying an Or condition. You will do this by entering two sets of criteria in two separate rows. You decide to save the filtered records by extracting them to a different location in the worksheet.

STEPS

1. **In cell** H3, **enter** TV, **then in cell** H4, **enter** Magazine
   The new criteria appear in two separate rows so you need to copy the previous filter criteria to the second row.

2. **Copy the criteria in** J3:K3 **to** J4:K4
   See Figure I-9. This time, you'll indicate that you want to copy the filtered list to a range beginning in cell A50.

TROUBLE
Make sure the criteria range in the Advanced Filter dialog box includes the field names and the number of rows underneath the names that contain criteria. If you leave a blank row in the criteria range, Excel filters nothing and shows all records.

3. **Click** Data **on the menu bar, point to** Filter, **then click** Advanced Filter

4. **Under Action, click the** Copy to another location option button **to select it, click the** Copy to **text box, then type** A50
   The last time you filtered the list, the criteria range included only rows 2 and 3, and now you have criteria in row 4.

5. **Edit the contents of the** Criteria range text box **to show the range** $A$2:$M$4, **click** OK, **then scroll down until row 50 is visible**
   The criteria range now includes row 4. The matching records now appear in the range beginning in cell A50. See Figure I-10. The original list, starting in cell A7, contains the records filtered in the previous lesson.

QUICK TIP
To print only the list data, click the List option button in the Print dialog box.

6. **Select the range** A50:M60, **click** File **on the menu bar, click** Print, **under Print what, click the** Selection option button, **click** Preview, **then click** Print
   The selected area prints.

7. **Press** [Ctrl][Home], **click** Data **on the menu bar, point to** Filter, **then click** Show All
   The original list is displayed starting in cell A7 and the extracted list remains in A50:M60.

8. **Save the workbook**

FIGURE I-9: Criteria in separate rows

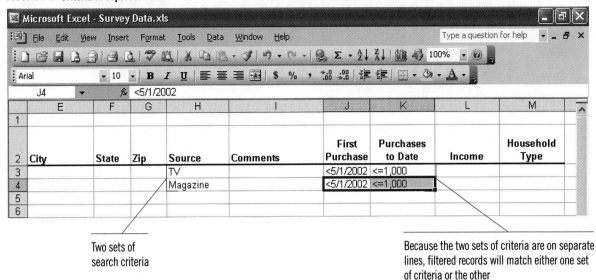

Two sets of
search criteria

Because the two sets of criteria are on separate
lines, filtered records will match either one set
of criteria or the other

FIGURE I-10: Extracted data records

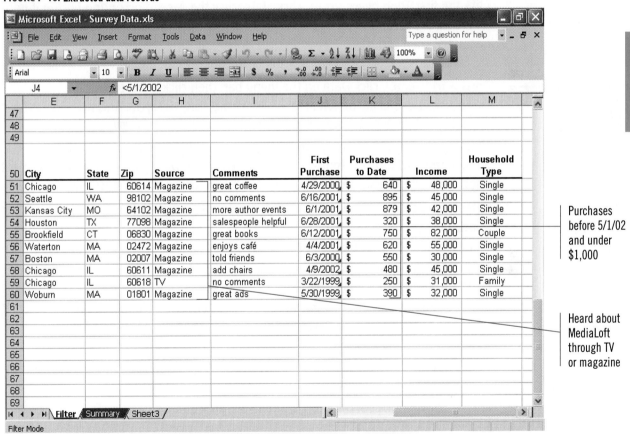

Purchases
before 5/1/02
and under
$1,000

Heard about
MediaLoft
through TV
or magazine

Clues to Use

Understanding the criteria range and the copy-to location

When you define the criteria range and the copy-to location in the Advanced Filter dialog box, Excel automatically creates the names Criteria and Extract for these ranges in the worksheet. The criteria range includes the field names and any criteria rows underneath them. The extract range includes just the field names above the extracted list. To extract a different list, select Extract as the copy-to location. Excel deletes the old list in the extract area and generates a new list under the field names. Make sure the worksheet has enough blank rows under the field names for your data.

Creating Subtotals Using Grouping and Outlines

The Excel Subtotals feature provides a quick, easy way to group and summarize data. Usually, you create subtotals with the SUM function, but you can also subtotal groups with functions such as COUNT, AVERAGE, MAX, and MIN. Before you can issue the Subtotal command, your list must have field names and be sorted, and the cell pointer must be within the data range.  Jim wants you to group data by advertising source, with subtotals for purchases to date and household income. You begin by sorting the data in ascending order, first by advertising source, then by state, and, finally, by city.

STEPS

1. **Click the** Summary sheet tab, **click** Data **on the menu bar, click** Sort, **click the** Sort by list arrow, **click** Source, **then click the** Ascending option button **if necessary**

2. **Click the first** Then by list arrow, **click** State, **click the** Ascending option button **if necessary, click the second** Then by list arrow, **click** City, **click the** Ascending option button **if necessary, then click** OK

   You have sorted the list in ascending order, first by advertising source, then by state, and, finally, by city.

QUICK TIP

If the Subtotal command is not available, click the Summary sheet tab.

3. **Press** [Ctrl][Home], **click** Data **on the menu bar, then click** Subtotals

   The range is selected, in this case, A1:M36, and the Subtotal dialog box opens. Here, you specify the items you want subtotaled, the function you want to apply to the values, and the fields you want to summarize.

4. **Click the** At each change in list arrow, **click** Source, **click the** Use function list arrow, **click** Sum; **in the Add subtotal to list, click the** Purchases to Date **and** Income **check boxes to select them, if necessary, click the** Household Type **check box to deselect it**

5. **If necessary, click the** Replace current subtotals **and** Summary below data **check boxes to select them**

   Your completed Subtotal dialog box should match Figure I-11.

6. **Click** OK, **then scroll to the right until columns K and L are visible, then scroll down so row 19 is at the top of your screen**

   The subtotaled data appears, showing the calculated subtotals and grand total in columns K and L. See Figure I-12. Notice that Excel displays an outline to the left of the worksheet, showing the structure of the subtotaled data.

7. **Save and preview the worksheet, place your name on the right side of the footer, then print the worksheet**

8. **Press** [Ctrl][Home], **click** Data **on the menu bar, click** Subtotals, **then click** Remove All

   You have turned off the Subtotaling feature. The subtotals are removed, and the Outline feature is turned off automatically.

Clues to Use

Converting a list to a range

You can only apply subtotals to data ranges. If you have converted your data to a list using the Create List command, the subtotal command will not be available. However, you can still use many list features with rows of contiguous data, even though you have not declared it as a list using the Create List command. In the remaining lessons of this unit, you will analyze list data that has not been formally declared as a list. As you use Excel, you may want to add subtotals to a declared list. In this case, you would need to convert the list to a range by clicking List on the List toolbar, clicking Convert to Range, then issuing the Subtotal command.

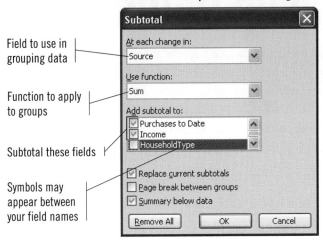

FIGURE I-11: Completed Subtotal dialog box

Field to use in grouping data

Function to apply to groups

Subtotal these fields

Symbols may appear between your field names

FIGURE I-12: Portion of subtotaled list

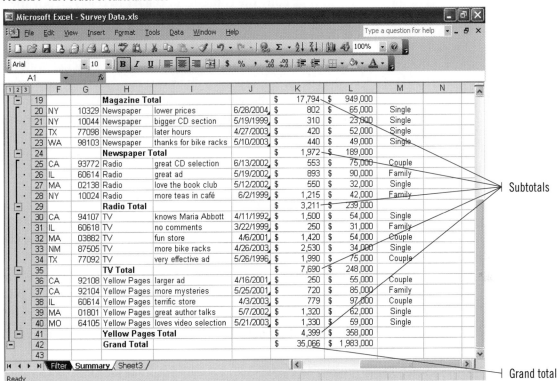

Subtotals

Grand total

Clues to Use

Using the Show Details and Hide Details buttons in an outline

Once you have generated subtotals, all detail records appear in an outline. See Figure I-13. You can then click the Hide Details button ⊟ of your choice to hide that group of records, creating a summary report. You can also create a chart that shows the summary data. Any chart you create is automatically updated as you show or hide data. You can also click the Show Details button ⊞ for the group of data you want to display. To show a specific level of detail, click the row or column level button for the lowest level you want to display. For example, to display levels 1 through 3, click ⒊.

FIGURE I-13: Subtotaled data with level 2 details

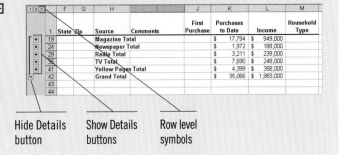

Hide Details button   Show Details buttons   Row level symbols

Looking up Values in a List

The Excel VLOOKUP function helps you locate specific values in a list. VLOOKUP searches vertically (V) down the far left column of a list then reads across the row to find the value in the column you specify, much as you might look up a number in a phone book: You locate a person's name then read across the row to find the phone number you want. Jim wants to be able to find out what type of household a particular customer lives in simply by entering his or her customer number. You will use the VLOOKUP function to accomplish this task. You begin by naming the list range so you can refer to it in a Lookup function.

STEPS

QUICK TIP

Excel also has a Lookup Wizard to help you perform lookups. It is an Excel add-in (or extra) program. Open the Tools menu and click Lookup to use the Lookup Wizard. If you don't see Lookup on the Tools menu, install the Lookup Wizard using the Add-Ins option on the Tools menu.

1. **Select the list range** A1:M36, **click the** Name Box **and type the name** List, **then press** Enter

2. **Press** [Ctrl][Home], **click cell** C2, **click** Window **on the menu bar, then click** Freeze Panes; **then scroll right until columns M through U and rows 1 through 15 are visible**

3. **Click cell** O1, **type** VLOOKUP, **press** [Alt][Enter], **type** Function, **click the** Enter button ☑, **click the** Bold button **B**; **copy the contents of cell** A1 **to cell** Q1, **copy the contents of cell** M1 **to cell** R1, **widen the columns as necessary to display the text neatly, then press** Esc

   See Figure I-14. You want to know the household type for customer number 3247.

4. **Click cell** Q2, **enter** 3247, **click cell** R2, **then click the** Insert Function button 𝑓𝑥

   The VLOOKUP function in the Insert Function dialog box lets you find the household type for customer number 3247, or for any customer whose number you enter in cell Q2.

5. **In the Search for a function text box, type** Lookup, **click** Go, **click** VLOOKUP **in the Select a function list, then click** OK

   The Function Arguments dialog box opens, with boxes for each of the VLOOKUP arguments. Because the value you want to find is in cell Q2, that is the Lookup_value. The list you want to search is the customer list, so its assigned name, List, is the Table_array.

6. **Drag the** Function Arguments dialog box **down so that at least rows 1 and 2 of the worksheet are visible; with the insertion point in the Lookup_value text box, click cell** Q2, **click the** Table_array text box, **then type** List

   The column you want to search (Household Type) is the 13th column from the left column in the list range, so the Col_index_num is 13. Because you want to find an exact match for the value in cell Q2, the Range_lookup argument is FALSE.

QUICK TIP

If you want to find only the closest match for a value, enter TRUE in the Range_lookup text box. However, this can give misleading results if you are looking for an exact match. If you use FALSE and Excel can't find the value, you see an error message.

7. **Click the** Col_index_num text box, **enter** 13, **click the** Range_lookup text box, **then enter** FALSE

   Your completed Function Arguments dialog box should match Figure I-15.

8. **Click** OK

   Excel searches down the far left column of the customer list until it finds a value matching the one in cell Q2. It finds the household type for that record, Single, then displays it in cell R2. You use this function to determine the household type for one other customer.

9. **Click cell** Q2, **type** 2125, **then click** ☑

   The VLOOKUP function returns the value of Family in cell R2.

10. **Press** [Ctrl][Home], **then save the workbook**

QUICK TIP

You can also use the DGET function to find a record in a list that matches specified criteria.

FIGURE I-14: Worksheet with headings for VLOOKUP

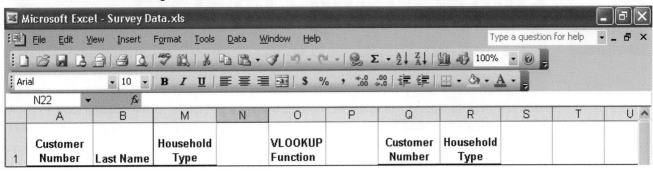

FIGURE I-15: Completed Function Arguments dialog box

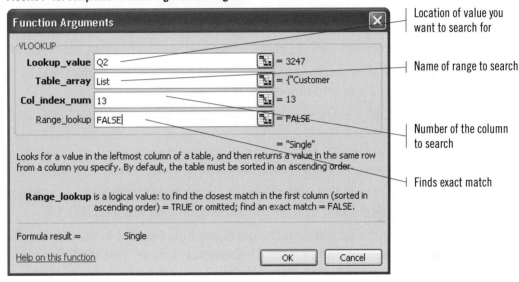

Location of value you want to search for

Name of range to search

Number of the column to search

Finds exact match

Clues to Use

Using the HLOOKUP and MATCH functions

The VLOOKUP (Vertical Lookup) function is useful when your data is arranged vertically, in columns. The HLOOKUP (Horizontal Lookup) function is useful when your data is arranged horizontally, in rows. HLOOKUP searches horizontally across the upper row of a list until it finds the matching value, then looks down the number of rows you specify. The arguments for this function are identical to those for the VLOOKUP function, with one exception. Instead of a Col_index_number, HLOOKUP uses a Row_index_number, which indicates the location of the row you want to search. For example, if you want to

search the fourth row from the top, the Row_index_number should be 4. You can use the MATCH function when you want the position of an item in a range. The MATCH function uses the syntax: MATCH (lookup_value,lookup_array,match_type) where lookup_value is the value you want to match in the lookup_array range. The match type can be 0 for an exact match, 1 for matching the largest value that is less than or equal to lookup_value or -1, for matching the smallest value that is greater than or equal to lookup_value.

Summarizing List Data

Database functions allow you to summarize list data in a variety of ways. For example, you can use them to count, average, or total values in a field for only those records that meet specified criteria. When working with a sales activity list, for example, you can use Excel to count the number of client contacts by sales representative or to total the amount sold to specific accounts by month. The format for the database function DSUM is shown in Figure I-16. Jim wants to explore the effect of yellow page and magazine ads in relation to advertising expenditures. He asks you to help by summarizing the information in his list in two ways. First, he wants you to find the total purchases to date for the advertising sources Yellow Pages and Magazine. He also wants you to count the number of records for these sources. You begin by creating a criteria range that includes a copy of the column label for the column you want to summarize, as well as the criterion itself.

STEPS

1. **With the panes still frozen, scroll down until row 31 is the top row underneath the frozen headings, then enter and format the five labels shown in Figure I-17 in the range H39:J41**

   The criteria range in H40:H41 tells Excel to summarize records with the entry Yellow Pages in the Source column. The functions will be in cells K39 and K41.

2. **Click cell K39, click the Insert Function button f_x, in the Search for a function text box, type database, click Go, click DSUM under Select a function, then click OK**

3. **In the Function Arguments dialog box, enter List in the Database text box, click the Field text box, and click cell K1, Purchases to Date**

   > **QUICK TIP**
   >
   > If you can't see the cell or range you need to select, you can move the dialog box or collapse it using the Collapse Dialog Box button to the right of the text box. Use the Redisplay Dialog Box button to re-open the dialog box.

4. **Click the Criteria text box and select the range H40:H41, then click OK**

   The result in cell K39 is 4399. For the range named List, Excel totaled the information in the column Purchases to Date for those records that meet the criterion of Source equals Yellow Pages. The DCOUNT function can help you determine the number of records meeting the criterion of Source equals Yellow Pages.

5. **Click cell K41, click f_x, in the Search for a function text box, type database, click Go, select DCOUNT from the Select a function list, then click OK**

6. **In the Function Arguments dialog box, type List in the Database text box, click the Field text box and click cell A1, Customer Number, click the Criteria text box and select the range H40:H41, then click OK**

   The result in cell K41 is 5, meaning that there are five customers who heard about MediaLoft through the Yellow Pages. This function uses the Customer Number field in the list to check for cells within the criteria range Source = Yellow Pages. You also want to see total purchases and a count for the magazine ads.

7. **Click cell H41, type Magazine, then click the Enter button**

   With total purchases of $17,794, it's clear that magazine advertising is a more effective way of attracting MediaLoft customers. Compare your results with Figure I-18.

8. **Press [Ctrl][Home], then save the workbook**

FIGURE I-16: Format of DSUM function

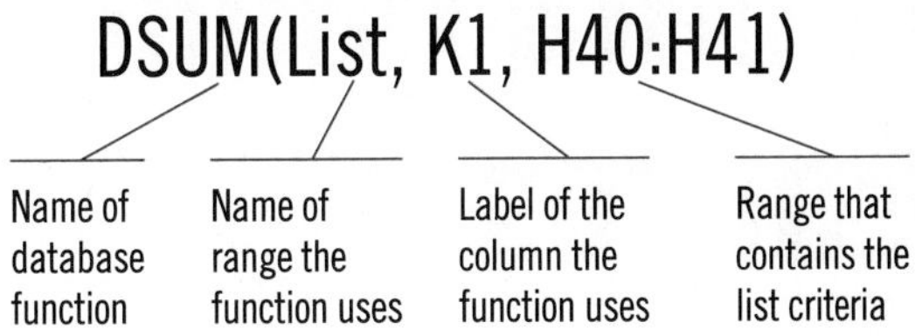

DSUM(List, K1, H40:H41)

| Name of database function | Name of range the function uses | Label of the column the function uses | Range that contains the list criteria |

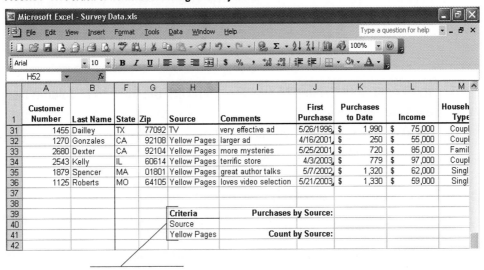

FIGURE I-17: Portion of worksheet showing summary area

Enter these labels to create a summary area

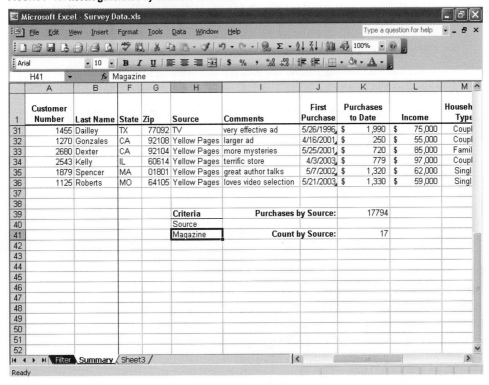

FIGURE I-18: Result generated by database functions

Using Data Validation for List Entries

The Excel Data Validation feature allows you to specify what data is valid for a range of cells. You can restrict data to whole numbers, decimal numbers, or text. You can also specify a list of acceptable entries. Once you've specified what data the program should consider valid for that cell, Excel displays an error message and can prevent users from entering any other data that it considers to be invalid. ▆▆▆▆ Jim wants to make sure that information in the Household Type column is entered consistently in the future. He asks you to restrict the entries in that column to three options: Couple, Single, and Family. First, you select the column you want to restrict.

STEPS

1. **Scroll right until Column M appears, then click the Column M column header**

   The entire column is selected.

2. **Click Data on the menu bar, click Validation, click the Settings tab if necessary, click the Allow list arrow, then click List**

   Selecting the List option lets you type a list of specific options.

   > **QUICK TIP**
   > To restrict entries to decimal or whole numbers, dates, or times, select the appropriate option in the Allow list. To specify a long list of valid entries, type the list in a column elsewhere in the worksheet, then type the address of the list in the Source text box.

3. **Click the Source text box, then type Couple, Single, Family**

   You have entered the list of acceptable entries, separated by commas. See Figure I-19. You want the data entry person to be able to select a valid entry from a drop-down list.

4. **Click the In-cell dropdown check box to select it if necessary, then click OK**

   The dialog box closes, and you return to the worksheet. The new data restrictions apply only to new or replacement entries in the Household Type column, not to existing entries.

5. **Click cell M37, then click the list arrow to display the list of valid entries**

   See Figure I-20. You could click an item in the list to have it entered in the cell, but you want to test the data restriction by entering an invalid entry.

6. **Click the list arrow to close the list, type Individual, then press [Enter]**

   A warning dialog box appears to prevent you from entering the invalid data.

7. **Click Cancel, click the list arrow, then click Single**

   The cell accepts the valid entry. The data restriction ensures that new records contain only one of the three correct entries in the Household Type column. The customer list is finished and ready for future data entry.

8. **Save the workbook, preview it, and compare your screen to Figure I-21**

9. **Print the worksheet and exit Excel**

Clues to Use

Adding input messages and error alerts

You can add an input message to cells in a worksheet to help with the data entry process by clicking the Input Message tab in the Data Validation dialog box. The message that you enter is displayed when the cell is selected. You can display error messages if invalid data is entered in a cell using the Error Alert tab in the Data Validation dialog box. The error message that you insert is displayed and the data entry stops if you choose the Stop style. Choosing the Warning or Information styles displays the error message, but allows the data entry to proceed.

FIGURE I-19: Creating data restrictions

Restricts entries to a list of valid options

List of valid options

Displays a list of valid options during data entry

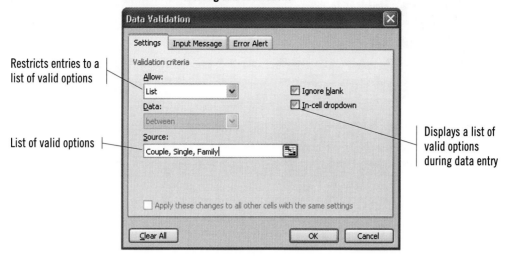

FIGURE I-20: Entering data in restricted cells

36	1125	Roberts	Yellow Pages	loves video selection	5/21/2003	$	1,330	$	59,000	Single
37										
38										Couple
39		**Criteria**		**Purchases by Source:**	17794					Single
40			Source							Family

FIGURE I-21: Print Preview of the final document

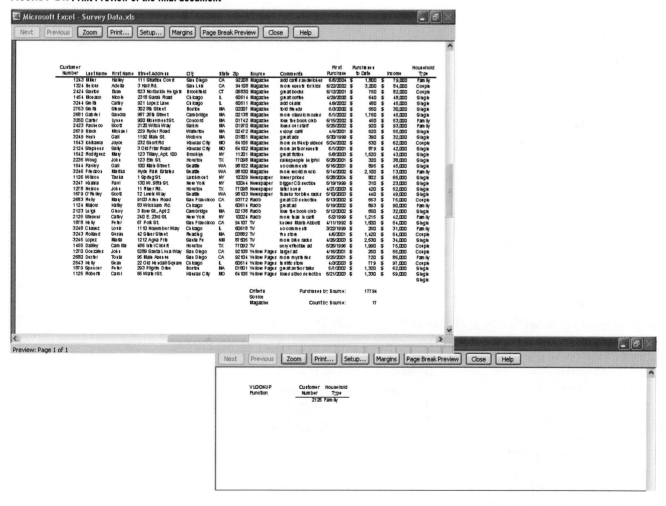

Practice

▼ CONCEPTS REVIEW

FIGURE I-22

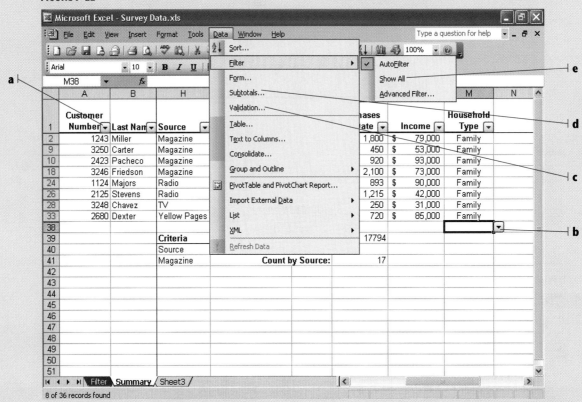

1. Which element points to an In-cell dropdown list arrow?
2. Which element points to an AutoFilter list arrow?
3. Which element would you click to remove a filter?
4. Which element do you click to group data and summarize data in a list?
5. Which element do you click to specify acceptable data for a list?

Match each term with the statement that best describes it.

6. **Table_array**	**a.** Cell range when Advanced Filter results are copied to another location
7. **Extracted list**	**b.** Range in which search conditions are set
8. **Criteria range**	**c.** Restricts list entries to specified options
9. **Data validation**	**d.** Name of the list searched in a VLOOKUP function
10. **DSUM**	**e.** Function used to total list values that meet specified criteria

Select the best answer from the list of choices.

11. The _____ logical condition finds records matching both listed criteria.
    a. And
    b. Or
    c. True
    d. False

12. What does it mean when you select the Or option when creating a custom filter?
    a. Either criterion can be true to find a match.
    b. Neither criterion has to be 100% true.
    c. Both criteria must be true to find a match.
    d. A custom filter requires a criteria range.

13. What must a list have before automatic subtotals can be inserted?
    a. Enough records to show multiple subtotals
    b. Grand totals
    c. Column or field headings
    d. Formatted cells

14. Which function finds the location of an item in a list?
    a. HLOOKUP
    b. VLOOKUP
    c. POSITION
    d. MATCH

▼ SKILLS REVIEW

1. **Retrieve records with AutoFilter.**
    a. Start Excel, open the Data File EX I-2.xls from the drive and folder where your Data Files are stored, then save it as **Compensation Summary**.
    b. With the Compensation sheet active, create a list from the data in cells A1:J11.
    c. Use AutoFilter to list records for employees in the Accounting Department.
    d. Redisplay all employees, then use AutoFilter to show the three employees with the highest annual salary.
    e. Redisplay all the records, then save the workbook.

2. **Create a custom filter.**
    a. Create a custom filter showing employees hired prior to 1/1/2002 or after 1/1/2004.
    b. Change the page setup to landscape orientation, fit to a single page, enter your name in the worksheet footer, save the workbook, preview, then print the filtered worksheet.
    c. Redisplay all records.
    d. Turn off AutoFilter.
    e. Save the workbook.

3. **Filter and extract a list with Advanced Filter.**
    a. You want to retrieve a list of employees who were hired prior to 1/1/2002 and who earn more than $100,000 a year. Define a criteria range by copying the field names in range A1:J1 to cell A14.
    b. In cell D15, enter the criterion <1/1/2002, then in cell J15 enter >100,000.
    c. Return to cell A1.
    d. Open the Advanced Filter dialog box.
    e. Indicate that you want to copy to another location, enter the criteria range A14:J15, then indicate that you want to copy it to cell A18.
    f. Confirm that the retrieved list meets the criteria.
    g. Save the workbook, preview, then print the worksheet.

4. **Create subtotals using grouping and outlines.**
   a. Click the Summary sheet tab, sort the list in ascending order by department, and in descending order by monthly salary.
   b. Group and create subtotals by department, using the SUM function; select Monthly Salary in the Add Subtotal to list box, deselect Annual Compensation. Widen the columns as necessary to display the subtotal information.
   c. Click the row level 2 button on the outline to display only the subtotals and the grand total.
   d. Enter your name in the worksheet footer, change the page orientation to landscape, save the workbook, preview, then print the first page of the worksheet displaying the subtotals and grand total.
   e. Remove the subtotals, then save the workbook.

5. **Look up values in a list.**
   a. Select A1:J11 and name the range List.
   b. You want to locate annual compensation information by entering an Employee Number. Scroll so that columns L through N are visible.
   c. In cell M2, enter 4439.
   d. In cell N2, use the VLOOKUP function and enter M2 as the Lookup_value; List as the Table_array, 10 as the Col_index_num, and FALSE as the Range_lookup.
   e. Enter another Employee Number, 8723, in cell M2, then view the annual compensation for that employee.
   f. Save the workbook.

6. **Summarize list data.**
   a. You want to enter a database function to average the annual salaries by department, using the Marketing Department as the initial criterion.
   b. Define the criteria area: in cell C14, enter Criteria; in cell C15, enter Department, then in cell C16, enter Marketing.
   c. In cell E14, enter Average Annual Salary by Department:.
   d. In cell H14, use the DAVERAGE function and enter List for the Database, click cell G1 for the Field and enter C15:C16 for the Criteria.
   e. Test the function further by entering the text Information Systems in cell C16. When the criterion is entered, cell H14 should display 67,900.
   f. Save the workbook.

7. **Use data validation for list entries.**
   a. Select column E and set a validation criterion specifying that you want to allow a list of valid options.
   b. Enter a list of valid options that restricts the entries to Accounting, Information Systems, and Marketing. Remember to use a comma between each item in the list.
   c. Indicate that you want the options to appear in an in-cell dropdown list, then close the dialog box.
   d. Go to cell E12, then select Marketing in the dropdown list.
   e. Select column F and indicate that you want to restrict the data entered to only whole numbers.
   f. In the Minimum text box, enter 1000. In the Maximum text box, enter 20000. Close the dialog box.
   g. Click cell F12, enter 25000, then press [Enter]. You should get an error message.
   h. Click Cancel, then enter 17000.
   i. Save, preview, then print the worksheet.
   j. Close the workbook, then exit Excel.

▼ INDEPENDENT CHALLENGE 1

As the owner of Olives, a gourmet food store located in Philadelphia, you spend a lot of time managing your inventory. To help with this task, you have created an Excel list of your olive oil inventory. You want to filter the list, and add subtotals and a grand total to the list. You also need to add data validation and summary information to the list.

   a. Start Excel, open the Data File EX I-3.xls from the drive and folder where your Data Files are stored, then save it as Olive Oil.

▼ INDEPENDENT CHALLENGE 1 (CONTINUED)

b. Create a list from the data on the Inventory sheet, then use AutoFilter to generate a list of extra virgin olive oil. Enter your name in the worksheet footer, save the workbook, then preview, and print the list. Clear the filter.

c. Use a Custom Filter to generate a list of olive oil with a quantity greater than 20. Preview, then print the list. Clear the filter.

d. Copy the labels in cells A1:F1 into A16:F16. Enter Extra Virgin in cell B17 and enter 2003 in cell C17. With cell A1 active, use the Advanced Filter with a criteria range of A16:F17 to extract a list of extra virgin olive oil with a vintage of 2003 to the range of cells beginning in cell A20. Save the workbook, preview, then print the list with the extracted information.

e. Click the Summary sheet tab, then sort the list in ascending order by type of olive oil. Insert subtotals by type of olive oil using the SUM function, then select Total in the Add Subtotal to list box. Click the row level 2 button on the outline to display only the subtotals and grand total. Save the workbook, enter your name in the worksheet footer, preview, then print the range containing the subtotals and grand total. Turn off subtotaling.

f. Select column B. Open the Data Validation dialog box, then select List in the Allow box. Enter Extra Virgin, Super Tuscan, Ultra Premium for the list of olive oil types in the Source text box. Make sure the In-cell dropdown check box is selected.

g. Test the data validation by entering valid and invalid data in cell B20. Delete your data from cell B20.

h. Sort the list range by vintage and then by unit price, both in ascending order.

i. Name the range A1:F13 List. Using Figure I-23 as a guide, enter a function in cell G17 that calculates the total quantity of Ultra Premium olive oil in your store.

j. Save the workbook, preview, then print the worksheet.

FIGURE I-23

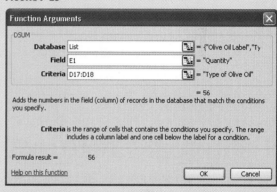

Advanced Challenge Exercise

- Copy the range A1:C1 and paste the column labels in cells A22:C22. Enter Tenno Ranch in cell A23, Ultra Premium in cell B23, 2003 in cell C23 and Price in cell F22.

- Using Figure I-24 as a guide, enter a database function in cell G22 that uses criteria in A22:C23 to find the price of the specified olive oil.

- Create a textbox and enter an explanation of the difference between the VLOOKUP and DGET functions. You can use the function dialog boxes or help topics. Move the text box to cell A26.

k. Save the workbook, preview then print the worksheet. Close the workbook, then exit Excel.

FIGURE I-24

▼ INDEPENDENT CHALLENGE 2

You recently started a business, called Custom Books. The business creates and sells personalized books for special occasions. After purchasing a distributorship from an established book company and the rights to use several of the company's titles, you started creating personalized books. Customers provide you with the name of the book's protagonist and the desired book title, and you generate the book text. You have put together an invoice list to track sales for the month of October. Now that you have this list, you would like to manipulate it in several ways. First, you want to filter the list to retrieve only books retailing for more than a particular price and ordered during a particular part of the month. You also want to subtotal the unit price and total cost columns by book title and restrict entries in the Order Date column. Finally, you would like to add database and lookup functions to your worksheet to efficiently retrieve data from the list.

a. Start Excel, open the Data File EX I-4.xls from the drive and folder where your Data Files are stored, then save it as Custom Books.

▼ INDEPENDENT CHALLENGE 2 (CONTINUED)

b. Without converting the data to a declared list, use the Advanced Filter to show books with a unit price of more than $11.99 ordered prior to 10/15/2005, using cells A27:B28 to enter your criteria and filtering the list in place. Enter your name in the worksheet footer, save the workbook, then print the filtered list in landscape orientation to fit on one page. Clear the filter, then save your work again.

c. Sort the list in ascending order by Book Title, then create subtotals in the Unit Price and Total Cost columns by book title. Save your subtotaled list, preview, then print the subtotaled list. Clear the subtotals.

d. Use the Data Validation dialog box to restrict entries to those with order dates between 10/1/2005 and 10/31/2005. Select Date in the Allow list, then enter the appropriate dates in the Start Date and End Date boxes. Test the data restrictions by attempting to enter an invalid date.

e. Name the range A1:J25 List. Enter 23721 in cell F28. Enter a VLOOKUP function in cell G28 to retrieve a customer's book title based on the invoice number entered in cell F28. Make sure you have an exact match with the invoice number. Test the function with another invoice number.

f. Enter the date 10/1/2005 in cell I28. Use the database function, DCOUNT, in cell J28 to count the number of invoices for the date in cell I28.

g. Save the workbook, preview, then print the Invoice worksheet.

Advanced Challenge Exercise

- Enter the label Average Sale in cell K27.
- Enter a database function in cell K28 that calculates the average sale (Unit Price) for the date in cell I28. (*Hint*: Use DAVERAGE.)
- Create a text box and enter an explanation of the DAVERAGE function. You can use the function dialog box or Help topics. Move the text box to cell F30.

h. Save the workbook, print the Invoice worksheet, close the workbook, then exit Excel.

▼ INDEPENDENT CHALLENGE 3

You are the manager of Readers, an independent bookstore located in San Francisco. You have created an Excel list that contains your book inventory, along with the sales figures for each book and the date it went on the bestseller list. You would like to manipulate this list to display product categories, and inventory items meeting specific criteria. You would also like to add subtotals to the list and add database functions to total sales. Finally, you want to restrict entries in the Category column.

a. Start Excel, open the Data File EX I-5.xls from the drive and folder where your Data Files are stored, then save it as Bestsellers.

b. Without converting the data to a declared list, create an advanced filter that retrieves, to its current location, records with dates before 9/10/2005 and whose sales were greater than $2500. Use cells A38:F38 to enter your criteria for the filter. Clear the filter.

c. Use cells A37:F39 to specify criteria for records with sales greater than $2500 having dates either before 9/10/2005 or after 9/24/2005. Use Figure I-25 as a guide in entering the criteria range. Create an advanced filter that extracts the records satisfying the criteria to a range starting in cell A42. Enter your name in the worksheet footer, preview, then print the worksheet.

FIGURE I-25

d. Subtotal the sales by category. Adjust column widths as necessary.

e. Use the outline to display only category names with subtotals and the grand total.

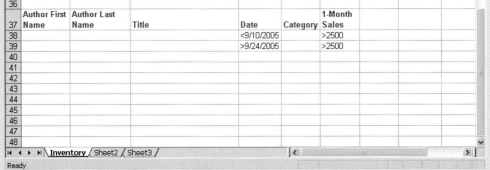

▼ INDEPENDENT CHALLENGE 3 (CONTINUED)

f. Redisplay the records and remove the subtotals.

g. Use the DSUM function in cell I2 to let worksheet users find the total sales for the category entered in cell H2, using a list name in the function. Format the cell containing the total sales appropriately, and test it with another category name.

h. Use data validation to restrict category entries to CD, Book, or Video, then test an entry with valid and invalid entries. Remove your test data.

i. Save the workbook, preview, then print the worksheet.

j. Close the workbook then exit Excel.

▼ INDEPENDENT CHALLENGE 4

You are a manager at Aussie Holidays, a travel agency that specializes in travel to Australia. You are organizing a group tour for the month of February and need to research the rates and amenities for hotels. The trip itinerary includes visiting the cities of Sydney and Cairns. You will research hotel accommodations on the Web, finding three hotels in each city. February is considered high season in Australia, and you want to find rates for a double room. You will enter information about hotel locations, prices and amenities in an Excel worksheet so you can manipulate it to determine hotels satisfying specific rate criteria that your clients select. You will also use a lookup function to locate a phone number when you provide a hotel name in your list. Finally, you will restrict the entries in certain fields to values in drop-down lists to simplify data entry and reduce errors.

a. Find information for three hotels in Cairns and three hotels in Sydney using the search engine of your choice.

b. Complete the table below with the information for six hotels you found in your search. The fields Pool, Room service, Gift shop, and AC will all have Yes/No entries. If you are using a listing from a hotel broker, you may need to search for the hotel's Web page to find some of the information.

c. Start Excel, open a new workbook, then save it as **Hotels** in the drive and folder where your Data Files are located.

d. Enter the information from the table into your Hotels workbook.

e. Create an advanced filter that retrieves records with hotels in Sydney charging less than $250 (Australian) per night. Place the filter criteria in cells A10:B11 and then extract the results of the filter to cell A13.

f. Restrict the city entries to Cairns or Sydney in cells C2:C9. Provide an in-cell dropdown list, allowing the selection of these two options. Test the dropdown list in cells C8 and C9, then remove your test data.

g. Restrict the Room Service entries to Yes or No in cells I2:I9. Provide an in-cell dropdown list, allowing the selection of these two options. Test the dropdown list in cells I8 and I9, then remove your test data.

h. Restrict the Rate to whole numbers between $100 and $400 (Australian) in cells G2:G9. Test the restriction by entering valid and invalid rates in cells G8 and G9, then remove your test data.

i. Enter **Hotel** in cell A17, and enter **Phone number** in cell B17.

j. Enter one of the hotel names you found in cell A18.

k. Enter a lookup function in cell B18 to locate the phone number for the hotel in cell A18. Make sure you match the hotel name exactly. (*Hint*: You can use a range name or range reference in the function.)

l. Enter your name in the right section of the worksheet footer, save the workbook, preview, then print the worksheet in landscape orientation on one page.

m. Close the workbook then exit Excel.

Hotel name	Street address	City	State	Phone	Fax	Rate Au$	Pool	Room service	Gift shop	AC

▼ VISUAL WORKSHOP

Open the file EX I-6.xls from the drive and folder where your Data Files are stored, then save it as **Schedule**. Complete the worksheet as shown in Figure I-26. Cells B18:E18 contain lookup functions that find the instructor, day, time, and room for the course entered in cell A18. Use CPS400 in cell A18 to test your lookup functions. Add your name to the worksheet footer, save the workbook, preview then print the worksheet in landscape orientation.

FIGURE I-26

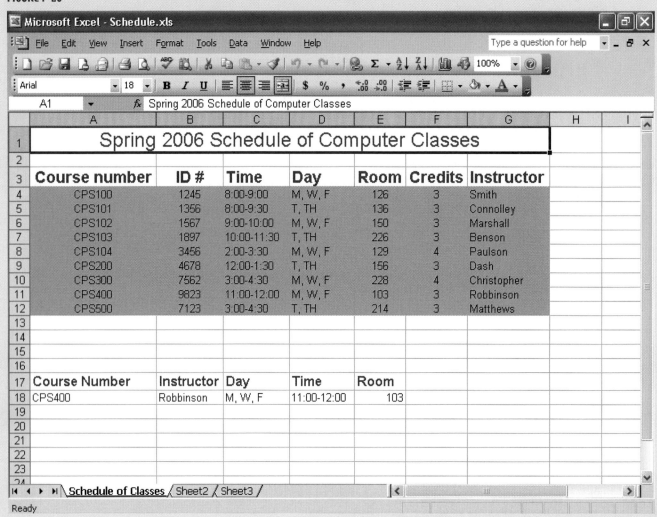

Enhancing Charts and Worksheets

OBJECTIVES

Select a custom chart type
Customize a data series
Format a chart axis
Add a data table to a chart
Rotate a chart
Enhance a chart with WordArt
Rotate text
Add a picture to a chart

If you have a SAM user profile, you may have access to hands-on instruction, practice, and assessment of the skills covered in this unit. Log in to your SAM account and go to your assignments page to see what your instructor has assigned.

There are many ways to revise a chart or a worksheet to present its data with greater impact. In this unit, you enhance both charts and worksheets by selecting a custom chart type, customizing a data series, formatting axes, adding a data table, and rotating a chart. You also add special text effects and rotate text. Finally, you enhance the appearance of a chart by adding a picture to its background. However, too much customization can be distracting; your goal in enhancing charts or worksheets is to communicate your data more clearly. MediaLoft's director of café operations, Jeff Shimada, has requested two charts showing the sales of pastry products in the first two quarters. You will produce these charts and enhance them to improve their appearance and make the worksheet data more accessible.

Selecting a Custom Chart Type

The Excel Chart Wizard offers a choice between standard and custom chart types. A **standard chart type** is a commonly used column, bar, pie, or area chart with several variations. For each standard chart type, you can choose from several subtypes, such as clustered column or stacked column. You can use the wizard to change the chart display and modify the formatting of any chart element. Excel also supplies 20 built-in **custom chart types**, with special formatting already applied. In addition, you can define your own custom chart type by modifying any of the existing standard or custom chart types. For example, you could define a chart type containing your company's logo and distribute it to other Excel users in your office.  Jeff wants you to create a chart showing the sales for each pastry type sold in January and February. To save time, you will use an Excel built-in custom chart.

STEPS

1. **Start Excel, open the Data File EX J-1.xls from the drive and folder where your Data Files are stored, then save it as** Pastry Sales

   The first step is to select the data you want to appear in the chart. In this case, you want the row labels in cells A6:A10 and the data for January and February in cells B5:C10, including the column labels. (You will add the data for March in the next lesson.)

2. **Select the range** A5:C10

3. **Click the** Chart Wizard button  **on the Standard toolbar, click the** Custom Types tab **in the Step 1 Chart Wizard dialog box, then under Select from, click the** Built-in option button **to select it if necessary**

   See Figure J-1. When the built-in option button is selected, all of the Excel custom chart types are displayed in the Chart type box, and a sample of the default chart appears in the Sample box.

4. **Click** Columns with Depth **in the Chart type box**

   A preview of the chart type appears in the Sample box. This custom chart type displays 3-D bars without gridlines.

5. **Click** Next

6. **Make sure =′TotalSales'!$A$5:$C$10 appears as the data range in the Data range box and the columns button is selected in the Step 2 Chart Wizard dialog box, then click** Next

7. **Click** Next **in the Step 3 Chart Wizard dialog box; if necessary, click the** As object in option button **in the Step 4 Chart Wizard dialog box to select it, then click** Finish

   The completed chart appears, covering part of the worksheet data.

   TROUBLE
   Remember that you can drag the Chart toolbar out of the way if it blocks your view of the chart.

8. **Scroll down the worksheet until rows 13 through 28 are visible, click the chart border and drag the chart left and down until its upper-left corner is at the top of cell** A13, **drag the** middle-right sizing handle **right to the border between column H and column I, then drag its bottom border to the bottom of row 25**

   The new chart fills the range A13:H25, as shown in Figure J-2.

9. **Save the workbook**

FIGURE J-1: Custom Types tab settings

Custom Types tab

Custom chart types

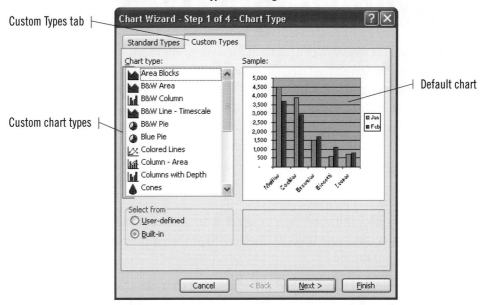

Default chart

FIGURE J-2: New chart using built-in custom type

Chart fills
range A13:H25

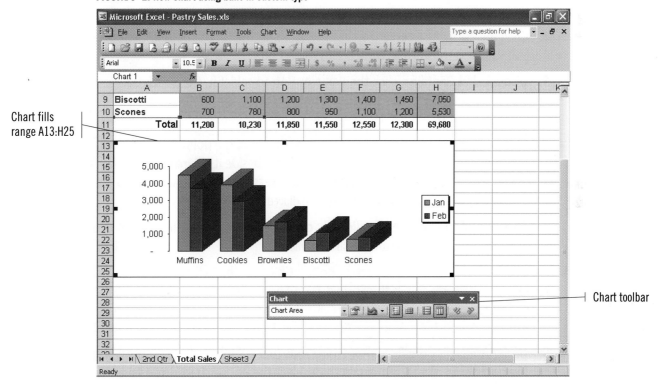

Chart toolbar

Clues to Use

Creating your own custom chart type

You can create your own custom chart type by starting with a standard chart then adding elements, such as a legend, color, or gridlines that suit your needs. After you have finished creating the chart, make sure it is selected, click Chart on the menu bar, click Chart type, click the Custom Types tab, then click User-defined. To make the chart available for later use, click Add, then type a name for your chart type in the Name text box. You can use your custom chart type to create additional charts by opening the Chart Wizard dialog box, then clicking the User-defined button in the Custom Types tab.

UNIT
J

Excel 2003

Customizing a Data Series

A **data series** is the sequence of values that Excel plots on a chart. You can customize the data series in a chart by altering the spreadsheet range that contains the chart data or by entering descriptive text, called a **data label**, which appears above a data marker in a chart. As with other Excel elements, you can change the borders, patterns, or colors of a data series. ▰▰▰▰▰ Jeff wants you to create a chart showing the amount of each type of pastry sold for the first quarter. You need to add the March data to your chart to make the chart reflect the first quarter sales. Jeff also wants you to customize the updated chart by adding data labels to one of the data series. You'll also change the color of a data series so its columns stand out more.

STEPS

1. If necessary, click the chart area to select it, scroll up until row 5 is the top row on your screen, select the range D5:D10, then position the pointer over the lower border of cell D10 until it changes to +↕+

2. Drag the selected range anywhere within the chart area, until the pointer changes to ▨⁺

   The chart now includes data for the entire first quarter: January, February, and March. Jeff wants to see more specific information about March sales.

   > **QUICK TIP**
   > The ScreenTip for the Format Selected Object button changes, depending on what chart object is selected.

3. Click the Chart Objects list arrow in the Chart toolbar, then click Series "Mar"

   See Figure J-3. Sizing handles appear on each of the columns representing the data for March.

4. Click the Format Selected Object button 📇 on the Chart toolbar, then click the Data Labels tab in the Format Data Series dialog box

   > **QUICK TIP**
   > To change the data series order of a chart, click any data series, click the Format Selected Object button on the Chart toolbar, click the Series Order tab and move the series up or down to the desired display location.

5. Under Label Contains, click the Value option to select it, then click OK

   The data labels appear on the data markers, as shown in Figure J-4. You want the value to appear above each selected data marker.

6. Click the 5000 data label to select it, move the tip of the pointer over the edge of the selected label, drag the label right to position it beside its March data marker, then move the other data labels above their March data markers; click the background to deselect the label

   The data labels would stand out if they were boldfaced.

7. Click one of the data labels, click 📇, click the Font tab, click Bold, then click OK

   You want the February data series to stand out more.

   > **QUICK TIP**
   > You can use the navigation arrows on the keyboard to select chart objects in succession.

8. Click the Chart Objects list arrow on the Chart toolbar, click Series "Feb", click 📇, then click the Patterns tab in the Format Data Series dialog box

   The maroon color in the Sample box matches the current color displayed in the chart for the February data series. See Figure J-5. You decide that the series would show up better in a brighter shade of red.

9. Under Area, click the Red color (third row, first column), click OK, press [Esc] to deselect the data series, press [Esc] again to deselect the entire chart, then save the workbook

   The February data series now appears in a brighter shade of red.

Clues to Use

Removing, inserting, and formatting legends

To insert or remove a legend, click the Legend button 📇 on the Chart toolbar to toggle the legend on or off. To format legend text,

click Legend in the Chart Objects list on the Chart toolbar, click 📇, and choose the options you want in the Font tab.

FIGURE J-3: Selected data series

Format Selected
Object button

Chart Objects
list arrow

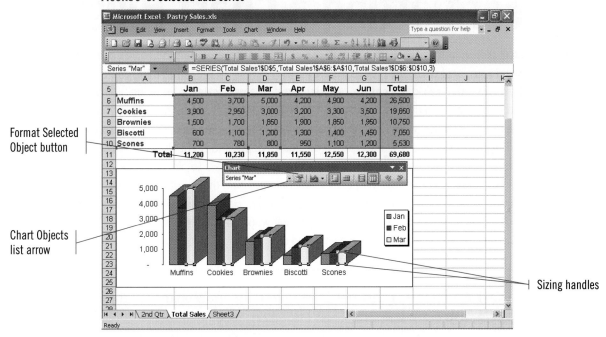

Sizing handles

FIGURE J-4: Chart with data labels

Data labels

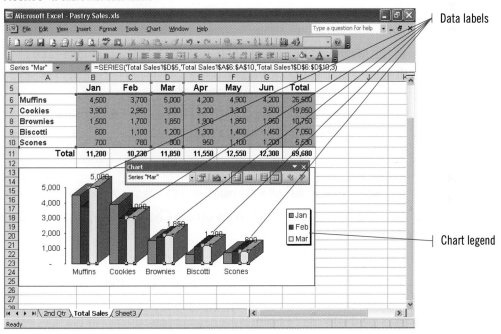

Chart legend

FIGURE J-5: Patterns tab settings

Red color choice

Current color of
February data series

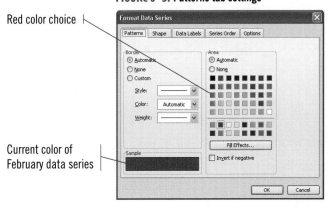

Excel 2003

Formatting a Chart Axis

Excel plots and formats chart data and places the chart axes within the chart's **plot area**. Data values in two-dimensional charts are plotted on the y-axis (often called the **value axis**) and categories are plotted on the x-axis (often called the **category axis**). Excel creates a scale for the value (y) axis based on the highest and lowest values in the series, and places intervals along the scale. A three-dimensional (3-D) chart, like the one in Figure J-6, has three axes:, the x-axis remains the category axis, but the z-axis becomes the value axis and the y-axis becomes the measure for the chart's depth and is not visible. In 3-D charts, the value (z) axis usually contains the scale. For a summary of the axes Excel uses to plot data, see Table J-1. You can override the Excel default formats for chart axes at any time by using the Format Axis dialog box. ▨▨▨ Jeff notices that the tallest column is very close to the top of the chart. He asks you to increase the maximum number on the value axis and change the axis number format. Jeff would also like you to change the font color of the pastry items on the horizontal axis to make them stand out.

STEPS

1. **Click the chart area, click the** Chart Objects list arrow **on the Chart toolbar, then click** Value Axis

    The vertical axis is selected. Because this is a 3-D chart, this is the z-axis.

2. **Click the** Format Selected Object button 🖼 **on the Chart toolbar, then click the** Scale tab

    The check marks under Auto indicate that the default scale settings appear in the text boxes on the right. You can override any of these settings by entering a new value.

3. **In the Maximum box select** 5000, **type** 6000, **then click** OK

    The chart adjusts so that 6000 appears as the maximum value on the value axis. Next, you want the minimum value to appear as a zero (0) and not as a hyphen (-).

4. **With the Value Axis still selected, click** 🖼 **on the Chart toolbar, then click the** Number tab

    Currently, a custom format is selected under Category, which instructs Excel to use a hyphen instead of zero as the lowest value.

5. **Under Category click** General, **click** OK

    The chart now shows zero (0) as the minimum value. Next, you want to change the font of the horizontal axis.

6. **Click the** Chart Objects list arrow **on the Chart toolbar, then click** Category Axis

    The horizontal axis is selected.

7. **Click** 🖼 **on the Chart toolbar, then click the** Font tab

8. **Click the** Color list arrow, **click the** Dark Blue color **(first row, third color from the right), click** OK, **press** [Esc] **twice, then save the workbook**

    The chart displays the pastry items on the horizontal axis in a dark blue font as shown in Figure J-7.

FIGURE J-6: Chart elements in a 3-D chart

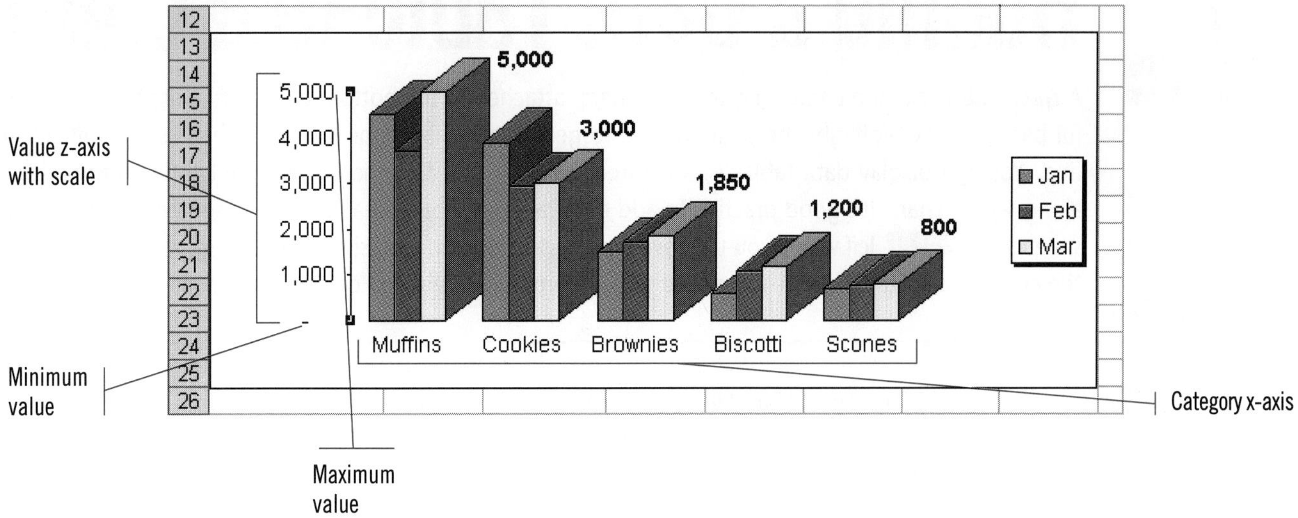

Value z-axis with scale

Minimum value

Maximum value

Category x-axis

FIGURE J-7: Chart with formatted axes

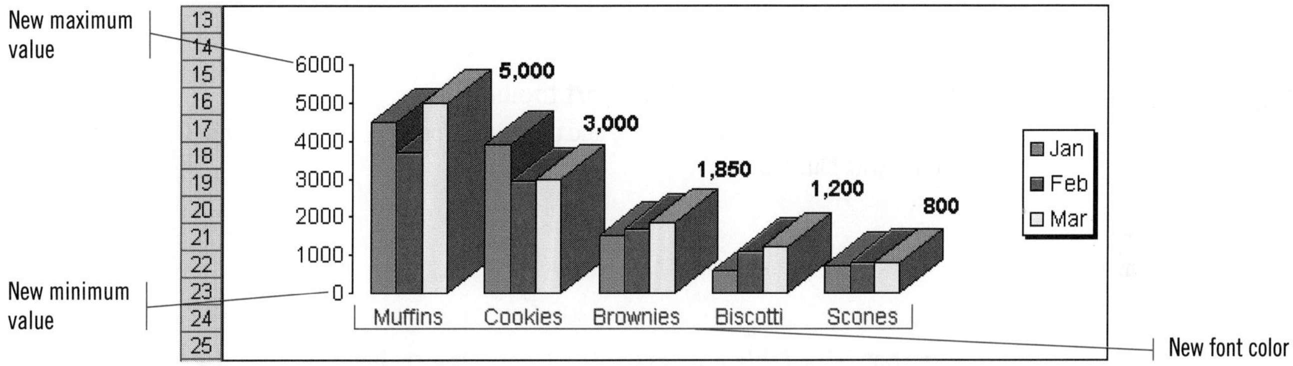

New maximum value

New minimum value

New font color

TABLE J-1: Axes used by Excel for chart formatting

axes in a two-dimensional chart	axes in a three-dimensional chart
Category (x) axis (horizontal)	Category (x) axis (horizontal)
Value (y) axis (vertical)	Series (y) axis (depth)
	Value (z) axis (vertical)

Adding a Data Table to a Chart

A **data table** is a grid containing the chart data, attached to the bottom of a chart. Data tables are useful because they highlight the data you use to generate a chart, which might otherwise be difficult to find. You can display data tables in line, area, column, and bar charts, and print them automatically along with a chart. It's good practice to add data tables to charts that are stored separately from worksheet data. ▰▰▰▰▰ Jeff wants you to move the chart to its own worksheet and change the orientation of the chart data. You decide to add a data table to emphasize the first quarter data in the chart.

STEPS

QUICK TIP
You can also move a chart to its own worksheet by clicking Chart on the menu bar, selecting Location, then clicking the As new sheet option button.

1. **Right-click the chart area, click** Location on **the shortcut menu, click the** As new sheet option button **under Place chart, then click** OK

   The chart now appears on a new sheet, named Chart1, where it is fully displayed in the worksheet window.

QUICK TIP
You can add a data table when creating a chart in Step 3 of the Chart Wizard.

2. **Click the** Data Table button 🖽 **on the Chart toolbar**

   A data table with the first quarter data appears at the bottom of the chart. See Figure J-8. Jeff wants to arrange the pastry sales data in rows instead of columns.

QUICK TIP
To hide a data table, click the Data Table button on the Chart toolbar to toggle it off.

3. **Click the** By Row button 🖽 **on the Chart toolbar**

   The months now appear on the category axis and the pastry types appear on the legend. The data table would look better in a dark blue font.

4. **Make sure that Data Table appears in the Chart Objects list box, click the** Format Selected Object button 🖼 **on the Chart toolbar, then click the** Font tab

5. **Click the** Color list arrow, **click the** Dark Blue color **(first row, third color from the right), then click** OK

   The data table is displayed in a dark blue font as shown in Figure J-9.

6. **Type your name in the left section of the sheet footer, save the workbook, then preview and print the chart sheet**

FIGURE J-8: Chart with data table

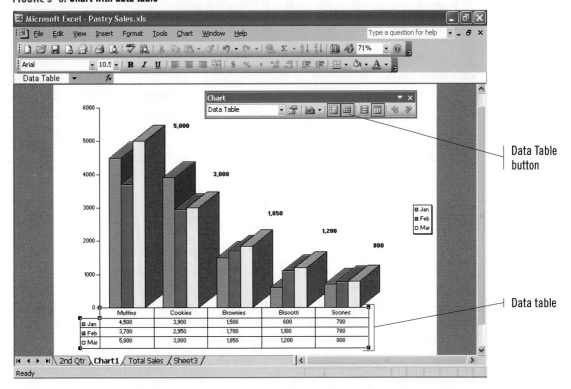

Data Table button

Data table

FIGURE J-9: Chart with formatted data table

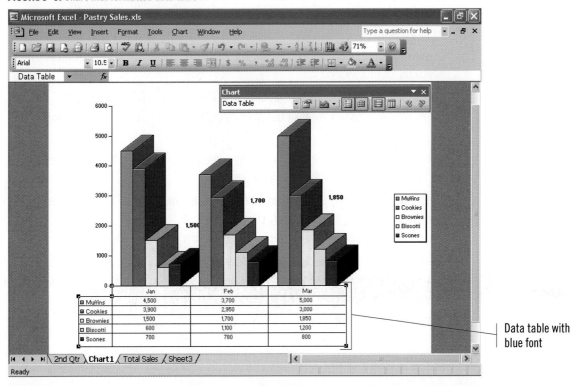

Data table with blue font

Clues to Use

Creating a trendline

Trendlines graphically represent data trends and can be added to data series in unstacked 2-D area, bar, column, line, stock, (xy) scatter, and bubble charts. To add a trendline to a data series, select the series and select the Add Trendline option on the Chart menu. You can specify the type of trendline you want in the Type tab of the Add Trendline dialog box. A trendline can be formatted by right-clicking it and selecting Format Trendline from the shortcut menu.

Excel 2003

Rotating a Chart

Three-dimensional (3-D) charts do not always display data in the most effective way. In many cases, a chart's data points can obscure the data. By rotating and/or elevating the axes, you can make the data easier to see. You can adjust the rotation and elevation of a 3-D chart by dragging it with the mouse or using the 3-D View command on the Chart menu.  Jeff has a workbook that already contains a 3-D chart illustrating the sales data for the second quarter. He wants you to rotate the chart so the June columns are easier to see.

STEPS

1. **Click the** 2nd Qtr sheet tab, **click the** Chart Objects list arrow **on the Chart toolbar, then click** Corners

   Sizing handles appear on the corners of the chart, as shown in Figure J-10.

2. **Click the** lower-front corner handle **of the chart, press and hold the left mouse button and drag left approximately 2" until it looks like the object shown in Figure J-11, then release the mouse button**

   The June columns may not be entirely visible. When using the dragging method to rotate a three-dimensional chart, you might need to make several attempts before you're satisfied with the view. It's usually more efficient to use the 3-D View option on the Chart menu.

> **TROUBLE**
> Your 3-D View dialog box settings may be different from the ones shown in Figure J-12.

3. **Click** Chart **on the menu bar, click** 3-D View, **then drag the** 3-D View dialog box **to the upper-right area of the screen**

   See Figure J-12. The preview box in the 3-D View dialog box allows you to preview changes to the chart's orientation in the worksheet.

4. **Click** Default

   The chart returns to its original position. You can also decrease the chart's elevation, which is the height from which the chart is viewed.

> **TROUBLE**
> If you have difficulty locating the Decrease Elevation button, refer to Figure J-12.

5. **To the left of the preview box, click the** Decrease Elevation button

   Notice how the preview image of the chart changes when you change the elevation.

6. **Click** Apply

   As the number in the Elevation box decreases, the viewpoint shifts downward. Next, you'll change the rotation and **perspective**, or depth, of the chart.

7. **In the Rotation box, select the current value, then type** 55; **in the Perspective box, select the current value, type** 0, **then click** Apply

   The chart is reformatted. You notice, however, that the columns appear crowded.

8. **In the Height box, select the current value, type** 70, **click** Apply, **then click** OK

   You have changed the height as a percentage of the chart base. The 3-D View dialog box closes. The chart columns now appear less crowded, making the chart easier to read.

9. **Save the workbook**

FIGURE J-10: Chart corners selected

Sizing
handles

Lower-front
corner handle

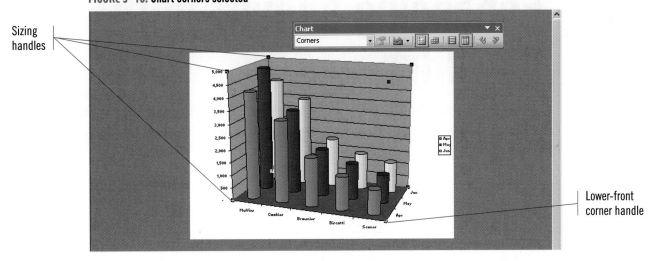

FIGURE J-11: Chart rotation in progress

Chart rotation
pointer

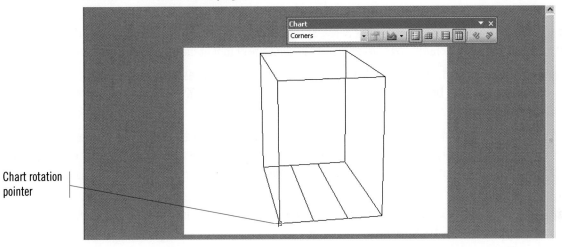

FIGURE J-12: Screen with chart and 3-D View dialog box

Increase Elevation button

Decrease Elevation button

Your settings may vary

Increase Rotation button

Preview box

Increase Perspective button

Decrease Perspective button

Your setting may be different

Decrease Rotation button

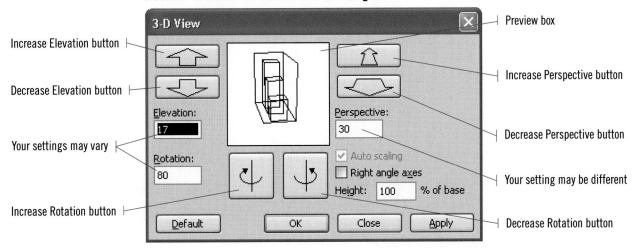

Enhancing a Chart with WordArt

You can enhance your chart or worksheet by adding **WordArt**, which is specially formatted text, using the WordArt tool on the Drawing toolbar. Once you've added a piece of WordArt to your worksheet or chart, you can edit or format it using the tools on the WordArt toolbar. WordArt text is a drawing object rather than text. This means that you cannot treat WordArt objects as if they were labels entered in a cell; that is, you cannot sort, use the spelling checker, or use their cell references in formulas. Jeff wants you to add a WordArt title to the second quarter chart.

STEPS

1. **If the Drawing toolbar does not already appear on your screen, click the** Drawing button **on the Standard toolbar**
   The Drawing toolbar appears at the bottom of the Excel window. The WordArt text will be your chart title.

2. **Click the** Insert WordArt button **on the Drawing toolbar**
   The WordArt Gallery dialog box opens. This is where you select the style for your text.

3. **In the second row, click the second style from the left, as shown in Figure J-13, then click** OK
   The Edit WordArt Text dialog box opens, as shown in Figure J-14. This is where you enter the text you want to format as WordArt. You also can adjust the point size or font of the text or select bold or italic styles.

> **QUICK TIP**
> To delete a WordArt object, click it to make sure it is selected, then press [Delete].

4. **Type** 2nd Quarter Sales, **click the** Bold button **B**, **if necessary select** Times New Roman **in the Font list box and** 36 **in the Size list box, then click** OK
   The new WordArt title appears in the middle of the chart.

> **QUICK TIP**
> To resize a WordArt object, drag any sizing handle. To rotate WordArt, drag the green rotation handle.

5. **Place the pointer over** 2nd Quarter Sales (the WordArt title) **until the pointer changes to ✛, then drag** 2nd Quarter Sales **up until it appears in the upper-right corner of the chart**
   The title is repositioned, as shown in Figure J-15. Next, you decide to edit the WordArt to change "2nd" to the word "Second."

6. **Click** Edit Text **on the WordArt toolbar, double-click** 2nd **in the Edit WordArt Text box, type** Second, **then click** OK
   The dialog box closes, and the edited title appears over the chart.

7. **Press** [Esc] **to deselect the WordArt object, then click** **to hide the Drawing toolbar**

> **QUICK TIP**
> To change the style of a WordArt object, click the WordArt Gallery button **on the WordArt toolbar, select a new style, then click OK.

8. **Enter your name in the Left section of the chart sheet footer, save the workbook, then preview and print the chart sheet**

FIGURE J-13: Selecting a WordArt style

New style to apply to text

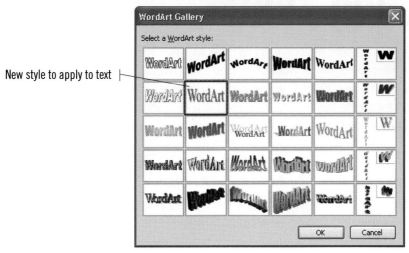

FIGURE J-14: Entering the WordArt text

Default font for this style

Default point size for this style

Italic button

Replace with your text

Bold button

FIGURE J-15: Positioning the WordArt object

New title location

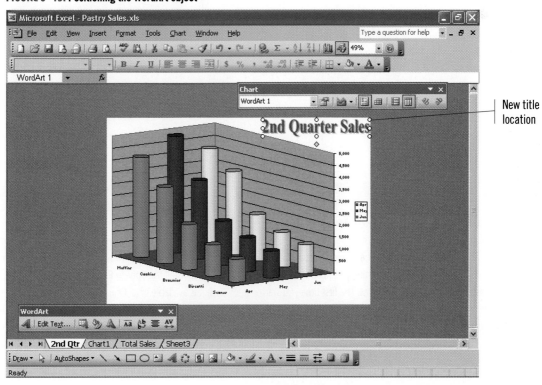

Rotating Text

By rotating text within a worksheet cell, you can draw attention to column labels or titles without turning the text into a drawing object. Unlike WordArt, rotated text retains its usefulness as a worksheet entry, which means you can still sort it, use the spelling checker, and use its cell reference in formulas. Now that you have finished enhancing the two charts in the workbook, Jeff wants you to improve the worksheet's appearance. You decide to rotate the column labels.

STEPS

1. **Click the** Total Sales sheet tab, **then select cells** B5:G5

2. **Click** Format **on the menu bar, click** Cells, **then click the** Alignment tab

    The Alignment tab of the Format Cells dialog box opens. See Figure J-16. The settings under Orientation allow you to change the rotation of cell entries. Clicking the narrow left box allows you to display text vertically in the cell. To rotate the text to another angle, you can drag the rotation indicator in the right box to the angle you want, or type the degree of angle you want in the Degrees text box.

3. **Double-click the** Degrees text box, **type** 45, **then click** OK

    The Format Cells dialog box closes and the column labels for January through June now appear at a 45-degree angle in their cells. You can also rotate a label by dragging the rotation indicator in the dialog box.

4. **Click cell** H5, **click** Format **on the menu bar, click** Cells, **then click the** Alignment tab

5. **Drag the red rotation indicator counterclockwise until the Degrees text box reads 45 degrees, click** OK, **then return to cell A1**

    The Total column label also appears at a 45-degree angle as shown in Figure J-17. The worksheet is now finished.

6. **Enter your name in the Right section of the sheet footer, save the workbook, then preview and print the worksheet**

Clues to Use

Using the Speech Recognition feature

Speech recognition technology lets you enter text and issue commands by talking into a standard microphone connected to your computer. To install the Speech Recognition feature, you need to answer some simple questions in several dialog boxes. The first time you start Speech Recognition, you step through the Training Wizard. The Training Wizard is a series of paragraphs that you read into your computer's microphone to teach the Speech program to recognize your voice and to help you learn the correct speed and clarity necessary to use the program. You can complete the training session more than once to improve the program's ability to understand your speech. Once you install the Speech Recognition component in Microsoft Word, it is available in all Office programs. To activate it, click Tools on the menu bar, point to Speech, then click Show Text To Speech Toolbar. When Speech Recognition is on, the language bar appears in the program title bar.

FIGURE J-16: Alignment tab settings

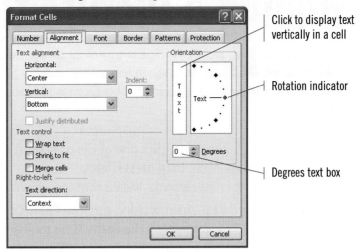

Click to display text vertically in a cell

Rotation indicator

Degrees text box

FIGURE J-17: Rotated column labels

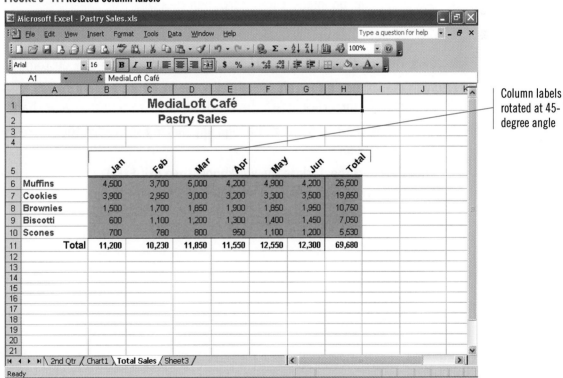

Column labels rotated at 45-degree angle

Clues to Use

Rotating chart labels

You can rotate the category labels on a chart by using the buttons on the Chart toolbar. First, select the Category Axis in the Chart Objects list box, then click either the Angle Clockwise button or the Angle Counterclockwise button on the Chart toolbar.

Adding a Picture to a Chart

You can enhance your chart by adding a picture to the data markers, chart area, plot area, legend, or chart walls and floors. ▦▦▦ Jeff wants you to improve the appearance of the second quarter chart by adding a picture to the chart walls. He also wants the MediaLoft logo to appear in the chart sheet header.

STEPS

1. **Click the 2nd Qtr sheet tab, click one of the gray chart walls, make sure the Chart Objects text box displays Walls, then press [Delete]**

   The chart wall formatting disappears, and the chart area remains selected.

2. **Select the chart walls again, making sure the Chart Objects text box displays Walls, click the Fill Color list arrow 🖌 ▾ on the Formatting toolbar**

   The fill options for the chart area appear, as shown in Figure J-18.

3. **Click Fill Effects, then click the Picture tab in the Fill Effects dialog box**

4. **Click Select Picture, click the Look in list arrow, then navigate to the drive and folder where your Data Files are stored**

   The available image files appear in the preview area of the Select Picture dialog box.

5. **Select the Cup.jpg image, click Insert, then click OK**

   A cup picture is inserted in each of the chart walls, as shown in Figure J-19. You also need the MediaLoft logo in the chart sheet header.

6. **Click View on the menu bar, click Header and Footer, then click Custom Header**

7. **With the pointer in the Left section, click the Insert Picture button 🖼, select the Logo.bmp picture, click Insert, then click OK twice to return to your chart**

8. **Preview the chart, verify that the logo appears in the header, then close the preview and save the workbook**

9. **Print the chart sheet, close the workbook, then exit Excel**

   The final Total Sales worksheet is shown in Figure J-17. The final 2nd Qtr chart sheet is shown in Figure J-19.

FIGURE J-18: Fill options

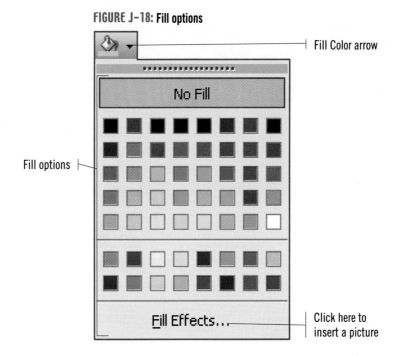

Fill Color arrow

Fill options

Click here to
insert a picture

FIGURE J-19: Chart with picture inserted

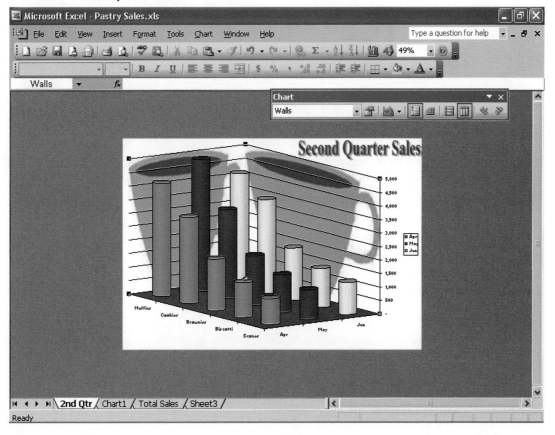

Practice

▼ CONCEPTS REVIEW

FIGURE J-20

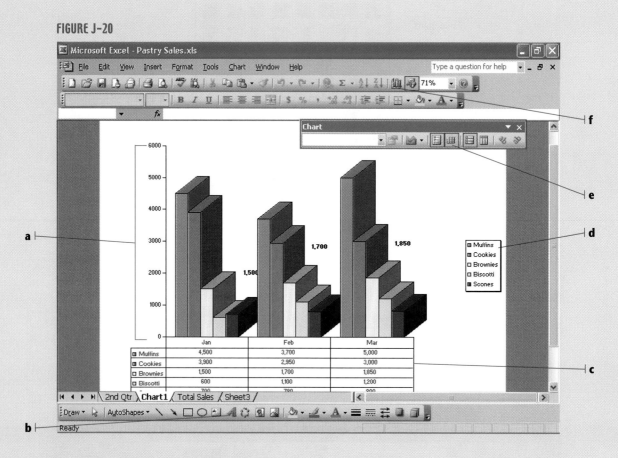

1. Which element points to the chart legend?
2. Which element points to a data table?
3. Which element do you click to add a data table to a chart?
4. Which element do you click to insert WordArt?
5. Which element points to the value axis?
6. Which element do you click to insert a chart in a worksheet?

Match each button with the statement that best describes it.

7.
8.
9.
10.
11.

a. Use to display the Drawing toolbar
b. Use to format the selected chart object
c. Use to change the style of a WordArt object
d. Use to rotate category labels on a chart clockwise
e. Use to add a data table to a chart

Select the best answer from the list of choices.

12. A chart's scale:

   a. Always appears on the x-axis.

   b. Always appears on the y-axis.

   c. Can be adjusted.

   d. Always appears on the z-axis.

13. In 3-dimensional charts, the z-axis is the:

   a. Category axis.

   b. Depth axis.

   c. 3-D axis.

   d. Value axis.

14. You can add WordArt to a chart by:

   a. Clicking the Insert WordArt button on the Standard toolbar.

   b. Clicking the Insert WordArt button on the Drawing toolbar.

   c. Clicking the Insert WordArt button on the Chart toolbar.

   d. Using the Format Cells dialog box.

15. In two-dimensional charts, the x-axis plots:

   a. Data values.

   b. The legend.

   c. Categories.

   d. Depth.

16. What is a data table?

   a. A three-dimensional arrangement of data on the y-axis.

   b. The data used to create a chart, displayed in a grid.

   c. Worksheet data arranged geographically.

   d. A customized data series.

17. Excel provides 20 built-in _____ chart types.

   a. Custom

   b. Standard

   c. Default

   d. 3-D

18. To rotate text in a worksheet cell:

   a. Click the Rotate button on the Standard toolbar.

   b. Select the text, then drag it to rotate it the desired number of degrees.

   c. Adjust settings on the Alignment tab of the Format cells dialog box.

   d. Format the text as WordArt, then drag the WordArt.

▼ SKILLS REVIEW

1. Select a custom chart type.

   a. Start Excel, open the Data File EX J-2.xls from the drive and folder where your Data Files are stored, then save it as **MediaLoft Coffee Sales**.

   b. With the 1st Quarter sheet active, select the range A4:B7.

   c. Open the Chart Wizard, and on the Custom Types tab in the Chart Wizard dialog box, make sure the Built-in option button is selected.

   d. Select Blue Pie in the Chart type box.

   e. Advance to the Step 2 Chart Wizard dialog box and make sure that the data range is correct and the data series is in columns, then proceed to Step 4 and make sure that the As object in button is selected. Finish the Wizard.

   f. Drag the chart to a location below row 10 in the worksheet, then resize it as necessary.

   g. Save the workbook.

2. Customize a data series.

    a. Display the 2nd Quarter sheet, move the June data in D4:D7 into the chart area. Increase the chart width to display all coffee types.

    b. Select the April data series and display its data labels as values on the chart.

    c. Move the April data labels above their data markers. Boldface the data markers and change the font color to red. (*Hint*: Use the Font tab of the Format Data Labels dialog box.)

    d. Use the Format Data Series dialog box to change the color of the May data series to a shade of green.

    e. Save the workbook.

3. Format a chart axis.

    a. With the 2nd Quarter sheet active, select the chart's value axis.

    b. Set the value axis maximum to 8000, minimum to zero (0), and major unit to 2000.

    c. Format the value axis with the Currency format and no decimal places using the Number tab in the Format Axis dialog box.

    d. Change the font color of the value axis to red using the Font tab in the Format Axis dialog box.

    e. Save the workbook.

4. Add a data table to a chart.

    a. Use the Location command on the Chart menu to move the chart to its own sheet.

    b. Add a data table to the chart.

    c. Click the 3rd Quarter sheet tab and select the chart.

    d. Use the Data Table button on the Chart toolbar to hide the data table.

    e. Use the Legend button on the Chart toolbar to remove the chart legend.

    f. Save the workbook.

5. Rotate a chart.

    a. Click the Chart1 sheet tab and use the Chart Objects list arrow to select the chart corners.

    b. Drag a chart corner to rotate the chart.

    c. Return the chart to its default rotation using the 3-D View command on the Chart menu.

    d. Change the rotation to 200.

    e. Change the elevation to 20.

    f. Deselect the chart corners. Move the April data labels to a location above their markers.

    g. Save the workbook.

6. Enhance a chart with WordArt.

    a. With the Chart1 sheet active, display the Drawing toolbar.

    b. Open the WordArt Gallery and select the second style from the left in the third row.

    c. In the Edit WordArt Text dialog box, enter the text Second Quarter Sales and format it in italic.

    d. Position the new title above the chart.

    e. Make sure the WordArt object is still selected, then use the WordArt Gallery button on the WordArt toolbar to select the second style from the right in the second row.

    f. Save the workbook.

    g. Close the Drawing toolbar.

7. Rotate text.

    a. Activate the 1st Quarter sheet, then select cells B4:E4.

    b. Change the orientation to 45 degrees.

    c. Activate the 2nd Quarter sheet, then select the range B4:E4.

    d. Change the orientation to 45 degrees.

    e. Save the workbook.

8. Add a picture to a chart.

    a. Activate the Chart1 sheet, then select the chart walls.

    b. Delete the formatting from the chart walls using the Delete key.

    c. With the chart walls selected, open the Fill Effects dialog box.

   d. Insert the Coffee cup.gif picture, from the drive and folder where your Data files are stored, into the chart walls.

   e. Insert the MediaLoft logo in the left section of the Chart1 sheet header.

   f. Enter your name in the footer of each worksheet.

   g. Preview each worksheet, then save the workbook.

   h. Print the four worksheets, then close the workbook.

   i. Exit Excel.

▼ INDEPENDENT CHALLENGE 1

You are the co-owner of Sandwich Express, a metropolitan delicatessen located in Baltimore, Maryland. Each week, you order several pounds of cheese: cheddar, Monterey Jack, Swiss, provolone, and American. Last month was especially busy, and you ordered an increasing amount of cheese each week in every category except American, which seems to be declining in popularity. Recently, your business partner suggested that using Excel could help you more efficiently forecast the amount of cheese to order each week. You developed a worksheet with a three-dimensional stacked bar chart to analyze last month's cheese orders. Now, you want to enhance the chart by adding data labels, reformatting the axes, increasing the elevation, and adding WordArt titles.

   a. Start Excel, open the Data File titled EX J-3.xls from the drive and folder where your Data Files are stored, then save it as **Cheese Order Tracking**.

FIGURE J-21

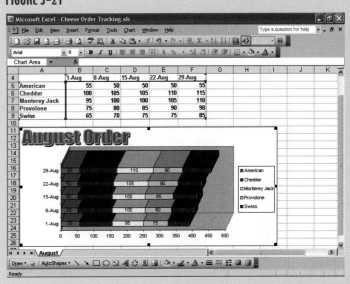

   b. Add the data for 8/22 and 8/29 to the chart.

   c. Use the Format Data Series dialog box to add values to all data markers.

   d. Use the Format Axis dialog box to reformat the value axis to display the scale in increments of 50, instead of 100 pounds.

   e. Use the 3-D View dialog box to increase the chart's elevation to 40.

   f. Add a WordArt title of **August Order** to the upper-left corner of the chart. Use the WordArt Gallery to apply the second style from the right in the second row. If necessary, resize the WordArt object so it does not overlap the data. See Figure J-21.

   g. Use the Chart menu to move the chart to its own sheet. Use the Chart toolbar to add a data table to the chart. Name the chart sheet **Cheese**.

Advanced Challenge Exercise

   ■ Modify the chart and data table so the data series are displayed in columns.

   ■ Rotate the Category Axis labels clockwise.

   ■ Change the series order on the chart to display from left to right: 29-Aug, 22-Aug, 15-Aug, 8-Aug, and 1-Aug. (*Hint*: Use the Series Order tab in the Format Data Series window.)

   ■ Change the font of the axes, legend, and data table to 12-point bold text.

   h. Enter your name in the footer of the Cheese sheet, save the workbook, preview, then print the Cheese sheet.

   i. Close the workbook and exit Excel.

▼ INDEPENDENT CHALLENGE 2

You are the assistant to the vice president of marketing at ProSoft, a software development company, located in Minneapolis, Minnesota. The vice president has asked you to chart some information from a recent survey of ProSoft customers. Your administrative assistant has entered the survey data in an Excel worksheet, which you will use to create two charts.

a. Start Excel, open the Data File titled EX J-4.xls from the drive and folder where your Data Files are stored, then save it as **Customer Survey**.

b. Using the data in A3:B8 of the Occupation data worksheet, create a pie chart on the worksheet. Select the 3-D visual effect from the standard pie chart types with the data series displayed in columns.

c. Add a WordArt title of **Occupation Data** to the chart, using the WordArt style of your choice. Move the title to the upper-left corner of the chart and resize the WordArt object as necessary so it does not overlap the chart data.

d. Move the chart to a separate sheet; name the sheet **Occupation chart**.

e. Select the Public Service pie slice by clicking the chart, then clicking the Public Service slice. Change the slice color to bright red. (*Hint*: Click the Format Selected Object button on the Chart toolbar and use the Format Data Point dialog box.)

f. On the Family data worksheet, use the Number of Children data to create a standard clustered bar chart with the data series displayed in columns.

g. Delete the legend. (*Hint*: Select the legend and press [Delete].)

h. Place the chart on a new sheet named **Family chart**.

i. Delete the chart title and add an appropriate WordArt title to the Family chart, using the style, fonts, colors, and font sizes of your choice. Move the title to the top center position on the chart.

j. Title the category axis title Number of Children. (*Hint*: Click Chart Options on the Chart menu.) Format the category axis title in 12-point bold.

k. Format the labels on both axes in 12-point bold type.

l. Enter your name in the footers of the Family chart and Occupation chart sheets.

m. Save the workbook, preview, then print the Family chart and the Occupation chart sheets.

n. Close the workbook and exit Excel.

▼ INDEPENDENT CHALLENGE 3

You were voted salesperson of the month for September at Galaxy Properties, a residential real estate company. Your sales manager has asked you to assemble a brief presentation on your sales activity during September to show to the new agents in the office. You decide to include a chart showing your sales in each of three areas: single-family homes, condominiums, and townhouses.

a. Start Excel, save a new workbook as **Real Estate Sales** in the drive and folder where your Data Files are stored.

b. Enter worksheet labels and your own data on a worksheet named **September Sales**. Format the sales data using the currency format with no decimals. Use the table below as a guide for the worksheet layout.

c. Create a bar chart on the worksheet showing your September sales figures for single-family homes, condominiums, and townhouses. Use the clustered bar with a 3-D visual effect from the standard bar types.

Galaxy Properties September Sales	
Property Type	**Sales in $**
Single-family	
Condominium	
Townhouse	

d. Add data values to the data series.

e. Delete the chart title and add a WordArt title of **September Sales**.

f. Add new data to the worksheet for multi-family homes, then add the data series to the chart.

g. Move the chart to a chart sheet named **September Chart** and add a data table. Resize the data table and WordArt title if necessary.

h. Rotate the category axis labels counterclockwise using a Chart toolbar button.

i. Change the value scale if necessary to fit your sales data and improve its readability.

j. Change the font of both axes and the data table to improve the readability.

k. Delete the chart legend. Add a value axis title of **Sales in Dollars**. (*Hint*: Click Chart Options on the Chart menu.) Format the value axis title in 12-point bold.

Advanced Challenge Exercise

- Create a custom chart type based on the modifications you made to the standard 3-D bar chart with which you started. Name the custom chart **Custom 3-D Bar** and verify that it appears in the user-defined Chart type list.
- Create a new worksheet named **October Sales** in the Real Estate Sales workbook with October sales figures. Use the format that you used for the September sales worksheet and your own data. Format the sales data using the currency format with no decimals.
- Use the custom chart, Custom 3-D Bar, to chart your October data. Place the chart on its own sheet named October Chart and add a WordArt title.
- Change the value axis scale to an appropriate value for your sales figures.

l. Enter your name in all the sheets' footers, save the workbook, then preview and print the four sheets.

m. Close the workbook and exit Excel.

▼ **INDEPENDENT CHALLENGE 4**

You are the beverage manager at Rosemont Market, a gourmet food store located in London, England. You meet twice annually with the store manager to discuss trends in departmental sales at the store. You decide to use charts to represent the sales trends for the department's beverage products. You begin by charting the tea sales for the first half of the year. Then you analyze the sales trend using a trendline. Lastly, you enhance the chart by adding a data table, reformatting the value axis, adding several titles, and adding a picture. You begin by searching the Web to find an appropriate picture for your chart.

a. Use the search engine of your choice to search the Web for photographs that are free for noncommercial use. Find a photograph that is appropriate for a chart displaying tea data. Save the picture in the drive and folder where your Data Files are stored.

b. Start Excel, open the Data File titled EX J-5.xls, then save the workbook as **Tea Sales**.

c. Create a line chart on the worksheet showing the January through May sales information. Use the standard line type for your chart with the data series in rows. Move the chart if necessary.

d. Add the June data from the table below to the worksheet, then add the data series to the chart.

e. Move the chart to its own sheet and add a data table.

f. Add a WordArt title and move it to the top center of the chart. Resize the title if necessary.

g. Move the legend to the upper-right edge of the chart area.

h. Remove the chart gridlines. (*Hint*: Select a gridline and press [Delete].)

i. Add the title, **Pounds of Tea Sold**, to the y-axis and change the font to 16-point bold.

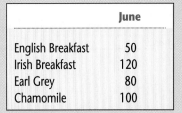

	June
English Breakfast	50
Irish Breakfast	120
Earl Grey	80
Chamomile	100

j. Change the value axis scale to increment by 40.

k. Add linear trendlines to the Irish Breakfast and English Breakfast data series. (*Hint*: Choose Add Trendline from the Chart menu, then select Linear as the type.)

l. Change the color of the trendlines to correspond to the color of the data series they represent. (*Hint*: Right-click the trendline and click Format Trendline.)

m. Add the photograph you downloaded from the Web as the background to the chart legend. Reformat the legend text if necessary for readability.

n. Enter your name in the footer of the chart sheet, save the workbook, preview, then print the chart.

o. Close the workbook and exit Excel.

▼ VISUAL WORKSHOP

Create the worksheet and accompanying custom chart shown in Figure J-22. Save the workbook as **The Dutch Garden**. Study the chart and worksheet carefully to make sure you select the displayed chart type with all the enhancements shown. (*Hint*: The source data series is charted in rows.) Enter your name in the sheet footer, preview, then print the worksheet and chart together in landscape orientation.

FIGURE J-22

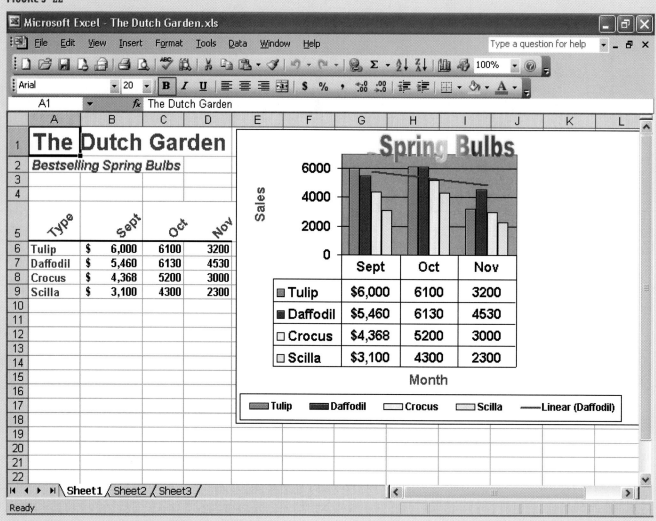

Using What-if Analysis

OBJECTIVES

Define a what-if analysis
Track a what-if analysis with Scenario Manager
Generate a scenario summary
Project figures using a data table
Create a two-input data table
Use Goal Seek
Set up a complex what-if analysis with Solver
Run Solver and generate an Answer Report

If you have a SAM user profile, you may have access to hands-on instruction, practice, and assessment of the skills covered in this unit. Log in to your SAM account and go to your assignments page to see what your instructor has assigned.

Each time you use a worksheet to explore different outcomes for Excel formulas, you are performing a **what-if analysis**. For example, what would happen to a firm's overall expense budget if company travel expenses decreased by 30%? Using Excel, you can perform a what-if analysis in many ways. In this unit, you will learn to track what-if scenarios and generate summary reports using the Excel Scenario Manager. You will design and manipulate one-input and two-input data tables to project multiple outcomes. Also, you will use the Goal Seek feature to solve a what-if analysis. Finally, you will use Solver to perform a complex what-if analysis involving multiple variables. The MediaLoft corporate office is considering the purchase of several pieces of capital equipment, as well as several vehicles. They have asked you to help analyze their options using Excel.

Defining a What-if Analysis

Excel 2003

By performing a what-if analysis in a worksheet, you can get immediate answers to questions such as "What happens to profits if we sell 30% more of a certain product?" or "What happens to monthly payments if interest rates rise or fall?" A worksheet you use to produce a what-if analysis is often called a **model** because it acts as the basis for multiple outcomes. To perform a what-if analysis in a worksheet, you change the value in one or more **input cells** (cells that contain data rather than formulas), then observe the effects on dependent cells. A **dependent cell** usually contains a formula whose resulting value changes depending on the values in the input cells. A dependent cell can be located either in the same worksheet as the changing input value or in another worksheet. ▓▓▓▓ Jim Fernandez has created a worksheet model to perform an initial what-if analysis of equipment loan payments. See Figure K-1. You will follow the guidelines below to perform a what-if analysis for him.

DETAILS

- **Understand and state the purpose of the worksheet model**

  The worksheet model is designed to calculate a fixed-rate, monthly equipment loan payment.

- **Determine the data input value(s) that, if changed, affect the dependent cell results**

  The model contains three data input values (labeled Loan Amount, Annual Interest Rate, and Term in Months), in cells B4, B5, and B6, respectively.

- **Identify the dependent cell(s), usually containing formulas, that will contain adjusted results as different data values are entered**

  There are three dependent cell formulas (labeled Monthly Payment, Total Payments, and Total Interest). The results appear in cells B9, B10, and B11, respectively.

- **Formulate questions you want the what-if analysis to answer**

  You want to answer the following questions with this model: (1) What happens to the monthly payments if the interest rate is 7%? (2) What happens to the monthly payments if the loan term is 60 months (five years) instead of 48 months (four years)? (3) What happens to the monthly payments if less-expensive equipment is purchased with a lower loan amount?

- **Perform the what-if analysis and explore the relationships between the input values and the dependent cell formulas**

  You want to see what effect a 7% interest rate has on the dependent cell formulas. Because the interest rate is located in cell B5, any formula that references cell B5 is directly affected by a change in interest rate—in this case, the Monthly Payment formula in cell B9. Because the formula in cell B10 references cell B9 and the formula in cell B11 references cell B10, however, a change in the interest rate in cell B5 affects these other two formulas as well. Figure K-2 shows the result of the what-if analysis described in this example.

FIGURE K-1: Worksheet model for a what-if analysis

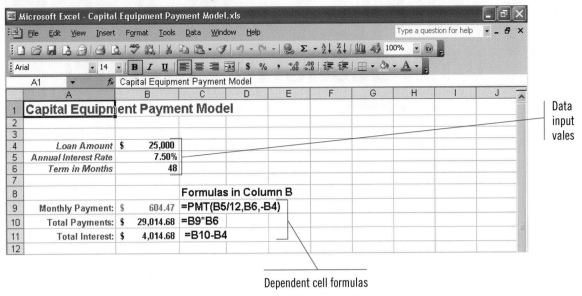

Data input vales

Formulas in Column B

Dependent cell formulas

FIGURE K-2: What-if analysis with changed input value and dependent formula results

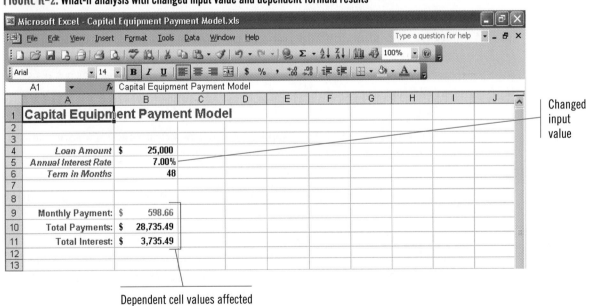

Changed input value

Dependent cell values affected by changed input value

UNIT
K
Excel 2003

Tracking a What-if Analysis with Scenario Manager

A **scenario** is a set of values you use to forecast worksheet results. The Excel Scenario Manager simplifies the process of what-if analysis by allowing you to name and save different scenarios with the worksheet. Scenarios are particularly useful when you work with uncertain or changing variables. If you plan to create a budget, for example, but are uncertain of your revenue, you can assign several different revenue values, then switch between the scenarios to perform a what-if analysis of the effects of each revenue figure on profits. Jim asks you to use Scenario Manager to consider three equipment loan scenarios: (1) the original loan quote, (2) a longer-term loan, and (3) a reduced loan amount.

STEPS

1. **Start Excel, open the Data File EX K-1.xls from the drive and folder where your Data Files are stored, then save it as Capital Equipment Payment Model**

   The first step in defining a scenario is choosing the cells that will vary in the different scenarios; these are known as **changing cells**.

2. **On the Single Loan sheet, select range B4:B6, click Tools on the menu bar, then click Scenarios**

   The Scenario Manager dialog box opens with the following message: "No Scenarios defined. Choose Add to add scenarios."

3. **Click Add, drag the Add Scenario dialog box to the right if necessary until columns A and B are visible, then type Original loan quote in the Scenario name text box**

   The range in the Changing cells box reflects your initial selection, as shown in Figure K-3.

4. **Click OK to confirm the Add Scenario settings**

   The Scenario Values dialog box opens, as shown in Figure K-4. The existing values appear in the changing cell boxes. Because this first scenario reflects the original loan quote input values ($25,000 at 7.5% for 48 months), these values are correct.

5. **Click OK**

   The Scenario Manager dialog box reappears with the new scenario listed in the Scenarios box. You want to create a second scenario, this one with a loan term of 60 months.

> **QUICK TIP**
> You can delete a scenario by selecting it in the Scenario Manager dialog box and clicking Delete.

6. **Click Add; in the Scenario name text box type Longer term loan, click OK; in the Scenario Values dialog box, select 48 in the third changing cell box, type 60, then click Add**

   You also want to consider a scenario that uses $21,000 as the loan amount.

7. **In the Scenario name text box, type Reduced loan amount, click OK; in the Scenario Values dialog box, change the 25000 in the first changing cell box to 21000, then click OK**

   The Scenario Manager dialog box reappears. See Figure K-5. All three scenarios are listed, with the most recent—Reduced loan amount—selected. Now that you have defined the three scenarios, you want to apply them and see what effect they have on the monthly payment.

8. **Make sure the Reduced loan amount scenario is still selected, click Show, notice that the monthly payment in the worksheet changes from $604.47 to $507.76; click Longer term loan, click Show, notice that the monthly payment is now $500.95; click Original loan quote, click Show to return to the original values, then click Close**

9. **Save the workbook**

FIGURE K-3: Add Scenario dialog box

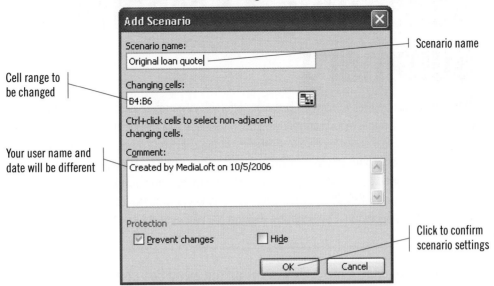

Scenario name → Scenario name

Cell range to be changed → Changing cells: B4:B6

Your user name and date will be different → Comment: Created by MediaLoft on 10/5/2006

Click to confirm scenario settings → OK

FIGURE K-4: Scenario Values dialog box

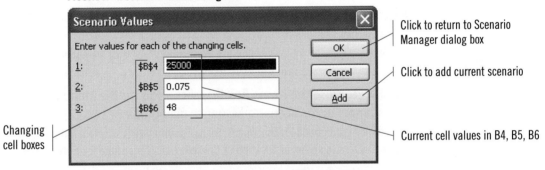

Click to return to Scenario Manager dialog box → OK

Click to add current scenario → Add

Changing cell boxes → Changing cell boxes

Current cell values in B4, B5, B6 → Current cell values in B4, B5, B6

FIGURE K-5: Scenario Manager dialog box with three scenarios listed

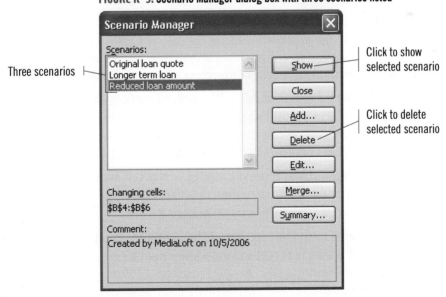

Three scenarios → Three scenarios

Click to show selected scenario → Show

Click to delete selected scenario → Delete

Clues to Use

Merging scenarios

To bring scenarios from another workbook into the current workbook, click the Merge button in the Scenario Manager dialog box. The Merge Scenarios dialog box opens, letting you select scenarios from other workbooks.

Generating a Scenario Summary

Although it may be useful to switch between different scenarios when analyzing data, in most cases you will want to refer to a single report summarizing the results of the scenarios in a worksheet. A **scenario summary** is an Excel table that compiles data from the changing cells and corresponding result cells for each scenario. You can use a scenario summary to illustrate the best, worst, and most likely scenarios for a particular set of circumstances. Naming the cells makes the summary easier to read because the names, not the cell references, appear in the report. Now that you have defined Jim's scenarios, he needs you to generate and print a scenario summary report. You begin by creating cell names in column B based on the labels in column A.

STEPS

QUICK TIP

To delete a range name, click Insert on the menu bar, point to Name, click Define, click the range name, then click Delete.

1. **Select the range** A4:B11, **click** Insert **on the menu bar, point to** Name, **click** Create, **click the** Left column check box **to select it if necessary, then click** OK
   Excel creates the names based on the labels in column A.

2. **Click cell** B4 **to make sure Loan_Amount appears in the Name box, then click the** Name Box list arrow
   All six labels appear in the Name Box list, confirming that they were created. See Figure K-6. Now you are ready to generate the scenario summary report.

3. **Press** [Esc] **to close the Name Box list, click** Tools **on the menu bar, click** Scenarios, **then click** Summary **in the Scenario Manager dialog box**
   The Scenario Summary dialog box opens. Scenario summary is selected, indicating that it is the default report type. Excel needs to know the location of the cells that contain the formula results.

4. **Select the** Result cells box, **if necessary, then select range** B9:B11 **in the worksheet**
   With the report type and result cells specified, as shown in Figure K-7, you are now ready to generate the report.

QUICK TIP

The scenario summary is not linked to the worksheet. If you change the cells in the worksheet, you must generate a new scenario summary.

5. **Click** OK
   The summary of the worksheet's scenarios appears on a new sheet titled Scenario Summary. The report appears in outline format so that you can hide or show report details. Because the Current Values column shows the same values as the Original loan quote column, you decide to delete column D.

6. **Right-click the** column D heading, **then click** Delete **in the shortcut menu**
   The column containing the current values is deleted, and the Original loan quote column data shifts to the left. Next, you want to delete the notes at the bottom of the report because they refer to the column that no longer exists. You also want to make the report title more descriptive.

7. **Select the range** B13:B15, **press** [Delete], **select cell** B2, **edit its contents to read** Scenario Summary for Equipment Loan, **then click cell** A1
   The completed scenario summary is shown in Figure K-8.

8. **Add your name to the left section of the Summary sheet footer, save the workbook, then preview and print the report in landscape orientation**

FIGURE K-6: List box containing newly created names

Name Box
list arrow

Names
match
labels in
column A

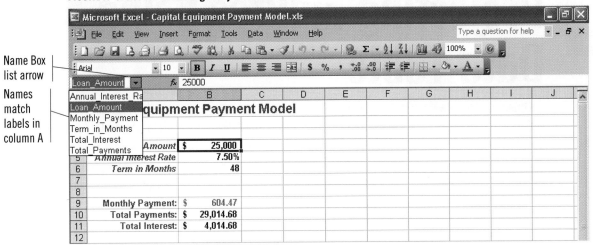

FIGURE K-7: Scenario Summary dialog box

Default report type

Cells to be recalculated when
a new scenario is applied

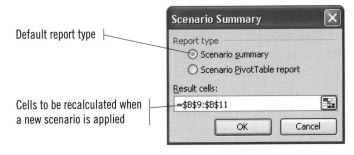

FIGURE K-8: Completed Scenario Summary report

Column D
now
contains
original
loan
quote

Report is
in outline
format

Input
cells

Result
cells

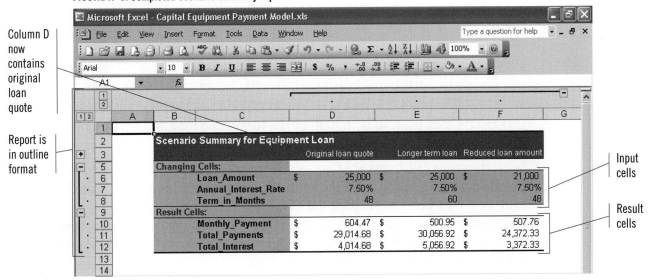

Excel 2003

Projecting Figures Using a Data Table

Another way to answer what-if questions in a worksheet is by using a data table. A **data table** is a range of cells that shows the resulting values when one or more input values is varied in a formula. For example, you could use a data table to calculate your monthly mortgage payment based on several different interest rates simultaneously. A **one-input data table** is a table that shows the result of varying one input value, such as the interest rate. ▰▰▰▰ Now that you have completed Jim's analysis, he wants you to find out how the monthly equipment payments would change as interest rates increased by increments of 0.25%. He estimates that the lowest interest rate would be about 7.00% and the highest 8.00%. You begin by creating a table structure, with the varying interest rates listed in the left column.

STEPS

1. **Click the** Single Loan sheet tab, **select cell** D4, **type** Interest, **select cell** D5, **type** 7.00%, **select cell** D6, **type** 7.25%; **select the range** D5:D6, **drag the fill handle to select the range** D7:D9, **then release the mouse button**

   With the varying interest rates (input values) listed in column D, you need to enter a formula reference to cell B9. This tells Excel to use the formula in cell B9 to calculate multiple results in column E, based on the changing interest rates in column D.

2. **Click cell** E4, **type** =B9, **then click the** Enter button ☑ **on the Formula bar**

   The value in cell B9, $604.47, now appears in cell E4, and the formula reference (=B9) appears in the formula bar. See Figure K-9. Because the value in cell E4 isn't a part of the data table (Excel only uses it to calculate the values in the table), you want to hide the contents of cell E4 from view.

3. **With cell E4 selected, click** Format **on the menu bar, click** Cells, **click the** Number tab **in the Format Cells dialog box if necessary, click** Custom **under Category, delete the codes in the Type box, type** ;;; **in the Type box, then click** OK

   The three semicolons hide the values in a cell. With the table structure in place, you can now generate the data table showing monthly payment values for the varying interest rates.

4. **Select range** D4:E9, **click** Data **on the menu bar, then click** Table

   You have highlighted the range that makes up the table structure. The Table dialog box opens, as shown in Figure K-10. This is where you indicate in which worksheet cell you want the varying input values (the interest rates in column D) to be substituted. Because the monthly payments formula in cell B9 (which you just referenced in cell E4) uses the annual interest rate in cell B5 as input, you enter a reference to cell B5. You place this reference in the Column input cell text box, rather than in the Row input cell text box, because the varying input values are arranged in a column in your data table structure.

5. **Click the** Column input cell text box, **click cell** B5, **then click** OK

   Excel generates the data table containing monthly payments for each interest rate. The monthly payment values appear next to the interest rates in column E. The new data and the heading in cell D4 need formatting.

6. **Click cell** D4, **click the** Bold button **B** **on the Formatting toolbar, then click the** Align Right button 🔳 **on the Formatting toolbar**

7. **Select the range** E5:E9, **click the** Currency Style button **$** **on the Formatting toolbar, select cell** A1, **add your name to the left section of the worksheet footer, save the workbook, then preview and print the worksheet**

   The completed data table appears as shown in Figure K-11. Notice that the monthly payment amount for a 7.50% interest rate is the same as the original loan quote in cell B9. You can use this information to cross-check the values that Excel generates in data tables.

FIGURE K-9: One-input data table structure

Reference to formula in cell D9

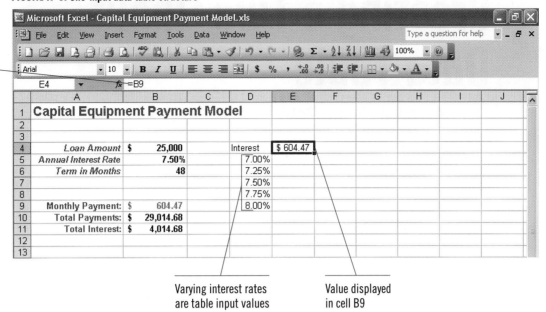

Varying interest rates are table input values

Value displayed in cell B9

FIGURE K-10: Table dialog box

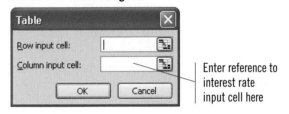

Enter reference to interest rate input cell here

FIGURE K-11: Completed data table with resulting values

Formatted heading

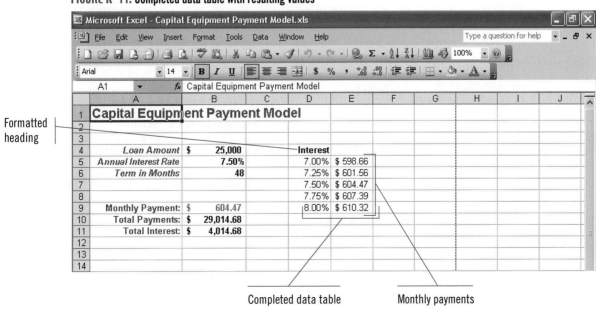

Completed data table

Monthly payments

Excel 2003

Creating a Two–input Data Table

A **two-input data table** shows the resulting values when two different input values are varied in a formula. You could, for example, use a two-input data table to calculate your monthly mortgage payment based on varying interest rates and varying loan terms. In a two-input data table, different values of one input cell appear across the top row of the table, while different values of the second input cell are listed down the left column of the table. ░░░░ Jim wants you to use a two-input data table to see what happens if the various interest rates are applied across several different loan terms, such as three, four, and five years. You begin by changing the structure of the one-input data table to accommodate a two-input data table.

STEPS

1. **With the Single Loan sheet activated, move the contents of cell D4 to cell C7; click cell C8, type Rates, click the Enter button ✓ on the Formula bar, click the Align Right button ▤ on the Formatting toolbar, then click the Bold button B on the Formatting toolbar**
   The left table heading is in place. You don't need the old data table values, and it is best to clear the cell formatting when you delete the old values.

2. **Select the range E4:E9, click Edit on the menu bar, point to Clear, then click All**
   Labels for the two types of input can make the table easier to read.

   > **TROUBLE**
   > If you do not see the value you entered in cell E4, make sure you cleared both values and formats in the correct range in Step 2.

3. **Click cell F3, type Months, click ✓, click B, click cell E4, type 36, click ✓, click cell F4, type 48, click cell G4, type 60, then click ✓**
   With both top row and left column values and headings in place, you are ready to reference the monthly payment formula. This is the formula Excel uses to calculate the values in the table. Because it is not part of the table (Excel uses it only to calculate the values in the table), it is best to hide the cell contents from view.

4. **Click cell D4, type =B9, click ✓, click Format on the menu bar, click Cells, in the Format Cells dialog box click the Number tab if necessary, click Custom, delete the codes in the Type box, type ;;; in the Type box, then click OK**
   The two-input data table structure is complete, as shown in Figure K-12. You are ready to have Excel calculate the table values.

5. **Select the range D4:G9, click Data on the menu bar, then click Table**
   The Table dialog box opens. The loan terms are arranged in a row, so you enter a reference to the loan term input cell (B6) in the Row input cell text box. The interest rates are arranged in a column, so you enter a reference to the interest rate input cell (B5) in the Column input cell text box.

   > **TROUBLE**
   > If the Table dialog box obstructs your view of the worksheet, drag it out of the way.

6. **With the insertion point positioned in the Row input cell text box, click cell B6 in the worksheet, click the Column input cell text box, then click cell B5**
   See Figure K-13. The row input cell (B6) references the loan term, and the column input cell (B5) references the interest rate. Now, you can generate the data table values and format the results.

7. **Click OK, select the range E5:G9, click the Currency Style button $ on the Formatting toolbar, then click cell F7**
   The resulting values appear, as shown in Figure K-14. The value in cell F7 matches the original quote: a monthly payment of $604.47 for a 48-month loan of $25,000 at a 7.50% interest rate.

8. **Save the workbook, then preview and print the worksheet**

FIGURE K-12: Two-input data table structure

Formula reference

Table headings

Varying input values

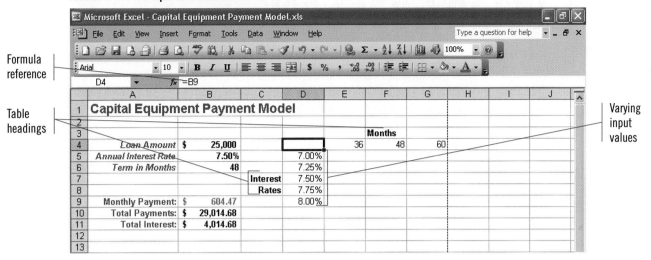

FIGURE K-13: Table dialog box

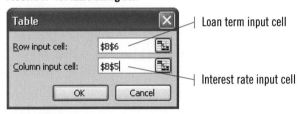

Loan term input cell

Interest rate input cell

FIGURE K-14: Completed two-input data table

Hidden reference to cell B9

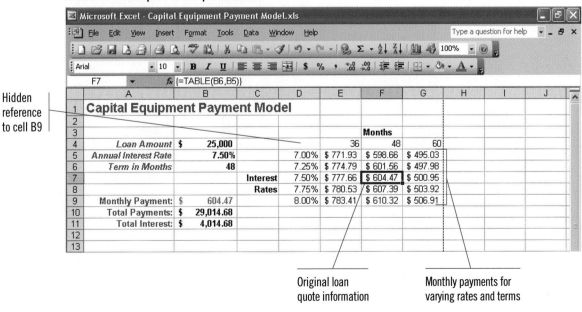

Original loan quote information

Monthly payments for varying rates and terms

Using Goal Seek

You can think of goal seeking as a what-if analysis in reverse. In a what-if analysis, you might try many sets of values to achieve a certain solution. To **goal seek**, you specify a solution, then find the input value that produces the answer you want. "Backing into" a solution in this way, sometimes referred to as **backsolving**, can save a significant amount of time. For example, you can use Goal Seek to determine how many units must be sold to reach a particular sales goal or to determine the expenses that must be cut to meet a budget. After reviewing his data table, Jim has a follow-up question: how much money could MediaLoft borrow if the company wanted to keep the total payment amount of all the equipment to $28,000? You use Goal Seek to answer his question.

STEPS

1. **On the Single Loan worksheet, click cell B10**

   The first step in using Goal Seek is to select a goal cell. A **goal cell** contains a formula in which you can substitute values to find a specific value, or goal. You use cell B10 as the goal cell because it contains the formula for total payments.

2. **Click Tools on the menu bar, then click Goal Seek**

   The Goal Seek dialog box opens. The Set cell box contains a reference to cell B10, the Total Payments cell you selected in Step 1. You need to indicate that the figure in cell B10 should not exceed 28000.

3. **Click the To value text box, then type 28000**

   The 28000 figure represents the desired solution you want to reach by substituting different values in the goal cell.

4. **Click the By changing cell box, then click cell B4**

   You have specified that you want cell B4, the loan amount, to change to reach the 28000 solution. See Figure K-15.

   > **QUICK TIP**
   > Before you select another command, you can return the worksheet to its status prior to the Goal Seek by pressing [Ctrl][Z].

5. **Click OK, then move the dialog box as necessary so that column B is visible**

   The Goal Seek Status dialog box opens with the following message: "Goal Seeking with Cell B10 found a solution." By changing the Loan Amount figure in cell B4 from $25,000 to $24,126, Goal Seek achieves a Total Payments goal of $28,000.

6. **Click OK**

   Changing the loan amount value in cell B4 changes all the values in the worksheet, including the data table. See Figure K-16.

7. **Save the workbook, then preview and print the worksheet**

FIGURE K-15: Completed Goal Seek dialog box

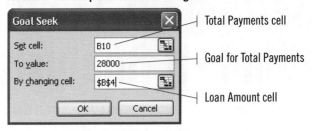

Total Payments cell

Goal for Total Payments

Loan Amount cell

FIGURE K-16: Worksheet with new values

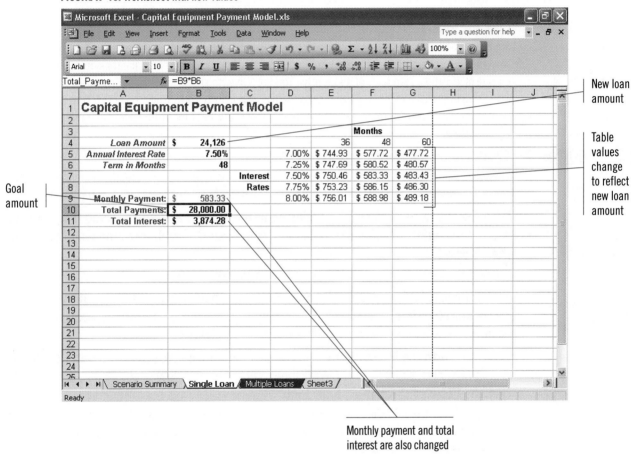

New loan amount

Table values change to reflect new loan amount

Goal amount

Monthly payment and total interest are also changed

Clues to Use

Using the Analysis ToolPak

The Analysis ToolPak is an add-in that contains many statistical analysis tools. To install the Analysis ToolPak, click Tools on the menu bar, click Add-Ins, select the Analysis ToolPak check box to select it, then click OK. To use the statistical tools, click Tools on the menu bar, click Data Analysis, click the tool that you want to use in the Data Analysis dialog box, then click OK. The Descriptive Analysis tool in the Data Analysis dialog box generates a statistical report including mean, median and mode for an input range you specify on your worksheet.

Setting up a Complex What-if Analysis with Solver

The Excel Solver finds the most appropriate value for a formula by changing the input values in the worksheet. The cell containing the formula is called the **target cell**. As you learned earlier, cells containing the values that change are called "changing cells." Solver is helpful when you need to perform a complex what-if analysis involving multiple input values or when the input values must conform to specific constraints. After seeing the analysis of interest rates and payments, Jim decides to review the vehicle purchase order for the MediaLoft shuttle service. He decides that the best plan is to purchase a combination of vans, sedans, and compact cars that can accommodate a total of 44 passengers. The total monthly payments for the vehicles should not exceed $3600. You use Solver to help Jim find the best possible combination of vehicles.

STEPS

TROUBLE

If Solver is not on your Tools menu, install the Solver add-in. Click Tools, click Add-Ins, then select the Solver Add-in check box.

1. **Click the** Multiple Loans sheet tab

   See Figure K-17. This worksheet is designed to calculate the total loan amount, total monthly payments, and total number of passengers for a combination of vans, sedans, and compact cars. It assumes an annual interest rate of 7% and a loan term of 48 months. You use Solver to change the purchase quantities in cells B7:D7 (the changing cells) to achieve your target of 44 passengers in cell B15 (the target cell). Your want your solution to include a constraint on cell B14, specifying that the total monthly payments must be less than or equal to $3600.

TROUBLE

If your Solver Parameters dialog box has entries in the By Changing Cells box or in the Subject to the Constraints box, click Reset All, click OK, then continue with Step 3.

2. **Click** Tools **on the menu bar, then click** Solver

   The Solver Parameters dialog box opens. This is where you indicate the target cell, the changing cells, and the constraints under which you want Solver to work. You begin by changing the value in the target cell.

3. **With the** Set Target Cell text box **selected in the Solver Parameters dialog box, click cell B15 in the worksheet, click the** Value of option button, **double-click the** Value of text box, **then type** 44

   You have specified a target value of 44 for the total number of passengers.

4. **Select the text in the By Changing Cells text box, then select cells** B7:D7 **in the worksheet**

   You have told Excel which cells to vary to reach the goal of 44 passengers. You need to specify the constraints on the worksheet values to restrict the Solver answer to realistic values.

5. **Click** Add, **with the insertion point in the Cell Reference text box in the Add Constraint dialog box, click cell** B14 **in the worksheet, click the list arrow in the dialog box, select <=, click the** Constraint text box, **type** 3600

   See Figure K-18. The Add Constraint dialog box specifies that cell B14 should contain total monthly payments that are less than or equal to 3600. Next, you need to add the constraint that the purchase quantities should be as close as possible to integers.

6. **Click** Add, **with the insertion point in the Cell Reference text box, select range** B7:D7 **in the worksheet, click the list arrow, then select** int

   Integer appears in the Constraint text box. Next, you need to specify that the purchase quantities should be greater than or equal to zero.

7. **Click** Add, **with the insertion point in the Cell Reference box, select cells** B7:D7, **select >=, type** 0 **in the** Constraint text box, **then click** OK

   The Solver Parameters dialog box reappears, with the constraints listed as shown in Figure K-19. In the next lesson, you run Solver and generate an Answer Report.

FIGURE K-17: Worksheet set up for a complex what-if analysis

Interest rate

Loan term

Changing cells

Amount must be less than $3600

Target cell

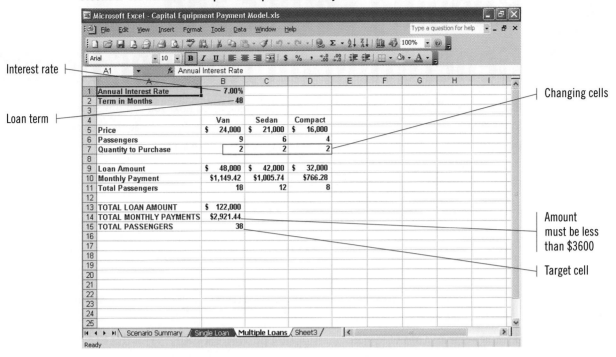

FIGURE K-18: Adding constraints

Constraints affect this cell

Cell containing total monthly payments

Less than or equal to symbol

Highest possible monthly payment

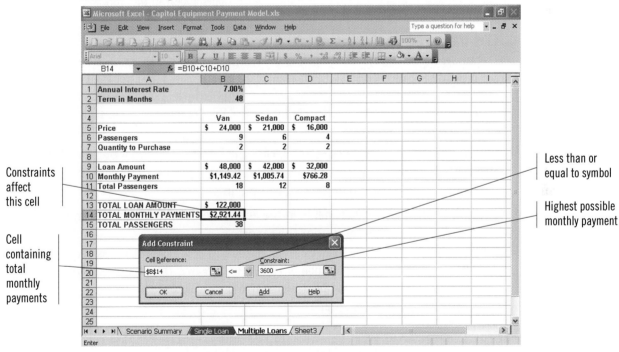

FIGURE K-19: Completed Solver Parameters dialog box

Target cell

Changing cells

Constraints on worksheet values

Target value

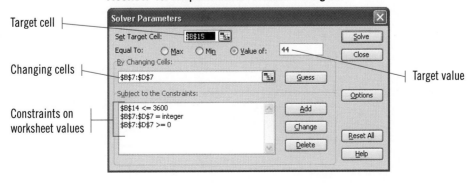

Running Solver and Generating an Answer Report

After entering all the parameters in the Solver Parameters dialog box, you can run Solver to find a solution. In some cases, Solver may not be able to find a solution that meets all of your constraints; then you would need to enter new constraints and try again. Once Solver finds a solution, you can choose to create a special report displaying the solution. ██████ You have finished entering the parameters in the Solver Parameters dialog box. Jim wants you to run Solver and create an Answer Report.

STEPS

1. **Make sure your Solver Parameters dialog box matches Figure K-19 in the previous lesson**

2. **Click** Solve

   After a moment, the Solver Results dialog box opens, indicating that Solver has found a solution. See Figure K-20. The solution values appear in the worksheet, but you decide to move them to a special Answer Report and display the original values in the worksheet.

3. **Click the** Restore Original Values option button, **click** Answer **in the Reports list box, then click** OK

   The Solver Results dialog box closes, and the original values appear in the worksheet. The Answer Report appears on a separate sheet.

4. **Click the** Answer Report 1 sheet tab

   The Answer Report displays the solution to the vehicle-purchasing problem, as shown in Figure K-21. To accommodate 44 passengers and keep the monthly payments under $3600, you need to purchase two vans, three sedans, and two compact cars. Solver's solution includes two long decimals, in cells E8 and E14, that are so small as to be insignificant. Additionally, the Original Value column in the Answer Report doesn't contain any useful information.

5. **Click cell** E8, **press** [Ctrl], **click cell** E14, **click the** Decrease Decimal button ⬚ **on the Formatting toolbar until the cells display no decimal places, right-click the** column D heading, **then click** Delete **in the shortcut menu**

6. **Return to cell A1, enter your name in the left section of the report footer, save the workbook, then preview and print the report**

   The Answer Report displays the Final Values for the number of vehicles as integers. See Figure K-22. You've successfully found the best combination of vehicles using Solver. The settings you specified in the Solver Parameters for the Multiple Loans worksheet are saved along with the workbook.

7. **Close the workbook and exit Excel**

FIGURE K-20: Solver Results dialog box

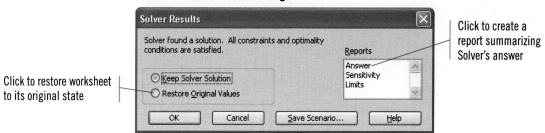

Click to create a
report summarizing
Solver's answer

Click to restore worksheet
to its original state

FIGURE K-21: Answer Report

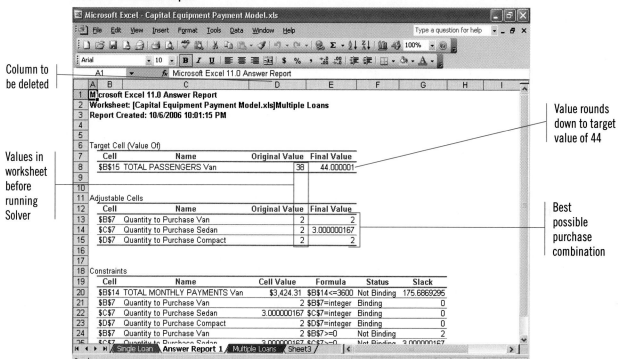

Column to
be deleted

Value rounds
down to target
value of 44

Values in
worksheet
before
running
Solver

Best
possible
purchase
combination

Excel 2003

FIGURE K-22: Completed Answer Report

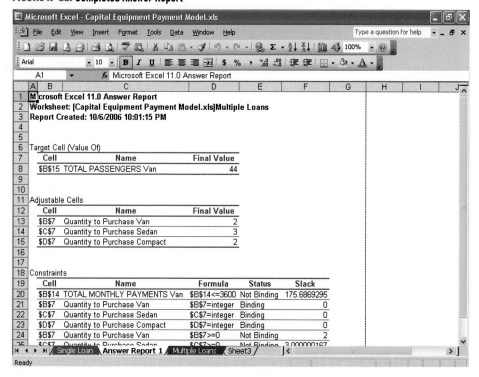

Practice

▼ CONCEPTS REVIEW

FIGURE K-23

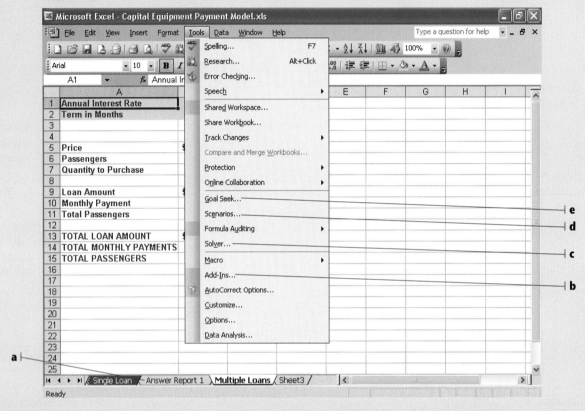

1. Which element do you click to perform a what-if analysis?
2. Which element do you click to find the input values that produce a specified result?
3. Which element is the result of running Solver?
4. Which element do you click to find a solution that meets certain constraints by changing input values in the worksheet?
5. Which element do you click to install Solver if it does not appear on the Tools menu?

Match each term with the statement that best describes it.

6. Goal Seek
7. Solver
8. Two-input data table
9. One-input data table
10. Scenario summary

a. Add-in that helps you solve complex what-if scenarios with multiple input values
b. Separate sheet with results from the worksheet's scenarios
c. Generates values resulting from varying two sets of changing values in a formula
d. Helps you backsolve what-if scenarios
e. Generates values resulting from varying one set of changing values in a formula

Select the best answer from the list of choices.

11. To hide the contents of a cell from view, you can use the custom number format:
   a. —
   b. ""
   c. ;;;
   d. Blank

12. The integer constraint can be added to cells in the Solver Parameters dialog box by choosing:
   a. int
   b. **.**
   c. **
   d. **.00

13. When you use Goal Seek, you specify a _____, then find the values that produce it.
   a. Solution
   b. Changing value
   c. Row input cell
   d. Column input cell

14. In Solver, the cell containing the formula is called the:
   a. Target cell
   b. Input cell
   c. Output cell
   d. Changing cell

▼ SKILLS REVIEW

1. **Define a what-if analysis.**
   a. Start Excel, open the Data File EX K-2.xls from the drive and folder where your Data Files are stored, then save it as **Capital Equipment Repair Model**.
   b. With the Cappuccino Machine Repair worksheet displayed, state the purpose of the worksheet model.
   c. Locate the data input cells.
   d. Locate any dependent cells.
   e. Write three questions that this what-if analysis model could answer.

2. **Track a what-if analysis with Scenario Manager.**
   a. Set up the most likely scenario with the current data input values. Select the range B3:B5, then create a scenario called **Most Likely**.
   b. Add a scenario called **Best Case** using the same changing cells, but change the Labor cost per hr. in the $B$3 text box to **70**, change the Parts cost per job in the $B$4 text box to **60**, then change the Hrs. per job value in cell $B$5 to **1**.
   c. Add a scenario called **Worst Case**. For this scenario, change the Labor cost per hr. in the $B$3 text box to **90**, change the Parts cost per job in the $B$4 text box **70**, then change the Hrs. per job in the $B$5 text box to 3.
   d. If necessary, drag the Scenario Manager dialog box to the right until columns A and B are visible.
   e. Show the Worst Case scenario results.
   f. Show the Best Case scenario results. Finally, display the Most Likely scenario results.
   g. Close the Scenario Manager dialog box.
   h. Save the workbook.

3. **Generate a scenario summary.**
   a. Create names for the input value cells and the dependent cell in the range A3:B7 (based on the left column).
   b. Verify that the names were created.
   c. Create a scenario summary report using the Cost to complete job value in cell B7 as the result cell.
   d. Edit the title of the Summary report in cell B2 to read **Scenario Summary for Cappuccino Machine Repair**.
   e. Delete the Current Values column.
   f. Delete the notes beginning in cell B11.
   g. Return to cell A1, enter your name in the left section of the Scenario Summary sheet footer, save the workbook, then preview and print the Scenario Summary sheet.

4. Project figures using a data table.

    a. Click the Cappuccino Machine Repair sheet tab.

    b. Enter the label Labor $ in cell D3.

    c. Format the label so that it is boldfaced and right-aligned.

    d. In cell D4, enter 70; then in cell D5, enter 75.

    e. Select range D4:D5, then use the fill handle to extend the series to cell D8.

    f. In cell E3, reference the job cost formula by entering =B7.

    g. Format the contents of cell E3 as hidden, using the ;;; Custom formatting type on the Number tab of the Format Cells dialog box.

    h. Generate the new job costs based on the varying labor costs: select range D3:E8 and create a data table. In the Table dialog box, make cell B3, the labor cost, the column input cell.

    i. Format range E4:E8 as currency.

    j. Enter your name in the worksheet footer, save the workbook, then preview and print the worksheet.

5. Create a two-input data table.

    a. Move the contents of cell D3 to cell C6.

    b. Delete the contents of range E4:E8, but do not clear the formatting.

    c. Format cell E3 using the General category on the Number tab of the Format Cells dialog box, then move the contents of cell E3 to cell D3.

    d. Format the contents of cell D3 as hidden, using the ;;; Custom formatting type on the Number tab of the Format Cells dialog box.

    e. Enter Hours per job in cell F2, and format it so it is boldfaced.

    f. Enter 1 in cell E3, enter 1.5 in cell F3, then enter 2 in cell G3.

    g. Select range D3:G8 and create a data table, making cell B5 the row input cell and cell B3 the column input cell.

    h. Format the range F4:G8 as currency.

    i. Save the workbook, then preview and print the worksheet.

6. Use Goal Seek.

    a. Click cell B7, and open the Goal Seek dialog box.

    b. Determine what the parts would have to cost so that the cost to complete the job is $160. Enter a job cost of 160 as the To value, and enter B4 (the Parts cost) as the By changing cell; write down the parts cost that Goal Seek finds.

    c. Click OK, then use [Ctrl][Z] to reset the parts cost to its original value.

    d. Enter the cost of the parts in cell B14.

    e. Determine what the labor would have to cost so that the cost to complete the job is $155. Use [Ctrl][Z] to reset the labor cost to its original value. Enter the labor cost in cell B15.

    f. Save the workbook, then preview and print the worksheet.

7. Perform a complex what-if analysis with Solver and generate an Answer Report.

    a. Click the Vehicle Repair sheet tab to make it active, then open the Solver dialog box.

    b. Make B14 (the total repair costs) the target cell, with a target value of 13000.

    c. Use cells B6:D6, the number of scheduled repairs, as the changing cells.

    d. Specify that cells B6:D6 must be integers and greater than or equal to zero.

    e. Use Solver to find a solution.

    f. Generate an Answer Report and restore the original values to the worksheet.

    g. Edit the Answer Report to delete the original values column.

    h. Enter your name in the left section of the report footer, save the workbook, then preview and print the Answer Report.

    i. Close the workbook then exit Excel.

▼ INDEPENDENT CHALLENGE 1

You are a sales representative for Ed-Toys, a toy company located in Minneapolis, Minnesota. Your sales territory includes five states in the Midwest. You submit a monthly expense report detailing car expenses calculated on a mileage basis. Your vehicle expenses have been increasing as your sales territory has grown. Your sales manager has asked you to research the monthly cost of purchasing a company car to see if it is more economical than expensing vehicle costs on your own car. You have created a preliminary worksheet model to determine the monthly payments for a $20,000 car, based on several different interest rates and loan terms using data from the company's bank. You will compare two-, three-, and four-year car loans. Using Scenario Manager, you create the following three scenarios: a four-year loan at 5.0%; a three-year loan at 4.75%; and a two-year loan at 4.5%. You prepare a scenario summary report for your manager showing the payment details.

a. Start Excel, open the Data File EX K-3.xls from the drive and folder where your Data Files are stored, then save it as **Car Loan Payment Model**.

b. Create cell names for the cells B4:B11 based on the labels in cells A4:A11, using the Name option on the Insert menu.

c. You use Scenario Manager to calculate the monthly payment on a $20,000 loan under three sets of loan possibilities. Create the following three scenarios, using cells B5:B6 as the changing cells for each one. Enter the interest rate in the first Scenario values text box and the number of months in the second Scenario values text box.

Scenario Name	Interest Rate	Term
5.0 percent	.05	48
4.75 percent	.0475	36
4.5 percent	.045	24

d. Show each scenario to make sure it performs as intended, then display the 5.0 percent scenario.

e. Generate a scenario summary titled **Scenario Summary for $20,000 Car Purchase**. Use cells B9:B11 as the Result cells.

f. Delete the Current Values column in the report. Delete the notes at the bottom of the report.

g. Enter your name in the left section of the Scenario Summary sheet footer. Save the workbook, preview, then print the scenario summary.

Advanced Challenge Exercise

- Create a copy of the Loan sheet using the Move or Copy Sheet option on the Edit menu. Delete the existing scenarios in the copied sheet.

- Create a new scenario in the copied sheet called **My Loan** using an interest rate and term available at a local lending institution.

- Merge the scenarios from the Loan sheet into the new sheet. (*Hint*: Use the Merge option in the Scenario Manager dialog box.)

- Generate a scenario summary titled **Advanced Scenario Summary** using cells B9:B11 as the Result cells. Delete the Current Values column in the report and the notes at the bottom.

- Enter your name in the left section of the Scenario Summary2 sheet footer, save the workbook, preview then print the Advanced Scenario Summary in landscape orientation.

h. Close the workbook, then exit Excel.

▼ INDEPENDENT CHALLENGE 2

You are a senior staff associate at Capital Adventures, a venture capital firm located in Albany, New York. One of the vice presidents has asked you to prepare a loan summary report for a software development company seeking capital for a business expansion. You need to develop a model to show what the monthly payments would be for a $900,000 loan, over 5- and 10-year terms, with interest rates ranging in 0.25% increments. You first create a two-input data table that shows the results of varying loan term and interest rates, then you use Goal Seek to specify a total payment amount for this loan application.

a. Start Excel, open the Data File EX K-4.xls from the drive and folder where your Data Files are stored, then save it as **Capital Loan Payment Model**.

b. Reference the monthly payment amount from cell B9 in cell D4, and format the contents of cell D4 as hidden.

▼ INDEPENDENT CHALLENGE 2 (CONTINUED)

c. Using cells D4:F13, create a two-input data table structure with varying interest rates for 5- and 10-year terms. Use cells D5:D13 for the interest rates, with 5% as the lowest possible rate and 7% the highest. Vary the rates in between by 0.25%. Use Figure K-24 as a guide.

d. Generate the data table that shows the effect of varying interest rates and loan terms on the monthly payments. Use cell B6, Term in Months, as the row input cell, and cell B5, the Annual Interest Rate, as the column input cell. Format cells E5:F13 as currency.

FIGURE K-24

	A	B	C	D	E	F	G
1	Capital Adventures						
2							
3					Terms		
4	Loan Amount	$ 900,000			60	120	
5	Annual Interest Rate	6.00%		5.00%			
6	Term in Months	60		5.25%			
7				5.50%			
8				5.75%			
9	Monthly Payment:	$ 17,399.52		6.00%			
10	Total Payments:	$ 1,043,971.28		6.25%			
11	Total Interest:	$ 143,971.28		6.50%			
12				6.75%			
13				7.00%			

e. Select cell B10 and use Goal Seek to find the interest rate necessary for a total payment amount of $1,000,000. Use cell B5, the Annual Interest Rate, as the By changing cell. Accept the solution found by Goal Seek.

f. Enter your name in the worksheet footer, save the workbook, then preview and print the worksheet.

g. Close the workbook, then exit Excel.

▼ INDEPENDENT CHALLENGE 3

You are the owner of Computer City, a small computer store, where you custom configure PCs to sell to the home and business markets. You have created a financial model to determine the costs and profits associated with your three most popular configurations: PC-1, PC-2, and PC-3. You want to show how the hourly labor cost affects the total profit for each PC model your company produces. To do this, you use Goal Seek. You also want to do a what-if analysis regarding the effect of hours per unit on total profit. You decide to solve the problem by using Solver, where you can specify multiple constraints for the solution. Finally, you produce an Answer Report summarizing your analysis.

a. Start Excel, open the Data File EX K-5.xls from the drive and folder where your Data Files are stored, then save it as **PC Production Model**.

b. Enter the labels shown in cells A12:A14 in Figure K-25.

c. Use Goal Seek to find the hourly labor cost that produces a total profit for model PC-1 of $15,000. In cell D12, record the labor cost next to the label in cell A12, then reset the labor cost to its original value.

FIGURE K-25

	A	B	C	D	E	F	G	H	I
1	Computer City								
2	Hourly labor cost	80							
3	Component cost	75							
4									
5		Hours per Unit	Components per Unit	Cost to Produce	Retail Price	Unit Profit	Units Produced	Total Profit	
6	PC-1	4.00	6	770	995	225	53	11,925	
7	PC-2	3.00	9	915	1,200	285	75	21,375	
8	PC-3	5.00	12	1,300	1,600	300	62	18,600	
9								51,900	
10									
11									
12	Labor cost for $15,000 profit for PC-1								
13	Labor cost for $25,000 profit for PC-2								
14	Labor cost for $20,000 profit for PC-3								
15									

d. Use Goal Seek to find the hourly labor cost that produces a total profit for model PC-2 of $25,000. In cell D13, record the labor cost next to the label in cell A13, then reset the labor cost to its original value.

e. Use Goal Seek to find the hourly labor cost that produces a total profit for model PC-3 of $20,000. In cell D14, record the labor cost next to the label in cell A14, then reset the labor cost to its original value.

f. Format your labor costs in cells D12:D14 as currency.

g. Use Solver to set the total profit of all configurations to $75,000. Use the hours per unit, cells B6:B8, as the changing cells. Specify that cells B6:B8 must be greater than or equal to 0 and less than or equal to 5.

h. Generate an Answer Report and restore the original values in the worksheet.

Advanced Challenge Exercise

- To complete this Advanced Challenge Exercise, you will need to use the Descriptive Analysis tool. If the Descriptive Analysis command does not appear on your Tools menu, install the Analysis ToolPak add-in: Click Tools on the menu bar, click Add-Ins, click to place a check mark next to Analysis ToolPak, then click OK.
- Return to the Model worksheet and use the Descriptive Statistics tool in the Data Analysis dialog box to produce a summary statistical analysis of the total profits for the three PC models. (*Hint*: Use the Data Analysis command on the Tools menu and select Descriptive Statistics. Use Figure K-26 as a guide to enter the Input Range. Notice that Grouped by Columns, Labels in First Row, New Worksheet, and Summary statistics are selected.)
- Adjust the column widths as necessary to display the statistical information. Use yellow as a fill color to emphasize the cells that contain mean and median profit information. Format the mean and median profit cells as currency with zero decimal places.

FIGURE K-26

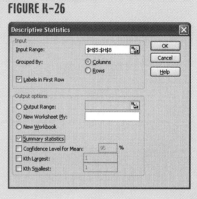

i. Enter your name in the left footer section of each worksheet. Save the workbook, then preview and print each sheet each on one page.

j. Close the workbook then exit Excel.

▼ INDEPENDENT CHALLENGE 4

You are the vice president of marketing for E-Learn, a distance learning consulting firm. You will be relocating to Toronto, Ontario, to set up the first Canadian office. You have sold your house and plan to use the $100,000 in equity to purchase a $200,000 home in Toronto. You will research mortgage rates for Toronto banks and mortgage brokers on the Web finding 7-year and 10-year interest rates. You'll enter the rates in a worksheet and use them to estimate monthly housing payments. You have created a preliminary worksheet model to determine these monthly payments and will investigate the effect of rate changes on your monthly payments.

a. Use the search engine of your choice to find 7-year and 10-year mortgage rates at a Toronto bank or mortgage broker.

b. Start Excel, open the Data File EX K-6.xls from the drive and folder where your Data Files are stored, then save it as **Mortgage Research**.

c. Use the Rates worksheet to enter one of the rates you found for a 7-year mortgage.

d. Create a data table structure for the worksheet with varying interest rates for 7-year and 10-year terms. Begin with a rate at least 1% lower than the 7-year rate you found as the lowest possible rate. Make the highest possible interest rate at least 1% greater than the 10-year rate you found, and vary the rates in between by 0.25%. Use Figure K-27 as a guide, using the rates you found. Use bold formatting as shown in the figure.

FIGURE K-27

	A	B	C	D	E	F	G
1	Mortgage Loan Payment Model						
2							
3	Home Price	$ 200,000			Term		
4	Down Payment	$ 100,000			84	120	
5	Loan Amount	$ 100,000		5.85%			
6	Annual Interest Rate	6.85%		6.10%			
7	Term in Months	84		6.35%			
8				6.60%			
9				6.85%			
10	Monthly Payment:	$ 1,501.95		7.10%			
11	Total Payments:	$ 126,163.46		7.35%			
12	Total Interest:	$ 26,163.46		7.60%			
13				7.85%			
14				8.10%			
15				8.35%			
16				8.60%			

e. Reference the monthly payment cell in the table and format it as hidden.

f. Generate a two-input data table for the worksheet. Use cell B7 as the row input cell and B6 as the column input cell.

g. You decide that you want to limit your housing payments to $1000 per month. You can accomplish this by using some of your savings to increase your down payment. Find the down payment amount that reduces your monthly payments to $1000 using the data and formulas in B3:B10 and Goal Seek. Make a note of the down payment amount then restore the worksheet to its original values. Record the answer found by Goal Seek in cell A20 of the worksheet.

h. Enter your name in the left section of the worksheet footer, save the workbook, then preview and print the worksheet.

i. Close the workbook, then exit Excel.

▼ VISUAL WORKSHOP

Create the worksheet shown in Figure K-28. Make sure to generate all three tables as data tables. Save the workbook as Notebook Payment Model. Add your name to the footer, then preview and print the worksheet in landscape orientation. Print the worksheet again with the formulas displayed.

FIGURE K-28

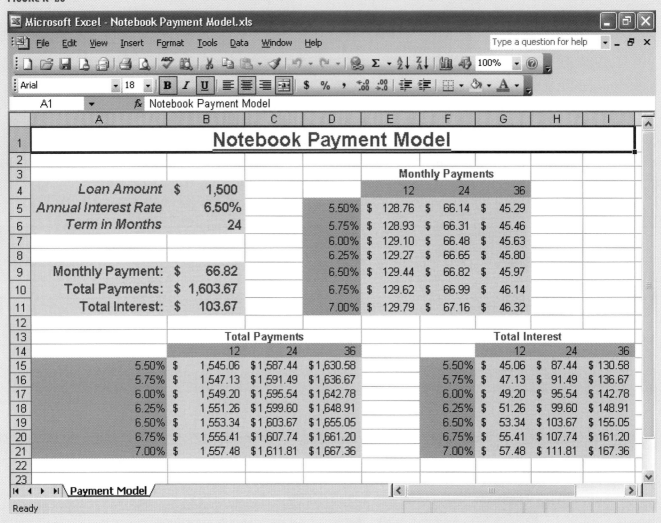

Microsoft Excel - Notebook Payment Model.xls

	A	B	C	D	E	F	G	H	I
1	Notebook Payment Model								
2									
3					Monthly Payments				
4	Loan Amount	$ 1,500			12	24	36		
5	Annual Interest Rate	6.50%		5.50%	$ 128.76	$ 66.14	$ 45.29		
6	Term in Months	24		5.75%	$ 128.93	$ 66.31	$ 45.46		
7				6.00%	$ 129.10	$ 66.48	$ 45.63		
8				6.25%	$ 129.27	$ 66.65	$ 45.80		
9	Monthly Payment:	$ 66.82		6.50%	$ 129.44	$ 66.82	$ 45.97		
10	Total Payments:	$ 1,603.67		6.75%	$ 129.62	$ 66.99	$ 46.14		
11	Total Interest:	$ 103.67		7.00%	$ 129.79	$ 67.16	$ 46.32		
12									
13			Total Payments				Total Interest		
14			12	24	36		12	24	36
15	5.50%	$ 1,545.06	$1,587.44	$1,630.58		5.50%	$ 45.06	$ 87.44	$ 130.58
16	5.75%	$ 1,547.13	$1,591.49	$1,636.67		5.75%	$ 47.13	$ 91.49	$ 136.67
17	6.00%	$ 1,549.20	$1,595.54	$1,642.78		6.00%	$ 49.20	$ 95.54	$ 142.78
18	6.25%	$ 1,551.26	$1,599.60	$1,648.91		6.25%	$ 51.26	$ 99.60	$ 148.91
19	6.50%	$ 1,553.34	$1,603.67	$1,655.05		6.50%	$ 53.34	$ 103.67	$ 155.05
20	6.75%	$ 1,555.41	$1,607.74	$1,661.20		6.75%	$ 55.41	$ 107.74	$ 161.20
21	7.00%	$ 1,557.48	$1,611.81	$1,667.36		7.00%	$ 57.48	$ 111.81	$ 167.36
22									
23									

Payment Model

Ready

EXCEL K-24 USING WHAT-IF ANALYSIS

Analyzing Data with PivotTables

OBJECTIVES

Plan and design a PivotTable report
Create a PivotTable report
Change the summary function of a PivotTable report
Analyze three-dimensional data
Update a PivotTable report
Change the structure and format of a PivotTable report
Create a PivotChart report
Use the GETPIVOTDATA function

If you have a SAM user profile, you may have access to hands-on instruction, practice, and assessment of the skills covered in this unit. Log in to your SAM account and go to your assignments page to see what your instructor has assigned.

The Excel **PivotTable** feature lets you summarize selected worksheet data in an interactive table format. You can freely rearrange, or "pivot," parts of the table structure around the data and summarize any data values within the table by category. You also can view data three-dimensionally, with data for each category arranged in a stack of pages. There are two PivotTable features in Excel: PivotTable reports and PivotChart reports. In this unit, you will plan, design, create, update, and change the layout and format of a PivotTable report. You will also add a page field to a PivotTable report, then create a PivotChart report. The Sales Department is getting ready for its annual meeting and the eastern regional sales manager has asked Jim Fernandez, the marketing director for MediaLoft, to develop an analysis of products sold in its Boston, New York, and Washington, DC, stores over the past year. Jim asks you to create a PivotTable to summarize the 2006 sales data by quarter, product, and city.

Planning and Designing a PivotTable Report

Creating a **PivotTable report** (often called a PivotTable) involves only a few steps. Before you begin, however, you need to review the data and consider how a PivotTable can best summarize it. ▰▰▰▰▰ Jim asks you to design a PivotTable to display MediaLoft's sales information for its eastern cities. You begin by reviewing guidelines for creating PivotTables.

DETAILS

Before you create a PivotTable, think about the following guidelines:

- **Review the source data**

  Before you can effectively summarize data in a PivotTable, you need to understand the source data's scope and structure. The source data does not have to be defined as a list, but should be in a list-like format. That is, it should not have any blank rows or columns, and should have the same type of data in each column. There should be repeated information in one or more fields in order for the PivotTable to effectively group it. There should also be numeric data that the PivotTable can total for each group. The data columns represent categories of data, which are called fields, just as in a list. You are working with product sales information that Jim received from MediaLoft's eastern region sales manager. This list is shown in Figure L-1. Notice that there is repeated information in the Item, City, and Quarter columns, so you will be able to summarize this data effectively in a PivotTable.

- **Determine the purpose of the PivotTable and write down the names of the fields you want to include**

  The purpose of your PivotTable is to summarize sales information by quarter across various cities. You will include the following fields in the PivotTable: Product ID, Item, City, Quarter, and Sales.

- **Determine which field contains the data you want to summarize and which summary function you want to use**

  You want to summarize sales information by summing the sales field for each product in a city by quarter. You'll do this by using the Excel SUM function.

- **Decide how you want to arrange the data**

  The layout of a PivotTable is crucial in delivering its intended message. Product ID will appear in the PivotTable columns, City, and Quarter will appear in rows, and the PivotTable will summarize Sales figures. See Figure L-2.

- **Determine the location of the PivotTable**

  You can place a PivotTable in any worksheet of any workbook. Placing a PivotTable on a separate worksheet makes it easier to locate, however, and prevents you from accidentally overwriting parts of an existing sheet. You decide to create the PivotTable as a new worksheet in the current workbook.

FIGURE L-1: Sales worksheet

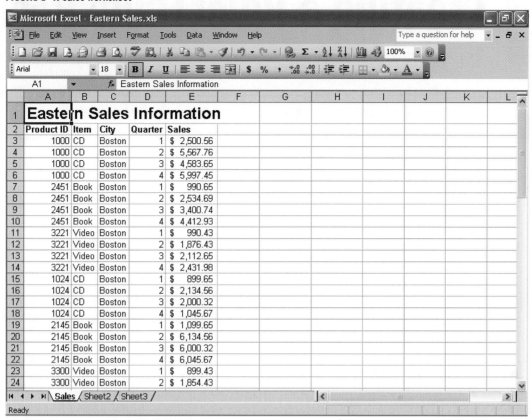

FIGURE L-2: Example of a PivotTable report

Product ID values appear in column area

Cities appear in row area

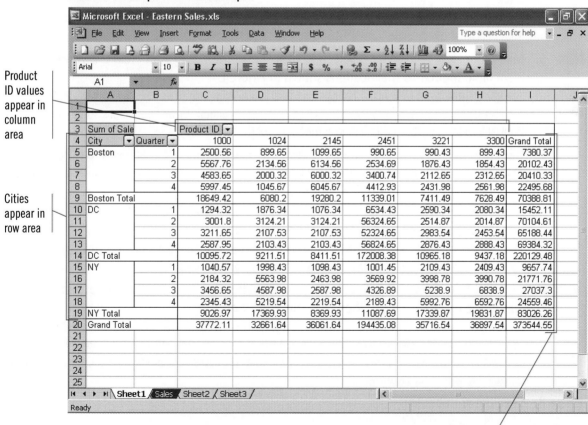

Sales figures are summarized in the data area

Excel 2003

Creating a PivotTable Report

Once you've planned and designed your PivotTable, you can create it. The PivotTable Wizard takes you through the process step by step. With the planning and design stage complete, you are ready to create a PivotTable that summarizes sales information. The sales managers in Boston, New York, and Washington, DC will use this information to develop a marketing plan for the coming year.

STEPS

1. **Start Excel if necessary, open the Data File EX L-1.xls from the drive and folder where your Data Files are stored, then save it as Eastern Sales**

   This worksheet contains the year's sales information for MediaLoft's eastern region, including Product ID, Item, City, Quarter, and Sales. Notice that the records are sorted by city.

2. **Select cell A1 if necessary, click Data on the menu bar, then click PivotTable and PivotChart Report**

   The first PivotTable and PivotChart Wizard dialog box opens, as shown in Figure L-3. This is where you specify the type of data source you want to use for your PivotTable: an Excel list or database, an external data source (for example, a Microsoft Access file), or multiple consolidation ranges (worksheet ranges). You also have the option of creating a PivotTable or PivotChart report.

3. **Make sure the Microsoft Office Excel list or database option button is selected, make sure PivotTable is selected, then click Next**

   The second PivotTable and PivotChart Wizard dialog box opens. Because the cell pointer was located within the list before you opened the PivotTable Wizard, Excel automatically completes the Range box with the table range that includes the selected cell—in this case, $A$2:$E$74.

4. **Click Next**

   The third PivotTable and PivotChart Wizard dialog box opens. You use this dialog box to specify where you want to place the PivotTable.

TROUBLE
To display the PivotTable toolbar, click View on the menu bar, point to Toolbars, then click PivotTable to select it.

5. **Make sure New Worksheet is selected, click Finish, then drag your Field List window and PivotTable toolbar to the locations shown in Figure L-4**

   The **PivotTable toolbar** contains buttons that allow you to manipulate data. The PivotTable Field List window contains field names that you can add to the PivotTable by adding them into various "drop areas" of the PivotTable or by using the Add To button at the bottom of the list window.

6. **Click the Product ID field in the PivotTable Field List, click the list arrow at the bottom of the window, choose Column Area, then click the Add To button; click the City field in the PivotTable Field List, click the list arrow at the bottom of the window, choose Row Area, then click the Add To button; click the Quarter field in the PivotTable Field List, verify that Row Area is selected, then click the Add To button**

   The Quarter field is added to the right of the City field in the Row Area. You have created a PivotTable with the Product IDs as column headers and Cities and Quarters as row labels.

QUICK TIP
To remove a field from a PivotTable, drag it outside of the PivotTable area.

7. **Click the Sales field in the PivotTable Field List, click the list arrow at the bottom of the window, choose Data Area, then click the Add To button**

   Because SUM is the Excel default function for data fields containing numbers, Excel automatically calculates the sum of the sales by product ID and by city and quarter. The PivotTable tells you that Product #1000 Boston sales were twice the New York sales level. Product 2451 was the best selling product overall, as you can see in the grand total row. See Figure L-5.

8. **Save the workbook**

FIGURE L-3: First PivotTable Wizard dialog box

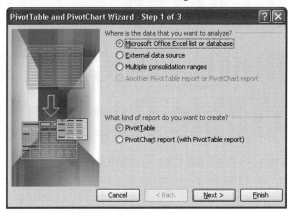

FIGURE L-4: New PivotTable ready to receive field data

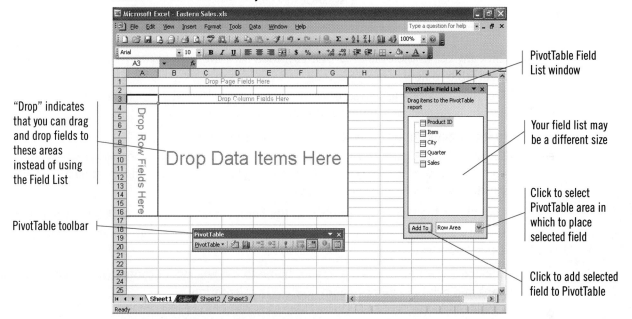

"Drop" indicates that you can drag and drop fields to these areas instead of using the Field List

PivotTable toolbar

PivotTable Field List window

Your field list may be a different size

Click to select PivotTable area in which to place selected field

Click to add selected field to PivotTable

FIGURE L-5: New PivotTable with fields in place

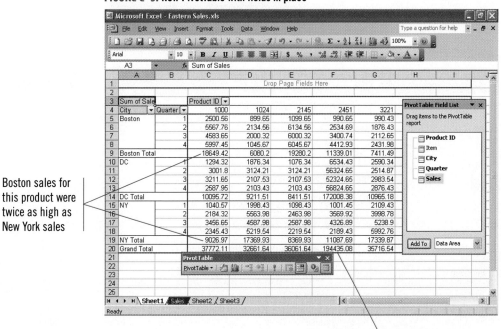

Boston sales for this product were twice as high as New York sales

Product 2451 outsold all products

Changing the Summary Function of a PivotTable Report

A PivotTable's **summary function** controls how Excel calculates the table data. Unless you specify otherwise, Excel applies the SUM function to numeric data and the COUNT function to data fields containing text. However, you can easily change the SUM function to a different summary function, such as AVERAGE, which calculates the average of all values in the field. ▰▰▰▰▰ Jim wants you to calculate the average sales for the northeastern cities using the AVERAGE function.

STEPS

1. **Click any cell in the data area (A3:I20), then click the Field Settings button 🖳 on the PivotTable toolbar**

   The PivotTable toolbar buttons are described in Table L-1. The PivotTable Field dialog box opens. The selected function in the Summarize by list box determines how the data is calculated.

2. **In the Summarize by list box, click Average, then click OK**

   The PivotTable Field dialog box closes. The data area of the PivotTable shows the average sales for each product by city and quarter. See Figure L-6. After reviewing the data, you decide that it would be more useful to sum the salary information than to average it.

   > **QUICK TIP**
   > When you name a PivotTable sheet, it is best to avoid using spaces in the name. If a PivotTable name contains a space, you must put single quotes around the name when you refer to it in a function.

3. **Click 🖳 on the PivotTable toolbar; in the Summarize by list box, click Sum, then click OK**

   The PivotTable Field dialog box closes and Excel recalculates the PivotTable—this time, summing the sales data instead of averaging it.

4. **Rename Sheet1 PivotTable, add your name to the worksheet footer, then save the workbook and print the worksheet in landscape orientation.**

TABLE L-1: PivotTable toolbar buttons

button	name	description
PivotTable ▾	PivotTable Menu	Displays menu of PivotTable commands
📄	Format Report	Displays a list of PivotTable AutoFormats
📊	Chart Wizard	Creates a PivotChart report
▤	Hide Detail	Hides detail in table groupings
▤	Show Detail	Shows detail in table groupings
↨	Refresh Data	Updates list changes within the table
📑	Include Hidden Items in Totals	Includes values for all items in totals, including hidden items
📋	Always Display Items	Turns on drop-down selections for PivotTable fields
🖳	Field Settings	Displays a list of field settings
📋	Show/Hide Field List	Displays/hides PivotTable Field List window; in a chart, displays or hides outlines and labels

FIGURE L-6: PivotTable showing averages

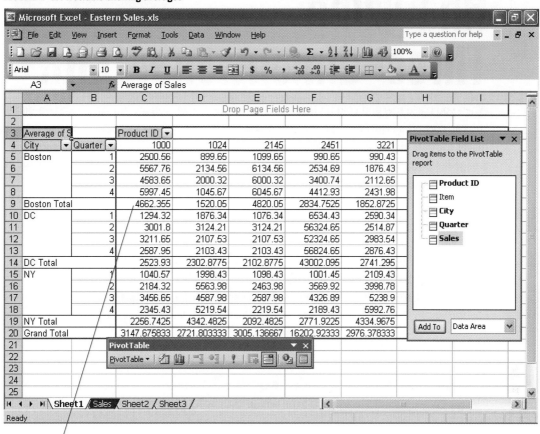

Boston Average for
Product ID 1000

Clues to Use

Changing PivotTable report field names

You can make your PivotTable report easier to read by changing the field names to more descriptive names. You can rename a field by double-clicking the field name to open the PivotTable Field List dialog box and entering the new field name in the Name textbox. This only changes the name in the PivotTable, not in the Field List. You can also rename a field by clicking the field name and then clicking the Field Settings button on the PivotTable toolbar to open the PivotTable Field dialog box.

Analyzing Three-dimensional Data

When you place row and column fields to create a PivotTable, you are working with two-dimensional data. You can convert a PivotTable to a three-dimensional data analysis tool by adding a page field. A **page field** makes the data appear as if it is stacked in pages, thus adding a third dimension to the analysis. When using a page field, you are in effect filtering data through that field. Jim wants you to filter the PivotTable so that only one quarter's data is visible at one time.

STEPS

TROUBLE
If the Quarter field was not added to the PivotTable, redo Step 1, making sure you click the Quarter field in the Field List.

1. **Click the** Quarter field name **in the PivotTable Field List, click the list arrow in the lower-right corner of the field list, select** Page Area, **click** Add To
   The PivotTable is re-created with a page field showing data for all the quarters. You can easily view the data for each quarter.

QUICK TIP
To display each page of the page field on a separate worksheet, click PivotTable on the PivotTable toolbar, click Show Pages, then click OK.

2. **In the PivotTable cell B1, click the** Quarter list arrow
   Each quarter is listed in addition to an option to show All quarters. See Figure L-7.

3. **Click** 1, **then click** OK
   The PivotTable summarizes the sales data for the first quarter only, as shown in Figure L-8.

4. **Click the** Quarter list arrow, **click** 4, **then click** OK
   The sales for the fourth quarter appear.

5. **Save the workbook**

Clues to Use

Customizing PivotTables

You can customize the default Excel PivotTable to show information in a format that is appropriate for your particular audience. To modify the order of items in the table, right-click a cell, then use the commands on the Order submenu to reorder the selected item(s).

To add or hide detail, right-click a cell, then use the commands on the Group and Show Detail submenu to expand, display, or hide more detail. When you show details of a selected area, Excel creates a new worksheet containing the detail you requested.

FIGURE L-7: PivotTable with Quarter as a page field

Click a quarter to view its data

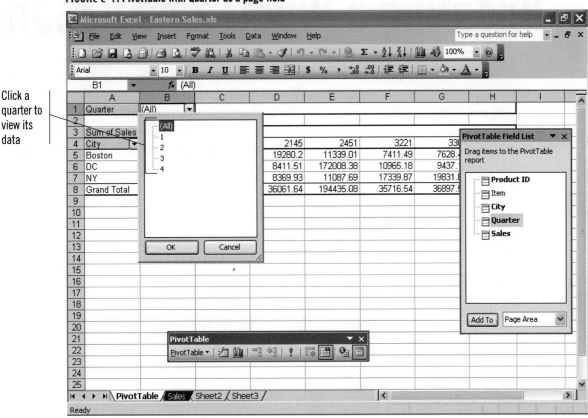

FIGURE L-8: PivotTable filtered to show only first quarter sales

Quarter field specifies that only the first quarter should be displayed

Sales for first quarter only

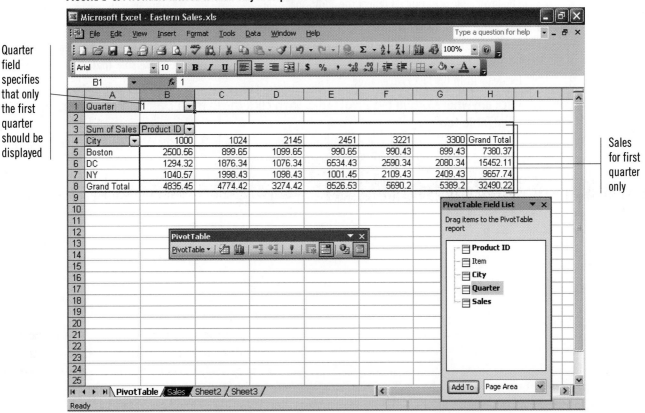

Updating a PivotTable Report

The data in a PivotTable report looks like typical worksheet data. Because the PivotTable data is linked to a **source list** (the list data you used to create the PivotTable), however, the values and results in the PivotTable are read-only values. That means you cannot move or modify a part of a PivotTable by inserting or deleting rows, editing results, or moving cells. To change PivotTable data, you must edit the items directly in the source list, and then update, or **refresh**, the PivotTable to reflect the changes. Jim just learned that sales information for a custom CD sold in Boston during the fourth quarter was never entered into the Sales worksheet. Jim asks you to add information about this CD to the current list. You start by inserting a row for the new information in the Sales worksheet.

STEPS

1. **Click the** Sales sheet tab

   By inserting the new row in the correct position by city, you will not need to sort the list again. Also, by adding the new information within the list range, the new row data is included automatically in the list range.

2. **Right-click the** row 27 heading; **then on the shortcut menu, click** Insert

   A blank row appears as the new row 27, and the data in the old row 27 moves down to row 28. You enter the CD data in the new row 27.

3. **Enter the data for the new CD using the following information**

Product ID	1924
Item	CD
City	Boston
Quarter	4
Sales	2600.68

   The PivotTable does not yet reflect the additional data.

4. **Click the** PivotTable sheet tab, **then make sure the** Quarter 4 **page is displayed**

   Notice that the fourth quarter list does not currently include this new CD information and that the grand total is $116439.46. Before you refresh the PivotTable data, you need to make sure that the cell pointer is located within the PivotTable range.

QUICK TIP

If you want Excel to refresh your PivotTable report automatically when you open the workbook in which it is contained, click the PivotTable list arrow on the PivotTable toolbar, click Table Options, under Data source options select Refresh on open, then click OK.

5. **Click anywhere within the PivotTable, then click the** Refresh Data button **on the PivotTable toolbar**

   The PivotTable now includes the new CD information in column H, and the grand total has increased by the amount of the CD's sales (2600.68) to 119040.14. See Figure L-9.

6. **Save the workbook**

FIGURE L-9: Updated PivotTable report

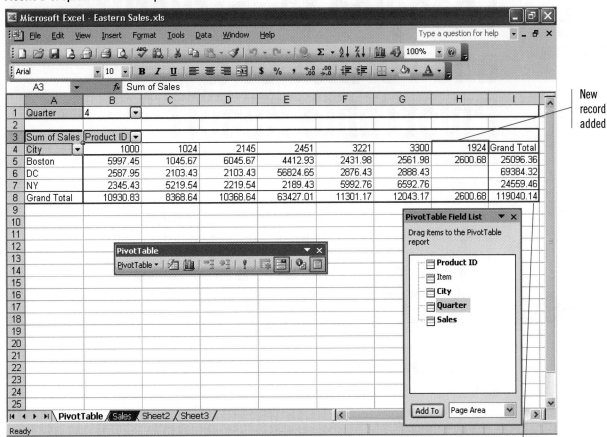

New record added

Total reflects new CD information

Clues to Use

Maintaining original table data

Once you select the Refresh Data command, you cannot undo the operation. If you want the PivotTable to display the original source data, you must change the source data list, then reselect the Refresh

Data command. If you're concerned about the effect refreshing the PivotTable might have on your work, save a second (working) copy of the workbook so that your original data remains intact.

Changing the Structure and Format of a PivotTable Report

Although you cannot change the actual data in a PivotTable, you can alter its structure and appearance at any time. You might, for example, add a column field, or switch the positions of existing fields. You can quickly change the way data is displayed in a PivotTable by dragging field buttons in the worksheet from a row position to a column position, or vice versa. Alternately, you may want to enhance the appearance of a PivotTable by changing the way the text or values are formatted. It's a good idea to format a PivotTable using AutoFormat, because once you refresh a PivotTable, any formatting that has not been applied to the cells through AutoFormat is removed. ▰▰▰▰ The eastern sales manager has asked Jim to include item information in the sales report. Jim asks you to add Item as a page field and then format the PivotTable.

STEPS

1. **Make sure that the** PivotTable sheet **is active, that the active cell is located anywhere inside the PivotTable, and that the PivotTable Field List is visible**

2. **Click the** Item field **in the PivotTable Field List, verify that** Page Area **is selected, then click** Add To

   You can move fields in a PivotTable by dragging and then dropping them at the desired location. When you drag a field, the pointer appears with a PivotTable outline attached to its lower-right corner.

3. **Drag the Item field up and drop it above the Quarter field**

   The PivotTable on the pointer displays a blue box in the Page area. When you drop the field, the Item field is placed in the Page area above the Quarter Page field. See Figure L-10. Jim asks you to display the book sales information for all quarters.

4. **Click the** Item list arrow, **click** Book, **click** OK, **click the** Quarter list arrow, **click** All, **then click** OK

   You are ready to format the PivotTable.

5. **Click any cell inside the PivotTable, click the** Field Settings button 🔲 **on the PivotTable toolbar, then click** Number **in the PivotTable Field dialog box**

6. **Under Category in the Format Cells dialog box, click** Accounting, **keep the Decimal places as** 2, **click** OK, **then click** OK **again**

   You have formatted the sales amounts with commas and dollar signs.

7. **Click the** Format Report button 🔲 **on the PivotTable toolbar bar; in the AutoFormat dialog box, scroll down and click the** Table 2 format, **click** OK, **then click outside the range to deselect it**

   You need to provide the eastern sales manager with sales information for all items.

8. **Click the** Item list arrow, **click** All, **then click** OK

   The completed PivotTable with the AutoFormat applied appears as shown in Figure L-11.

9. **Save the workbook, preview the PivotTable, then print it in landscape orientation**

FIGURE L-10: Revised PivotTable structure

Item field is now in the Page area

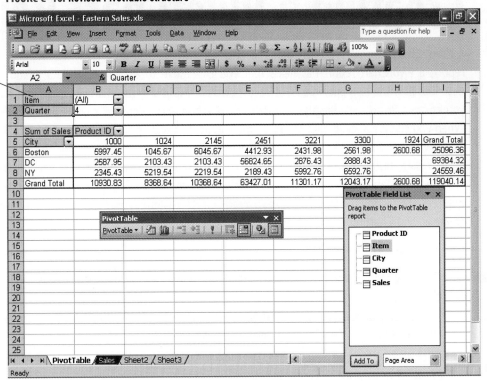

FIGURE L-11: Completed PivotTable report

AutoFormat has applied shading and blue headings

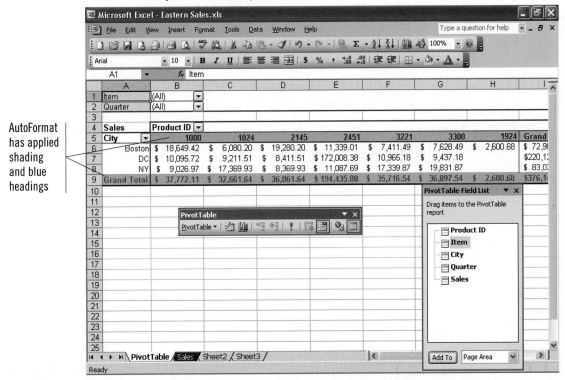

Excel 2003

Creating a PivotChart Report

A **PivotChart report** is a chart that you create from data or from a PivotTable report. Like a PivotTable report, a PivotChart report has fields that you can move to explore new data relationships. Table L-2 describes how the elements in a PivotTable report correspond to the elements in a PivotChart report. When you create a PivotChart directly from data, Excel automatically creates a corresponding PivotTable report. When you change a PivotChart report by moving fields, Excel updates the corresponding PivotTable report to show the new layout. You can create a PivotChart report from any PivotTable report to reflect that view of your data, but if you use an indented PivotTable report format, your chart will not have series fields; indented PivotTable report formats do not include column fields. Jim wants you to chart the fourth quarter CD sales and the yearly CD sales average for the eastern sales manager. You use the Chart Wizard to create a Pivot Chart report from the PivotTable data.

STEPS

QUICK TIP
If your PivotTable report is an indented format, move at least one field to the column area before you create a PivotChart report to display a series field on the chart.

1. **Click the** Item list arrow, **click** CD, **click** OK, **click the** Quarter list arrow, **click** 4, **then click** OK

   The fourth quarter CD sales information appears in the PivotTable. See Figure L-12. You want to create the PivotChart from the PivotTable information you have displayed.

2. **Click any cell in the PivotTable, then click the** Chart Wizard button 📊 **on the PivotTable toolbar**

   A new chart sheet opens with the fourth quarter CD sales displayed as a bar chart, as shown in Figure L-13. The Chart toolbar also appears. Jim wants you to change the chart to show the average sales for all quarters.

3. **Click the** Quarter list arrow **on the chart sheet, click** All, **then click** OK

   The chart now represents the sum of CD sales for the year. As with a PivotTable, you can change a PivotChart's summary function to display averages instead of totals.

QUICK TIP
You can also double-click the Sum of Sales cell to change the PivotTable's summary function.

4. **Click** Sum of Sales **above the PivotChart, click the** Field Settings button 📊 **on the PivotTable toolbar, click** Average **in the Summarize by list, then click** OK

   The PivotChart report recalculates to display averages. The chart would be easier to understand if it had a title.

5. **Click** Chart **on the menu bar, click** Chart Options, **click the** Titles **tab if necessary, enter** Average CD Sales **in the Chart title text box, then click** OK

6. **Rename the chart sheet** PivotChart, **place your name in the chart sheet footer, save the workbook, then preview and print the PivotChart report**

   The final PivotChart report displaying the average CD sales for the year is shown in Figure L-14.

TABLE L-2: PivotTable and PivotChart elements

PivotTable items	PivotChart items
row fields	category fields
column fields	series fields
page fields	page fields

FIGURE L-12: PivotTable displaying fourth quarter CD sales

4th quarter CD sales selected

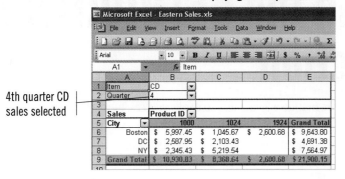

FIGURE L-13: New chart sheet displaying fourth quarter CD sales

Chart toolbar

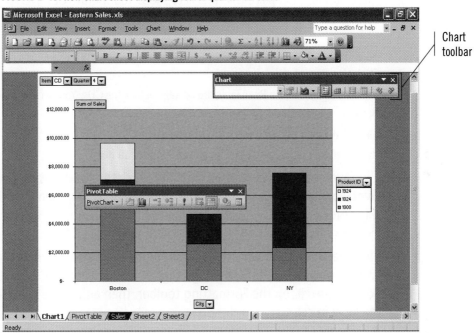

FIGURE L-14: Completed PivotChart report

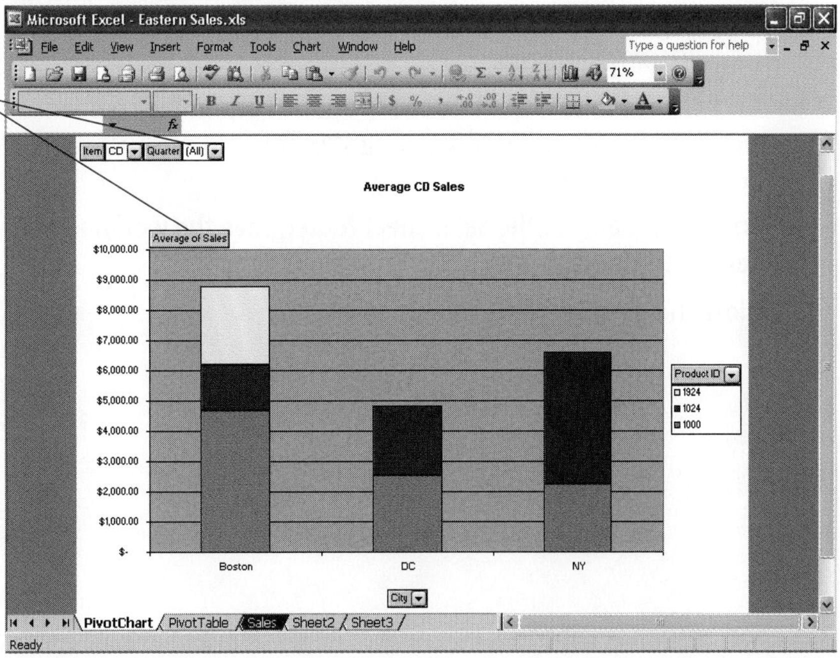

Chart now shows average sales for the year

Using the GETPIVOTDATA Function

Because you can rearrange a PivotTable so easily, you can't use an ordinary cell reference when you want to reference a PivotTable cell in another worksheet. If you change the way data is displayed in a PivotTable, the data moves, rendering an ordinary cell reference incorrect. Instead, to retrieve summary data from a PivotTable, you need to use the Excel GETPIVOTDATA function. See Figure L-15 for the GETPIVOTDATA function syntax. █████ In preparing for the Boston sales meeting, the eastern sales manager asks Jim to include the yearly sales total for the Boston store in the Sales sheet. Jim asks you to retrieve this information from the PivotTable and place it in the Sales sheet. You use the GETPIVOTDATA function to retrieve this information.

STEPS

1. **Click the** PivotTable sheet tab

   The sales figures in the PivotTable are average values for CDs. You decide to show sales information for all items and change the summary information back to Sum.

2. **Click the Item list arrow, click** All, **then click** OK

   The PivotChart report displays sales information for all items.

3. **Click** Average of Sales **on the PivotTable, click the** Field Settings button 📊 **on the PivotTable toolbar, click** Sum **in the Summarize by list, then click** OK

   The PivotChart report is recalculated to display sales totals. Next, you want to include the total for sales for the Boston store in the Sales sheet by retrieving it from the PivotTable.

4. **Click the** Sales sheet tab, **click cell** G1, **type** Total Boston Sales:, **click the** Enter button ✔ **on the Formula bar, click the** Align Right button ▤ **on the Formatting toolbar, click the** Bold button **B** **on the Formatting toolbar, then adjust the width of column G to display the label in cell G1**

   You want the GETPIVOTDATA function to retrieve the total Boston sales from the PivotTable.

5. **Click cell** H1, **type** = , **click the PivotTable tab, click cell** I6 **on the PivotTable, then click** ✔

   Cell I6 on the PivotTable contains the data you want to return to the Sales sheet. The GETPIVOTDATA function along with its arguments is inserted into cell H1 of the Sales sheet. Review Figure L-15 for the GETPIVOTDATA arguments.

6. **Click the** Currency Style button **\$** **on the Formatting toolbar**

   The current sales total for the Boston store is $72,989.49, as shown in Figure L-16. This is the same value displayed in cell I6 of the PivotTable.

7. **Enter your name in the Sales sheet footer, save the workbook, then preview and print the Sales worksheet**

8. **Close the file and exit Excel**

FIGURE L-15: Syntax of GETPIVOTDATA function

GETPIVOTDATA("Sales",PivotTable!$A$4,"City","Boston")

Field where data   PivotTable name and a cell   Field and item pair
is extracted from   in the report that contains   that describe the data
                          the data you want to retrieve   you want to retrieve

FIGURE L-16: Completed Sales worksheet showing total Boston sales

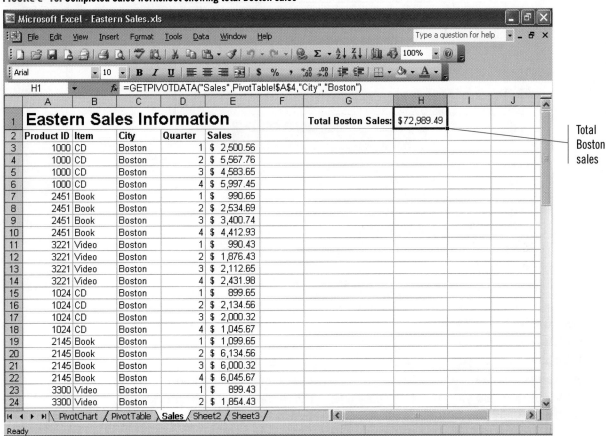

Total
Boston
sales

Practice

FIGURE L-17

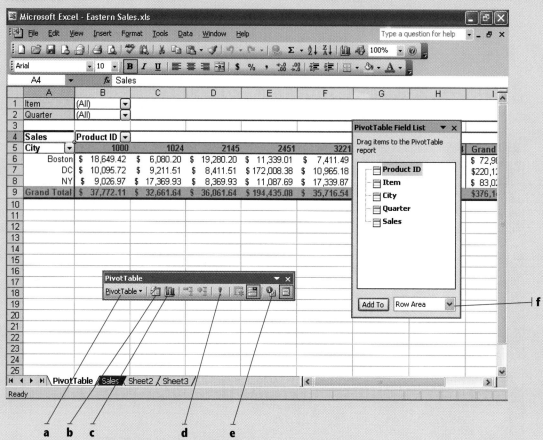

1. Which element do you click to display a list of field settings?
2. Which element do you click to update list changes within a table?
3. Which element do you click to create a PivotChart report?
4. Which element do you click to display a menu of PivotTable commands?
5. Which element do you click to display a list of PivotTable AutoFormats?
6. Which element do you click to display the areas of a PivotTable where fields can be added?

Match each term with the statement that best describes it.

7. GETPIVOTDATA function
8. COLUMN area
9. Summary function
10. PivotTable page
11. DATA area

a. Retrieves information from a PivotTable
b. Displays fields as column labels
c. Shows data for one item at a time in a table
d. Displays values
e. Determines if data is summed or averaged

Select the best answer from the list of choices.

12. **Which dialog box allows you to enter a title for a PivotChart?**
    a. PivotChart
    b. PivotTable
    c. Field Items
    d. Chart Options

13. **Which PivotTable report field allows you to average values?**
    a. Data field
    b. Page field
    c. Row field
    d. Column field

14. **To make changes to PivotTable data, you must:**
    a. Create a page field.
    b. Edit cells in the source list and then refresh the PivotTable.
    c. Edit cells in the PivotTable and then refresh the source list.
    d. Drag a column header to the column area.

15. **The PivotTable _____ helps you to create a PivotTable.**
    a. Assistant
    b. Wizard
    c. Designer
    d. Menu

16. **The default summary function for data fields containing numbers in an Excel Pivot table is:**
    a. Average
    b. Sum
    c. Count
    d. Max

17. **A two-dimensional PivotTable can be converted to a three-dimensional PivotTable by adding a:**
    a. Row field
    b. Column field
    c. Page field
    d. Three-dimensional field

18. **Refreshing a PivotTable removes any formatting that was not applied through:**
    a. AutoFormat
    b. PivotTable Format
    c. Format Paragraph
    d. Format Cells

19. **Report formats 1-10 for a PivotTable are _____ formats.**
    a. Database
    b. Indented
    c. Currency
    d. Numerical

20. **The default summary function for data fields containing text in an Excel Pivot table is:**
    a. Min
    b. Max
    c. Count
    d. CountA

1. **Plan and design a PivotTable report.**
   a. Start Excel, open the Data File titled EX L-2.xls from the drive and folder where your Data Files are stored, then save it as July CDs.
   b. You'll create a PivotTable to show the sum of sales across regions and stores. Study the list, then write down the field names you think should be included in the PivotTable.
   c. Determine which fields you think should be column fields, row fields, and data fields.
   d. Sketch a draft PivotTable.

2. **Create a PivotTable report.**
   a. Open the PivotTable Wizard and create a PivotTable report on a new worksheet using an Excel list.
   b. Add the Product field in the PivotTable List window to the Column Area.
   c. Add the Sales $ field in the PivotTable List window to the Data Area.
   d. Add the Store field in the PivotTable List window to the Row Area.
   e. Add the Sales Rep field in the PivotTable List window to the Row area.
   f. Drag the Store field to the left of the Sales Rep field in the Row Area if necessary.

3. **Change the summary function of a PivotTable report.**
   a. Change the PivotTable summary function to Average using the Field settings button.
   b. Rename the new sheet July PivotTable.
   c. Enter your name in the left section of the PivotTable report footer, then save the workbook.
   d. Print the PivotTable report in landscape orientation on one page.
   e. Change the Summary function back to Sum.

4. **Analyze three-dimensional data.**
   a. Add the Region field to the Page Area of the PivotTable.
   b. Display sales for only the West region.
   c. Display sales for all regions.
   d. Display sales for only the East region.
   e. Save the workbook, then print the worksheet.

5. **Update a PivotTable report.**
   a. With the July PivotTable sheet active, note the NY total for Pops Holidays.
   b. Activate the Sales List sheet and change L. Smith's sales of Pops Holidays in cell D8 to 10,843.
   c. Refresh the PivotTable so it reflects the new sales figure.
   d. Note the NY total for Pops Holidays in the East and verify that it increased by 3000.
   e. Save the workbook, preview then print the PivotTable.

6. **Change the structure and format of a PivotTable report.**
   a. With the July PivotTable active, redisplay data for all regions.
   b. Drag the Product field from the Column Area to the Row Area of the PivotTable.
   c. Drag the Sales Rep field from the Row Area to the Column Area of the PivotTable.
   d. Drag the Store field from the Row Area to the Page Area of the PivotTable.
   e. Remove the Region field from the PivotTable. (*Hint*: To remove a field, drag it back over to the field area in the PivotTable Field list window, or drag it outside the PivotTable area.)
   f. Use the Field Settings button on the PivotTable toolbar to change the numbers to Currency format with no decimal places.
   g. Use the Format Report button on the PivotTable toolbar to apply the Table 4 AutoFormat, save the workbook, then print the PivotTable.

7. Create a PivotChart report.

   a. Use the existing PivotTable data to create a PivotChart report on a new worksheet.

   b. Rename the chart sheet PivotChart.

   c. Change the chart to display average sales.

   d. Change the chart to display average sales for the LA store only.

   e. Add your name to the left section of the PivotChart sheet footer.

   f. Save the workbook, preview then print the chart.

   g. Change the summary function on the PivotChart sheet back to Sum.

8. Use the GETPIVOTDATA function.

   a. Change the store field on the July PivotTable sheet to show information for all stores.

   b. In cell D26 of the Sales List sheet enter = , click the July PivotTable sheet, click the cell that contain the grand total for T. Thomas, then press [Enter].

   c. Review the GETPIVOTDATA function that you entered in cell D26, then format the value as currency with no decimal places.

   d. Enter your name in the Sales List sheet footer, save the workbook, then preview and print the worksheet.

   e. Close the workbook and exit Excel.

▼ INDEPENDENT CHALLENGE 1

You are the bookkeeper for the small accounting firm of Chavez, Long, and Doyle. Until recently, the partners had been track-ing their hours manually in a log. You have created an Excel list to track basic information: billing date, partner name, client name, nature of work, and billable hours. It is your responsibility to generate a table summarizing this billing information by client. You will create a PivotTable that sums the hours by partner and date for each project. Once the table is completed, you will create a column chart representing the billing information.

   a. Start Excel, open the Data File titled EX L-3.xls from the drive and folder where your Data Files are stored, then save it as **Partner Billing Report**.

   b. Use the PivotTable Wizard to create a PivotTable on a separate worksheet that sums hours by partner and dates accord-ing to client. Use Figure L-18 as a guide.

   c. Name the new sheet **PivotTable** and use the Format Report button on the PivotTable toolbar to apply the Table 3 AutoFormat to the table.

   d. Use the Chart Wizard button on the PivotTable toolbar to create a PivotChart showing the PivotTable informa-tion. Name the chart sheet **PivotChart**.

   e. Use the Field Settings button on the PivotTable toolbar to change the summary function in the chart to **Average**.

   f. Add your name to the left section of the PivotTable and PivotChart footers, then save the workbook. Preview and print both the PivotTable and the PivotChart.

   g. Close the workbook and exit Excel.

FIGURE L-18

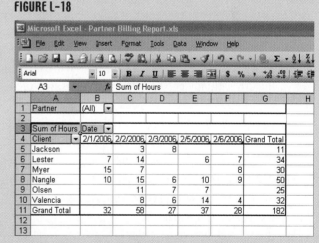

Excel 2003

▼ INDEPENDENT CHALLENGE 2

You are the owner of three midsized computer stores called PC Assist. One is located downtown, one is in the Plaza Mall, and one is in the Sun Center shopping center. You have been using Excel to maintain a sales summary list for the second quarter sales in the following three areas: hardware, software, and miscellaneous items. You want to create a PivotTable to analyze and graph the sales in each category by month and store.

a. Start Excel, open the Data File titled EX L-4.xls from the drive and folder where your Data Files are stored, then save it as **Second Qtr Sales**.

b. Rename the Sheet 1 worksheet **Sales**.

c. Create a PivotTable on a new worksheet that sums the sales amount for each store across the rows and each category of sales down the columns. Add a page field for month. Use Figure L-19 as a guide.

d. Change the summary function in the PivotTable to Average.

e. Format the PivotTable using the Table 6 AutoFormat.

f. Format the amounts as Currency with no decimal places.

g. Rename the sheet **PivotTable**.

h. On a separate sheet, create a PivotChart report for the May sales data in all three stores. (*Hint*: Create the PivotChart, then use the Page field list arrow to select May.) Name the chart sheet **PivotChart**.

FIGURE L-19

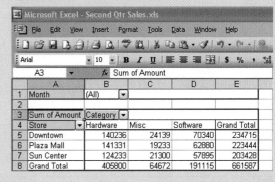

i. Add a descriptive title to your chart, using the Chart Options dialog box.

j. Add your name to the left section of the PivotTable and PivotChart worksheet footers, save the workbook, then print the PivotTable and the PivotChart.

k. Close the workbook and exit Excel.

▼ INDEPENDENT CHALLENGE 3

You manage a group of sales offices in the Western region for a cellular phone company called Digital West. Management has asked you to provide a summary table showing information on your sales staff, including their locations and their titles. You have been using Excel to keep track of the staff in the San Francisco, Phoenix, and Portland offices. Now you will create a PivotTable and PivotChart summarizing this information.

a. Start Excel, open the Data File titled EX L-5.xls from the drive and folder where your Data Files are stored, then save it as **Western Sales Employees**.

b. Create a PivotTable on a new worksheet that lists the number of employees in each city, with the names of the cities listed across the columns and the titles listed down the rows. (*Hint*: Remember that the default summary function for cells containing text is Count.) Use Figure L-20 as a guide.

c. Rename the new sheet **PivotTable**.

d. Create a PivotChart using the PivotTable information that shows the number of employees in each store by position. Rename the new chart sheet **PivotChart**.

e. Add a chart title of **Western Sales Staff**.

FIGURE L-20

	A	B	C	D	E
1		Drop Page Fields Here			
2					
3	Count of Last Name	City			
4	Title	Phoenix	Portland	San Francisco	Grand Total
5	Sales Manager	2	1	1	4
6	Sales Representative	3	6	3	12
7	Grand Total	5	7	4	16
8					

f. Insert a new row in the Employee List worksheet above row 7. In the new row, add information reflecting the recent hiring of Cathy Connolly, a sales manager, at the Phoenix office. Update the PivotTable to display the new employee information.

▼ INDEPENDENT CHALLENGE 3 (CONTINUED)

g. Add the label Total Phoenix Staff: in cell C20 of the Employee List sheet. Right-align and boldface the label in cell C20.

h. Enter a function in cell D20 that retrieves the total number of employees located in Phoenix from the PivotTable.

Advanced Challenge Exercise

- Rename the Title field name on the PivotTable to Position.
- Rename the Count of Last Name field to Number of Employees.
- Check the PivotChart to be sure that the new field names have been added.

i. Add your name to the left section of all three worksheet footers, save the workbook, then print the PivotTable, the Employee List, and the PivotChart.

j. Close the workbook and exit Excel.

▼ INDEPENDENT CHALLENGE 4

You are a member of an investment group that meets weekly on Thursday evenings. You need to prepare a report for this week's meeting showing the performance of three stocks over the past five business days. You decide to use a PivotTable and a PivotChart to represent the market trends for the stocks you are researching. You will begin by researching stock prices on the Web and charting each stock for the past five business days. Then you will use a PivotTable function to display each stock's weekly high. Last, you will use a PivotChart to represent each stock's five-day performance.

a. Start Excel, create a new workbook, then save it as Stock Prices in the drive and folder where your Data Files are stored.

b. Use the search engine of your choice to research stock prices. (*Hint*: You may want to enter stock price history as your search fields. If your search engine requires a + sign between fields be sure to enter them also.)

c. Record prices for three stocks of your choice over the past five days, then create a list that contains your stock research data. Name the list worksheet Price. Use Figure L-21 as a guide.

d. Create a PivotTable on a new worksheet that sums the stock prices for each stock across the rows and each day down the columns. Rename the PivotTable sheet PivotTable.

e. Format the sales figures as currency with two decimal places and apply the Table 6 AutoFormat.

f. Change the summary function in the PivotTable to MAX to show the highest stock price.

g. Create a PivotChart report from your data on a separate sheet. Change the Column chart to a Bar chart. (*Hint*: Use the Chart Type dialog box). Rename the sheet PivotChart.

h. Enter the label Highest Price in cell F1 of the Price sheet. Right-align and bold-face the label in cell F1.

i. Enter a function in cell G1 that retrieves the highest price for one of your stocks over the past five days from the PivotTable. Add the stock name to the label in cell F1.

FIGURE L-21

Stock	Day	Price
Stock 1	1	
Stock 1	2	
Stock 1	3	
Stock 1	4	
Stock 1	5	
Stock 2	1	
Stock 2	2	
Stock 2	3	
Stock 2	4	
Stock 2	5	
Stock 3	1	
Stock 3	2	
Stock 3	3	
Stock 3	4	
Stock 3	5	

Advanced Challenge Exercise

- Change the structure of the PivotTable, moving the Day field to the Row Area and Stock to the Column Area. Verify that the highest price for a stock is still correct on the Price worksheet.
- Move the stock information in the first column of the PivotTable to the last column.
- Change the Grand Total label in cell A10 of the PivotTable to Highest Price.

j. Add your name to the left section of each worksheet footer, save the workbook, then print the PivotTable, the Price sheet, and the PivotChart.

k. Close the workbook and exit Excel.

Excel 2003

▼ VISUAL WORKSHOP

Open the workbook titled EX L-6.xls from the drive and folder where your Data Files are stored, then save it as Photo Store. Using the data in the workbook, create the PivotTable shown in Figure L-22. (*Hint*: There are two data summary fields and the table has been formatted using the Table 4 AutoFormat.) Add your name to the PivotTable sheet footer, then preview and print the PivotTable. Save the worksheet, then close the workbook.

FIGURE L-22

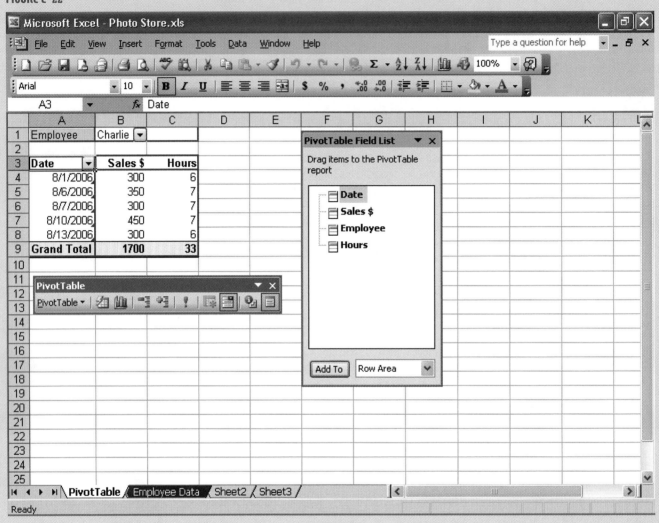

Exchanging Data with Other Programs

OBJECTIVES

Plan a data exchange
Import a text file
Import a database table
Insert a graphic file in a worksheet
Embed a worksheet
Link a worksheet to another program
Embed an Excel chart into a PowerPoint slide
Import a list into an Access table

If you have a SAM user profile, you may have access to hands-on instruction, practice, and assessment of the skills covered in this unit. Log in to your SAM account and go to your assignments page to see what your instructor has assigned.

In a Windows environment, you can freely exchange data among Excel and most other Windows programs, a process known as **integration**. In this unit, you will plan a data exchange between Excel and other Microsoft Office programs. ▆▆▆▆ MediaLoft's upper management has asked Jim Fernandez, the marketing director, to research the possible purchase of CafeCorp, a small company that operates cafés in large businesses, hospitals, and, more recently, drug stores. Jim is reviewing the broker's paper documents and electronic files and developing a presentation on the feasibility of acquiring this company. To complete this project, Jim asks you to help set up the exchange of data between Excel and other programs.

Planning a Data Exchange

Because the tools available in Microsoft Office programs are designed to be compatible, exchanging data between Excel and other programs is easy. The first step involves planning what you want to accomplish with each data exchange.  Jim asks you to use the following guidelines to plan data exchanges between Excel and other programs in order to complete the business analysis project.

DETAILS

To plan an exchange of data:

- **Identify the data you want to exchange, its file type, and, if possible, the program used to create it**

  Whether the data you want to exchange is a graphics file, a database file, a worksheet, or consists only of text, it is important to identify the data's **source program** (the program used to create it) and the file type. Once you identify the source program, you can determine options for exchanging that data with Excel. Jim needs to analyze a text file containing the CafeCorp product data. Although he does not know the source program, Jim knows that the file contains unformatted text. A file that consists of text but no formatting is sometimes called an **ASCII** or **text** file. Because ASCII is a universally accepted file format, Jim can easily import an ASCII file into Excel. See Table M-1 for a partial list of other file formats that Excel can import. For more information on importable file formats, see the Help topic "File format converters supplied with Excel".

- **Determine the program with which you want to exchange data**

  Besides knowing which program created the data you want to exchange, you must also identify which program will receive the data, called the **destination program**. This determines the procedure you use to perform the exchange. You might want to insert a graphic object into an Excel worksheet or add a spreadsheet to a Word document. Jim received a database table of CafeCorp's corporate customers created with the Access database program. After determining that Excel can import Access tables and reviewing the import procedure, he imports that database file into Excel so he can analyze it using Excel tools.

- **Determine the goal of your data exchange**

  Although it is convenient to use the Office Clipboard to cut, copy, and paste data within and between programs, you cannot retain a connection with the source program when using these methods. However, there are two ways to transfer data within and between programs that allow you to retain some connection with the source program. These data transfer methods use a Windows feature known as **object linking and embedding**, or **OLE**. The data to be exchanged, called an **object**, may consist of text, a worksheet, or any other type of data. You use **embedding** to insert a copy of the original object in the destination document and, if necessary, to subsequently edit this data separately from the source document. This process is illustrated in Figure M-1. You use **linking** when you want the information you inserted to be updated automatically when the data in the source document changes. This process is illustrated in Figure M-2. Embedding and linking are discussed in more detail later in this unit. Jim has determined that he needs to use both object embedding and object linking for his analysis and presentation project.

- **Set up the data exchange**

  When you exchange data between two programs, it is often best to start both programs prior to starting the exchange. You might also want to tile the program windows on the screen either horizontally or vertically so that you can see both during the exchange. You will work with Excel, Word, Access, and PowerPoint when exchanging data for this project.

- **Execute the data exchange**

  The steps you use will vary, depending on the type of data you want to exchange. Jim is ready to have you start the data exchanges for the business analysis of CafeCorp.

FIGURE M-1: Embedded object

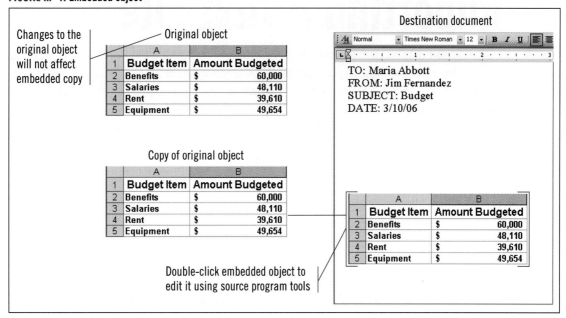

Changes to the original object will not affect embedded copy

Original object

Copy of original object

Double-click embedded object to edit it using source program tools

Destination document

FIGURE M-2: Linked object

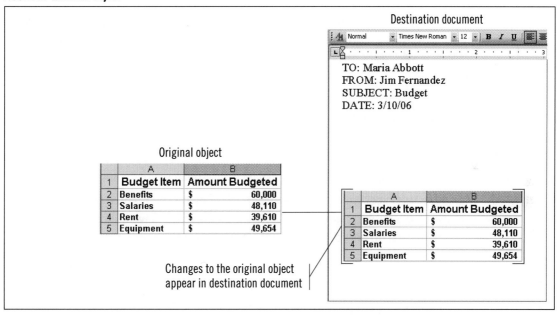

Destination document

Original object

Changes to the original object appear in destination document

TABLE M-1: Importable file formats and extensions

file format	file extension(s)	file format	file extension(s)
dBASE 2,3,4	.dbf	CSV (comma separated values)	.csv
Excel 97–XP	.xls, .xlt (template), .xlw (workspace)	DIF (Data Interchange Format)	.dif
Quattro/Quattro Pro	.wq1, .wb1, .wb3	Formatted text (Space or column delimited)	.txt, .prn
Lotus 1-2-3	.wks, .wk1, .wk3, .wk4	Text (Tab delimited)	.txt
HTML	.htm	XML	.xml
Web page	.mht	SYLK (Symbolic Link)	.slk
Microsoft Works	.wks		

UNIT
M

Excel 2003

Importing a Text File

You can import data created in other programs into Excel by opening the file, as long as Excel can read the file type. After importing the file, you use the Save As command on the File menu to save the data in Excel format. Text files use a tab or space as the **delimiter**, or column separator, to separate columns of data. When you import a text file into Excel, the Text Import Wizard automatically opens and describes how text is separated in the imported file. ▓▓▓▓ Now that Jim has planned the data exchange, he wants you to import a tab-delimited text file containing product cost and pricing data from CafeCorp.

STEPS

1. **Start Excel if necessary, click the** Open button 📂 **on the Standard toolbar, click the** Look in list arrow, **then navigate to the folder containing your Data Files**

   The Open dialog box shows only those files that match the file types listed in the Files of type box—usually Microsoft Excel files. In this case, however, you're importing a text file.

TROUBLE

In the Preview window, small squares may separate the field. You can continue with the lesson.

2. **Click the** Files of type list arrow, **click** Text Files, **click** EX M-1.txt, **then click** Open

   The first Text Import Wizard dialog box opens. See Figure M-3. Under Original data type, the Delimited option button is selected. In the Preview of file box, line 1 indicates that the file contains three columns of data: Item, Cost, and Price. No changes are necessary in this dialog box.

3. **Click** Next

   The second Text Import Wizard dialog box opens. Under Delimiters, Tab is selected as the delimiter, indicating that tabs separate the columns of incoming data. The Data preview box contains lines showing where the tab delimiters divide the data into columns.

4. **Click** Next

   The third Text Import Wizard dialog box opens with options for formatting the three columns of data. Under Column data format, the General option button is selected. This is the best formatting option for text mixed with numbers.

5. **Click** Finish

   Excel imports the text file into the blank worksheet as three columns of data: Item, Cost, and Price.

QUICK TIP

If you do not specify Excel as the file type, you will be asked if you want to proceed. Click No, then choose Excel in the Save as type list box.

6. **Maximize the Excel window if necessary, click** File **on the menu bar, click** Save As, **make sure the folder containing your Data Files appears in the Save in box, click the** Save as type list arrow, **scroll up and click** Microsoft Office Excel Workbook (*.xls), **change the filename to** CafeCorp, **then click** Save

   The file is saved as an Excel workbook, and the new name appears in the title bar. The sheet tab automatically changes to the name of the imported file, EX M-1. The worksheet information would be easier to read if it were formatted and if it showed the profit for each item.

7. **Double-click the border between the headers in** Columns A **and** B, **click cell** D1, **type** Profit, **click cell** D2, **type** =, **click cell** C2, **type** -, **click cell** B2, **click the** Enter button ✔ **on the Formula bar, then copy the formula in cell D2 to the range** D3:D18

8. **Rename the sheet tab** Product Information, **center the column labels, apply bold formatting to them, format the data in columns B, C, and D using the Number style with two decimal places, then click cell** A1

   Figure M-4 shows the completed worksheet, which analyzes the text file data you imported into Excel.

9. **Add your name to the left section of the worksheet footer, save the workbook, preview and print the worksheet, then close the workbook**

FIGURE M-3: First Text Import Wizard dialog box

Original data type is delimited

Three column headings

Preview of file contents

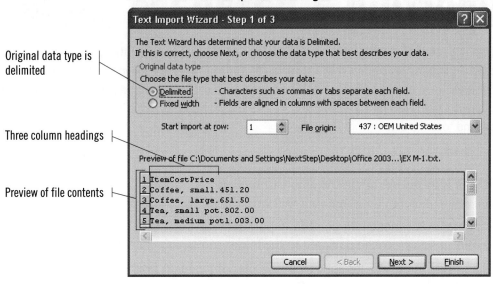

FIGURE M-4: Completed worksheet with imported text file

Columns from text file

Added column with new profit data

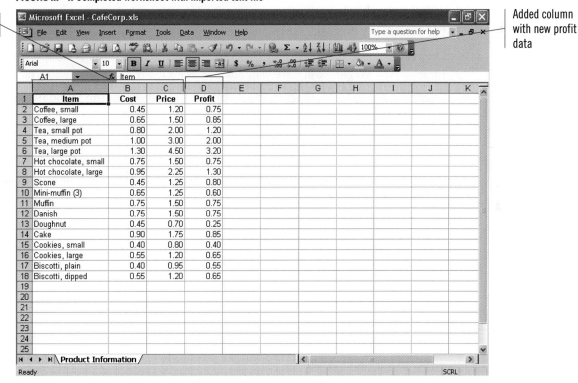

Clues to Use

Other ways to import files

Another way to open the Text Import Wizard is by pointing to Import External Data on the Data menu, clicking Import Data, then selecting a data source. Although the Text Import Wizard gives you the most flexibility, there are other ways to import text files. For example, on the Windows desktop, you can drag the icon representing a text file into a blank worksheet window, and Excel will create a worksheet from the data without going through the wizard.

Importing a Database Table

In addition to importing text files, you can also use Excel to import files from other programs or from database tables. To import files that contain importable file formats, open the file in Excel, then work with the data and save it as an Excel workbook. ▰▰▰ Jim received a database table containing CafeCorp's corporate customers, which was created with Access. He asks you to import this table into the workbook, then format, sort, and total the data.

STEPS

1. **Click the** New button ▢ **on the Standard toolbar**
   A new workbook opens, displaying a blank worksheet to which you can import the Access data.

2. **Click** Data **on the menu bar, point to** Import External Data, **click** Import Data, **then click the** Look in list arrow **and navigate to the folder containing your Data Files**

QUICK TIP
You can move the External Data toolbar if you can't see your worksheet data.

3. **Make sure** All Data Sources **appears in the Files of type text box, click** EX M-2.mdb, **click** Open, **then click** OK **in the Import Data dialog box**
   Excel inserts the Access data into the worksheet starting in cell A1 and displays the External Data toolbar. See Figure M-5.

4. **Rename the sheet tab** Customer Information, **then format the data in** columns F **and** G **with the Number format, using commas and no decimal places**
   You are ready to sort the data in columns F and G.

5. **Click cell** G1, **then click the** Sort Descending button ⬇ **on the Standard toolbar**
   The records are reorganized in descending order according to the amount of the 2006 orders.

6. **Select the range** F19:G19, **click the** AutoSum button Σ **on the Standard toolbar, then return to cell A1**
   Your completed worksheet should match Figure M-6.

7. **Add your name to the left section of the worksheet footer, save the workbook as** Customer Information, **then preview and print the worksheet in landscape orientation**

Clues to Use

Using smart tags

When Excel recognizes certain data types, it marks the cell with a smart tag, a small, purple triangle in the lower-right corner of the cell. For example, if you type a name that matches a name in an Outlook address book, you can use the smart tag to send an e-mail to that person from within Excel. To see a list of what actions you can take, point to the smart tag, then click the Smart Tag Actions button ⓘ that appears. To turn smart tags on or off, click Tools on the menu bar, click AutoCorrect Options, click the Smart Tags tab, then select or deselect "Label data with smart tags."

FIGURE M-5: Imported Access table

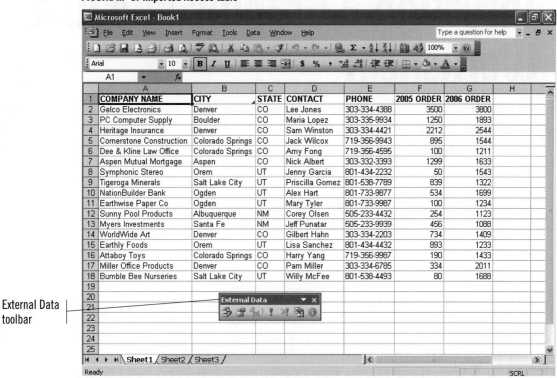

External Data toolbar

FIGURE M-6: Completed worksheet containing imported data

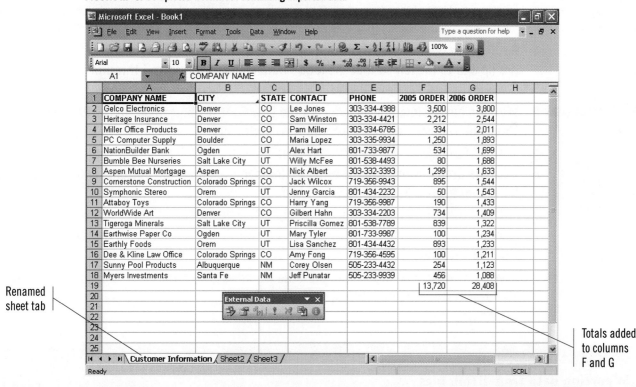

Renamed sheet tab

Totals added to columns F and G

Clues to Use

Exporting cell data

Most of the file types that Excel can import (listed in Table M-1) are also the file types which Excel can export, or deliver data. Excel can also export HTML and XML formats for the Web. To export an Excel worksheet, use the Save As command on the File menu, click the Save as type list arrow, then select the desired format. Saving in a non-Excel format might result in the loss of formatting that is unique to Excel.

Inserting a Graphic File in a Worksheet

A graphic object (such as a drawing, logo, or photograph) can greatly enhance a worksheet's visual impact. The Picture options on the Insert menu make it easy to insert graphics into an Excel worksheet. Once you've inserted a picture, you can format it using the tools on the Picture toolbar. ▰▰▰▰ Jim wants you to insert the upper part of the MediaLoft logo at the top of the customer worksheet. The company's Marketing Department has created the graphic and saved it in JPG format. You insert and format the image on the worksheet. You start by creating a space for the logo on the worksheet.

STEPS

1. **Select rows 1 through 5, click Insert on the menu bar, then click Rows**
   Five blank rows appear above the header row, leaving space to insert the picture.

2. **Click cell A1, click Insert on the menu bar, then point to Picture**
   The Picture submenu opens. See Figure M-7. This menu offers several options for inserting graphics. You want to insert a picture that you already have in a file. The file you will insert has a .jpg file extension, so it is called a "jay-peg" file. JPEG files can be viewed in a Web browser.

   > **TROUBLE**
   > If the picture toolbar is not displayed, right-click any toolbar, then click Picture from the shortcut menu.

3. **Click From File, make sure the folder containing your Data Files appears in the Look in box, click EX M-3.jpg, then click Insert**
   Excel inserts the graphic and opens the Picture toolbar. The small circles around the picture's border are sizing handles. Sizing handles appear when a picture is selected; you use them to change the size of a picture.

4. **Position the pointer over the sizing handle in the logo's lower-right corner, drag the corner up and to the left so that the logo's outline fits within rows 1 through 5**
   Compare your screen to Figure M-8. You will lower the picture's contrast and brightness.

   > **QUICK TIP**
   > You can rotate a picture using the Rotate Left 90° button 🔄 on the Picture toolbar. For more rotating options, click the Format Picture button 🎨 on the Picture toolbar, then click the Size tab and enter a value in the Rotation textbox.

5. **With the picture image selected, click the Less Contrast button 🔲 on the Picture toolbar three times, then click the Less Brightness button 🔲**
   You will crop the image to remove the text at the bottom.

6. **Click the Crop button ⊹ on the Picture toolbar, then drag the bottom-center cropping handle up to crop out the MediaLoft text**
   The logo will look better on the worksheet without the blue background.

7. **Click the Set Transparent Color button ✎ on the Picture toolbar, then click anywhere on the blue background of the logo**

8. **Save the workbook, preview then print the worksheet, close the workbook, then exit Excel**
   Your completed worksheet should match Figure M-9.

Clues to Use

Importing data from HTML files

You can import information from HTML files and Web pages into Excel by using drag and drop or the Insert Object command. To use drag and drop, open Internet Explorer, then open the HTML file or Web page that contains the data you want to import. Resize the Explorer window so it covers only half of the screen. Open the Excel file to which you want to import the data, then resize the Excel window so it covers the other half of the screen. In the Explorer window, highlight the table or information you want to import, then drag it over to the Excel window. When the pointer changes to the Copy Pointer ⬚, release the mouse button. The information will appear in your Excel document, ready for analysis. You can also open an HTML file from your intranet or a Web site in Excel and modify it. To retrieve data from a particular Web page on a regular basis, use a Web query, which you'll learn about in the next unit.

FIGURE M-7: Picture menu

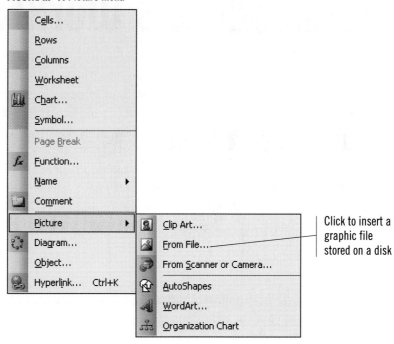

Cells...
Rows
Columns
Worksheet
Chart...
Symbol...
Page Break
Function...
Name ▶
Comment
Picture ▶
Diagram...
Object...
Hyperlink... Ctrl+K

Clip Art...
From File... ◄ Click to insert a graphic file stored on a disk
From Scanner or Camera...
AutoShapes
WordArt...
Organization Chart

FIGURE M-8: Picture toolbar

Less Brightness button
Less Contrast button
Sizing handle
Crop button
Set Transparent Color button

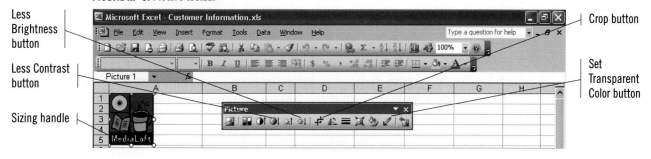

FIGURE M-9: Worksheet with formatted picture

Formatted picture

	A	B	C	D	E	F	G
1							
2							
3							
4							
5							
6	COMPANY NAME	CITY	STATE	CONTACT	PHONE	2005 ORDER	2006 ORDER
7	Gelco Electronics	Denver	CO	Lee Jones	303-334-4388	3,500	3,800
8	Heritage Insurance	Denver	CO	Sam Winston	303-334-4421	2,212	2,544
9	Miller Office Products	Denver	CO	Pam Miller	303-334-6785	334	2,011
10	PC Computer Supply	Boulder	CO	Maria Lopez	303-335-9934	1,250	1,893
11	NationBuilder Bank	Ogden	UT	Alex Hart	801-733-9877	534	1,699
12	Bumble Bee Nurseries	Salt Lake City	UT	Willy McFee	801-538-4493	80	1,688
13	Aspen Mutual Mortgage	Aspen	CO	Nick Albert	303-332-3393	1,299	1,633
14	Cornerstone Construction	Colorado Springs	CO	Jack Wilcox	719-356-9943	895	1,544
15	Symphonic Stereo	Orem	UT	Jenny Garcia	801-434-2232	50	1,543
16	Attaboy Toys	Colorado Springs	CO	Harry Yang	719-356-9987	190	1,433
17	WorldWide Art	Denver	CO	Gilbert Hahn	303-334-2203	734	1,409
18	Tigeroga Minerals	Salt Lake City	UT	Priscilla Gomez	801-538-7789	839	1,322
19	Earthwise Paper Co	Ogden	UT	Mary Tyler	801-733-9987	100	1,234
20	Earthly Foods	Orem	UT	Lisa Sanchez	801-434-4432	893	1,233
21	Dee & Kline Law Office	Colorado Springs	CO	Amy Fong	719-356-4595	100	1,211
22	Sunny Pool Products	Albuquerque	NM	Corey Olsen	505-233-4432	254	1,123
23	Myers Investments	Santa Fe	NM	Jeff Punatar	505-233-9939	456	1,088
24						13,720	28,408

Embedding a Worksheet

Microsoft Office programs work together to make it easy to copy an object (such as text, data, or a graphic) in a source program and then insert it into a document in a different program (the destination program). If you insert the object using a simple Paste command, however, you retain no connection to the source program. That's why it is often more useful to embed objects rather than simply paste them. Embedding allows you to edit an Excel workbook from within a different program using Excel commands and tools. If you send a Word document with an embedded worksheet to another person, you do not need to send a separate Excel file with it. All the necessary information is embedded in the Word document. When you embed information, you can either display the data itself, or an icon representing the data; users double-click the icon to view the embedded data. Jim decides to update Maria on the project status. He asks you to prepare a Word memo, including the projected sales worksheet embedded as an icon. You begin by starting the Word program and opening the memo.

STEPS

1. **Start Word, click the** Open button 🖻 **on the Standard toolbar, make sure the folder containing your Data Files appears in the Look in box, click** EX M-4.doc, **then click** Open
   The memo opens in Word.

2. **Click** File **on the menu bar, click** Save As, **make sure the folder containing your Data Files appears in the Save in box, change the file name to** CafeCorp Sales Memo, **then click** Save
   You want to embed the worksheet below the last line of the document.

> **QUICK TIP**
> You can also use the Object dialog box to embed an HTML file in an Excel worksheet.

3. **Press** [Ctrl][End], **click** Insert **on the menu bar, click** Object, **then click the** Create from File tab **in the Object dialog box**
   See Figure M-10. You need to indicate the file you want to embed.

4. **Click** Browse, **make sure the folder containing your Data Files appears in the Look in box, click** EX M-5.xls, **click** Insert, **select the** Display as icon check box
   You will change the icon to a more descriptive name.

> **QUICK TIP**
> To display a different icon to represent the file, scroll down the icon list and select any icon.

5. **Click the** Change Icon button, **delete the text in the Caption textbox and type** Projected Sales, **then click** OK **twice**
   The memo contains an embedded copy of the sales projection worksheet, displayed as an icon. See Figure M-11.

6. **Double-click the** Projected Sales worksheet icon **on the Word memo then maximize the Excel window and the worksheet window if necessary**
   The Excel program starts and displays the embedded worksheet, with its location displayed in the title bar. See Figure M-12. Any changes you make to the embedded object using Excel tools are not reflected in the source document. Similarly, if you open the source document in the source program, changes you make are not reflected in the embedded copy.

7. **Click** File **on the Excel menu bar, click** Close & Return to CafeCorp Sales Memo.doc, **close Excel, then click the** Save button 🖫 **on the Word toolbar to save the memo**

FIGURE M-10: Object dialog box

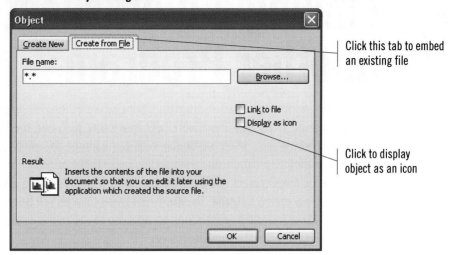

Click this tab to embed an existing file

Click to display object as an icon

FIGURE M-11: Memo with embedded worksheet

Memo is a Word document

Icon representing the embedded Excel worksheet

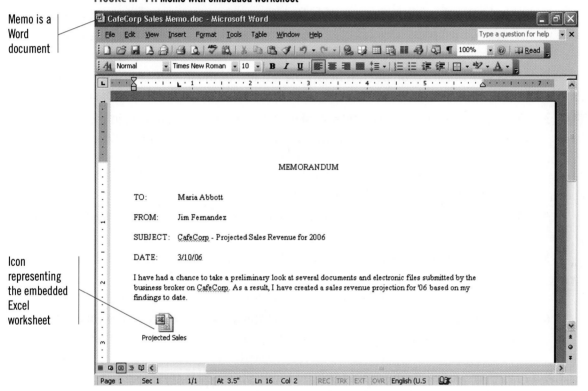

FIGURE M-12: Embedded worksheet opened in Excel

Location of the embedded worksheet

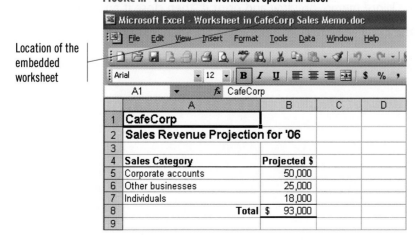

Excel 2003

Linking a Worksheet to Another Program

Linking a worksheet into another program retains a connection with the original document as well as the original program. When you link a worksheet to another program, the link contains a connection to the source document so that, when you double-click it, the source document opens for editing. Once you link a worksheet to another program, any changes you make to the original worksheet (the source document) are reflected in the linked object. Jim realizes he may be making some changes to the workbook he embedded in the memo to Maria. To ensure that these changes will be reflected in the memo, he feels you should use linking instead of embedding. He asks you to delete the embedded worksheet icon and replace it with a linked version of the same worksheet.

STEPS

1. **With the Word memo still open, click the Microsoft Excel Worksheet icon to select it if necessary, then press [Delete]**
   The embedded worksheet is removed. The linking process is similar to embedding.

2. **Make sure the insertion point is below the last line of the memo, click Insert on the Word menu bar, click Object, then click the Create from File tab in the Object dialog box**

> **QUICK TIP**
> If you want to insert part of an existing worksheet into another file, you can copy the information that you want to link and then use the Paste Special option on the Edit menu to paste a link to the source file.

3. **Click Browse, make sure the folder containing your Data Files appears in the Look in box, click EX M-5.xls, click Insert, select the Link to file check box, then click OK**
   The memo now displays a linked copy of the sales projection worksheet. See Figure M-13. In the future, any changes made to the source file, EX M-5, will also be made to the linked copy in the Word memo. You verify this by making a change to the source file and viewing its effect on the Word memo.

4. **Click the Save button 🖫 on the Standard toolbar, then close the Word memo and exit Word**
   The sales projection for other businesses has changed to $20,000.

5. **Start Excel, open the file EX M-5.xls from the drive and folder where your Data Files are stored, click cell B6, type 20,000, then press [Enter]**
   You want to verify that the same change was made automatically to the linked copy of the worksheet.

6. **Start Word, open CafeCorp Sales Memo from the drive and folder where your Data Files are stored, then click Yes if asked if you want to update the document's links**
   The memo displays the new value in cell B6 and an updated total. See Figure M-14.

7. **Click View on the menu bar, click Header and Footer, type your name in the header box, then click Close on the Header and Footer toolbar**

8. **Save the Word memo, preview and print it, then close it and exit Word**

9. **Close the Excel worksheet without saving it, then exit Excel**

FIGURE M-13: Memo with linked worksheet

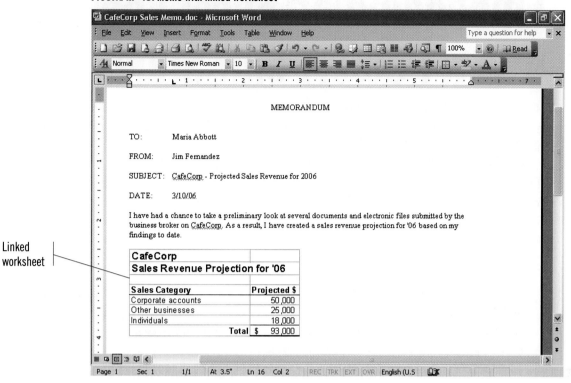

Linked worksheet

FIGURE M-14: Memo with link updated

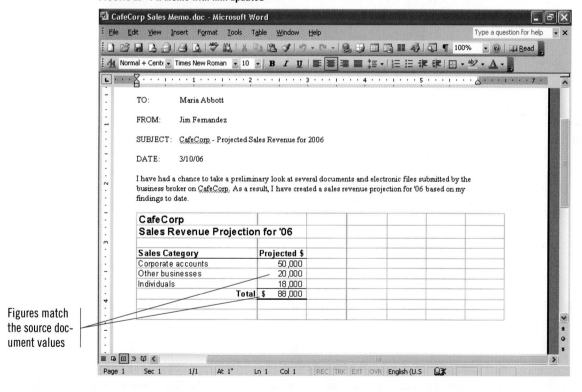

Figures match the source document values

Clues to Use

Managing links

When you change a source file, the link is updated automatically each time you open the destination document. You can manage linked objects further by choosing Links on the Edit menu. This opens the Links dialog box, which allows you to update a link or to change the source file of a link. You can also break a link by selecting the source file in the Links dialog box and clicking Break Link.

UNIT
M
Excel 2003

Embedding an Excel Chart into a PowerPoint Slide

Microsoft PowerPoint is a **presentation graphics** program that you can use to create slide show presentations. For example, you could create a slide show to present a sales plan to management or to inform potential clients about a new service. PowerPoint slides can include a mix of text, data, and graphics. Adding an Excel chart to a slide can help to illustrate data and give your presentation more visual appeal. ▓▓▓▓ Upper management asks Jim to brief the Marketing Department on the possible acquisition of CafeCorp, based on his analysis so far. Jim will make his presentation using PowerPoint slides. He decides to add an Excel chart to one of the presentation slides, illustrating the 2006 sales projection data. He begins by starting PowerPoint.

STEPS

1. **Click the** Start button **on the task bar, point to** All Programs, **point to** Microsoft Office, **click** Microsoft Office PowerPoint 2003, **click the** More button 🖼 **in the Open section of the Getting Started task pane, make sure the folder containing your Data Files appears in the Look in box, click** EX M-6.ppt, **then click** Open

    The presentation appears in Normal view and contains three panes and the Drawing toolbar, as shown in Figure M-15.

2. **Click** File **on the menu bar, click** Save As, **make sure the folder containing your Data Files appears in the Save in box, change the file name to** Marketing Department Presentation, **then click** Save

    The outline of the presentation in the Outline pane on the left shows the title and text for each slide. You will add an Excel chart to Slide 2, "2006 Sales Projections." To add the chart, you first need to select the slide on which it will appear.

3. **Click the** Slide 2 icon ▓ **in the Outline pane**

    The slide appears in the Slide pane on the right.

4. **Click** Insert **on the menu bar, then click** Object

    The Insert Object dialog box opens. You want to insert an object (the Excel chart) that has already been saved as a file.

5. **Click the** Create from file option button, **click** Browse, **click the** Look in list arrow, **navigate to the folder containing your Data Files, click** EX M-7.xls, **click** OK, **then in the Insert Object dialog box click** OK **again**

    After a moment, a pie chart illustrating the 2006 sales projections appears in the slide with resizing handles. The chart would look better if it was larger.

QUICK TIP
If you need to move the selected chart to center it, you can use the arrow keys on the keyboard.

6. **Drag the lower-right corner sizing handle down and to the right to increase the chart size, then press** [Esc] **to deselect the chart**

    Slide Show view displays the slide on the full screen the way the audience will see it.

7. **Click the** Slide Show from current slide button 🖳 **in the lower-left corner of the screen**

    The finished sales projection slide appears, as shown in Figure M-16. The presentation for the Marketing Department is complete.

8. **Press** [Esc] **to return to Normal view, in the Outline pane click at the end of the Slide 2 text: "2006 Sales Projections"; press** [Spacebar], **type** by **followed by your name, then click the** Save button 🖫 **on the PowerPoint Standard toolbar**

9. **Click** File **on the menu bar, click** Print, **under Print Range select the** Current slide **option, click** OK, **close the presentation, then exit PowerPoint**

FIGURE M-15: Presentation in Normal view

Slide 2 icon

Outline pane

Slide pane

Notes pane

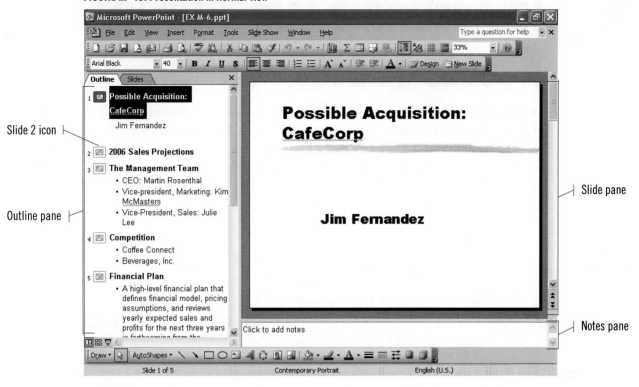

FIGURE M-16: Completed Sales Projections slide in Slide Show view

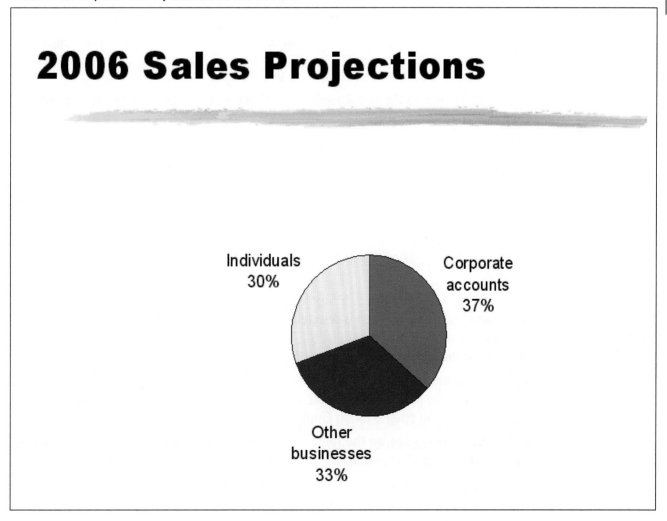

UNIT
M
Excel 2003

Importing a List into an Access Table

If you need to analyze an Excel list using the more extensive tools of a database, you can import the list into Microsoft Access, a database program. Column labels in Excel become field names in Access. Once converted to Access format, a data list is called a **table**. In the process of importing an Excel list, Access specifies a primary key for the new table. A **primary key** is the field that contains unique information for each record (row) of information. ▰▰▰▰▰ Jim has just received a workbook containing salary information for the managers at CafeCorp. He asks you to convert the list to a Microsoft Access table.

STEPS

1. **Click the** Start button **on the task bar, point to** All Programs, **point to** Microsoft Office, **click** Microsoft Office Access 2003, **click** Create a new file **in the Getting Started task pane, then click** Blank database **in the task pane**

2. **Click the** Save in list arrow, **navigate to the disk and folder containing your Data Files, change the filename in the File name text box to** CafeCorp Management, **then click** Create

   The database window for the CafeCorp Management database opens. You are ready to import the Excel list.

QUICK TIP

You can also use the Microsoft AccessLinks Add-in program, available on the Web, to convert an Excel list to an Access table from within Excel.

3. **Click** File **on the menu bar, point to** Get External Data, **click** Import, **make sure the folder containing your Data Files appears in the Look in box, select** Microsoft Excel (*.xls) **in the Files of type box, click** EX M-8.xls, **then click** Import

   The First Import Spreadsheet Wizard dialog box opens. See Figure M-17. The top section of the dialog box shows the sheets in the workbook. The Compensation worksheet is selected by default, and a sample of the sheet data appears in the lower section. In the next dialog box, you indicate that you want to use the column headings in the Excel list as the field names in the Access database.

4. **Click** Next, **make sure the** First Row Contains Column Headings check box **is selected, then click** Next

   You want to store the Excel data in a new table.

5. **Make sure the** In a New Table option button **is selected, then click** Next

   The wizard has converted the column headings from the Excel list into field names. Your completed Import Spreadsheet Wizard dialog box should match Figure M-18. The table's primary key field contains unique information for each record; the Employee field is unique for each person in the list.

QUICK TIP

Specifying a primary key allows you to retrieve data more quickly in the future.

6. **Click** Next, **select the** Choose my own primary key option, **make sure Employee Number appears in the list box next to the selected option button, click** Next, **click** Finish, **then click** OK

   The icon and name of the new Access table ("Compensation") appears in the database window.

7. **Make sure that** Compensation **is selected, click** Open **in the Database toolbar, then maximize the table window**

   The data from the Excel worksheet is displayed in a new Access table. See Figure M-19.

8. **Double-click the border between the Employee Number and First Name column headings, then use the last row of the table to enter** your name **in the First Name and Last Name columns and enter** 0 **for an Employee Number**

9. **Click the** Save button 🖫 **on the Table Datasheet toolbar, click the** Print button 🖨 **on the Table Datasheet toolbar to print the table, close the table, then exit Access**

FIGURE M-17: First Import Spreadsheet Wizard dialog box

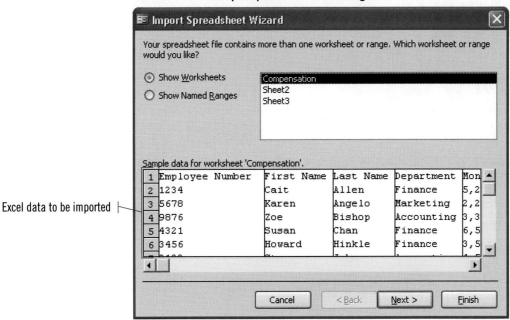

Excel data to be imported

FIGURE M-18: Completed Import Spreadsheet Wizard dialog box

Field names

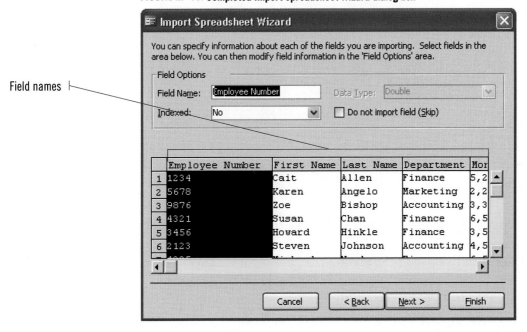

FIGURE M-19: Completed Access table

Primary key

Access table

Practice

▼ CONCEPTS REVIEW

FIGURE M-20

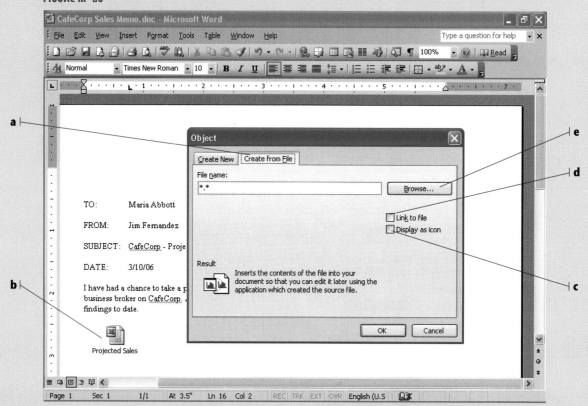

1. **Which element do you click to insert an existing object rather than creating a new file into a Word document?**
2. **Which element do you click to embed information that can be viewed by double-clicking an icon?**
3. **Which element do you double-click to display an embedded Excel worksheet?**
4. **Which element do you click to insert an object that maintains a connection to the source document?**
5. **Which element do you click to find a file to be embedded or linked?**

Match each term with the statement that best describes it.

6. **Destination document**
7. **Embedding**
8. **Source document**
9. **Linking**
10. **Table**
11. **Presentation graphics program**

a. File from which the object to be embedded or linked originates
b. Copies an object and retains a connection with the source program and source document
c. Document receiving the object to be embedded or linked
d. An Excel list converted to Access format
e. Copies an object and retains a connection with the source program
f. Used to create slide shows

Select the best answer from the list of choices.

12. An ASCII file:

   a. Contains text but no formatting

   b. Contains an unformatted worksheet

   c. Contains a PowerPoint presentation

   d. Contains formatting but no text

13. An object consists of:

   a. Text, a worksheet, or any other type of data

   b. Text only

   c. A worksheet only

   d. Database data only

14. A purple triangle in the lower-right corner of a cell is a:

   a. Field tag

   b. Table tag

   c. Smart tag

   d. Information tag

15. To view a worksheet that has been embedded as an icon in a Word document, you need to:

   a. Click View, then click Worksheet.

   b. Drag the icon.

   c. Double-click the worksheet icon.

   d. Click File, then click Open.

16. A field that contains unique information for each record in a database table is called a:

   a. Header key

   b. ID Key

   c. First key

   d. Primary key

▼ SKILLS REVIEW

1. Import a text file.

   a. Start Excel, open the tab-delimited text Data File titled EX M-9.txt from the drive and folder where your Data Files are stored, then save it as a Microsoft Office Excel workbook with the name **CafeCorp New Products**.

   b. Widen the columns as necessary so that all the data is visible.

   c. Format the data in columns B and C using the Accounting style with two decimal places.

   d. Center the column labels and apply bold formatting.

   e. Add your name to the left section of the worksheet footer, save the workbook, print the list in portrait orientation, then close the workbook.

2. Import a database table.

   a. In the Excel program, use the Import External Data command on the Data menu to import the Access Data File EX M-10.mdb from the drive and folder where your Data Files are stored, then save it as a Microsoft Office Excel workbook named **CafeCorp January Budget**.

   b. Rename the sheet **Budget**.

   c. Change the column labels so they read as follows: **Budget Category**, **Budget Item**, **Month**, and **Amount Budgeted**.

   d. Center the column labels and adjust the column widths as necessary.

   e. Use AutoSum to calculate a total in cell D26.

   f. Format range D2:D26 using the Accounting style with no decimal places.

   g. Save the workbook.

3. **Insert a graphic file in a worksheet.**
   a. Add four rows above row 1 to create space for a graphic.
   b. In rows 1 through 4, insert the picture file EX M-11.jpg from the drive and folder where your Data Files are stored.
   c. Resize and reposition the picture as necessary to make it fit in rows 1 through 4.
   d. Lower the contrast and the brightness of the picture.
   e. Remove the light blue background in the picture by making it transparent.
   f. Add your name to the left section of the worksheet footer, save the workbook, then print the worksheet.

4. **Embed a worksheet.**
   a. In cell A33, enter For details on CafeCorp salaries, click this icon:.
   b. In cell D33, use the Object dialog box to embed the worksheet object EX M-12.xls from the drive and folder where your Data Files are stored, displaying it as an icon with the caption Salary Details.
   c. Reposition the icon as necessary, double-click it to verify that the worksheet opens, then close it.
   d. Save the workbook, print the Budget worksheet, then close the workbook.

5. **Link a worksheet to another program.**
   a. Start Word, create a memo header addressed to your instructor, enter your name in the From line, enter January Salaries as the subject, and enter the current date in the Date line.
   b. In the memo body, link the spreadsheet object EX M-12.xls, displaying the worksheet, not an icon.
   c. Save the document as January Salaries in the drive and folder where your Data Files are stored, note that John Kelley's salary is $6,800. Close the document.
   d. Open the EX M-12 workbook in Excel and change John Kelley's salary to $7,000.
   e. Open the January Salaries document in Word, updating the links, and verify that John Kelley's salary has changed to $7,000 and that the new total salaries amount is $49,940.
   f. Save the January Salaries document, print the memo, then close the document and exit Word.
   g. Close the EX M-12 workbook without saving changes, then exit Excel.

6. **Embed an Excel chart into a PowerPoint slide.**
   a. Start PowerPoint.
   b. Open the PowerPoint Data File EX M-13.ppt from the drive and folder where your Data Files are stored, then save it as Monthly Budget Meeting.
   c. Display Slide 2, January Expenditures.
   d. Embed the Excel file EX M-14.xls from the drive and folder where your Data Files are located into Slide 2.
   e. View the slide in Slide Show view.
   f. Press [Esc] to return to Normal view.
   g. Replace the name Anna Smith with your name on the first slide.
   h. Save the presentation, print slides one and two as a handout (two slides to a page), then exit PowerPoint. (*Hint*: In the Print dialog box change Slides in the Print what section to Handouts, then select 2 in the slides per page section under Handouts.)

7. **Import a list into an Access table.**
   a. Start Access.
   b. Create a blank database named Budget List on the drive and folder where your Data Files are stored.
   c. Use the Get External Data option on the File menu to import the Excel list in the January Budget of EX M-15.xls from the drive and folder where your Data Files are stored. Use the first row as column headings, store the data in a new table, let Access add the primary key, and use the default table name January Budget.
   d. Open the January Budget table in Access and widen the columns as necessary to fully display the field names and field information.
   e. Enter your name in the Budget category column of row 25 in the table, save the database file, print the table, then exit Access.

▼ INDEPENDENT CHALLENGE 1

You are a loan officer for the Naples, Florida, branch of EastWest bank. You have been asked to give a presentation to a group of bank vice presidents about the types and number of loan applications your branch has received in the past year. To illustrate your loan data, you will add an Excel chart to one of your slides, showing the most popular loan types and the number of applications received this year for each type.

TABLE M-2

Loan type	Number of applications
Fixed home loans	1600
New car loans	7000
Used car loans	5400
Adjustable home loans	970
Boat loans	400

a. Start Excel, create a new workbook, then save it as **Consumer Loans** in the drive and folder where your Data Files are stored.

b. Enter the loans and the corresponding number of applications shown in Table M-2 into the Consumer Loans workbook. Name the sheet with the loan data **Loans**.

c. Create a 3-D pie chart from the loan data on a new sheet. Increase the font size to 20 in the legend. If a title appears on the chart, delete it. Your chart should look like Figure M-21.

d. Save the workbook with the chart sheet as the active sheet, then close the workbook.

e. Start PowerPoint, open the PowerPoint Data File EX M-16.ppt from the drive and folder where your Data Files are stored, then save it as **Loan Presentation**.

f. Embed the Excel chart from the Consumer Loans workbook into Slide 2.

g. View the slide in Slide Show view, then press [Esc] to end the show.

h. Edit Slide 1 to replace Allen Oles with your name, then save the presentation.

i. Print Slides 1 and 2 as a handout with two slides to a page, then close the presentation and exit PowerPoint.

FIGURE M-21

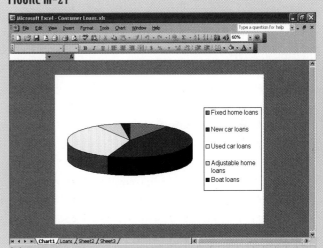

▼ INDEPENDENT CHALLENGE 2

You are opening a new store, Bridge Blades, that rents in-line skates in San Francisco, California. The owner of Gateway In-line, a similar store in San Francisco, is retiring and has agreed to sell you a text file containing his list of supplier information. You need to import this text file into Excel so that you can manipulate the data. Later you will convert the Excel file to an Access table, so that you can give it to your partner who is building a supplier database.

a. Start Excel, open the Data File titled EX M-17.txt from the drive and folder where your Data Files are stored, then save it as an Excel file named **Skate Supplier List**. (*Hint*: This is a tab-delimited text file.)

b. Adjust the column widths as necessary. Rename the worksheet **Supplier List**.

c. Center the column labels and apply bold formatting.

d. Sort the worksheet data in ascending order, first by Item, then by Supplier. (*Hint*: Open the Sort dialog box by clicking Sort on the Data menu, select Item in the first Sort by text box and Supplier in the second Then by text box.) Your worksheet should look like Figure M-22.

FIGURE M-22

▼ INDEPENDENT CHALLENGE 2 (CONTINUED)

e. Add your name to the left section of the worksheet footer, print the worksheet in landscape orientation, save and close the workbook, then exit Excel.

f. Start Access, create a new blank database on the drive and folder where your Data Files are stored. Name the new database **Supplier List**.

g. Use the Get External Data option on the File menu to import the Excel file **Skate Supplier List** from the drive and folder where your Data Files are stored. Use the column labels as the field names, store the data in a new table, let Access add the primary key, and accept the default table name.

h. Open the Supplier List table and AutoFit the columns.

i. Enter your name in the Supplier column in row 13, save and print the table in landscape orientation so it fits on one page (adjust column width as necessary), then close it and exit Access.

▼ INDEPENDENT CHALLENGE 3

You are the newly hired manager at ReadIt, an independent bookstore in your town. An employee, Joy Yee, has complained that she is underpaid and would like a raise. You have examined the salaries of the employees of the company and agree with Joy. You will present this information to the owner of the bookstore and request permission to grant Joy Yee an increase in salary.

a. Start Word, open the Word file EX M-18.doc from the drive and folder where your Data Files are stored, then save it as **Salary Adjustment**.

b. Add your name to the From line of the memo and change the date to the current date.

c. At the end of the memo, embed the worksheet object EX M-19.xls as an icon from the drive and folder where your Data Files are stored, then double-click the icon to verify that the worksheet opens.

d. Return to Word, delete the icon for EX M-19 and link the spreadsheet object EX M-19 to the memo, displaying the worksheet, not an icon.

e. Save the Salary Adjustment memo and close the file.

f. Open the EX M-19 workbook and change Joy Yee's salary to $7000.

g. Open the Salary Adjustment memo, updating the links, and make sure Joy Yee's salary is updated.

Advanced Challenge Exercise

- Delete the worksheet at the bottom of the Salary Adjustment memo. Copy the range A1:C10 from Sheet1 of the EX M-19 workbook to the Clipboard.
- Return to the Salary Adjustment memo and use the Paste Special dialog box to paste a link to the range A1:C10 from EX M-19 that is on the Clipboard. Use Figure M-23 as a guide.
- Change Joy Yee's salary to $8000 in EX M-19. Update the links to display the new salary information in the Salary Adjustment memo.

FIGURE M-23

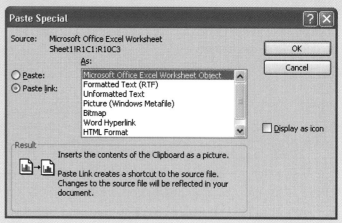

h. Save and print the memo.

i. Close the memo and exit Word.

j. Close EX M-19 without saving the change to Joy Yee's salary, then exit Excel.

▼ INDEPENDENT CHALLENGE 4

You are an assistant to the vice president of Sunshine Temporary, a temporary agency located in Winnipeg, Manitoba. Presently, Sunshine Temporary contracts with local companies to staff temporary secretarial and data entry positions. Management is considering adding permanent and temporary technical positions to the job titles it currently helps its clients fill. The vice president has asked you to prepare an Excel workbook showing the current open positions in the Sunshine Temporary database; she also wants you to include information about professional positions for which companies in the United States and Canada are recruiting. You will import a database list of current openings at Sunshine Temporary into an Excel workbook. Then you will use the Web to research professional positions in the United States and Canada and enter that information in the workbook.

a. Start Excel, import the Access file titled EX M-20.mdb from the drive and folder where your Data Files are stored, then save it as an Excel workbook titled **Temp Jobs**.

b. Rename the sheet tab **Open Positions**.

c. Format the data in column C using the Accounting style with two decimal places.

d. Sort the worksheet data in ascending order by Position.

e. Enter **Average Hourly Rate** in cell B14, then use the AutoSum list to enter a function in cell C14 that averages the Hourly Rates in column C.

f. Add four rows above row 1 to create space for a picture, and insert the file EX M-21.bmp from the drive and folder where your Data Files are stored. Resize the graphic as necessary to fit in rows 1 through 4.

g. Apply the List 1 AutoFormat to the range A5:C16. Compare your worksheet to Figure M-24.

h. Open your Web browser and go to the search engine of your choice. Search for job postings for six technical positions in the United States and Canada. Note the following information from the job postings: job title, city, state or province, and country.

i. Rename Sheet2 **Technical Positions**. On the Technical Positions sheet, enter the label **Position** in cell A1, **City** in cell B1, **State/Province** in cell C1, and **Country** in cell D1. Resize the columns as necessary. Use the information from your Web search to enter six records on the sheet.

FIGURE M-24

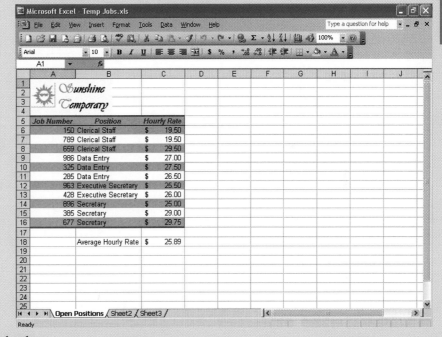

j. Apply the List 3 AutoFormat to the range A1:D7.

Advanced Challenge Exercise

- Add four rows above row 1 in the Technical Positions worksheet and insert the picture EX M-21.bmp.
- Resize the picture as necessary to fit in rows 1 through 4.
- Crop the right side of the picture to remove the text. Crop the picture to remove the borders.
- Rotate the picture ten degrees.

k. Enter your name in the left section of both sheet footers, save the workbook, then print both worksheets.

l. Close the workbook, then exit Excel.

▼ VISUAL WORKSHOP

Create the worksheet shown in Figure M-25. Insert the graphic file EX M-22.jpg and embed the workbook file EX M-23.xls as an icon with the caption shown. Both files are located in your Data Files folder. Resize both objects as necessary. Enter your name in the left section of the worksheet footer, save the workbook as **Atlantic Price List**, then print the worksheet and exit Excel.

FIGURE M-25

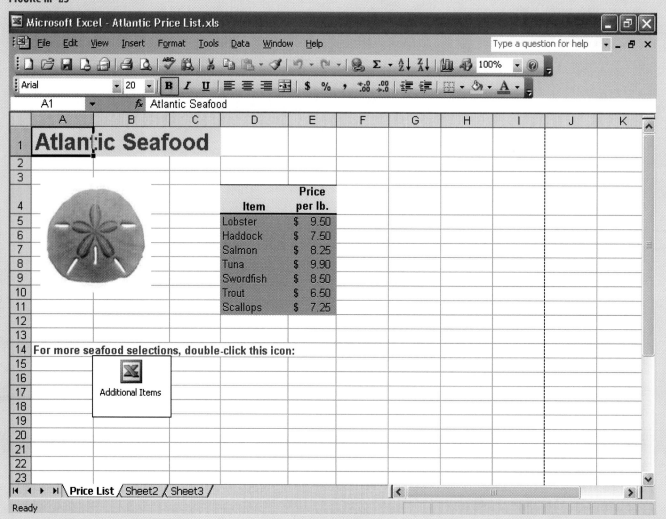

UNIT
N
Excel 2003

Sharing Excel Files and Incorporating Web Information

OBJECTIVES

Share Excel files
Set up a shared workbook for multiple users
Track revisions in a shared workbook
Apply and modify passwords
Create an interactive worksheet for the Web
Create a PivotTable list for the Web
Work with XML data
Run Web queries to retrieve external data

If you have a SAM user profile, you may have access to hands-on instruction, practice, and assessment of the skills covered in this unit. Log in to your SAM account and go to your assignments page to see what your instructor has assigned.

With the recent growth of networks, company intranets, and the World Wide Web, people are increasingly sharing electronic spreadsheet files with others for review, revision, and feedback. They are also incorporating information from intranets and the Web into their worksheets. Jim Fernandez, the marketing director for MediaLoft, has some MediaLoft corporate information he wants to share with corporate office employees and store managers.

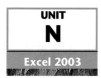

UNIT N
Excel 2003

Sharing Excel Files

Microsoft Excel provides many different ways to share spreadsheets electronically with people in your office, in your company, or anywhere on the Web. You can post workbooks for users to interact with on a company intranet or on the Web. When you share workbooks, however, you have to consider how you will protect information that you don't want everyone to see. You can also use Excel workbooks to run queries to retrieve data from the Web. ▇▇▇ Jim considers the best way to share his Excel workbooks with corporate employees and store managers. He also thinks about how to import Web and XML data to use in his workbooks. He discusses the following issues with you:

DETAILS

- ### Allowing others to use a workbook

  When you share Excel files with others, you need to set up your workbooks so that several users can **share** them, which means they can simultaneously open them from a network server, modify them electronically, and return their revisions to you for incorporation with others' changes. You can view each user's name and the date each change was made. Jim wants to obtain feedback on selected store sales and customer information from MediaLoft corporate staff and store managers.

- ### Controlling access to workbooks on a server

  When you set up a workbook on a network server, you might want to control who can open and change it. You can do this easily using Excel passwords. Jim assigns a password to his workbook and gives the workbook to the corporate staff and store managers, along with the password, so only they can open the workbook and revise it.

- ### Distributing workbooks to others

  There are several ways of making workbook information available to others. You can send it to recipients simultaneously as an e-mail attachment or as the body of an e-mail message; you can **route** it, or send it sequentially to each user, who then forwards it on to the next recipient using a **routing slip**, or list of recipients. You can also save the file in HTML format and post it on a company intranet server or on the Web, where people can view it with their Web browsers. Jim decides to make an Excel workbook available to others by putting it on a company server.

- ### Publishing a worksheet for use on an intranet or the World Wide Web

  When you save a workbook as a Web page, you can save the entire workbook or a single worksheet. You can specify that you want to make it **interactive**, meaning that users can make changes to it when they view it in their browsers. They do not need to have the Excel program on their computer. See Figure N-1. The changes remain in effect until users close their browsers. Jim decides to publish the worksheet with the MediaLoft café pastry sales information on the company intranet.

- ### Interactive PivotTables

  You can save a PivotTable in HTML format so people can only view it, but the data is much more useful if people can interact with it using their browsers, just as they would in Excel. To make an Excel PivotTable interactive, you need to save it as a PivotTable list. Jim wants corporate staff to explore sales data relationships using their browsers just as they would with Excel.

- ### Working with XML data

  You can import XML data from different sources and merge the information in an Excel workbook. Once the data is in a workbook you can manage it using Excel tools. Jim decides to merge XML files that contain sales information from the east and west regions to get a summary of the total sales at MediaLoft.

- ### Using an Excel query to retrieve data from the Web

  You can use Microsoft Query to import data from the Web into an Excel workbook. Then you can organize and manipulate the information using Excel spreadsheet and graphics tools. Jim decides to use a query to get currency rate information for a MediaLoft project in Canada. See Figure N-2.

FIGURE N-1: Interactive worksheet in a Web browser

Toolbar allows users to manipulate and format worksheet data

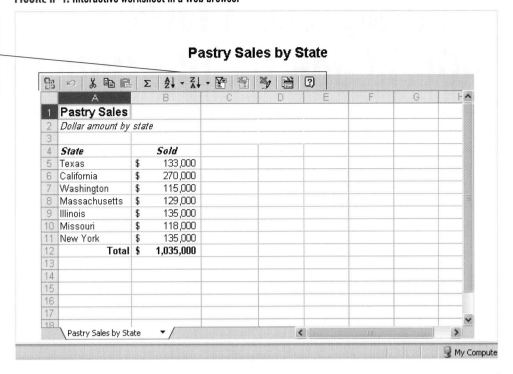

FIGURE N-2: Data retrieved from the Web using a Web query

Excel worksheet with imported currency data

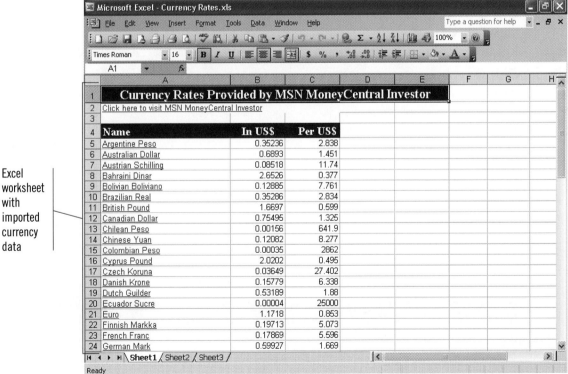

Setting up a Shared Workbook for Multiple Users

You can make an Excel file a **shared workbook** so that several users can open and modify it at the same time. This is very useful for workbooks that you want others to review on a network server. The workbook is equally accessible to all network users. When you share a workbook, you can have Excel keep a list of all changes to the workbook, which you can view and print at any time. ▰▰▰ Jim asks you to help him put a shared workbook containing customer and sales data on the company's network. He wants to get feedback from selected corporate staff and store managers before presenting the information at the next corporate staff meeting. You begin by making his workbook containing customer and sales data a shared workbook.

STEPS

QUICK TIP
The Advanced tab of the Share Workbook dialog box allows you to specify the length of time the change history is saved and when the file will be updated with the changes.

1. **Start Excel, open the Data File** EX N-1.xls **from the drive and folder where your Data Files are stored, then save it as** Sales Info

   The workbook with the sales information opens, displaying three worksheets. The first is the chart of MediaLoft pastry sales for the first quarter, the second contains data about pastry sales by state, and the third contains a listing of sales for selected stores and sales representatives for the last four quarters.

2. **Click** Tools **on the menu bar, then click** Share Workbook

   The Share Workbook dialog box opens. See Figure N-3.

3. **Click the** Editing **tab, if necessary**

   The dialog box lists the names of people who are currently using the workbook. You are the only user, so your name, or the name of the person entered as the computer user, appears, along with the current date and time.

QUICK TIP
You can remove users from the list by clicking their names and clicking Remove User.

4. **Click to select the check box next to** Allow changes by more than one user at the same time, **then click** OK

   A dialog box appears, asking if you want to save the workbook. This will resave it as a shared workbook.

5. **Click** OK

   Excel saves the file as a shared workbook. The Title bar now reads Sales Info.xls [Shared]. See Figure N-4. This version replaces the unshared version.

QUICK TIP
You can return the workbook to unshared status. To do so, click Tools, click Share Workbook, then deselect the Allow changes by more than one user at the same time option on the Editing tab.

Clues to Use

Merging workbooks

Instead of putting the shared workbook on a server, you may want to distribute copies to your reviewers via e-mail. Once everyone has entered their changes, you can merge the changed copies into one master workbook that will contain all the changes. Each copy you distribute must be designated as shared, and the Change History feature on the Advanced tab of the Share Workbook dialog box, must be activated. Once you get the changed copies back, open the master copy of the workbook, click Tools on the menu bar, then click Compare and Merge Workbooks. The Select Files to Merge Into Current Workbook dialog box opens. Select the workbooks you want to merge (you can use the [Ctrl] key to select more than one workbook), then click OK.

FIGURE N-3: Share Workbook dialog box

Select to allow multiple users of the workbook at the same time

Current users of the workbook

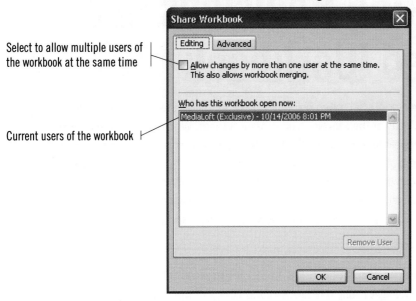

FIGURE N-4: Shared workbook

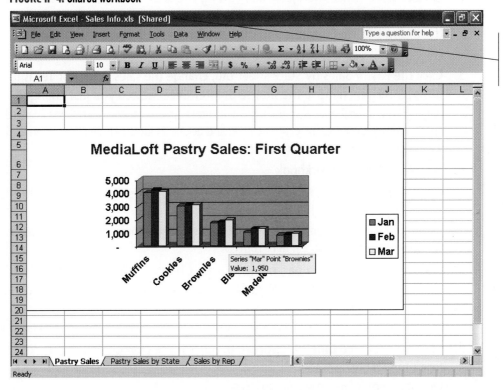

Title bar indicates the workbook is shared

Excel 2003

Clues to Use

Comparing workbooks side by side

Placing workbooks side by side allows you to easily compare changes made to workbooks by many users. To review the workbooks in this way, you need to first open the workbooks, click Window, then click Compare Side by Side. The workbooks will be vertically tiled on your screen and the Compare Side by Side toolbar will be displayed. You can scroll through the workbooks simultaneously by making sure the Synchronous Scrolling button is selected. To reset the workbooks to their original positions, click the Reset Window Position button on the Compare Side by Side toolbar. To end the workbook comparison, click the Close Side by Side button on the Compare Side by Side toolbar.

Tracking Revisions in a Shared Workbook

When you share workbooks, it is often helpful to **track** modifications, or identify who made which changes. If you disagree with any of the changes, you can reject them. When you activate the Excel change tracking feature, changes appear in a different color for each user. Each change is identified with the username and date. In addition to highlighting changes, Excel keeps track of all changes in a **change history**, a list of all changes that you can place on a separate worksheet so you can review them all at once. ▰▰▰ Jim asks you to set up the shared Sales Info workbook so that all future changes will be tracked. You will then open a workbook that has been on the server and review the changes and the change history.

STEPS

1. **Click Tools on the menu bar, point to Track Changes, click Highlight Changes**

   The Highlight Changes dialog box opens, allowing you to turn on change tracking. You can also specify which changes to highlight and whether you want to display changes on the screen or save the change history in a separate worksheet. See Figure N-5.

2. **Click to select Track changes while editing check box if necessary, remove check marks from all other boxes except for Highlight changes on screen, click OK, then click OK in the dialog box that informs you that you have yet to make changes**

   Leaving the When, Who, and Where check boxes blank allows you to track all changes.

3. **Click the Pastry Sales by State sheet tab, change the sales figure for Texas to 140,000, press [Enter], then move the mouse pointer over the cell you just changed**

   A border with a small triangle in the upper-left corner appears around the cell you changed, and a ScreenTip appears with your name, the date, the time, and details about the change. See Figure N-6. Cells that other users change will appear in different colors.

4. **Save and close the workbook**

5. **Open the Data File EX N-2.xls from the drive and folder where your Data Files are stored, then save it as Sales Info Edits**

   Jose Mendel has made changes to a version of this workbook. You want to view the details of these changes and accept the ones that appear to be correct.

6. **Click Tools on the menu bar, point to Track Changes, click Accept or Reject Changes, click the When check box in the Select Changes to Accept or Reject dialog box to deselect it, then click OK**

   You will accept the first three changes that Jose made to the workbook and reject his last change.

7. **Click Accept three times to approve the first three changes, then click Reject to undo Jose's fourth change**

   Jim wants a printed record of Jose's changes.

8. **Click Tools on the menu bar, point to Track Changes, click Highlight Changes, click the When check box in the Highlight Changes dialog box to deselect it, click to select the List changes on a new sheet check box, then click OK**

   The History sheet appears, as shown in Figure N-7, with a record of each change made by Jose in the form of a filtered list.

   QUICK TIP

   Because saving the file closes the History sheet, you need to print it before saving the workbook.

9. **Enter your name in the left section of the History sheet footer, print the History sheet in landscape orientation on one page, save the workbook, observe that the History sheet closes automatically, then close the workbook**

   The change history printout shows all of Jose's changes to the workbook.

FIGURE N-5: Highlight Changes dialog box

Select to show changes on the worksheet

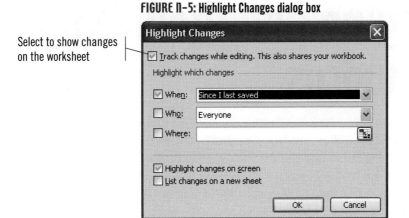

FIGURE N-6: Tracked change

Triangle in corner indicates cell has been changed

ScreenTip provides details of changes to the cell

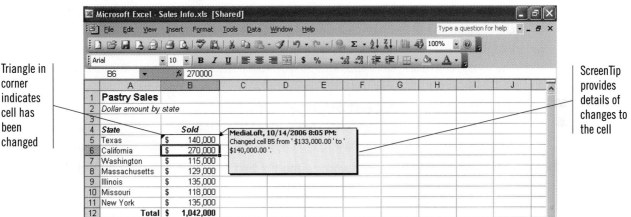

FIGURE N-7: History sheet tab with change history

Details of changes to the worksheet

History tab

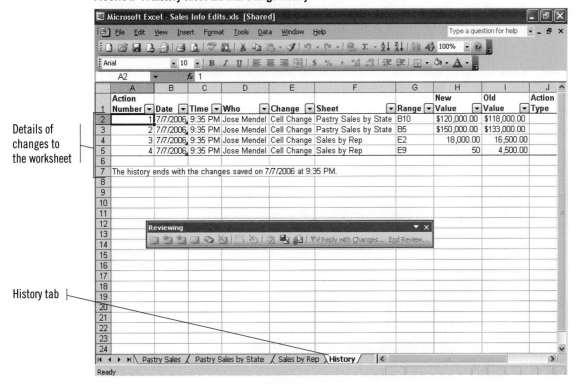

Applying and Modifying Passwords

When you place a shared workbook on a server, you may want to use a password so that only authorized people will be able to open it or make changes to it. *If you lose your password, you will not be able to open or change the workbook.* Passwords are case sensitive, so you must type them exactly as you want users to type them, with the same spacing and using the same case. It is a good idea to include both letters and numbers in a password. 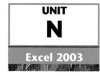 Jim wants you to put the workbook with sales information on one of the company's servers. You decide to save a copy of the workbook with two passwords: one that users will need to open it, and another that they will use to make changes to it.

STEPS

1. **Open the Data File** EX N-1.xls **from the drive and folder where your Data Files are stored, click** File **on the menu bar, click** Save As, **click the** Tools list arrow **in the Save As dialog box, then click** General Options

   The Save Options dialog box opens, with two password boxes: one to open the workbook, and one to allow changes to the workbook. See Figure N-8.

2. **In the Password to open text box, type** saturn654

   Be sure to type the letters in lowercase. This is the password that users must type to open the workbook. When you enter passwords, the characters you type are masked with asterisks (***) for security purposes.

   > **QUICK TIP**
   > You can press [Enter] rather than clicking OK after entering a password. This allows you to keep your hands on the keyboard.

3. **Press** [Tab] **twice, in the Password to modify text box, type** atlas321, **then click** OK

   This is the password that users must type to make changes to the workbook. A dialog box asks you to verify the first password by reentering it.

4. **Enter** saturn654 **in the first Confirm Password dialog box, click** OK, **enter** atlas321 **in the second Confirm Password dialog box, then click** OK

5. **Edit the filename so it reads** Sales Info PW, **click** Save, **then close the workbook**

   > **QUICK TIP**
   > To protect cell ranges with a password, click Tools, point to Protection, then click Allow Users to Edit Ranges. Click New, then specify a range to protect and assign a password.

6. **Reopen the workbook** Sales Info PW, **enter the password** saturn654 **when prompted for a password, click** OK, **then enter** atlas321 **to obtain write access**

   The Password dialog box is shown in Figure N-9. Obtaining write access for a workbook allows you to modify it.

7. **Click** OK, **click the** Pastry Sales by State Sheet tab, **change the sales figure for Texas in cell B5 to** 150,000, **then press** [Enter]

   You were able to make this change because you obtained write access privileges using the password "atlas321."

8. **Save and close the workbook**

FIGURE N-8: Save Options dialog box

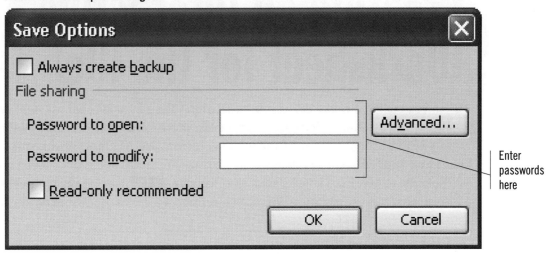

Enter
passwords
here

FIGURE N-9: Password entry prompt

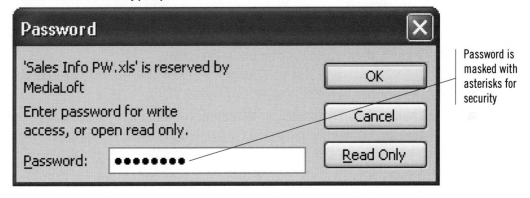

Password is
masked with
asterisks for
security

Clues to Use

Removing passwords

You can change or delete a workbook's password if you know what it is. Open the workbook, click File on the menu bar, then click Save As. In the Save As dialog box, click the Tools list arrow, then click General Options. Double-click to highlight the symbols for the existing passwords in the Password to open or Password to modify text boxes, press [Delete], click OK, change the filename if desired, then click Save.

Creating an Interactive Worksheet for the Web

When you publish a worksheet with **interactivity**, users can modify, format, sort, and analyze data using their Web browsers. To create an interactive workbook or worksheet, you must open it in Excel, save it in HTML format then **post** (place) it in a shared location. To work with interactive data, users must have installed Internet Explorer version 4.01 or later as well as the Office Web Components. Users do not need to have Excel installed on their computers. ▰▰▰▰ Jim asks you to save the Pastry Sales by State worksheet as an interactive Web page that managers can manipulate using Internet Explorer.

STEPS

1. **Open the Data File** EX N-1.xls **from the drive and folder where your Data Files are stored, then save it as** Sales Info 2

2. **Click the** Pastry Sales by State sheet tab, **click** File **on the menu bar, click** Save as Web Page
   The Save As dialog box opens. See Figure N-10. This dialog box allows you to specify what workbook components you want to publish, the title of the published file, and whether you want users to be able to modify the published document.

> **QUICK TIP**
> You need to select Single File Web Page as the File Type before selecting any options in the Save As dialog box.

3. **Click the** Save as type list arrow, **click** Single File Web Page, **edit the filename to read** pastry.mht, **make sure the folder containing your Data Files appears in the Save in text box**
   Recall that an MHT file is an HTML file with page and graphical elements in a single file.

4. **Click the** Selection: Sheet option button, **select the** Add interactivity check box, **click** Change Title, **enter** Pastry Sales by State, **click** OK, **then click** Publish

> **QUICK TIP**
> If you select the AutoRepublish every time this workbook is saved check box, the Web page is updated automatically every time you save the Excel file.

5. **Click to select the** Open published web page in browser check box **if necessary, click** Publish, **then maximize your browser window**
   The HTML version of your worksheet opens in your browser. See Figure N-11. You can make temporary changes to the worksheet using Internet Explorer.

6. **Change the Sold number for Washington in cell B7 to** 120,000, **then press** [Enter]
   The total updates automatically to 1,040,000. Changes you make using your browser remain in effect until you close your browser.

7. **Select the range B5:B12, click the** Commands and Options button 🗔 **on the toolbar above the worksheet, on the Format tab click the** Number format list arrow, **click** Currency, **then close the dialog box**

8. **Select the range** A5:B11, **click the** Sort Ascending button ⬇ **on the toolbar above the worksheet**
   The data is sorted according to state name. You can also remove the total.

9. **Select the range** A4:B11, **click the** AutoFilter button 🖺 **on the toolbar above the worksheet, click the** State list arrow, **click the** Total check mark **to remove it, then click** OK

> **TROUBLE**
> Your browser's Print dialog box may show an OK button instead of a Print button.

10. **Enter your name in cell A15 of the worksheet, click** File **on the menu bar, click** Print, **click** Print, **then close your browser**

FIGURE N-10: Save As dialog box

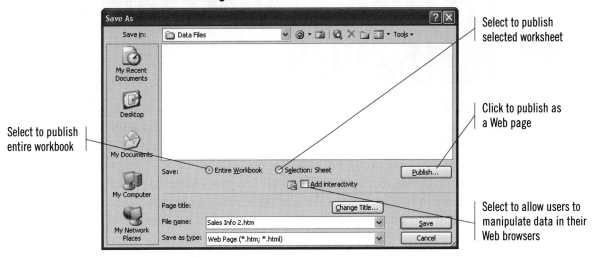

Select to publish entire workbook

Select to publish selected worksheet

Click to publish as a Web page

Select to allow users to manipulate data in their Web browsers

FIGURE N-11: Pastry Sales by State worksheet as Web page

Toolbar allows you to manipulate and analyze worksheet data

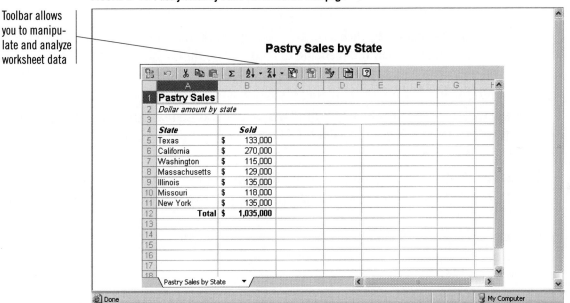

Clues to Use

Adding Web hyperlinks to a worksheet

In Excel worksheets, you can create hyperlinks to information on the Web. Every Web page is identified by a unique Web address called a Uniform Resource Locator (URL). To create a hyperlink to a Web page, click the cell for which you want to create a hyperlink, click the Insert Hyperlink button 🌐 on the Standard toolbar, under Link to make sure Existing File or Web Page is selected, specify the target for the hyperlink (the URL) in the Address text box, then click OK. The link text on your worksheet changes to blue, underlined text, indicating that it is a hyperlink.

Creating a PivotTable List for the Web

Not only can you create interactive worksheets that users can modify in their Web browsers, but you can also create interactive PivotTables that users can analyze by dragging fields to get different views of the data. An interactive PivotTable for the Web is called a **PivotTable list**. Users cannot enter new values to the list, but they can filter and sort data, add calculations, and rearrange data to get a different perspective on the information. As the PivotTable list creator, you have complete control over what information is included from the source data, which could be an Excel worksheet, a PivotTable, or external data (for example, an Access database). You can include only selected columns of information if you wish. You can also include charts with your PivotTable data. As with spreadsheets you publish in HTML format, users view PivotTable lists in their browsers, and changes they make to them are retained only for that browser session. The HTML file remains in its original form. Jim has compiled some sales information about sales representatives at selected stores for the last four quarters. He asks you to save it as a PivotTable list so he and selected corporate staff and store managers can review and analyze the information using their Web browsers.

STEPS

1. **Click the** Sales by Rep tab **in the** Sales Info 2 **workbook**

   You create the PivotTable list directly from the data, rather than creating an Excel PivotTable first.

2. **Click** File **on the menu bar, click** Save as Web Page, **click the** Save as type list arrow, **click** Single File Web Page, **edit the filename to read** repinfo.mht, **make sure the folder containing your Data Files appears in the Save in text box, click the** Selection: Sheet option button, **click the** Add interactivity check box **to select it, then click** Publish

3. **Make sure** Items on Sales by Rep **is displayed in the Choose text box and that** Sheet - All contents of Sales by Rep **appears in the Choose list**

   All items on the Sales by Rep sheet will appear in the PivotTable list.

4. **Click the** Add interactivity with list arrow, **then select** PivotTable functionality

   PivotTable functionality allows users to manipulate items on the PivotTable list in the same way they would on a PivotTable in Excel.

   > **QUICK TIP**
   >
   > To return the PivotTable to its original state, click the Address box containing the URL and press [Enter].

5. **Make sure** Open published web page in browser **is checked**

   You are ready to publish the PivotTable list. See Figure N-12.

6. **Click** Publish, **then maximize your browser window if necessary**

   The new PivotTable list opens in Internet Explorer. Its layout looks similar to a PivotTable report in Excel, with row and column fields and field list arrows. As with an Excel PivotTable, you can change the layout to view the data in different ways. You use the toolbar above the PivotTable to change the position of the field headings.

   > **QUICK TIP**
   >
   > You can also drag the field headings to the desired drop areas.

7. **Click the** Field List button 🗔 **on the toolbar above the PivotTable, in the PivotTable Field List window, click the** Store **field, click the** list arrow **at the bottom of the window, choose** Row Area **if necessary, then click** Add To; **click the** Department **field in the PivotTable Field List, click the** list arrow **at the bottom of the window, choose** Column Area, **click** Add To, **then close the PivotTable Field List**

   The layout of the PivotTable list has changed. Now, the data is organized by department and store. This rearrangement of data allows you to see, for example, that Barnard sold the most books in the Boston store, while Haile sold the most books in the Seattle store. See Figure N-13.

8. **Click** File **on the menu bar, click** Print, **click** Print, **close your browser, then save and close the workbook**

FIGURE N-12: Publish as Web Page dialog box

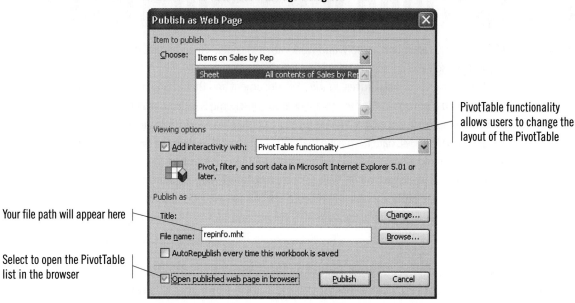

PivotTable functionality allows users to change the layout of the PivotTable

Your file path will appear here

Select to open the PivotTable list in the browser

FIGURE N-13: PivotTable list with new layout

Department field is in the column area

Store field is in the row area

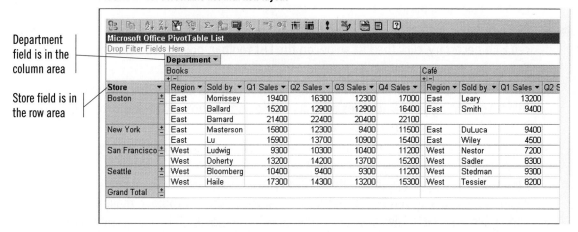

Clues to Use

Exporting a PivotTable list from a Web page to an Excel workbook

Changes that you make to a PivotTable list are lost when you close your browser. However, you can use the Export to Microsoft Office Excel button on the toolbar above the PivotTable list to save your PivotTable list changes in an Excel file. Some of the formatting features applied using the Commands and Options dialog box will not be exported with the data. Also, if your PivotTable list included calculated fields such as totals and statistical values, only those values will be displayed in the worksheet until you click the Show Detail button of the PivotTable toolbar.

Working with XML Data

Using Excel you can import, export, and work with XML data. To bring XML data into a workbook, Excel requires a file called a schema or map that describes the structure of the XML file. A **schema** lists all of the fields, defined as either **elements** or **attributes**, in the XML document and their characteristics, such as the type of data they contain. Once a schema is attached to a workbook, a schema is called a **map**. When you **map** an element to a worksheet, you place the element name on the worksheet in a specific location. Mapping XML elements allows you to choose the XML data from a file that you want to work with in the worksheet. After the mapping is complete, you can import any XML file with a structure that conforms to the workbook schema and the mapped elements on the worksheet will fill with (or be **populated** with) data from the XML file. Once you import the XML data, you can analyze it using Excel tools. ▒▒▒▒▓ Jim asks you to combine the east and west sales rep information for MediaLoft and total the sales for the company.

STEPS

1. **Create a new workbook, save it as** Sales Rep Info **in the drive and folder where your Data Files are stored, click** Data **on the menu bar, point to** XML, **then click** XML Source

   The XML Source pane opens. This is where you specify a schema, or map, to import. A schema has an extension of .xsd. Jim has provided you with a schema describing the XML file structure.

2. **Click** XML Maps **at the bottom of the task pane, click** Add **in the XML Maps dialog box, make sure the folder containing your Data Files appears in the Look in box of the Select XML Source dialog box, click** EX N-3.xsd, **click** Open, **then click** OK

   The schema elements appear in the XML Source task pane. You choose the elements that you want to work with and map them to the worksheet.

3. **Click the** REGION **element in the XML Source task pane and drag it to cell A1 on the worksheet, then use Figure N-14 as a guide to drag the** FNAME, LNAME, SALES, **and** ENUMBER **fields to the worksheet**

   The blue border around the cell indicates that it is mapped to an XML element. You decide to remove the ENUMBER field from the list.

4. **Right-click the** ENUMBER **element in the XML Source task pane, click** Remove Element, **click cell** E1 **if necessary, click the** List arrow **on the List toolbar, point to** Delete, **then click** Column

   You use the List toolbar to import XML data into the worksheet.

5. **Click cell** A1, **click the** Import XML Data button 🗗 **on the List toolbar, make sure the folder containing your Data Files appears in the Look in box of the Import XML dialog box, click** EX N-4.xml, **then click** Import

   The worksheet is populated with data from the XML file that contains the eastern sales rep information. You decide to add the sales rep data for the western region to the worksheet.

6. **Click the** XML Map Properties button 🗗 **on the List toolbar, click the** Append new data to existing XML lists option button, **click** OK, **click** 🗗 **on the List toolbar, make sure the folder containing your Data Files appears in the Look in box, click** EX N-5.xml, **then click** Import

   The western region sales rep data is added to the eastern region data. You total the sales figures for all sales reps.

7. **Click the** Toggle Total Row button 🟰 Toggle Total Row **on the List toolbar, select the range of cells** D2:D13, **click the** Currency Style button 💲 **on the Formatting toolbar, return to cell A1, enter your name in the left section of the worksheet footer, then click the** Print List button 🗗 **on the List toolbar**

   Compare your completed list to Figure N-15. You will export the complete sales rep data as an XML file.

8. **Click the** Export XML Data button 🗗 **on the List toolbar, make sure the folder containing your Data Files appears in the Save in box of the Export XML dialog box, enter the name of** allreps **in the File name text box, then click** Export; **save and close workbook**

   The sales data is saved in your Data File location in XML format, in the file called allreps.xml.

FIGURE N-14: XML elements mapped to the worksheet

Mapped elements

List toolbar

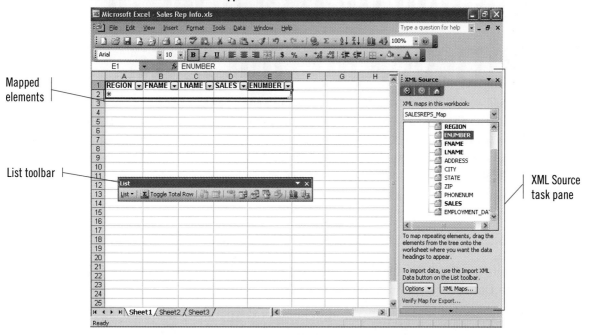

XML Source task pane

FIGURE N-15: Completed list of sales rep information

Imported data

Total of all sales

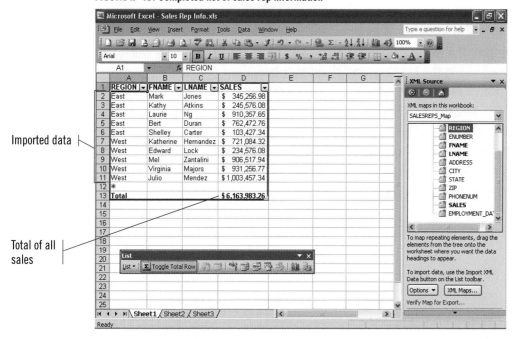

Clues to Use

What is XML?

XML is a universal data format for business and industry information sharing. Using XML you can store structured information related to services, products, or business transactions and easily share and exchange that information with others. XML provides a way to express structure in data. Structured data is tagged, or marked up, to indicate its content. For example, an XML data marker (tag) that contains an item's cost might be named COST.

Excel's ability to work with XML data allows you to access the large amount of information stored in the XML format. For example, there are many XML applications developed by organizations with a specific focus like MathML (Mathematical Markup Language) and RETML (Real Estate Transaction Markup Language).

Running Web Queries to Retrieve External Data

Often you'll want to incorporate information from the Web into an Excel worksheet for analysis. Using Excel, you can obtain data from a Web site by running a **Web query**, then save the information in an existing or new Excel workbook. You must be connected to the Internet to run a Web query. You can save Web queries so you can use them again later; a saved query has an .iqy file extension. Several Web query files come with Excel. As part of a special project MediaLoft is working on in Canada, Jim needs to obtain currency rate information for the Canadian dollar. He asks you to run a Web query to obtain the most current currency rate information from the Web.

STEPS

1. **Create a new workbook, then save it as Currency Rates in the drive and folder where your Data Files are stored**

2. **Click Data on the menu bar, point to Import External Data, then click Import Data**
   The Select Data Source dialog box opens, with the My Data Sources folder contents displayed. The queries that come with Excel are in this folder.

3. **Click MSN MoneyCentral Investor Currency Rates.iqy, then click Open**
   The Import Data dialog box opens. See Figure N-16. Here you specify the worksheet location where you want the imported data to appear.

4. **Make sure the Existing worksheet option button is selected, click cell A1 if necessary to place =$A$1 in the Existing worksheet text box, then click OK**
   Currency rate information from the Web is placed in the workbook. See Figure N-17. Jim wants you to obtain the previous closing exchange rate of the Canadian dollar.

5. **Click the Canadian Dollar link**
   A Web page opens in your browser, with currency rate details for the Canadian dollar. See Figure N-18.

6. **Click File on the menu bar, click Print, click Print, close the browser, save and close the workbook, then exit Excel**

Clues to Use

Creating your own Web queries

To retrieve data from a particular Web page on a regular basis, it's easiest to create a customized Web query. Click Data on the menu bar, point to Import External Data, then click New Web Query. In the New Web Query dialog box, type the address of the Web page from which you want to retrieve data, then click Go. Click the Import table arrows ➡ next to the information you want to bring into a worksheet or click the upper-left Import table arrow to import the entire page, then click Import. The Import Data dialog box opens and allows you to specify where you want the imported data placed in the worksheet. You can save a query for future use by clicking the Save Query button 🖫 in the New Web Query dialog box before you click Import. The query is saved as a file with an .iqy file extension.

FIGURE N-16: Import Data dialog box

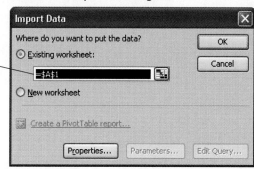

Location on worksheet where imported data will appear

FIGURE N-17: Currency rates quote

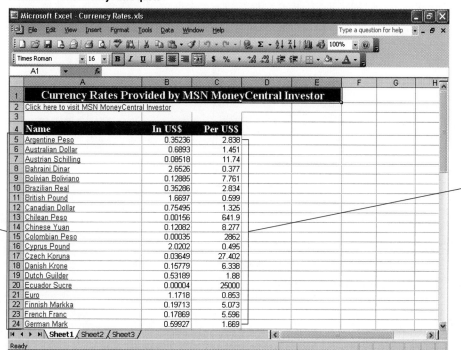

Currency rates from the Web

Your numbers will differ depending on the date you run the query

FIGURE N-18: Rate details for the Canadian dollar

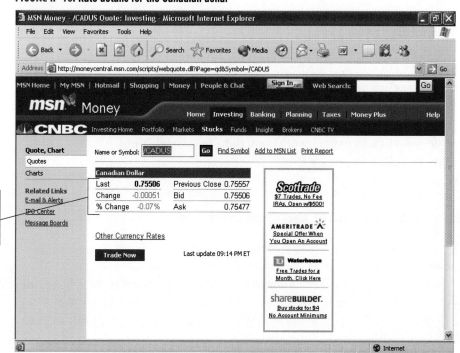

Your values will differ depending on the date you run the query

Practice

▼ CONCEPTS REVIEW

FIGURE N-19

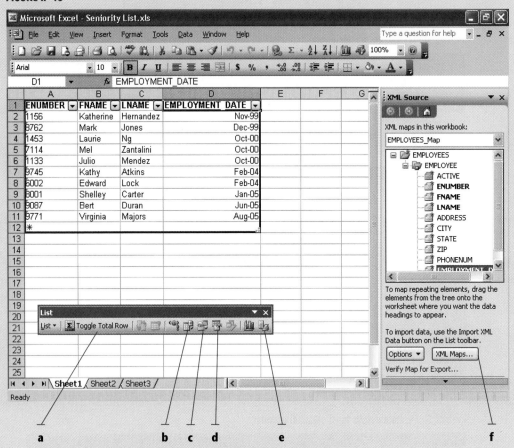

1. **Which element do you click to add a schema to an Excel workbook?**
2. **Which element do you click to add totals to a worksheet list?**
3. **Which element do you click to import XML data into a workbook?**
4. **Which element do you click to change the XML Map properties?**
5. **Which element do you click to export workbook data to an xml file?**
6. **Which element do you click to print a list?**

Match each item with the statement that best describes it.

7. **PivotTable list**   a. A unique address on the Web
8. **Shared workbook**   b. Used by many people on a network
9. **Web query**   c. Data on a worksheet with fields that can be repositioned using Web browser tools
10. **Change history**   d. Used to access and import information from the Web
11. **URL**   e. A record of edits others have made to a worksheet

Select the best answer from the list of choices.

12. **A list of recipients to whom you are sending a workbook sequentially is called a:**
    a. Routing slip
    b. PivotTable
    c. Hypertext document
    d. Shared workbook

13. **Which of the following can be saved in HTML format and then manipulated on the Web?**
    a. A worksheet
    b. A PivotTable
    c. A workbook
    d. All of the above

14. **Which of the following allows you to obtain data from the Web?**
    a. Web Wizard
    b. PivotTable
    c. Web query
    d. Data query

15. **The process of selecting XML elements to include on a worksheet is called:**
    a. Sharing
    b. Selecting
    c. Loading
    d. Mapping

16. **A file that describes the structure of XML data is called a:**
    a. Layout
    b. Schema
    c. Query
    d. Detail File

▼ SKILLS REVIEW

1. **Set up a shared workbook for multiple users.**
    a. Start Excel, open the Data File EX N-6.xls from the drive and folder where your Data Files are stored, then save it as Ad Campaigns.
    b. Use the Share Workbook option on the Tools menu to set up the workbook so that more than one person can use it at one time.
    c. Use the Advanced tab in the Share Workbook dialog box to specify that the change history should be maintained for 1000 days.
    d. Make sure the Advanced tab in the Share Workbook dialog box specifies changes will be made when the file is saved.

2. **Track revisions in a shared workbook.**
    a. In the Ads Q1 All Stores worksheet, change the Billboards amounts to $45,000 for each month.
    b. Save the file.
    c. Display the History sheet by opening the Highlight Changes dialog box, clicking the When check box to deselect it, then selecting the option for List changes on a new sheet.
    d. Enter your name in the History sheet footer, then print the History sheet.
    e. Save and close the workbook.

3. **Apply and modify passwords.**
    a. Open the Data File EX N-6.xls from the drive and folder where your Data Files are stored, open the Save As dialog box, then open the General Options dialog box.
    b. Set the password to open the workbook as ads987 and the password to modify it as spring654.
    c. Save the password-protected file as Ad Campaigns PW.
    d. Close the workbook.
    e. Use the assigned passwords to reopen the workbook and verify that you can change it by adding your name in the left section of the Ads Q1 All Stores sheet footer.

4. **Create an interactive worksheet for the Web.**
    a. Save the Ads Q1 All Stores worksheet as an interactive Web page in single-file Web page format, with spreadsheet functionality. (*Hint*: Select Single File Web Page as the File Type before selecting any options in the Save As dialog box.) Set the title to Ad Campaign Forecast, and save it to the folder containing your Data Files with the filename campaign.mht. Open the Web page in Internet Explorer.
    b. Using the toolbar above the worksheet, add totals for each month in B11:D11, then add a grand total to cell E11.
    c. Use the Commands and Options dialog box to apply the currency format to the range B3:E11.
    d. Sort the list in ascending order by ad type. (*Hint*: Select the range A3:E10 before clicking the Sort Ascending button.)
    e. Add your name to cell A13, print the worksheet from Internet Explorer, then close Internet Explorer.

5. Create a PivotTable list for the Web.

   a. In the Ad Campaigns PW workbook, save the worksheet Ad Detail in MHT format as an interactive Web page with PivotTable functionality. (*Hint*: Select Single File Web Page as the file type before selecting any options in the Save As dialog box.)

   b. Add a title of Ad Forecast, and save it as storeads.mht in the folder containing your Data Files; open the file in your Web browser.

   c. Use the PivotTable Field list to add the Region field to the Row Field area.

   d. Use the PivotTable Field list to add the Department field to the Column Field area.

   e. Print the Web page from Internet Explorer showing the changed data orientation, then close Internet Explorer and close the workbook.

6. Work with XML data.

   a. Create a new workbook, then save it as Phone List in the drive and folder where your Data Files are stored.

   b. Open the XML Source task pane and add the XML map EX N-3.xsd to the workbook.

   c. Map the FNAME element to cell A1 on the worksheet, LNAME to cell B1, PHONENUM to cell C1, and EMPLOYMENT_DATE to cell D1.

   d. Remove the EMPLOYMENT_DATE element and delete the field from the list.

   e. Import the XML file EX N-4.xml into the workbook.

   f. Sort the worksheet list in ascending order by LNAME.

   g. Enter your name in the left section of the worksheet footer, save the workbook, then print the list.

   h. Export the worksheet data to an XML file named phone, then close the workbook.

7. Run Web queries to retrieve external data.

   a. Create a new workbook, then save it as Stock Quotes in the drive and folder where your Data Files are stored.

   b. Use the Select Data Source dialog box to select the Web query MSN MoneyCentral Investor Major Indices.iqy.

   c. Specify that you want to place the data to cell A1 of the current worksheet.

   d. Place your name in the worksheet footer, save the workbook, then preview and print the worksheet in landscape orientation on one page.

   e. Close the workbook, then exit Excel.

▼ INDEPENDENT CHALLENGE 1

Blantyre Consulting helps small businesses become profitable by having their consultants monitor their sales and expense information. The consultants work together on projects using shared Excel workbooks. As a Blantyre consultant, you are setting up information for a new client, Boston Touring Company, which specializes in giving trolley and bus tours in Boston and the surrounding area. You are preparing a shared workbook for the three consultants working on the first quarter data for this project. They will each make changes to the first quarter figures, then you will review all three workbooks and accept their changes.

   a. Start Excel, open the Data File EX N-7.xls from the drive and folder where your Data Files are stored, then save it as Boston Touring. The workbook has been shared so the other consultants can modify it. Notice the current figures for each month on the Q1 Sales worksheet. Close the workbook.

   b. Open the Data File EX N-8.xls from the drive and folder where your Data Files are stored, then save it as Boston Touring1. This workbook is a copy of the original that Wanda Merlanson has reviewed and changed.

   c. Use the Select Changes to Accept or Reject dialog box to accept the change Wanda made to the workbook. Save and close the workbook.

   d. Open the Data File EX N-9.xls from the drive and folder where your Data Files are stored, then save it as Boston Touring2. Keith Long has reviewed this workbook and made a change.

   e. Use the Select Changes to Accept or Reject dialog box to accept the change Keith made. Save and close the workbook.

   f. Open the Data File EX N-10.xls from the drive and folder where your Data Files are stored, then save it as Boston Touring3.

   g. Use the Select Changes to Accept or Reject dialog box to accept the change made to the workbook by Mary Lee.

▼ INDEPENDENT CHALLENGE 1 (CONTINUED)

h. Use the Highlight Changes dialog box to highlight Mary Lee's change on the screen. Review the ScreenTip details.

i. Use the Highlight Changes dialog box to create a History worksheet detailing Mary Lee's change to the workbook. Add your name to the left section of the History sheet footer, then print the History worksheet. Save and close the workbook.

Advanced Challenge Exercise

- Open the Data File EX N-7.xls from the drive and folder where your Data Files are stored, then save it as **Merged Tours**.

- Merge the files EX N-8.xls, EX N-9.xls, and EX N-10.xls into the Merged Tours workbook. Notice the new values in the worksheet. Compare your merged values with Figure N-20.

- Enter your name in the Q1 Sales worksheet footer, then save the workbook.

- Print the merged Q1 Sales worksheet, then close the workbook,

j. Exit Excel.

FIGURE N-20

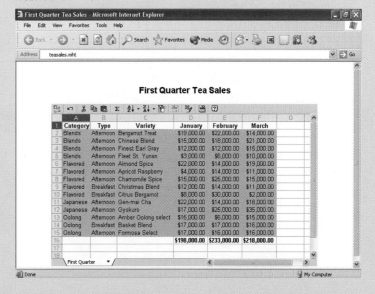

▼ INDEPENDENT CHALLENGE 2

Tuckerman Teas is an import and export firm with offices in Tokyo and London. They distribute specialty teas to shops in the United States and Canada. Tuckerman wants the employees in both offices to be able to analyze sales data using their Web browsers. The sales information for the first two quarters is stored in an Excel file. You have been asked to prepare the sales data to be published on the Web.

a. Start Excel, open the Data File EX N-11.xls from the drive and folder where your Data Files are stored, then save it as **Tuckerman Teas**.

b. Add a password of **tealeaves** to open the workbook and **infuser** to modify it.

c. Save the First Quarter worksheet as an interactive Web page with spreadsheet functionality. (*Hint*: Select Single File Web Page as the File Type before selecting any options in the Save As dialog box.) Add a title of **First Quarter Tea Sales** and save it to the folder containing your Data Files with the filename **teasales.mht**. Open the Web page in Internet Explorer.

d. Add totals for each month and apply bold formatting to the total values.

e. Apply the currency format to the sales values and the totals.

f. Sort the list in ascending order by Category.

g. Change the text color of the column headers to a dark blue color. (*Hint*: Use the Commands and Options dialog box.)

h. Add fill color to the cells to separate the categories. (*Hint*: Use the Commands and Options dialog box.) Use Figure N-21 as a guide.

FIGURE N-21

▼ INDEPENDENT CHALLENGE 2 (CONTINUED)

i. Filter the list using AutoFilter to show only the Blends and Flavored categories, then widen columns as necessary to fully display the column headings.

j. Add your name to cell A23, print the worksheet from Internet Explorer, then close Internet Explorer.

k. Save the Second Quarter worksheet as a single-file Web page with PivotTable functionality. (*Hint*: Remember to choose Single File Web Page as the file type first.) Have **Second Quarter Sales** appear as the title, and save it to the folder containing your Data Files with the filename **teasales2.mht**. Open the Web page in Internet Explorer.

l. Use the AutoFilter arrows to display only the Oolong and Japanese tea categories.

m. Add the Category field to the Row Field area and the Type field to the Column Field area.

n. Print the Web page from Internet Explorer, using Landscape orientation.

Advanced Challenge Exercise

- Use the Export to Microsoft Office Excel button on the toolbar above the PivotTable to save your PivotTable changes in an Excel file.
- Add the fields April, May, and June to the data area of the PivotTable.
- Add your name to the left section of the PivotTable footer.
- Save the PivotTable as an Excel workbook with the name **Tuckerman Teas2**.
- Print the PivotTable in landscape orientation on one page, then close the workbook.

o. Close Internet Explorer, close the Tuckerman Teas workbook, then exit Excel.

▼ INDEPENDENT CHALLENGE 3

You are the director of Human Resources for a company that is in the process of downsizing. To help make the decisions regarding employee layoffs, you have been asked by your supervisor to prepare a seniority list of all employees in the organization. The employee data is available in an XML file. You will bring the XML data into Excel where you will arrange it in ascending order by employees' hire dates.

a. Start Excel, create a new workbook, then save it as **Seniority List** in the drive and folder where your Data Files are stored.

b. Add the map EX N-12.xsd from the drive and folder where your Data Files are stored, to the workbook.

c. Map the ENUMBER element to cell A1, FNAME to cell B1, LNAME to cell C1, and EMPLOYMENT_DATE to cell D1. Widen the columns as necessary to see the full field names.

d. Import the XML data in file EX N-13.xml from the drive and folder where your Data Files are stored.

e. Sort the list in ascending order by EMPLOYMENT_DATE. Compare your sorted list to Figure N-22.

f. Export the worksheet data to an XML file named **hiredata**.

FIGURE N-22

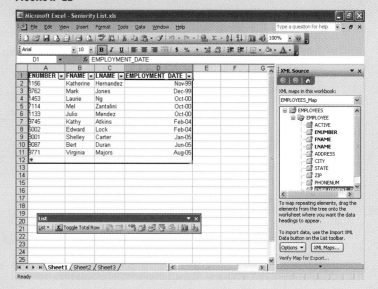

▼ INDEPENDENT CHALLENGE 3 (CONTINUED)

Advanced Challenge Exercise

- Add the map EX N-14.xsd from the drive and folder where your Data Files are stored to the workbook.
- Using the HRINFO_MAP, map the ENUMBER element to cell A20, and EVALUATION to cell B20.
- Import the XML data in file EX N-15.xml from the drive and folder where your Data Files are stored.
- Delete the HRINFO map from the workbook.

g. Enter your name in the left section of the worksheet header, save the worksheet then print the worksheet.

h. Close the workbook and exit Excel.

 # INDEPENDENT CHALLENGE 4

You belong to an investment group that meets regularly to discuss investment topics and manage a small stock portfolio. Next week it is your turn to present a stock to recommend to the group. You will use the MSN MoneyCentral Investor Stock Quotes Web query to research a stock that you are interested in. You will prepare a worksheet that tracks the history of the stock and you will also create a chart that shows the stock price history for the past three years.

a. Start Excel, create a new workbook, then save it as Trend Analysis in the drive and folder where your Data Files are stored.

b. Run the Web Query MSN MoneyCentral Investor Stock Quotes to obtain a stock quote for the stock that you are interested in. Enter the symbol for your stock in the Enter Parameter Value dialog box as shown in Figure N-23. (*Hint*: Microsoft's symbol is MSFT and IBM's symbol is IBM. Once you run the query, you can use the Symbol Lookup hyperlink to find symbols of companies that you are interested in researching.)

c. Display the chart of this data by clicking the Chart link on the worksheet.

d. Print the Chart page showing the stock price history from your browser.

e. Close your browser and return to the workbook.

f. Place the name of the company that you are researching in cell A20. Use the name in cell A20 to add a hyperlink to the company's Web site. (*Hint*: Use the Insert Hyperlink button on the Standard toolbar.)

g. Test the link, then close the browser to return to the workbook.

h. Enter your name in the left section of the worksheet footer, save the workbook, then preview and print the worksheet in landscape orientation on one page.

i. Close the Trend Analysis workbook, saving your changes, exit Excel, then close your browser.

FIGURE N-23

▼ VISUAL WORKSHOP

Start Excel, open the Data File EX N-16.xls from the drive and folder where your Data Files are stored, then save it as **Percussion**. Save the worksheet as a Web page with spreadsheet functionality using the title shown in Figure N-24. Save the Web file with the name **percsale.mht** and open it in your browser. Use the Internet Explorer tools to obtain totals for each quarter and to apply formatting to totals, column headers, and the company name as shown in Figure N-24. Adjust column widths as shown. Enter your name in cell A9, then print the Web page from Internet Explorer with your modifications and calculations applied.

FIGURE N-24

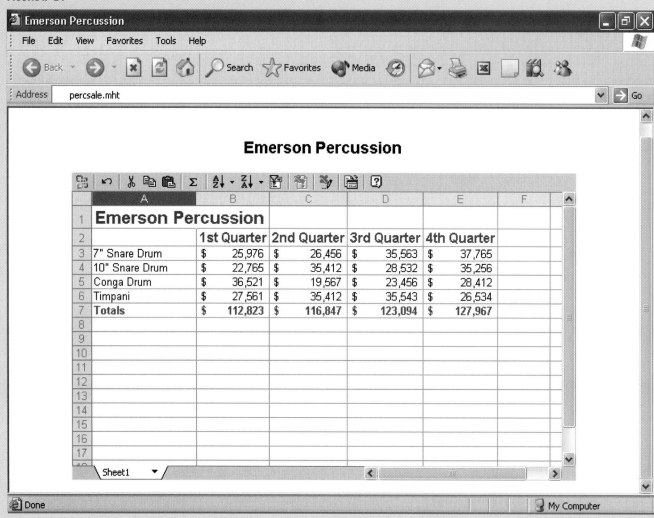

Customizing Excel and Advanced Worksheet Management

OBJECTIVES

Find files
Audit a worksheet
Outline a worksheet
Control worksheet calculations
Create custom AutoFill lists
Customize Excel
Add a comment to a cell
Create a template

If you have a SAM user profile, you may have access to hands-on instruction, practice, and assessment of the skills covered in this unit. Log in to your SAM account and go to your assignments page to see what your instructor has assigned.

Excel includes numerous tools and options designed to help you work as efficiently as possible. In this unit, you will learn how to use some of these elements to find errors and hide unnecessary detail. You'll also find out how to eliminate repetitive typing chores, save calculation time when using a large worksheet, and customize basic Excel features. Finally, you'll learn how to document your workbook and save it in a format that makes it easy to reuse. ▰▰▰ MediaLoft's assistant controller, Lisa Wong, routinely asks Jim Fernandez, MediaLoft's marketing manager, to help with a variety of spreadsheet-related tasks. You will use the numerous tools and options available in Excel to help Jim perform his work quickly and efficiently.

Finding Files

The Search task pane in Excel contains powerful searching tools that make it easy for you to find files. You can search for a file in several ways, such as by name or according to specific text located within a particular file. When searching for a file, you must specify one or more **criteria**, or conditions that must be met, to find your file. For example, you can specify that Excel should find only files that have the word "Inventory" in the filename and/or that were created after a particular date. Recently, Jim created a workbook that tracks the number of overtime hours employees worked in each MediaLoft store. He can't remember the exact name of the file, so he asks you to search for it by the first few letters of the filename.

STEPS

1. **Start Excel, click** File **on the menu bar, then click** File Search

   The Basic File Search task pane offers both basic and advanced search features. You can switch between the Basic and Advanced panes by using the first link at the bottom of the pane.

> **QUICK TIP**
> You can also search for text within Excel files. For example, if you know that your worksheet contains the text "Overtime hours," you can specify this in the "Search text:" text box of the Basic File Search task pane.

2. **In the Search pane, if Basic File Search appears in the title bar, click the** Advanced File Search **link; click** Remove All **to remove previous search criteria**

   All previous search conditions are cleared. You think the filename Jim needs starts with the prefix EX O but you're not sure of the remaining filename characters.

3. **Click the** Property list arrow, **click** File name, **make sure the Condition text box displays** includes, **click in the Value text box, then type** EX O*

   Be sure you type the letter "O" and not a zero. You use the **wildcard symbol** (*), or asterisk, to substitute for the remaining unknown characters. You need to specify where you want Excel to search for the file.

4. **Under Other Search Options, click the** Search in list arrow, **click the** Everywhere **check box to clear it if necessary, use the** ⊞ **sign to navigate to and select the check box next to the drive and folder that contains your Data Files, then click any cell in the worksheet**

5. **Click the** Results should be list arrow, **select** Excel Files **if it's not already selected, deselect any other files types, then click any cell in the worksheet**

   Compare your Advanced File Search task pane to Figure O-1.

> **QUICK TIP**
> If the search doesn't locate your file, click Modify, then try changing the Search in location to My Computer.

6. **Click** Go, **then click** Yes **to add the "File name" property to the search criteria**

   Five files are displayed that begin with "EX O". See Figure O-2. Once you have found the file you want, you can open and edit the file, create a new document based on the file, copy a link to the file to the Office Clipboard, or view the file's properties.

7. **Move the pointer over the** EX O-1.xls filename, **then click its** list arrow

   The options for file EX O-1 are listed, including an option to open the Properties dialog box.

8. **Click any cell in the worksheet, then click the file EX O-1.xls in the Search pane**

   The EX O-1 workbook opens.

9. **Close the Search Results pane, then save the workbook as** Overtime Hours **in the drive and folder where your Data Files are stored**

FIGURE O-1: Advanced File Search pane

Clicking this dislays
lower part of task pane

Link to Basic
File Search

FIGURE O-2: Search results

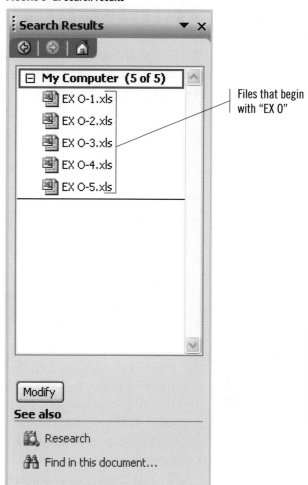

Files that begin
with "EX O"

Clues to Use

Using file properties

Excel automatically tracks specific file properties, such as author name, file size, and file type, and displays them when you display file properties. To display a file's properties, right-click its name in the Search Results task pane or the Open dialog box and click Properties. In the [Filename] Properties dialog box, click the General tab to view general file information, the Custom tab to enter customized properties, and the Summary tab to enter a descriptive title, a subject, or keywords you can use in future searches. See Figure O-3. To search for a file by a specific property, in the Advanced File Search pane, select Text or property in the Property list, then enter the property text in the Value box.

FIGURE O-3: EX O-1 Properties dialog box

Auditing a Worksheet

The Excel **auditing** feature helps you track errors and check worksheet logic. The Formula Auditing toolbar contains many error-checking tools to help audit a worksheet. Because errors can occur at any stage of worksheet development, it is important to include auditing as part of your workbook-building process. Jim asks you to help audit the worksheet that tracks the number of overtime hours at each store to verify the accuracy of the year-end totals. He also asks you to check for invalid overtime hours, which has been previously defined in the Data Validation dialog box to be any store's monthly amount that exceeds 60 hours. You will use the buttons on the Formula Auditing toolbar to identify errors in your worksheet.

STEPS

1. **Click View on the menu bar, point to Toolbars, click Formula Auditing, then click the Error Checking button 🕹 on the Formula Auditing toolbar**
   The Error Checking dialog box alerts you to an error in cell S6. The formula reads =R6/$R$16, indicating that the value in cell R6 will be divided by the value in cell R16. In Excel formulas, blank cells have a value of zero. That means the value in cell R6 cannot be divided by the value in cell R16 (zero) because division by zero is not mathematically possible. To correct the error, you must edit the formula so that it references cell R15, the grand total of overtime hours, not R16.

2. **Click Edit in Formula Bar in the Error Checking dialog box, edit the formula to read =R6/$R$15, click the Enter button ✔ on the formula bar, then click Resume In the Error checking dialog box**
   The edited formula produces the correct result, 9%, in cell S6. The Error Checking dialog box indicates an error from an inconsistent formula. Since this formula is correct you will ignore the warning.

3. **Click Ignore Error, then click Ignore Error three more times to ignore other inconsistent formula errors.**
   The Error Checking dialog box finds another division by zero error in cell S14. You decide to use another tool on the formula auditing toolbar to get more information about this error.

4. **Close the Error Checking dialog box, then click the Trace Error button 🕹 on the Formula Auditing toolbar**
   Tracer arrows, or **tracers**, point from cells that might have caused the error to the active cell containing the error, as shown in Figure O-4. The tracers extend from cells R14 and R16 to cell S14. To correct the error, you must edit the formula so that it references cell R15, the grand total of overtime hours, not R16.

5. **Edit the formula in the formula bar to read =R14/$R$15, then click ✔ on the formula bar**
   Notice that the total for the Boston store in cell R5 is unusually high compared with the totals of the other stores. You can investigate this value by tracing the cell's **precedents**—the cells on which cell R5 depends.

6. **Click cell R5, click the Trace Precedents button 🔣 on the Formula Auditing toolbar, then scroll left until you see the tracer's starting point**
   The tracer arrow runs between cells B5 and R5, indicating that the formula in cell R5 reflects the quarterly *and* monthly totals of overtime hours. Only the quarterly totals should be reflected in cell R5.

7. **Click the Remove Precedent Arrows button 🔣 on the Formula Auditing toolbar, with cell R5 selected, click the AutoSum button Σ on the Standard toolbar, then press [Enter]**
   The tracer arrow disappears, the formula changes to sum only the quarterly totals, and the correct result, 524, appears in cell R5. Correcting the formula in cell R5 also adjusts the Grand Total percentage in cell S5 to 12%. You decide to check for invalid overtime hours that may have been entered in the worksheet.

8. **Click the Circle Invalid Data button ⊞ on the Formula Auditing toolbar, then scroll to the left to display the May hours**
   The cells containing overtime hours exceeding 60 (the criterion previously defined for invalid data) are circled. See Figure O-5.

9. **Click the Clear Validation Circles button 🔣, return to cell A1, then save the workbook**
   Now that all the errors have been identified and corrected, you are finished auditing the worksheet.

> **QUICK TIP**
> To find cells to which a formula refers, click the cell containing the formula, then click the Trace Dependents button 🔣 on the Formula Auditing toolbar. To remove the Dependent tracer arrows, click the Remove Dependent Arrows button 🔣.

> **QUICK TIP**
> To add validation criteria to selected worksheet cells, click Data, click Validation, then enter your validation criteria on the Settings tab of the Data Validation dialog box.

FIGURE O-4: Worksheet with traced error

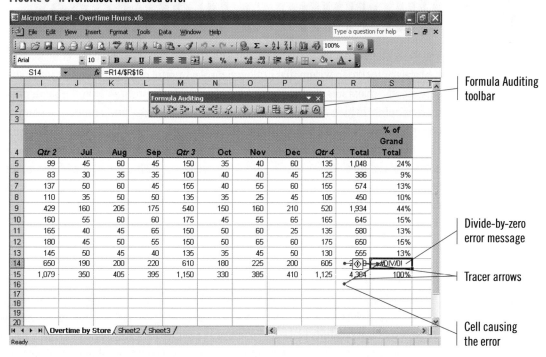

Formula Auditing toolbar

Divide-by-zero error message

Tracer arrows

Cell causing the error

FIGURE O-5: Worksheet with invalid data circled

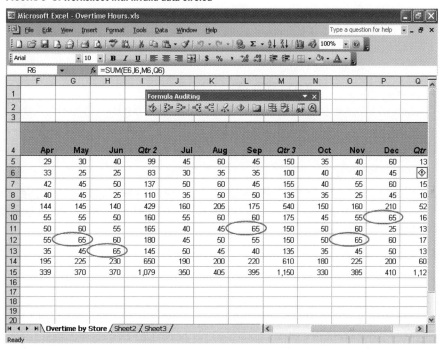

Clues to Use

Watching and evaluating formulas

As you edit your worksheet, you can watch the effect cell changes have on worksheet formulas. Select the cell or cells that you want to watch, click the Show Watch Window button ⊞ on the Formula Auditing toolbar, click Add Watch, then click Add. The Watch Window appears with the workbook name, worksheet name, the cell address you want to watch, the current cell value and its formula. As cell values that "feed into" the formula change, the resulting formula value in the Watch Window changes. You can also step through the evaluation of a formula, selecting the cell that contains a formula and clicking the Evaluate Formula button ⊞ on the Formula Auditing toolbar. The formula appears in the Evaluation Window and as you click the Evaluate button, the cell references are replaced with their values and the formula result is calculated.

Outlining a Worksheet

The Excel Outline command displays symbols that let you show only the critical rows and columns, such as subtotals or totals. To ensure that outlining displays useful results, it is important to structure your worksheet consistently: make sure that worksheet formulas "point" consistently in the same direction: Summary rows, such as subtotal rows, must be located below related data, and summary columns, such as grand total columns, must be located to the right of related data. (If you're not sure which way your formulas point, click the Trace Precedents button on the Formula Auditing toolbar.) You can outline an entire worksheet or a range of cells in a worksheet. 🖼️ Jim needs to give Lisa Wong, the MediaLoft assistant controller, the first and second quarter totals. He asks you to outline the first and second quarter information on the worksheet and to emphasize the subtotals for the East and West regions.

STEPS

QUICK TIP

You can group or ungroup a range of cells if the Auto Outline feature doesn't organize the worksheet data the way you want. Select the rows or columns you want to group, click Data on the menu bar, point to Group and Outline, then click Group or Ungroup.

1. **Select the cell range** A1:I15, **click** Data **on the menu bar, point to** Group and Outline, **then click** Auto Outline

   The first and second quarter information is displayed in Outline view, as shown in Figure O-6. There are several ways to change the amount of detail in an outlined worksheet, but the easiest is to use the column and row **outline symbols** in the upper-left corner of the worksheet, which hide varying levels of detail. The Row Level 1 symbol hides everything in the worksheet except the most important row or rows—in this case, the Grand Total row.

2. **Click the** Row Level 1 button [1]

   Only the heading and grand total appear. This selection doesn't display enough information, so you try the Row Level 2 button, which hides everything except the second most important rows—in this case, the subtotal rows and the Grand Total row.

3. **Click the** Row Level 2 button [2]

   Now you can see the rows you want. Next, you decide to display only the Qtr 1 and Qtr 2 columns.

QUICK TIP

If your summary information appears above your detail rows or to the left of your detail columns, you need to change the outline settings. Click Data on the menu bar, point to Group and Outline, then click Settings. The Settings dialog box will let you change the outline criteria.

4. **Click the** Column Level 1 button [1]

   The first and second quarter totals appear, and the monthly figures are no longer visible. You need a printed copy of the totals.

5. **Place your name in the left section of the worksheet footer, click** File, **click** Print, **click the** Selection option button **in the Print what area of the Print dialog box, then click** Preview

   The preview should look like Figure O-7.

6. **Click** Print, **click the** Row Level 3 button [3], **then click the** Column Level 2 button [2]

   The first and second quarterly monthly figures for each store reappear. You are finished using the outlining feature.

7. **Click** Data **on the menu bar, point to** Group and Outline, **then click** Clear Outline

   The Outline view closes, and the column and row level symbols are no longer visible. The worksheet returns to Normal view.

FIGURE O-6: Range in Outline view

Column outline symbols

Row outline symbols

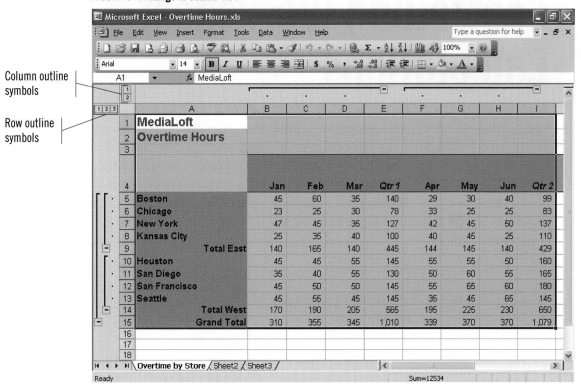

FIGURE O-7: Preview of outlined range

Subtotal rows

Total row

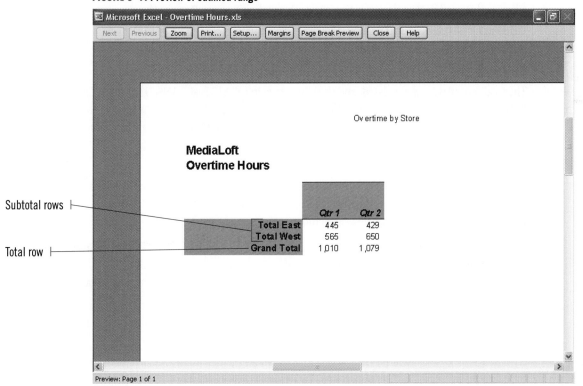

Controlling Worksheet Calculations

Whenever you change a value in a cell, Excel automatically recalculates all the formulas in the worksheet based on that cell. This automatic calculation is efficient until you create a worksheet so large that the recalculation process slows down data entry and screen updating. Worksheets with many formulas, data tables, or functions may also recalculate slowly. In these cases, you might want to selectively determine if and when you want Excel to perform calculations automatically. You do this by applying the **manual calculation** option. Once you change the calculation mode to manual, Excel applies manual calculation to all open worksheets. ███████ Because Jim knows that using specific Excel calculation options can help make worksheet building more efficient, he asks you to change from automatic to manual calculation.

STEPS

1. **Click Tools on the menu bar, click Options, then click the Calculation tab**

   The Calculation tab of the Options dialog box opens, as shown in Figure O-8.

QUICK TIP

To automatically recalculate all worksheet formulas except one- and two-input data tables, under Calculation, click Automatic except tables.

2. **Under Calculation, click to select the Manual option button**

   When you select the Manual option, the Recalculate before save box automatically becomes active and contains a check mark. Because the workbook does not recalculate until you save or close and reopen the workbook, you must make sure to recalculate your worksheet before you print it and after you make changes.

3. **Click OK**

   Jim informs you that the December total for the San Francisco store is incorrect. You decide to freeze the worksheet panes and adjust the entry in cell P12 accordingly.

4. **Click cell B5, click Window on the menu bar, click Freeze Panes, then scroll right to bring columns P through S into view**

   Notice that, in cell S12, San Francisco's percentage of the Grand Total is 15%.

5. **Click cell P12, type 10, then click the Enter button ☑ on the formula bar**

   The total formulas are *not* updated, and the percentage in cell S12 is still 15%. The word "Calculate" appears in the status bar to indicate that a specific value in the worksheet did indeed change and that the worksheet must be recalculated. See Figure O-9. You can press [F9] at any time to calculate all the open worksheets manually or [Shift][F9] to calculate just the active worksheet.

QUICK TIP

If a worksheet formula is linked to a worksheet that you have not recalculated and you update that link, you will see a message informing you of the situation. To update the link using the current value, click OK. To use the previous value, click Cancel.

6. **Press [Shift][F9], then save the workbook**

   The percentage in cell S12 is now 14% instead of 15%. The other formulas in the worksheet affected by the value in cell P12 changed as well. See Figure O-10. Because this is a relatively small worksheet that recalculates quickly, you will return to automatic calculation.

7. **Click Tools on the menu bar, click Options, click the Calculation tab if necessary, under Calculation click the Automatic option button, then click OK**

   Now any additional changes you make will automatically recalculate the worksheet formulas.

FIGURE O-8: Calculation tab of the Options dialog box

Calculation tab ⊢

Manual option button

Your settings may be different

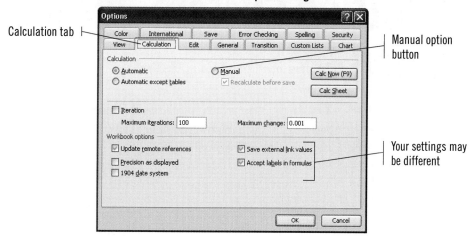

FIGURE O-9: Worksheet in manual calculation mode

Changed value ⊢

Indicates that the worksheet needs to be recalculated

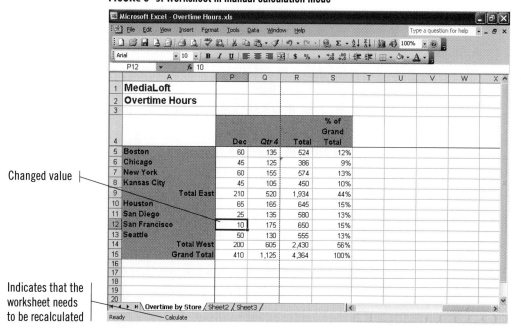

FIGURE O-10: Worksheet with updated values

Changed values

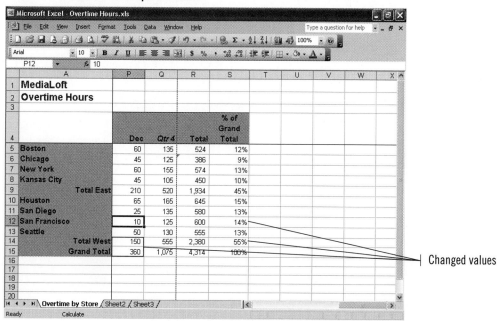

Creating Custom AutoFill Lists

Whenever you need to type a list of words regularly, you can save time by creating a custom AutoFill list. Then you need only to enter the first value in a blank cell and drag the AutoFill handle. Excel will enter the rest of the information for you. Figure O-11 shows some examples of AutoFill lists built into Excel and of Custom AutoFill lists. ▰▰▰▰▰ Jim often has to repeatedly enter MediaLoft store names and regional total labels in various worksheets. He asks you to create an AutoFill list to save time in performing this task. You begin by selecting the names and total labels in the worksheet.

STEPS

1. **Select the range** A5:A15

QUICK TIP

If a list of store locations already appears in the Custom lists box, the person using the computer before you forgot to delete it. Click the list, click Delete, then proceed with Step 3. It isn't possible to delete the four default lists for days and months.

2. **Click** Tools **on the menu bar, click** Options, **then click the** Custom Lists tab

   See Figure O-12. The Custom Lists tab shows the custom AutoFill lists that are already built into Excel. You want to define a custom list using the store information you selected in column A. The Import list from cells box contains the range you selected in Step 1.

3. **Click** Import

   The list of names is highlighted in the Custom lists box and appears in the List entries box. You will test the custom AutoFill list by placing it in a blank worksheet.

4. **Click** OK, **click the** Sheet2 tab, **type** Boston **in cell A1, then click the** Enter button ☑ **on the formula toolbar**

5. **Position the pointer over the AutoFill handle in the lower-right corner of cell A1**

   Notice that the pointer changes to ✚, as shown in Figure O-13.

QUICK TIP

You can also drag the AutoFill handle to the right to enter a custom list.

6. **Click and drag the pointer down to cell** A11, **then release the mouse button**

   The highlighted range now contains the custom list of store locations and total rows you created. You've finished creating and applying your custom AutoFill list, and you will delete it from the Options dialog box in case others will be using your computer.

7. **Click** Tools **on the menu bar, click** Options, **click the** Custom Lists tab **if necessary, click the list of store and region names in the Custom lists box, click** Delete, **click** OK **to confirm the deletion, then click** OK **again**

8. **Save and close the workbook**

FIGURE O-11: Sample AutoFill lists

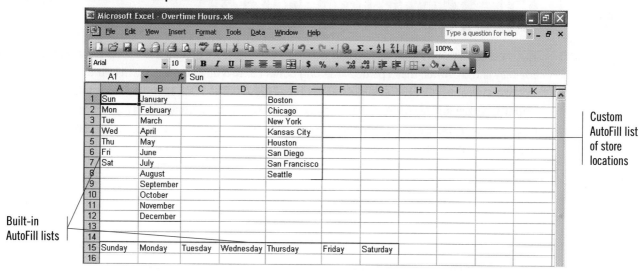

Built-in AutoFill lists

Custom AutoFill list of store locations

FIGURE O-12: Custom Lists tab

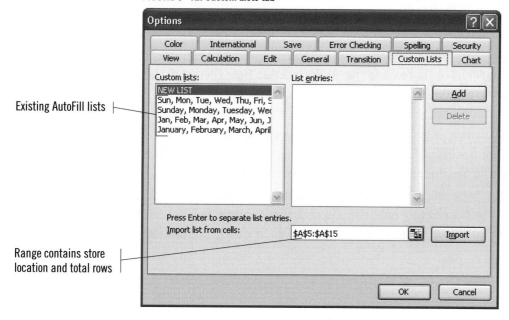

Existing AutoFill lists

Range contains store location and total rows

FIGURE O-13: Applying a custom AutoFill list

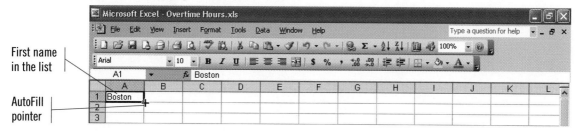

First name in the list

AutoFill pointer

Excel 2003

Customizing Excel

The Excel default settings for editing and viewing a worksheet are designed with user convenience in mind. You may find, however, that a particular setting doesn't always fit your needs, such as the default number of worksheets in a workbook. The thirteen tabs of the Options dialog box allow you to customize Excel to suit your work habits and needs. You've already used the Calculation tab to switch to manual calculation and the Custom Lists tab to create your own AutoFill list. The most commonly used Options dialog box tabs are explained in more detail in Table O-1. ▰▰▰▰ Jim is curious about how he might customize Excel to allow him to work more efficiently. He asks you to use a blank workbook to explore some of the features of Excel available in the Options dialog box.

STEPS

1. **Click the** New button 🗋 **on the Standard toolbar, click** Tools **on the menu bar, click** Options, **then click the** General tab
   You would like to have five worksheets displayed rather than three when a new workbook is opened.

2. **Select** 3 **in the** Sheets in new workbook text box, **then enter** 5
   See Figure O-14. You can change the standard (default) font Excel displays in new workbooks.

3. **Click the** Standard font list arrow, **then select** Book Antiqua
   You can also change the standard workbook font size.

4. **Click the** size list arrow, **then select** 12
   These default settings take effect after you exit and restart Excel. Next, you'll check the default security settings.

5. **Click the** Security tab, **click** Macro Security, **click the** Medium **radio button if necessary, click** OK, **click** OK **to close the Options dialog box, then click OK to the message about quitting and restarting Excel**
   The Medium setting allows you to choose whether to enable macros when you open your workbooks.

6. **Close the workbook, exit Excel, then start Excel again**
   A new workbook opens with five sheet tabs and a 12-point Book Antiqua font. See Figure O-15. Now that you have finished exploring the Options dialog box, you need to reestablish the original Excel settings.

7. **Click** Tools **on the menu bar, click** Options, **click the** General tab, **select** 5 **in the** Sheets in new workbook text box, **enter** 3, **click the** Standard font list arrow, **select** Arial, **click the** size list arrow, **select** 10, **click** OK **twice, then close the workbook and exit Excel**

FIGURE O-14: General tab in the Options dialog box

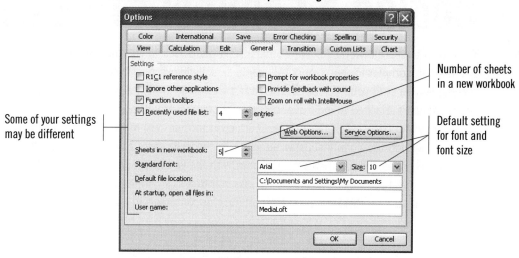

Some of your settings may be different

Number of sheets in a new workbook

Default setting for font and font size

FIGURE O-15: Workbook with new default settings

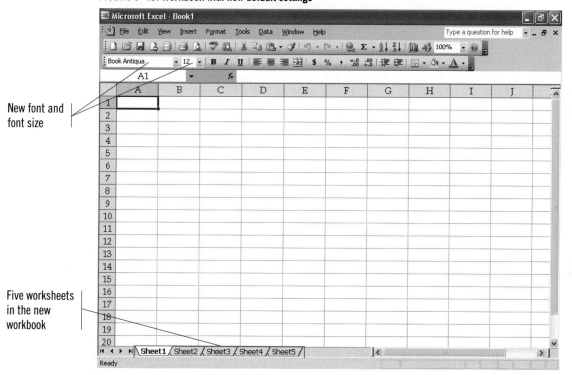

New font and font size

Five worksheets in the new workbook

TABLE O-1: Selected Options dialog box tabs

tab	description
Calculation	Controls how the worksheet is calculated; choices include automatic and manual
Chart	Controls how empty cells are treated in a chart and whether chart tips are displayed
Color	Allows you to copy a customized color palette from one workbook to another
Custom Lists	Allows you to add or delete custom AutoFill lists
Edit	Controls the direction in which the cell selector moves after you press [Enter]; also contains other editing features
General	Controls the option to display the Properties dialog box when saving a workbook, the number of sheets in a new workbook, the default font in a workbook, and the drive and folder used in the Save dialog box by default; user name is also listed here
Transition	Provides options useful for users familiar with Lotus 1-2-3, and sets the default file type for saved worksheets
View	Controls the visibility of the formula bar, startup task pane, windows in taskbar, comments, status bar, gridlines, row and column headers, and scroll bars; also controls the option to display formulas in a worksheet

Adding a Comment to a Cell

If you plan to share a workbook with others, it's a good idea to **document**, or make notes about, basic assumptions, complex formulas, or questionable data. Reading your documentation, a coworker can quickly become familiar with your workbook. The easiest way to document a workbook is to use **cell comments**, which are notes attached to individual cells that appear when you place the pointer over a cell. When you sort or copy and paste cells, any comments attached to them will move to the new location. In PivotTable reports, however, the comments stay attached to the cell where they are entered. If the layout of the PivotTable changes, the comments do not move with the worksheet data. Jim thinks one of the figures in the worksheet may be incorrect. He asks you to add a comment for Lisa, pointing out the possible error. You will start by checking the default settings for comments in a workbook.

STEPS

1. **Start Excel, open Overtime Hours.xls from the drive and folder where your Data Files are stored, click Tools on the menu bar, click Options, click the View tab, click the Comment indicator only option button to select it if necessary, then click OK**

   The View tab allows you to display the comment and its indicator, the comment indicator only, or no comments. See Figure O-16.

QUICK TIP
You can also insert a comment by clicking the Comment option on the Insert menu or by clicking the New Comment button on the Reviewing or the Formula Auditing toolbar.

2. **Right-click cell P12 on the Overtime by Store sheet, then click Insert Comment on the shortcut menu**

   The Comment box opens, as shown in Figure O-17. Excel automatically includes the computer's username at the beginning of the comment. The username is the name that appears on the General tab of the Options dialog box. Notice the white sizing handles on the border of the Comment box. You can drag these handles to change the size of the box.

3. **Type Is this figure correct? It looks low to me.**

   The text automatically wraps to the next line as necessary.

4. **Click outside the Comment box**

   A red triangle appears in the upper-right corner of cell P12, indicating that a comment is attached to the cell. People who use your worksheet can easily display comments.

5. **Place the pointer over cell P12**

   The comment appears next to the cell. When you move the pointer outside of cell P12, the comment disappears. The worksheet is now finished and ready for printing.

6. **Click File on the menu bar, click Page Setup, click the Page tab if necessary, specify landscape orientation and fit the worksheet to one page**

   On a second printed page, you'll print only the cell comment along with its associated cell reference.

7. **Click the Sheet tab, under Print click the Comments list arrow, click At end of sheet, click Print, then click OK**

   Your comment is printed on a separate page after the worksheet.

8. **Save the workbook**

FIGURE O-16: View tab in the Options dialog box

Comment indicator only button

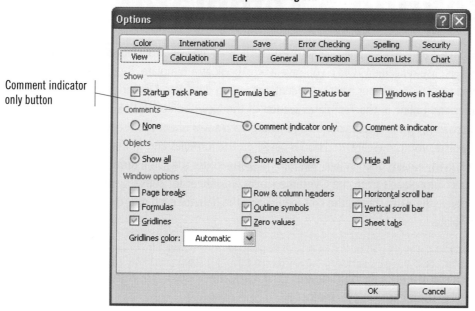

FIGURE O-17: Comment box

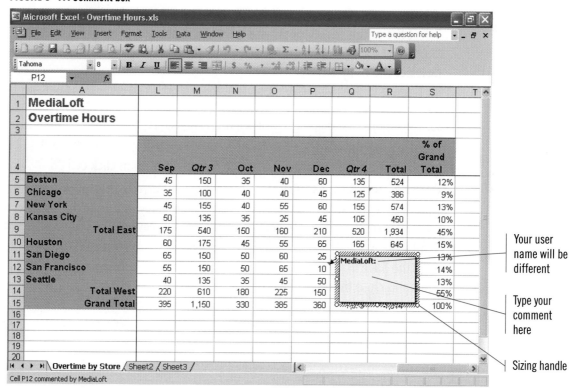

Your user name will be different

Type your comment here

Sizing handle

Clues to Use

Editing, copying, and deleting comments

To edit an existing comment, select the cell to which the comment is attached, click Insert on the menu bar, then click Edit Comment. You can also right-click a cell with a comment and click Edit Comment from the shortcut menu. To copy only comments, copy the cell contents, right-click the destination cell, select Paste Special, click Comments, then click OK. You can delete a comment by right-clicking the cell it is attached to, then selecting Delete Comment.

Creating a Template

A **template** is a workbook that contains text (such as column and row labels), formulas, macros, and formatting you use repeatedly. Once you save a workbook as a template, it provides a model for creating a new workbook without your having to reenter standard data. Excel provides access to templates on your computer and online in the Templates section of the New Workbook task pane. In most cases, though, you'll probably want to create your own template from a worksheet you use regularly. When you save a file as a template, you can create workbooks based on the formulas and formatting in the template and the template itself remains unchanged.  Jim plans to use the same formulas, titles, frozen panes, and row and column labels from the Overtime Hours worksheet for subsequent yearly worksheets. He asks you to delete the extra sheets, the comments, and the data for each month, and then save the workbook as a template.

STEPS

1. **Click the** Sheet2 tab, **hold down** [Ctrl], **click the** Sheet3 tab, **right-click the** Sheet3 tab, **click** Delete, **then click** Delete **again**

2. **Right-click cell** P12, **then click** Delete Comment

    Now that you've removed the extra sheets and the comment, you'll delete the data on overtime hours. You'll leave the formulas in rows 9, 14, and 15, and in columns E, I, M, Q, R, and S, however, so that another user can simply begin entering data without having to re-create the formulas.

3. **Select the range** B5:D8, **press and hold** [Ctrl], **select the ranges** B10:D13, F5:H8, F10:H13, J5:L8, J10:L13, N5:P8, **and** N10:P13, **press** [Delete], **then click any cell in the worksheet to deselect the ranges**

    See Figure O-18. The hyphens in the subtotal and total rows and columns indicate that the current value of these cells is zero. The divide-by-zero error messages in column S are only temporary and will disappear as soon as you open the template, save it as a workbook, and begin to enter next year's data. To make the template easier to use, it's best to have the first data entry cell selected when you save it.

4. **Scroll left to bring columns B through G into view, then click cell** B5

5. **Click** File, **click** Save As, **click the** Save as type list arrow, **then click** Template

    Excel adds the .xlt extension to the filename and automatically switches to the Templates folder, as shown in Figure O-19. If you are using a computer on a network, you may not have permission to save to the Templates folder. You'll save your template to the drive and folder where your Data Files are stored instead.

6. **Click the** Save in list arrow, **click the drive and folder containing your Data Files, click** Save, **print and close the workbook, then exit Excel**

    Next year, when Jim needs to compile the information for overtime hours, he can simply open a document based on the Overtime Hours template (apply the template) and begin entering data.

Clues to Use

Applying and editing templates

To create a document based on a template (that is, to **apply** a template to a new document) you have saved in the Templates folder, open the New Workbook task pane, then under Templates, click On my computer. In the Templates dialog box, click the General tab, click the template you want to use, then click OK. Excel creates a new document named [Template Name]1. Save it as you would any new Excel document. The Spreadsheet Solutions tab lets you access several ready-made templates designed for business-related tasks.

The Templates section of the task pane also contains links to templates you might have previously stored on the Web and to templates on the Microsoft Office Web site. To edit a template, you must open the template itself (the .xlt file), change it, then save it under the same name. The changes are applied only to new documents you create; the changes do not affect documents you've already created using the template.

FIGURE O-18: Preparing the template

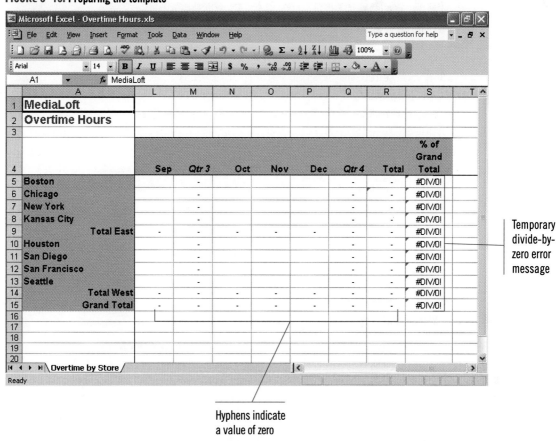

Temporary divide-by-zero error message

Hyphens indicate a value of zero

FIGURE O-19: Saving a template

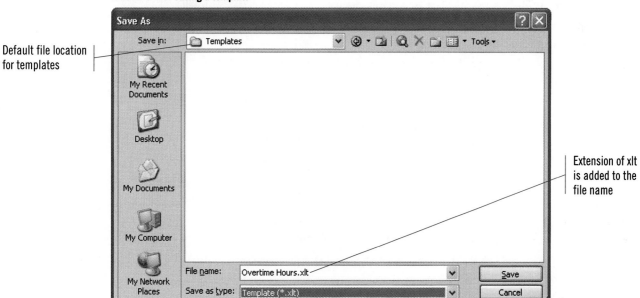

Default file location for templates

Extension of xlt is added to the file name

Practice

FIGURE O-20

Which element do you click to:

1. Evaluate a formula in a selected cell?
2. Trace the precedents of a selected cell?
3. Trace an error in a formula?
4. Watch the changes to a cell on a worksheet?
5. Circle invalid worksheet data?

Match each term with the statement that best describes it.

6. Note that appears when you place the pointer over a cell
7. Contains settings for customizing Excel
8. Calculates the worksheet manually

9. A workbook that contains text, formulas, and formatting
10. Automatically enters a list in a worksheet

a. Options dialog box
b. [Shift][F9]
c. Template
d. Comment
e. AutoFill

Select the best answer from the list of choices.

11. When searching for a file, which of these characters can substitute for unknown characters in a filename?
   a. #
   b. &
   c. *
   d. !

12. The _____ tab in the Options dialog box allows you to control the display of comments in a workbook.
   a. Properties
   b. Edit
   c. General
   d. View

13. The _____ automatically hides everything in the worksheet except the most important row or rows.
   a. Row Level 2 button
   b. Row Level 3 button
   c. Row Level 1 button
   d. Trace Error button

14. To apply a custom AutoFill list you:
   a. Press [Shift][F9].
   b. Click the AutoFill tab in the Edit dialog box.
   c. Select the list in the worksheet.
   d. Type the first cell entry and drag the AutoFill handle.

▼ SKILLS REVIEW

1. Find files.

  a. Start Excel, open the Advanced Search pane.

  b. Use the wildcard character (*) to enter the search criterion for all filenames that include EX O. Search in the drive and folder containing your Data Files. Limit the search to Excel files only. (*Hint*: Remember to clear previous search criteria.)

  c. Display the properties for file EX O-2.xls.

  d. Open the workbook EX O-2.xls from the Search Results task pane.

  e. Close the Search Results task pane, then save the workbook as Cafe Budget.

2. Audit a worksheet.

  a. Display the Formula Auditing toolbar and drag it to the bottom of the worksheet.

  b. Select cell B10, then use the Trace Dependents button to locate all the cells that depend on this cell.

  c. Clear the arrows from the worksheet using the Remove All Arrows button on the Formula Auditing toolbar.

  d. Select cell B19, use the Trace Precedents button on the Formula Auditing toolbar to find the cells on which that figure is based, then correct the formula in cell B19. (*Hint*: It should be B7-B18.)

  e. Use the Trace Error button on the Formula Auditing toolbar to trace the error in cell G6, then correct the formula. (*Hint*: It should be F6/F7.)

  f. Use the Error Checking button on the Formula Auditing toolbar to check the worksheet for any other errors.

  g. Use the Circle Invalid Data button on the Formula Auditing toolbar to locate any invalid data on the worksheet, then clear any validation circles.

  h. Remove any arrows from the worksheet, close the Formula Auditing toolbar, then save the workbook.

3. Outline a worksheet.

  a. Group the income information in rows 5 through 7. (*Hint*: Select rows 5 through 7, click Data on the menu bar, point to Group and Outline, then click Group.)

  b. Hide the income information in rows 5 through 7 by clicking ⊟ to the lower left of row 7.

  c. Enter your name in the worksheet header, then print the Budget worksheet with the income information hidden.

  d. Redisplay the income rows by clicking ⊞.

  e. Remove the row grouping. (*Hint*: With the grouped rows selected, click Data on the menu bar, point to Group and Outline, then click Ungroup.)

  f. Click cell A1, then display the worksheet in Outline view.

  g. Use the Row outline symbols to display only the Net Profit value in the budget.

  h. Print the outlined worksheet.

  i. Use the Row outline symbols to display all the rows in the budget.

  j. Clear the outline from the worksheet.

4. Control worksheet calculations.

  a. Open the Options dialog box.

  b. Change the worksheet calculations to manual.

  c. Change the figure in cell B6 to 33,000.

  d. Recalculate the worksheet manually, using the appropriate key combination.

  e. Turn off manual calculation and save the workbook.

5. Create custom AutoFill lists.

  a. Select the range A4:A19.

  b. Open the Custom Lists tab in the Options dialog box. Delete any custom lists except the four default day and month lists.

  c. Import the selected text into the dialog box.

  d. Close the dialog box.

  e. On Sheet2, enter Income in cell A1.

  f. With cell A1 selected, drag its fill handle to cell A15.

  g. Select cell A1, and drag its fill handle to cell O1.

  h. Enter your name in the Sheet2 footer, change the orientation to landscape, fit it to one page, then print it.

  i. Open the Options dialog box again, delete the custom list you just created, then save the workbook.

6. Customize Excel.

    a. With Sheet2 still selected, open the Options dialog box.

    b. On the General tab, change the number of sheets in a new workbook to 4.

    c. On the General tab, change the default font of a new workbook to 14-point Times New Roman.

    d. On the Security tab, set the macro security level to medium.

    e. Close the workbook and exit Excel.

    f. Start Excel and verify the new workbook's font is 14-point Times New Roman and that it has four worksheets.

    g. Reset the default number of worksheets to 3 and the default workbook font to 10-point Arial.

    h. Close the workbook and exit Excel.

7. Add a comment to a cell.

    a. Start Excel, open the Cafe Budget workbook from the drive and folder where your Data Files are stored. In the Budget sheet, select cell E12.

    b. Insert a comment in cell E12 using the shortcut menu.

    c. Type Does this include TV and radio spots, or only newspaper and magazine advertising? It is very important to include these.

    d. Drag the resize handles on the borders of the Comment box until you can see the entire comment.

    e. Click anywhere outside the Comment box to close it.

    f. Display the comment by moving the pointer over cell E12, then check it for errors.

    g. Edit the comment in cell E12 so it ends after the word spots, with a question mark at the end.

    h. Print the worksheet and your comment, with the comment appearing at the end of the sheet.

    i. Save the workbook.

8. Create a template.

    a. Delete Sheet2 and Sheet3.

    b. Delete the comment in cell E12.

    c. Delete the budget data for all four quarters. Leave the worksheet formulas intact.

    d. Select cell B5, then save the workbook as a template named Budget Template, in the folder where your Data Files are stored.

    e. Close the template, then open a document based on the template using the New Workbook task pane. (*Hint*: Use the From existing workbook option under New, click the Budget Template, then click Create New.)

    f. Enter your own data for all four quarters and in every budget category.

    g. Save the workbook as Cafe Budget 2.xls to the folder where your Data Files are stored.

    h. Print the Budget worksheet, then close the workbook and exit Excel.

▼ INDEPENDENT CHALLENGE 1

You are a manager at Life Skills, a nonprofit agency devoted to helping people with severe learning disabilities become proficient computer users. Your department specializes in hands-on instruction for software programs. During the month of October, you created a check register in Excel for department expenses. Before you begin generating a November register, however, you want to check the October register for errors. In your worksheet audit, you will look for miscalculated totals and formula errors. You will also add a comment to document the worksheet.

    a. Start Excel, open the Data File titled EX O-3.xls from the drive and folder where your Data Files are stored, then save it as Check Register.

    b. Select cell F16 and use the Trace Precedents button on the Formula Auditing toolbar to show the cells used in its formula.

    c. The balance in cell F16 does not reflect the hardware purchase on October 15th. Edit the formula to subtract the hardware expense from the previous balance. (*Hint*: The formula should be F15-E16.)

    d. Due to illness, your Excel instructor taught only two hours of a six-hour course. Create a comment indicating this in cell C19 to remind you that he owes you four hours.

    e. Use the Error Checking button to locate and fix any other errors in the worksheet. (*Hint*: Check cell E24.)

▼ INDEPENDENT CHALLENGE 1 (CONTINUED)

Advanced Challenge Exercise

- Evaluate the formula in cell F21 using the Evaluate Formula button on the Formula Auditing toolbar.
- In the Evalute Formula dialog box, click Evaluate three times to see the process of substituting values for cell addresses in the formula and the results of those formula calculations. Close the Evaluate Formula window.
- Open the Watch Window using the Show Watch Window button on the Formula Auditing toolbar. Click Add Watch to add cell E23 to the Watch Window and observe its value in the window as you change cell E6 to 1600. Close the Watch Window.

f. Add your name to the left section of the worksheet footer, preview the worksheet, then save the workbook. Use the Page Setup command on the File menu to print the worksheet and the comments. Close the workbook, then exit Excel.

▼ INDEPENDENT CHALLENGE 2

You are a manager at EarthSchool, a nonprofit agency located in Toronto, Ontario. Your agency's mission is to educate students in elementary school about environmental issues. One of your responsibilities is to keep track of your department's regular monthly expenses. Your assistant has compiled a list of fixed expenses in an Excel workbook but can't remember the filename. Once you find the file by using the search tools in the Search pane, you want to create a custom AutoFill list including each expense item to save time in preparing similar worksheets in the future. You will also temporarily switch to manual formula calculation, check the total formula, and document the data.

Excel 2003

a. Start Excel, then use the Advanced File Search pane to find a file in the drive and folder where you Data Files are stored with the text **EarthSchool** in the workbook. (*Hint*: Choose **Text or property** in the Property text box, make sure the Condition text box displays **includes**, and enter **EarthSchool** in the Value text box. Make sure that you clear any previous search conditions.) Open the workbook.

b. Save the workbook as **Monthly Budget** in the drive and folder where your Data Files are stored, then close the Search Results task pane.

c. Select the range of cells **A6:A17** on the Fixed Expenses sheet, then open the Options dialog box and import the list into the Custom Lists tab.

d. Close the Options dialog box and use the AutoFill handle to insert your list in cells C1:C12 in Sheet2.

e. Add your name to the Sheet2 footer, save the workbook, then preview and print Sheet2.

f. Return to the Fixed Expenses sheet and delete your custom list from the Options dialog box.

g. Use the Options dialog box to switch to manual calculation.

h. Change the expense for Printer paper to 39.00. Calculate the worksheet formulas manually.

i. Turn on automatic calculation again.

j. Use the View tab on the Options dialog box to display comments and their indicators in a worksheet.

k. Add the comment **This may increase** to cell B6.

l. Trace the precedents of cell B18. Compare your worksheet to Figure O-21.

m. Remove the arrow from the worksheet, change the comments settings back to display comment indicators only.

FIGURE O-21

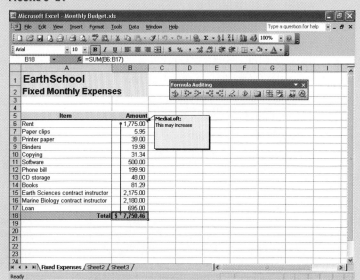

Advanced Challenge Exercise

- Edit the comment in cell B6 to **This may increase next month**.
- Paste the comment in cell B6 to cell B11.
- Delete the comment in cell B6.

n. Add your name to the left section of the worksheet footer, save the workbook, then print the Fixed Expenses worksheet with the comment appearing at the end of the sheet.

o. Close the workbook and exit Excel.

▼ INDEPENDENT CHALLENGE 3

Your business, Kidcare, helps parents find high-quality, in-home childcare. In exchange for a one-time fee, you recruit and interview potential nannies, confirm references, and conduct thorough background checks. In addition, once a nanny has been hired, you provide training in child development and infant first aid. Currently, you are preparing your budget for the next four quarters. After you enter the data for each expense and income category, you will create a condensed version of the worksheet using Excel outlining tools.

a. Start Excel, create a new workbook, then save it as Kidcare in the drive and folder where your Data Files are stored.

b. Using Figure O-22 as a guide, enter and format a title of Yearly Budget, then enter the following column labels: Description, 1st Qtr, 2nd Qtr, 3rd Qtr, 4th Qtr, and Total.

c. Enter labels for the following income items: Nanny Fee, Child Development Course, CPR Course, and Income Total. Enter labels for at least six office expense items and the Expenses Total. Create a row for net cash flow calculations. Format the worksheet appropriately.

d. Enter expenses and income data for each quarter. Total the income items and the expenses. Create formulas for the total column and the cash flow row (income minus expenses).

e. Check the outline settings to make sure the summary rows are below the detail rows and the summary columns are to the right of the detail columns. (*Hint*: Click Data, point to Group and Outline, then click Settings.)

f. Display the worksheet in Outline view.

g. Use the Row Level 1 button on the outline to display only the Net cash flow row, as shown in Figure O-22. Your net cash flow data and formatting will be different.

FIGURE O-22

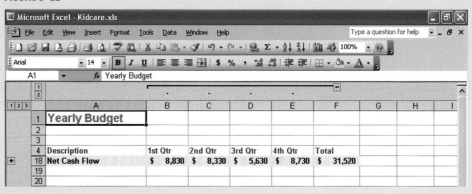

h. Add your name to the left section of the worksheet footer, save the workbook, then print the outlined worksheet.

i. Redisplay all the rows, then clear the outline.

j. Select the Yearly Budget title, the row labels, and the first and second quarter data and display them in Outline view.

k. Use the Row outline symbols to show only the Income Total, Expenses Total, and Net Cash Flow rows and their headings.

l. Preview the outlined first and second quarter information. Compare your preview to Figure O-23. Your data will be different.

m. Print the outlined first and second quarter information.

n. Clear the outline. Close the workbook and exit Excel.

FIGURE O-23

Yearly Budget

Description	1st Qtr	2nd Qtr
Income Total	$ 11,200	$ 10,700
Expenses		
Expenses Total	$ 2,370	$ 2,370
Net Cash Flow	$ 8,830	$ 8,330

▼ INDEPENDENT CHALLENGE 4

As the marketing manager of products at NewSite, a Web development firm, you frequently travel to customer sites. After every trip, you submit an expense report for reimbursement of your travel expenditures. A template containing the input fields and formulas would speed up the process of preparing this report. You decide to research the templates available in the Microsoft Office template gallery to see if any are suitable for recording your travel expenses.

a. Start Excel, then use the link for Templates on Office Online in the New Workbook task pane to view the templates available on Microsoft Online. You must have an open Internet connection to connect to Microsoft Online and to download templates.

b. Search for an expense statement that might be suitable for recording your travel expenses. (*Hint*: Search on Expense statement.)

c. Download the template named Expense Report (with the Excel icon) in the list of links. (*Hint*: When you can see the template preview, you need to minimize your browser, close any open workbooks, exit from Excel, then maximize the browser window with the template preview and click Download Now. You need to exit Excel before downloading the template because Excel automatically starts during the download process.

d. Accept the licensing agreement and click continue on any dialog box if necessary. When the download is complete, Excel will start and the template will be displayed as a worksheet. Close the task pane.

e. Save the downloaded worksheet as a template to the folder containing your Data Files and name it **Expense Statement**.

f. Edit the template to change the font color of the text in cell A2 to blue, delete row 1, and delete column B. Compare your edited template to Figure O-24.

g. Save the edited template then close the template.

h. Open a workbook based on the Expense Statement template. (*Hint*: Use the From existing workbook link on the New Workbook task pane.) Save the workbook as **My Expense Statement**.

i. Enter two lines of your own expense data for a business trip. Enter your name in the Name field. Widen columns as necessary.

j. Add **Includes all taxes** as a comment in cell C10.

FIGURE O-24

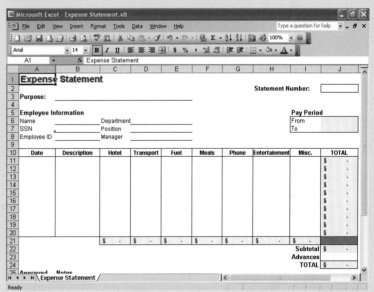

k. Outline the worksheet and use the Row outline symbols to display only your employee information and the expense totals.

l. Print the outlined worksheet showing the total information. Clear the outline.

m. Save and close the workbook. Exit Excel and your browser.

▼ VISUAL WORKSHOP

Open the Data File EX O-5.xls from the drive and folder where your Data Files are stored, then save it as Zoo Count. Use the auditing and error correction techniques you have learned to correct any errors in the worksheet. Your calculated results should match Figure O-25. Make sure to include the comment in cell E21. Add your name to the left section of the worksheet footer, save the workbook, then preview and print the worksheet and comment. Close the workbook and exit Excel.

FIGURE O-25

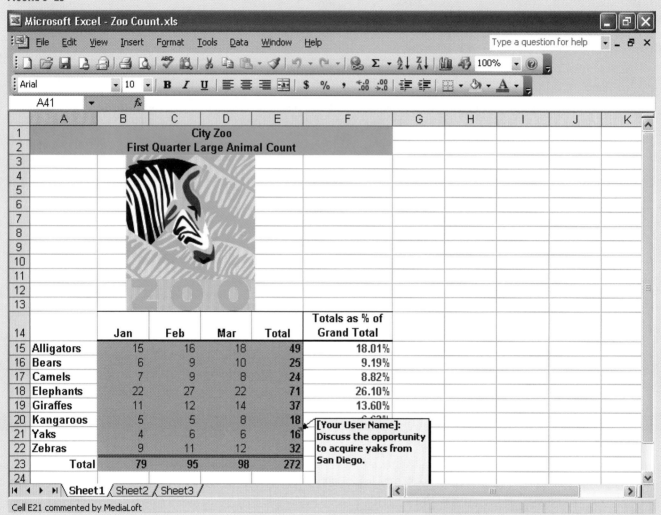

Programming with Excel

OBJECTIVES

View VBA code
Analyze VBA code
Write VBA code
Add a conditional statement
Prompt the user for data
Debug a macro
Create a main procedure
Run a main procedure

If you have a SAM user profile, you may have access to hands-on instruction, practice, and assessment of the skills covered in this unit. Log in to your SAM account and go to your assignments page to see what your instructor has assigned.

All Excel macros are written in a programming language called Visual Basic for Applications, or simply, **VBA.** When you create a macro with the Excel macro recorder, the recorder writes the VBA instructions for you. You can also create an Excel macro by entering VBA instructions manually. The sequence of VBA statements contained in a macro is called a **procedure**. In this unit, you will view and analyze existing VBA code; then you will write VBA code on your own. You will learn how to add a conditional statement to a procedure, as well as how to prompt the user for information while the macro is running. You will also find out how to locate any errors, or bugs, in a macro. Finally, you will combine several macros into one main procedure. MediaLoft's marketing manager, Jim Fernandez, would like to automate some of the division's time-consuming tasks. You will help Jim by creating five Excel macros for the Marketing Department.

Viewing VBA Code

Before you can write Excel macro procedures, you must become familiar with the VBA (Visual Basic for Applications) programming language. A common method of learning any programming language is to view existing code. To view VBA code, you open the **Visual Basic Editor**, which contains a Project window, a Properties window, and a Code window. The VBA code for macro procedures appears in the Code window. The first line of a procedure, called the **procedure header**, defines the procedure's type, name, and arguments. Items that appear in blue are **keywords**, which are words Excel recognizes as part of the VBA programming language. **Comments**, which are notes explaining the code, appear in green, and the remaining code appears in black. You use the Visual Basic Editor to view or edit an existing macro as well as to create new ones. ▚▚▚▚ Each week, MediaLoft receives a text file from the radio station KHOT, containing information about weekly radio ads. Jim has already imported the text file into a worksheet, but it still needs to be formatted. He asks you to work on a macro to automate the process of formatting this imported text file.

STEPS

TROUBLE

If you get a security error message when attempting to open your workbook, the security level may be set too high in the workbook. You can enable macros for the workbook by pointing to Macro on the Tools menu then clicking Security. Set the security level to Medium, then close and reopen the workbook.

1. **Start Excel, if necessary, open the Data File EX P-1.xls from the drive and folder where your Data Files are stored, click** Enable Macros, **then save it as** KHOT Procedures

   The security warning, shown in Figure P-1, alerts you that the worksheet contains macros. The KHOT Procedures workbook displays a blank worksheet. This is the workbook that you will use to create and store all the procedures for this lesson.

2. **Click** Tools **on the menu bar, point to** Macro, **then click** Macros

   The Macro dialog box opens with the FormatFile macro procedure in the list box. If you have any macros saved in your Personal Macro workbook they will also be listed in the Macro dialog box.

3. **If it is not already selected, click** FormatFile, **click** Edit, **then in the Project Explorer window shown in Figure P-2, under Modules click** Format **if it is not already selected**

   Because the FormatFile procedure is contained in the Format module, clicking Format selects the Format module and displays the FormatFile procedure in the Code window. See Figure P-2. See Table P-1 to make sure your screen matches those in the unit.

4. **Make sure both the Visual Basic window and the Code window are maximized to match Figure P-2**

5. **Examine the top three lines of code, which contain comments, and the first line of code beginning with Sub FormatFile( )**

   Notice that the different parts of the procedure appear in various colors. The first two comment lines give the procedure name and tell what the procedure does. The third line of comments explains that the keyboard shortcut for this macro procedure is [Ctrl][F]. The keyword Sub in the procedure header indicates that this is a **Sub procedure**, or a series of Visual Basic statements that perform an action but do not return a value. In the next lesson, you will analyze the procedure code to see what each line does.

TABLE P-1: Matching your screen to the unit figures

if...	do this...
The Properties or Project Explorer window is not displayed	Click the Properties Window button 🖼 then click the Project Explorer button 📑 on the toolbar
You see only the Code window	Click Tools on the menu bar, click Options, click the Docking tab, then make sure the Project Explorer and Properties Window options are selected
You do not see folders in the Explorer window	Click the Toggle Folders button 🗔 on the Project Explorer window Project toolbar

FIGURE P-1: Security warning dialog box

Click here to open workbook with the ability to run macros

FIGURE P-2: Procedure displayed in the Visual Basic Editor

Procedure header

Comments in green

Project Explorer window

Code window

Keywords in blue

Properties window

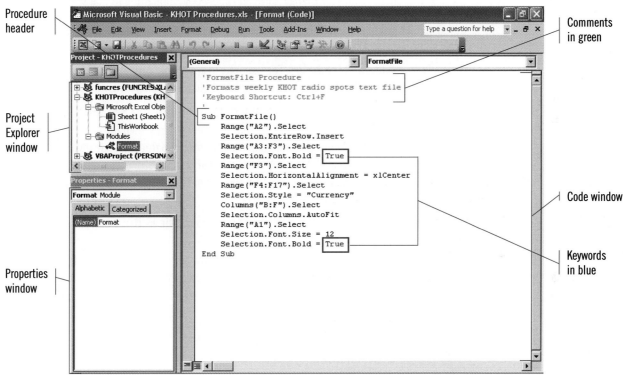

Clues to Use

Understanding the Visual Basic Editor

A **module** is the Visual Basic equivalent of a worksheet. In it, you store macro procedures, just as you store data in worksheets. Modules, in turn, are stored in workbooks (or projects), along with worksheets. A **project** is the collection of all procedures in a workbook. You view and edit modules in the Visual Basic Editor, which is made up of three windows, Project Explorer (also called the Project window), the Code window, and the Properties window. Project Explorer displays a list of all open projects (or workbooks) and the worksheets and modules they contain. To view the procedures stored in a module, you must first select the module in Project Explorer (just as you would select a file in Windows Explorer). The Code window then displays the selected module's procedures. The Properties window displays a list of characteristics (or properties) associated with the module. A newly inserted module has only one property, its name.

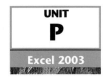
Analyzing VBA Code

You can learn a lot about the VBA language simply by analyzing the code generated by the Excel macro recorder. The more VBA code you analyze, the easier it is for you to write your own programming code. Before writing any new procedures, you will analyze a previously written one that applies formatting to a worksheet, then you will open a worksheet that you want to format and run the macro.

STEPS

1. **With the FormatFile procedure still displayed in the Code window, examine the next four lines of code, beginning with** `Range("A2").Select`

   See Figure P-3. Every element of Excel, including a range, is considered an **object**. A **range object** represents a cell or a range of cells. The statement Range("A2").Select selects the range object cell A2. Notice that several times in the procedure, a line of code (or **statement**) selects a range, and then subsequent lines act on that selection. The next statement, Selection.EntireRow.Insert, inserts a row above the selection, which is currently cell A2. The next two lines of code select range A3:F3 and apply bold formatting to that selection. In VBA terminology, bold formatting is a value of an object's Bold property. A **property** is an attribute of an object that defines one of the object's characteristics (such as size) or an aspect of its behavior (such as whether it is enabled). The properties of an object are listed in the Properties window. To change the characteristics of an object, you change the values of its properties. For example, to apply bold formatting to a selected range, you assign the value True to the range's Bold property. To remove bold formatting, assign the value False.

2. **Examine the remaining lines of code, beginning with** `Range ("F3").Select`

   The next two statements select the range object cell F3 and center its contents, then the following two statements select the F4:F17 range object and format it as currency. Column objects B through F are then selected and their widths set to AutoFit. Finally, the range object cell A1 is selected, its font size is changed to 12, and its Bold property is set to True. The last line, End Sub, indicates the end of the Sub procedure and is also referred to as the **procedure footer**.

3. **Click the View Microsoft Excel button ⊠ on the Visual Basic Editor Standard toolbar to return to Excel**

   Because the macro is stored in the KHOT Procedures workbook, Jim can open this workbook and use the macro stored there repeatedly each week after he receives that week's data. He wants you to open the workbook containing data for January 1–7 and run the macro to format that data. You must leave the KHOT Procedures workbook open to use the macro stored there.

4. **Open the workbook EX P-2.xls from the drive and folder where your Data Files are stored, then save it as KHOT Advertising**

   This is the workbook containing the data you want to format.

5. **Press [Ctrl][F] to run the procedure**

   The FormatFile procedure formats the text, as shown in Figure P-4.

6. **Save the workbook**

   Now that you've successfully viewed and analyzed VBA code and run the macro, you will learn how to write your own code.

FIGURE P-3: VBA code for the FormatFile procedure

Selects range object cell A2

Applies bold formatting to range A3:F3

Sets widths of columns B-F to AutoFit

Adjusts font size and bolds cell A1

Inserts a row above cell A2

Centers contents of cell F3

Formats range F4:F17 as currency

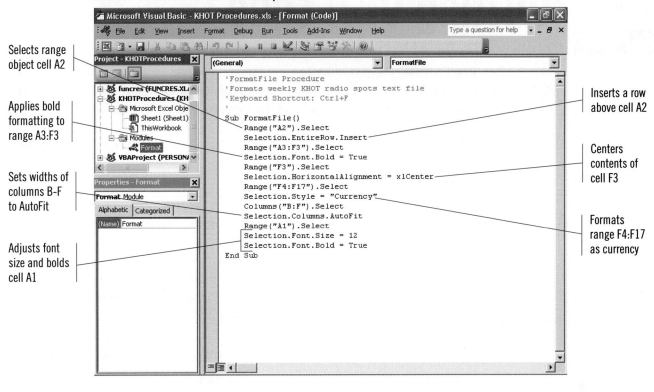

```
'FormatFile Procedure
'Formats weekly KHOT radio spots text file
'Keyboard Shortcut: Ctrl+F
'
Sub FormatFile()
    Range("A2").Select
    Selection.EntireRow.Insert
    Range("A3:F3").Select
    Selection.Font.Bold = True
    Range("F3").Select
    Selection.HorizontalAlignment = xlCenter
    Range("F4:F17").Select
    Selection.Style = "Currency"
    Columns("B:F").Select
    Selection.Columns.AutoFit
    Range("A1").Select
    Selection.Font.Size = 12
    Selection.Font.Bold = True
End Sub
```

FIGURE P-4: Worksheet formatted using the FormatFile procedure

Formatted title

Row inserted

Columns widened

Formatted column headings

Range formatted as currency

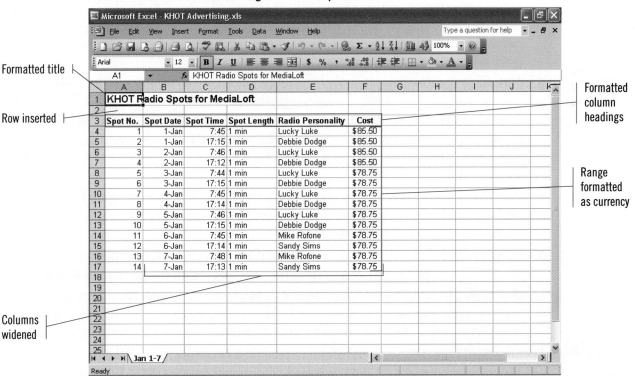

	A	B	C	D	E	F
1	KHOT Radio Spots for MediaLoft					
2						
3	Spot No.	Spot Date	Spot Time	Spot Length	Radio Personality	Cost
4	1	1-Jan	7:45	1 min	Lucky Luke	$85.50
5	2	1-Jan	17:15	1 min	Debbie Dodge	$85.50
6	3	2-Jan	7:46	1 min	Lucky Luke	$85.50
7	4	2-Jan	17:12	1 min	Debbie Dodge	$85.50
8	5	3-Jan	7:44	1 min	Lucky Luke	$78.75
9	6	3-Jan	17:15	1 min	Debbie Dodge	$78.75
10	7	4-Jan	7:45	1 min	Lucky Luke	$78.75
11	8	4-Jan	17:14	1 min	Debbie Dodge	$78.75
12	9	5-Jan	7:46	1 min	Lucky Luke	$78.75
13	10	5-Jan	17:15	1 min	Debbie Dodge	$78.75
14	11	6-Jan	7:45	1 min	Mike Rofone	$78.75
15	12	6-Jan	17:14	1 min	Sandy Sims	$78.75
16	13	7-Jan	7:48	1 min	Mike Rofone	$78.75
17	14	7-Jan	17:13	1 min	Sandy Sims	$78.75

Writing VBA Code

To write your own code, you first need to open the Visual Basic Editor and add a module to the workbook. You can then begin entering the procedure code. In the first few lines of a procedure, you typically include comments indicating the name of the procedure, a brief description of the procedure, and short-cut keys, if applicable. When writing Visual Basic code for Excel, you must follow the formatting rules, or **syntax**, of the VBA programming language exactly. A misspelled keyword or variable name causes a procedure to fail. Jim would like to total the cost of the radio ads. You will help him by writing a procedure that automates this routine task.

STEPS

TROUBLE
If the Code window is empty, verify that the workbook that contains your procedures (KHOT Procedures) is open.

1. **With the Jan 1-7 worksheet still displayed, click** Tools **on the menu bar, point to** Macro, **then click** Visual Basic Editor

   Two projects are displayed in the Project Explorer window, KHOT Procedures (which contains the Format macro) and KHOT Advertising Jan 1-7 (which contains the weekly data). The FormatFile procedure is again displayed in the Visual Basic Editor. You may have other projects in the Project Explorer window.

2. **Click the** Modules folder **in the KHOT Procedures project**

   You will store all of the procedures in the KHOT Procedures project, which is in the KHOT Procedures workbook. By clicking the Modules folder, you have activated the workbook, as you can see in the title bar.

3. **Click** Insert **on the Visual Basic Editor menu bar, then click** Module

   A new, blank module, with the default name Module1, is inserted in the KHOT Procedures workbook. The property name of the module could be more descriptive.

QUICK TIP
As you type, you may see words in drop-down lists. This optional feature is explained in the Clues to Use titled "Entering code using the scrollable word list" on the next page. For now, just continue to type.

4. **Click** (Name) **in the Properties window, then type** Total

   The module name is Total. The module name should not be the same as the procedure name (which will be AddTotal). In the Figure P-5 code, comments begin with an apostrophe, and the lines of code under Sub AddTotal( ) have been indented using the Tab key. When you enter the code in the next step, after you type Sub AddTotal( ) (the procedure header) and press [Enter], the Visual Basic Editor automatically enters End Sub (the procedure footer) in the Code window.

5. **Click in the** Code window, **then type the procedure code exactly as shown in Figure P-5**

   The lines that begin with ActiveCell.Formula insert the information enclosed in quotation marks into the active cell. For example, ActiveCell.Formula = "Weekly Total:" inserts the words Weekly Total: into cell E18, the active cell. The With clause near the bottom of the procedure is used to repeat several operations on the same object. As you type each line, Excel adjusts the spacing. Press [Tab] to indent text and [Shift][Tab] to move the insertion point to the left.

6. **Compare the procedure code you entered in the Code window with Figure P-5; if necessary, make any corrections, then click the** Save KHOT Procedures.xls button 🖫 **on the Visual Basic Editor Standard toolbar**

7. **Click the** View Microsoft Excel button 🖾 **on the toolbar, if necessary, click** KHOT Advertising.xls **on the taskbar to display the worksheet; with the Jan 1-7 worksheet displayed, click** Tools **on the Excel menu bar, point to** Macro, **then click** Macros

   Macro names have two parts. The first part ('KHOT Procedures.xls'!) indicates the workbook where the macro is stored. The second part (AddTotal or FormatFile) is the name of the procedure, taken from the procedure header.

QUICK TIP
If an error message appears, click Debug. Click the Reset button 🔳 on the toolbar, correct the error, then repeat Steps 6–8.

8. **Click** 'KHOT Procedures.xls'!AddTotal **to select it if necessary, then click** Run

   The AddTotal procedure inserts and formats the ad expenditure total in cell F18, as shown in Figure P-6.

9. **Save the workbook**

FIGURE P-5: VBA code for the AddTotal procedure

Save button

View Microsoft Excel button

New module name

In the xl terms, be sure to use a lowercase letter l, not the number 1

Comments begin with apostrophes

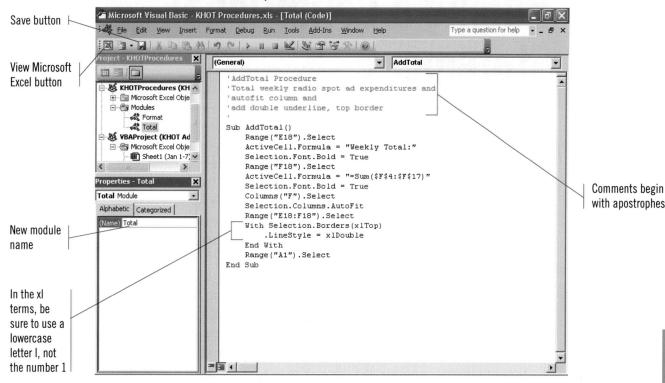

```
'AddTotal Procedure
'Total weekly radio spot ad expenditures and
'autofit column and
'add double underline, top border
'
Sub AddTotal()
    Range("E18").Select
    ActiveCell.Formula = "Weekly Total:"
    Selection.Font.Bold = True
    Range("F18").Select
    ActiveCell.Formula = "=Sum($F$4:$F$17)"
    Selection.Font.Bold = True
    Columns("F").Select
    Selection.Columns.AutoFit
    Range("E18:F18").Select
    With Selection.Borders(xlTop)
        .LineStyle = xlDouble
    End With
    Range("A1").Select
End Sub
```

FIGURE P-6: Worksheet after running the AddTotal procedure

Result of AddTotal procedure

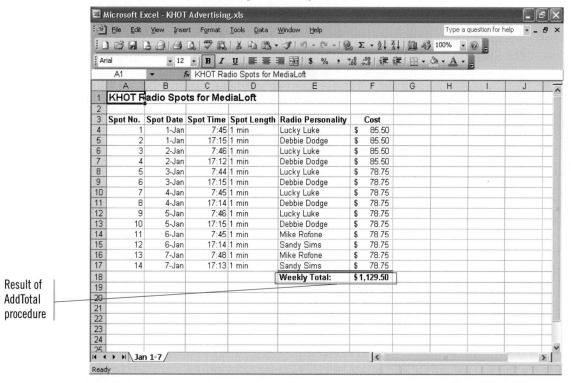

Clues to Use

Entering code using the scrollable word list

To assist you in entering the VBA code, the Editor often displays a list of words that can be used in the macro statement. Typically, the list appears after you press [.] (period). To include a word from the list in the macro statement, select the word in the list, then double click it or press [Tab]. For example, to enter the Range("E12").Select instruction, type Range(" E12"), then press [.] (period). Type s to bring up the words beginning with the letter s, select the Select command in the list, then press [Tab] to enter the word Select in the macro statement.

Adding a Conditional Statement

Sometimes, you may want a procedure to take an action based on a certain condition or set of conditions. For example, *if* a salesperson's performance rating is a 5 (top rating), *then* calculate a 10% bonus; otherwise (*else*), there is no bonus. One way of adding this type of conditional statement in Visual Basic is by using an **If...Then...Else statement**. The syntax for this statement is: "If *condition* Then *statements* Else [*else statements*]." The brackets indicate that the Else part of the statement is optional. Jim wants the worksheet to point out if the amount spent on radio ads stays within or exceeds the $1000 budget. You will use Excel to add a conditional statement that indicates this information. You start by returning to the Visual Basic Editor and inserting a new module in the KHOT Procedures project.

STEPS

> **QUICK TIP**
> You can also return to the Visual Basic Editor by clicking its button on the taskbar.

1. **With the Jan 1-7 worksheet still displayed, click** Tools **on the menu bar, point to** Macro, **click** Visual Basic Editor, **verify that KHOT Procedures is the active project in the Project Explorer window, click** Insert **on the Visual Basic Editor menu bar, then click** Module
   A new, blank module named Module1 is inserted in the KHOT Procedures workbook.

2. **In the Properties window click** (Name), **then type** Budget

3. **Click in the Code window, then type the code exactly as shown in Figure P-7**
   Notice the comment lines (in green) in the middle of the code. These lines help explain the procedure.

> **QUICK TIP**
> The If...Then...Else statement is similar to the Excel IF function.

4. **Compare the procedure you entered with Figure P-7; if necessary, make any corrections, click the** Save KHOT Procedures.xls button ⊞ **on the Visual Basic Editor Standard toolbar, then click the** View Microsoft Excel button ⊠ **on the toolbar**

5. **If necessary, click** KHOT Advertising.xls **in the taskbar to display it; with the Jan 1-7 worksheet displayed, click** Tools **on the menu bar, point to** Macro, **click** Macros, **in the Macro dialog box, click** 'KHOT Procedures.xls'!BudgetStatus, **then click** Run
   The BudgetStatus procedure indicates the status—over budget—as shown in Figure P-8.

6. **Save the workbook**

FIGURE P-7: VBA code for the BudgetStatus procedure

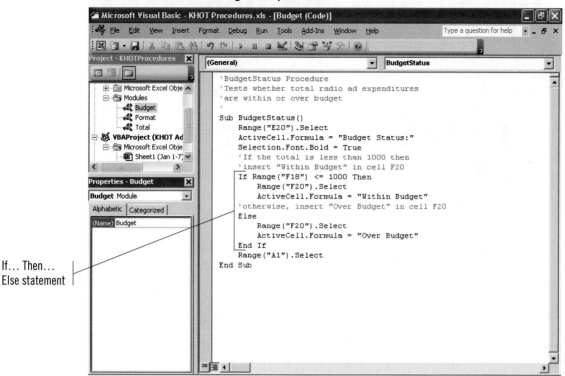

If... Then... Else statement

```
'BudgetStatus Procedure
'Tests whether total radio ad expenditures
'are within or over budget
'
Sub BudgetStatus()
    Range("E20").Select
    ActiveCell.Formula = "Budget Status:"
    Selection.Font.Bold = True
    'If the total is less than 1000 then
    'insert "Within Budget" in cell F20
    If Range("F18") <= 1000 Then
        Range("F20").Select
        ActiveCell.Formula = "Within Budget"
    'otherwise, insert "Over Budget" in cell F20
    Else
        Range("F20").Select
        ActiveCell.Formula = "Over Budget"
    End If
    Range("A1").Select
End Sub
```

FIGURE P-8: Result of running the BudgetStatus procedure

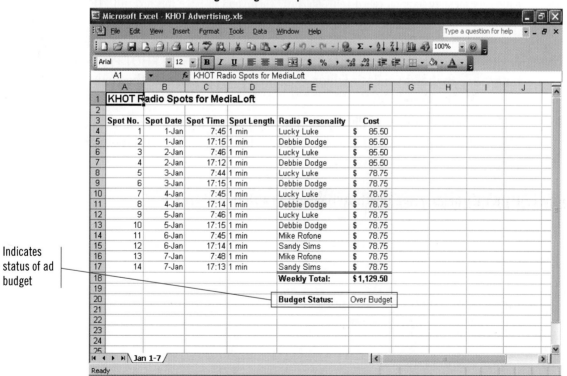

Indicates status of ad budget

	A	B	C	D	E	F
1	KHOT Radio Spots for MediaLoft					
2						
3	Spot No.	Spot Date	Spot Time	Spot Length	Radio Personality	Cost
4	1	1-Jan	7:45	1 min	Lucky Luke	$ 85.50
5	2	1-Jan	17:15	1 min	Debbie Dodge	$ 85.50
6	3	2-Jan	7:46	1 min	Lucky Luke	$ 85.50
7	4	2-Jan	17:12	1 min	Debbie Dodge	$ 85.50
8	5	3-Jan	7:44	1 min	Lucky Luke	$ 78.75
9	6	3-Jan	17:15	1 min	Debbie Dodge	$ 78.75
10	7	4-Jan	7:45	1 min	Lucky Luke	$ 78.75
11	8	4-Jan	17:14	1 min	Debbie Dodge	$ 78.75
12	9	5-Jan	7:46	1 min	Lucky Luke	$ 78.75
13	10	5-Jan	17:15	1 min	Debbie Dodge	$ 78.75
14	11	6-Jan	7:45	1 min	Mike Rofone	$ 78.75
15	12	6-Jan	17:14	1 min	Sandy Sims	$ 78.75
16	13	7-Jan	7:48	1 min	Mike Rofone	$ 78.75
17	14	7-Jan	17:13	1 min	Sandy Sims	$ 78.75
18					Weekly Total:	$1,129.50
19						
20					Budget Status:	Over Budget

Prompting the User for Data

When automating routine tasks, you sometimes need to pause a macro to allow user input. You use the VBA InputBox function to display a dialog box that prompts the user for information. A **function** is a predefined procedure that returns (creates and displays) a value; in this case the value returned is the information the user enters. The required elements of an InputBox function are as follows: *object*.InputBox("*prompt*"), where "*prompt*" is the message that appears in the dialog box. For a detailed description of the InputBox function, use the Visual Basic Editor's Help menu. ██████ You decide to create a procedure that will insert the user's name in the left footer area of the workbook. You'll use the InputBox function to display a dialog box in which the user can enter his or her name. You will also type an error into the procedure code, which you will correct in the next lesson.

STEPS

1. **With the Jan 1-7 worksheet displayed, click** Tools **on the menu bar, point to** Macro, **click** Visual Basic Editor, **verify that KHOT Procedures is the active project, click** Insert **on the Visual Basic Editor menu bar, then click** Module

   A new, blank module named Module1 is inserted in the KHOT Procedures workbook.

2. **In the Properties window, click** (Name), **then type** Footer

3. **Click in the Code window, then type the procedure code exactly as shown in Figure P-9**

   Like the Budget procedure, this procedure also contains comments that explain the code. The first part of the code, Dim LeftFooterText As String, **declares**, or defines, LeftFooterText as a text string variable. In Visual Basic, a **variable** is a location in memory in which you can temporarily store one item of information. Dim statements are used to declare variables and must be entered in the following format: Dim *variablename* As *datatype*. The datatype here is "string." In this case, you plan to store the information received from the input box in the temporary memory location called LeftFooterText. Then you can place this text in the left footer area. The remaining statements in the procedure are explained in the comment line directly above each statement. Notice the comment pointing out the error in the procedure code. You will correct this in the next lesson.

4. **Review your code, make any necessary changes, click the** Save KHOT Procedures.xls **button** 🔲 **on the Visual Basic Editor Standard toolbar, then click the** View Microsoft Excel **button** 🔳 **on the toolbar**

5. **With the Jan 1-7 worksheet displayed, click** Tools **on the menu bar, point to** Macro, **click** Macros, **in the Macro dialog box click** 'KHOT Procedures.xls'!FooterInput, **then click** Run

   The procedure begins, and a dialog box generated by the InputBox function appears, prompting you to enter your name. See Figure P-10.

6. **With the cursor in the text box, type your name, then click** OK

7. **Click the** Print Preview button 🔍 **on the Standard toolbar**

   Although the customized footer with the date is inserted on the sheet, because of the error, your name does *not* appear in the left section of the footer. In the next lesson, you will learn how to step through a procedure's code line by line. This will help you locate the error in the FooterInput procedure.

8. **Click** Close **then save the workbook**

   You return to the Jan 1-7 worksheet.

FIGURE P-9: VBA code for the FooterInput procedure

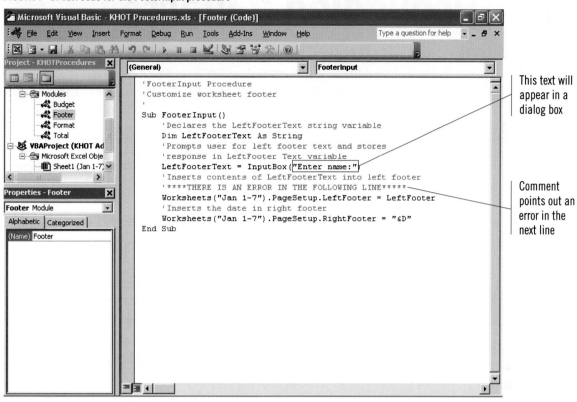

This text will appear in a dialog box

Comment points out an error in the next line

FIGURE P-10: InputBox function's dialog box

User prompt

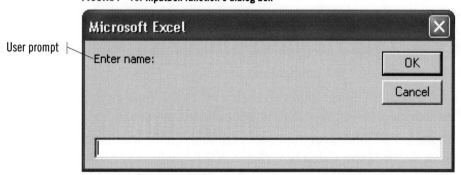

Debugging a Macro

When a macro procedure does not run properly, it can be due to an error, referred to as a **bug**, in the code. To assist you in finding the bug(s) in a procedure, the Visual Basic Editor helps you step through the procedure's code, one line at a time. When you locate the error, you can then correct, or **debug**, it. 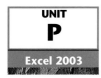 You decide to debug the macro procedure to find out why it failed to insert your name in the worksheet's footer.

STEPS

1. **With the KHOT Advertising Jan 1-7 worksheet displayed, click** Tools **on the menu bar, point to** Macro**, click** Macros**, in the Macro dialog box click** 'KHOT Procedures.xls'!FooterInput**, then click** Step Into

   The Visual Basic Editor appears with the statement selector positioned on the first statement of the procedure. See Figure P-11.

2. **Press** [F8] **to step to the next statement**

   The statement selector skips over the comments and the line of code beginning with Dim. The Dim statement indicates that the procedure will store your name in a variable named LeftFooterText. Because Dim is a declaration of a variable and not a procedure statement, the statement selector skips it and moves to the line containing the InputBox function.

3. **Press** [F8] **again; with the cursor in the text box in the Microsoft Excel dialog box, type your name, then click** OK

   The Visual Basic Editor reappears. The statement selector is now positioned on the statement that reads Worksheets ("Jan 1-7").PageSetup.LeftFooter = LeftFooter. This statement should insert your name (which you just typed in the text box) in the left section of the footer. This is the instruction that does not appear to be working correctly.

4. **If necessary, scroll right until the end of the LeftFooter instruction is visible, then place the mouse pointer I on** LeftFooter**, as shown in Figure P-12**

   Rather than containing your name, the variable LeftFooter at the end of this line is empty. That's because the InputBox function assigned your name to the LeftFooterText variable, not to the LeftFooter variable. Before you can correct this bug, you need to turn off the Step Into feature.

5. **Click the** Reset button ☑ **on the Visual Basic Editor toolbar to turn off the Step Into feature, click at the end of the statement containing the error, then replace the variable LeftFooter with** LeftFooterText

   The revised statement now reads Worksheets("Jan 1-7").PageSetup.LeftFooter = LeftFooterText.

6. **Delete the comment line pointing out the error**

7. **Click the** Save KHOT Procedures.xls button ☑ **on the Visual Basic Editor Standard toolbar, then click the** View Microsoft Excel button ☒ **on the toolbar**

8. **With the Jan 1-7 worksheet displayed, click** Tools **on the menu bar, point to** Macro**, click** Macros**; in the Macro dialog box, click** 'KHOT Procedures.xls'!FooterInput**, click** Run **to rerun the procedure, when prompted, type your name, then click** OK

9. **Click the** Print Preview button ☑ **on the Standard toolbar**

   Your name now appears in the left section of the footer.

10. **Click** Close**, save the workbook, then print the worksheet**

FIGURE P-11: Statement selector positioned on first procedure statement

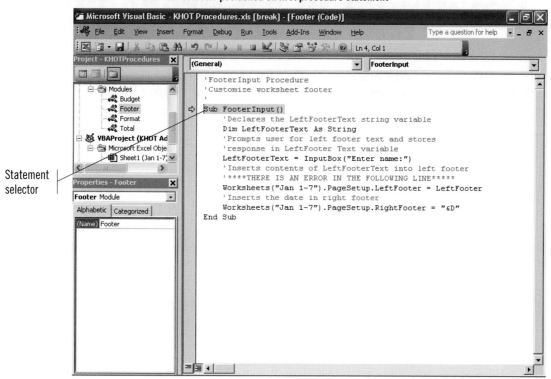

Statement selector

FIGURE P-12: Value contained in LeftFooter variable

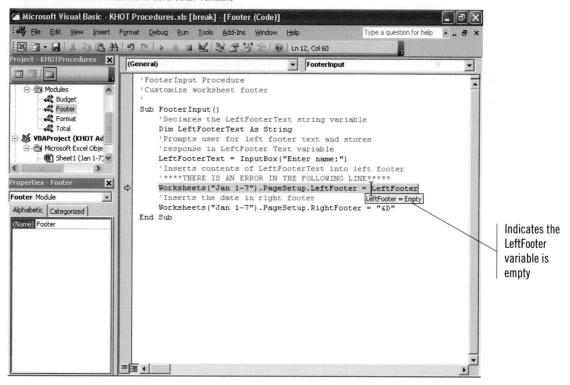

Indicates the LeftFooter variable is empty

Creating a Main Procedure

When you routinely need to run several macros one after another, you can save time by combining them into one procedure. The resulting procedure, which processes (or runs) multiple procedures in sequence, is referred to as the **main procedure**. To create a main procedure, you type a Call statement for each procedure you want to run. The syntax of the Call statement is Call *procedurename*, where *procedurename* is the name of the procedure you want to run. To avoid having to run his macros one after another every month, Jim asks you to create a main procedure that will run (or call) each of the procedures in the KHOT Procedures workbook in sequence.

STEPS

1. **With the Jan 1-7 worksheet displayed, click** Tools **on the menu bar, point to** Macro, **then click** Visual Basic Editor

2. **Verify that KHOT Procedures is the active project, click** Insert **on the menu bar, then click** Module
   A new, blank module named Module1 is inserted in the KHOT Procedures workbook.

3. **In the Properties window, click** (Name), **then type** MainProc

4. **In the Code window, enter the procedure code exactly as shown in Figure P-13**

5. **Compare your main procedure code with Figure P-13, correct any errors, if necessary, then click the** Save KHOT Procedures.xls button 🖫 **on the Visual Basic Editor Standard toolbar**
   To test the new main procedure you need an unformatted version of the KHOT radio spot workbook.

6. **Click the** View Microsoft Excel button 🖾 **on the toolbar, then close the KHOT Advertising workbook**
   The KHOT Procedures workbook remains open.

7. **Open the Data File titled EX P-2.xls from the drive and folder where your Data Files are stored, then save it as** KHOT Advertising 2
   In the next lesson, you'll run the main procedure.

FIGURE P-13: VBA code for the MainProcedure procedure

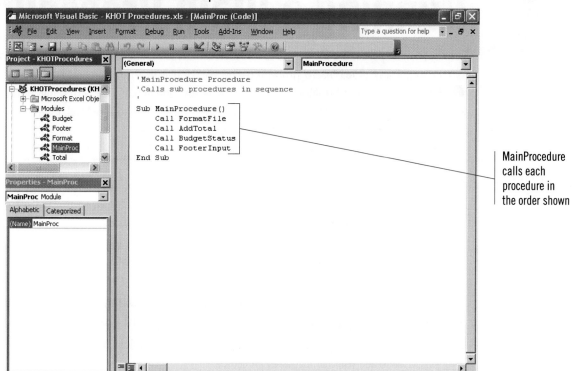

MainProcedure
calls each
procedure in
the order shown

Running a Main Procedure

Running a main procedure allows you to run several macros in sequence. You can run a main procedure just as you would any other macro procedure—by selecting it in the Macro dialog box, then clicking Run. You have finished creating Jim's main procedure, and you are ready to run it. If the main procedure works correctly, it should format the worksheet, insert the ad expenditure total, insert a budget status message, and add your name to the worksheet footer.

STEPS

1. **With the Jan 1-7 worksheet displayed, click** Tools **on the menu bar, point to** Macro, **then click** Macros; **in the Macro dialog box, click** 'KHOT Procedures.xls'!MainProcedure, **click** Run, **when prompted, type your name, then click** OK

   The MainProcedure runs the FormatFile, AddTotal, BudgetStatus, and FooterInput procedures in sequence. You can see the results of the FormatFile, AddTotal, and BudgetStatus procedures in the worksheet window. See Figure P-14. To view the results of the FooterInput procedure, you need to switch to the Preview window.

2. **Click the** Print Preview button **on the Standard toolbar, verify that your name appears in the left footer area and the date appears in the right footer area, then click** Close

3. **Click** Tools **on the menu bar, point to** Macro, **then click** Visual Basic Editor

   You decide to add your name to each procedure.

4. **In the Project Explorer window, double-click each module and add a comment line after the procedure name that reads** Written by [your name], **then click the** Save KHOT Procedures.xls button **on the toolbar**

5. **Click** File **on the Visual Basic Editor menu bar, then click** Print

   The Print - KHOTProcedures dialog box opens, as shown in Figure P-15. You could print each procedure separately, but it's faster to print all the procedures in the workbook at one time. Recall that all procedures in a workbook are known as a project.

6. **In the Print - KHOTProcedures dialog box, click the** Current Project option button, **then click** OK

   Each procedure prints on a separate page.

7. **Click the** View Microsoft Excel button **on the toolbar**

8. **Save the KHOT Advertising 2 workbook and close it; close the KHOT Procedures workbook, then exit Excel**

FIGURE P-14: Result of running MainProcedure procedure

Total cost calculated

Budget status message inserted

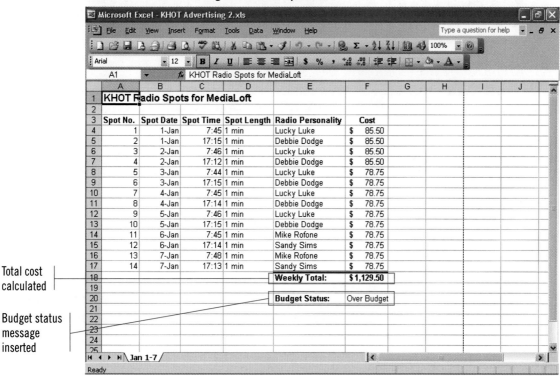

FIGURE P-15: Printing the macro procedures

Current Project option button

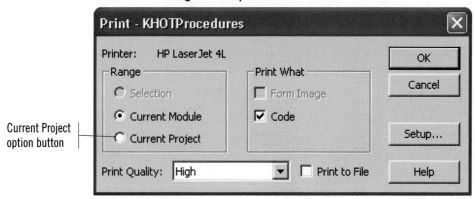

Excel 2003

Practice

▼ CONCEPTS REVIEW

FIGURE P-16

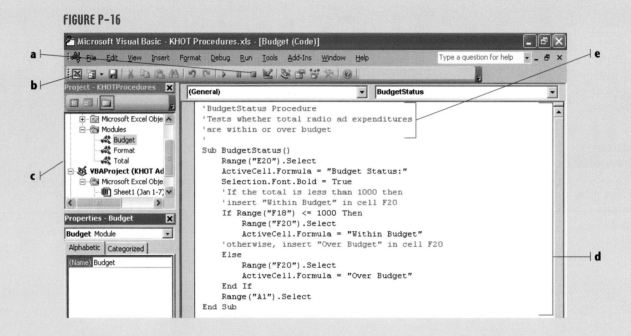

1. Which element do you click to turn off the Step Into feature?
2. Which element do you click to return to Excel from the Visual Basic Editor?
3. Which element points to the Project Explorer window?
4. Which element points to the Code window?
5. Which element points to comments in the VBA code?

Match each term with the statement that best describes it.

6. Keywords
7. Comments
8. Procedure
9. Sub procedure
10. Function

a. Another term for a macro in Visual Basic for Applications (VBA)
b. A procedure that returns a value
c. Words that are recognized as part of the programming language
d. A series of statements that perform an action but don't return a value
e. Descriptive text used to explain parts of a procedure

Select the best answer from the list of choices.

11. A location in memory where you can temporarily store information is a(n):
    a. Function
    b. Procedure
    c. Sub procedure
    d. Variable

12. You enter the statements of a macro in:

   a. The Macro dialog box   **c.** The Properties window of the Visual Basic Editor

   b. The Code window of the Visual Basic Editor   **d.** Any blank worksheet

13. If your macro doesn't run correctly, you should:

   a. Create an If...Then...Else statement.   **c.** Select the macro in the Macro dialog box, click Step Into,

   b. Click the Properties button.   and then debug the macro.

   d. Click the Project Explorer button.

14. Comments are displayed in _____ in VBA code.

   a. Green   **c.** Red

   b. Blue   **d.** Black

15. Keywords are displayed in _____ in VBA code.

   a. Red   **c.** Green

   b. Black   **d.** Blue

▼ SKILLS REVIEW

1. View and analyze VBA code.

   a. Start Excel, open the Data File titled EX P-3.xls from the drive and folder where your Data Files are stored, enable macros, then save it as **Northeast Sales**.

   b. Review the unformatted January 2006 worksheet.

   c. Open the Visual Basic Editor.

   d. Select the ListFormat module and review the FormatList procedure.

   e. Insert comments in the procedure code describing what action you think each line of code will perform. (*Hint*: One of the statements will sort the list alphabetically by city.)

   f. Save the macro, return to the worksheet, then run the FormatList macro.

   g. Compare the results with the code and your comments.

   h. Save the workbook.

FIGURE P-17

```
'SalesTotal Procedure
'Totals January sales
Sub SalesTotal()
    Range("E17").Select
    ActiveCell.Formula = "=SUM($E$3:$E$16)"
    Selection.Font.Bold = True
    With Selection.Borders(xlTop)
        .LineStyle = xlSingle
    End With
    Range("A1").Select
End Sub
```

2. Write VBA code.

   a. Open the Visual Basic Editor and insert a new module named **Total** in the Northeast Sales project.

   b. Enter the code for the SalesTotal procedure exactly as shown in Figure P-17.

   c. Save the macro.

   d. Return to the January 2006 worksheet and run the SalesTotal macro.

   e. Save the workbook.

FIGURE P-18

```
'SalesGoal Procedure
'Tests whether sales goal was met
Sub SalesGoal()
    'If the total is >=185000, then insert "Met Goal"
    'in cell E18
    If Range("E17") >= 185000 Then
        Range("E18").Select
        ActiveCell.Formula = "Met goal"
    'otherwise, insert "Missed goal" in cell E18
    Else
        Range("E18").Select
        ActiveCell.Formula = "Missed goal"
    End If
End Sub
```

3. Add a conditional statement.

   a. Open the Visual Basic Editor and insert a new module named **Goal** in the Northeast Sales project.

   b. Enter the SalesGoal procedure exactly as shown in Figure P-18.

   c. Save the macro.

   d. Return to the January 2006 worksheet and run the SalesGoal macro. The procedure should enter the message **Missed goal** in cell E18.

   e. Save the workbook.

4. Prompt the user for data.

a. Open the Visual Basic Editor and insert a new module named **Header** in the Northeast Sales project.

b. Enter the HeaderFooter procedure exactly as shown in Figure P-19. You will be entering an error in the procedure that will be corrected in Step 5.

c. Save the macro then return to the January 2006 worksheet and run the HeaderFooter macro.

d. Preview the January 2006 worksheet. Your name should be missing from the left section of the footer.

e. Save the workbook.

FIGURE P-19

```
'HeaderFooter Procedure
'Procedure to customize the header and footer
Sub HeaderFooter()
    'Inserts the filename in the header
    Worksheets("January 2006").PageSetup.CenterHeader = "&F"
    'Declares the variable LeftFooterText as a string
    Dim LeftFooterText As String
    'Prompts user for left footer text
    LeftFooter = InputBox("Enter your full name:")
    'Inserts response into left footer
    Worksheets("January 2006").PageSetup.LeftFooter = LeftFooterText
    'Inserts the date into right footer
    Worksheets("January 2006").PageSetup.RightFooter = "&D"
End Sub
```

5. Debug a macro.

a. Open the Visual Basic Editor.

b. The error occurs on the line:

LeftFooter = InputBox("Enter your full name:")

(The variable that will input the response text into the worksheet footer is LeftFooterText.)

c. Correct the error by changing the line with the error to:

LeftFooterText = InputBox("Enter your full name:")

d. Save the macro, then return to the January 2006 worksheet and run the HeaderFooter macro again.

e. Verify that your name now appears in the left section of the footer.

f. Save the workbook.

6. Create and run a main procedure.

a. Return to the Visual Basic Editor, insert a new module, then name it **MainProc**.

b. Begin the main procedure by entering comments in the code window that provide the procedure's name (MainProcedure) and explain that its purpose is to run the FormatList, SalesTotal, SalesGoal, and HeaderFooter procedures.

c. Enter the procedure header: **Sub MainProcedure()**.

d. Enter four Call statements that will run the FormatList, SalesTotal, SalesGoal, and HeaderFooter procedures in sequence.

e. Save the procedure and return to Excel.

f. Open the EX P-3.xls workbook, then save it as Northeast Sales 2.

g. Run the MainProcedure macro, entering your name when prompted. (*Hint*: In the Macro dialog box, the macro procedures you created will now have *'Northeast Sales.xls'!* as part of their names. That's because the macros are stored in the Northeast Sales workbook, not in the Northeast Sales 2 workbook.)

h. Verify that the macro ran successfully, save the Northeast Sales 2 workbook, print the January 2006 worksheet, then close the Northeast Sales 2 workbook.

i. Return to the Visual Basic Editor, enter your name in a comment line in each procedure, print the current project's code, then close the Visual Basic Editor.

j. Return to Excel, close the Northeast Sales workbook, then exit Excel.

▼ INDEPENDENT CHALLENGE 1

You work at an art supply store. Your coworker is on vacation for two weeks, and you have taken over her projects. The information systems manager asks you to document and test the Excel procedure Qtr1, which your coworker wrote for the company's accountant. You will run the macro procedure first to see what it does, then you will add comments to the VBA code to document it. Lastly, you will enter data to verify that the formulas in the macro work correctly.

▼ INDEPENDENT CHALLENGE 1 (CONTINUED)

a. Start Excel, open the Data File titled EX P-4.xls from the drive and folder where your Data Files are stored, enable macros, then save it as **First Quarter Income**.

b. Run the Qtr1 macro, noting anything that you think should be mentioned in your documentation.

c. Review the Qtr1 procedure in the Visual Basic Editor. It is stored in the Quarter 1 module.

d. Document the procedure by annotating the printed code, indicating the actions the procedure performs and the objects (ranges) that are affected. (*Hint*: The month names are entered into cells B1, C1, and D1. The income row headers are entered into cells A2, A4, A5, and A6. The Total Income header is entered into cell A8. The column headers are bolded. The row headers are bolded. Columns A through D are AutoFitted. Totals are entered into cells B8, C8, and D8.)

e. Enter your name in a comment line.

f. Save the procedure, then print the procedure code.

g. Return to the First Quarter Income workbook and use Figure P-20 as a guide to enter data in cells B4:D6 of Sheet1. The totals will be displayed as you enter the income data.

h. Check the total income calculations in row 8 to verify that the macro is working correctly.

i. Enter your name in the Sheet1 footer, save the worksheet, then print the worksheet.

j. Close the workbook, then exit Excel.

FIGURE P-20

	A	B	C	D	E
1		January	Feburary	March	
2	Income				
3					
4	Supplies	600	500	480	
5	Classes	800	675	650	
6	Consulting	300	700	900	
7					
8	Total Income				

▼ INDEPENDENT CHALLENGE 2

You work in the sales office of an automobile dealership called Team Motors. Each month you are required to produce a report stating whether sales quotas were met for the following three vehicle categories: compacts, sedans, and sports/utility. This quarter, the sales quotas for each month are as follows: compacts 65, sedans 50, and sports/utility 65. The results this month were 45, 65, and 75, respectively. You decide to create a procedure to automate your monthly task of determining the sales quota status for the vehicle categories. You would like your assistant to take this task over when you go on vacation next month. Because he has no previous experience with Excel, you decide to create a second procedure that prompts a user with input boxes to enter the actual sales results for the month.

a. Start Excel, open the Data File titled EX P-5.xls from the drive and folder where your Data Files are stored, then save it as **Sales Quota Status**.

b. Use the Visual Basic Editor to insert a new module named **Quotas** in the Sales Quota Status workbook. Create a procedure in the new module named **SalesQuota** that determines the sales quota status for each vehicle category and enters Yes or No in the Status column. The VBA code is shown in Figure P-21.

c. Add comments to document the SalesQuota procedure, including your name, then save it.

FIGURE P-21

```
Sub SalesQuota()

    If Range("C4") >= 65 Then
        Range("D4").Select
        ActiveCell.Formula = "Yes"
    Else
        Range("D4").Select
        ActiveCell.Formula = "No"
    End If

    If Range("C5") >= 50 Then
        Range("D5").Select
        ActiveCell.Formula = "Yes"
    Else
        Range("D5").Select
        ActiveCell.Formula = "No"
    End If

    If Range("C6") >= 65 Then
        Range("D6").Select
        ActiveCell.Formula = "Yes"
    Else
        Range("D6").Select
        ActiveCell.Formula = "No"
    End If

End Sub
```

▼ INDEPENDENT CHALLENGE 2 (CONTINUED)

d. Insert a new module named **MonthlySales**. Create a second procedure named **Sales** that prompts a user for sales data for each vehicle category, enters the input data in the appropriate cells, then calls the SalesQuota procedure. The VBA code is shown in Figure P-22.

FIGURE P-22

```
Sub Sales()

    Dim Compact As String
    Compact = InputBox("Enter Compact Sales")
    Range("C4").Select
    Selection = Compact

    Dim Sedans As String
    Sedans = InputBox("Enter Sedan Sales")
    Range("C5").Select
    Selection = Sedans

    Dim SportsUtility As String
    SportsUtility = InputBox("Enter SportsUtility Sales")
    Range("C6").Select
    Selection = SportsUtility


    Call SalesQuota

End Sub
```

e. Insert your name in a **Created by** comment below the procedure name. Enter comments to document the macro actions. Save the procedure.

f. Run the Sales macro and enter 45 for compact sales, 65 for sedan sales, and 75 for sports/utility sales. Correct any errors in the VBA code.

g. Print the current project's code, then return to the workbook.

Advanced Challenge Exercise

- Assign a shortcut of [Ctrl][w] to the Sales macro. Insert a line on the worksheet that tells the user to press [Ctrl][w] to enter sales data.
- Delete the data in cells C4:D6.
- Run the macro using the shortcut key combination entering 70 for compact sales, 30 for sedan sales, and 60 for sports/utility sales.

h. Add your name to the left section of the worksheet footer, save the workbook, then print the worksheet. Close the workbook, then exit Excel.

▼ INDEPENDENT CHALLENGE 3

You own a flower store named Tulips. You have started to advertise your business using a local magazine, billboards, cable TV, radio, and local newspapers. Every month you prepare a report with the advertising expenses detailed by source. You decide to create a macro that will format the monthly reports. You add the same footers on every report, so you will create another macro that will add a footer to a document. Finally, you will create a main procedure that will call the macros to format the report and add a footer. You begin by creating a workbook with data you can use to test the macros. You will save the macros you create in this workbook.

a. Use Figure P-23 as a guide to create a workbook containing the January advertising expenses. Save the workbook as **Tulips** in the drive and folder where your Data Files are stored.

FIGURE P-23

	A	B	C	D	E	F	G
1	Tulips						
2	Ad Campaign						
3	Advertising Type	Source	Cost				
4	Magazine	What's Happening	500				
5	Newspaper	Times	450				
6	Billboard	First Street	550				
7	TV	Cable TV	300				
8	Radio	Public Radio	550				
9							

b. Insert a module named **Format**, then create a procedure named Formatting that:
- Selects a cell in row 3 and inserts a row in the worksheet above it
- Selects the cost data in column C and formats it as currency. (Hint: After the row is inserted, this range is C5:C9.)
- Selects cell A1 before ending

▼ INDEPENDENT CHALLENGE 3 (CONTINUED)

c. Save the Formatting procedure.

d. Insert a module named **Foot**, then create a procedure named Footer that:

- Declares a string variable for text that will be placed in the left footer
- Uses an input box to prompt the user for his or her name and places the name in the left footer
- Places the date in the right footer

e. Save the Footer procedure.

f. Insert a module named **Main**, then create a procedure named MainProc that calls the new Footer procedure and the Formatting procedure.

g. Save your work, then run the MainProc procedure. Debug each procedure as necessary.

h. Insert your name in a comment line under each procedure name, then print the code for the current project.

i. Return to the January worksheet, save the workbook, then print the worksheet.

j. Close the workbook, then exit Excel.

▼ INDEPENDENT CHALLENGE 4

You are working as an assistant currency trader for an international bank based in London. To keep on top of the fluctuating world currencies, you create a daily report using data imported from the Web to an Excel spreadsheet. Since you perform the same formatting and place the same header and footer on each report, you decide to write a macro that will do this automatically.

a. Start Excel, create a new workbook, then save it as **Currency Rates** in the drive and folder where your Data Files are stored.

b. Use the search engine of your choice to search for world currency rates. Find a Web site that displays the rate information in a table.

c. Copy the currency rate information from the Web page into Sheet1 of your Currency Rates workbook, then save the workbook.

d. Use the Visual Basic Editor to create a procedure named Formatting that does the following:

- Inserts a blank row after the column headers
- Changes the font size of the column and row headers to 14
- Bolds the currency data
- Adds a footer with your name in the left section and the date in the right section

e. Enter your name as a comment in the procedure.

f. Save your work, then return to the worksheet and test the new macro.

g. Debug the macro as necessary, print the module, then close the Visual Basic Editor.

h. Return to the Currency Rates workbook, then resize the columns on Sheet1 as necessary. Save the workbook, then print the worksheet.

Advanced Challenge Exercise

FIGURE P-24

- Use the Visual Basic Editor to create a procedure named Printdata that prints a worksheet. Use Figure P-24 as a guide. Note that your range depends on the amount of data on your worksheet.

```
Sub Printdata()

'Your range will be different on the next two lines

Range("A1:C17").Select
ActiveSheet.PageSetup.PrintArea = "$A$1:$C$17"
ActiveWindow.SelectedSheets.PrintOut Copies:=1

End Sub
```

- Save the macro and return to the worksheet.
- Assign the macro Printdata to a button on the worksheet. (*Hint*: Use the Rectangle tool to create the button, label the button **Print**, select the button and then right-click one of the button's edges to assign the macro.)
- Test the button.

i. Save the workbook, close the workbook, then exit Excel.

▼ VISUAL WORKSHOP

Open the Data File titled EX P-6.xls and save it as **Strings** in the drive and folder where your Data Files are stored. Create a macro procedure that will format the worksheet as shown in Figure P-25. Run the macro and debug it as necessary to make the worksheet match Figure P-25. Insert your name in a comment line under the procedure name, then print the procedure code.

FIGURE P-25

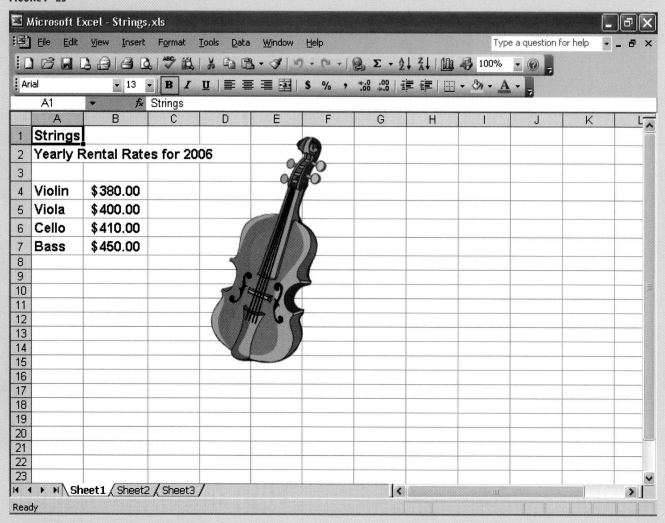

Glossary

3-D reference A reference that uses values on other sheets or workbooks, effectively creating another dimension to a workbook.

Absolute cell reference A cell reference that contains a dollar sign before the column letter and/or row number to indicate the absolute, or fixed, contents of specific cells. For example, the formula $A$1+$B$1 calculates only the sum of these specific cells no matter where the formula is copied in the workbook.

Active cell The current location of the cell pointer.

Alignment The placement of cell contents; for example, left, center, or right.

Analyze To manipulate data, such as a list, with Excel or another tool.

AND condition A filtering feature that searches for records by specifying that all entered criteria must be matched.

Apply To open a document based on an Excel template.

Area chart A line chart in which each area is given a solid color or pattern to emphasize the relationship between the pieces of charted information.

Argument Information that a function needs to calculate an answer. In an expression, multiple arguments are separated by commas. All of the arguments are enclosed in parentheses; for example, =SUM(A1:B1).

Argument ScreenTip The yellow box that appears as you build a function. As you build the function using different elements, the box displays these elements. You can click each element to display its online help.

Arithmetic operator A symbol used in a formula (such as + or -, /, or *) to perform mathematical operations.

ASCII file A text file that contains data but no formatting; instead of being divided into columns, ASCII file data are separated, or delimited, by tabs or commas.

Ascending order In sorting worksheet records, the order that begins with the letter A or the number 1.

Attribute The styling features such as bold, italics, and underlining that can be applied to cell contents. In XML, the component that provides information about the document's elements.

Auditing An Excel feature that helps track errors and check worksheet logic.

AutoCalculate value Value displayed in the status bar that represents the sum of values in the selected range.

AutoComplete A feature that automatically completes entries based on other entries in the same column.

AutoFill A feature that creates a series of text entries or numbers when a range is selected using the fill handle.

AutoFill Options button Allows you to specify what you want to fill and whether or not you want to include formatting.

AutoFilter An Excel list feature that lets you click a list arrow and select criteria by which to display certain types of records.

AutoFilter list arrows Small triangles that appear next to field names in an Excel list; used to display portions of your data.

AutoFit A feature that automatically adjusts the width of a column to accommodate its widest entry when the boundary to the right of the column selector is double-clicked.

AutoFormat Preset schemes that can be applied to format a range instantly. Excel comes with 16 AutoFormats that include colors, fonts, and numeric formatting.

AutoSum A feature that automatically creates totals using the SUM function when you click the AutoSum button.

Background color The color applied to the background of a cell.

Backsolving A problem-solving method in which you specify a solution and then find the input value that produces the answer you want; sometimes described as a what-if analysis in reverse. In Excel, the Goal Seek feature performs backsolving.

Bar chart A chart that shows information as a series of horizontal bars.

Border The edge of a cell, an area of a worksheet, or a selected object; you can change its color or line style.

Bug In programming, an error that causes a procedure to run incorrectly.

Category axis The x-axis (horizontal axis) of a chart.

Cell The intersection of a column and row in a worksheet, datasheet, or table.

Cell address The location of a cell expressed by the column and row coordinates; the cell address of the cell in column A, row 1, is A1.

Cell comments Notes you've written about a workbook that appear when you place the pointer over a cell.

Cell pointer A highlighted rectangle around a cell that indicates the active cell.

Cell reference The address or name that identifies a cell's position in a worksheet; it consists of a letter that identifies the cell's column and a number that identifies its row; for example, cell B3. Cell references in worksheets can be used in formulas and are relative or absolute. *See also* Absolute cell reference and Relative cell reference.

Change history A worksheet containing a list of changes made to a shared workbook.

Changing cells In what-if analysis, cells that contain the values that change in order to produce multiple sets of results.

Chart A graphic representation of worksheet information. Types include 2-D and 3-D column, bar, pie, area, and line charts.

Chart sheet A separate sheet that contains only a chart linked to worksheet data.

Chart Wizard A series of dialog boxes that helps you create or modify a chart.

Clip An individual media file, such as art, sound, animation, or a movie.

Clip art An image such as a corporate logo, a picture, or a photo.

Clipboard A temporary storage area for cut or copied items that are available for pasting. *See also* Office Clipboard.

Clipboard task pane A task pane that shows the contents of the Office Clipboard; contains options for copying and pasting items.

Code *See* Program Code.

Code window In the Visual Basic Editor, the window that displays the selected module's procedures, written in the Visual Basic programming language.

Column chart The default chart type in Excel, which displays information as a series of vertical columns.

Column heading The gray box containing the letter above the column in a worksheet.

Combination chart Combines a column and line chart to compare data requiring different scales of measure.

Comments In a Visual Basic procedure, notes that explain the purpose of the macro or procedure; they are preceded by a single apostrophe and appear in green. *See also* cell comments.

Complex formula An equation that uses more than one type of arithmetic operator.

Conditional format A cell format that is based on the cell's value or the outcome of a formula.

Conditional formula A formula that makes calculations based on stated conditions, such as calculating a rebate based on a particular purchase amount.

Consolidate To combine data on multiple worksheets and display the result on another worksheet.

Control menu box A box in the upper-left corner of a window used to resize or close a window.

Criteria Conditions that must be met when searching for files.

Criteria range A cell range containing one row of labels (usually a copy of column labels) and at least one additional row underneath it that contains the criteria you want to match.

Custom chart type A specially formatted Excel chart.

Data entry area The unlocked portion of a worksheet where users are able to enter and change data.

Data form In an Excel list (or database), a dialog box that displays one record at a time.

Data label Descriptive text that appears above a data marker in a chart.

Data marker A graphical representation of a data point, such as a bar or column.

Data point Individual piece of data plotted in a chart.

Data series The selected range in a worksheet that Excel converts into a graphic and displays as a chart.

Data table A range of cells that shows the resulting values when one or more input values are varied in a formula; when one input value is changed, the table is called a one-input data table, and when two input values are changed, it is called a two-input data table. In a chart it is a grid containing the chart data.

Data validation A feature that allows you to specify what data is allowable (valid) for a range of cells.

Database An organized collection of related information. In Excel, a database is called a list.

Debug In programming, to find and correct an error in code.

Declare In the Visual Basic programming language, assigning a type, such as numeric or text, to a variable.

Delimiter A tab or space used in text files to separate columns of data.

Dependent cell A cell, usually containing a formula, whose value changes depending on the values in the input cells. For example, a payment formula or function that depends on an input cell containing changing interest rates is a dependent cell.

Descending order In sorting an Excel list, the order that begins with the letter Z or the highest number in a list.

Destination program In a data exchange, the program that will receive the data.

Document To make notes about basic worksheet assumptions, complex formulas, or questionable data. In a macro, to insert comments that explain the Visual Basic code.

Drag-and-drop technique Method in which you drag the contents of selected cells to a new location.

Dummy column/row Blank column or row included at the end of a range that enables a formula to adjust when columns or rows are added or deleted.

Dynamic page breaks In a larger workbook, horizontal or vertical dashed lines that represent the place where pages print separately. They also adjust automatically when you insert or delete rows or columns, or change column widths or row heights.

Electronic spreadsheet A computer program that performs calculations on data and organizes information into worksheets. A worksheet is divided into columns and rows, which form individual cells.

Element An XML component that defines the document content.

Embedded chart A chart displayed as an object in a worksheet.

Embedding Inserting a copy of data into a destination document; you can double-click the embedded object to modify it using the tools of the source program.

Exploding pie slice A slice of a pie chart that has been pulled away from the whole pie to add emphasis.

Extensible Markup Language (XML) A system for defining languages using tags to structure data.

External reference indicator The exclamation point (!) used in a formula to indicate that a referenced cell is outside the active sheet.

Extract To place a copy of a filtered list in a range you specify in the Advanced Filter dialog box.

Field In a list (an Excel database), a column that describes a characteristic about records, such as first name or city.

Field name A column label that describes a field.

File properties Attributes of a file, such as author name, file size, and file type.

Fill color The cell background color.

Fill handle A small square in the lower-right corner of the active cell used to copy cell contents.

Filter To display data in an Excel list that meet specified criteria.

Font The typeface or design of a set of characters.

Font size The size of characters, measured in units called points (pts).

Footer Information that prints at the bottom of each printed page; on screen, a footer is visible only in Print Preview.

Format The appearance of text and numbers, including color, font, attributes, borders, and shading. *See also* Number format.

Format Painter A feature used to copy the formatting applied to one set of text or in one cell to another.

Formatting toolbar A toolbar that contains buttons for frequently used formatting commands.

Formula A set of instructions used to perform numeric calculations (adding, multiplying, averaging, etc.).

Formula bar The area below the menu bar and above the Excel workspace where you enter and edit data in a worksheet cell. The formula bar becomes active when you start typing or editing cell data. It includes the Enter button and the Cancel button.

Formula prefix An arithmetic symbol, such as the equal sign (=), used to start a formula.

Freeze To hold in place selected columns or rows when scrolling in a worksheet that is divided in panes. *See also* panes.

Function A special, predefined formula that provides a shortcut for a commonly used calculation; for example, AVERAGE.

Getting Started task pane Lets you quickly open new or existing workbooks.

Goal cell In backsolving, a cell containing a formula in which you can substitute values to find a specific value, or goal.

Goal Seek A problem-solving method in which you specify a solution and then find the input value that produces the answer you want; sometimes described as a what-if analysis in reverse; also called backsolving.

Gridlines Horizontal and/or vertical lines within a chart that make the chart easier to read.

Header Information that prints at the top of each printed page; on screen, a header is visible only in Print Preview.

Help system A utility that gives you immediate access to definitions, steps, explanations, and useful tips.

Hide To make rows, columns, formulas, or sheets invisible to workbook users.

Hotspot An object that, when clicked, will run a macro or open a file.

HTML Hypertext Markup Language, the format of pages that a Web browser such as Internet Explorer or Netscape Navigator can read.

Hyperlink An object (a filename, a word, a phrase, or a graphic) in a worksheet that, when you click it, will display another worksheet or a Web page called the target.

If...Then...Else statement In the Visual Basic programming language, a conditional statement that directs Excel to perform specified actions under certain conditions; its syntax is "If *condition* Then *statements* Else [*elsestatements*].

Input Information that produces desired results, or output, in a worksheet.

Input cells Spreadsheet cells that contain data instead of formulas and that act as input to a what-if analysis; input values often change to produce different results. Examples include interest rates, prices, or other data.

Insert row The last row in an Excel list, where a record can be entered.

Insertion point The blinking vertical line that appears in the formula bar or in a cell during editing in Excel.

Integration A process where data is exchanged among Excel and other Windows programs; can include pasting, importing, exporting, embedding, and linking.

Interactivity A feature of a worksheet saved as an HTML document and posted to an intranet or Web site that allows users to manipulate data using their browsers.

Intranet An internal network site used by a particular group of people who work together.

Keyword A representative word on which the Help system can search to find information on your area of interest. In a macro procedure, words that are recognized as part of the Visual Basic programming language.

Label Descriptive text or other information that identifies the rows and columns of a worksheet. Labels are not included in calculations.

Label prefix A character, such as the apostrophe, that identifies an entry as a label and controls the way it appears in the cell.

Landscape orientation A print setting that positions the worksheet on the page so the page is wider than it is tall.

Legend A key explaining how information is represented by colors or patterns in a chart.

Line chart A graph of data that is mapped by a series of lines. Line charts show changes in data or categories of data over time and can be used to document trends.

Linking Inserting an object into a destination program; The information you insert will be updated automatically when the data in the source document changes.

List The Excel term for a database, an organized collection of related information.

Lock To secure a row, column, or sheet so that data in that location cannot be changed.

Logical condition A filtering feature that searches for records using And and Or conditions; the conditions can include operators such as greater than or less than.

Logical test The first part of an IF function; if the logical test is true, then the second part of the function is applied, and if it is false, then the third part of the function is applied.

Macro A set of instructions recorded or written in the Visual Basic programming language used to automate worksheet tasks.

Main procedure A procedure containing several macros that run sequentially.

Manual calculation option An option that turns off automatic calculation of worksheet formulas, allowing you to selectively determine if and when you want Excel to perform calculations.

Map An XML schema that is attached to a workbook.

Map an XML element A process where XML element names are placed on an Excel worksheet in a specific locations.

Menu bar The bar beneath the title bar that contains the names of menus, that when clicked, open menus from which you choose program commands.

Minor gridlines Gridlines that show the values between the tick marks.

Mixed reference A formula containing both a relative and absolute reference.

Mode indicator A box located in the lower-left corner of the status bar that informs you of a program's status. For example, when Excel is performing a task, the word "Wait" appears.

Model A worksheet used to produce a what-if analysis that acts as the basis for multiple outcomes.

Module In Visual Basic, a module is stored in a workbook and contains macro procedures.

Moving border The dashed line that appears around a cell or range that is copied to the Clipboard.

Name box The left-most area in the formula bar that shows the cell reference or name of the active cell. For example, A1 refers to cell A1 of the active worksheet. You can also display a list of names in a workbook using the Name list arrow.

Named range A range of cells given a meaningful name; it retains its name when moved and can be referenced in a formula.

Number format A format applied to values to express numeric concepts, such as currency, date, and percentage.

Object A chart or graphic image that can be moved and resized and contains handles when selected. In object linking and embedding (OLE), the data to be exchanged between another document or program. In Visual Basic, every Excel element, including ranges.

Object Linking and Embedding (OLE) A Microsoft Windows technology that allows you to transfer data from one document and program to another using embedding or linking.

Office Clipboard A temporary storage area shared by all Office programs that can be used to cut, copy and paste multiple items within and between Office programs. The Office Clipboard can hold up to 24 items collected from any Office program. *See also* Clipboard and Clipboard task pane.

OLE *See* Object Linking and Embedding.

One-input data table A range of cells that shows resulting values when one input value in a formula is changed.

Order of precedence The order in which Excel calculates parts of a formula: (1) operations in parentheses (2) exponents, (3) multiplication and division, and (4) addition and subtraction.

Outline symbols In outline view, the buttons that, when clicked, changes the amount of detail in the outlined worksheet.

Output The end result of a worksheet.

Page field In a PivotTable or a PivotChart report, a field area that lets you view data as if it is stacked in pages, effectively adding a third dimension to the data analysis.

Panes Sections into which you can divide a worksheet when you want to work on separate parts of the worksheet at the same time; one pane freezes, or remains in place, while you scroll in another pane until you see the desired information.

Paste Function A series of dialog boxes that helps you build functions; it lists and describes all Excel functions.

Personal macro workbook A workbook that can contain macros that are available to any open workbook. By default, the personal macro workbook is hidden.

Pie chart A circular chart that represents data as slices of a pie. A pie chart is useful for showing the relationship of parts to a whole; pie slices can be extracted for emphasis. *See also* Exploding pie slice.

PivotChart report An Excel feature that lets you summarize worksheet data in the form of a chart in which you can rearrange, or "pivot," parts of the chart structure to explore new data relationships.

PivotTable Field List A window containing fields that can be used to create or modify a PivotTable.

PivotTable list An interactive PivotTable on a Web or intranet site that lets users explore data relationships using their browsers.

PivotTable report An Excel feature that allows you to summarize worksheet data in the form of a table in which you can rearrange, or "pivot," parts of the table structure to explore new data relationships; also called a PivotTable.

PivotTable toolbar Contains buttons that allow you to manipulate data in a PivotTable.

Plot area The area of a chart that contains the chart itself, its axes, and the legend.

Point A unit of measure used for fonts and row height. One inch equals 72 points, or a point is equal to ½ of an inch.

Pointing method Specifying formula cell references by selecting the desired cell with the mouse instead of typing its cell reference; it eliminates typing errors. Also known as Pointing.

Populate a worksheet with XML data The process of importing an XML file and filling the mapped elements on the worksheet with data from the XML file.

Portrait orientation A print setting that positions the worksheet on the page so the page is taller than it is wide.

Post To place an interactive workbook in a shared location.

Precedents In formula auditing, the cells that are used in the formula to calculate the value of a given cell.

Presentation graphics program A program such as Microsoft PowerPoint that you can use to create slide show presentations.

Preview A view of the worksheet exactly as it will appear on paper.

Primary Key The field in a database that contains unique information for each record.

Print area A portion of a worksheet that you can define using the Print Area command on the File menu; after you define a print area, clicking the Print icon on the Standard toolbar prints only that worksheet area.

Print title In a list that spans more than one page, the field names that print at the top of every printed page.

Procedure A sequence of Visual Basic statements contained in a macro that accomplishes a specific task.

Procedure footer In Visual Basic, the last line of a Sub procedure.

Procedure header The first line in a Visual Basic procedure.

Program Task-oriented software (such as Excel or Word) that enables you to perform a certain type of task, such as data calculation or word processing.

Program code Macro instructions, written in the Visual Basic for Applications programming language.

Project In the Visual Basic Editor, the equivalent of a workbook; a project contains Visual Basic modules.

Project Explorer In the Visual Basic Editor, a window that lists all open projects (or workbooks) and the worksheets and modules they contain.

Property In Visual Basic, an attribute of an object that describes its character or behavior.

Properties window In the Visual Basic Editor, the window that displays a list of characteristics, or properties, associated with a module.

Publish To place an Excel workbook or worksheet on a Web site or an intranet in HTML format so that others can access it using their Web browsers.

Range   A selected group of adjacent cells.

Range finder   A feature that outlines an equation's arguments in blue and green.

Range object   In Visual Basic, an object that represents a cell or a range of cells.

Record   In a list (an Excel database), data about an object or a person.

Refresh   To update a PivotTable so it reflects changes to the underlying data.

Relative cell reference   A type of cell reference used to indicate a relative position in the worksheet. It allows you to copy and move formulas from one area to another of the same dimensions. Excel automatically changes the column and row numbers to reflect the new position. Also known as Relative reference.

Research services   Reference information available through the Research task pane that can be inserted into your document.

Retrieve   In Autofilter, to search for and list records.

Route   To send an e-mail attachment sequentially to each user in a list, who then forwards it to the next user on the list.

Routing slip   A list of e-mail users who are to receive an e-mail attachment.

Row height   The vertical dimension of a cell.

Row heading   The gray box containing the row number to the left of the row.

Run   To play, as a macro.

Scenario   A set of values you use to forecast results; the Excel Scenario Manager lets you store and manage different scenarios.

Scenario summary   An Excel table that compiles data from various scenarios so that you can view the scenario results next to each other for easy comparison.

Schema   In an XML document, a list of the fields, called elements or attributes, and their characteristics.

Search criterion   The specification for data that you want to find in an Excel list, such as "Brisbane" or "is greater than 1000."

Series of labels   Preprogrammed series, such as days of the week and months of the year. They are formed by typing the first word of the series, then dragging the fill handle to select and fill the desired range of cells.

Shared workbook   An Excel workbook that several users can open and modify.

Sheet   A term used for a worksheet.

Sheet tab   A description at the bottom of each worksheet that identifies it in a workbook. In an open workbook, move to a worksheet by clicking its sheet tab. Also known as Worksheet tab.

Sheet tab scrolling buttons   Buttons that enable you to move among sheets within a workbook.

Single-file Web page   A Web page that integrates all of the worksheets and graphical elements from a workbook into a single file in the MHTML file format, making it easier to publish to the Web. Users who have IE 4.0 or higher can open a Web page saved in MHTML format.

Sizing handles   Small boxes appearing along the corners and sides of charts and graphic images that are used for moving and resizing.

Sort   To change the order of records in a list according to one or more fields, such as Last Name.

Sort keys   Criteria on which a sort, or a reordering of data, is based.

Source list   The list on which a PivotTable is based.

Source program   In a data exchange, the program used to create the data you are embedding or linking.

Standard chart type   A commonly used column, bar, pie, or area chart in the Excel program; each type has several variations. For example, a column chart variation is the Columns with Depth.

Standard toolbar   A toolbar that contains buttons for frequently used operating and editing commands.

Statement   In Visual Basic, a line of code.

Status bar   The bar at the bottom of the Excel window that provides information about various keys, commands, and processes.

Style   A named combination of formatting characteristics, such as bold, italic, and zero decimal places.

Sub procedure   A series of Visual Basic statements that performs an action but does not return a value.

SUM   The most frequently used function, this adds columns or rows of cells.

Summary function   In a PivotTable, a function that determines the type of calculation applied to the PivotTable data, such as SUM or COUNT.

Syntax   In the Visual Basic programming language, the formatting rules that must be followed so that the macro will run correctly.

Table   In an Access database, a list of data. In Excel, a special list containing worksheet data that can be searched using Excel features.

Target   The location that a hyperlink displays after you click it.

Target cell   In what-if analysis (specifically, in Excel Solver), the cell containing the formula.

Task pane   A window area to the right of the worksheet that provides worksheet options, such as creating a new workbook, conducting a search, inserting Clip Art, and using the Office Clipboard.

Task pane list arrow   Lets you switch between 11 different task panes.

Template A workbook containing text, formulas, macros, and formatting you use repeatedly; when you create a new document, you can open a document based on the template workbook. The new document will automatically contain the formatting, text, formulas, and macros in the template.

Text annotations Labels added to a chart to draw attention to a particular area.

Text color The color applied to text in a cell or on a chart.

Text file A file that consists of text but no formatting. It is also called an ASCII file.

Tick marks Notations of a scale of measure on a chart axis.

Title bar The bar at the top of the program window that indicates the program name and the name of the current file.

Toggle button A button that turns a feature on and off.

Toolbar A bar that contains buttons that you can click to perform commands.

Toolbar Options button A button you click on a toolbar to view toolbar buttons not currently visible.

Tracers In Excel worksheet auditing, arrows that point from cells that might have caused an error to the active cell containing an error.

Track To identify and keep a record of who makes which changes to a workbook.

Trendline A chart that represents trends in a data series.

Truncate To shorten the display of cell information because a cell is too wide.

Two-input data table A range of cells that shows resulting values when two input values in a formula are changed.

Type a question for help box Area on the menu bar in which you can query the Excel help system by typing a question.

URL *See* Uniform Resource Locator.

Uniform Resource Locator (URL) A unique Web address that identifies a Web page.

Validation *See* Data Validation.

Validation Circles In formula auditing, the circles that identify invalid data.

Value A number, formula, or function used in calculations.

Value axis Also known as the y-axis in a 2-dimensional chart, this area often contains numerical values that help you interpret the size of chart elements. In a 3-dimensional chart, the z-axis.

Variable In the Visual Basic programming language, an area in memory in which you can temporarily store an item of information; variables are often declared in Dim statements such as *DimNameAsString*.

View A set of display or print settings that you can name and save for access at another time. You can save multiple views of a worksheet.

Virus Destructive software that can damage your computer files.

Visual Basic Editor A program that lets you display and edit macro code.

Visual Basic for Applications (VBA) A programming language used to create macros in Excel.

Web discussion Comments attached to an Excel worksheet that you will save as an HTML document, allowing people viewing your worksheet on the Web to review and reply to your comments.

Web query An Excel feature that lets you obtain data from a Web, Internet, or intranet site and places it in an Excel workbook for analysis.

What-if analysis A decision-making feature in which data is changed and formulas based on it are automatically recalculated.

Wildcard A special symbol you use in defining search criteria in the data form or Replace dialog box. The most common types of wildcards are the question mark (?), which stands for any single character, and the asterisk (*), which represents any group of characters.

Window A rectangular area of a screen where you view and work on the open file.

WordArt Specially formatted text, created using the WordArt button on the Drawing toolbar.

Workbook A collection of related worksheets contained within a single file.

Worksheet An electronic spreadsheet containing 256 columns by 65,536 rows.

Worksheet tab *See* Sheet tab.

Worksheet window Includes the tools that enable you to create and work with worksheets.

Workspace An Excel file with an .xlw extension containing information about the identity, view, and placement of a set of open workbooks. Instead of opening each workbook individually, you can open the workspace file instead.

X-axis The horizontal axis in a chart; because it often shows data categories, such as months, it is also called the category axis.

X-axis label A label describing a chart's x-axis.

XML (Extensible Markup Language) A system for defining languages using tags to structure data.

XY (scatter) chart Compares trends over uneven time or measurement intervals; used in scientific and engineering disciplines for trend spotting and extrapolation.

Y-axis The vertical axis in a chart; because it often shows numerical values in a 2-dimensional chart, it is also called the value axis.

Y-axis label A label describing the y-axis of a chart.

Zoom A feature that enables you to focus on a larger or smaller part of the worksheet in Print Preview.

Index

hiding/unhiding, EXCEL F-8, EXCEL F-9

multiple operators, EXCEL E-2–3

names, EXCEL E-4–5

order of precedence, EXCEL B-8, EXCEL E-2

predefined. *See* function(s); *specific functions*

printing, EXCEL B-17

watching and evaluating, EXCEL O-5

Formula Auditing Mode, EXCEL E-16

formula bar, EXCEL A-6, EXCEL A-7

formula prefix, EXCEL B-6

Forward button, Standard Buttons toolbar, WINDOWS XP B-11

Free-Form Select but, WINDOWS XP B-5

freezing worksheet columns and rows, EXCEL F-2, EXCEL F-3

function(s), EXCEL B-10–13, EXCEL P-10. *See also specific functions*

copying between worksheets, EXCEL E-12

statistical, EXCEL E-12–13

Function Arguments dialog box, EXCEL B-12, EXCEL B-13, EXCEL I-12, EXCEL I-13

future value, PMT function, EXCEL E-15

FV function, EXCEL E-15

▶G

General option, Options dialog box, EXCEL O-13

GETPIVOTDATA function, EXCEL L-16–17

Getting Started task pane, EXCEL A-6, EXCEL A-7, EXCEL A-8

displaying, EXCEL A-8

Go To command, EXCEL A-11

Go to New Workbook task pane button, EXCEL A-8

Goal Seek dialog box, EXCEL K-12, EXCEL K-13

goal seeking, EXCEL K-12–13

graph(s). *See* chart(s)

graphic files, inserting in worksheets, EXCEL M-8–9

greater than operator (>), EXCEL E-10

Greater than option, Conditional Formatting dialog box, EXCEL C-14

Greater than or equal to option, Conditional Formatting dialog box, EXCEL C-14

gridlines in charts, EXCEL D-10, EXCEL D-11

grouping

cell ranges, EXCEL O-6

creating subtotals, EXCEL I-10, EXCEL I-11

worksheets, EXCEL F-4

▶H

hard disks, WINDOWS XP APP-1

header(s), worksheets, EXCEL F-5

Header dialog box, EXCEL F-5

Help system, EXCEL A-16–17

Help task pane, EXCEL A-16, EXCEL A-17

displaying, EXCEL A-16

Help window, EXCEL A-16, EXCEL A-17

Hide command, EXCEL C-8

Hide Detail button, PivotTable toolbar, EXCEL L-6

Hide Details button, outlines, EXCEL I-11

hiding

columns and rows, EXCEL C-10

data tables, EXCEL J-8

formulas, EXCEL F-8, EXCEL F-9

Highlight Changes dialog box, EXCEL N-6, EXCEL N-7

highlighted items, WINDOWS XP A-4

Highlighted text, WINDOWS XP B-2

History button, WINDOWS XP A-16

History sheet, saving, EXCEL N-6

HLOOKUP function, EXCEL I-13

Home button, task panes, EXCEL A-6

horizontal resizing pointer, charts, EXCEL D-7

horizontal scroll bar, WINDOWS XP A-14, WINDOWS XP A-15

hotspots, running macros, EXCEL G-11

HTML (Hypertext Markup Language), EXCEL F-16

importing data from HTML files, EXCEL M-8

hyperlinks. *See also* Internet Explorer

deleting, EXCEL F-14

between Excel files, EXCEL F-14–15

Web, to worksheets, EXCEL N-11

▶I

I-beam pointer, EXCEL A-11

icons, WINDOWS XP A-1, WINDOWS XP A-3

changing, EXCEL M-10

IF function, EXCEL B-12, EXCEL E-10–11

If...then...else statements, EXCEL P-8–9

Import Data dialog box, EXCEL N-16, EXCEL N-17

importing

data from HTML files, EXCEL M-8

database tables, EXCEL M-6–7

importable file formats and extensions, EXCEL M-3

lists into Access tables, EXCEL M-16–17

text files, EXCEL M-4–5

inactive programs, WINDOWS XP A-10

Include Hidden Items in Totals button, EXCEL L-6

indenting cell entries, EXCEL C-6

input, worksheets, EXCEL B-2

input messages, EXCEL I-16

Insert dialog box, EXCEL B-21, EXCEL C-10, EXCEL C-11

Insert Function dialog box, EXCEL B-12, EXCEL B-13, EXCEL E-2, EXCEL E-3

Insert Hyperlink dialog box, EXCEL F-14, EXCEL F-15

insert row, lists, EXCEL H-6

Some of the exercises in this book require that you begin by opening a Data File. Follow one of the procedures below to obtain a copy of the Data Files you need.

Instructors
- A copy of the Data Files is on the Instructor Resources CD under the category Data Files for Students, which you can copy to your school's network for student use.
- Download the Data Files via the World Wide Web by following the instructions below.
- Contact us via e-mail at reply@course.com.
- Call Course Technology's Customer Service Department for fast and efficient delivery of the Data Files if you do not have access to a CD-ROM drive.

Students
- Check with your instructor to determine the best way to obtain a copy of the Data Files.
- Download the Data Files via the World Wide Web by following the instructions below.

Instructions for Downloading the Data Files from the World Wide Web

1. Start your browser and enter the URL www.course.com.
2. When the course.com Web site opens, click Student Downloads, and then search for your text by title or ISBN.
3. If necessary, from the Search results page, select the title of the text you are using.
4. When the textbook page opens, click the Download Student Files link, and then click the link of the compressed files you want to download.
5. If the File Download dialog box opens, make sure the Save this program to disk option button is selected, and then click the OK button. (NOTE: If the Save As dialog box opens, select a folder on your hard disk to download the file to. Write down the folder name listed in the Save in box and the filename listed in the File name box.)
6. The filename of the compressed file appears in the Save As dialog box (e.g., 3500-8.exe, 0361-1d.exe).
7. Click either the OK button or the Save button, whichever choice your browser gives you.
8. When a dialog box opens indicating the download is complete, click the OK button (or the Close button, depending on which operating system you are using). Close your browser.
9. Open Windows Explorer and display the contents of the folder to which you downloaded the file. Double-click the downloaded filename on the right side of the Windows Explorer window.
10. In the WinZip Self-Extractor window, specify the appropriate drive and a folder name to unzip the files to. Click Unzip.
11. When the WinZip Self-Extractor displays the number of files unzipped, click the OK button. Click the Close button in the WinZip Self-Extractor dialog box. Close Windows Explorer.
12. Refer to the Read This Before You Begin page(s) in this book for more details on the Data Files for your text. You are now ready to open the required files.

Macintosh users should use a program to expand WinZip or PKZip archives. Students, ask your instructors or lab coordinators for assistance.

Keep Your Skills Fresh with Quick Reference CourseCards!

Thomson Course Technology CourseCards allow you to easily learn the basics of new applications or quickly access tips and tricks long after your class is complete.

Each highly visual, four-color, six-sided CourseCard features:

- **Basic Topics** enable users to effectively utilize key content.

- **Tips and Solutions** reinforce key subject matter and provide solutions to common situations.

- **Menu Quick References** help users navigate through the most important menu tools using a simple table of contents model.

- **Keyboard Shortcuts** improve productivity and save time.

- **Screen Shots** effectively show what users see on their monitors.

- **Advanced Topics** provide advanced users with a clear reference guide to more challenging content.

Over 75 CourseCards are available on a variety of topics! To order, please visit *www.courseilt.com/ilt_cards.cfm*

IF THIS BOOK DOES NOT HAVE A COURSECARD ATTACHED TO THE BACK COVER, YOU ARE NOT GETTING THE FULL VALUE OF YOUR PURCHASE.